MANAGING AND ORGANIZATIONS

An Introduction to Theory and Practice

Stewart Clegg,
Martin Kornberger, and Tyrone Pitsis

SAGE Publications

London • Thousand Oaks • New Delhi

ISBN 0-7619-4388-9 (hbk)
ISBN 0-7619-4389-7 (pbk)

© Stewart Clegg, Martin Kornberger and Tyrone Pitsis 2005

First published 2005
Reprinted 2005

SAGE Publications Ltd
1 Oliver's Yard
55 City Road
London EC1Y 1SP

SAGE Publications Inc
2455 Teller Road
Thousand Oaks
California 91320

SAGE Publications India Pvt. Ltd
B-42 Panchsheel Enclave
PO Box 4109
New Delhi 110 017

British Library Cataloguing in Publication data

A catalogue record for this book is available from the British Library

Library of Congress Control Number: 2004094412

Typeset by C&M Digitals Pvt. Ltd., Chennai, India
Printed and bound in Great Britain by
Cromwell Press Limited, Trowbridge, Wiltshire

MANAGING AND ORGANIZATIONS

CONTENTS

FIGURES

TABLES

IMAGES

Gentlemen, he said,
I don't need your organization, I've shined your shoes,
I've moved your mountains and marked your cards
But Eden is burning, either brace yourself for elimination
Or else your hearts must have the courage for the changing of the guards.

Bob Dylan (1978), "The Changing of the Guards"

INTRODUCTION

Welcome to the new world of management and organization theory! We will take you on a trip through some main roads, back streets, secret places, and exciting viewpoints, to explore management thinking and practice. But let us begin at the beginning . . .

THE GENESIS

As with so many great ideas, this book had its genesis in a pub. One day, Stewart had just given a lecture to students new to management. In preparation, he looked at a number of management theory and organizational behavior textbooks, as well as at some that were more critically oriented. Afterwards, Stewart met up with Martin and we walked to the pub, where we had arranged to see Tyrone. We talked about the lecture. We were wondering why textbooks did not always communicate the fascination, the passion, and the excitement that we find in doing our own thing. Over a few beers, we found the answer: Although the established textbooks provide a lot of information, sometimes it's too much. Although they offer an account of established theories, they often leave out new, cutting-edge thinking, and although they teach you, they do not always help you to explore. So we resolved to do something different by building creatively on our various strengths. We had already written lots of papers together for academic journals and had heaps of fun doing this work— so why not write a book? We needed to get out of the pub and start working!

THE IDEA

We have written a textbook that introduces management as we conceive of it. It is a realist's guide to management, and this is what makes it so different from many other books. It is not a work of desiccated science fiction, creating an "as if" world where technical dreams come true and the reality of life lived in organizations rarely intrudes. We tell it like it is, but we also tell you how to do it better; thus, we offer a book that proposes a new approach to management and treats it in an open and refreshing way.

The book is not only intended to be a learning resource, not only an account of theories, but also an introduction to their practice, one that we hope you will find enjoyable. To make it more so, we have used examples from everyday life and culture, such as surfing and skating, as well as discussions of management and organization theories. The book is intended to be a resource for making connections, a book that will connect with you and will connect you to lots of other interesting ideas and people. It is a book that is meant to be serious but also fun. It is undoubtedly scholarly, but it is also accessible. We think that while the graphics are aesthetically elegant, they are also to the point. In short, we think that you will find this book challenging but also engaging.

THE GUIDE

The idea that structures the book is quite simple: Think of a travel guide. It provides you with all the necessary information you need to know to enjoy your trip. Of course, sometimes it is tricky to read, with lots of details and comparisons, maps, and tables. But it also gives you a flavor of the country you will visit, its lifestyle, culture, and attractions. To package this into a formula, what a guidebook does is provide you with necessary information, but it also fascinates, inspires, and motivates you to explore more and to see things from different perspectives. So we decided that we wanted to write a travel guide to the world of management, containing reliable maps of the terrain, highlighting some critical viewpoints, and outlining ways forward, as well as exploring some of the nooks and crannies and byways while observing the main thoroughfares. We wanted to provide you with a resource book that helps you to navigate through this world and encourages you to explore not only new, exciting, and brilliant aspects but also some dark sides as well.

THE CONTENT

The structure of the book reflects the idea of navigating, and its journey is divided into three main parts. Part I is called Making Sense of Management. It outlines the history of the field and the origins of management thinking. It also focuses on some of the classic theories that inform debate. Part I contains three chapters:

1. "Making Sense of Management" is a basic introduction to the field, exploring why it became so popular in the first place.
2. "Managing Rationalities" focuses on the ideas, the theoretical constructs that informed the way people thought of and acted in organizations in the last century.
3. "Managing Realities" shows how influential empirical work makes us aware of the plurality of possibilities and realities coexisting in organizations.

Part II is called Managing Organizations and is concerned with the present, with the day-to-day life of and in organizations. It focuses on how we enact organizations, how we are embedded in them. It's all about emerging issues, the glue that holds an organization together. Part II is made up of six chapters:

4. "Managing Organization Design" looks at organizational structures as the skeleton that keeps the organization in shape.
5. "Managing Power and Politics in Organizations" explores how organizations are kept together and how they achieve compliance.
6. "Managing Organizational Behavior" shows the importance of human factors in the enterprise.
7. "Managing Leadership" explores how you actually can manage these "soft" issues—which are not always quite as soft as they might appear.
8. "Managing Cultures" looks at the importance of everyday practices and belief systems that are the value basis of organizations.
9. "Managing Communications" picks up a central yet neglected theme and explores how communication shapes the practices of organizing and managing.

The last part of the book, Part III, deals with Managing Change. Here the emphasis is on future developments, on how to change organizations. Whereas Part II was concerned with present realities, this part is all about moving boundaries and shaping the future. The topics discussed are the most current challenges that management faces:

10. "Managing Knowledge and Learning" looks at how organizations can manage and sustain one of the most valuable assets—knowledge.
11. "Managing Innovation and Change" explores one of the most lively and fascinating areas of management: How do new practices come into being?
12. "Managing Strategy" looks at how organizations try to navigate through stormy seas and move forward with a compass.
13. "Managing Globalization" addresses the changing conditions and the emerging challenges of thinking globally while acting locally.

THE STRUCTURE

With such a lot of information, we thought that it was important to think carefully about how to package the book so that it was balanced between providing information that you need to know, information that is necessary, and the fascinating, inspiring parts that will motivate and encourage you to find out more. Although we knew there was much that we had to address, we also agreed with the editors of the *Harvard Business Review* that sometimes "questioning the unquestionable" is the only way to move forward. Thus, we wanted to build this questioning into the structure of the book. Sometimes thinking critically sparks off innovation as well as criticisms of existing practice. For instance, Taylor, one of the founding fathers of management, criticized everyday practices that had been established before him, and argued that common sense was often non-sense. Thus, we tried to keep the balance between what you *need* to know and what you might *like* to know. You don't always know what you need and you don't always need what you want. Put simply, the first half of every chapter covers business as usual in management and organization theory, whereas the second half explores business as unusual. And each chapter has just the same structure as every other chapter. We think that this strongly framed structure will work as an important tool to assist your learning.

The structure of the chapters is designed to be enticing. The chapter heading, the three words beneath it, and the first section, Objectives and Learning Outcomes, give you a glimpse of what you will find out and learn in the chapter. Section 2, Outline of the Chapter, provides what it says: It tells you what the structure will be. Setting the Scene provides background information and puts the content of the chapter into a broader context. The fourth section, Central Approaches and Main Theories, introduces you to the most important theories and approaches. Sometimes we managed to summarize and boil these down to one or two theories, but at other times we covered several approaches. Basically, this section covers what you need to know to gain a good idea about the different fields. It does not, of course, tell you every little detail, but it will provide enough information to give you an overview of current debates. In the fifth section, Critical Issues, we introduce more cutting-edge thinking or thought-provoking research that challenges the mainstream approaches presented in Section 4. We hope that this section will inspire you to think outside the box and question what is taken for granted. Section 6 focuses on ideas qualifying mainstream thinking. As every product description has fine print explaining the hidden downsides and dangers, we call this section The Fine Print. It explores the tacit knowledge that mainstream approaches often cover uncritically. A Summary and Review at the end of each chapter recaptures the most important issues discussed. One More Time . . . provides you with a simple exercise to assess your own understanding of the content (before someone else assesses you!). Finally, Additional Resources lists further readings as well as movies and other sources of inspiration that relate to the material covered in the chapter.

THE DESIGN

We paid special attention to the graphic design of the book. Why do we enjoy reading magazines but not so much textbooks? Because textbooks are like the telephone yellow pages: full of information but with little graphic design—or sometimes really bad graphic design! When you browse this book, you'll see that there are lots of images, tables, and graphic devices that should make life easier or at least reading more fun. For instance, you will find (1) graphical figures, such as models, with arrows and boxes representing the way a particular theorist sees the issues in question, (2) tables, with columns and rows, representing a way of summarizing some ideas or data, and (3) cross-references and images. Within each chapter, we cross-reference other chapters in order to direct you to where a topic is covered more fully, or where related topics and issues are located. The images are there to make the book more appealing and to make you think. We had a reason for putting each image in the book, and we provide some clues as to why we did so in the titles of the images! (Sometimes we have been elliptical in our choices. This is deliberate, because we think it is best if you work out what each might mean. You might come up with a better explanation than we could anyway.) In each case where we have used images, we have received permission to do so or have done our best to contact the person or organization that we thought is the copyright holder to gain permission. (In many cases, the copyright holder is Stewart; sometimes it is Jonathan Clegg, or Jessica Ferguson, who graciously allowed us to use some of their images. For the other images, should anyone whom we have overlooked feel that they wish us to acknowledge copyright in any subsequent edition, please contact us and we will rectify the omission.)

THE WEB SITE

Books are dinosaurs (but make great pets, nonetheless): They are heavy, quickly age, and can expire rapidly. Thus, we decided to use the Web as a complementary resource for our project, as a place where we could host material that needed more frequent updates and change. Developing the site was an exciting adventure in itself. As their research project, students from the University of Technology, Sydney's, Interdisciplinary Media and Learning program found out what other students liked about Web sites and what they did not like, and how to design them accordingly. We ended up with an impressive list of exciting features that will help you to understand management and organization theory.

The Web site that the book relates to is **www.ckmanagement.net.** You will find additional material, arranged on a chapter-by-chapter basis, that enables you to extend your research, connect with other users of the book around the world, do case studies, and view videos of interviews with top management thinkers talking about the topics the book covers, such as strategy, communications, and culture. In addition, there will be downloadable PDF files of articles from top Sage journals, such as *Organization Studies* and *Human Relations,* that are related to the chapters. Using these you can have access to up-to-date resources to immediately broaden and deepen your understanding of the contents of the chapters. As there is no necessity to make the textbook bulkier than it needs to be, we have placed all the case study material on-line as well.

We are interested in what you think of the book, its features, and the associated products such as the Web site, so there are feedback links that invite you to become involved. And there will be other material and links relating to other projects that Stewart, Martin, and Tyrone are involved in.

THE INSTRUCTOR'S CD

We have also produced an instructor's CD, available to instructors when ordering the book as a set text from Sage. On this CD you will find all the resources that you need to build great teaching and learning, using the book. These include material such as multiple choice questions (a test bank of about 50 per chapter); short essay questions with assessment guides, longer essay topics, and integrated essay questions that embed the material of the chapter in broader practical and theoretical concerns. Also, there is a complete set of PowerPoint slides for the chapters; all the tables, figures, and images used in the book (the latter in full color—plus some that we decided not to use but have left on the disc anyway). Using these resources, lectures can be enlivened with illustrative material, tests and assessments can be rapidly administered, and the slides customized as required. In addition, an image of the book's cover is included.

THE ACKNOWLEDGMENTS

All book authors need good friends, patient colleagues, and great loves. Starting with the last first, Stewart had Lynne, Jonathan, and William, Martin had Jessica, and Tyrone had Sharon. The good friends and patient colleagues' list has to start with Cleusa Lester. Everyone who knows Cleusa (or Cleo) realizes, even if they cannot imagine all of the incredibly important roles she plays, that she is absolutely fabulous. Being Brazilian is not the least! Among the patient friends, good colleagues, and others who have helped us, provided feedback, or just been supportive, we would like to mention, alphabetically, Anjana Anandakumar, Emma Bowyer, Geoff Breach, Chris Carter, Andrew Chan, Jonathan Clegg, Lynne Clegg, William Clegg, Chris Coupland, David Courpasson, Miriam Dornstein, Dan Evans, Jessica Fergusson, Kevin Foley, John Garrick, Ranjan George, Ray Gordon, John Gray, Julie Gustavs, Winton Higgins, Simon Hoerauf, Brian Hunt, Joan S. Ingalls, Emanuel Josserand, Ken Kamoche, Kevin Keough, Robert van Krieken, Karl Kruselniscki, Linda Leung, Adam Morgan, Michael Muetzelfeldt, Katherine Peil, Bruce Petty, Paul O. Radde, Tim Ray, Carl Rhodes, Anne Ross-Smith, John Sillince, David Silverman, John Stokes, Emanuela Todeva, Marc Tyyrell, Johannes Weissenbaeck, Adam Yazxhi, Joanne Young, and also the members of the Friends of Positive Psychology listserve.

It seems almost unfair to single out anyone in particular from this list, but we should acknowledge some specific contributions: Anjana Anandakumar's proofreading, alerting us to continuity problems, as well as giving us insight into what should go into our glossary, and her help in preparing the PowerPoint slides; Emma Bowyer's knowledge was a great help in keeping us focused on our readers; Chris Carter, for providing the very careful and thorough reading, as well as the many small word-sketches of ideas and input to the material on culture and strategy, especially; David Courpasson and Dan Evans, for providing an opportunity to first test out some of the ideas from the book in the classroom with the 2003 MBA Summer School at EM Lyon in Managing with Power and Politics, as well as the students who took the subject; Miriam Dornstein's panoptic capability for telling us where we were getting lost in our text; Kevin Foley's ability to detect structural weaknesses and omissions—not all of which might have been rectified to his "standards"; Ranjan George, for inviting Stewart to Sri Lanka to develop curriculum material for the Open University of Sri Lanka, which formed an initial challenge within which some of the convictions that shaped this book were gestated; Ray Gordon, for the Police case; John Gray's alertness to our occasional lapses into a particular type of metaphysical bathos; Julie Gustavs's sharp eye for detail; Emanuel Josserand's assistance in researching the current state of play in the French bread industry; Michael Muetzelfeldt, for the photo of the Virgin; Carl Rhodes's support and enthusiasm; John Sillince's identification of a number of theoretical absences in our arrangement of the material; and Joanne Young's detailed commentary on early drafts and suggestions for the title. We would also like to thank all the IML students who presented ideas for the Web site, especially Antoine Tremoulet and Ian Tanedo, whose ideas we enjoyed most and who have built the Web site for us. Without the great images that Jonathan Clegg and Jessica Fergusson made available, the book would not have been as interesting. Penultimately, a very special thanks to Johannes and Simon from PLAY, with whom Martin thought a lot about why so many books are so boring and, as a result, started thinking about some new ideas that are reflected in the underlying structure for this book, and finally, from Stewart to Jonathan, because, through working with his visual creativity, he learned to be more fluent with words.

We also appreciate the great support and guidance that we have had at Sage from many people, including Ian Eastment, Seth Edwards, Ben Sherwood, Alison Mudditt, Sanford Robinson (not forgetting the great copyediting job done by Barbara Coster and Meredith L. Brittain), and especially Kiren Shoman. She is a persistent editor who was able to persuade Stewart to do something that he had agreed, in principle and in contract, to do a long time ago with some other potential collaborators (for both Sue Jones and Rosemary Nixon, who should also be acknowledged as earlier editors) but which, for various reasons, he never got around to doing. As it transpired, Stewart is delighted to have written the book with Martin and Tyrone. He doesn't think he could have had a more enjoyable partnership for the project. Finally, there may have been some other people we should have thanked and acknowledged but have overlooked. Sorry if that is the case. We'll fix it in the next edition if you let us know.

Stewart, Martin, and Tyrone
University of Technology, Sydney, Australia

PART I
MAKING SENSE OF MANAGEMENT

CHAPTER 1

MAKING SENSE OF MANAGEMENT

History, Science, Perspectives

Objectives and learning outcomes

By the end of this chapter, you will be able to

- Appreciate the issues for which management ideas were developed as solutions

- Understand the contributions of some foundational management thinkers

- Explain key themes in thinking about organizations and management

- Understand the historical development of management thinking

- Discuss the differences and the continuities in early management thought

- Distinguish between the ideas articulated by the key foundational thinkers and be able to engage with them critically

Before you get started . . .

Improvising on a statement by the English landscape painter John Constable:
"Remember that management is a science of which organizations are but the experiments!"

OUTLINE OF THE CHAPTER

Understanding management thinking is easier than many people might think, especially when a textbook is structured in such a way that it allows one to follow the progression of management thinking as a coherent story. That is the aim of this textbook. In this chapter, you will read about some of the early issues that had to be confronted and some of the solutions that thinkers contributed to management thinking. Their thought helped to design the underlying practices of management and organization, as well as frame thinking about them. In addition, you will also be able to reflect on the legacy of the work bequeathed by these foundational management thinkers to gain some more historical context on the question, What is the origin of modern management and organization thinking? The question is important since these early management thinkers set the scene for contemporary discussions. They designed the cornerstones of the map that we (still) use when we try to navigate through the world of management and organization theory. We will set the scene by turning the clock back to a time before modern management emerged, so you can grasp its singularity.

SETTING THE SCENE

Traditionally, management and organization were a concern principally of rulers, such as princes, lords, and monarchs, as well as religious orders. For most ordinary people, just working to live and being able to buy and sell or otherwise acquire necessities in the market was the major focus of life. However, despite what many economists imagine, organizations did not just emerge as a secondary form that provided alternatives to market transactions when there were market failures (Williamson 1985).

The origins of modern organizations were not quite as mundane as the idea of there being a migration from markets to hierarchies might suggest. They had sacred and spiritual antecedents in the emphasis on rules that was characteristic of the medieval monastery, which became the template for later forms of bureaucratic organization (Keiser 2002; also see Eco 1994 for a literary example of similar points). If we want to find historical compass points for the emergence of modern organizations in Western Europe, we should look to the great religious institutions of its past. The rational qualities that could inspire

Image 1.1   *The market in everyday life: scenes from Taxco, Mexico*

Image 1.2   *Inspirational spaces within which complex rules flourished*

architects to design great naves and spires and allow its administrators to write complex rules are a more useful point of reference than the uncertainties of actors in the markets. Markets played their role, but, as we shall see shortly, that role was quite specific and limited.

The earliest architects of modern business organizations needed little learning to run their affairs.

The earliest architects of modern business organizations needed little learning to run their affairs, at least until increasing scale complicated the picture. It was then that the model of bureaucracy, as rule by rules, was adopted, the idea that first emerged in the monasteries of Western Europe, among the few literates in medieval society. From there it went out and conquered the state, especially the administration of its civil and military affairs, and became, in the nineteenth century, the model for all areas of civil administration:

infirmaries, asylums, schools, railways, colonial administration. Hardly any area escaped the reforming zeal of rationalizing bureaucracy.

Initially, there was no straight transfer of organization form from church to secular society. As feudal society gave way to industrial capitalism in Western Europe, new rulers emerged on the scene whose wealth was built on commerce and industry rather than the landed estates that had sustained both church and state. With new rulers emerged new issues. In the past, the central management issue for the state had been the occasional extraction of monies and taxes from a reluctant citizenry in order to support feudal wars and a noble lifestyle. With respect to the church, an alliance between religious conviction and supernatural fear could ensure revenues and estates for the church in the here and now as a comfort for their better endowed parishioners against the future uncertainties of heaven, hell, and purgatory. The state would occasionally loot, plunder, and tax but cared little for how what it took was produced. For the inmates of the monasteries, what was important was organizing the day so as to maximize time for prayer and devotion, so of all those who mattered on the medieval scene, it was the monks, or at least some among their orders, who had the best organization designs.

The new men of property steered by a different compass, one that did not immediately lead to rational organization designs. For them the central issue was the maximization of private profit. The way in which revenue was produced was their central concern because they had to be able to exercise regular and routine dominion and sway over the working lives of those who produced these revenues: those who labored on land and sea, in mines and factories. Two types of laborer were involved: freemen and slaves. Freemen were found in cities everywhere, whereas slaves were, by and large, confined to the economies of the New World, where significant profits were to be made from plantations.

On the plantations, the central issue was how to produce disciplined labor in the service of those who owned the land. The combination of black bodies, fertile fields, and cash crops proved lucrative indeed for the owners of these properties. The good management of their assets was a major concern. Just as no prudent investors would want to run down the value of their investments needlessly, so the slave owners did not want to exhaust the usefulness of their slaves through overwork. They would have to meet the costs of premature wasting of these human resources. In everyday practice, discipline was settled through the employment of tight surveillance, the use of exemplary harsh punishment to keep the mass in line, together with routine management enacted on these recalcitrant bodies owned as property (Cooke 2003).

Cooke suggests that the management of slaves in plantations anticipated many ideas later associated with F. W. Taylor (1911), whom we shall meet shortly. Others suggest that the main basis of Taylor's ideas came from the lessons learned in the assembly and disassembly of muskets in the military and the drilling of soldiers in the use of these and other weapons on the parade ground (Dandeker 1990). One suggestion is that, in fact, these methods were first applied to muskets by French gunsmiths, and brought from France to the

United States at the time of the American Revolution. French techniques, in turn, have been seen as arising centuries later than the methods pioneered by the masters of the Venetian arsenal in warship building and crossbow manufacture. Other accounts suggest that the important thing to realize about Taylor was that he was an engineer; his ideas merely applied an engineering logic to the management and disposition of relations between men and machines (Miller and O'Leary 2002; Shenhav 1999). The balance of the history, whether it lies in dealing with slaves, muskets, or machines, remains contested. One fact is evident, however: In Britain, the first industrial society, slavery was not a legally available mode of production, having been outlawed by the British Parliament early in the development of modern industry, on March 25, 1807.

Industrial property owners preferred able and willing bodies in their service rather than slaves. The employers could not rely on feudal fealty or obligation to deliver these bodies to them, as did the lords of old; however, it was a matter of record that they often found religious observance, with its deference and piety, to be an invaluable asset (Thompson 1965). That authority, which could claim that it had God on its side, stood a better chance of success, as Weber (1947) realized when he noted that deeply held Protestant religious convictions produced not only industrious capitalists but also sober and disciplined workers (see also pp. 49–50). As Anthony (1977: 43) notes, the "engagement of God as the supreme supervisor was a most convenient device," one whose omnipotence more secular methods sought to emulate (see also pp. 16–18). If God alone could not be relied on to provide sober and industrious employees to bring order, enforce discipline, and construct authority, what could they turn to?

In the early days of industrialism, a combination of heavy doses of paternalism, rough discipline, and an "efficient" labor market (one that could send young children, as well as their fathers and mothers, out to labor, mine, and chimney-sweep) buttressed less secular sources of moral authority with sheer necessity. More traditional relations could often overlie the wage relations that mostly bound production. However, unlike feudal serfs, these men, women, and children who were employed in the new industries were "formally free"; they were not obliged to work where and when they did by virtue of being bound to a feudal estate but because of the sheer necessity of selling their labor in order to survive in a market economy.

In lieu of internalized religious ritual or deference to feudal hierarchy, management control seemed best assured through the routine disciplining of those employed. In small workshops, discipline was relatively easy to enact, especially where these workshops had a craft basis and were organized around mastery of a specific knowledge, such as how to make barrels, fabricate metal, or weave wool. In such a structure, the master was presumed to know the craft, which apprentices were presumed not to know and had every motive for learning, so that they too could become skilled workers. The master exercised power by getting the apprentice to do things the way that he favored. The basis of the master's authority was a possession of power unified with the knowledge that they not only owned the workshop but also the knowledge of how to work in it. On this basis, they were easily able to enforce rules, to say when work was done correctly or incorrectly. The major mechanism for enforcing the rules was effective oversight by *direct control* of people in the workshop.

CENTRAL APPROACHES AND MAIN THEORIES

Management and scale: Legislation, internal contracts, and bureaucracies

The early days of modern management and organizations were bootstrapped. Primitive methods of surveillance and drill were adapted, and elements from preindustrial craft relations were incorporated. As one of the most significant economic historians of management suggested:

> The pioneers of the industrial revolution were forced to lay the foundations of the practices of labour management themselves, involving a subject as complex, novel and full of pitfalls as the other applied sciences they had to master. . . . We can hazard a guess as to how many of the survivors were successful . . . largely because they mastered . . . the tasks of management, [but] we shall probably remain forever ignorant of the number of those who failed because they did not. (Pollard 1965: 160)

Pollard puts his finger on a pervasive problem with the bases of management knowledge: It is much more likely to be about the successes at any particular time than the failures—although, in many ways, knowing the reasons for failure may be more important than learning the lessons of success. And success is always temporal, anyway. Yesterday's success can easily become tomorrow's failure.

Bootstrapped solutions worked appropriately for as long as the scale of enterprise remained small. However, the issue of surveillance was about to be made a whole lot more complicated because of institutional innovations that led to an increase in scale. There was a synergy between simple control and small scale, for as long as organizations remained somewhat limited in size because of the financial means available, questions of managerial control could be resolved through simple and direct supervision. The numbers to be supervised were not great. As late as the early 1850s in the British cotton industry, a factory of 300 people could still be considered very large (Hobsbawm 1975: 21), and as late as 1871, the average British cotton factory employed only 180 people, whereas engineering works averaged only 85.

There were two distinct shortcomings associated with expanding the scale of these small-scale arrangements. The first was the supply of finance.

> By and large the characteristic enterprise of the first half of the century had been financed privately—e.g., from family assets—and expanded by reinvesting profits, though this might well mean that, with most of capital tied up in this way, the firm

Image 1.3   *A woolen textile mill, Holywell Green, West Yorkshire, U.K., circa 1965*

might rely a good deal on credit for its current operations. But the increasing size and cost of such undertakings as railways, metallurgical and other expensive activities requiring heavy initial outlays, made this more difficult, especially in countries newly entering upon industrialization and lacking large accumulations of private investment capital. (Hobsbawm 1975: 214)

To grow large meant expending capital. Not that much was available. The capital in circulation in the early industrial economy was relatively small compared to that invested in more aristocratic ventures, such as real estate. Mostly it was raised through credit. Merchants combined credit with rented buildings and machinery, together with cheap sources of labor, important mechanisms in an age of unlimited liability for the debts of the enterprise, because if the enterprise were to fail, the liability and exposure of the emergent entrepreneurs would be limited (Tribe 1975). By keeping these commitments small, fortunes might be better insured.

It was a particular institutional innovation, pioneered first in Britain in 1856, but widely copied internationally almost immediately thereafter, that enabled enterprises to grow beyond the financial capacities of their owners. The legislation was known as limited liability legislation. The intention and consequence of this legislation was to separate the private fortunes of entrepreneurs from their investments in business, so that if the latter failed, the personal fortune was sequestered and the debtors' prison avoided (see Charles Dickens's [1982] novel, *Little Dorrit*). Before 1856, the situation was quite different. If the business failed, the owner's personal fortune could be seized against debtors. Not surprisingly, this limited the size of the enterprise, because a prudent investor would not want to be overexposed. As Marx (1959: 436) predicted, being able to risk the savings of investors freed up entrepreneurial energies and did much to prepare the ground for a widespread share-market in which individuals might invest their savings in productive enterprises. Contemporary observers anticipated that there would be an increasing concentration of capital (Marx 1959: 440), that is, the development of many fewer organizations employing much greater numbers of workers. The scale effects were dramatic. The Krupp works at Essen in Germany had a mere 72 workers in 1848, but by 1873 it employed almost 12,000. Whole regions became dominated by huge commercial ventures.

If limited liability legislation solved the problem of how to raise capital and increase scale, it did not resolve the problem of how to manage the vastly expanded enterprise. It was the "'master' rather than the impersonal authority of the 'company'" that held sway in "the enterprise, and even the company was identified with a man rather than a board of directors" (Hobsbawm 1975: 214). But how could a single master exercise mastery over so many? How was the master to achieve effective governance over a vastly increased scale of operations? Two resolutions of the puzzle of how to ensure mastery were proposed: One adopted a market solution, whereas the other copied what had already occurred in the large-scale public service of the day and threw in its lot with bureaucracy. The market solution was based on the owners of previously independent business being reemployed as internal contractors to oversee the processes of labor in firms that were taken over by financiers. These were individuals skilled more in the art of raising capital than executing the mundane command of work. One consequence of internal contracting—where the contractor used materials, plant, and equipment supplied by the owners but managed the labor contracted to deliver a certain quantity of product—was that quite different methods of internal control could flourish in different plants in the same industry. Standards were highly variable. Here a benign and benevolent despot might be master, there the master might be acting on behalf

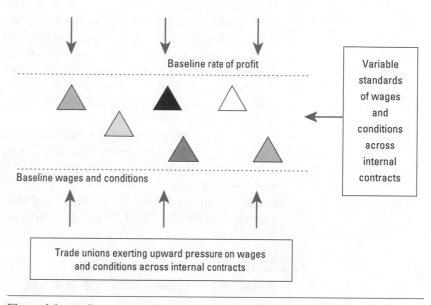

Figure 1.1   *Pressures tending to standardize internal contracts*

of a labor-managed cooperative, while in another plant the master might be a ruthless and vicious tyrant, exploiting family members or those too weak in the market to resist downward pressure on their wages.

Given that the internal contract was a fixed sum agreed between the internal contractor and the employers of capital, then the middleman, the internal contractor, stood to gain the most by paying the least for the quantity contracted, so there was plenty of opportunity for downward pressure to occur. Not surprisingly, this was a fact that the trade unionism of the day (the system of internal contracting flourished from the late nineteenth through to the early twentieth century, with variable lags in different countries, being developed earliest and superseded fastest in the United States) eagerly latched onto in efforts to improve the lot of their members by standardizing conditions and wages (Clawson 1980; Littler 1982). Unionism exercised an upward pressure, standardizing the conditions of work, whereas, from the business owners and employers of finance, there was a downward pressure beginning to be exercised in the name of an efficient rate of return.

The downward pressure from finance and the upward pressure from the unions led, inexorably, to an increased standardization of workplace routines. It was not the market but the military model that provided the best template for this organization design. By the early twentieth century, the most percipient observer, Max Weber (1976), noted that bureaucracy had become the fate of our times. It was a fate modeled unambiguously on the military. As the economic historian Hobsbawm (1975: 216) put it, "Paradoxically, private enterprise in its most unrestricted and anarchic period tended to fall back on the only available model of large-scale management, the military and bureaucratic," noting the railway companies, with their "pyramid of uniformed and disciplined workers, possessing job security, often promotion by security and even pensions," as an extreme example. Weber (1948: 261) put it even more sharply: "No special proof is necessary to show that military discipline is the ideal model for the modern capitalist factory."

The result of processes working toward standardization was that the blueprint for designing modern organizations was increasingly inherited from the design of professional armies, shaped within a framework of military discipline, even while being applied to market-based enterprises. Being disciplined and being visible were the key themes. Order, discipline, and authority were to become the organizational watchwords of the new world under construction.

Management and hands: The importance of being confined in space

The spatially enclosed world of the factory offered unique opportunities for management as well as being the place in which many of its standard terms were first stabilized in meaning. Long before there were formal theorists of management, managers managed. What they managed were "hands."

Stewart, one of the authors of this book, grew up in a small town in the North of England, at a time when many people worked in one or other of the numerous textile mills built in the nineteenth century. Outside each mill, high on a sandstone wall, soot-darkened from the smoke that poured out from mill and domestic chimneys alike, were black painted signboards bearing the legend, "Following Hands Wanted," usually in gold lettering. In the board, position descriptions could be slotted in, such as leading charge hand, or carding hand, using the term for an employee, a *hand,* that had been passed down in common usage from the old Anglo-Saxon English, derived from the Norse. Sometimes overseers or supervisors were advertised. That employees were known as hands was not only etymologically derived but also descriptively accurate, because they were employed largely for what they did with their hands—hands that were interchangeable, provided they had machine-minding skills and manual dexterity. Hands were overseen and supervised, literally. Hence, frontline managers were overseers or supervisors. The terms betray their origin; those in positions of authority were there because they exercised surveillance over others whose skilled hands were engaged in work—the one employed to exercise oversight, the other to use their hands.

Not all hands were subject to systematic surveillance, however. If we follow etymology west, to the frontier society of the United States in the nineteenth century, we see an interesting shift in the definition of a hand. As the cattle industry developed, those who worked in it became known as ranch hands. However, the ranch hand, riding through the High Sierra or prairies, worked in a situation enviable to any factory worker—he was *out of sight.* The ranch hand could freely roam the range, whereas the factory hand was confined to a small space, both physically and in task terms. The freedom of a ranch hand on a horse roaming the prairies in search of steers that had cut loose from the herd could only be a dream to a factory hand under the watchful eye of a supervisor. The one was free to ride as the spirit took him; the other was always under a watchful eye.

Although the idea of being a hand (for instance, a hired hand) passed into common currency, the contexts in which the term was used differed widely. The designation of being a hand need not mean tight supervision and close control. What was crucial was the nature of the context in which work was done. Something about the factory lent itself to close supervision—and this something was its boundedness, its spatial concentration and encasing. Space could be used to become an adjunct to supervision and control. It also enabled lessons to be transmitted not only about the development of skills and aptitudes but about the authority of the master and the overseer, foreman, or supervisor. The mills contained small and relatively self-contained workshops, which the hiring boards described perfectly. Managing involved supervision, overseeing, surveillance, and superintendence, whereas working involved hands. Managing was premised on simple and direct supervision, on knowing what was going on through seeing and understanding the nature of the action performed by the hands being watched. It is a method of management that we still find today in many small-scale enterprises. The union of insight and oversight is, indeed, powerful.

In factory work, as Adam Smith (1961) extolled in *An Enquiry Into the Nature and Causes of the Wealth of Nations,* the division of labor formally done by one person, when divided into many parts, each specialized in by different individuals, caused great increases in productivity. Consequently, mill hands tended to be specialized workers, whereas ranch hands were jacks-of-all-trades. The point is not just the shifting use of English; it is also that being treated as a hand was not in itself sufficient to ensure a loss of autonomy, diminished personal scope, and enhanced control. It was being confined and under surveillance that was important. Various methods of fusing discipline and surveillance were tried. The earliest of these relied on architecture before there was a general shift to engineering. Systematic architecture that concentrated surveillance and control was developed in the late eighteenth century by the famous English philosopher Jeremy Bentham, when he sought to make oversight more efficient.

Management and surveillance: Jeremy Bentham's design for the Panopticon

Bentham was a utilitarian philosopher. Utilitarianism elevated the principle of usefulness above all else. When Bentham began to think about how one might design a rational enterprise, one in which the utility of oversight could

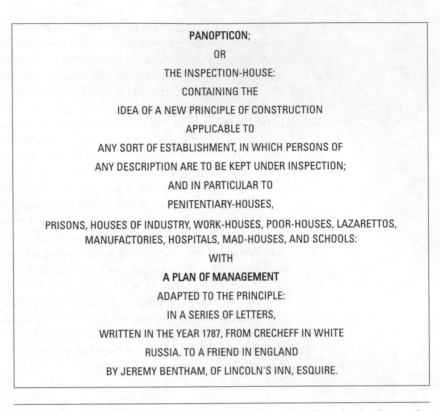

PANOPTICON;

OR

THE INSPECTION-HOUSE:

CONTAINING THE

IDEA OF A NEW PRINCIPLE OF CONSTRUCTION

APPLICABLE TO

ANY SORT OF ESTABLISHMENT, IN WHICH PERSONS OF

ANY DESCRIPTION ARE TO BE KEPT UNDER INSPECTION;

AND IN PARTICULAR TO

PENITENTIARY-HOUSES,

PRISONS, HOUSES OF INDUSTRY, WORK-HOUSES, POOR-HOUSES, LAZARETTOS,
MANUFACTORIES, HOSPITALS, MAD-HOUSES, AND SCHOOLS:

WITH

A PLAN OF MANAGEMENT

ADAPTED TO THE PRINCIPLE:

IN A SERIES OF LETTERS,

WRITTEN IN THE YEAR 1787, FROM CRECHEFF IN WHITE

RUSSIA. TO A FRIEND IN ENGLAND

BY JEREMY BENTHAM, OF LINCOLN'S INN, ESQUIRE.

Figure 1.2   *Bentham's cover from 1787, introducing his ideas for the design of the Panopticon*

be maximized, he came up with a design for something that he called a Panopticon. Its ingenuity resided in the economy of effort required to administer it, once it was designed and built. Figure 1.2 shows the text in his first proposal for the Panopticon.

The Panopticon, literally, is a means for making work as visible as it could be, by virtue of the supervisor (note the term: literally, it means the exercise of superordinate vision) seeing as much as possible. Notice that Bentham's concept could apply to almost every situation! It is the particular relation between the seer and the seen that is significant in the Panopticon. Those who are being seen are scrutinized in ways that do not enable them to see that they are under surveillance.

As you can see from Image 1.4, the Panopticon was a complex architectural design. It consisted of a central observation tower (which you can see clearly in the cutaway section) from which any supervisor, without being seen, could see the bodies arranged in the various cells of the building. In each cell, the occupants were backlit, isolated from one another by walls and subject to scrutiny by the observer in the tower. Control was to be maintained by the

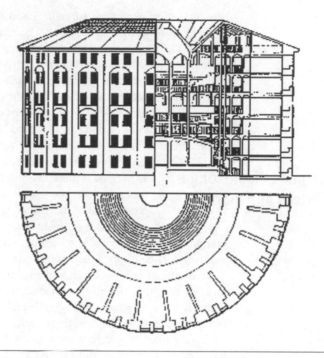

Image 1.4   *The Panopticon*

constant sense that unseen eyes might be watching those under surveillance. You had nowhere to hide, nowhere to be private, and no way of knowing if you were being watched at any particular time. The situation was structured such that obedience in and through productive activity seemed the worker's only rational option, not knowing whether or not they were being watched but obliged to assume that they were (see also pp. 176–178).

For Bentham, the Panopticon was designed as a progressive replacement for current penal methods. Moreover, as a pioneering "best practice," the Panopticon could equally be applied to schools, hospitals, and poorhouses, as well as factories (where Bentham got the idea in the first place—from his brother's Russian manufactory). It was a project to be applied to everything. It was not only panoptical but also had wide applications (explored in McKinlay and Starkey 1979).

The French historian of ideas, Michel Foucault (1979), is responsible for the modern interest in Bentham's Panopticon as a unique instrument of reform and governance. No prison was ever built exactly to the model—although many show its influence—but the principles embodied in the Panopticon had widespread influence. The key principle was *inspection* by an all-seeing but unseen being—rather like a secular version of God. And it did not matter if the inmates were actually being watched at any specific time—they would never know—*but they did know that they were always at risk of being watched.* The principle of inspection or surveillance instilled itself in the moral conscience of those who were being overseen. The aim was to produce a self-disciplining subject. The asymmetrical nature of seeing but not being seen, of knowing you were possibly being watched but not when or if you were, was designed to produce employees predisposed to be socialized into submitting their will to the task at hand, under the threat of constant supervision.

The Panopticon was not just a system of surveillance but also a system of records and rules. The authorities would have a complete file on the behavior of each inmate. There would be rules governing timetables, the nature of work,

The Panopticon is no longer built of bricks and mortar.

and the authority to exercise surveillance. Again, the Panopticon is not just a mere historical curiosity. We all live in a surveillance culture now, with cameras watching us constantly at work, even if that's for "security" reasons. The Panopticon is no longer built of bricks and mortar but is recorded by video, computer monitoring, audio recording—making us all accountable to controls we may only be dimly aware of (see also pp. 170–172).

If Bentham saw the origins of modern management residing in architecture, on the other side of the Atlantic, a little later, in the nineteenth century, a much more economical, rational, and efficient design for managing was being produced. While buildings were expensive and inflexible once built, designing rules to govern work was relatively cheap and more flexible. New work designs and rules did not require a specific arrangement of bricks and mortar, only a certain engineering of the body and the relations between people and machines, based upon an empirical time-based assessment of the most efficient ways to achieve the maximum productivity.

Management and engineering: F. W. Taylor and scientific management

Engineers had long been fascinated by work. The English engineer Charles Babbage made many contributions to early work study and, in fact, designed an early form of the computer as well as writing extensively *On the Economy of Machinery and Manufactures* (1971). Engineering had a natural affinity with work in a profit-based economy, because it was oriented to getting more output from less input as its definition of efficiency. Although early ideas of efficiency were important, it took an engineer to systematize these with the separate concern of surveillance and discipline. Armed with a checklist and a stopwatch, F. W. Taylor developed scientific management around a set of ideas for making people's work more visible. He observed and timed work, and then redesigned it, so that tasks could be done more efficiently. Taylor, an engineer, proposed that "scientific management" could design the best way of performing any set of tasks on the shop floor, based on detailed observation, selection, and training. Time was of the essence.

Image 1.5   *Clocking in*

Taylor's system survives today in the way many semiskilled machine-tending tasks are designed in organizations. Elements of Taylorism survive as deeply vestigial organs within modern organizations, but it is not just history. Every time "lean production," "methodologies for total quality management," or "business process reengineering" are introduced into contemporary firms, then an element of Taylorism is being reproduced, because these approaches define the most efficient "one best way" to organize. As we shall see shortly, other important writers, such as the Frenchman Henri Fayol, also saw the potential to expand similar ideas to the whole organization—not just the shop floor.

Rationality, defined in engineering terms, became a new source of scientific legitimation for management. The science resided in knowledge of how to use

Image 1.6   *F. W. Taylor, founder of scientific management*

specific means to achieve given ends. Management would be a new breed of practical scientists. Engineering was an innovating discipline with great authority. It was being constructed by popular engineering journals and magazines of the day as *the* locus of professional managerial expertise (Shenhav 1999). According to the new engineering approaches to management, corporations and organizations could be managed empirically, on the basis of facts and techniques, rather than experience, privilege, or an arbitrary position. Functions and responsibilities should be aligned in a scientifically proven manner by engineers trained in the management of things and the governance of people working with and on them.

Engineering and opposing scientific management

Taylor articulated an essentially engineering view of the role of management in his book *Principles of Scientific Management,* first published in 1911. It was not very popular with many existing people who fulfilled management roles. Contesting Taylor were a number of forces. First were internal contractors—people who provided and supervised labor to work within factories owned by remote financiers, entrepreneurs, and industrialists—who stood to lose their livelihoods if scientific management triumphed and replaced them with systematic managers. Second were the owners of capital, particularly those with small workshops, who were already fearful of the risk of being swallowed up or driven out of business by big businessmen gobbling up small enterprises into new centers of financial control, the men who became known as the robber barons (such as Andrew Carnegie and Theodore Vanderbilt). Also, they were fearful of the dilution of the power of ownership. Third were the workers, increasingly organizing in unions, who railed against the loss of craft skills that the project of standardization and systematization of work entailed (Shenhav 1999). Standardization became a wedge that opened the door for a wider adoption of systematic scientific management through linking individual remuneration to individual effort in scientifically framed tasks. Much of the opposition to Taylor's ideas came to a head when the U.S. Congress, in 1912, held an inquiry into the use of his system of management, due to association of its adoption with strikes. For the workers, the fact that there were layoffs, due to available work being completed sooner, appeared particularly threatening to their jobs. Taylor's ideas had the advantage of being quite easy to grasp (see Taylor 1995; Wrege 1995) and so were as easily adopted as they were opposed. However, it is worth noting that employers tended to adopt his ideas piecemeal; they were keen on the efficiencies from the time measurement but not as keen on the rewards in the form of bonuses that Taylor proposed under his recommendations for the use of piece rates (Taylor 1895).

Four principles of scientific management

Taylor proposed what he called "four great principles of management":

1. *Developing a science of work.* This would be achieved by observing and measuring norms of output, using a stopwatch, and detailed observation of human movements. On this basis, improvements could be made to the design of workstations and tools, which could improve effectiveness. Given improvements in effectiveness, pay would be improved.
2. *Scientifically selecting and training the employee.* Not just anybody could earn the higher rates of pay—they had to be people scientifically selected and trained. Taylor believed that everyone had different aptitudes—it was really a question of fitting the worker to the job, and this was the task of management. When management did this job properly, all human resources would be developed to their utmost potential.
3. *Combining the sciences of work and selecting and training of employees.* The workers would easily perceive the good sense of doing this, thought Taylor. They would benefit from higher wages. Resistance was more likely to come from managers—who also had to learn new systems of work and to give up privileges that they had, in Taylor's view, no right to.
4. *Management and workers must specialize and collaborate closely.* Management must focus on mental labor: on setting up systems, designing

them, and supervising them. Workers must concentrate on manual labor and leave the higher-order mental labor to the managers. If everyone keeps to one's assigned tasks, roles, and methods, then conflict in the workplace between management and workers will be eliminated, he thought. That is because science will show the one best way of doing things.

Taylor had a very limited view of science. He regarded it as equivalent to making systematic measurement and observation, after which work would be redesigned on the basis of the data generated and inferences made about existing procedures and how they might be improved. A famous example, which is discussed critically by Braverman (1974), was the example of the Dutch worker Schmidt and the art of shoveling pig iron. Taylor established that even a rather dumb worker, with a carefully designed tool, could increase productivity significantly, as long as whatever scientific management said should be done was done.

Management could be designed as a series of functions. These could actually be scientifically disaggregated and redefined so that different functional specialists would do different aspects of the task. Taylor was the founding father of work-study—fitting the person to the job and work design—and the pioneer of productivity-related pay systems, though few managers were prepared to accept this element of his system (they preferred the efficiency outcomes without the costs of wages designed to achieve them). His views have been subject to severe criticism. For instance, Braverman (1974) provides a highly critical perspective on Taylor that has been very influential in terms of rethinking the effects of Taylorism as profoundly exploitative and alienating (see also pp. 101–108).

Taylorism after Taylor: Sedimenting scientific management deep into organizations

Taylorism did not die with Taylor—it became sedimented deep inside organizations. His ideas became a part of the way that a great deal of routine process work was designed and measured in industry. Eventually, in such assembly plants, people would be replaced with robots, in which scientific management would find far better raw material—there were no sources of uncertainty in designing and calibrating pure machines rather than the person/machine interface. Of course, you don't have to go to a factory to find Taylorism. Check out the system for manufacturing fast food in any burger restaurant such as McDonald's (see also pp. 108–110).

Management and authority: Henri Fayol and systematic authority

Foundations of administrative science

It was another engineer, Henri Fayol, who is often regarded as the most significant European founder of modern management, because he provided a basis for systematic authority in the fledgling occupation. He published *Administration Industrielle et Generale* in 1916 (see Fayol 1949), in which he argued that better management is not merely concerned with improving output and disciplining subordinates but also must address the training of the people at the top.

Fayol was important for his stress on management training. Without training, it was too much to expect that either legitimacy or rationality would follow. The training should focus on preparing management to plan, organize, command, coordinate, and control for optimal performance. To outperform Taylor's idea of scientific management, presented in only four principles, the core of Fayol's training program offered fourteen principles to provide a manual for proper management, efficient organizations, and happy employees:

1. *Specialization of labor:* to encourage continuous improvement in skills and the development of improvements in methods
2. *Authority:* establishing the right to give orders and the power to exact obedience
3. *Discipline:* there was to be obedience
4. *Unity of command:* each employee was to have one and only one boss
5. *Unity of direction:* a single mind should generate a single plan
6. *Subordination of individual interests* to the interests of the organization
7. *Remuneration policy:* employees should receive fair payment for services
8. *Centralization:* consolidation of management functions so that decisions will be made from the top
9. *Scalar chain:* a clear line of authority and formal chain of command running from top to bottom of the organization, as in the military
10. *Order:* all materials and employees have a prescribed place, where they should be found
11. *Equity:* there should be a principle of fairness involved in the way that the organization treats employees
12. *Personnel tenure:* limited turnover of personnel was a good thing, and lifetime employment should be offered to good employees
13. *Initiative:* this requires designing a plan and doing what it takes to make it happen
14. *Esprit de corps:* there should be harmony and cohesion among organization members

Fayol was an especially important figure in the francophone world, as one might expect. In France, his ideas received endorsement from leading industrialists and politicians of the time. Although Fayol developed his work about the same time as the era of scientific management, it is a different approach, one that focuses on positions rather than people. It is noteworthy that Fayol worked for a mining company with substantial interests in Decazeville, a French locale with strong traditions of labor dissent and proletarian solidarity.

The relation of these traditions to Fayol's ideas is not discussed in the literature. Fayol was not translated into English until the 1940s, so his impact on American management was delayed.

Management and counseling: Elton Mayo's management of collaboration

Not all of the early management thinkers saw the solutions to problems of managing and organizing in terms of engineering. Rather, some theorists, such as Elton Mayo, saw engineering as a part of the problem rather than the solution. Following the rise (and fall) of his ideas helps us to understand some other foundations of management that are still at work today.

Collaboration, not conflict

Although the prosperous 1920s had seen modern corporate bureaucracies become legitimate, by the 1930s their legitimacy came into question as so many productive assets and people were rendered idle in the Depression era. How could organizations be efficient and legitimate, when they also caused so much unemployment and turmoil? Now the focus switched to a rationalization for management as an antidote for the presently troubled times. As Miller and O'Leary put it:

> The depression had pressed the rationality of individuals beyond its limits. Traditional institutions had crumbled in the course of industrialization, and new institutions had not emerged to maintain their disciplinary effects. Driven by their emotions, individuals had a proclivity to engage in socially destructive acts. They became unfit for cooperation. The catastrophic proportions of the depression stood as a pressing exemplar of that unfitness. (Miller and O'Leary 2002)

In the middle of this Depression, the Australian-born Elton Mayo entered the stage of management and organization theory as one of the most influential of the interwar and postwar theorists. Mayo did not arrive in the United States until he was forty-two; not surprisingly, many of his views about organizations and management had already been formed by the experience that he had in Australia, which he left in 1922, never to return. In Brisbane, where he was the first professor of social philosophy at the University of Queensland, he had been exposed to the militant traditions of the Australian labor movement, traditions formed in the great shearing strikes of the 1890s, hardened in the battle against conscription in World War I, and exemplified for Mayo by the rail strikes of 1917. His fundamental model of society was one of social integration rather than the conflict that he encountered at Trades Hall in Brisbane and in some of his Workers Educational Association students, especially those who were members of the International Workers of the World. Work for Mayo should not be the source of class conflict but the opposite:

> It must be possible for the individual to feel, as he works, that his work is socially necessary; he must be able to see beyond his group to the society. Failure in this respect will make disintegration inevitable. Social unity must be conscious unity, known and recognised by every group and individual; the alternative is disruption. The occupational aspect of social activity is, therefore, fundamental. (Mayo 1919: 37, cited in Bourke 1982: 220)

Mayo discussed his ideas with British anthropologists, notably Bronislaw Malinowski, and later, in the United States, he was to add explicit social science references to his ideas. But there was another ingredient born out of his early Australian experience that was decisive for his later work in the United States: He had been a medical student. He used ideas from contemporary psychology and psychiatry in an informal collaboration with a Brisbane physician in the aftermath of the Great War to develop therapeutic treatments for patients with shell shock and other "nervous" conditions. From the treatment of maladjustment on the part of veterans, it was a small step to the treatment of industrial malaises: "Industrial unrest is not caused by mere dissatisfaction with wages and working conditions but by the fact that a conscious dissatisfaction serves to 'light up' as it were the hidden fires of mental uncontrol" (Mayo 1922: 64, cited in Bourke 1982: 226). Treating conflict at work meant treating industrial neuroses. Most people's actions were driven by the unconscious, and this was as true of people at work as at war. Agitators and radicals were victims of neurotic fantasies that could be traced, invariably, to infantile history. If individuals could be guided by therapy in work, they would be healed of their agitational neuroses. When he arrived in the United States, he brought these ideas with him as a highly successful public speaker on the lecture circuit. He eventually found a congenial home at Harvard, where he was invited in 1926.

Human relations, not mechanic determination

At Harvard, Mayo became associated with what are known as the Hawthorne Studies. These studies have become a classic of modern management and were named thus because they were carried out in the Hawthorne Plant of the Western Electric organization in the suburbs of Chicago between 1924 and 1927. After the data had been collected and the experiments ended, he joined the project in April 1928 (Henderson and Mayo 2002). In a range of experiments concerning the physical determinants of productivity, illumination and other physical variables were manipulated, with the surprising result that productivity kept rising even when unexpected—when the illumination was lowered rather than increased. Why was this so? Eventually, the question was answered by Mayo in terms of what became known as the Hawthorne Effect:

When a group realizes that it is valued and forms social relations among its members, productivity rises as a result of the group formation. It was this finding for which the study became famous. The Hawthorne Effect is what happens when informal organization formation occurs. In this instance, it was presumed that the effect was an unanticipated consequence of the experimental interest taken in workers. Such formation will often be an unanticipated consequence of academic interest in people in organizational settings: Research may have unanticipated effects. (His experiments have been widely criticized. See Carey 2002 and O'Connor 2002 for the criticisms.)

Among the major presuppositions that Mayo brought to interpretation of the Hawthorne data were the following:

- Work should be seen as a group rather than individual activity.
- Work is a central life interest for most people.
- With Follett, he agreed that the lack of attention to human relationships was a major flaw in other management theories.
- In work, people find a sense of belonging to a social group and seek a need for recognition, satisfaction of which is vital for their productivity.
- When workers complain, it may be a manifestation of some more fundamental and psychologically located issue.
- Informal social groups at work have a profound influence on the worker's disposition and well-being.
- Management can foster collaboration within informal groups to create greater cohesion and unity at work, with positive organizational benefits.
- The workplace should be viewed as a social system made up of interdependent parts.

Many of Mayo's ideas addressed the failure of modern management to seriously consider social relations, social order, and the collaboration that sustained them as integral to modern enterprise. They were also developed in the context of his membership of the Pareto Circle. This was a group of scholars dedicated to disseminating and exploring the ideas of the Italian political economist/scientist Vilfredo Pareto, who, among many other things, was the originator of the famous Pareto Curve in economics. The group met at Harvard University, from 1926 onward (see Heyl 2002), where Mayo worked closely with the influential biologist L. J. Henderson and his ideas developed further during his wartime studies of absenteeism and labor turnover in war-related industries, especially aircraft plants in Southern California. He came to the conclusion that the real problems encountered in work were the lack of "well-knit human groups." Too much attention was being paid to technical relations at work and not enough to social relations, especially those that enable people to get on well and cooperate with others. More training in social skills is required. Organizational authority depends on individual members having a cooperative attitude, together with the organization having an effective system of communications to foster social skills (see also Chapter 9). Organizations should organize teams and use personnel interviews to aid members, as Mayo (1985) put it, to get "rid of useless emotional complications," "to associate more easily, more satisfactorily with other persons—fellow workers or supervisors—with whom he is in daily contact," and to develop in the worker a "desire and capacity to work better with management."

Mayo developed what became known as the Human Relations School. The emphasis of this approach was on informal work group relations, the importance of these for sustaining the formal system, and the necessity of the formal system meshing with the informal system. In the informal system, special attention was to be paid to the satisfaction of individual human needs, focusing on what motivates different people, in order to try to maximize their motivation and satisfaction. Mayo thought the manager had to be a social clinician, fostering the social skills of those with whom she or he worked. Workers who argued with their managers and supervisors were expressing deep-seated neuroses lodged in their childhood history. Therapeutic interviews were recommended as a management tool to create better adjusted workers, and training in counseling and personnel interviews was touted as an essential management skill. The advice was simple: Pay full attention to the intervie- wee and make it clear that this is the case; listen carefully to what they have to say; don't interrupt; don't contradict them; listen carefully for what is being said as well as any ellipses in terms of what is left unspoken; try to summarize carefully what has been said by the speaker as feedback for the interviewee; and treat what has been said in confidence (Trahair 2001).

Mayo emerged from his wartime studies strengthened in his belief in the importance of human relations theory. Together with other Harvard academics, he contributed to an emergent consensus around the centrality of notions of social order, conformism, and the necessity of building rational normative commitments. These became a key part of the Cold War consensus about the nature of American society. The central theme of his work was that the rushed implementation of new technologies gave rise to most of the problems experienced at work. These problems were seen as manifested psychologi- cally. Hence, it was not surprising if these workers founded unions, went on strike, became irrational, and endangered the social order with demands not for reform but radical change (Trahair 2001; see also Trahair 1984 for much more on Mayo). It was an agreeable message for many managers.

> What, after all, could be more appealing than to be told that subordinates are non- logical; that their uncooperativeness is a frustrated urge to collaborate; that their demands for cash mark a need for your approval [as a manager]; and that you have a historic destiny [as a manager] as a broker of social harmony? (Rose 1975: 124)

Mayo undoubtedly believed that the technical competencies of managers had to be buttressed by social competencies. People had to be shown how to collaborate in the new complex organizations, and management's task, par excellence, was to aid this. Managers were to be the new conciliators and arbitrators of an accord with rational workers. While the workers would draw

The managers would draw on the rationality of science.

on local rationalities, variants of cultures of solidarity rooted in family, church, and community experience, the managers would draw on the rationality of science. In Mayo's view, it would be a one-sided contest where the reason of management should be self-evident. Later researchers, however, were to see the traditional resources that the Hawthorne workers could draw on as strong and sustaining, quite able to provide a basis for resistance to the rationalization of Mayo's rationality (Hogan 1978; Weiss 1981).

Management and leadership: Chester Barnard and the functions of the executive

For Chester Barnard (1936), the key issue was leadership, of which he had considerable experience, having been the president of New Jersey Bell Telephone and the Rockefeller Foundation. Barnard communicated his ideas about leadership in a book that had a major impact, *The Functions of the Executive* (1936). In those situations where people do not have to obey but only choose to do so out of self-interest, then leadership is required, said Barnard, to ensure both managerial authority and employee obedience. He knew that people were frequently capable of being, from an executive's point of view, mistaken about what they took their interests to be. Leaders should make followers' self-interest apparent, and this interest should be service to authority. Leaders created moral codes for subordinates to live by; subordinates needed tutelage in strong moral values, which it was management's duty to provide.

Good management requires emotional work, and it is the task of the managerial elite to configure others as servants of responsible authority through guiding them, emotionally. That these managerial elites have achieved their position, and their organizations survived, is sufficient evidence of their fitness for leadership, maintained Barnard. His key principles, based on his own executive experience, were the following:

- Individual behavior was always variable and could never be easily predicted.
- All individuals will have a "zone of indifference" within which compliance with orders will be perceived in neutral terms without any questioning of authority. Managers should seek to extend the borders of this zone through material incentives but more especially through providing others with status, prestige, and personal power.
- Communications, especially in informal organization, are absolutely central to decision making. Everyone should know what the channels of communication are and should have access to formal channels of communications. Lines of communication should be as short and direct as possible.

- Management's responsibility is to harness informal groupings and get them working for the organization, not against it.
- Authority only exists insofar as the people are willing to accept it.

Barnard was the first really significant modern executive to write on management and organization. In that sense, he was the genesis of the "been there, done that, profited from the experience" type of text that executives are prone to write when they want to record how they did it "my way." From the vantage point of his experience, he saw the managers' key task as ensuring that organizational systems motivated employees toward organization goals—because where individuals worked with common values rather than common orders, they would work much more effectively. The real role of the manager, he wrote, is to manage the values of the organization, which should be set by the chief executive (see also Chapter 7).

Barnard proposed a moral role for management. He did so at a time when, in American society, its moral authority was not great. The Depression of the 1930s saw many millions of people unemployed, reduced to welfare and soup kitchens. If managers were such great leaders, how come they had gotten American firms into such a mess? Barnard's answer to this question was that those lucky enough to still have jobs should buckle down to the leadership of superior moral agents—their managers—for it was only the good judgment of these leaders that stood between them and the misery of unemployment.

CRITICAL ISSUES: MANAGEMENT AND SOCIAL JUSTICE—THE WORK OF MARY PARKER FOLLETT

Social responsibility and democracy

Taylor and Fayol were very much engineers, and the stamp of that discipline was evident in their thought. However, the management theory that began to develop during the 1920s saw management becoming professionalized as something separate from engineering. Optimism about management was widespread and captured in management texts, most notably by Mary Parker Follett (1918, 1924). Born into a wealthy and privileged Boston family, Follett was passionately committed to democratic ideals. After graduating from the Women's College at Harvard, she became involved in social work in a diverse Boston neighborhood. Follett never lost her commitment to democracy and local group organization, which she honed in her community work in Boston. What she learned in making community centers work for people lacking in the obvious resources of a wealthier society was that, with experience in "modes of living and acting which shall teach us how to grow the social consciousness" (Follett 1918: 363), many people were far more capable than they or others might have imagined. Follett sought to establish conditions in which management and workers cooperated together to achieve not only productivity but also social justice. She suggested that Taylor's ideas were incomplete. In particular, they had not been thought through for their democratic potential; Taylor's lone individuals, in a massive functional structure, under strict control, did not accord with American ideas of democracy. Something had to change in management thinking if this were to be the case. Mary Parker Follett signaled the changes. Her work still continues to excite contemporary interest (Boje and Rosile 2001; Calás and Smircich 1996; Fox 1968; O'Connor 1999, 2002).

Mary Parker Follett was the first woman to have had a book on management published, called *Dynamic Administration* (1941), albeit after her death. In this book, she argued that organizations, like communities, could be approached as local social systems involving networks of groups. Not for her the image of the all-knowing scientific engineer in control. Unlike scientific management, she believed in the full collaboration of employees and managers, and she sought their willingness to make these values compatible.

Central to Follett's worldview was the concept of power. Organizations organize power and they create power. She saw power as legitimate and inevitable. But because power is so central, it does not mean that it need be authoritarian. She was concerned to democratize power, distinguishing between power-with and power-over (or coercive power rather than coactive power). She argues that it is the former that needs developing and the latter that needs diminishing. Organizations must be developed democratically as places where people learn to be cooperative in power with others, especially managers and workers (see also pp. 184–186). In a democracy, Follett believed that people had to be able to exercise power themselves, at the grassroots level. Democratic diversity had great advantages, she said, over more authoritarian homogeneity. We should welcome difference because it feeds and enriches society, whereas differences that are ignored feed *on* society and eventually corrupt it (Follett 1918). Given democratic opportunities, she thought that people could make the most of their situation, even if they seemed relatively impoverished in their access to resources. Her view of democracy was that it should be participatory, because the experience of being participative was empowering and educative.

More modest than her male colleagues, she formulated her ideas in only three principles:

1. Functions are specific task areas within organizations, which should be allocated the appropriate degree of authority and responsibility necessary for task accomplishment.
2. Responsibility is expressed in terms of an empirical duty: People should manage their responsibility on the basis of evidence and should integrate this effectively with the functions of others.
3. Authority flows from an entitlement to exercise power, which is based upon legitimate authority.

Mary Parker Follett was a unique management academic. She saw that the central questions of organization revolved on questions of power, legitimacy, and authority in a way that few of her contemporaries did. She was also a woman, in a world of men, and a committed democrat in a world of macho managers. Notions of legitimate authority and civic responsibility were important to Follett's thinking. Thus, not surprisingly, when she turned her attention to organizations and management, she saw the concept of power as the essential basis for understanding business. She separated power from hierarchy, shunning the idea that some were born to rule and others to follow, which Taylor's ideas legitimated. She produced a rationale for authority distinct from Taylor's "scientific" approach. Management is a responsible discharge of necessary functions, not the privilege of elites, she maintained. Authority and responsibility derive from function, not privilege. Both politics and business require an understanding of how to produce collaborative action between different people integrated in a common enterprise rather than creating their mutually assured destruction through incivility and nondemocracy.

Rationality **and** civility

It seemed to Follett that Taylor's system of scientific management might have achieved rationality within the firm, but it had also eroded the civility within which employees were once bound in the quintessential small-scale communities of American democracy. Mass production and large scale were made possible through efficiency in the division of labor, but this division had gone too far. It had removed the social bonds that constrained individuals and now pitted them ruthlessly and relentlessly against each other in a highly competitive individualism. What was required was a reinstitution of civility, society, and fellowship in and through work and its organization if the corrosive effects of competitive individualism on the moral character of the American employee were to be halted. People needed to think not just of themselves and the individual benefit to be gained through competition at work but how they fitted into an overall pattern of functions, responsibilities, and authoritative entitlements to command and to obey.

The meaning of management?

Hard-fought and bitter battles were waged over the meaning of management as it first emerged. These were battles of the intellectual will, practical authority, and professional power. Despite Bentham's designs for architecture, bricks and mortar were never going to provide a flexible means of managing. Designing control into buildings is less economical than designing it around how people should do what they are asked to do. It was the emphasis on rules and appropriate ways of doing things that really offered hope for efficiency—not the buildings that activities were housed in so much as the design of the activities themselves. As a root metaphor for management, architecture was to prove much less useful than engineering. The roots of modern management were fed from engineering as a profession.

Although in the nineteenth century organizations were largely entre-preneurially founded, to far greater extent in the United States than elsewhere, by the twentieth century this was no longer the case. Deferring to the moral authority of the successful entrepreneur was no longer a plausible basis for legitimacy, when the relation between success and entrepreneurship had been so thoroughly uncoupled in the new corporate empires. Such uncoupling raised highly contentious issues for a liberal democracy. How were relations inside these corporate empires not to be simply capricious domination by the new robber barons? How could robber barons not be the new Lords of the Corporate Manor, with wage-slaves rather than serfs at their beck and call? In a country as fiercely and proudly democratic as the United States professed to be, this was an uncomfortable question ill at ease with the rhetoric of polit-ical democracy. How could a moral ethos pervade the relations of command and control in large public and private sector bureaucracies? The notion of political democracy became the normal basis for citizenship in advanced soci-eties in the twentieth century. Yet, at the same time that men and women were embracing political democracy and equal citizenship, they were being increas-ingly employed in large-scale organizations in which their basic civil rights as equals were routinely abrogated to claims of managerial prerogative and supe-rior authority. Follett dedicated her work to attempting to resolve these issues.

THE FINE PRINT: THE CHANGING
THEORY AND PRACTICE OF MANAGEMENT

The Depression of the 1930s and the widespread unemployment that ensued tested notions of managerial responsibility as mass layoffs became the norm in much of U.S. industry. It was at this time that the work of authors such as Chester Barnard and Elton Mayo rose to prominence. The post-World War I years had seen the decline of many of the huge corporations that had domi-nated U.S. economic life, particularly as effective antitrust legislation took shape from 1932. A concern with the concentration of power and the disper-sion of share ownership was to become allied with the view that there had been a "managerial revolution" in U.S. corporate life (Berle and Means 1932; Burnham 1942). Power had shifted to the stewards of capital—the managers—and the major concentrations of capital held by the dominant stockholders. But if there had been a managerial revolution, then where did that leave the many individuals who were not or never would be managers, those who toiled cease-lessly, at management's command? Fortunate indeed, argued Mayo and

Barnard, because modern management was the authority best able to hold society together, even in the face of overall macroeconomic irrationality. Within the rational organization, employees were sheltered against adversity, could rely on each other, and above all, rely on their managers to manage them in their best interests. Their organization was a closed haven in an uncertain world and so, not surprisingly, was conceived in what would later be seen as closed system terms. In such a system, it was in the self-interest of individuals to submit to authority as part of an implicit contract. Assent was conditional upon management being efficient and delivering benefits to the individuals and, as Mayo was at pains to stress, the groups that inhabited this anthropological space. Of course, people frequently were deluded about their interests, said Mayo and Barnard. It was the task of effective managerial leadership to align individual values, sentiments, and emotions with the organization, through providing moral codes and leadership, and Mayo argued that the recognition and support of informal groups and organizations within the formal structure were effective ways of achieving this. For responsibilities to be discharged, sentiments had to be engaged; the rationality of functions alone could not be relied on. Authority, similarly, was insufficient in itself; it had to be buttressed by moral leadership that could produce cooperation and collaboration within organizations.

In the Depression-torn 1930s, the legitimating and authoritative sentiments expressed by writers such as Mayo and Barnard were largely produced for domestic consumption. They were not to achieve large-scale export success until after World War II. With the exception of Fayol, the influential debates came from the United States and were exported globally, with variable market penetration. In Britain, the titled and wealthy defined rationality largely in terms of aristocratic rather than managerial values. Engineers were regarded as lowly individuals with dirty hands, and were thus hardly in a position to carry a societal project. Indeed, British engineers have been remarkably unsuccessful in attaining occupational status and power. The term *engineer* is stretched to refer both to professional engineers with formal qualifications as well as to people who use tools to do manual labor. In France or Germany, such a stretch would be unimaginable. Despite the early impact of approaches to industrial management (Littler 1982), managerialism was slow to become really established. (In fact, Prime Minister Thatcher was still railing against the complacent inefficiency of British management in the 1980s when she was promoting "efficiency in government," much as had Prime Minister Wilson in the 1960s when he was spreading the "white heat of the technological revolution.")

Elsewhere, in France, the interwar state, under Clemenceau, introduced some elements of technocratic rationalization from above, befitting both the elite status of engineering and Fayol's eminence in its application to management. In Germany, although America became increasingly an inspiration for engineers from the early years of the century, it was not until the rise of the National Socialist state that a management project premised on efficiency was widely adopted and diffused. In Italy, scientific management ideas were sponsored by notable industrialists, such as Gino Olivetti, in a counter-argument to ideas emergent from the workers' movement (Clegg and Dunkerley 1980: 110–111), and also became espoused by Mussolini's Fascist state—whose achievements, for many, were summed up in the idea that it "got the trains running on time."

In the aftermath of World War II, with the end of Fascism among the combatant countries and the bankruptcy of most of Europe, the overwhelming superiority of U.S. know-how and management were all too clear. The impact of U.S. institutions on postwar Europe through the Marshall Plan, and in Japan under postwar occupation, ensured a process of widespread dissemination of U.S. management and organization theory. In Europe business schools were created on explicitly American lines. Curricula were developed, and *Writers on Organizations* (Pugh, Hickson, and Hinings 1971) studied, most of whom were American, although a few who were not, such as the French Fayol or British Urwick, were admitted to the pantheon. Even in relatively underindustrialized countries, such as Australia, a national school of management was established in the late 1970s. American management had, by and large, become institutionalized as *the* template for modern management (see Locke 1984).

It is not a static model of American management that has been exported but one subject to dynamic change, with some suggestion that it has been subject to long-wave cyclical changes. It was an economist named Kondratieff (1935) who pioneered the idea of long-wave cycles. Although originally imported into the discussion of management by Harvie Ramsay (1977), these ideas have recently been taken up by U.S. theorists of management, such as Barley and Kunda (1992) and DeGreene (1988). The most recent and empirically sophisticated proponent of these is Eric Abrahamson (1997), who has coupled an account of long waves with an explanation as to why management theories and practices change.

Long-wave theory proposes that the world economy displays a rhythmical pattern, as rapid expansion and stagnation alternate with a periodicity of about fifty years. A single long wave is estimated to have about a fifty-year cycle through initial growth to decline. The causes of the seismic changes that long waves represent are seen as the result of massive investments in, and the subsequent depreciation of, major aspects of infrastructure such as canals, railways, and roads. Others follow Schumpeter (1934) and think that it is less the decline in infrastructure that is responsible and more the fact that clusters of innovation bunch together, creating new and discontinuous leading-edge sectors in the world economy, driving macroeconomic growth. Periodic "gales of creative destruction" wipe out preexisting innovations. Eventually, further innovation restarts the whole cycle around further discontinuous innovation bunches. Innovations precipitate system changes across firms, industries, and countries. New eras are ushered in by innovations like the steam engine, automobile, computer, and Internet.

Substantial economic restructuring and organizational redesign accompany each phase. The impact is variable across countries, industries, and organizations, and each of these adds their own level of indetermination to the picture, producing a highly contingent outcome. Each innovation-led system change, related to key factors, such as steel, oil, and electronics, crystallized new patterns of rational management in the upstream swing, according to Abrahamson (1997). The advent of mass production bureaucracy contingent upon the dawn of the automobile era would be one example. Today, the corollary would be the impact of the digital revolution that accompanied the growth and importance in computers and the emergence of new organizational forms (see also pp. 92–101). Thus, new rhetoric for management theory and practice emerges around the onset of each expansionary upswing of the long wave, a wave of economic activity that takes approximately twenty-five years to crest and twenty-five years to recede.

There are two types of management rhetoric that organize theory and practice, suggests Abrahamson (1997): rational and normative rhetoric. Rational rhetoric is associated with upswings and normative rhetoric with downswings. Rational rhetoric stresses technical aspects of work organization, whereas normative rhetoric stresses the orientations of the employees. Rational rhetoric stresses the formalization and rationalization of management and organizations, such as Taylor's (1911) scientific management. It uses engineering-type analogies and metaphors to make its rhetorical points, thinking of organizations as if they were machines. Although such thinking clearly characterized scientific management, it also marked the systems rationalism of the 1950s and 1960s, although now the mechanistic analogy was less with a machine and more with the organization as a type of cybernetic system. Normative rhetoric stresses that it is the orientation and attitude of employees that is most important. The stress is on the needs of the employees and their satisfaction in the firm, modeled as a community. Managers must meet employee needs (human relations) and simultaneously unleash their creative energies (corporate culture) (see Chapter 8). While the rational rhetoric is stronger in the upswing and the normative rhetoric is stronger in the downswing, neither is ever wholly dominant. They coexist with greater or lesser emphasis.

The writers we have dealt with in this chapter span a fifty-year long wave, from the early twentieth century when Taylor's ideas first gained currency. It was a rational innovation, the continuous production line, coupled with systematic scientific management, placing workers under the discipline of Fordism, which permitted successive gains in productivity. Economies of scale under mass production allowed the mental and physical injuries of work to be compensated for by the pleasures of consumption. It is easy to see that the upswing could be said to have ended with the Wall Street crash of 1929 and that the theory developed subsequent to this would be classified as being in the downstream and, according to the hypothesis, normative theory. Mayo clearly fits into this category. Thus, by the early 1940s, the paradigm of human relations had increasingly overlain scientific management in the United States, especially during World

War II. The human relations paradigm represented a set of images and means to complete the Taylorist dream, proposing rhetoric for inventing a new identity at work, allowing management to try to produce satisfied workers. Though ameliorative in many circumstances, this did not in itself provide the competitive efficiency required, despite the evidence of the Hawthorne Effect.

Why is a new rhetoric of management theory and practice innovated? Performance gaps open up when the targets that managers wish to meet, and their performance in meeting them, do not coincide—when the targets are out of reach. Consequently, managers become interested in rhetoric that holds the promise that they can bridge the gap. Should management or environmental changes narrow these gaps, then interest will shift to other rhetoric that seems better able to address other gaps that have been ignored or have opened up more recently. Also, as rational innovations recede in importance, then the pendulum swings toward normative innovations in the rhetoric of management theory and practice because they seem capable of squeezing better performance out of the rational technologies in use. Again, this seems plausible as an account of the change from scientific management to human relations, and Abrahamson (1997) would argue that it accounts for subsequent shifts in emphasis as well.

SUMMARY AND REVIEW

Persistent and central themes have organized this chapter. Bentham designed an early form of spatial control called the Panopticon, which became a model for asylums, prisons, and factories. Early management theorists were divided in their accounts of the nature of management rule and what it should be. Taylor, notably, was an authoritarian, and believed that management's right to rule could be established scientifically, whereas for Fayol it seemed indubitable that the more rational and enlightened should lead—and lead wisely with care. In management theory circles, the contributions of F. W. Taylor have been both overlauded as well as overdemonized (Braverman 1974), as David Stark (2002) argues. The Taylor system was simply one aspect of a widespread movement of systematization, articulated by engineers, that was afoot in late nineteenth- and early twentieth-century management, initially in the United States and then, in the post–World War I era, throughout Europe (Maier 1970), Japan (Littler 1982), and China (Morgan 2003), as well as elsewhere (Dunford 1988). Owners, managers, and employees alike frequently resisted, and it was by no means a smooth path to a more rational future, as Taylor hoped. However, Taylor delivered the template for both a systematic practice of management based on universal principles and management science. Disguised, refined, and altered, his ideas are at work in many contemporary approaches.

Mayo's human relations school contributed significantly to the development of management and organization theory. It manifests itself today in initiatives such as the "learning organization" (see also pp. 349–354), and "empowerment" (see also pp. 170–174). Although this type of theory focuses on the soft, human side of business, it is often seen as the oil that is necessary to run smoothly the machine that Taylor designed. Follett and Mayo disagreed markedly with Taylor. Follett was much more of a democrat than Mayo, however. Mayo drew on his early experiences in Australia of a radicalized labor movement to point to the necessity of social integration and collaboration to overcome what he saw as the irrationality, the hatreds, and the futility of class struggle. Follett's experiences were more positive. She had seen at a community level what could be achieved by education, grassroots action, and social networks, and believed that these could deliver similar results in business. Until her revival with the publication of Graham's (1995) edited volume *Mary Parker Follett—Prophet of Management: A Celebration of Writings from the 1920s,* she was largely ignored, although there are signs that her unique contribution and connection to current issues is being recognized (Boje and Rosile 2001). Mayo's star faded similarly, although there was some critical interest in the 1970s and 1980s (Clegg 1979; Clegg and Dunkerley 1980), and a renewed appreciation of his importance for contemporary human resource management in the work of writers such as O'Connor (1999, 2002).

The account of the early years of U.S. management thought that has been sketched here owes a great deal to the work of Miller and O'Leary (2002) and Shenhav (1999), as well as Abrahamson (1997). It stresses the interconnection between the larger canvas of changing political concerns and economy with the innovations that were registered in management thinking. The relationship between management theories and the society that nourished them was open, such that, as the broader political culture changed, ideas about management changed in consequence. We doubt that the relations were quite as deterministic as Abrahamson portrays them, but there is no doubt they were linked. Often management ideas are presented in the literature as if they were something abstracted, similar to physics, something for which the social context in which they were developed is largely irrelevant, merely a context from which translation anywhere can flow effortlessly. It should be apparent that this is not the case. Ideas about social arrangements—and management and organizations are undoubtedly social arrangements—are always highly bounded by the contexts in which these ideas were developed.

ONE MORE TIME . . .

Getting the story straight

- What was Bentham's unique contribution to management?
- What was innovative about Taylor's scientific management?
- What did Fayol add to scientific management?

- According to Follett, what were the unanticipated consequences of highly rational (scientific) management practices?
- What aspects of management and organization did Mayo highlight?
- How did Barnard conceptualize leadership?

Thinking outside the box

- How did its changing environment shape management thinking?
- To what extent is management mostly an American invention? If its knowledge is context-dependent, that is, it sprang from American soil, what is likely to happen when it is exported?

ADDITIONAL RESOURCES

1. The classic crammer on *Writers on Organizations,* edited by Derek Pugh and David Hickson (1997, although it has been in print in various editions for over thirty years), should be a staple resource for all introductory students. It provides thumbnail sketches of the life, times, and ideas of many of the key thinkers of management and covers almost all of those addressed here, plus plenty who were not.

2. Although very detailed, the book by Yehouda Shenhav (1999), *Manufacturing Rationality: The Engineering Foundations of the Managerial Revolution,* is an excellent analysis of the engineering auspices of so many influential ideas and people in the early career of modern management.

3. As Boje and Rosile (2001) argue, Follett was the first advocate of situational models of leadership and cooperation—models that avoided general theories and approaches in favor of those that were contextually sensitive, that appreciated the detail of the situation that they were to be applied in. Other appreciations by distinguished management academics of Mary Parker Follett can be found in work such as *Prophet of Management: A Celebration of Writings from the 1920s,* which Pauline Graham (1995) edited, including commentary by Peter Drucker, Rosabeth Moss Kanter, and Henry Mintzberg, among others.

4. In his book *Recreating Strategy,* Stephen Cummings (2002: 79–131) "deconstructs" management's history, and it is well worth reading for those who want to gain some idea of how the modern idea of management was socially constructed.

5. An earlier account by one of the present authors was published as *Organization, Class and Control* (Clegg and Dunkerley 1980), and it contains detailed accounts of some other founding fathers of early management, of a more sociological bent, who have been omitted here.

6. We would recommend also the account by Peter Miller and Ted O'Leary (2002: 1989) of "Hierarchies and American Ideals, 1900–1940," from which we have drawn to frame this chapter.

7. In films, there are plenty of examples of satire of various aspects of management, from Charles Chaplin's 1936 *Modern Times,* with its critique of the moving production line and associated efficiencies, through the 1948 John Farrow film *The Big Clock,* which is savage in its depiction of how one man's megalomania finds expression through a ruthless and amoral concern with efficiency centered on mastery of time.

8. In more contemporary films, science fiction classics such as the 1982 *Blade Runner* (there is a director's cut from 1992 as well) and the 1997 *Gattaca,* provide a bleak view of a future where modern management has become institutionalized as wholly corporate and in control, able to fit the person to the job almost perfectly, such that life outside its requirements can only be nasty, bleak, and poor. Both movies show the dark side of meritocracy wed to bureaucracy and science.

In addition to these suggested additional resources, don't forget to look at what is also available on the Web site **www.ckmanagement.net,** including free PDF files of recent papers related to this chapter, which you can download; video interviews with famous academics talking about related themes; as well as many other resources, such as connections to interesting Web sites.

CHAPTER 2

MANAGING RATIONALITIES

Modernity, Postmodernity, Embeddedness

Objectives and learning outcomes

By the end of this chapter, you will be able to

- Understand the contributions of Max Weber to management thought

- Appreciate how Weber's ideas have been influential for much subsequent debate

- Be able to see that there are different forms of rationality

- Discuss rationalities from institutional theory and postmodern approaches

- Understand how and why management action is embedded

Before you get started . . .

Remember that rationality is like a lamppost to a drunken man—more for leaning on than illumination.

OUTLINE OF THE CHAPTER

As we have seen in the previous chapter, management theories were first formed around 1900. Although Taylor, Mayo, and the other thinkers we have surveyed got the credit for opening up inquiry into management and organizations, Max Weber, a German scholar active in the late nineteenth and early twentieth centuries, was easily a more significant thinker. Weber's work was part of a broad comparative inquiry into human civilization. He was the first to focus on the totality of the organizational forms that were becoming significant when he wrote—the model for which was bureaucracy. Bureaucratic organization, seen at the turn of the nineteenth century as the hallmark of modern organization, depended above all else on the application of what Weber termed "rational" means for the achievement of specific ends. Techniques would be most rational where they were designed purely from the point of view of fitness for purpose: The better they fit their purpose, the more rational they were. However, the stress on rationality symptomatic of Taylor and the engineers was analyzed critically by Weber. His interest was in the link between rationality, rules, and their social impact, which we illuminate in more detail in this chapter.

SETTING THE SCENE

Although Weber wrote on bureaucracy in the first twenty years of the twentieth century, he was not much read by anglophone management theorists until after World War II, when his works were widely translated into English. Weber wrote on rationality at roughly the same time as Taylor, yet his contributions were unheralded in English at that time. He was familiar with the work of Taylor and other scientific management writers, but they were not familiar with him, although their conceptions of rationality were clearly related. However, Weber's conceptions of rationality were not purely instrumental. Relating a set of means as mechanisms to achieve a given end was certainly one version of rationality, but Weber recognized it as only one of a number of ways of being rational. Although Weber believed that instrumental means–end rationality would become dominant, he did not believe that it would be the only basis for rationality.

Weber (1976, 1978) focused also on the substantive effects of instrumental rationality, which the writers on management did not. For instance, at the end of his study of *The Protestant Ethic and the Spirit of Capitalism* (1976), he noted that, although it would be instrumentally rational to consume resources till the last ton of fossil fuel was exhausted, such industry would be something only a fool bent on environmental folly would do. In substantive or real terms, this kind of rationality was idiocy.

As management thinking developed, its notion of rationality became much more complex. Decision making, rather than being a simple matter of rational calculation, was seen to be something marked by incomplete knowledge, irrational preferences, limited search, and a disposition to accept satisfactory rather than maximally utilitarian and efficient outcomes. The context within which the process of making decisions occurred became likened to a garbage can. Various solutions were tossed into the garbage with other trash; there they attached themselves to those problems that they had an affinity for, like a ripe banana skin spreading and oozing onto yesterday's used tissues. The tissues' absorptive capacity becomes the solution to the problem of the ooze.

What counts as a solution and what is reckoned to be a problem is culturally contingent. For instance, in the United States, a president who enjoyed the brief attentions of a female intern risked the rationality of his presidency. Other achievements were consumed by the garbage that attached to the statement "I did not have sexual relations with that woman." In France they do things differently. When President Mitterrand died, what the whole political and journalistic establishment had known for years became news: that the President maintained a mistress as well as a wife, and had fathered a daughter with her. In the United States, a small indiscretion and a big mouth spelled heaps of trouble; in France, the trash was not exposed but left in the garbage can of a private life.

To insist on a singular rationality, a rationality ensured by science, a single story, proves to be an exemplification of modern rationality, espoused by modern management. Postmoderns do it differently. They accept a plurality of plausible stories; entertain the possibility of different rationalities for different people—different strokes for different folks, as the old adage has it.

In the early foundations of modern management, these insights were articulated clearly by Weber. He realized that different interests in modern organizations would have different conceptions of what comprised rationality. Postmodern managers need to be able to understand these different rationalities and manage them accordingly. In this respect, they can learn much from stories of humble folk—simple bread makers—presented later in this chapter.

CENTRAL APPROACHES AND MAIN THEORIES

Bureaucracy

Bureaucracy was important for Weber because it seemed to be the repository of a powerful kind of formal rationality. The rationality in question was

Australia has government of the people by the departments for the cabinet. Its political philosophy is to keep the water on and the foreigners off, at the same time ensuring that the economic confusion is shared as democratically as possible. Although the woolsack in the House of Lords is symbolically stuffed with top grade merino, many believe it should be more appropriately stuffed in the Statue of Liberty.

Image 2.1   *Bruce Petty's view of authority*

constituted in the formal rules of the bureaucracy. When we think of bureaucracy, we often think of red tape strangling individualism or the individual being stamped on by some superior authority that they have to obey. To be labeled a bureaucrat is about as strong an insult as an entrepreneurially minded manager can throw at a contemporary. Bureaucrats are the type of people who say, "I'm from the government and I'm here to help you"—something no red-blooded entrepreneur is supposed to find believable. Bruce Petty, an Australian cartoonist, captures the popular sense of bureaucracy wittily in the drawing in Image 2.1.

Although the rubber stamp is often the symbol of authority, despite this popular perception, bureaucracy has not always been regarded so negatively.

The career of bureaucracy

Bureaucracy as a concept has had an interesting career. It begins in France in the eighteenth century by compounding the French word for an office—a *bureau*—with the Greek word for rule. By the nineteenth century, Germany provided the clearest examples of its success. The German state constructed by its first chancellor, Bismarck, was a model bureaucracy in both its armed forces and civil administration. The origins of the modern German state were innovations pioneered in Prussia, the heart of modern Germany. Weber realized that the creation of the modern state of Germany had only been possible because of the development of a disciplined state bureaucracy and standing army—inventions that became the envy of Europe. In the military, nothing exhibited bureaucratic discipline better than goose-stepping, which the Prussians invented in the seventeenth century. The body language of goose-stepping transmitted a clear set of messages. For the generals, it demonstrated the absolute obedience of their recruits to orders, no matter how painful or ludicrous these might be. For civilians, the message was that when men were drilled as if they were a collective machine that would ruthlessly crush insubordination and eliminate individualism, a formidable apparatus was created (Davies 1998). Not surprisingly, as modern industrial organizations emerged in Germany in the late years of the century, they incorporated some of the forms of rule whose success was everywhere around them. Although the workers did not goose-step into the factory, they were drilled in obedience to rules.

By the twentieth century, economic ascendancy passed to the United States, especially in the wake of World War I. Corporations increasingly came to be taken as the model of modern management. Increasingly, they too developed bureaucratic forms as a superstructure on the rationalized basis produced by systems such as that of Taylor (see also pp. 18–22). It was these rational superstructures that triggered Max Weber's prolific research inquiries into the nature of rationality, rules, and bureaucracy.

Authority and rules

At the core of Weber's (1978) conception of organization as bureaucracy was the notion that members of an organization adhere to the rules of that organization. He contrasted three types of authority, based upon the rule of *charisma*, the rule of *tradition*, and the rule of *rational, legal precepts*.

Three sources of authority

Thus, there were three major bases of authority, thought Weber:

1. *Charismatic authority* means that deference and obedience will be given because of the extraordinary attractiveness and power of the person. The person is owed homage because of his or her capacity to project personal magnetism, grace, and bearing. For instance, management gurus such as Jack Welch, politicians such as Nelson Mandela, or popular characters such as Princess Diana have all been seen as charismatic authorities. People follow them because of what they believe to be the special nature of their personalities and the success they have achieved.

Image 2.2   *Max Weber*

2. *Traditional authority* occurs where deference and obedience are owed because of the bloodline. The title held is owed homage because the person who holds it does so by birthright—they are in that position by right of birth. Prince Charles, for instance, is not so much an authority because of his charisma but because of tradition: As oldest son of the queen, he is the future king of England.

3. *Rational-legal authority* signifies that deference and obedience are owed not to the person or the title they hold but to the role they fill. It is not the officer but the office that is owed homage because it is a part of a rational and recognized disposition of relationships in a structure of offices. Examples are easy to find—just think of passport control or police. They are authorities although you don't know the people acting in the roles. The people who are actually acting are secondary; what is important is the office they represent.

Rational organizations

The third source of authority, based on rational-legal precepts, is exactly what Weber identified as the heart of bureaucratic organizations. People obey orders rationally because they believe that the person giving the order is acting in accordance with a code of legal rules and regulations (Albrow 1970: 43). Members of the organization obey its rules as general principles that can be applied to particular cases and which apply to those exercising authority as much as those who must obey the rules. People do not obey the rules because of traditional deference or submission to charismatic authority; they do not obey the person but the office holder. Members of the organization "bracket" the personal characteristics of the office holder and respond purely to the demands of office. Whether you like the office holder or not is supposed to be unimportant. Police officers may be disagreeable personally, but they hold an office that enables them to do what they do, within the letter of the law. The rule of law is the technical basis of their ability to take appropriate action, in terms of the definitions laid down in law. Weber's view of bureaucracy was as an instrument or tool of unrivaled technical superiority. He wrote that "[p]recision, speed and unambiguity, knowledge of the files, continuity, discretion, unity, strict subordination, reduction of friction, and of material and personal cost. These are raised to the optimum point in the strictly bureaucratic administration" (Weber, 1948: 214). Bureaucracy was a rational machine.

Weber saw modern bureaucratic organizations as resting on a number of "rational" foundations. These include the existence of a "formally free" labor force; the appropriation and concentration of the physical means of production as disposable private property; the representation of share rights in

Image 2.3   *Rational machines?*

organizations and property ownership; and the "rationalization" of various institutional areas such as the market, technology, and the law.

The outcome of this process of rationalization, Weber suggests, is the production of a new type of person: the specialist or technical expert. Such experts master reality by means of increasingly precise and abstract concepts. Statistics, for example, began in the nineteenth century as a form of expert codified knowledge of everyday life and death, which could inform public policy. The statistician became a paradigm of the new kind of expert, dealing with everyday things but in a way that was far removed from everyday understandings. Weber sometimes referred to the results of this process as disenchantment, meaning the process whereby all forms of magical, mystical, traditional explanation is stripped away from the world. The world stripped bare by rational analysis is always open and amenable to the calculations of technical reason. It holds no mystery. New disciplines colonize it (Clegg 1995).

Rationality and values

Although things may be done in formally rational ways, they may also be done for substantively rational reasons. Substantive rationality refers to the reasons for rational action—its substance, its meaningfulness and value. These matters "cannot be measured in terms of formal calculation alone, but also involve a relation to the absolute values or to the content of the particular ends to which it is oriented" (Weber 1947: 185). For instance, the "absolute values" that initially sanctified capitalist activity were the religious values of Calvinism, especially the stress on "this-worldly" asceticism: the renunciation of luxury and pleasure for a simple, disciplined, and ordered life dedicated to the glory of the Calvinist God—a stern taskmaster (Weber 1976). Indirectly, suggested Weber (1976), these beliefs were responsible for the rise of early capitalism. Early Calvinists sought religious meaning in a sober and disciplined approach to life—especially in their work—rather than in Catholic religious rituals, ceremonies, and saints' days. The application of sobriety and discipline meant that they were often successful in creating a profit. However, earning profits provoked a moral quandary: What to do with the profits made? If they gave it to the poor, in charity, they would be encouraging idle hands, the devil's work. If they spent it on fine living, they would be damning themselves. If they could not maintain their life as a preserve of strict discipline, order, and sobriety, how could they be worthy of the Spirit of God that they ached to know moved through them? In fact, they had little choice. Luxurious consumption—the equivalents of sex, drugs, and rock 'n' roll—was clearly out of the question, as was the encouragement of idleness in others. Work was what they did best; it was what gave their life meaning, because their dedication and discipline in all things demonstrated their evident fitness to be servants of God. Hence, the least censorious and most religiously faithful thing that they could do was to invest any profit or surplus back into their life's work—into the business—in order to demonstrate their piety and readiness to be one of the elect who would join the heavenly host on judgment day.

Weber believed that ultimate values would be in inexorable decline with the development of modernity, which he defined in terms of an increasing rationalization of the world and a concomitant decline in beliefs in enchantment, magic, and fatalism. In large part this would be because the "calculability" contained in the formal rationality of the disciplines that the Puritans embraced—such as double-entry bookkeeping—would progressively replace the role of values with that of technique. As techniques increasingly achieved what previously only great value commitments could ensure, then the necessity for these values would diminish. Value-based belief systems no longer sustained the technical rationality of contemporary life. Above all, Weber believed that this technical rationality would find expression in bureaucratic organization—a form of organization that would increasingly require no meaning or ultimate values beyond those of its necessity as a ceaseless round:

> Since asceticism undertook to remodel the world and to work out its ideals in the world, material goods have gained an increasing and finally an inexorable power over the lives of men [*sic*] as at no previous period in history. Today the spirit of religious asceticism—whether finally, who knows?—has escaped from the cage. But victorious capitalism, since it rests on mechanical foundations, needs its support no longer. . . . [T]he idea of duty in one's calling prowls about in our lives like the ghost of dead religious beliefs." (Weber 1976: 181–182)

Weber wrote these words at the dawn of the twentieth century, foreseeing a future in which we would strive ceaselessly in jobs and organizations that held no charm for us. Their lack of charm was denoted by the fact that they served no ultimate values but were merely machines for processing people and things in which the formal rationality of existence would be all we had to hold on to. In such a world no ultimate values would guide or anchor us; there would just be a future of unending activity in the service of prosaic, utilitarian ends—such as making money, processing data, or applying rules. Interestingly, today many people are turning their backs on these kinds of work and organizations, making more space for themselves and their families in their lives, perhaps embracing new nonmaterialist values, such as those of the green movement, and trying to apply these in their working lives—the growth of the concern with "sustainability," for instance (see Dunphy, Griffiths, Beneviste, and Sutton (2000).

Bureaucracy

Bureaucracy is an organizational form consisting of differentiated knowledges and many different forms of expertise, with their rules and disciplines arranged not only hierarchically in regard to each other but also in parallel. If you moved through one track, in theory, you need not know anything about how things were done in the other tracks. Whether the bureaucracy was a public or private sector organization would be largely immaterial. Private ownership might enable you to control the revenue stream, but day-to-day control would, however, be done through the intermediation of experts. And expertise is always fragmented.

The notion of a career is essential to the practice of bureaucracy, but progression through the ranks could never bring you close to overall mastery. There is differentiation of both expertise and careers.

At the heart of bureaucracy's moral purpose is a belief in the legitimacy of its protocols, its personnel, and its policies. Given these beliefs, and serving to reproduce them, there exists a specific form of administration and organization, which Weber defined in terms of fifteen major characteristics.

Max Weber's fifteen dimensions of bureaucracy

1. Power belongs to an office and is not a function of the office holder.
2. Power relations within the organization structure have a distinct authority configuration, specified by the rules of the organization.
3. Because powers are exercised in terms of the rules of office rather than the person, organizational action is impersonal.
4. Disciplinary systems of knowledge, either professionally or organizationally formulated, rather than idiosyncratic beliefs, frame organizational action.
5. The rules tend to be formally codified.
6. These rules are contained in files of written documents that, based on precedent and abstract rule, serve as standards for organizational action.
7. These rules specify tasks that are specific, distinct, and done by different formal categories of personnel who specialize in these tasks and not in others. These official tasks would be organized on a continuous regulated basis in order to ensure the smooth flow of work between the discontinuous elements in its organization. Thus, there is a tendency toward specialization.
8. There is a sharp boundary between what is bureaucratic action and what is particularistic action by personnel, defining the limits of legitimacy.
9. The functional separation of tasks means that personnel must have authority and sanction available to them commensurate with their duties. Thus, organizations exhibit an authority structure.
10. Because tasks are functionally separated, and because the personnel charged with each function have precisely delegated powers, there is a tendency toward hierarchy.
11. The delegation of powers is expressed in terms of duties, rights, obligations, and responsibilities. Thus, organizational relationships tend to have a precise contract basis.

12. Qualities required for organization positions are increasingly measured in terms of formal credentials.

13. Because different positions in the hierarchy of offices require different credentials for admission, there is a career structure in which promotion is possible either by seniority or by merit of service by individuals with similar credentials.

14. Different positions in the hierarchy are differentially paid and otherwise stratified.

15. Communication, coordination, and control are centralized in the organization.

Institutionalizing rationalities

There are a limited number of explanations as to why so many organizations adopted the bureaucratic form. One explanation would stress biological necessity: It might be genetic to create and order life according to hierarchies, and thus unavoidable: something imprinted in the species way of doing things. Another explanation might stress efficiency: It might be functional, simply the one best way to organize large-scale activities under uncertain conditions. Finally, it might be that bureaucracy has become conventional, that we find it normal to mimic the bureaucratic form because it has become so widely institutionalized. The reasons for its institutionalization (that it was associated with actions widely admired) have faded with time, such that it now seems natural, normal, and necessary. The last argument is now widely accepted and is known as institutional theory.

Much modern institutional theory was developed from Berger and Luckmann's (1967) adaptation of some elements of Weber's social action approach into a generic "social constructionist" perspective. Reality, they say, is socially constructed. This sounds more confusing than it actually is. Just think of yourself as a student, enrolled in a first-year subject called Management. As a student, you are assigned a number, and then you have to enroll. The process of enrolling in a subject means choosing a code, standing in line on a particular day between 8 A.M. and 12 noon, then attending classes on a regular basis, passing assignments, until you either accumulate enough credits to graduate or pass final exams. You will not do these things just as you please but through skillful work in constructing answers to questions that are acceptably "academic." You must construct an academic persona and reality. All these things shape your reality as a student, but none of them are facts of nature—they do not have to be designed the way they actually are. At a certain point in history, universities simply decided to organize higher education in such a way. Thus, much of what we take for granted as reality is, in fact, socially constructed.

Institutional theorists puzzle about why, for instance, almost all public sector organizations in the Western world apply such similar models. To put it a bit more abstractly, what is at issue is the process by which actions are repeated and given similar meaning by oneself and others, which they define as institutionalization. Meyer and Rowan (2002) argued that modern societies consist of many institutionalized rules, providing a framework for the creation and elaboration of formal organizations. Many of these rules are rationalized myths that are widely believed but rarely if ever tested. They originate and are sustained through public opinion, the educational system, laws, or other institutional forms. Thus, many of the factors shaping management and organization are not based on efficiency or effectiveness but on social and cultural pressures to conform to already legitimated practices. For instance, there is a lot of pressure on organizations to adapt to new tools invented by fashionable management gurus. Buzzwords such as TQM, Kaizen, BPR, and so on are by no means proven to lead to success but are concepts that challenge organizations, since, if they don't apply them (and pay large fees to not always so great consultants who are implementing them), they are seen as inert, reactive, and increasingly anachronistic. Institutional theory analyzes the impact of this pressure on organizations and management decisions.

Isomorphism

A leading example of the institutional focus is the work of DiMaggio and Powell (2002), who explain why organizations adopt similar forms and practices. They termed this process of copying "isomorphism"; the effect of institutional pressures is to constrain an organization's choice of structures to a set of arrangements that are acceptable within its field. There are three main mechanisms of transmission of isomorphism: normative, coercive, and mimetic forms. Phenomena can become widespread because they are regarded as culturally positive norms, such as teamwork. Not meeting the expectations of what is regarded as a culturally positive norm would be regarded as either stupid or deviant. Where the adoption of norms is forced by powerful agencies, such as the state, this is coercive isomorphism, which we associate with legal requirements. As an example, think why it is the case that all commercial airplanes have the same little speech and demonstration of safety features before you take off (including pointing out a whistle with which to attract attention in the unlikely event of an accident!). Because international aviation law says they must do so, because they are in breach of the law if they do not perform the ritual, they do it so as to be seen to observe the law. The state coercively shapes institutions by enforcing certain forms of legislation. For instance, in most advanced societies, there are usually legal rules outlawing discrimination on various grounds that mandate organizations to collect data and present profiles of their activities. They do so to show the ways the organizations are in accord with these laws. Hence, organizations develop an equal employment opportunity officer and programs—not necessarily because they want to or they think it is a good idea to do so but because they are obliged, by law, to do so.

Sometimes organizations and their managers desire, consciously, to be similar to a particularly highly regarded exemplar, and when they copy it in this way, it is a case of mimetic isomorphism. In this type of action, something is regarded as so normatively attractive that it is desired to be like it because being similar easily defines what is proper, correct, and legitimate. Think of the prestige of a business school such as Harvard, whose approach is admired around the world. Or ask yourself the question, Why do all nation-states have a flag, an anthem, and a head of state? Anderson (1982) answers this question in terms of institutional theory by providing a fascinating account of the spread of the idea of the nation-state as an organizational form, with its appropriate modes of style, dress, and address, almost everywhere during the nineteenth century. The idea of the state continued to shape post-colonial policy after World War II when decolonizing territories were imagined into existence as if they were nation-states, whereas, often, there was precious little in the way of precedents to suggest that they ever had been. The legitimacy of the nation-state as the appropriate organizational form—even for tiny territories with a few thousand people or vast tracts of land containing tribal and linguistically distinct, defined groups—was so overwhelming that no other organizational form could be considered. Once produced, the state becomes subject to the normal pressures of economic growth and recession, demographic changes, civil war, policies of structural adjustment, and struggles to control it. Sometimes the state in question succeeds by surviving these struggles. For instance, if we think about the long period from the U.S. Civil War to the civil rights struggles of the post-1960s, it is clear that although there have been major struggles to control and use the state for different and contradictory purposes, through it all something that is recognizable as the state of the United States has survived intact. Sometimes states fail, as was the case in Rwanda and the neighboring Great Lakes Region of Africa during its postcolonial history, most notably in the 1990s (Jefremovas 2002). What is interesting is that the failing state is never held as the normative model. When states fail, rather than weakening the normative ideal, they strengthen it: that is how "normative isomorphism" works—as an ideal metric. Failing the isomorphic test simply becomes further fuel for endorsing the normative model more strongly.

Mimetic isomorphism is demonstrated when a particular organizational practice, such as professors and teachers dressing up in academic gowns and making a procession as a part of the ceremony of awarding a degree to new graduates, becomes widely diffused because people identify it as a central part of an institution. We know of no university that has dispensed with this ceremony for, as vice chancellors have frequently been known to remark, such a ceremony is symbolically representative of the university. So the ritual is widely adopted and diffused even in the newest universities. Stewart, coauthor of this book, once worked somewhere in which many of the students who did the MBA were from overseas countries. Often, they had returned home prior to being awarded their degrees in order to return to careers and families and friends. Hence, they missed the ceremony and its photo opportunities, but nonetheless they clamored for an opportunity to gain these mementos. The problem was that they did not want to have the expense of flying back to Australia from India or China, for instance, to get their pictures taken. Consequently, the university instituted a predegree ceremony, where a senior university dignitary would speak some formal words, during which the students would be told that this was not a degree ceremony, and then hand them something that was not a degree certificate but looked just like one. The students wore gowns that they were not yet entitled to wear—as they had not graduated—but the all-important pictures could be taken "proving" that they had been at the university and had been "awarded" their "degree." The pictures proved it! Thus, in this way their social reality was constructed. They had the pictures to prove they were graduates of, and belonged to, a specific university, with its appropriate ceremonies, rituals, and photo opportunities, even though none of it had really happened.

Postmodern rationalities

For early modern management theorists such as Fayol (1949: 181), "the soundness and good working order of the body corporate depend on a certain number of conditions termed indiscriminately, principles, laws, rules." Such principles relate to that unity of direction and command centrally exercised by (top) management. These principles, says Fayol, belong "to the natural order; this turns on the fact that in every organism, animal or social, sensations converge towards the brain or directive part, and from the brain or directive part orders are sent out which set parts of the organism in movement" (Fayol 1949: 193). Fayol clearly makes an argument by genetic extension; the organization is a giant organism, similar to the human body writ large, in which some people will have the function of "brain" and others the function of "hands." These ordinary members of the organization are conceived as if they were a body of limbs and organs controlled and directed by the managerial brain. In practice, however, such metaphor-laden language becomes troublingly literal, as, for example, when a desperate Henry Ford once asked why he always got stuck with the whole person rather than with just a pair of hands. Hands were what he hired, but troublesome bodies with querulous minds were what he so often got (see also pp. 373–374). The metaphorical body corporate easily reduces to the literal body of the worker who will only be regarded as exemplary if he or she behaves as a puppet to the commands issued through the managerial pulling of strings.

> **A desperate Henry Ford once asked why he always got stuck with the whole person rather than with just a pair of hands.**

Image 2.4   *Hands or brain at work?*

Decision making

Theorists like Fayol and industrialists such as Henry Ford were not singularly unusual in their stress on the well-oiled worker. Their sentiments were shared by that father of modern management, Frederick Winslow Taylor, when he insisted that "all of the planning which under the old system was done by the workman, as a result of his personal experience, must out of necessity under the new system be done by management" (Taylor 1911/1967: 38). Here, decision making is taken to be the domain of the superior intellect of the manager such that he (usually) can deploy a scientific rationality in order to find the one best way proposed by Taylor's approach. Management makes decisions in such a way that the managerial brain, in a mixed metaphor, is both at the center and the top of the organization. As Taylor (1911/1967: 59) wrote of one of his favorite workers:

> Now one of the very first requirements for a man who is fit to handle pig iron as a regular occupation is that he shall be so stupid and so phlegmatic that he more nearly resembles in his mental make-up the ox than any other type. . . . [T]he work-man who is best suited to handling pig iron is unable to understand the real science of doing this class of work. He is so stupid that the word "percentage" has no meaning to him, and he must consequently be trained by a man more intelligent than himself into the habit of working in accordance with the laws of this science before he can be successful.

Indeed, by defining workers as brainless and unthinking hands following orders determined elsewhere, the notion of decision making became both elitist *and* rational. Rational in that it must lead to optimum decisions because it is based, in every sense of the word, on *superior* intelligence, and rational also in that it applies *scientific method,* "the hallmark of superior intelligence, in order to result in the optimal achievement of desired organizational ends." Summarizing, this concept of management can be illustrated with the image of organizations as hierarchies: The more or less inert body (the structure) of the organization has to have its "hands" informed and directed (and, if necessary, corrected) by its "head," the top management. Management develops the vision that tells the organization where to go, the strategic intent that gives organization its direction (see also pp. 442). Just think of everyday language—it is in *head*quarters where decisions are made, by *heads* of departments, which the organization is supposed to follow.

Decision making expresses this concept of rationality most precisely. Decision making is understood as management's task par excellence—the bureaucratic *cogito* (the thinking brain) whose decisions the corporate body should follow. Management makes decisions on strategic directions, action plans to implement them, and forms of control to evaluate their effect. Usually, the model of decision making is described as a perfectly well-organized, rational, and logical process. First, the problem is defined. Second, all the relevant information that leads to an optimal solution is collected. Third, reviewing the data, management (perhaps with the help of technocratic "experts") develops several possible solutions. Fourth, evaluating the possible solutions carefully, management makes a decision regarding the optimal solution. Fifth, this solution is implemented in a top-down approach and evaluated constantly by management.

Such constant processes of rational decision making, supported by the latest IT equipment and an army of analysts and consultants, are meant constantly and incrementally to refine and improve an organization's processes and products.

The problem of recalcitrant hands is solved by turning them into disciplined and reflexive extensions of the corporate body, able to exercise discretion, but in corporately prescribed ways.

Raising doubts . . .

Although still in powerful circulation in today's organizations, the model of managerial decision making discussed above has been challenged by various contributions in management and organization theory. Almost half a century ago, James March and Herbert Simon (1958) doubted whether decision makers really look for optimal solutions. They suggested that they look for "satisficing" solutions. Because of the limited capacity of human information processing, no

Image 2.5   *Rational planning?*

one could really consider all solutions and then decide which one was the best one—not even a top manager. But top managers, because of their wide experiences, have a raft of comparable cases to draw on for most decision situations, and on the basis of that limited search are able to be rational within the bounds of their own experiences. However, having more experience, these bounds are less constraining than would be the case were lower-order members to do the deciding. In organizational life, a careful analysis of all available information would be impossibly time-consuming, given that time (and motivation for such use of time) is a scarce resource. It is for this reason that satisfactory decisions will be made rather than optimal ones. Simon and March saw people as having "bounded rationality." By this they meant to establish a distinction with the conception of economic rationalism that was inherent to the orthodox views of economics. The economic view of rationality assumed that the person would make rational decisions based on perfect knowledge about the nature of the phenomenon. This perfect knowledge would be contained in what economists call "price signals," because all that you would need to know about broadly similar goods in perfectly competitive markets is how much they cost. A rational person would always buy the cheapest product, all other things being constant. This would be the optimal decision. But in complex organizations, Simon and March argued, decision makers work under constraints that make optimal decisions impossible. They have imperfect knowledge because there is insufficient time to collect all the data they need, their information processing capacities are subject to cognitive limitations, they are not sure what they need to know, and so on. The result is that rationality is "bounded" and decision makers cannot optimize but must "satisfice"—make the best decisions that they can—those that are most satisfactory, based on the information available there and then.

Cohen, March, and Olsen (1972) pushed March and Simon's critique one step further, announcing that the decision-making process in organizations is organized according to the logic of what they call the *garbage can*. As they argue provocatively, decisions are made when solutions, problems, participants, and choices flow around and coincide at a certain point. Like garbage in a can, these adjacencies are often purely random. Yesterday's papers end up stuck to today's dirty diapers just as downsizing attaches itself to profit forecasts. William Starbuck (1983), to mention a third critical spirit, turned this logic completely upside down and argued that organizations are not so much problem solvers as action generators. Instead of analyzing and deciding rationally how to solve problems, organizations spend most of their time generating problems to which they already have the solutions. It's much more economical that way. They know how to do what they will do, so all they have to do is work out why they will do it. Just think of any consulting business—its solutions to whatever problems occur will be what it

Decisions are made when solutions, problems, participants, and choices flow around and coincide at a certain point.

currently offers. Products such as TQM, BPR, and so on are solutions to almost every problem, and thus it is not so much the problem that drives the solution but the solution already at hand that is waiting to be applied to a variety of different issues.

... and postmodern rationalities

It is exactly this criticism that is nicely packaged and successfully branded under the label of postmodernism. As Martin Parker (1992: 3) argues, modernism is essentially the belief in rationality:

> Modernism is described as having elevated a faith in reason to a level at which it becomes equated with progress. The world is seen as a system, one that comes increasingly under human control as our knowledge of it increases. The common terms for this kind of belief system are positivism, empiricism and science. All share a faith in the power of the mind to understand nature; that which is "out there." . . . [At the core of versions of modernism] is a rationalism that is unchallengeable and a faith that it is ultimately possible to communicate the results of enquiry to other rational beings. In contrast, the postmodernist suggests that this is a form of intellectual imperialism that ignores the fundamental uncontrollability of meaning. *The "out there" is constructed by our discursive conceptions* of it and these conceptions are collectively sustained and continually renegotiated in the process of making sense.

Put simply, modernism is the belief in progress through the rigorous application of rationality to different arenas of life—regardless of whether it is mathematics, organization of people, or decision making that shapes the future of the community. The belief in progress is the essence of early management theory, even up to much theory today. However, criticisms by Simon, March, Cohen, Olsen, and Weick prepared the ground for postmodernism with its central idea of substituting the concept of rationali*ties* for that of a singular rationality.

What a group of French philosophers and writers, who have been labeled as postmodernists, show is that commonly accepted concepts of rationality are, in fact, just one possible concept, and that there are many other forms of rationality lurking underneath the smooth surface of textbook knowledge and scientific jargon. For instance, Jean-François Lyotard emphasized that we make sense of the world through the use of narratives. In modern times, the dominant narrative was the narrative of science. As we saw in Chapter 1, Taylor and the engineering movement around 1900 was an expression of this belief. However, as Lyotard argues, through this one dominant story we forget and actively repress other potential narratives. As each of these narratives is constituted through different rationalities, we too easily find ourselves in a unified, homogenous universe. But instead of keeping on writing (which we have done elsewhere—see Clegg and Kornberger 2003), an example can illustrate the point more easily.

Martin, coauthor of this book, visited the Genolian caves, a cave system hundreds of thousands of years old in the Blue Mountains, near Sydney. Being interested in the history of the caves, he joined a guided tour. What he heard in the scientific treatise that followed in the next two hours was hardly exciting. The guide started a monologue on stalagmites and how they are formed over many million years, and how earth movements over the last couple of million years—and microorganisms kept hidden deep inside in the waterholes in the cave, and so forth—made them possible. With Lyotard, this becomes understandable. What the guide did (and what probably most visitors expect from a guide) was to use the scientific template to make sense of what one can see in the caves. Using this dominant rationality, the caves turned almost into a lab, a showcase of how much the guide knew. But a whole other reality got buried. The guide could also have told stories about indigenous people and the meaning of the cave for them, about the changes of use of the cave over the years, about the tragedies witnessed and comedies hosted over the centuries, about the local people and how they used the caves, about myths, secrets, and stories that evolved around the cave. In short, the guide could have told many different stories about the cave, and the scientific story would have been just one. All these stories enact different rationalities, none per se is superior to the other. But through the domination of one story—the story of science—all the other stories get subordinated.

Postmodernism tries to criticize (deconstruct, as they say) the dominant story and to re-find those other stories marginalized by the dominant mode of thinking. Normally, these marginal accounts are branded as "irrational," but as we have seen with the critique of rational decision making, rationality in organizations is in itself just a form of pattern making. And a pattern does not necessarily have to be a variation on just one theme to display rationality. Look at the two images on page 62 and think about this: Are they both rational?

CRITICAL ISSUES: RULES AND RATIONALITIES

Different perspectives, different rationalities

The early history of management involved attempts at making work visible and transparent and its management legitimate. The Panopticon provided a simulacrum (an imagined copy of a presumed original) of an all-seeing capacity by constituting the overseen in a relation where they could never be sure that they were not being held visibly to account by those who oversaw. The founders drew on different disciplines to legitimate management's claims to managerial prerogative and superior authority. Taylor drew on engineering, Fayol on his experience in mining, Mayo on psychological

Image 2.6   *Rational patterns?*

counseling after World War I, and Barnard on the experience of executive leadership after the managerial revolution. Of the founding theorists, only Follett seemed to sense the necessity of combating managerial elitism and arbitrary authority with a real commitment to and stress on democracy and its accountabilities.

Bureaucracy's formulation of explicit rules of conduct raised the possibility of decisions being made about the conformance or nonconformance of those actions that were enacted in their name. Those who either implemented or internalized the rules could be seen to have done so more or less correctly—they could be held to account in terms of the rules. At the time that the bureaucratic model began to emerge in the United States as an appropriate model for organizational management, there was considerable concentration of power. In such a setting, rules that limited and framed unfettered prerogative could be an essential element of a liberal polity, which was a central aspect of the message that Max Weber sought to instill in students of bureaucracy. Value-neutral rules, applied technically, without fear or favor, are a bulwark against prejudice, discrimination, and the concentration of power, as well as being rational because they remain the same irrespective of context or time. They have a strongly moral quality. Of course, as we shall see, Weber was at pains to stress that the rationality of technically and legally defined bureaucracy was just one mode of rationality among several. Its success depended on its domination.

In the original German, one of Weber's central concepts was *herrschaft,* which literally translates as "domination." For Weber, domination occurs in organizations when lower-order members are obliged to obey commands from those above them in the hierarchy. However, where domination was tempered by legitimacy, then, almost as alchemy, the base metal of domination could be transformed into the pure gold of authority, legitimated by principles and rules that were widely accepted. At the end of the day, that was bureaucracy's promise. It could cool out the politics of organizations, because if its formal rules held sway, only those who had legitimately striven, worked with, and obeyed the rules would advance up its hierarchy. It would be domination accorded legitimacy because it was based on transparent, meritocratic, and accountable norms.

Transparent, meritocratic, and accountable norms were easier to establish in a purely public bureaucracy than a private one, where familial wealth and inheritance might skew the upper echelons of domination, but they do provide an ideal that could be aspired to, even in shareholder-based organizations. The principal owners of capital—individual shareholders, institutions, and some employees, such as the top managers themselves—could at least expect those agents who were managing these assets to be accountable in terms of their formal authority and all it entailed. Legitimacy through rules thus sought to resolve a tricky problem: how to align the interests of principals—whether ministers or shareholders—and agents—the managers. Weber also addressed this issue in terms of the relation between what the formal rules authorized and what actually occurred, between what organizations might formally record as rational and what actual employee actions displayed as being substantively rational.

Formal and substantive rationality

The second chapter of Max Weber's (1978) *Economy and Society* deals with the relationship between formal and substantive rationality. For Weber, economic action is *formally* rational to the extent that it rests on the best technically possible practice of quantitative calculation or accounting. By contrast, *substantive* rationality denotes a concept of goal-oriented action where whatever the goals may be will vary according to the context within which they work. Hence, they are indivisible from the real substance of specific settings. For instance, economic action may be substantively rational to the extent that it is motivated and assessed according to an ultimate goal, even while it is technically irrational. Family businesses often fit this case. Family firms know what it would be technically rational to do, such as raising capital by diluting family equity, but the preservation of the family holdings, even if it means less efficiency, growth, and profits, is held in higher esteem. Such a substantive orientation, Weber notes from the start, may lead the actor to see formal, quantitative calculation as unimportant, or even inimical to the achievement of ultimate ends.

Put simply, people will not necessarily be instrumentally rational managers, applying means-end rationality to the calculation of an economic bottom line, unless either they are in structured situations in which they have no choice other than to achieve this end, or they really want to achieve this end. Where their preferences are for other ends, such as the maintenance of tradition or the family business under family control or the design and creation of something that they love dearly, even when it is economically irrational in instrumental terms to do so, they orient themselves to other forms of rationality, such as affective or traditional conceptions of rationality. Think of an entrepreneur who invests a fortune in a football team with which he or she has a sentimental affinity, even when the team remains a bunch of expensive losers.

The more the world approximates to a formally rationalized ideal of capitalist accounting in which ultimate ends hardly figure, the more chance that rationality will be wholly instrumental, says Weber (1978: 165). In the characteristic form of a modern market economy, defined as "a complete network of exchange contracts in deliberate planned acquisitions of powers of control and disposal" (Weber 1978: 67), organizations are most likely to be instrumentally rational. The formal categories of a purely accounting notion of efficiency are the dominant element shaping organization design and top management judgments. In such a situation, a specific cultural value—efficiency, defined in terms of the categories of a particular form of knowledge—is raised to the status of an "ultimate value" to be culturally prized for its own sake, as an end in itself. The organizations that exist under these conditions do so because, in all probability, "certain persons will act in such a way as to carry out the order governing the organization" (Weber 1978: 49). In other words, organization is premised on an expectation of trust in the obedience of others. Trust and obedience function as resources in creating effectively functioning organization (as some central contributions by Fox 1974, Gambetta 1988, Granovetter 2002, Kramer 2003, and Sievers 2003 argue).

Weber (1978: 108) isolates three circumstances where "irrationality" can arise from the instrumental rationality of capital accounting as the perfect expression of means-end relations. First, where there are autonomous and antagonistic enterprises, producing only according to the criterion of arbitrarily distributed demand. Here what people want gets produced. It may be what they want, but it is not necessarily what they need. For instance, high-cholesterol, sweet, salt-ridden junk food. Lots of people want to eat it despite its adverse effects on their diet, health, and weight. Second, capital accounting presupposes absolute property rights over capital goods and a purely commercial orientation of management, which favors speculative behavior. Capital accounting is technically most optimal under ideal economic-liberal conditions, where there are unfettered proprietorial prerogatives and absolute market freedom. Conditions supporting this will include free labor markets, complete freedom of contract, mechanically rational technology, a formally rational administration and legal system, and a complete divorce between enterprise and household organization. Weber singles out the exclusion of workers from control over capital ownership as well as from its returns, together with their subordination to entrepreneurs, as a specific source of substantive irrationality (Weber 1978; also Clegg, Boreham, and Dow 1986: 60–61). Workers are expected to exert themselves for the ultimate value of the capital owners—the shareholders—who will, in the appropriate circumstances, have no compunction about "letting them go" if it will boost the share price.

The third circumstance in which Weber sees formal rationality being compromised is where economic organization becomes prey to competing and contradictory calculations. Such a situation can occur when share ownership becomes the subject of a takeover battle. Where control is concentrated in proprietorial interests, credit and financial institutions, acting as predators, can acquire the issued share capital for speculative purposes. Either way, the outside interests pursue their own business interest, "often foreign to those of the organisation as such" and "not primarily oriented to the long-term profitability of the enterprise" (Weber 1978: 139; also see the discussion in Clegg et al. 1986: 61–62). The implications become acute when such interests "consider their control over the plant and capital goods of the enterprise . . . not as a permanent investment, but as a means of making a purely short-run speculative profit" (Weber 1978: 140). Weber recognized that rationality was not purely instrumental. Rather, people rationalized their own versions of rationality based upon contextual pressures and interests. Sometimes these would reward short-term rather than long-term rationality.

In praise of bureaucracy

Despite being forensically analytic in his appreciation, Weber saw that bureaucracy had several positive attributes with much to recommend it. Organizations constructed in this way could be sources of satisfaction for those working within them. They were fairly predictable, and they offered opportunities for careers and for individual members to specialize in what they most enjoyed and to develop these skills. The benefits of bureaucracy can be enumerated:

- It limits arbitrary power and privilege. To the extent that the bureaucracy treats you as merely a case, the more you could expect to be treated according to precedents established by rules, rather than the whim of an officer.
- You have a right of appeal in a bureaucracy. If the application of rules to cases were illegitimate, then you have rational recourse to an appeal mechanism.
- None were above the law, none could escape rules, and every office was accountable. In short, bureaucracy was a bulwark of civil liberty.

A cornerstone of bureaucracy for Weber was that it operated "without regard for persons." Reading this phrase for the first time may resonate with what you already know about bureaucracy: that it is heartless, soulless, and cruel. It doesn't have a human face—it makes everybody a number. But Weber was arguing something far more fundamental. Essentially, Weber was saying that it doesn't matter if you are black or white, Muslim or Jew, gay or straight, rich or poor. It doesn't matter who or what you are. You are entitled to be judged not on the prejudices of the community or the person applying a rule but strictly according to the rules, without regard for the specificities of whatever might be your identity.

You are entitled to be judged ... without regard for the specificities of whatever might be your identity.

Impersonal rules without regard for persons are a fundamental bulwark of a decent, civil, liberal society. In the service of impersonal rules, devised without prejudice for specific categories of persons (an example of such prejudice would have been the apartheid regime's notorious "Pass Laws" in the era prior to Nelson Mandela assuming the presidency of the new Republic of South Africa), the impersonality of bureaucracy applied properly is a guarantee of civil rights and liberty.

In bureaucracy, if *everyone* was subject to abstract, impersonal rules, this quality could be something menacing rather than comforting, something to dread rather than celebrate for its guarantee of liberal freedom, if one did not understand the rules being applied or where the rules were not transparent, serving not liberty, equality, and fraternity but tyranny. As Kafka (1956) imagined modern bureaucracies in *The Trial,* they were inscrutable and unknowing to those who became caught up in their machinations, and obsessive in their detail for those who dispatched their business—or those parts of it that they were privy to.

It was not only novelists such as Kafka who voiced reservations about bureaucracy. Weber, too, had his doubts about this new instrument. Because of its "purely technical superiority" as a mechanism for accomplishing complex tasks, bureaucracy seemed almost irresistible, Weber thought, and this irresistibility alarmed him. Rational calculation had become a monstrous discipline. Everything seemingly had to be put through a calculus, irrespective of other values or pleasures. It was a necessary and unavoidable feature of organizing in the modern world. If you want modernity, suggests Weber, then you have to have bureaucracy. The two go together. Thus, while Weber admired the achievements of bureaucracy greatly, he was also pessimistic about their long-term impact. On the one hand, bureaucracies would free people from arbitrary rule by powerful patrimonial leaders—those who personally owned the instruments and offices of rule. They would do this because they were based on rational legality—the rule of law contained in the files that defined practice in the bureaus. On the other hand, however, they would create an "iron cage of bondage," a hierarchy of offices that interlocked and intermeshed, through whose intricacies you might seek to move, with the best hope for your future being that you would shift from being a small cog in the machine to one that was slightly bigger, in a slow but steady progression. Nonetheless, most modern organizations for most of the twentieth century were based on some variant or other of these principles. We were, Weber thought, destined to live inside the metaphorical iron cage.

THE FINE PRINT: WEBER, HIS HEIRS, AND CONSEQUENCES

Dominant rationality or plural rationalities?

Weber's analysis took emergent terms and ideas that were current in actual bureaucracies at the time when he was writing and used them as the basis for theoretical construction. They were a reconstruction of ordinary language in use into the ideal type. A certain normative slippage occurs in this process, because he is using ordinary language terms, as defined by members of organizations, to describe what it is that these members do. The members in question were those of the Prussian and German bureaucracies of the state and

Image 2.7 *Iron cages*

military. They were bounded by a ferociously strong sense of duty and conformance in service to the state. Generalizing from this case, it might appear as if the norms of organizations are invariably shaped by a singular rationality rather than by rationalities: a dominant rather than competing sense of what "should" be done rather than a grasp of the multiple rationalities that might be in play, even in contest, in a specific situation. In the hands of subsequent approaches less historically subtle and sensitive than those of Weber, it was hardly surprising that a narrow focus on bureaucracy as what should happen was the prevalent conception (see also Chapters 3 and 4). It was a perspective that became, ultimately, much more compatible with an instrumental concern with "efficiency" overshadowing the cultural, historical, institutional, political, and economic analysis of the market that Weber (1978) pioneered. It also became an analysis that presumed the security of that which it also investigated: rationality. Rationality became identified with top managerial prerogative and irrationality with deviations from it. Explicitly, the management analysts who followed this route were taking sides in what were highly political games (see also pp. 162–165).

Engineering rationality

Taylor and the engineers argued that if engineering knowledge was applied appropriately, then it would not only legitimate the manager as a new class of highly skilled employee, who planned and designed rationally, but would also justify the entire structures of control in which they were inserted. It would make these structures authoritative—for what could be a better basis for authority in the New World than the legitimacy of science?

Engineering rationality replaced older legitimations grounded in the Protestant ethic or ideas about the survival of the fittest, flourishing as Social Darwinism. The last twenty years of the nineteenth century had seen the rise of vast empires of agglomerated enterprise in key areas such as steel, building the fortunes of entrepreneurs such as Andrew Carnegie and his contemporaries, men like John D. Rockefeller and Andrew Mellon. The emergence of these vast financial empires made traditional, religious, and moral justifications for property ownership seem quite hollow when confronted with corrupt monopoly power. And this monopoly was such that it made nonsense of any ethic of ruthless competition and the survival of the fittest. It became a central tenet of progressive political thought that the power of the large corporations should be curbed somehow, and the new science of management seemed one way to do it. Emerging out of the institutional sponsorship of the American Society of Mechanical Engineers, scientific management was able to position itself as a rational and irrefutable bastion against the privileges that ownership allowed. Installing scientific management, it was claimed, would eradicate arbitrary and socially destructive domination, tame it, and make it authority. It would make a certain model of hierarchy and management legitimate and not just the expression of a dilettante or capricious will. It was based, protagonists said, on facts and technical analysis of the organizational situation. It was grounded in functional analysis of necessity rather than the random exercise of will by an overseer or master. It would fit the person to the job, after the job had first been scientifically analyzed. Thus, people were not to be slotted into their positions on the basis of their class, their history, their destiny—but their aptitudes and abilities. Individual responsibilities could and would match what was functionally required. Above all, management would be the harbinger and hallmark of efficiency. With efficiency installed, all would benefit in a commonwealth of enterprise, whether toilers or shareholders. Indeed, that rewards should flow to each according to the value of his or her inputs was a dogma of the new rationalism. And the rationalism had a cadre who would ensure its probity. The engineers become managers who would ensure the visibility, accountability—in a word, the rationality—of the new hierarchies of merit, function, and efficiency.

Not all of this panegyric to engineering rationality was swallowed without some bile. Unbeknownst to these early management writers, one of the most brilliant minds of the twentieth century, Max Weber, had already wrestled with these questions and come up with an analysis whose insights far exceeded their own. But as he had published only in German, few English writers knew. However, there were other writers in English who had been widely read by the 1930s. Clearly, writers such as Follett and those who came after her, including Mayo and Barnard, found an analysis composed purely in terms of engineering rationality somewhat incomplete. Taylor's science had disastrous unanticipated consequences: It destroyed democratic accountability, said Follett. For Mayo, it invited resistance and an excess of individualism, while Barnard couldn't see how following engineering really allowed executives to exercise leadership.

The rational and "the other": keeping chaos at bay

Although they might oppose narrow engineering conceptions of rationality, the second-generation theorists did not want to throw out the baby of rationality per se with the bathwater soiled by the engineers. With the engineers, they could accept that if rationality was predicated on instrumental control, then chaos threatened where control of the instruments, whether human or machine, could not be achieved. Questions of rationality, once established in an instrumental mode, were to remain central to emerging management and organization theory. If rationality dealt with the predictable, the systematic, and the known, then opposed to it was the unpredictable, the chaotic, and the uncertain. Indeed, in subsequent theoretical constructions, after the emergence of the theory of the firm (Cyert and March 1963; March and Simon 1958) and especially after the work of James D. Thompson (1967), uncertainty took on an almost metaphysical quality in the theory of management and organizations.

It was the evil to be opposed, the anxiety to be tamed, and the phenomenon to be reduced. Organizations were to become thought of as systems erected against an uncertain world. Organizations were forms of rationality that minimized the dangerous chances of irrational surprise. Central to the new rationality were the appropriate rules defining the function, responsibility, and authority of the new managerial cadre and those they managed. Their task was systematically to extend rationality, minimize uncertainty, and reproduce those designs that best achieved these outcomes. Calibrating relations that could achieve this end was precisely management's peculiar genius, as scientific management's rationalist foundations sought to establish.

From rationality to rationalities

Rationality can be whatever it is defined as being by those who have the authoritative resources to define it. That this is the case is a central claim of this book, integrating knowledge with power. The assumed rationality of organization operates as a disciplinary mechanism, which can be used by those who occupy positions of authority. They do so to judge, normatively, the actions of those other members of the organization expected to be using the same constructs in their orientation to action. Hence, the rationality of organizations, when used as a judgmental concept, already presumes the possibility of plural and competing rationalities. There will usually be a plural and potentially conflicting use of rationalities at work in any actual organization setting because there will be a "negotiable relationship between policy and politics" (Bittner 2002: 85). In other words, there is many a slip twixt the definition and the implementation of what is rational.

Organizations are an arena that individuals and other collective interests attempt to dominate in concert with others. Their attempts at capture involve coalitions competitively bargaining to control organizational resources and positions, to enforce their ends on the organization. These may be organized collectively through share raids by other firms, or they may be individual or shared attempts to gain power internally. Organizationally dominant coalitions, whether internal or external, appropriate power through various forms of strategy. Different coalitions struggle to constitute the organization in terms that represent their interests, bargaining with whatever resources they can constitute as strategic. More or less abstract cultural values can be used, such as the pursuit of "innovation," "profit," or even "fun," which become the basis for organizationally situated actions and vocabularies of motive (Mills 2002) as the public complexes of reasons through which we might seek to justify organizational action. (In the British TV comedy *The Office,* for instance, "fun" is a dominant value through which the characters act out their aggressions and hostilities, as well as their attractions, to each other. Enjoying business is a common ideology of highly competitive teams, often expressed in terms of sporting team metaphors.)

What survives organizationally may not be most efficient but survives because at some time in the past of the organization it became instilled with value.

What survives organizationally may not be most efficient but survives because at some time in the past of the organization it became instilled with value. Things, forms, and practices may be valued for and in themselves, irrespective of their contribution to the efficiency of the organization. Historically, one might think of the place that the Latin mass once had in the Roman Catholic Church, or the role that the confessional still plays. They are constitutive parts of a ceremonial fabric with an explicable past cultural context rather than norms established for efficiency purposes.

Organizations are constructions, concocted out of whatever knowledge their members deem salient in specific locales. What is considered appropriate in a specific locale is subject to shifting and ever more global definition (see also pp. 478–482), in which the limits of possibility are most likely to be purely cultural and institutional. For instance, research by Child and Kieser (1979) found that a sample of German organizations was consistently more centralized than was a comparable sample of British firms, which they put down to local cultural difference. These proved to be even more important than the impact of models of best practice retailed by international consulting agencies. These models did not produce convergence by eroding the value basis of a German cultural predisposition for more centralized control. Such findings, of a "societal effect," are widely established (see Maurice and Sorge 2002).

The structure of capital markets, interest rate regimes, and accounting conventions all provide specific institutional frameworks within which managerial judgment forms. While the trick of a successful management team is to achieve appropriate consensus, such consensus may well form around inadequate strategies, or subsequently come to be defined as such when a new rational metric is introduced. Think of what happens when the opposition wins an election. The new government will reconceptualize all the policies of the recent past as errors and foolishness. New policies require new priorities and new measures of their achievement, which the new government will introduce. Something similar often happens when there is a contested takeover of a firm or a merger; sometimes it also happens when, as a result of the appointment of a new CEO, there is a change in the top management team. In with the new, out with the old—politics is a major mechanism of organizational change.

In theory, there is actually little point, analytically, in running some preferred model of action like a metric over the organization's actions. To do so would not tell us whether they are rational or not, because it will all depend on the normative presuppositions that are implicit in the conception of rationality being used to measure as well as what is being measured. Of course, if you are a manager, then these considerations hardly matter. You will be held accountable and hold others accountable in terms of whatever metrics are constructed as rational in a specific context—irrespective of how irrational they might actually be. Hence, as we shall see in Chapter 5, rationality, or at least what counts as rationality (and we would say the two conceptions are indivisible), is utterly implicated with power; knowledge of what is rational is embedded in institutionalized practices of power.

Rationalities are historically structured differently in varying periods, as different kinds of knowledge dominate. This is the lesson we learn from post-modernism. As the rules of the game shift historically, then different issues become critical for organization strategy. As these issues shift, different forms

> **Rationalities are historically structured differently in varying periods, as different kinds of knowledge dominate.**

of occupational knowledge give personnel an advantage in terms of the shifting rules of the game. Think of the major Hollywood studios, which are largely formula driven. Although there are exceptions, such as an innovative movie not made to formula that becomes successful despite or because of this, such as *Pulp Fiction, Trainspotting,* or *The Blair Witch Project,* how many movies can you think of that were hits, and because they were hits, then a sequel gets made? Sometimes many sequels! And the other studios copy the successes of their competitors.

Rationality concerns not just technical efficiency, because it is always culturally framed. Managers seek to make their organizations similar to models that are already institutionalized as positive examples. They do not want to deviate too far from the forms that are already culturally valued. Thus, organizations end up being similar not because it is *rationally efficient* for them to be so but because it is *institutionally rational.* Sticking to legitimate forms bestows legitimacy. Hence, organizations in similar fields of activity tend to be similar in their design, functioning, and structure. These are the basic insights of institutional approaches to organization analysis. Together with the insights of postmodern critiques, and Weber's thoughts on bureaucracy, they give raise to the idea that we do not deal with rationality but rationalit*ies*. The example of French bread illustrates this more tangibly.

Institutionalizing French bread

Stewart once wrote about French bread in the context of an earlier book, drawing on wonderful work by Daniel Bertaux and Isabelle Bertaux-Wiame (1981). In their research into "Artisanal Bakery in France: How It Lives and Why It Survives," Bertaux and Bertaux-Wiame (1981) wrote, disparagingly, about industrial bread as "industrial food wrapped in a shroud of cellophane which is sold in the supermarkets of the western world under the somewhat euphemistic label of 'bread.'" Industrial bread accounts for most of the bread sold in the Anglo-Saxon countries of the United States, Canada, Australia, New Zealand, and Britain. The reasons for the supremacy of this industrial bread are evident from what we can learn from Chandler (1962). Bread is usually produced from within a division of a giant food conglomerate based around vertical integration from flour milling to bread and related food retailing.

Chandler's (1962) thesis is that efficient, successful organizations in similar industries, cross-culturally, should adopt the same type of strategy and structure, irrespective of their location (see also Chapter 13).

Visitors to and residents of France know that the typical French bread is a crusty baguette or half pound loaf. It looks good and it tastes good. However, to describe it does not tell us what French bread is. It is clearer, perhaps, if we determine what it is not. First, it is not a standardized, easily transportable, mass-produced product. It is not a heavily marketed, brand-identified, size-invariant, shrink-wrapped, and sliced product sold identically in virtually similar super-market chains throughout the country. It possesses an inherent quality of "fresh-ness." It is perishable, its value being that it is fresh, does perish, and cannot be bought other than on a daily basis. It incorporates everything that industrial bread could never be. So how is French bread possible? How has the market dominance of conglomerate oligopoly bread been avoided? Why should it be that in France and a number of Latin countries most of the bread consumed is made by artisans rather than in factories, and only a small percentage of the market is for industrial bread, whereas in other countries, such as Britain and the United States, it is industrial bread that wins the market?

In France there is about one bakery for every thousand people, a decentral-ized scattering of small, independent bakeries that manufacture and sell bread, cakes, and croissants from the same premises. The shopkeeper is usually the baker's wife, and the couple is the real economic unit, the man as an artisan and the woman as a shopkeeper. On average, each bakery employs fewer than three workers, usually less than twenty years old. Most of these young men leave the trade sometime between twenty and twenty-five. Many of these very small bakeries are in decline in depopulating urban areas and villages. Newer, larger (employing ten to fifteen people) bakeries making bread for large chains, such as Carrefour, have developed in suburban areas. However, these are still the same kind of artisan bakeries, making the same kind of artisan bread, using the same methods of production. They are just larger.

In 1966, however, traditional methods of making French bread did seem to be under threat. The largest flour-milling group in France, which had a virtual monopoly on the supply of flour to the Paris market, was rumored to be prepar-ing a huge bread factory close to the Seine in order to supply industrial bread to the French market. One day, without warning, the flour-milling company changed the terms of trade. Henceforth, only full truckloads would be deliv-ered, a crippling blow to bakers who had neither the market nor the storage capacity to warrant such an amount. However, after a week of panic, when it looked as if what the big millers desired—the eclipse of the small bakers— might occur, the small bakers discovered some independent mills still func-tioning in the regions outside Paris, which were on the verge of closing down, due to a lack of work, that were delighted to receive the orders of the small bak-ers. The new network functioned quite smoothly after a month or so, at which point the "big flour-milling company understood it had lost the fight; it went

Image 2.8   *Artisanal bread*

back to its previous policy of retail delivery, lowered its prices to get back its former customers, and put the plans for the factory back in the safe where they are waiting for the next opportunity" (Bertaux and Bertaux-Wiame 1981: 161).

Baking bread has always been, and remains, hard work, sometimes for relatively small returns. Before World War II, the working day would often start at midnight, or earlier, with the preparation of the first batch of dough. The oven had to be warmed next, so wood had to be cut, the fire lit, and so on. At around two in the morning, the first batch had to be cooked, and so on, in successive batches through to noon. Lunch and sleep followed till four, when the baker and the young apprentice would attend to their rural rounds delivering bread to the farms. Returning home from this later that evening, they would have time for a few hours of sleep until midnight rolled around again.

The shop opens from eight in the morning, or seven in working-class districts; it may shut from one till four, and then reopen, closing finally at eight, a long day's work to which the shopkeeper-wife "must add the work of any housewife and mother. The closing day is used not for rest or leisure, but in making up for the accumulated backlog of cleaning, washing, shopping" (Bertaux and Bertaux-Wiame 1981:163). The wives are the street-level workers, the frontline marketers. Good bakers bake good bread, but it is good wives who sell it, who create a regular customer attracted to a particular bread and a particular shop. In addition, wives are also the accountants, cashiers, and trusted confidantes. Wives who become widows can hire bakery workers to continue the business, but husbands who have become widowers, or whose wives have left them, find it difficult to continue in the business without an unpaid and trustworthy partner. Good wives are good investments in more ways than one. It is to the wives' judgment that the reproduction of this whole enterprise falls.

Given the nature of the trade, only someone who had been apprenticed in it could possibly run the business, and, indeed, most present-day bakers were formerly workers who had become self-employed at an early age. Initially, this discovery was puzzling for the researchers. Where would a lowly paid worker in a low-status trade, in all probability with no collateral, raise the significant sums necessary to buy even one of the smallest going concerns? Redefining the problem from the other end of the age spectrum solved the puzzle. Consider an old couple whose life has been their bakery and who want to retire, with no children to hand on the business to. How can they retire? Only if they can sell the business as a going concern, complete with goodwill, to someone who will continue to use the premises as a bakery. For any other purpose, it is just a small shop and workshop, with no intrinsic value over and above that of the market value as real estate. Anyway, premises are invariably rented. All there is to sell is the baker's ovens and machines unless the bakery continues as a bakery, in which case goodwill (stable customer relationships with a specific local population) can return an appropriate monetary value, which the machinery, frequently worn out, will not. The only people who can take over the trade are the young men who have been apprenticed in it. They are the only ones to know the trade intimately. Becoming a self-employed baker consummates the hard union of an apprenticeship, with long hours and low pay. It is this possibility that makes being a lowly worker bearable.

How bakery workers become proprietors and old couples retire from the trade are inextricably linked. The retiring couple lend the necessary money to the bakery worker and his wife. For the incoming couple, its acceptance means eight years of relative hardship and privation as they save to repay the value of the goodwill (based on the value of an average month's sale of bread). For the retiring couple it means placing tremendous trust in the new couple, for the turnover may be a risky business. If they do not succeed in the trade, then they cannot repay the loan. Actually, the trust is placed not so much in the couple—the bakery worker is trusted to know the trade on the basis of his ten years or so of service—the trust has to be placed in the young woman who is entering the trade, for she is the key to the whole enterprise. She is the secret of the future success of the *boulangerie*. Has she got what it takes to be a good shopkeeper? Can she tolerate the long hours of work during the day and the emptiness of the nights as her husband toils in the bakery? Does she know what being a baker's partner means and entails? Will she resent the customers who, arriving after hours, will nonetheless disturb her because they want, expect, fresh bread? A good baker needs a good partner in life and business as well as money to succeed. If he does not have the former, it is unlikely he will make the latter.

A baker's marriage is not just a transaction between marital partners—it is also a transaction between an artisan and a shopkeeper who are bonded together.

When we checked with our French colleague and friend Emanuel Josserand, he updated the story for us. It is apparent from what we learned that the artisan form is not in present danger of extinction from industrial bread. There has been a renaissance of artisanal techniques in the late 1980s and early 1990s. The big mills seem to have completely given up the "all-industrial" strategy. Interestingly, at least two of them offer increased services to the *boulangeries,* including a brand of bread using specifically selected flours. They provide wrapping papers and bags, signs, and the flour to make a specific baguette as well as some more upmarket baguettes and other breads. This builds up on a tendency to buy more sophisticated breads with, for example, seeds, olives, and cereals, at least in the big towns, from the specialist bakers. Indeed, the latest figures that we were able to find suggest as much. According to data from the French Ministry of Foreign Affairs (*Le Magazine* 26: 12/1996), the independent shops of artisan bakers comprise 75% of the volume (probably more in value), industrial bread has an 18% market share, and retailers like Carrefour (bread produced most of the time in big artisanal units) have 7%. There are still 35,000 *boulangeries artisanales,* and despite a tendency to uniformization that dates back to the 1940s, there are still eighty-one regional breads, with the baguette representing 80% of the purchases. Each shop serves an average 1,570 inhabitants per shop. A new tendency is an increase in the quality of frozen uncooked bread, cooked on demand in small franchise shops with a small oven (such as *Brioche Doré*). They take part of the market in the big towns, for immediate consumption during a lunch break or at teatime. More recent figures for 2000 from the *Confédération nationale de la boulangerie-patisserie Française* show that 71.3% of the market is still serviced by artisanal bakeries. The share of franchise and industrial bread has increased but very slowly and not very significantly. We can hardly talk about a paradigm shift in French bread. In some small towns or big villages, although a *boulangerie* can be a very profitable business in the long run, and one will find quite a few Mercedes in the backyards, at the other end, the prospects are modest in small villages and remote areas.

The tale is long and complex, yet it teaches us some profoundly important things. First, these organizations are composed around a core of "value imperatives," as institutional theory argues. At every stage where the *boulangerie* might have been annihilated at the hands of industrial bread and its organizational form, the resources of deeply held cultural values were there to keep it going. For the *boulangerie* of France, these resources were a supply of potential shopkeepers and the culturally legitimate value of a model whereby the social structuring of the organizational form could reproduce itself. Second, these organizations are constituted within culturally defined ways of doing, ways of being, and ways of becoming. To be sure, there are pressures for rationalization and efficiency. We saw how the industrial flour millers sought to exercise power and dispense with the preferences of French consumers not to purchase the kind of industrial bread that they could make. The transaction costs are expensive and inefficient for all concerned. The customers had to shop for bread both in the morning and again in the afternoon. With industrial bread, just one weekly supermarket trip would suffice. For the bakers, the costs are even higher. They have to endure a long, arduous, and unremunerative apprenticeship; they borrow heavily at the beginning to become proprietors and lend heavily at the end to become retirees; they have to take extraordinary risks so that at the end of their lives the costs associated with retirement will be recouped; they leave themselves open, when they are most vulnerable to opportunistic or foolish behavior. They place their fate in the hands of a party they can never be sure to trust in a transaction that has no guarantees. Yet they choose to be bakers. In addition, their customers choose to eat baker's bread rather than its industrial counterpart.

The lesson we learn is simple: These bakers act rationally, as do their industrial counterparts equipped with methods of rational management seeking economies of scale, even though they each act radically differently. Thus, do not expect a singular scientific rationality to be played out in an industry; rather, rationalities exist in plural, each based and legitimized in its own logic. No rationality is *necessarily* "more rational" than another.

Embedding economic action in social action

The preceding analysis of French bread is a testament to what Granovetter (2002: 363) has termed the "embeddedness" of economic action: "The argument that the behaviour and institutions to be analysed are so constrained by ongoing social relations that to construe them as independent is a grievous misunderstanding." Granovetter attempts to correct this misunderstanding by focusing on the central role of networks of social relations in producing trust in economic life. Seen from this perspective, the reproduction of the *boulangerie* is not only a mode of organization but also a complex of cultural and economic practices. It is a classic case of embeddedness. One consequence of an embedded analysis is a perceptible transformation in the object studied. It enables one to appreciate that "small firms in a market setting may persist . . . because a dense network of social relations is overlaid on the business relations connecting such firms" (Granovetter 2002: 385).

Granovetter's emphasis on embeddedness is quite at odds with the conventional perspective on a singular rationality of market efficiency. Such theories operate with an "undersocialized" conception of action in their models and analysis, one modeled on the abstractions of economic rationality. The people who inhabit the theories of singular economic rationality are truly one-dimensional characters—they can calculate but not do much else. In Oscar Wilde's phrase, they know the price of everything and the value of nothing. They have been reduced to a calculus, while every other aspect of their social being has been stripped away. The reductionism of an undersocialized view of economic action has been dealt an effective counter-factual blow with the case of French bread, with its insistence on the institutionalization of value and the centrality of culturally framed economic mechanisms in ensuring the survival of a seemingly archaic form into contemporary times.

SUMMARY AND REVIEW

In Chapter 1, we encountered the idea that management was concerned with instilling rationality into organization, where engineers largely conceived that rationality in instrumental and efficiency terms. There were objections raised at the time, of course, by writers such as Mayo, Barnard, and Follett, all of whom wished to point to the importance of either irrational elements (Mayo and Barnard) or the importance of quite different factors, such as community (Follett) that the new forms of rationality seemed to be destroying.

None of the writers encountered earlier had any fundamental criticisms of the conceptions of rationality that were in use. However, this was not the case for Max Weber, with his distinction between substantive and formal types of rationality and his idea that there were more ways of being rational than merely calculating in the manner of an engineer. At heart, what was most important in Weber was the injunction to research how values became institutionalized in organization and management. Subsequently, many theorists have developed this perspective into institutional theory to explain that organizations and the management action that occurs within them are culturally embedded, culturally framed, culturally reproduced, and culturally changed. In a word, whatever passes for rationality is culturally defined (rather than something that can be settled by reference to some external standard, of engineering or economic efficiency), a topic to which we return in Chapter 6.

ONE MORE TIME . . .

Getting the story straight

- What are the central features of bureaucracy?
- What does isomorphism mean? What are its major variants?
- From a postmodern perspective, how does the concept of rationality differ from a modernist account such as Taylor's?

Thinking outside the box

- What are some of the ways that different rules define different rationalities?
- What are the main competing rationalities at work in the story of French bread?
- What are some of the ways in which purely economic accounts of organizational action are inadequate?

ADDITIONAL RESOURCES

1. There is no intellectual substitute for reading great scholars in the original, and Weber is a case in point. Many of his books are very difficult to read today, as they are very formal and rather heavy going. However, *The Protestant Ethic and the Spirit of Capitalism* (1976) is probably the most accessible of his books, and has wonderfully prescient conclusions pointing to the world in which we live today.

2. For those who find the ideas of institutional theory intriguing, then there is a wealth of materials from which to choose. Probably most thorough and useful are the contributions of Greenwood and Hinings (2002), which address "old" and "new" institutionalism, bringing them together.

3. A fascinating institutional account is provided of how the changes from there being an East and West Germany to a unified Germany had significant effects on the organization and survival of symphony orchestras from the two territories by Allmendinger and Hackman (2002).

4. Finally, Scott (2002) provides a synoptic overview of the wide variations in different types of institutional theory.

5. In terms of institutional theory, there is one recent film that illustrates the general points particularly well. In *Down with Love,* the 2003 romantic comedy of sexual manners, starring Renée Zellweger and Ewan McGregor, when the female lead character starts up a magazine in opposition to the one that the male lead character is employed on, it is almost a clone of *KNOW*—the men's magazine—even to the name, which is *NOW*—the only difference being that *NOW* is pitched at a female demographic whereas *KNOW* is aimed at men. The crucial point is that in establishing the magazine, the successful form is copied. In fact, the whole film is a witty and extended scripting of institutional theory in its premises—all the main plot moves on the part of the two lead actors are generated by character mimesis.

6. In addition, there is also an excellent film of Kafka's *The Trial* from 1993, starring Kyle MacLachlan and Anthony Hopkins, which illustrates the dread and oppressiveness of bureaucracy at its worst.

In addition to these suggested additional resources, don't forget to look at what is also available on the Web site **www.ckmanagement.net,** including free PDF files of recent papers related to this chapter, which you can download; video interviews with famous academics talking about related themes; as well as many other resources, such as connections to interesting Web sites.

CHAPTER 3

MANAGING REALITIES

Pathologies, New Forms, Dialectics

Objectives and learning outcomes

By the end of this chapter, you will be able to

- Understand how some central ideas relate to different processes of organizing

- Appreciate how specific features of different contexts within which managing and organizing occurs can give rise to different ways of making sense of these

- Discuss the strengths and limitations of both bureaucratic and postbureaucratic organizations and be familiar with the debates about them

- Explain the key issues involved in the management of the labor process

OUTLINE OF THE CHAPTER

In the postwar era, the first generation of classical theories of management, with their strong story lines about how things ought to be organized in one best way, lost out to more nuanced typologies of organizations and more empirically grounded analyses. A concern with processes began to be developed that undercut the previous emphasis on prescription of the classical management theorists such as Fayol and Taylor. These provided a third generation of theory following the second generation dominated by theorists such as Mayo, Barnard, and Follett. The third-generation focus was not only more hands-on empirical than their predecessors, but it was also informed by the translations of Max Weber's work into English. Thus, it was more attuned to the actual nature of Weber's concern with "social action" as something that happens than was the case in the rather static emphasis on bureaucracy and its structure, which was later taken to be the central Weberian contribution.

We call this chapter "Managing Realities" because it deals with a more realist and empirically robust basis that was constructed by a number of significant researchers in the mid-twentieth century. We focused in the previous chapter on how different rationalities made sense of management. Now we will turn to surprising and challenging research that shows some more specific ways in which reality differs from what you might expect after having read Chapter 1. The ground we cover in this chapter reflects the sometimes messy, sometimes exploitive, and sometimes pathological realities found when studying real-life organizations.

In this chapter, there is only sufficient space to review a few of many notable studies, namely those by Blau and Scott, Etzioni, Merton, Selznick, Gouldner, and Blau once again. We shall then move on to review how, in recent years, many theorists have sought to think outside the bureaucratic envelope and imagine what "new organizational forms" might be like. Although there are a number of options available, one influential critic suggests that the future for many people will be little more than McJobs in McOrganizations, while others are more optimistic about a new era of empowerment.

SETTING THE SCENE

In the immediate post–World War II climate, bureaucracy was a representative experience of just about everyone who had been involved in either civilian or military mobilization. All who had served in the armed forces or been mobilized in the civilian war economy knew about bureaucracy! Mostly, they knew about its faults, red tape, and rigidities, and much of this was reflected in postwar work. Weber's work, translated immediately after the war, made a significant impact on the development of the nascent study of organizations and management. It helped generate a number of influential research programs that sought to extend Weber's ideal type of bureaucracy to a wider range of organizations.

Weber's type was only ever a model. It had no predictive or representational value. Its function was to sharpen the researchers' gaze so that they would be alert to the features that they thought could generally be seen as significant in, and definitive of, the bureaucratic form. It selects empirical data inductively—that is, on the basis of the researchers' best-informed hunches—and conceptualizes these as a model. The model is an abstraction and exaggeration of the features that we might find in reality. It represents a logically coherent model that accentuates some features for the purpose of making the focus of analysis clear. Weber's model was not a moral one. He was not saying that bureaucracy *is* an ideal, that it is the most efficient or effective type of organization (Albrow 1970). Bureaucracy is an analytic concept: Actual organizations represent sources of empirical data that we may make sense of through using the concept. Thus, rules need not translate into action. Image 3.1 is a witty instance that confirms this precept.

In fact, bureaucracies are far from ideal vehicles for rational action and efficient outcomes. A number of studies suggested that breaking the rules rather than following them could often produce more efficient outcomes. Rules were seen to be, despite their promulgation in formal and official documents, something indissoluble from the ways in which they were actually constituted and exemplified in everyday organizational life by those who worked there. They made the meaning, not the rules—although they were quite skilled and sophisticated enough to use these rules in different ways to assist in making their meaning. Normal pathologies were not unusual in everyday organizational life. Not surprisingly, if bureaucracies are seen, routinely, not to produce the outcomes that they are supposed to guarantee, a number of organizations have tried to evolve to a postbureaucratic design, one in which they can both exploit what they already know as well as explore new horizons.

As if to make the point more sharply, it was toward the end of the dominance of the normal bureaucratic form that its most trenchant critic emerged. Harry Braverman was an American Marxist who saw the system of scientific

Image 3.1   *Keep these toilets clean!*

management as the foundation of much of what was rotten in the organization of work. When he wrote about exploitation, it was not knowledge that was being leveraged when it was exploited. Instead, he saw exploitation in terms of craft knowledge either being denied or ripped out of shape by management as they wrought violence to workers' everyday stock of knowledge, pride, and sense of well-being. Braverman emerged as an articulate voice on behalf of those whom he saw as the downtrodden, the wretched, and the put upon: those whose historic legacies of craft knowledge were systematically undercut by a management bent on efficiency on its own terms at any human cost. As a later observer was to observe, this amounted to a kind of wholesale McDonaldization of organizational life, as standardization drove efficiency into every task that could be routinized, every burger that could be flipped, and every job that could be dumbed down.

CENTRAL APPROACHES AND MAIN THEORIES

Weber's legacy

It is not surprising that Weber's work was initially influential in the postwar era. It offered a unifying frame within which to research organization processes. Consider the alternatives. The problem for those who stressed the principles of management that we looked at in Chapter 1 was that none of them really agreed with each other; they all stressed different aspects of management and organization, often depending on the values that they held. The principles were often prescriptive, but they did not prescribe the same things!

For instance, Taylor abhorred the craft control that workers were able to exercise and the way that they could evade effective supervision of their activities; Mayo's preferences for psychoanalytical theory and his antipathy to militant labor struggles predisposed him to see the workplace as a place where deep-seated malaises needed to be cured as a part of effective management. Mayo's prescriptions for management were very different from those of Taylor; indeed, they were fundamentally opposed. Where these predecessors were taken, literally, as "founders," then the problem was that empirical case studies kept throwing up instances of a reality that did not consistently confirm their principles one way or the other.

Weber was by far the more scholarly and disciplined of the early contributors. He was producing not a representational model of reality but an accentuated one, composed of mental constructs. Early case study researchers, as we shall see, made their names by finding some principle that Weber had overlooked. But as Gouldner was to show, what really mattered was not so much the patterns that the theorist drew but the patterns that were in use by the people working in organizations. Followed literally, Weber's approach was based on an analysis of how members of organizations use their sense of the organization and its rule as a resource in their everyday management (see Bittner 2002). Weber's account merely sought to systematize and accentuate elements of what had become ordinary bureaucratic practice by the beginning of the twentieth century. The model was neither prescriptive nor predictive: If these practices changed, then typologies would need to change. If the typologies were assumed to be descriptive of reality, how did they relate to each other, especially where the principles or types around which they were constructed differed from case to case?

Bureaucracies and their normal pathologies

Typically, researchers first started to interpret organizations using Weber's ideas, which they then revised as they attended to features of reality that were not captured in his model.

Who benefits?

Blau and Scott (1963) focused on the relation of the organization to its members and beneficiaries. As they argued, there were at least four types of organizations that could be distinguished on the basis of "who benefits?":

1. Member-beneficent organizations, such as cooperatives
2. Owner-beneficent organizations, such as businesses
3. Client-beneficent organizations, such as schools or hospitals
4. Public-beneficent organizations, such as a public postal service, which serves all members of a community

The notion of "who benefits?" captures a dimension that Weber had not focused on. It assumed that organizations served the person or persons who were their ostensive beneficiaries. However, this is not always the case. Many organizations seem to be run for the benefit of those who manage them rather than those who are, ostensively, being served. Have you seen the John Cleese comedy *Fawlty Towers* in which he plays Basil Fawlty? Basil is authoritarian and incompetent, arrogant to those whom he despises, deferential to those whom he admires, and prone to making judgments and assumptions that are invariably managerially inappropriate and wrong. Nonetheless, the customers and the staff are always to blame, in his view. One reason why this show is so funny is that it is so easy to relate it to real-life situations. Most of us, to be sure, have encountered organizations similar to Fawlty Towers, where the managers seem to think that if they didn't have to serve pesky customers (or students, patients, passengers, pupils, citizens, etc.), they could run a tightly managed organization.

Why compliance?

Other writers took different tacks. Etzioni (1961) focused on what he thought was the key issue in Weber's account—the relations of compliance. Why do people do what other people in organizations tell them to do when these people hold more powerful positions? What is the motivational basis for their compliance? Why do we obey directives? Two factors explain these questions, suggests Etzioni: subordinate involvement and management resources. Essentially, there are three types of power and three types of involvement, which tend to be internally consistent with each other.

1. Coercive power elicits alienated involvement: "I do this because I have no option other than to do so."
2. Remunerative power elicits calculative involvement: "I do this because I am being paid to do it and thus it is in my interests to do so."
3. Normative power elicits moral involvement: "I do this for the good of a greater cause, a higher glory."

Trying to use the different types of power without the corresponding type of involvement will lead to unstable organizations and incongruent involvement, Etzioni suggests. You cannot run a business organization primarily on calculative involvement if you neglect to pay wages, as many formerly Soviet enterprises found after the fall of communism. Hence, these three types of relations will tend to be the coherent points about which actual organizations are organized. The more coherent the power/involvement relations, the more efficient the organizations will be, he suggests. There will be a tendency for coherence to emerge in the long run, so that misaligned organizations will tend to realign themselves.

Things are rarely as simple and as clear cut as the schema might lead us to believe. Organizations typically use all three patterns variably at different times. They try to increase moral involvement as well as paying wages; they try to coerce people while at the same time trying to maintain moral involvement. Nonetheless, empirical investigation has tended to support the consistency thesis that Etzioni puts forward (Hall, Haas, and Johnson 1966).

How maladjusted?

Bureaucracies might be technically superior in many respects, but it has been suggested that they make people sick. Merton (2002), for instance, argued that bureaucracies make those who work in them pathologically, psychologically maladjusted. He claimed it was normal to become cranky in a bureaucracy. Why? The answer resided in the normal processes of bureaucracy. Bureaucracies achieve an orderly transmission of instructions from top to bottom. Instructions are the major mechanism of control, and reliable obedience to instructions is the major mechanism of consent. Reliable subordinates perform accountably and predictably, according to the rules. Organization members realize that if they follow rules, they can't be formally criticized. They can always "cover their backs," even if following the rules produces a less good result. Rule-following becomes the reason for people to adopt defensive behavior, such as saying, "I can't do that; it's more than my job is worth," meaning it's not part of my duty statement, job description, or responsibility.

> **Bureaucracies might be technically superior in many respects, but it has been suggested that they make people sick.**

Nobody wins through excessive rule-following, says Merton. In such organizations, members show signs of what he calls rule tropism—following rules for their own sake. When they do adapt to rule tropism, an unanticipated consequence is that the psychological maturity of organization members as adults capable of healthy learning and development is arrested. They learn only to follow the rules, for they can never be held to be irresponsible when doing this. Thus, organizational dysfunctions develop from organizations designed to create efficiency through rule-following behavior.

Merton identified the phenomenon of "trained incapacity," which he describes as "that state of affairs in which one's abilities function as inadequacies or blind spots. Actions based upon training and skills that have been successfully applied in the past may result in inappropriate responses under changed conditions. An inadequate flexibility in the application of skills will, in a changing milieu, result in more or less serious maladjustment" (Merton 2002: 358).

Strict adherence to rules often leads to a displacement of goals, because the aims of the organization become identified with following the rules that are only intended as means to achieving the goals. Filling in forms correctly can quickly substitute for whatever action the forms were supposed to achieve. Formalism and ritualism develop as behavioral traits in consequence. The upshot of rigid adherence to bureaucratic rules is inefficiency. Merton captures this process in four steps:

1. Effective bureaucracy demands reliability of response and strict devotion to regulations.
2. Rules become absolutes rather than means to an end.
3. Adaptation is minimized as rules are rigorously followed.
4. Elements designed in principle to enhance efficiency end up generating inefficiency as the letter of the law is observed rather than the spirit of the mission.

Why delegation?

Philip Selznick (1943, 1949) was interested in how authority could be delegated. Delegation tends to increase the need for training in specialized competencies in order to ensure that people are accountable for what has been delegated to them. It opens up opportunities for discretionary action on the part of delegates. Delegation occurs through defining different functional responsibilities, bifurcating organizational interests. Increased conflict can often occur between different responsibilities, in consequence; suboptimal goals will become paramount as departmental interests overrule overall organizational interests. Consequently, a gap opens between the goals set by organizational elites and the performance delivered by departmental delegates. The normal workings of bureaucracies produce dysfunctional and counterproductive results.

Whose meaning?

Organization rules mean different things to different people in different contexts at different times. The meaning of rules is not fixed by what they say but how they are used. Gouldner (1954) tells a story illustrating this point. Briefly,

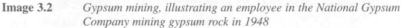

Image 3.2   *Gypsum mining, illustrating an employee in the National Gypsum*
Company mining gypsum rock in 1948

the story was that a new and younger manager more focused on the bottom line
replaced a traditional CEO in a remote gypsum mine. Mining gypsum is hard,
dirty, and dangerous work. The wonderful photograph in Image 3.2 illustrates
the conditions under which the mining occurred.

From the perspective of the new mine manager, when he took over the
plant, what he saw was considerable slackness. Employees "borrowed" plant
materials and used them at home. Safety regulations were violated. Authority
relations were very familiar and flexible. The situation was one of "mock
bureaucracy," where the rules were seen as a result of external industry regulations that could be ignored for all practical purposes. Neither management's
nor workers' values were aligned with the rules, so they were widely regarded
as lacking legitimacy. The rules simply got in the way of customary means of
doing things. Informality reigned in the relations between management and the
workers. Gouldner called this an "indulgency pattern." Everyone knew what
the rules were but no one took them seriously. The new manager resolved to
tighten control.

Tightening control didn't solve the problem. Employees had become used to a slack regime. They saw the enhanced control as an imposition, and failed to accept the legitimacy of the written rules over the customary ways of doing things. The consequence was an escalating resistance to increased managerial control by employees used to slackness as a norm. With the tighter policing of the rules, power relations became much more visible, raising the level of tension and resistance. Now management defined rule infringements as deliberate, given that the formal rules were being emphasized. The management response was to tighten supervision still further. Now, getting away with rule infringements became a serious game for the employees and a means of enhancing their prestige as successful larrikins or rebels in the workplace, free and independent spirits whom management couldn't tame. The situation escalated out of control in a dynamic, unstable, and vicious cycle, as management saw such noncompliant behavior as simply further warrant for rule enforcement. The final result was a sudden and illegal wildcat strike. The organization moved from a pattern of indulgency to one that was "punishment centred." After the strike, there was a concerted attempt to reinterpret and use the rules to create legitimate boundaries for action. During the whole cycle, the rules remained the same; it was their interpretation that changed. Managing the organization is less about knowing what the rules are per se and more about managing their meaning.

Whose interpretation?

Peter Blau (1955) studied two U.S. government agencies, in one of which rule-following was widely policed and observed, whereas in the other, the rules were creatively and interpretively followed. In the latter agency, rules were often bent or locally adjusted to ensure that a desired outcome was achieved. Performance assessment was premised on competition between officials. Blau found that those officials who collaborated rather than competed and who were more flexible in their reporting were more productive. Thus, the creative rule users performed better than the rule followers. Where individuals were given more discretionary delegation in organizations, they performed better than when they worked according to rule. (Of course, working to rule is a classic industrial relations strategy for putting pressure on management.) In fact, in one of the two agencies, a federal office, Blau found that persistent and patterned infringement of the rules by officials made the organization more effective in achieving its formal goals. Local tacit knowledge and ways of doing things produced better outcomes than those ways that were formally mandated. More decentralized organization and less authoritarian management seemed a better bet if you wanted better practice outcomes. Tightly stipulating rules and procedures did not produce best practice. Instead, best practice outcomes occurred where there was room for flexibility within a frame of employment security, a professional orientation, collegiality in work

Image 3.3   *Normal or pathological factory life?*

groups, an absence of entrenched conflicts within the hierarchy, and evaluation by results rather than pressure to conform to processes.

When we think of the organizations in which we would want to work, we probably would prefer not to be in normally pathological forms of bureaucracy. Of course, the pathologies we have covered here are but what goes on inside the organization. We might, perhaps, also wish to consider the impact that the organization may have, pathologically, on its immediate environment, illustrated in Image 3.3, a theme that will recur in this book.

CRITICAL ISSUES: NEW FORMS OF POSTBUREAUCRATIC ORGANIZATION

Questioning bureaucracy

Against bureaucracy

In management today, Weber's concern with bureaucracy seems resolutely old-fashioned, indeed pathologically so. Few care for bureaucracy now, with the exception of Paul du Gay (2000a, 2000b), who makes a robust defense of the concept and practice. Against the defense of bureaucracy, as many theorists argue, we now live in postbureaucratic times, where a concern with efficiency predominates over issues of equity or justice. Organizations have become sleek, shiny, and modern in such a way that the dusty old recesses of bureaucracy have all been eliminated. No more dusty files and laborious clerks, but bright shiny new machines.

Efficiency is often narrowly defined and often confused with effectiveness and economy (see Ransom and Stewart 1994). However, organizations focused solely on cost reduction may be economical in their use of resources but not

Image 3.4   *Bright, shiny, new modernity*

necessarily efficient. Efficiency is the accomplishment of predetermined goals. By using given means to achieve prescribed ends, it does not matter what the ends are as long as they are achieved. Short-term goals will tend to be favored since they are easier to measure (Clarke and Newman 1997: 147). Efficiency rules these days, and everyone seems now to be against bureaucracy. Even the public service, the heartland of bureaucracy, is dominated by "the twin rubrics of business planning and the building of corporate commitment to a specific organizational 'mission' and purpose, linked to survival in a competitive environment" (Clarke and Newman 1997: 147).

The criticism of bureaucracy most frequently cited in the mainstream literature is that which Peters and Waterman (1982) outlined in their version of the "excellent" organization (see also pp. 275–276). Drawing on the research of March and Olsen (1976) and Karl Weick (1979), they argue that following bureaucratic rules produces unimaginative outcomes. Instead, employees must share a managerial vision of their organization's culture and be prepared to go to extraordinary lengths to achieve it, not just follow rules. Organizational members can be liberated from the bondage of bureaucracy by increasing their responsibility and autonomy. Bureaucracy delimits the employee to being a cog in the organizational machine with a limited set of responsibilities. Peters (1994) advocates a broader sort of person, one with nothing to lose but the chains that connect the gears of bureaucracy. The chains of organizational hierarchy were to be smashed through encouraging individual responsibility. It was revolutionary rhetoric. What it sought to overthrow, much as had Mao in 1966-76 in China, was bureaucracy by "cultural revolution."

Weber identified bureaucracy with a growing pervasiveness of rational calculation in all spheres of life. He made a moral case for bureaucracy as rule without regard for persons as a positively democratic ideal, robust against the blandishments of power and privilege. Against Weber, a number of well-known critiques emerged: Bureaucracy is not rational but produces action oriented to past precedents (Lindblom 1959); it generates warped decisions (Cockett 1995) and enables exploitation of uncertainty for sectional benefits (Crozier 1964); bureaucratic personalities are individually and organizationally pathological (Merton 2002). Kanter (1984) wanted to reform bureaucracy through freeing creativity, broadening the individuals' understanding of the overall organization, connecting them to others in it. The corollary of this process would be to improve management. Other writers saw even more reasons for distrusting bureaucracies. For instance, Peters and Waterman (1982) argue that bureaucratic rules privilege past precedents, freezing them for situations that could not have been anticipated. Often these rules remain in existence because they served sectional interests, as Mao had diagnosed.

Beyond bureaucracy

If the classical bureaucracy was a triangle with a broad base, it was superseded in the minds of many management writers by the multidivisional form

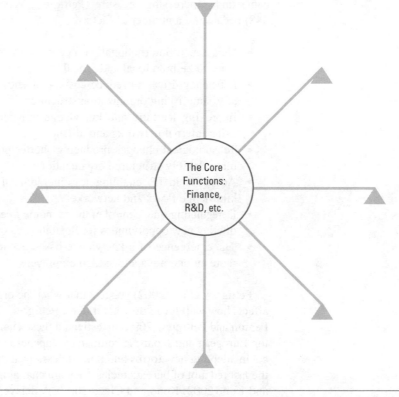

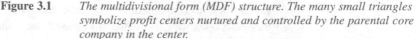

Figure 3.1   *The multidivisional form (MDF) structure. The many small triangles symbolize profit centers nurtured and controlled by the parental core company in the center.*

or MDF, which emerged in the 1930s to become the dominant U.S. form by the 1950s (Fligstein 2002) and became dominant in Western Europe during the 1960s and 1970s. Put simply, this was a hub-and-spokes model with a hub of central services serving spokes with profit centers at their end, which were based usually on either product or regional specialization. Each profit center had to meet centrally fixed performance criteria or else be axed. The MDF consisted of a multiplicity of smaller triangles connected by umbilical cords of financial control to the parental core company. The structure of 3M, with a division for every product, became the classic case of such an organization.

Bureaucracy was located in the MDF in either the product- or region-centered divisions, which related as satellites to core centralized functions, such as finance. The devolved geographical or product-based divisions had to perform according to criteria fixed centrally—for instance, a certain return on investment (ROI). Thus, the rules were more oriented to *outcomes* rather than to processes, unlike the classic bureaucracy. From the 1990s onward, the MDF came under increasing pressure (Pettigrew, Massini, and Numagami 2002: 348) because of a number of factors:

- Heightened international competition through globalization, forcing firms to be both local and global
- Efficiency drives to reduce costs, concentrating manufacturing regionally, simplifying organization structures
- Improving learning and knowledge transfer in international firms, by using internal networks and alliances
- Technological changes producing shorter product life cycles, requiring more flexibly structured organizations
- Advances in IT, enabling less hierarchical controls and more lateral knowledge flows and networks
- Deregulating state control of the economy freed up state-run bureaucracies, offering new opportunities for flexibility, innovation, and radical change
- The emergence of a knowledge-based economy as the norm, requiring more autonomous and skilled employees

Pettigrew et al. (2002) suggest that what the organization is designed to be affects how well it can do what it does. Pettigrew (2003; Pettigrew et al. 2002; Fenton and Pettigrew 2000) investigated these changes during the 1990s in the top European and Japanese companies. Japanese organizations were less radical in adopting new forms but, nonetheless, even though they are often seen as the last redoubt of bureaucracies, they are changing in significant ways (Clegg and Kono 2002; Kono and Clegg 2001). A delayering of middle-management hierarchies, accompanied by increased decentralization, both operational and strategic, is creating more incentive-based and leaner management, often organized in cross-functional and cross-boundary project teams. Organizations are becoming much more interactive, both vertically and horizontally, as a result of IT investments and the development of associated new knowledge and learning capabilities (see also pp. 349–354). These new capabilities are not only intraorganizational but also interorganizational, involving suppliers and customers through supply chains and enhanced human resource management (HRM) functions. Such activities aim to foster horizontal relationships both internally and with external stakeholders, through conferences, seminars, interactions with business schools, and sometimes with rival firms, to create a "boundaryless organization" (Nohria and Ghoshal 1997). The hierarchy of large-scale vertical organization is being replaced with more horizontal relationships, focused more narrowly on core competencies. What is not core can be outsourced to some other organization that can provide the service cheaper, faster, and more innovatively—because it is their core business—or it can be delivered through an alliance (see also pp. 373–374).

Relatively simple mass production technologies gave rise to bureaucratic patterns of managing. Where technologies changed to become more flexible, more flexible styles of managing become possible. Fulk and DeSanctis (2002: 279–280) suggest that it is technologies that make these new styles more flexible. Technologies that offer a dramatic increase in the speed of communication; decrease its cost; increase its bandwidth; vastly expanded connectivity; enhance integration of communication with computing technologies; and open up communal, collaborative capabilities for communication help create alternatives to traditional bureaucratic organizations, making more decentralized and flexible approaches to organization design imaginable (Daft and Lewin 1993).

New organizational forms

Many new forms of organization are emerging these days: the network and cellular form (Miles, Snow, Matthews, and Coleman 1997), the federal organization (Handy 1993), the creative compartment (Fairtlough 1994), the postmodern and flexible firm (Clegg 1990; Volberda 2002), the virtual organization (Goldman, Nagel, and Preiss 1995), and the individualized corporation (Ghoshal and Bartlett 1997). Clarke and Clegg (1998) review the mainstreams in the literature of these "post" organizations—all of which have in common that they are conceived in terms that are opposed to and seen as superseding bureaucratic models of structure. Often, in a generic sense, these post organizations are referred to as "new organizational forms." In Table 3.1 we indicate some of the terms and sources of new organizational forms.

Concepts of new organizational forms are characterized by being less sure about what they are than what they are not; they are opposed to bureaucracy because of its variously diagnosed pathologies. All point the way to some version or other of a postbureaucratic future (Heckscher 1994), but no one term, other than the generic "new organizational forms" (Lewin, Long, and Carroll 2002) and "virtual organization" (Ahuja and Carley 1999; Black and Edwards 2000; Davidow and Malone 1992; De Sanctis and Monge 1999), has captured the imagination in the way that the term *bureaucracy* once did. Palmer and Dunford (2001) provide a succinct account of the relationships between design and form. That there are strong organizational relationships between design and form is evident. Think of the image of a central business district and contrast a traditional townscape with a corporate cityscape, crowding out the small-scale domestic architecture in its surrounds. Could the corporates be easily headquartered in the townscape? Could the townspeople easily live in or adapt to the corporatescape? The literature on new organizational forms suggests that modern corporations can become similar to high-tech cottage industries, as everyone is wired from anywhere. Working virtually, there may be no need to concentrate in a few blocks of central business district real estate. Not every organizational form is as tangible as those which are housed in city skyscrapers. In its most virtual new form, organization will be composed of networks of interdependent but independent

TABLE 3.1   Concepts of new organizational forms

Concept	Characteristics	Author and Year
Adhocracy	Lack of structure and formal rules	Mintzberg 1983b
Technocracy	Organization structure enabled by technological innovations	Burris 1993
Internal market	Flexible markets and internal contracts within an organization structure	Malone, Yates, and Benjamin 1987
Clans	Organization that is based on shared culture rather than formal rules	Ouchi 1980
Heterarchy	A form of organization resembling a network or fishnet	Hedlund 1986
Virtual organization	An organization linked through virtual networks rather than formal rules, often involving several ostensibly separate organizations, often project-organized	Davidow and Malone 1992
Network organization	An organization formed by intersecting and crosscutting linkages between several ostensibly separate organizations	Biggart and Hamilton 1992 Ghoshal and Bartlett 1997 Powell 1990 Rockart and Short 1991
Postbureaucratic organization	An absence of formal rules and hierarchy and more networked structure	Heckscher 1994
Postmodern organization	De-differentiation of structure	Clegg 1990

knowledge-based teams working in different continents and time zones. Such work can be organized on a rolling twenty-four-hour process and often involves multiple global collaborators (Clarke and Clegg 1998: 293). The work activities are often associated with digital databased projects, such as film or copy editing, computer programming, or graphic designing. We even produced a lot of this book in such a way! Some of the time, Stewart was in Europe while Martin and Tyrone were in Sydney, so in twenty-four hours we could do two shifts of drafting and revision instead of one. The book was copy edited in California, sent digitally by e-mail to be reviewed in Sydney, and was back in California for the next workday. From this perspective, designing work in these new ways and hanging on to the old bureaucratic paradigms would be pathological. However, as we shall see, there are those of a strongly "scientific" bent in management who think that abandoning the formal models of the past is equally as pathological (see also pp. 123–124)—at least for the development of a modern, cumulative, and scientific approach to management. We investigate the pathologies of science in Chapter 4, but for now we consider how a constant stress on change may well be inappropriate, if not pathological, for the reality of organizations.

Rhetoric of change?

Given that writing about new organizational forms has proliferated considerably in recent years, we might be seduced into thinking that changing paradigms is easy to do (Clarke and Clegg 1998). That we live in a new age of uncertainty due to enhanced political uncertainty from stressed political systems ("the war on terror" being only the most recent manifestation) further contributes to a sense of unease and change. The rhetoric of change as escalating, increasing momentum and movement rapidly and unpredictably, and creating more volatile organization environments than ever before is widespread. The proximate causes are usually seen as globalization and shifts to digital technology, as well as the development of competition based less on exploitation of existing knowledge and more on exploration and innovation of new knowledge.

But is the rhetoric really useful? Is change as easy as the literature of "changing paradigms" suggests? March (2002) suggests, in a small statement with some big implications, that organizations are essentially adaptive systems. To be adaptive can mean both preserving elements of what is as well as adopting elements of what is not part of the organization's makeup. Making up managers and organizations as radically different may not be so easy, because organizations that seek to change radically are hampered both by remembering and forgetting. Organizations forget some of what they know when their managers presume they can ditch the past for a new future. In order to survive in any changing present, organizations have to remember a great deal of what they have been if they are to maintain cohesion and routine. But too much routine can be lethal for organizations, just as can too much change. Simultaneously, organizations have to exploit what they know and explore what they do not if they are to be adaptive.

> **Organizations that seek to change radically are hampered both by remembering and forgetting.**

Exploitation and exploration

March stresses that adaptiveness involves both the exploitation of what is known as well as the exploration of what is not yet known and might come to be so. Exploitation refers to the routinization, standardization, and formalization of what is already known and done: doing it more cheaply, quickly, efficiently. It focuses attention on repetition, precision, discipline, and control in and of existing capabilities. Its hallmark is process improvement, deepening and refining existing knowledge about ways of doing things. It is risk averse and measurement oriented; it seeks measurable improvement in performance as a result of systematically identifiable causal factors. Exploitation is aided by strongly legitimated and uncontested organization cultures where people know and perform in highly institutionalized appropriate ways. Exploitative initiatives include phenomena such as downsizing, reengineering, and total quality management. By contrast, exploration thrives on accident, randomness, chance, and risk taking. It requires more relaxed attitudes to controls and institutional norms. Risky behavior is more likely to occur when organizations are failing to meet targets than when they are achieving them, when they are failing rather than succeeding. However, risks are best taken when there is sufficient slack or surplus resources that the organization can afford to risk different ways of doing things. In many respects, however, it is least likely that risks will be taken at this time because the grooves of success are already directing the organization.

Evolving and adaptive organizations need to be able to exploit and explore simultaneously. If they are only good at exploitation, they will tend to become better and better in increasingly obsolescent ways of doing things; they will find themselves outflanked. And if they are only specialists in star trekking, in exploration, they are unlikely to realize the advantages of their discoveries, as they lack the exploitative capacities to be able to do so. Organizations have to learn to balance search and action, variation and selection, and change and stability (March 2002: 271).

Two traps confront organizations seeking to achieve this balance. One is the failure trap, the other is the success trap. In the failure trap, organizations explore too much, always trying new ideas; when they fail, they try something else new, which fails again, and so on. A culture of failure develops impatience with new ideas that don't work immediately, as well as an excess of exploration. The success trap arises from being too good at exploitation. It keeps on repeating actions that mimic what was successful previously, and consequently develops highly specific capabilities that new ideas do not match in action, thus encouraging aversion to exploration. The moral of this story is that organizations should never be where they do not belong: Being in too deep a groove is just as dangerous as always searching for innovative futures. Organizations need both exploration and exploitation but not too much of either. But how are they to be designed to achieve this?

March suggests that those organizations that become specialists at short-run efficiency in exploitation will fail in the long run because of their inability to explore. Where a rigid organization fails to explore sufficiently, another will replace it by successfully mutating through exploiting what the previous one failed to explore. March is less confident than the revolutionaries of management such as Peters (1994). From March's perspective, organizations that abandon what they know best in search of the new will be led only to error and failure. Only those few organizations that were able genuinely to exploit novelty—paradoxically by driving the unknown out of exploration rapidly—would survive, although not for too long. It might be instructive to reflect on the dot-com boom and bust through this perspective. The imagined futures and alternative new forms generated in those heady days have been largely abandoned in the debris of the tech wrecks.

In what might stand as a pithy and beautifully expressed epigraph to the dot-com boomers, with their commitment to new ways of organizing, not all of which were necessarily wiped out in 2001, March (2002: 275) states that "[i]maginations of possible organizations are justified by their potential not for predicting the future (which is almost certainly small) but for nurturing the uncritical commitment and persevering madness required for sustained organizational and individual rigidity in a selective environment." The many organizations must fail so that the few models of difference may survive "in a system that sustains imaginative madness at the individual organizational level in order to allow a larger system to choose among alternative insanities" (March 2002: 276). Empirical research thus far suggests that the majority of new organization practices remain incorporated within traditional organizational forms, that organizations may embrace new technologies and practices but do not necessarily change their forms in consequence (Palmer and Dunford 2001).

In fact, March offers a good diagnosis of why efficient forms of exploitation are likely to continue to be reproduced as the dominant organization form. Where innovation does occur, then it is likely to be rewarded only where its exploration rapidly becomes exploited. While particular organizations may come and go, the forms that they exhibit are much less likely to display the radical discontinuities that some of the gurus of management, such as Peters, would suggest. As March says, it is tenacity more than awareness that most revolutions require. Interestingly, while the revolutionaries of the New Right such as Peters were critiquing the old bureaucracy, so were the revolutionaries of the Old Left. For exploitation, which March sees in such matter-of-fact terms, had always been the dark side of the dialectic of modern capitalism and its organizations, from the point of view of radical critics.

March (2002) thinks that the framework of increasingly rapid organizational change will be more likely to create rapid incremental turnover in organization forms than radical discontinuities. In an environment demanding greater flexibility and change of organizations, these changes will tend to play out not just in individual organizations but also in terms of the population of organizations. Some organizations will be selected as efficient, adaptive, and legitimate, whereas others will not survive because they do not match what the environment requires. He foresees a future of short-term organizations that are effectively disposable. These organizations will efficiently exploit what they know how to do until some other organizations emerge to do this better. Then they will die. Adaptability will occur at the population level rather than necessarily at the specific organizational level. Overall, efficiency will be served, although specific organizations may not survive. Not every organization can be a survivor.

THE FINE PRINT: THE DARK SIDE OF THE DIALECTIC

In many ways, when reading writers such as Peters, we are reminded of that point where the libertarian Right meets the radical Left in critique. Of course, they differ markedly in their diagnoses. Peters sees bureaucracies as dinosaurs from an earlier age whose extinction he wishes to hasten. The left wing critiques did not see the errors of bureaucracies in their failure to evolve to a smarter form of life. For the Left, bureaucracies were too efficient, because in contrast to Peters, they enabled ruthless exploitation of labor. The Left were less interested in how the structure of authority relations stifles initiative and enterprise but were more concerned with exploitation in the economic sense. Just as the theory of bureaucracy served as a foil for the new theorists of enterprise and postbureaucracy, the Left theorists who sought to critique exploitation also went back to basics. As a result of a book by Harry Braverman (1974), *Labor and Monopoly Capital: The Degradation of Work in the Twentieth Century,* F. W. Taylor's work was revived in such a way that a contribution that had seemed dead had life transfused into it by virtue of new debates being joined. Braverman, a member of the Socialist Party of America, intended his book to be a Marxist critique of how modern management had deliberately designed junk jobs into which most workers were expected to slot. The book became, in some parts of the world, one of the two or three most influential contributions to organization theory in the last quarter of the twentieth century. Mostly it was read and used by writers who could relate to a socialist tradition of analysis. One consequence was that Europeans and Antipodeans read Braverman much more widely than Americans. The United States has few current traditions of political leftism, in the way that is represented by Social Democratic and Labor Parties elsewhere. While writers close to these parties seized on Braverman as a way of connecting political commitments and analysis, the absence of such commitments among most U.S. academics in management and organization theory meant that Braverman was largely neglected. Elsewhere, however, his work lived on after his untimely death in 1976.

Harry Braverman and the labor process

Harry Braverman lived a full life quite different from the other writers we have encountered thus far. He started out in Brooklyn, New York, where he was born into a poor family in December 1920. In his teens, during the Depression years when Barnard and Mayo were penning their accounts of management, Braverman became a socialist. He was educated at City College in Brooklyn but was forced to leave after just one year and become an apprentice in the Brooklyn Naval Yards from 1937 to 1941. He became a craftsman coppersmith who, with the decline of the trade, later worked in several other jobs where his craft skills were useful, eventually ending up managing the New York-based socialist journal *Monthly Review,* a position that suited a man who was a lifelong socialist. In part his socialism was a response to a working life in which he had seen technological change undercut and dilute his craft skills on many occasions: most recently, making knowledge of machine-based print technology redundant.

(In the days before computers, print was set manually, using lead letters slotted into a frame to compose the text. This was then stamped in ink, which transmitted the image to paper. Later, the technology shifted to electrotype. Extreme skill and considerable handwork were required. Plates had to be leveled, trued up, and carefully checked for high and low "spots." Halftone finishing was even more delicate and exacting. When completed, each plate had to be accurate in thickness and the printing surface uniformly true and sharp. As a final step, the nonprinting sections of the plate were routed for the sure prevention of smudges on the printed sheet. The finishing of electrotype plates required the skill of a watchmaker—and just as much patience.)

Braverman knew very little about contemporary organization and management theory, and what little he knew he disliked intensively. He saw it as a form of apology for a profoundly exploitative system of working relations. In understanding these relations, he took his cue from Karl Marx's (1976) analysis of the labor process in his book *Capital*. The centerpiece of this analysis was the notion of unequal exchange: When laborers exchanged their labor for a wage, then the capitalist must gain more from the exchange than the workers—otherwise there would be no way that a profit could be produced from the labor hired. Marx referred to this profit as "surplus value." Surplus value was achieved by exploiting labor: working them for a greater return than they received and retaining the surplus value that they produced over and above that which they received.

Managers fitted into this schema of capital and labor by being seen as the delegates of capital. Their job was to ensure the efficient extraction of surplus value. They did this by constantly seeking to increase productivity by simplifying jobs, by "de-skilling" them (making them less craft-based and thus less likely to be controlled by a craft worker, using their specialist craft knowledge, and more likely to be controlled by the manager who could insist that managerial rather than craft-approved methods be followed). The result was not only a "degradation of labour" but also an increase in specialization (albeit at a lower level of skill), and thus the division of labor. It also contributed to longer organizational hierarchies, as organizations now needed supervisors to oversee routine de-skilled work in order to see that it was done correctly, according to management plans (see also pp. 18–21).

Against Taylor

There was a villain in Braverman's story and that villain was F. W. Taylor (1911). Taylor was seen as simply an agent of principals who were capital holders. These holders of capital—capitalists—were seen as ruthlessly needing to exploit as much value from the labor process of those they hired as was possible. In the interest of exploitation, they required control. Scientific management was the epitome of the methods that managers instituted to de-skill and control labor. Braverman distilled Taylor's system down to three principles:

1. The unity of knowledge of the labor process under management control
2. The radical separation of "mental" (managerial) labor from "manual" (worker) knowledge
3. The total control of the labor process by management through mechanisms of de-skilling

Braverman's biography, as a craft worker successively de-skilled, as a socialist, and as an author, achieved a remarkable degree of unity. He saw monopoly capitalism (Braverman's expression for the large oligopolies that dominated the U.S. Fortune 500 lists and in which many millions of Americans worked) as a conspiracy against the interests of ordinary employees, the working class. Managers were aligned in their interests with the capitalists, the ruling class, as a "new middle class" of people delegated to do the job of operating surveillance systems on the workers.

Braverman's book was clearly polemical, and written from a definite point of view: that capitalism was a rotten system that routinely denied people freedom, autonomy, and creativity at work. The real villain was "Monopoly Capital." If the principal capital-owners of these firms were shareholders—who ranged from institutional funds, through ordinary investors, and, of course, the top management teams in these companies—then the agents who acted on their behalf were the managers. Although these people were not, strictly speaking, capitalists in the way that a nineteenth-century proprietor may have been, they were, Braverman insisted, indubitably the agents of those whose capital was invested. As such, he believed that they had to operate on the basis of interests that were clearly different from and opposed to the workers they employed—because it was only through the exploitation of these workers that capitalists could make their profits. Like many Marxists, Braverman argued that human labor is the source of all value; therefore, profit must be a form of surplus value extracted from the worker in the labor process. From a Marxist premise, given these assumptions, then it would be only rational for workers to resist the exploitation of their labor power.

To illustrate the thesis, we have chosen to contrast two images of fishing. The first is craft fishing, which is usually done either at dawn or dusk, when the fish are feeding, and entails considerable tacit knowledge that is a part of the craft of fishing. Industrial fishing, by contrast, is equivalent to a process where the brute strength of industrial machinery substitutes for craft and the fish are basically dredged rather than caught with skill. Braverman has been criticized for being too "romantic" about the nature of work, harking back to a gilded age of craft, before the fall, when the worker was less alienated and had more autonomy. Of course, many jobs are industrial or postindustrial, and we cannot compare these with craft jobs—they have not derived from them but were newly born with technological change. Braverman's analysis would best fit jobs such as those he once had—ancient crafts radically transformed or superseded by changes in technology, for which we use fishing as an illustration.

Image 3.5   *The craft and industry of fishing*

One could argue that Braverman stated his case too one-dimensionally. The control that management achieves over workers is never "total"; there is always space for resistance, either individually or collectively. Many subsequent studies were devoted to cases of this resistance and the ever more ingenious ways in which it might be organized. Braverman did not place sufficient stress on the many ingenious ways in which workers can resist managerial control, but nonetheless, his work sparked new and interesting debates around the issue of resistance.

The labor process debate

Braverman's work enjoyed a popular critical reception among many sociologists and some organization and management theorists. Textbooks were written, developing the labor process perspective (Clegg and Dunkerley 1980; Thompson and McHugh 1995). Admirers of Braverman's approach inaugurated an annual Labour Process Conference. A key theme centered on de-skilling, initially seen as the result of Taylorism but which became a theme in itself, irrespective of the historical argument. Wherever jobs could be argued to be undergoing a process of fragmentation and where mental elements involved in the conception of work were being separated from their manual execution, a dynamic of de-skilling would be in process. The result would be increasingly routine and fragmented tasks, where individual employees lacked understanding of the principles underlying their relation with others. In a word, they would be alienated. The introduction of newer, simpler technologies would be used to transfer control over the labor process from workers to management (Braverman 1974: 194). The result would be a downward pressure on wages and conditions of work, both within nation-states and globally. Junk jobs would emerge that had been de-skilled into easily learned low-paid tasks. Although these might initially open up a divide between those who held such jobs and those who were in more demanding work in particular countries, the long-term effect would be experienced in an international division of labor. Junk jobs could be set up anywhere in the world where there was compliant, cheap labor (see also pp. 470–474).

The thesis of the "degradation of work" had as its fulcrum the need for control by capital exercised through its delegates, management. Friedman (1977: 78) argued that the limitations of direct control as a strategy for management could be partially counteracted by developing "responsible autonomy" for some employees, such as highly skilled and creative types, whose discretion management needed in work. Not all jobs could or would be de-skilled to the furthest point. Edwards (1979) extended Braverman's analysis by highlighting that management also controlled employees through machinery and technological innovations such as assembly lines as well as through the rules of "bureaucratic control," as Weber's account had developed. The effects of technology, in particular, were much elaborated by labor process writers (e.g., see the contributions of Knights and Willmott 1988; also Friedman 1990).

Other researchers rapidly amended Braverman's ideas. Burawoy (1979) noted the prevalence of cooperation in most workplaces much of the time, which he saw as arising from participation in local "games" on the shop floor—where the immediate elements of management control (such as a supervisor or payment system) became the object of worker ingenuity designed to beat the rules. He argued that the opportunity to gain small victories in local struggles over things close at hand to the immediate concerns of the employees softened the fundamentally skewed nature of the game in which any employee cooperates.

Some writers insisted that the important issues did not occur in these local struggles at work but in the way that the labor market was structured. In fact, to see labor as subject to inexorable degradation was to simplify the nature of reality hugely. It assumed that all workers competed in a single swelling labor market, when in fact there were many labor markets, often exhibiting characteristics of "dual labor market segmentation."

Rubery (1978) developed a theory of dual labor market segmentation. She argued that labor markets were structured not just by the actions of employers but also by the ability of workers "to maintain, develop, extend and reshape their organisation and bargaining power" (Rubery 1978: 34). Characteristically, dual labor markets divide between those segments that have some degree of career prospects, are full-time and better paid, and enjoy better conditions. The other segment is composed of less-skilled jobs, often casual and part-time, with worse pay, prospects, and conditions. Often, labor market dualism was argued to have a gender dimension to it, that is, the pool of employees divided into those who had secure, better-paid full-time work, largely men, whereas those who were in part-time, less secure, and lower paid work were disproportionately women (see Clegg and Dunkerley 1980: 400–422 and Knights and Willmott 1986 for earlier labor process treatments of these themes).

Divisions in the broad class of labor, between different market segments and genders, made the task of control much easier. According to these accounts, this was because such divisions concentrated employees' minds on the fact that they slotted into a huge hierarchy of labor, with the long-term unemployed at the bottom, and everyone competing for the minor qualitative differences available from shifting from one segment to the next—what Braverman called divide and rule prevailed. Hence, as Clegg (1981) argued, different types of control, using different principles, would be targeted at different categories of employees. Organizations were sedimented structures, revealing a complex layering of controls stratified both in terms of their emergences, as a temporal phenomena, and in terms of the organizational hierarchy. Taylorism might persist in detailed definitions and prescriptions underneath many subsequent accretions, but to concentrate only on it and to miss these other elements would be to fail to deal adequately with the multifaceted phenomena of organization control. It would miss the effects of job redesign as these had sedimented over time (also see the contributions in Knights, Willmott, and Collinson 1988).

According to an influential school of critique, the labor process debate was constructed around a theoretical dualism (Knights 1990; Knights and Vurdubakis 1994; Knights and Willmott 1988). Braverman and traditional labor process theorists were structuralist and determinists. They minimized the capacity of ordinary people to exercise their human agency through resistance to control at work. They saw control as almost total, in a fatalistic way. Those human beings who were workers became ciphers in these views, shaped almost entirely by external agencies—which, correlatively, were granted an almost total power as against the almost total subordination of those they controlled. Knights and Willmott (1989: 554) argued that everyone has some power and that we all have subjectivity. It is not the case that some are ciphers and some are agents, that some can only do what only others can demand. It is not a case of power and autonomy on the one hand and subjection and control on the other. With this move, the labor process debate was linked with Foucault's (1979) emphases in the study of surveillance (see also pp. 366–367). In this vein, many case studies were conducted that demonstrated the ingenious sources of resistance that workers could use to ensure that they did not fall under total managerial control (see also pp. 170; 165–170).

Knights and Willmott's (1989) interventions suggested that if the labor process theorists had a too pessimistic view of the strategies for resistance available to employees through resistant subjectivities—such as Burawoy (1979) found—they also had an inflated view of the strategic abilities of capitalists. Certainly, if capitalists were so clever and capable, and exploiting the workers was all they needed to do to thrive and prosper, we might well ask why so many companies seemed to be so badly managed that they went bankrupt with such frequency. Didn't they know how to exploit labor?

Braverman started the debate in opposition to Taylor, drawing on his experience as a craft worker. In such work, the human element is a high part of the cost structure. But in many industries, the costs of human labor are quite marginal, so there is little need to focus strategy exclusively on them. Most enterprises use a range of simultaneous strategies targeted at different elements in the strategic mix. However, some organizations do concentrate on exploitation in both Braverman's and March's sense by developing a one-dimensional focus on cost cutting and systematization. The most obvious example comes from the fast-food industry, for which McDonald's has become both the metaphor and an icon.

McDonaldization

The American sociologist George Ritzer (1993) coined the term "McDonaldization." It refers to the application of goal-oriented rationality to

The model of McDonald's is a metaphor for a highly rationalized and "cheap as chips" approach to business processes.

all areas of human life. The model of McDonald's is a metaphor for a highly rationalized and "cheap as chips" approach to business processes "by which the principles of the fast-food restaurants are coming to dominate more and more sectors of American society as well as the rest of the world" (Ritzer, 1993: 1). However, McDonaldization does not stop at the fast-food store—it spreads to all areas of everyday life: to recreation, informal and interpersonal relationships, and even love and intimacy—think of "speed dating." As Ritzer says, even those places and activities that used to offer some release from a routinized world have now been rationalized through four major mechanisms:

1. *Efficiency* means utilizing the least output to gain the highest return. In mechanics, where the term comes from, efficiency is defined in terms of minimizing losses to extraneous physical activities, such as heat or friction in the transmission of energy. In business, efficiency implies instrumental rationality, that is, given a goal, such as to maximize profits, what is the most instrumentally efficient way of achieving this outcome? Or in simple terms, if the organization is a tool that is managed to achieve specific purposes, how can waste of resources be minimized around the tool's use? One way is to transfer the costs to the consumer. The McDonald's model dispenses with waitresses and offers only preformatted menus. The same is true of call centers, where you, the customer, pay to be lined up to wait on the telephone, often interminably, to speak to someone about your problem. But then when you do speak to someone, you might as well be at a McDonald's, because the person at the other end knows nothing in particular about your problem—but they do know how to read a pre-programmed script from a menu of options on the computer in front of them.

2. *Calculability* means cheapening the assembly costs of the standard product. It is calculably cheaper to make reality TV shows where there is no script development cost, no actors and agents' fees, just a bunch of people happy to try to grab their fifteen minutes of "fame"—or notoriety.

3. *Predictability* means that a McDonaldized service or product should be the same anywhere in the world every time. There should be no surprises. It means leaving nothing to the imagination; scripting everything—"You want French fries with that?"—and using standardized procedures to produce always standardized outputs. Every day at Disneyland should be just the same experience, irrespective of the "team members" inside the suits, on the rides, or serving in the cafeteria. And the team members are always young, cheap, and interchangeable.

4. *Control* means minimizing variation in every ingredient in the organizational assembly of people and things: customers and employees, raw materials, labor processes, and markets. It often means substituting machine processes that are utterly controllable for people who are not. Where people can't be

substituted, they can be drilled—just like the call center operators and McDonald's staff—to always perform the same routines. And the organization can try to ensure that even physical appearance is controlled. Ritzer cites the example of the Euro Disney employees who had strict rules applied about their weight-to-height ratios, facial appearance, hair length, jewelry, makeup, and underwear. Control means learning to do and to be as one is told, even down to smiling on cue, as Mills (1996) demonstrates in his analysis of flight attendants.

McDonald's may be instrumentally rational as a profit center but is not very rational in other terms. It uses enormous quantities of grain to grow cereals to feed to cattle to kill in rationalized slaughterhouses (which were the original basis for Ford's idea of the moving production line). It packs the burgers in sweet bread that is unhealthy and serves it in containers that will be discarded and added to the planet's waste. Ritzer's McDonaldization kills spontaneity, creativity, and joy in discovery. When most things are reduced to the cheapest way of making them the same, there will be few surprises in store.

McDonaldization may be seen as a soulless prefiguring of the kind of hell—the endless repetition of being in the frying pan of life as if one were already in the fire of purgatory—that is usually served from the pulpit (with apologies to James Joyce's [1986] *Portrait of the Artist as a Young Man*). However, as it mostly employs young people, part-time, and students, many put up with it because they know that it is not a life sentence. Not everyone working in a McDonaldized organization is so fortunate. For some people, the segmentation of the labor market condemns them to a lifetime of junk jobs.

March thinks much of the world will become more McDonaldized, producing efficient firms that last for a while, but which are then disposable. For March's scenario to be realized, however, there has to be a pool of organizations that are discontinuously exploring learning through active imagining. Of course, without the pioneering of new forms and structures, there would be no new and more efficient mutations of organization forms to succeed those that already exist. Now, if March is right, what this probably means is a double-edged movement: McDonaldization of the efficient but relatively disposable exploiters of knowledge, with the exercise of imagination reserved for those organizations that seek to explore new forms of knowledge. What is foreseen is a type of *Blade Runner* scenario: highly innovative science-based knowledge organizations in gleaming towers for the highly paid, skilled, and educated, on the one hand, and on the other hand, lots of street-level organizations that are exploitive and relatively impoverished, providing a poor working environment.

SUMMARY AND REVIEW

One star from the founding firmament—in many ways the least likely—has shone brightly since his death and that is F. W. Taylor. Taylor was the least likely of the founding figures to have been remembered because he was, in almost every respect, the most limited and one-dimensional in his thinking. However, perhaps for this reason, he has been the management thinker most seized on as an object of critique, especially in the wake of Braverman pinning responsibility on him for the degradation of work in the twentieth century. The denigration of Taylor and the elevation of the labor process and its control to the central conceptual topic for analysis privileged the contributions of Marx and those who followed in his tracks. In many ways, this was odd. Weber, who was far more a founder of organization theories than Marx ever was, became somewhat neglected by comparison, as did those who followed in the typological tracks that he laid down. Much that was insightful and interesting in the main currents that were available in the twentieth century became neglected in consequence. Relatively mundane figures such as Taylor were elevated to an intellectual importance that they probably did not deserve, despite the fact that the practical implementation of ideas that they helped popularize was enormously influential in the twentieth century. Weber and those who followed his typological path were in many ways far more encompassing and creative in their concerns than was the case with those who followed Braverman in reconsidering Taylor and the centrality of the labor process. Shop-floor sociology leaves out a great deal of what is important and interesting about the way organizations are constructed and the way that people are managed within them. Indeed, the most significant debates in terms of their impact on the way that organizations are structured today has probably come from those for whom Weber's bureaucracy was more the object of attention than the time and motion studies of Taylor. Weber's star went down as bureaucracies came under increasing criticism—especially through the populist antibureaucratic theorizing by recent gurus that has contributed to much of the privatization and restructuring of public sectors around the world. As March suggests, radical reformism is not as easy as the revolutionaries would have it—and that goes for the revolutionaries of the Right (the antibureaucrats), just as much as those of the Left (the anticapitalists). If March is right, McDonaldization does seem to be confirmed as the fate of many of us for much of our time. Maybe Weber was right after all?

ONE MORE TIME . . .

Getting the story straight

- What were the main criticisms of Weber's model of bureaucracy?
- Why did classical management prescriptions not produce efficiency in the way theorists have anticipated, according to the empirical studies of organizational typologists?

Thinking outside the box

- What are the main drivers of new organizational forms?
- How do exploitation and exploration link to organizational forms?
- According to Braverman, what role do managers play in capitalist society?
- What are the central processes of McDonaldization?

ADDITIONAL RESOURCES

1. Weber is important—but not easy to read. He wrote at a time, nearly a hundred years ago, when only a small elite was well educated. Today we live in a very different world with a much wider but quite different set of cultural resources at our disposal. Perhaps if you were to read the extract on "Bureaucracy" in *From Max Weber* (1948), this would be as good as any place to start. It is reasonably self-contained.

2. If you wanted to gain a better understanding of the typologies that followed on Weber's work, then a 1980 book by Stewart Clegg (with David Dunkerley) called *Organization, Class and Control* would probably be a good place to gain an overview. It provides synopses and criticisms in Chapter 4.

3. Pugh and Hickson's (1997) *Writers on Organizations* is ever reliable, providing brief and clear thumbnail sketches of many of the characters encountered in this and the preceding chapters.

4. If the "labor process debate" interests you greatly, then, along with Braverman (1974), good and critical overviews are to be found in articles by Stark (2002) and Meiksins (2002).

5. Finally, the writer who has done most to alert us to the trade-offs between dumbed-down efficiency and human dignity is probably George Ritzer (1993), the person responsible for the McDonaldization thesis, in his entertaining book *The McDonaldization of Society*.

6. Films on bureaucracy are many. We particularly like the film directed by Terry Gilliam, of Monty Python fame, that is simply called *Brazil,* and the Ealing classic, directed by Henry Cornelius, to which it owes so much, *Passport to Pimlico*.

7. We also mentioned the Ridley Scott film *Blade Runner,* which is a science fiction depiction of a world where exploration and exploitation of knowledge are only too institutionalized and separated.

8. Finally, there is an excellent film of Kafka's *The Trial* from 1993, starring Kyle MacLachlan and Anthony Hopkins, which illustrates the dread and oppressiveness of bureaucracy at its worst, which we have already mentioned in the Additional Resources for Chapter 2.

In addition to these suggested additional resources, don't forget to look at what is also available on the Web site **www.ckmanagement.net,** including free PDF files of recent papers related to this chapter, which you can download; video interviews with famous academics talking about related themes; as well as many other resources, such as connections to interesting Web sites.

PART II
MANAGING ORGANIZATIONS

CHAPTER 4

MANAGING ORGANIZATION DESIGN

Structure, Environment, Fit

Objectives and learning outcomes

By the end of this chapter, you will be able to

- Define organizations in terms of their structures

- Discuss size, technology, and environment as the key contingencies associated with organization structures

- Link organizational contingencies to organizational design

- Join issues of organizational structure to questions of organizational strategy

- Understand the promises and premises of positivism

Before you get started . . .

A little thought by Jean Cocteau:
"I look at the scaffold for the king from the carpenter's perspective: The structure of the scaffold is of more interest to me than the actual execution." (Cocteau 1988: 99 [our translation])

OUTLINE OF THE CHAPTER

In this chapter, we follow Cocteau's carpenter. Instead of focusing on the sometimes glamorous, sometimes messy actions that take place in the organizational arena, we analyze the structures that provide the framework for organizational action. Although they are not always visible to the spectators, they are the core of organizations.

Contingency theory emerged out of disgruntlement with the multiplicity of typologies and a desire to find a singular basis for comparing organizations. Recent discussion of the management of organizations has focused on how the goodness of fit between an organization's structure and its *contingencies*— the inescapable things that it has to deal with—can change over time. As these become misaligned, because contingencies change, a process of structural readjustment is required. The process emerged out of studies that focus on the relation between mechanisms such as technology and size and organization structure.

One consequence of thinking of organizations as more-or-less effective designs for dealing with a number of contingencies is that certain aspects of the historical design of organizations become privileged. It becomes really hard to think about how we might design organizations without hierarchies that require controlling and a division of labor that requires coordinating. Therefore, most of the contingencies literature deals with organizations as imperfect designs that can be improved to deal more effectively with predictable contingencies; thus, in a shorthand way, one might say that if we want to know why the design is as it is, we should first know what the main contingencies are that the organization has to deal with. For instance, does it deal with an environment that is stable and predictable or one that is changing and uncertain? Does it have a routine or nonroutine technology? Is the organization small—that is, one in which communication can be largely face-to-face, and where coordination and control are fairly straightforward? Or is it a large and much more impersonal organization, where managers cannot rely on face-to-face meetings to reach most people—there are simply too many people— and where, in consequence, the amount of planning dedicated to dealing with coordination and control issues is much greater? The latter type of organization, suggests contingency theory, is likely to be much more bureaucratic, requiring far more planned routines, formalized structures, centralized meetings and communications than the smaller, more personal organization.

Most contingency models of organizations offer variations on an underlying bureaucratic organization form. Moreover, adherents of the theory suggest that, in principle, all types of organizations, irrespective of their specificities—big or small, profit or not-for-profit, technologically complex or simple—can be compared using a contingency approach.

SETTING THE SCENE

Mainstream organization and management theory poses a central issue: how to best design a structure specifically suited to the circumstances with which an organization has to deal. Whereas earlier writers such as Taylor (see also pp. 18–22) had presumed there was one best way to organize, the contingency theorists suggest that how to organize depends on what the central factors are that management faces. Structure becomes one of the most important issues because it is structure that holds the whole organization together, keeps it afloat, and separates the inside from the outside.

Prior to the development of contingency perspectives, most theorists had either written up case studies of particular organizations or focused on some specific substantive aspect of organizations, such as "who benefits?" Contingency theory developed in tandem with what is known as the *open systems* conception of the organization. In this approach, organizations were viewed as systems that were open to inputs from their environments and that sent outputs to their environments as a result of their internal transformation processes. The advantage of this model was that any and every organization could be conceptualized as a system, with system properties of inputs, throughputs, and outputs. However, persistent disagreements occurred between major theorists regarding what the major determinants shaping the structures of these organization systems were. For some, the most critical factor was the number of employees the organization employed. Some thought it was the technology the organization used, whereas others focused on the environments in which the organizations operated. Some theorists came to the conclusion that focusing on such factors was too deterministic—it left no role for top management to exercise strategic choice. All management had to do was periodically redesign the organization structure to fit changing contingencies. Such a conception of top management work hardly squared with the very complex work carried out by strategic managers.

One of the problems with contingency approaches was that, although they developed robust measures with which to capture data on organization structures, the assumptions upon which these measures were based were less robust. The approaches assumed bureaucracy. This would not be a problem if the world of organizations were always a world of bureaucracy. However, many theorists have suggested that, from the 1980s onward, the organizational world has increasingly seen development of new organization forms that are alternatives to bureaucracy (see also pp. 97–101). If, indeed, they are alternatives

Image 4.1   *Structure*

and not just variants on the form, where does this leave theory that developed out of reflection of and on bureaucratic models?

Contingency theory assumes that changes in contingencies render variation around an essential organization form, but what if there is no essence to the organizational form? What if the form of organization is itself a historically contingent device, something that may not outlive its fifteen metaphorical minutes of fame? Modern organizations are a relatively recent historical device; we should not assume that, like other nineteenth century innovations such as the internal combustion energy, they will go on forever. And if the empirical correlates of the science of modern organizations are temporally contingent, we need a different model of science than one that assumes the eternal verity and stability of its objects of analysis.

Science is full of cases of random variation; the impact of meteorites or of volcanic-induced climate changes (through the blanket effect of volcanic ash) on the ecosystem would be cases in point. Random and arbitrary variation in the contextual conditions need not come from just some exogenous source of change, such as a meteorite or geological activity. Although these are clearly important, there are other, more mundane, sources of variation to consider. For instance, in the sphere of organizations, all attempts at organized corporate sensemaking rely on the organization's power to secure this sense. Potentially, any organization's power to do this may be subject to *erosion,* defined as a diminished capacity on the part of the organization to maintain the set of conditions that, contextually, structure its action episodes. Erosion may derive from the failure of existing organization imagination (such as in the former Soviet Union), success in implementing its imagination on the part of some other power (such as the images of prosperity and the good life beamed through Hollywood TV dramas around the world), as well as random and arbitrary acts that serve to destabilize the existing context (such as the impact of 9/11 on many of the policies and procedures of the U.S. government).

The historical constitution of bureaucratic rules provides a concrete organizational example. These rules may no longer make sense for some powerful actors who had traditionally framed them. For instance, their security might be undercut by the imagination of other possibilities by actors elsewhere—competitors or influential consultants. If actors choose to make organizational sense using some other rules, such as rules for new organization forms" (see also pp. 97–99), the new organizations will not necessarily be a variant on the same bureaucratic theme as before. As sense changes, themes may change, too.

CENTRAL APPROACHES AND MAIN THEORIES

One problem with the typological approach that developed in the wake of Weber's translation into English, which we reviewed briefly in Chapter 3, was a lack of accumulation and coherence; how could one accumulate research in which each study had a different principle for typological formation? If one study focused on control and involvement, another on who benefits, and a third on the meaning of rules in different contexts at different times, how could one synthesize the undoubtedly useful knowledge that each produced?

Strengthening the science

The study of organizational structure and design bridges the gap inherent in the typological approach and supposedly creates useful knowledge for practice. Just reflect on the developments we have outlined so far; as you might have noticed, all the studies that were previously considered were either theoretical studies, such as those of Weber (1978) and Merton (2002), or case studies, such as those of Gouldner (1954) and Blau (1955). As such, they conformed to what Crozier (1976: 194) termed a "dominant paradigm"—a model that was widely used—in which he saw a number of weaknesses:

- A focus on organizational processes rather than the structural characteristics of organizations themselves
- Too much reliance on cases and an inability to generalize and theory build
- An over-functionalist approach, where it was assumed that organization mechanisms contributed to consensus and harmony as a norm

Against these weaknesses, Crozier noted the development of newer approaches that used statistical analysis of samples of data for testing hypotheses expressed in terms of variables. The case study approach, he implied, was increasingly seen as passé, superseded by newer approaches focused on variables rather than cases. The aim was to make studies comparable to each other and, in doing so, to build up knowledge that would provide clear advice for managers on how to design their organizations. A particular method, known as *positivism,* guided their inquiries.

Positivism

Postivism, the model of science that underpins contingency theory, argues that although theoretical constructions such as organization structure may be unobservable, hypotheses concerning the properties of these constructs may be tested. The results of these tests tend either to confirm or to refute the theories in question. For instance, in Chapter 3, we discussed Braverman's labor process theory. The theory argued that exploitation was the prime mechanism that drives changes to organization structuring. The result of exploitation would be the degradation of labor through breaking down the skill basis of craft labor—called "de-skilling" by Braverman (1974). Hence, if it could be established that de-skilling had not been the dominant trend in particular organizations during the twentieth century, then the hypothesis would be refuted for those cases.

Positivism models itself on natural science.

Positivism models itself on natural science; it seeks theoretical generalizations of a broad scope through explanations that address objective mechanisms in terms of their causal regularities. Proponents of positivism argue that organizations, and the behavior that we may observe within them, are a patterned and regulated result of causal mechanisms. These mechanisms include factors such as the environment of the organization and the organization's size.

The mechanisms are conceptualized as *social facts*—as real things that cannot be ignored or imagined away, just as their effects cannot be withstood by the assertion of willpower. In all probability, given specific contingencies, organizations will have certain characteristics. In a related vein, organizations express *brute facts*—that is, regardless of what you and I might want to be the case, something predictable actually will occur as a result of given conditions, whether we like it or not. For example, we might not want our organizations to become more bureaucratic as we increase their size but, in all probability, they will become so, according to contingency theory. Increased competition will put a premium on efficiency in management; those organizations that do not have efficient practices will lose market share to those that do (Donaldson 2003: 118). Managers exposed to extreme competition have to become more efficient if their organizations are to survive.

Some analysts would argue that contingency theories of organizations do express general causal laws—the theories express conjectures about the behaviors and structure of organizations, and those hypotheses have been repeatedly tested through observations of empirical patterns. When the hypotheses that are deduced are not confirmed, these hypothetical elements of the theory are rejected, or a competing theory, which is more hypothetically robust, is accepted.

Simply because a hypothesis is not refuted does not mean that the theory behind it is valid. The hypothesis may be confirmed, but the theory that it is derived from may later prove to be false because some other mechanism is at work that the theory did not stipulate. For instance, we might hypothesize that lightning will invariably be associated with thunder, in probabilistic terms. However, it would be wrong to think the lightning caused the thunder; they are both the effects of atmospheric mechanisms, which a more adequate theory would stipulate.

Positivism is a very cautious approach, which is one of its great strengths. It does not allow for any theory to attain the status of a self-evident truth because it is always possible that it might be refuted in the future. Donaldson (2003: 119) expresses this idea very clearly:

> Thus a theory is never proven or established as the truth, but rather is a fallible human conjecture that constitutes valid scientific knowledge until it is in turn falsified and replaced by a new conjecture that is better able to resist falsification. No theory is absolutely true, but rather it is truer than the theories that preceded it. In this way progress in science consists of refuting untruths and replacing them with theories that are less untrue.

In organizational terms, the mechanisms that regulate organizations are seen to be an interactive effect between the structure of the organization and the organization's functions—what it does. The usual name for this approach is *structural functionalism*. Briefly, proponents of this model argue that more functionally effective practices tend to be selected in the long term because they are more efficient; because they are more efficient, the organizations that exhibit these characteristics tend to have better survival rates than those that do not. Organizations whose structures are best adapted to their functioning are those that have a good fit between their design and the contingencies that they have to deal with. Less efficient organizations are those with a mismatch between design and contingencies. Hence, organizations take a relatively small number of forms because the ones that survive and become widely reproduced are those that are functionally most efficient. These forms comprise a particular set of patterns formed around certain key variables.

What is a variable?

If one thinks of a class of students, height, weight, shoe size, and waistband size would all be variables—that is, one would expect a degree of variance in the empirical results for any of these measures. A variable is represented by data collected on measures that capture a range of values using a standard metric. (Of course, if the sample was representative enough, one would expect the data on any of these to be normally distributed.) Organization variables are similar; they represent properties that one would expect to find in any population of organizations but which one would not expect to be distributed in the same manner in each organization. Some organizations would have more of the property, others less—or, to put it another way, if we were using some standard measures of the extent of the distribution of these properties across a sample of organizations, some organizations would have a higher, and others a lower, score. With the term *contingency,* organizational theorists capture the most important environmental influences that determine those organizational variables that build up its structure.

What is a contingency?

Dictionaries usually define a *contingency* as an event that may occur; it is a possibility that must be prepared for or a future emergency that might arise depending on chance and uncertainty. In management and organization theory, the term takes on a different meaning. For management, a *contingency* is something that managers cannot avoid. Contingencies arise from routines rather than from emergencies, as facts of organizational life, and have to be acknowledged and dealt with. Different organizations face different contingencies. How they handle these contingencies is reflected in their organizational design. Thus, contingencies have a significant impact on the main variables in organizational design.

Key contingencies

On the basis of correlations between contingencies and organization structural variables, established through large-scale, survey-based studies, contemporary organization theorists argue, much as Etzioni (1961) did, that there is a tendency toward consistency. Those organizations whose structures are not well aligned with the contingencies that they currently deal with have to undertake structural adjustment to regain fit with those contingencies. The contingencies of environment, technology, and size have been seen as theoretically important:

- *Environment:* The more certain and predictable the environments in which organizations operate, the more probable it is that they will have bureaucratic structures.
- *Technology:* As organizations adopt more *routinized technologies*— technologies with repetition and routines associated with them—they tend to become more bureaucratic.
- *Size:* As organizations become bigger, they become more bureaucratic, in the sense of being characterized by higher scores on scales that measure the degree of formalization, standardization, and centralization.

Burns and Stalker: The environment matters

Burns and Stalker (1961) were Scottish researchers who envisioned organizations as variable structures related to differences in the key contingency of the external environment that they had to deal with. Firms operating in stable business environments in which there was little discontinuous innovation were much more mechanistic than firms operating in more rapidly changing and uncertain environments. In these more dynamic environments, firms had much more organic, looser, less bureaucratic structures. Basically, the model depicted a world of mechanistic, stable organizations for routine environments. If the environment changed to one that was dynamic, the structure of the organization would need to change to become more organic. To see how various management dimensions change depending on whether an organization follows a mechanistic or organic design, see Table 4.1.

Woodward: Technology matters

Joan Woodward (1965), an English researcher, studied about 80 industrial firms in the southeast of England and focused on technology to make sense of the data that she collected. She argued that the more routinized the technology, the more the firm had a structured set of organizational authority relations. Technology meant, simply, the production methods in use in the firms in question. Technologies were classified into a number of types: *small batch and unit production* (where the products were largely tailored designs for different customers with small runs) *large batch and mass production* (where the production runs were much larger and the customers usually many fewer) and *process production* (where the system was a continuous flow on a twenty-four-hour,

TABLE 4.1 Burns and Stalker's structures

	Design	
Dimension	**Mechanistic**	**Organic**
Standardization	High	Low
Formalization	High	Low
Centralization	Concentrated	Diffuse
Discretion	Small	Extensive
Authority levels	Many	Few
Administrative component	Large	Small
Specialization	Depth	Breadth
Communication	Minimal	Extensive
Source: Pennings (2002: 6)		

seven-day-a-week basis, with the major requirement being that the system stay to specifications and standards). These distinctions were made on the basis of the technical complexity of the operations, defined in terms of the degree of controllability of the production process and the extent to which results were predictable.

Woodward found out, to her surprise, that firms with similar production systems were organized in a similar manner and that the degree of technical complexity was related to the number of levels in the organization, the span of control of front-line supervisors, and the ratio of managers and administrative staff to the total work force. Organizations using the least and the most complex technologies—unit and process production, respectively—showed a number of similarities. These organizations had a low level of specialization compared with the managers in the mass production firms.

The reason that specialists were less evident in unit and process firms differed in each case. Small batch and unit production firms employed fewer specialists because these organizations required more generalist skills for more variable production runs; also, these firms tended to be smaller than mass production organizations, so staff had to be technically more competent. In process production, staff specialists had a very high status and were sometimes difficult to distinguish from management, who also had to have a high level of technical expertise. Both process and unit and small batch production had relatively low levels of bureaucracy compared to mass production.

Woodward related these differences in organization structure and technology to the central problems that each category of organization dealt with. For unit and small batch production, it was product development—meeting specific customer requirements for single or small batches of a specialist pro

For the process organizations, the central issue was marketing—they had to ensure that the continually flowing output from the production process met sufficient immediate demand. Thus, the type of innovation that was central depended on the type of organization. A formally bureaucratic structure, such as was common in a mass production technology-centered firm, seemed inimical to innovation; instead, the central issue was efficiency in administering standardized production.

It is not only the central organizational problem that is significant but also the time span of the discretion exercised in making decisions. In batch and unit production, many decisions are made, but they typically have short-term consequences because they relate to an immediate design or production issue that will not necessarily have implications for the next, probably different, job. Decisions tend to be made on the line with little need for authorization from on high. In mass production, however, there are fewer decisions to be made because the process is so much more routinized and predictable, but those decisions have much longer implications because production runs are long-lasting and repeating. Because decisions about production have major resource and related implications, they tend to be referred up the management line to the level of the functional specialist responsible for the arena within which the decision issue falls. In process production, although fewer policy decisions are made, they have both longer-term and more interdependent implications. In a continuous process, any change to any parameter may affect all others, so decision making has to be pooled because of the sequential and reciprocal nature of the issues involved. Hence, a strongly bureaucratic structure would be inappropriate because it would place functional specialists in separate silos of knowledge rather than integrating and pooling them. In Woodward's research, technology is a crucial contingency because it enables her to construct a detailed narrative about the nature of organizational structuring and decision making.

The Aston project: Size matters

One approach above all others reflected the new emphasis on contingencies: the work of the Aston School (Pugh and Hickson 1976). A group of researchers at the University of Aston applied techniques developed in the analysis of personality structure to the analysis of organization structure. Psychology had developed a central concept—that of the personality—but had little consensus on what it encompassed. Different schools held different views. Literary speculation mingled with armchair theorizing and the occasional case study. Organization structures, the researchers reasoned, were not too dissimilar. They agreed that organization structure mattered, but they were unable to agree on what the term meant.

The matter had been more urgent for psychologists interested in personality structure. From their experiences screening individuals during World War

I, psychologists were well aware of the important impact that personality type might have on fitness for particular types of military service. Put bluntly, you wouldn't want people with highly emotional personalities, who might become hysterical under fire and lose control, in charge of troops. Thus, in the 1940s, spurred on by the necessity to develop well-designed instruments for selection of enlisted men for particular aptitudes and tasks in the U.S. armed forces, psychologists developed a solution to the problem of a lack of agreement on what comprised personality structure. The solution began with a good dictionary. Allport and Odbert (1936) discovered that there were about 18,000 adjectives that appeared to be descriptive of personality in the English language. About 4,000 words seemed to correspond to particular traits such as "humility" or "arrogance." Subsequently, psychologists collected systematic data on these traits, coming up with 4,504 potential personality traits. They constructed questions using these terms and asked about people's dispositions and how well these terms seemed to describe them. In this way, subsequent psychologists reduced these traits to a list of only 171 items and then produced a data bank of responses across a large sample of people who identified themselves more or less strongly with these traits (Cattell 1946).

After Cattell and his team collected a large data set, they were able statistically to test the data for association between terms. Starting with a list of 171 terms culled from the dictionary, and then using a simple statistical technique known as *factor analysis,* they identified sixteen *factors*—clusters of closely related traits—that seemed to be highly intercorrelated. These factors represented an economical way of describing the data collected.

The Aston researchers followed this approach faithfully. Instead of regarding Freud as the fountainhead, they looked to Weber and early management theorists such as Taylor (1911), Fayol (1949), Urwick (1947), and Gouldner (1954), as well as theorists who focused on more informal organizational and social psychological characteristics, such as Argyris (1960) and McGregor (1960). Thus, they read everything relevant that had been produced by writers on organizations, looking for convergence and divergence in the literature (Hickson 2002; Pugh, Hickson, and Hinings 1971). At the same time that they were involved in the literature review, they were also conducting interviews with practicing managers about the relevant dimensions of organization structure. From these key informants, they learned what the most salient aspects of the manager's role seemed to be for those who practiced it. Between the literature review and the focal discussions with the managers, "the concepts slowly crystallized" (Pugh and Hickson 1976) to indicate the appropriate research procedures.

The Aston researchers assumed that all organizations were variants of a unitary but multidimensional concept. They used factor analysis to search statistically for patterns of variations in the data. These common factors could then be used to refine the data collection instruments to more closely align them with those factors that were statistically robust. These statistically tested questions are said to form *scales,* which are seen as a way of representing the real features of the empirical world as they are defined in terms of the conceptual constructs one is using. In the case of the Aston project, the scales coalesced around a contingency perspective.

The researchers' discussions and reflections finally focused on five variables drawn from Weber's initial list of fifteen (which was discussed in Chapter 2):

- *Specialization:* The extent to which the organization had highly specialized job descriptions and designs
- *Standardization:* The extent to which the organization has many standard manuals of procedure
- *Formalization:* The extent to which the organization's total range of actions and procedures are covered by formal policies and agreements
- *Centralization:* The extent to which the organization ensures that decision making is referred to the apex of the organization or distributed to lower levels
- *Configuration:* The shape of the authority structured as a system of role relationships

Having made what they thought was an accurate assessment of the main features of organizations on the basis of their predecessors in the literature and the managers who were their contemporaries, they were ready to *operationalize* these dimensions. They accomplished this task by asking questions that they had designed to collect information on the distribution of data in terms of the presumed dimensions. *Operationalization* simply means deciding that the meaning of a concept can be best determined by proxy measures. For example, to determine the degree of centralization, researchers can ask how many people directly report to senior managers; the higher the number of people that do so, the more centralized the organization is. Other questions inquired about the nature of the rules that were written down and filed away: the job descriptions, standard manuals of procedures, and operating principles.

Earlier researchers such as Gouldner emphasized what the phenomena of everyday organizational life meant, such as the changing meaning of the organization rulebook. The Aston researchers were less interested in meaning and more concerned with collecting considerable amounts of statistical data on a large number of organizations. They could correlate such data with the hypothetical dimensions and come up with some well-grounded empirical answers to the question they had set for themselves: What were the determinants of organization structure? The answer was that structure is determined by situational contingency.

For the Aston researchers, the crucial contingency turned out to be that "size matters." They had collected extensive data on the dimensions of organization structures for forty-four organizations from the West Midlands of England. After analysis, they concluded that the variable that best explained why these organization dimensions had a certain shape or pattern of association between them was the size of the organization. Basically, the larger the organization, the more it seemed to be patterned in ways that could be characterized as bureaucratic.

Size matters for three variables in particular. One sees more specialization, standardization, and formalization as organizations become larger. In short, the Aston project findings suggested that, regardless of all other factors, the bigger an organization was in terms of the number of people that it employed, the more likely it would be organizationally highly structured or be bureaucratic. The smaller it was, the less likely that this would be the case. Plenty of additional research supports the central proposition, including work by Peter Blau (Blau and Schoenherr 1971) conducted in a similar mode to that of the Aston researchers. Collectively, this style of work is often referred to as *structural contingency theory*.

The findings of the structural contingency theorists nicely unsettle some common misconceptions, the best known of which is Parkinson's Law (Parkinson 1957). Parkinson was a civil servant who, on the basis of his experience and observations, argued that work expands proportionately with the time available for its completion. Following from this assertion, he argued that organizations therefore increase the number of administrators that they require disproportionately with their increases in size. Structural contingency theory demonstrates that this argument is not correct. For instance, Blau (2002) measured differentiation in terms of the number of organization levels in the hierarchy, the number of departments, and the number of job titles. He found that increasing size is associated with increasing differentiation but that the rate of differentiation decreased with increasing size. Administrative overheads are lower in larger organizations, and the span of control for supervisors is greater. Administrative overheads are inversely related to size, whereas the span of control is positively related to size. Thus, larger organizations are able to achieve economies of scale *if* they can distribute delegation of authority efficiently and effectively in the organization. If they can do so, they can handle the costs of differentiation—an increased necessity for control and coordination of the differentiated activities—without piling a weighty administrative overhead on top of the hierarchy to control the complex differentiation. Thus, the larger the organization, *given that it is able effectively to delegate authority and line control of workflow,* the less necessity there is for centralized control and administrative overheads. This concept helps to explain the lack of association between size and concentration of authority/line control of workflow that the Aston researchers found. Size increases overhead costs but also increases the scope for economies of scale, which can be deepened further by effective delegation of authority and control.

Mintzberg: Fit matters

Henry Mintzberg, a prolific writer with guru attributes, published a seminal paper in 1981 summarizing and systematizing some of the main issues in the debate on organization design. He argued that five natural configurations fit the different tasks organizations have to accomplish. Like an ill-cut piece of clothing, some structures don't fit the purpose organizations want to achieve. This misfit leads to trouble and inefficiencies. Consistency and coherence between organizational structure and tasks, says Mintzberg, is the key to success. Rather like an organic structure that evolves in its environment, some organization structures should simply fit, naturally. They don't need to be chopped to size.

Structuring devices such as span of control, forms of decentralization and hierarchy, degrees of job enlargement, and so on must be chosen in a way that is consistent with an organization's specific situation (its size, strategy, competitors, production technology, and so on). Imagine a large manufacturing company that has experience and know-how in mass production buying a small supplier known for its innovation potential. Should management of the large company put its bureaucratic structure (suitable for mass production) into the smaller innovative daughter company? What effects would this have on its innovation potential?

Mintzberg argues that, for every situation and task an organization is facing, there is a specific structure that fits best. He distinguishes between five such structures:

- *Simple structure:* This configuration, the most basic structure, consists of top management, a few middle managers, and a task force. Power is centralized; management knows and supervises the whole company. According to Mintzberg, this structure is typical for entrepreneurial companies that are small and innovative but that work on relatively simple products. Most organizations start off as simple structures but struggle when they grow.

- *Machine bureaucracy:* This structure puts the emphasis on standardization and employs low-skilled but highly specialized staff. It is a structure for mass production that focuses on simple products in a fairly stable environment. Taylor's scientific management ideas derived from such structures. In contrast to the simple structure, this design requires management of administration; the organization needs detailed planning and standardization, which leads to a bureaucratic system. The more bureaucratic the system is, the easier it can grow; the organization continues to do the same things, but instead of making 100,000 hamburgers a day, it produces 1,000,000 a day. McDonald's is Mintzberg's example for such a machine bureaucracy—very efficient in what it does but not very flexible and not very interesting to work for (see also pp. 108–110).

- *Professional bureaucracies:* In contrast to machine bureaucracies, professional bureaucracies rely on standardized skills, not processes. Universities, large consulting firms, or hospitals are examples of this structure; they work like bureaucracies, but they need highly trained staff to deliver their services. Thus, employees in professional bureaucracies have more autonomy than workers

Image 4.2   *Organic fit or misfit?*

Image 4.3   *Organic or mechanic?*

in machine bureaucracies. Professional bureaucracies have relatively flat hierarchies, where professionals accredited through external institutions (having earned certificates from universities, and so on) do the central work. However, parallel to the professional staff, a large number of support staff back up the professionals. Their jobs are simpler, more routinized, and normally less well paid. (Think of a hospital with well-paid doctors, nurses who are not as well paid, and poorly paid auxiliaries, such as porters and cleaners, laundry staff and ward orderlies.) These structures fit best into a complex but fairly stable environment. They are good at executing state-of-the-art tasks but not as adept when it comes down to changing them. Hospitals, for instance, develop great expertise in operating, but when they are challenged by alternative herbal medicines or natural therapies, they don't know how to integrate them, and their normal professional strategy is one of exclusion.

• *Divisionalized form:* In contrast to the professional bureaucracy, this structure does not rely on highly trained professional individuals; instead, it uses expert units called *divisions*. Each division runs its own business by producing specialized products for a particular market. Hence, these divisions are relatively autonomous and enjoy a certain degree of freedom. But how does management make sure that the divisions are on track? Headquarters (HQ) normally measures their performance (the standardization of outputs, as Mintzberg puts it). Each division's performance is measured and compared with that of the other divisions. This arrangement keeps the division managers busy and HQ in charge. Put simply, top management imposes goals on divisions, which forces divisions to plan their activities properly, ultimately leading to the bureaucratization of the single divisions. As we saw previously in this chapter, machine bureaucracies are appropriate when standards are imposed and clear objectives need to be achieved. However, because the divisional form was chosen so that organizations can respond to a flexible environment, the dynamic that leads them to bureaucratization has a negative effect on the organization. Also, it has important consequences regarding ethical behavior; because the goals the division must achieve are mostly formulated in terms of monetary targets for sales, rate of return, and so on, the social consequences (because they are hard to measure) tend to be ignored.

• *Adhocracy:* None of the previous four structures really fits when put into a highly turbulent environment where constant innovation is the key to success. The *adhocracy,* a structure of interacting project teams, is the solution. Creative think tanks such as advertisting agencies (see also pp. 402–403) for the example of St. Luke's) need lots of experts who create products that cannot be standardized. With every job they do, they have to deliver the standards to be able to measure them. In those project teams that make up the adhocracy, power is distributed; everybody is a decision maker, and strategies are not implemented top-down but emerge while the teams explore new terrain (see also pp. 170–174; 209–214).

All these configurations have strengths and weaknesses. Each type represents a structure that best fits a certain environment. The consistency and coherence between structure and task is, above all, the most important thing.

CRITICAL ISSUES: GETTING THE THEME RIGHT

Contingency theory, given its association with open systems theory, seemed to carry the promise of unifying organization researchers in a common program in which the key contingencies could be identified and the patterns of variance associated with them elaborated. This proved not to be the case. In fact, disputes among structural contingency theorists about the appropriate way of conceiving contingencies flourished almost from the start.

The theme is technology

The American sociologist Howard Aldrich (2002; Mindlin and Aldrich, 2002) suggested that technology rather than size is the crucial variable. He reached this conclusion after reanalyzing the Aston data using a different logic of analysis. Whereas the Aston researchers relied primarily on factor analysis (a statistical technique that establishes high degrees of intercorrelational coherence and variance in a data set), Aldrich used causal path analysis to model the relations between variables. *Causal path analysis* makes theoretical assumptions that it seeks to justify, theoretically, about the likely explanation for structural relations. These assumptions can then be tested through various models. The Aston approach differed in that those researchers simply looked for the correlations that existed and then imagined how they might have come into being as a result of cross-sectional casual relations. For instance, if they had counted kitchen sinks, and the number of sinks had been shown to correlate highly with structure, they would have imagined a story that explained the relation. Aldrich wouldn't do this unless he had some prior reason in theory for thinking that kitchen sinks were important.

Aldrich gives external dependence and technology high priority in his hypothetical story. *External dependence* occurs where top management depends on parent organizations for key resources. *Technology* is what the organization's top management chooses to use as its method for doing what it does. It can be thought of, as suggested by Perrow (2002), as the number of exceptions that an organization has to deal with in its workflow and the extent to which it has to engage in nonstandardized search behavior to deal with them. More highly structured firms—those that seem more bureaucratic—need to employ more people, he suggests. Size is an effect rather than a cause, a dependent rather than an independent variable, and the major causes of the degree of structure, according to Aldrich's reanalysis, are the technologies in use in the organization. From these flow the specifications, job descriptions, and so on, that compose the structural measures. The number of people employed does not precede the technologies used. The casual path that would assume so seems nonsensical. Technologies and people evolve together, and the structure adapts accordingly.

In brief, the development of an organization proceeds from its initial founding and capitalization in response to perceived market opportunities, through its design based on copying and modifying other organizations' structures, and finally to the employment of a workforce to staff the nearly completed organization. This obviously oversimplified view of the development of an organization leads to specific predictions about the causal ordering of observed organizational variables. Technology is causally prior to the size of the workforce, and organizational structure is at least initially usually prior to size (Aldrich 2002: 355).

Essentially, Aldrich has a more plausible story to tell than the Aston researchers, who, as pioneers, made up the story as they went along, testing their *cross-sectional data*—data collected at the same time and place—in terms of the degree of its intercorrelation. Whereas the Aston narrative was driven by the correlations—the story was fitted to the variance observed in the data—Aldrich sought to refine the narrative structure and then model these assumptions in the causal path analysis.

The theme is control

Etzioni (1961) identified commitment and power as the interlocking basis of organization control (see also pp. 87–88; 136–137). Control was a key element in early theoretical accounts of business organizations because it was assumed that, as managers were hired to control the organization in the interest of its stakeholders (a group that would often include themselves, of course, because their interests were aligned with those of shareholders through stock options), managerial control of the organization was a fundamental phenomenon. Through controlling costs, overheads can be reduced, profits increased, and shareholder value enhanced.

A narrative of control structured one of the most influential critiques of the Aston studies, that of John Child (2002), who emphasized the role of *strategic choice*. Simply put, he says that managers in positions of control make strategic choices about how they will configure the organizations they are responsible for. They will choose work plans, resources, and equipment. This is the nature of their work—it is what their plans and orders are meaningfully oriented toward. The technologies and structures that ensue will be the result of these managers making decisions that link available resources with necessary tasks. The top-management team that constitutes the dominant coalition will constantly be evaluating the organization's competitive position. They will do so in terms of the values that they share—the organization's dominant culture or ideology—from which they derive goal preferences for the organization. For example, will the organization be innovative with respect to new technology, copy innovations developed elsewhere, or be a cost-cutting exercise to minimize the costs associated with innovation? What the managers do on behalf of the organization is its strategic action (see also pp. 136–139; 410; 414). It is this strategic choice that influences structural features. Hence, management decisions shape organizational design more powerfully than purely environmental influences because, to an extent, they choose the conditions under which they operate.

The theme is metaphysical pathos

One percipient writer, Alvin Gouldner (2002), identified what he referred to as a "metaphysical pathos" of pessimism and fatalism endemic to writing on organizations. The overall impression recalled Weber's remarks on the iron cage (see also p. 67), which seemed to suggest that bureaucracy was inescapable if organizations grew in scale, such that there was no alternative. It seemed beyond the wit and wisdom of humans to make organizations much better or different than they are. It appeared that we just have to accept them as we find them. Such an attribution of pathos seems singularly apt when we consider some of the later Aston work on comparative organization structure. It is centered especially on the relation between size and the other structural contingencies. The results show that increasing size always leads to more bureaucratization, a relationship generalized across many organizations and sixteen countries (Donaldson 1996 cites the relevant studies). The big comparative questions seem to boil down to only one issue: that size really matters and nothing much else does:

Size really matters and nothing much else does.

> In all countries, big organizations will be the most formalized and specialized in structure. This is because everywhere growth means reaping economies of scale and expertise by dividing labor still further, and as the knowledge possessed by any one person of what is happening in the organization becomes a smaller part of the whole, so more formalized documentation of action and intended action is required for control. Non-formalized custom is inadequate to control large numbers in organizations with a turnover of personnel. (Hickson, McMillan, Azumi, and Horvath 1979: 37)

Or, as it was put on another occasion:

> Simply stated, if Indian organization were found to be less formalized than American ones, bigger Indian units would still be more formalized than smaller Indian units. (Hickson, Hinings, McMillan, and Schwitter 1974: 59)

Notice how this view is an echo of Weber's cultural pessimism—certain consequences are inevitable if certain contingencies prevail—but without the culture and without the pessimism! What remains is a sense of the inexorable, the undebatable—of something that cannot be opposed because it is almost as if it were nature.

The theme is SARFIT

There is lack of dynamism to the contingency models that the Aston researchers developed because of the historical specificity of the assumptions that framed them. One writer who appreciated that this was the case, while still remaining wedded to the basic contingency framework, was Lex Donaldson (2002), who argued that, periodically, because any organization design would slip out of kilter with the contingencies with which it had to deal, organizations had to undergo a structural change to regain fit with their contingencies—especially those in their environment. He calls this approach the SARFIT model. *SARFIT,* which stands for "structural adjustment to regain fit," is a theoretical approach that Donaldson champions against both the contingency determinism of the earlier Aston School as well as Child's strategic choice approach. SARFIT blends insights from the strategy literature with themes from the literature on organization structure and its determination, and develops the sociological theory of structural functionalism.

Strategic choice views organizational configuration as the result of actions taken by the dominant coalition. This elite group may choose to adapt to changing contingencies by protecting the present structure of the organization—for instance, by withdrawing from an arena in which there is a particular contingency challenge to deal with, such as a specific market or technology. The coalition will do this because of the role that their values, perceptions, and political influences play in creating a cultural comfort zone. Donaldson argues that changing contingencies to fit an extant structure, while feasible, is more difficult than changing structure so that it is better aligned with the changing contingencies, especially in a competitive business environment where a firm's position is always going to be judged in relation to its competitors. Organizations and their dominant coalitions, he suggests, are more likely to readjust their structure than their contingencies to regain fit between it and the contingencies that they are obliged—by competitive pressures—to handle.

Donaldson (2002) draws on the well-known strategy/structure literature, sparked by the studies of Chandler (1962). The essential insight was that

> as companies move from being undiversified to being diversified in their product range so they move from the functional to the product divisional form. Similarly, the shift from single to various geographic areas leads to a move from functional structure to geographic divisions, *ceteris paribus* (Egelhoff, 1982) . . . There is a cycle of change in strategy leading to mismatch and low performance, then structural adjustment to a new match. There are relatively few cases where adjustment comes about by the alteration of the contingency to fit the structure. (Donaldson 2002: 383; 389)

The causal path that shows how strategy and structure are matched is the motif for the structural adjustment literature.

How strategy and structure come together

As product diversity expands, the HQ of a functionally structured organization finds that its decision making becomes increasingly complex because it has to manage greater product diversity with corresponding requirements to know about more products, materials, technologies, markets, competition, and so on. The HQ that does not delegate its decision making to the divisions will soon become overwhelmed by more information than it is able to process. In product divisional form organizations, the divisions are given relative autonomy by the corporate office. Control by corporate HQ is accomplished through comparisons of profitability across divisions. Low-performing divisions are axed or restructured. Delegated decisions should be better decisions because they are made closer to market knowledge and organizationally specific know-how. They should be quicker and better quality because they are more specialized and expert-based. Decentralizing in this way gives the top-management team at corporate HQ more scope for strategic rather than for operational decision making. It allows the division's top managers to have more autonomy in decision making on matters such as design, manufacture, and marketing. The HQ no longer has to assimilate so much information and has only to coordinate the decisions made at divisional level. The costs of this increased efficiency are some measure of duplication of certain administrative functions in each division, which adds costs. The functional form is best for more homogenous product offerings because its unified control structure is cheaper. Thus, the functional form matches low product diversification; the product divisional form matches high product diversification.

Donaldson's reanalyses of a number of well-known longitudinal studies of structural changes test whether the straightforward contingency determinism model, the strategic choice model, or the SARFIT model best explains the data. He finds that the story predicted by SARFIT best explains the changes that occur. Changes in contingency, such as moving to new markets or products, initially lower performance. This leads to a structural adjustment to regain fit and a new cycle of matched contingencies. Periodically, he suggests, the organization will still require additional changes to stay in match as contingencies continue to change. Structures overwhelmingly adjust to contingencies rather than contingencies to structures. For instance, after a company diversifies, it needs to adjust its structure. Diversification disequilibriates the organization's fit with its contingencies, so it has to structurally readjust to regain fit. The top-management dominant coalition will make choices to regain fit, but they are quite limited in the choices that they can make. Misfit from diversification leads to poor performance; poor performance is tackled by making some structural adjustments, and in this way fit is regained. Strategy leads to structure, just as, in modern architecture, function was supposed to determine form—although, given the rise of postmodernist architecture, you can't count on t'

Strategy leads to structure.

Image 4.4   *Eggs or beehives as inspiration for innovation?*

dictum anymore. Why should the organizations that fill the structure shown in Image 4.4 not be as innovative in their own design as was the architect who designed the space (in London) in which they work?

Design inspirations

Organization design assumes certain things about structure. For instance, structures originate more from engineering analogies, with their rational principles of straight lines and form following function, than they do from nature, with its more riotous examples. From within engineering, they tend to focus on spatial conceptions of structure, replete with straight lines rather than curves, spirals, and helixes. Overleaf (Image 4.5) is an example of a structure that, although it is still straight lines, composes an ascending spiral. What kind of organizations might it inspire?

Of course, structure is to be found everywhere, in many shapes, sizes, and forms. Nature, for instance, rarely favors straight lines, yet straightness dominates management thinking about organizational design, with its stress on unity of direction, scalar chains, and order. Organization and management theorists express a distinct preference for the clean lines of machines and mechanistic structures as sources for design. By contrast, look at Image 4.6: a detail from the structure of what is the world's largest tree, the Arbol del Tule, to be found at Santa Maria del Tule, in the State of Oaxaca in Mexico.

Image 4.5   *Spiral staircase*

The tree is a structure; it is clearly efficient and effective, for the tree is very old and still flourishes with the application of science and care, yet it is hardly what would be called a "rational structure" in organization and management theory terms—it is too wild and anarchic. It is not the kind of tree to appeal to an engineer. Architects, however, are another matter. Not all architects follow modernist metaphors exclusively, engineering structures purely as machines for living in. For example, Gaudí, the famous Catalan, found inspiration in the structures of nature. The limbs of a great tree inspire Gaudí's design for the structure of the nave in the famous Sagrada Familia cathedral in Barcelona.

The pyramid is the oldest, simplest design for constructing large structures. We find it in the Middle East and in the pre-Colombian Americas. It is the

Image 4.6   *Arbol del Tule*

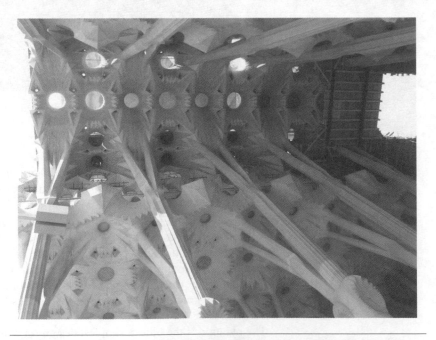

Image 4.7   *Detail from the Sagrada Familia, by Gaudí, in Barcelona*

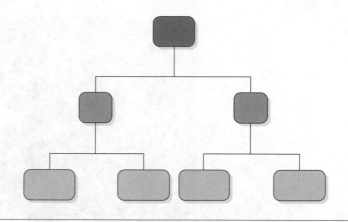

Figure 4.1   *Pyramidal representation of organization structure*

classic organization structure of a bureaucracy, shown in Figure 4.1, in a highly simplified and stylized form.

Pyramids need not just be straight lines, of course, although they are easier to represent that way. Image 4.8 provides the detail of a chimney from one of Gaudí's domestic designs. It seems to refer to a pile of fruit in the market—the organic and the mechanical in unison and, indeed, in harmony with representations of organization structure in its pyramidal form. However, a chimney of fruit both defines and defies organization design. Ranged linearly and spatially in an ascending pyramid, the organization of the fruit captures both the mechanistic and the organic in one image. In this respect, the artistic metaphor is more accurate than the representations that management and organization theory allows, for it is simultaneously united in its opposites and fused in its contrariness in a way that organization science has failed to engineer as well as art and architecture can represent.

The heyday of contingency theory, with its modernist straightness, its dedicated engineering, was the 1960s through the early 1980s. Since that time, other approaches have captured the imagination of many of the best research journals, but it is fair to say that contingency theory, although it may not be at the cutting edge of current research, is constitutive of much of our normal understanding of contemporary management and organizations as machines within which we work.

THE FINE PRINT: WHAT KIND OF SCIENCE?

Contingency thinking and measurement was historically framed by its own contingencies. We can explain this point best through an analogy. Typically, insurance companies classify events such as floods or droughts in terms of the

Image 4.8   *The fruitful chimney*

probability of the severeness of their occurrence. For instance, some floods are referred to as a one-in-a-hundred-year event—meaning that the probability is that a flood of this severity will occur only every hundred years or so. However, after the severe drought that afflicted the east coast of Australia in 2002, the insurance companies are not so sure about these probabilities. They realize that their old projections have failed to take account of the way that climate change is occurring, probably as a result of human activity contributing to global warming. The reality on which measures of normalcy and deviations from it were based no longer accurately mirror the world in which we live. The world has changed. If nature can change, then the assumptions that we might have made about it in the past may not be as good a basis for generalization in the future.

If even nature changes, how much more changeable is social reality? Organizations and their management are, after all, social constructions.

For instance, it is normal to assume that products are something held in proprietary relation by specific organizations. Hence, if you wanted to understand how the Microsoft Windows operating systems have evolved, you would need to understand how Microsoft is organized. However, what about Linux?

If even nature changes, how much more changeable is social reality?

It has not been developed inside any specific organization in the way that Windows has developed. It is open-source software—it follows the successful model pioneered in the nineteenth century in the development of the Oxford English Dictionary. To try to relate the innovative properties of Linux to the organization structure of a parent firm would be a grievous error of specification of the appropriate object for analysis. Linux is an emergent product of a loosely coupled network, not an organization. In the early twenty-first century, products can be produced in the absence of an enveloping organization. It would be difficult to see Linux as just an organization with a low score on bureaucracy because of its distributed nature; the distributed nature is the essence.

In the early 1960s, when the Aston researchers first started to think about organizations, they had no reference point other than what existed at that time. And what existed were, by and large, variations on bureaucracy, so the measures that they devised to capture empirical data on the structure of organizations were largely normalized on these assumptions. Thus, their questions were all oriented toward capturing data that demonstrated whether there was more or less bureaucracy, as measured by the constructs of standardization, formalization, and so on in any specific organizations in a given sample.

But the world has changed. Forty years later, in the early twenty-first century, we not only have many new forms of organization but also technologies, environments, and strategies to sustain them that were unimaginable all those years ago. Of course, one can still go out and use the Aston measures to collect data on organizations, and, because of the questions one asks, one will still pick up a distribution of data around these bureaucratic constructs. However, is their saliency still the same? If the world has changed sufficiently, the assumptions on which these questions were constructed will no longer be the central issues but will have become more marginal. Continuing to ask these questions—although doing so will deliver a distribution of data on them, and thus result in social facts concerning the constructs—may miss the more salient issues for the design and management of organization structures that have emerged in the meantime. To continue with the old assumptions is similar to continuing to work with climatic models that preceded global warming after global warming has changed the rules of climate prediction.

The trouble with contingency theory

The contingencies play the key causal role in the functional argument. They are conceptualized and measured through regularities that they are, theoretically, seen to produce—we know the contingencies through their regular, predictable effects. Thus, for instance, organization size is a matter of the number of people employed by an organization: as this number increases, the organization tends to become bureaucratic. If an organization shrinks in size, then, hypothetically, it should become less bureaucratic.

But what happens if an organization lays off workers, develops outsourcing of previously internal functions, and focuses on its core competencies? It has certainly become smaller in terms of the number of employees, but is it a real change in form? If you were a maintenance employee on Friday, and on Monday you come in to work as an outsourced subcontractor doing the same sort of job, has anything really changed that much? The organization still has an Operations and Maintenance (O&M) function, but instead of being remunerated through the payroll, it is now paid for through a contract with another firm, which pays the labor. Why should the change in contractual form through which a function is delivered change the overall nature of the organization? Certainly, the change means that there is one less area to manage in terms of day-to-day administration, but the effects of moving to an O&M outsourcing contract do not mean an end to responsibilities; instead, they are simply shifted to other areas of the organization and different mechanisms of control.

One problem with the positivist approach to organizational contingencies is that there are some pretty shaky everyday assumptions framing the mechanisms that they rely on so heavily in their theories. Size, for instance, is a construct that made great sense in bureaucracies where virtually everything was internalized; however, as organizations become more virtual in form or shift from employment to other forms of contracts, the simple assumption that their size equals the number of labor contracts they have written seems misguided. And if the fundamental mechanisms are not self-evident, the theories built on their basis will not be as secure as they seem.

One place where the basis of structural contingency theory becomes especially problematic is in considering new forms of organization. Given that these are designed around new and virtual contingencies, will they be consistent in their behavior with those organizations designed around the bureau and written files of rules? Will the same categories apply? The answer is fairly simple: If we have ways of asking questions that already assume that organizations have certain properties, we will collect data based on these assumptions. Think of it in these terms: In the nineteenth century, scientists believed that by studying the shape of the skull and its bumps, they could build taxonomies of skull types that could then be related to behavioral traits such as criminality. The practice was called *phrenology*. Phrenology is now regarded as a mistaken theory, and structural contingency theory may eventually be seen in the same terms. Positivism allows for that possibility, but we should not expect the theoretical renunciation to come from within the contingency theory framework. Just as phrenology could always construct taxonomies from within its assumptions, so can structural contingency theory, because, in each case, the questions it asks are embedded in the assumptions made. Or, in other words, ask the right questions, and you get answers whose assumptions you have already framed in the presuppositions that underlie the asking.

SUMMARY AND REVIEW

Bureaucracy was the initial point of departure for empirical studies of organizations. Theorists studied organizations and analyzed them in terms of their degree of difference from the ideal type model that Weber had constructed. Clearly, they would differ, and they did. Although a number of classic and interesting studies were completed in this vein, there was a problem with the knowledge generated: How could it be made comparable and cumulative? The Aston program of research sought to make this scientific goal a centerpiece of their inquiry and shifted analysis to a more sophisticated plane—that of contingency theory. However, the findings that they launched were contested almost from the start. Aldrich accused them of drawing obvious conclusions on the basis of inference that was guided purely by jumping to conclusions from the variance found in the data rather than considering deeply how plausible was the story that underlay the connections presumed. To build a more plausible narrative, he reanalyzed their data using causal path analysis. Child also questioned the narrative; for him, it downplayed the role of the top-management dominant coalition being able to exercise strategic choice. Donaldson does not deny that such strategic choice occurs but thinks it most probable, on the basis of empirical enquiry, that the choice will tend to be exercised in favor of the organization structure being adjusted to regain fit with changing contingencies rather than the contingencies being changed to suit the existing structure. Much recent debate has centered on the emergence of new organization forms. From the perspective of contingency theory, whose classic conceptual dimensions were modeled on bureaucratic organizations, the emergence of new organization forms may be challenging because their premises are less bureaucratic and written rules, and more IT and virtual designs.

ONE MORE TIME . . .

Getting the story straight

- Why was it important for the development of organization and management theory to develop a general theory?
- According to Burns and Stalker, why do organizations in stable environments have different structures than those in fast-changing and innovative environments?

- According to the Aston School, why does an organization become more bureaucratic as its size increases?
- According to Mintzberg, what are the five most feasible configurations of organization structure?

Thinking outside the box

- How do assumptions about science and reality interact in different accounts of the determinants of organization structure?
- How factual are social facts in the Aston schema?

ADDITIONAL RESOURCES

1. The debates that surround a somewhat arcane area of organization and management theory—namely, why organization structures are as they are—can sometimes be quite passionate. Topics that evoke lively discussion include the appropriate methodologies that researchers should use and the appropriate assumptions that they should make about the nature of organizational reality. Most analysts of organization structures regard these methodologies and assumptions as objectively real, as social facts, rather than as social constructions that analysts use to make sense of what they assume is reality. The strongest proponent of this approach, which insists that organization structures are real things that are representable in terms of a limited number of variables, is Lex Donaldson, who has been a prolific and robust debater. A clear statement of his views is to be found in Donaldson (2002), an article titled "Strategy and Structural Adjustment to Regain Fit and Performance: In Defence of Contingency Theory."

2. Clegg has elsewhere criticized Donaldson for the tendency in his work to leave little or no room for any evolution in organizations' forms in other than a bureaucratic mode; see Stewart Clegg (1990), *Modern Organizations*, Chapter 2.

3. You might want to consult the overview of structural contingency theory offered by Pennings (2002).

4. Films about organization structure do not easily spring to mind, although several demonstrate bureaucracy in use. One that is situated in the domestic bureaucracy of an Edwardian manor house is *Gosford Park* (Altman 2001). Each servant is assigned a role and authority "beneath stairs" that is contingent on that assumed by their masters above.

5. Films about the military often demonstrate bureaucracy in action. Think of all those films about prisoners of war seeking to escape but first

having to gain permission from the officers in captivity who run the escape committee. *The Great Escape* (Sturges 1963) is one of the best of the genre.

6. Finally, another military film worth looking at is *A Few Good Men* (Reiner 1992). In this film, Dawson and Downey are two Marines stationed in the United States naval base at Guantanamo Bay in Cuba. They follow orders that cause harm to another Marine, resulting in his death. They are put on trial for murder. The basis of their defense is that they were only following orders—a line that we will also encounter in the next chapter. Dawson and Downey were trained to exist strictly in terms of the hierarchy and structure of the corps. Even though they knew that what they were doing to the other Marine was wrong and that they were endangering him, their life code was to follow orders from their senior officers without question. The contingency that the Marine Corps had established in its structure and authoritarian culture (see also pp. 45–47; 176–179; 215–216) resulted in them being able to commit and to rationalize certain acts that most people would ordinarily consider inhumane. By not using their own reason, they ultimately acted against the best interests of the Marines. The colonel is imprisoned for giving the order, and the two Marines are dismissed from duty. We see in this movie that the hierarchy and order in organizations such as the Marines Corps and the Army, when followed unquestioningly, have the potential to result in a sequence of events that are not only immoral but against the best interests of the institution that they were designed to protect. We explore these themes further in the next chapter.

In addition to these suggested additional resources, don't forget to look at what is also available on the Web site **www.ckmanagement.net,** including free PDF files of recent papers related to this chapter, which you can download; video interviews with famous academics talking about related themes; as well as many other resources, such as connections to interesting Web sites.

CHAPTER 5

MANAGING POWER AND POLITICS IN ORGANIZATIONS

Resistance, Empowerment, Ethics

Objectives and learning outcomes

By the end of this chapter, you will be able to

- Appreciate that the central task of any manager is to manage people and that managing people means managing power relations

- Understand how power is played out in organizational structures

- Evaluate what might be bases for authority in organizations

- Grasp some of the central ethical issues involved in managing power and authority relations

Before you get started . . .

A famous thought by Lord Acton:

"Power tends to corrupt and absolute power corrupts absolutely. Great men are almost always bad men, even when they exercise influence and not authority: still more when you superadd the tendency or the certainty of corruption by authority."

—Lord Acton, letter, 5 April 1887,
to Bishop Mandell Creighton (Acton 1972)

OUTLINE OF THE CHAPTER

Organizations are made up of formal and informal rules that coordinate actions of different people. But how can organizations make sure that people—who have diverse backgrounds, particular interests, and different understandings—comply with these rules? Raising these questions means addressing the fine line between the exercise of power and ethics. *Power* is the concept that encompasses the mechanisms, processes, and dispositions that try, not always successfully, to ensure that people act according to the rules of the game. Hence, power is one of the central concepts in both management practice and theory. Ethics, on the other hand, is concerned with doing the right things in the right way. Of course, the whole issue of ethics depends in the first place on the ethicality of the business proposition that underlies the organization. Is it ethical, for example, to build a business on cheating?

Researchers in organization theory and management in the era after World War II had developed a set of expectations about the exercise of power in organizations that they had derived from the formal structure of bureaucratic authority (Bennis, Berkowitz, Affinito, and Malone 1958). However, a number of case studies refuted these expectations. Surprisingly, these case studies discovered bases of power outside the formal structure of authority and described the games they sanctioned and the rules that made them possible. More recently, interest in discussions of power has shifted to issues of resistance—how people in organizations resist formal organizational authorities. However, perhaps of more pressing concern is not the question of why people resist but why they might obey, particularly where there are ethical issues attached to what it is that they are obeying, issues that come into particular focus when considering examples of extreme organizations that are known as *total institutions*. Although we can learn a great deal from the concentration of power that occurs in total institutions, in fact, most organizational power is neither so total nor so hard edged. Instead of making people do what they wouldn't otherwise do, this power is subtler—it operates through modes of *soft domination*.

Image 5.1   *Ethics at work?*

SETTING THE SCENE

We spend at least one third of our adult lives working in organizations. Another third disappears in sleep and replenishment, and a further third in things we choose to do. Therefore, for one third of our lives, we cede control to others and enter into complex relations of power that range from others getting us to do things we would not otherwise do, to us doing the same to others. We will spend that third of our lives in different organizations. At best, these will be warm, friendly, welcoming, open places in which we can do our jobs with pride, growth, and achievement. At worst, however, they may be akin to places of concentrated power that frames and shapes our hours there.

As organization theorists began studying the empirical workings of organizations rather than simply constructing abstract models, they noticed that some members of organizations were able to exploit and use seemingly impersonal rules for their own ends. The prevalent conception of organization hierarchy identified it with legitimacy; thus, when actions were identified that seemed to subvert or bypass the official hierarchy of authority, they were labeled "illegitimate"—they were not authorized. In this way, power came to be seen as illegitimate, whereas authority was legitimate. Certain resources within organizations seemed to provide bases for illegitimate expressions of power.

At various times, several key resources have been promoted as the basis for expert power in organizations. The most pervasive basis for arguing a special relationship between power and a specific resource relate to the ability to control uncertainty in bureaucratic organizations. More recently, there has been a shift in focus from bureaucracy to consideration of more empowered alternatives. But, as we shall see, empowerment is not necessarily all it is cracked up to be—it can mean even tighter control.

The world of organization power is complex—full of shifting alliances, words that mean something other than they say, and actions that do more than they proclaim. It is impossible to escape power in organizations, if only because organization means yoking together people with multiple and complex interests whose search for satisfaction is structured through a set of organizational relations with people that one would not necessarily choose to spend time with. If you had a choice, would you spend eight hours a day with the passing parade of megalomaniacs, incompetents, and cruelly brutal gossips that people most offices and other organizations? When the boss tells you that he wants everyone to work as one happy family, look around. Would you choose any or all of these people as partners with whom to make a family?

Power is more profound than just the push and pull of attraction and repulsion, command and control. It also involves the structuring of dispositions and capacities for action as well as action itself. We explore these themes in this chapter, looking at the good, the bad, and the ugly in power relations. We take care to concentrate not only on the negatives but also to accentuate the positives. After all, if power is inescapable, we might as well learn how to use it wisely.

CENTRAL APPROACHES AND MAIN THEORIES

Sources of power

If an organization makes people do things they normally wouldn't do, power must be the central issue. Many potential sources or bases of power have been listed, including information; expertise; credibility; stature and prestige (Pettigrew 1973); uncertainty (Crozier 1964); access to top-level managers and the control of money, sanctions, and rewards (French and Raven 1968; Benfari, Wilkinson, and Orth 1986); and control over resources (Pfeffer and Salancik 2002). We consider some of the more important of these bases of power in this section.

Legitimacy

Power works best when it is seen least. Power as legitimation needs to do nothing to secure its will if people already want to do what is expected of them. If legitimacy can be created for individual actions, it greatly reduces the

Power works best when it is seen least.

chance of opposition to them because it creates a meaningful context in which they can be accepted and justified (Edelman 1964, 1971). Legitimation lowers the probability of resistance, as Blau (1964: 199) recognized when he noted that "stable organizing power requires legitimation. . . . The coercive use of power engenders resistance and sometimes active opposition." Legitimation is achieved through what Pettigrew (2002) called the "management of meaning"— a double action because it seeks both to create legitimacy for one's initiatives as it simultaneously seeks to delegitimize those it opposes.

Some of the main sources of legitimacy are symbolic. Images can represent a great deal of power in simple ways. For example, the law is often portrayed as an institution that impartially weighs justice in its scales. That the common symbol of this power is blindfolded while holding the scales of justice is meant to represent it as a legitimate authority; it shows that an impartial judiciary resides over a mass population that is weighed equally in the scales.

Some of the most potent sources of power and its symbolism are the many remnants of imperialism that dot the globe. We have chosen one from our city, Sydney, where one of the most famous nineteenth century buildings is a beautiful old structure that now contains some of the most popular and best retail outlets in the city. The Queen Victoria Building is named after the monarch who, during the latter half of the nineteenth century, was Queen of Britain and all her colonies, as well as Empress of India. When the building was renovated during the 1980s into one of the city's premier retail sites, an appropriate statue was found and placed immediately in front of it. Once upon a time, there were thousands of similar monuments scattered around what used to be the British Empire. What is interesting about this particular statue is that it was acquired and unveiled in Sydney in 1987, so the statue and the building enjoyed unrelated biographies until that point.

When the City of Sydney was searching for a spare statue of the building's namesake, Ireland was the logical place to look because it had been a colony and had become a free state. The statue used to stand in Dublin outside the Parliament Building. Such statues, especially in the contexts in which they were originally placed, made power that was remote and abstract present and material in a symbolic sense. (Which is, perhaps, why the Irish got rid of it. Having been a republic for some time, the Parliamentarians presumably had little present use for it.)

Of course, although Queen Victoria was the monarch of the colony of New South Wales (NSW) and the colony of Ireland, she did not rule in person. In NSW in the nineteenth century, the governor ruled on her behalf. But in NSW's limited parliamentary democracy, he did not really rule. There was considerable uncertainty about the governor's exact powers, given their derivation from an abstract authority that he served at such a distance.

Such a situation of rule was not at all organizationally unusual. Weber (1978) noted the uncertainty that the elected members of a legislative assembly had in

Image 5.2   *Queen Victoria, imperial symbol of authority*

terms of parliamentary, budgetary, and other procedures of rule compared to the far more detailed and certain knowledge of their senior permanent public servants. He saw the uncertainty—a lack of knowledge of the precise rules of the bureaucracy—of elected politicians as their undoing in power terms when compared with permanent civil servants. However, the generation of empirical researchers in organization theory after World War II reversed this analysis. For them, uncertainty increasingly became seen as a source of power rather than a constraint on its exercise.

Uncertainty

As we have seen, uncertainty and power are not strange bedfellows, and their proximity has been much explored in organization theory. The view for the last fifty years has been that when an organization experiences uncertainty in areas of organizational action, if a person has organizational skills that can reduce that uncertainty, he or she will derive power from such expertise. In other words, this view states that despite formal hierarchies, prescribed organizational communications, and the relations that they specify, people will be able to exercise power when they control or have the necessary knowledge to master uncertain zones in the organizational arena.

One of the earliest proponents of these views conducted research in one of the most clearly prescribed of organizations: a military bureaucracy. Thompson (1956) researched two U.S. Air Force bomber wing commands, comprising both flight and ground crew personnel. The flight crew had greater formal authority, but the role of the ground crew was central for the safety of the flight crew. Their need for safety conferred a degree of power on the ground crew that was not evident in formal authority relations. Their technical competency vis à vis safety issues put them in a strategic position to secure their own interests—to exercise "unauthorized or illegitimate power" (Thompson 1956: 290), which they were able to rationalize in terms of a need for safety. Hence, the maintenance workers controlled the key source of uncertainty in an otherwise routinized system.

In a study conducted by Michel Crozier (1964) in a French state-owned tobacco factory, uncertainty also proved to be a central resource. The female production workers, at the technical core of the organization, were highly central to its workflow-centered bureaucracy. The male maintenance workers were marginal, at least in the formal representation of the organization design. The production workers were paid on a piece-rate system in a bureaucracy designed on scientific management principles. Most workers were effectively de-skilled. The bureaucracy was a highly formal, highly prescribed organization, except for the propensity of the machines to break down. The effect of them doing so was to diminish the bonus that the production workers could earn. To maintain earnings, the production workers needed functional machines.

Work stoppages made the production workers extraordinarily dependent on the maintenance workers, whose expertise could rectify breakdowns. Consequently, the maintenance workers had a high degree of power over the other workers in the bureaucracy because they controlled the remaining source of uncertainty in the system. Management and the production workers were aware of the situation, and they had made attempts to try to remedy it. Management had introduced planned preventive maintenance to be done by the production workers, but manuals disappeared and sabotage occurred. Maintenance workers were indefatigable in defense of their relative autonomy, privilege, and power. Through their technical knowledge, they could render the uncertain certain and the nonroutine routine. The benefit of maintaining routine was a degree of autonomy and relative power for the maintenance workers in excess of that formally designed. There was also an issue of gender; the male maintenance workers used their expert knowledge as a masculine device over and against the female production workers.

Crozier's (1964) study was a major landmark. He had taken an underexplicated concept—power—and attached it to the central concept of uncertainty. After this study, the field developed rapidly. A theory called the "strategic contingencies theory of intra-organizational power" (Hickson, Hinings, Lee, Schneck, and Pennings 2002) emerged; it sought to build a theory from existing ideas, particularly that power was related to the control of uncertainty and that, following Tannenbaum (1968), it could be measured. Tannenbaum had developed a measurement of power, the *control graph*. The graph maps the means of the perceived power of each level in the formal hierarchy of an organization by averaging the sum of the perceptions of people in the organization of the amount of power vested at various levels within it. In this way, intersubjective measures of power may be achieved. It became apparent that power was not something that was fixed—it could be increased. Organizations that were quite similar structurally could design power quite differently.

Strategic contingencies theory

Hickson et al. (2002) sought to measure power in organizations. One of their theoretical innovations was to use a formal model. The organization was conceptualized as being composed of four functional subsystems or subunits. The subunits were seen as interdependent. Some were more or less dependent and produced more or less uncertainty for other subunits. What connected them was the major task of the organization, coping with uncertainty. The theory ascribes the differing power of subunits to imbalances in the way in which these interdependent subunits cope with and handle uncertainty. The most powerful are the least dependent subunits that cope with the greatest systemic uncertainty, although there are certain qualifications—namely, that the subunit is not easily substitutable with any other subunit and that it is central to the organization system. Note the absence of a vertical dimension and the assumption that each subunit is quite contained and unitary.

To conceptualize an organization as composed of subunits is to flatten out the normal hierarchical representation of it as a "structure of dominancy," to use Weber's (1978) terms. This perspective views the organization on a horizontal rather than vertical axis. To view organizations as more horizontal than vertical is to make a number of assumptions about the unitary and functionally cohesive nature of subunits. In reality, each subunit is typically a hierarchy with a more or less problematic culture of consent or dissent. For it to be treated as if it were unitary, there needs to exist some internal mechanisms of power that allow for such a representation. In other words, there must be a hierarchy of order that is effectively reinforced through everyday organizational actions.

Strategic contingencies theory assumes that management's definitions prevail. Indeed, sometimes they do, in which case management has exercised power. When they do not, management is outmaneuvered. Being outmaneuvered is a fate that most managers are familiar with. Thus, the strategic contingencies theory of power unfortunately explains very little that is important in understanding hierarchical power. Indeed, it refrains from such an explanation, given its tacit assumptions. And these tacit assumptions mean that it explains very little that is useful because it is assumed that the organizational configuration will be simply bureaucratic. Indeed, in the later empirical analysis

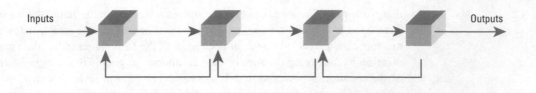

Figure 5.1   *An organization conceived as made up of subunits*

conducted using the framework, the researchers deliberately sought out a simple and tightly regulated bureaucracy to test the theory (Hinings, Hickson, Pennings, and Schneck 1974). It worked.

Resources

Similar to strategic contingencies theory is the resource dependency view, derived from the work of social psychologists such as Emerson (1962) and related work by French and Raven (1968). All resource dependence theorists view a certain resource as key in organizations, but they differ in which resource is regarded as key.

Pfeffer and Salancik (2002) argued that power could be both vertical and horizontal in organizations, and their focus, like Hickson et al.'s (2002), was on subunit power. They hypothesized that power would be used in organizations to try to influence decisions about the allocation of resources (Pfeffer and Salancik 2002). Subunits may be thought of as departments in the organization. To the extent that subunits contributed critical resources, including knowledge, that the organization needs, other subunits submitted to their demands and ceded power to them.

The similarities to strategic contingencies theory are striking. Using archival data on university decision making in the University of Illinois, they confirmed their hypotheses, suggesting that power is a positive-sum game for those that have control of critical resources—using the power these resources bestow, they can acquire yet more resources, to leverage more power. Those that have resources attract more resources and thus more power. From this perspective, power is often conceptualized as if it were a zero-sum game in which, rather like being on a seesaw, more resources on the part of one party outweigh those of another party because they can be gained only at the expense of the other party. It is assumed that there is a fixed amount of power to go around.

Crozier subsequently revisited the links between power and uncertainty as a critical resource (Crozier and Friedberg 1980). Members of an organization meet each other in spaces that offer relatively open opportunities for control of rules and resources. People do not adapt passively to the circumstances that they meet; they use these circumstances creatively to enhance the scope of

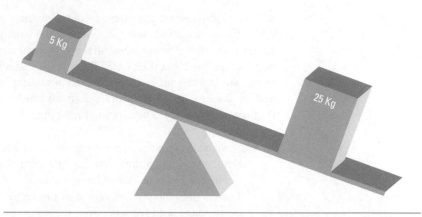

Figure 5.2   *A zero-sum conception of power*

their own discretion, through shaping and bending rules and colonizing resources. Power is still seen in terms of the control of uncertainty as it is played out in daily struggles over the rules of an uncertain game.

Contexts for power games

There is no doubt that uncertainty—as well as the other contenders for strategic resource status—can be a source of power, but not in a context-independent way. What counts as a resource can be made to count only in specific contexts. For instance, box cutters, which are used for cutting paper and cardboard, are not usually thought of as powerful resources—or at least they were not until September 11, 2001. Then, in the hands of determined terrorists, they were responsible for what has now passed into history as 9/11. So, if information, uncertainty—or box cutters—are to count as resources for power, they will do so only in specific contexts.

To the extent that specific resources are related to power in a general way, without regard for context, they are not very helpful. Anything can be a resource in the right context—the context is what is important. Thus, possessing scarce resources is not enough to deliver power over and above that formally authorized; one also needs to have an explicit knowledge of context (Hickson, Butler, Cray, Mallory, and Wilson 1986; Pettigrew 1973, 2002) and how to use resources accordingly.

Politics

The process of mobilizing power is the process of politics. Given the stress on authority and formal organization in the literature, politics are what happens when members of organizations behave in ways that are potentially authoritatively illegitimate. Pettigrew (2002: 45) sees the mobilization of power as what happens when either individuals or subgroupings within organizations make a claim against the extant resource-sharing system of the organization. As Pettigrew suggests, power is central to the strategy process in organizations because decisions about what strategy to maintain or innovate will always be political. Such decisions are "likely to threaten the existing distribution of organizational resources as represented in salaries, in promoting opportunities, and in control of tasks, people, information, and new areas of business" (Pettigrew 2002: 45). These politics are generated by the following:

- *Structural cleavages* in the organization between different component elements and identities, and the *different values, affective, cognitive and discursive styles* associated with these
- The *complexity and the degree of uncertainty attached to the dilemma* (as we have seen from previous theory)
- The *salience of the issues* for different actors and identities in the organization
- The *external pressure coming from stakeholders or other actors or organizations in the environment*
- The *history of past politics* in the organizations in question

Consequently, power and organizational politics are absolutely central to a great deal of what normally goes on in organizations. This would have to be the case because, according to Pettigrew (2002: 47), organization politics fundamentally concern the management of meaning, as protagonists in these politics seek to legitimate the ideas, values, and demands that they espouse while simultaneously denying or decrying those that they seek to oppose. Hence, power ultimately is deployed in games of organizational symbolism, wrapped up in myths, beliefs, language, and legend—the stuff of organizational culture. As we will see later, whenever discussion switches to organization culture, organizational politics are not far behind (see also pp. 278–286).

The most crucial issue, as Lord Acton noted at the outset of the chapter, is the potential for power to corrupt those who have it. Another way of addressing this issue is to ask, "Who controls the controllers?" These are not just academic issues; in many countries around the world, the ethicality and controllability of major and politically important public sector organizations is very much at issue. How clean is your police force? Does it use symbolic reminders, such as those in Images 5.4 and 5.5, of the necessity for local communities and other organization members to maintain eternal vigilance against the possibilities of corrupt behavior?

Organizations as political arenas

In Mintzberg's (1983a, 1984, 2002) terms, the organization is a political arena, one in which the system of politics comes into play whenever the systems of authority, ideology, or expertise may be contested in various

Image 5.3   *The community policing the police in Bangkok*

Image 5.4   *Fighting corruption in a public sector organization in Mexico*

political games—that is to say, almost always. Mintzberg identifies various commonly occurring political games, including the following:

- *Insurgency games:* Played by lower-status participants against the dominant elites.
- *Counter-insurgency games:* Played by the dominant elites against the insurgents.
- *Sponsorship games:* Played by patrons and clients.
- *Alliance-building games:* Played among peers who implicitly seek reciprocal support.
- *Empire-building games:* A political actor or subsystem seeks to capture others and enroll them as subordinate to its interests.
- *Budgeting games:* The objective is to secure resources.
- *Expertise games:* The games of strategic contingency.
- *Lording games:* Relatively powerless players seek to "lord it" through using their legitimate power over those supplicant or lower in status.
- *Line vs. staff games:* Each side uses legitimate power in illegitimate ways in games of rivalry.
- *Rival camps games:* Alliance or empire-building games develop into rival blocks that face each other in zero-sum games.
- *Strategic candidate games:* Those in power seek to ensure the succession of preferred candidates as vacancies arise.
- *Whistle-blowing games:* Participants, usually lower-status ones, seek to expose malfeasance or illegitimacy outside the organization to effect internal policy or strategy changes.
- *Young Turks games:* Organizational authority is preserved, but a coup unseats its present incumbents to institute a regime change

In organizations, politics are normal and serve many orderly functions. They can be the harbinger of a need for realignment (Donaldson 1999), the midwife to change (Pettigrew, Ferlie, and McKee 1992), the source of refreshing innovation (Frost and Egri, 2002) or, sometimes, the instrument of death (Havemann 1993). Thus, political games are to be expected—they are neither aberrant nor deviant. The types that Mintzberg specifies are not mutually exclusive, of course, and may often overlap and interlink, but they typically find expression in four major forms in the political arena:

- *Confrontation:* Characterized by intense, confined, and unstable conflict, as in a takeover or merger
- *Shaky alliances:* Characterized by conflict that is moderate, confined, and relatively stable, as in professional organizations subject to public accountability, such as public hospital or education systems
- *Politicized organizations:* Characterized by conflict that is moderate, pervasive, and relatively stable, such as large public sector bodies or regulatory agencies

- *Complex political arenas:* Characterized by intense, pervasive, and brief unstable conflict, such as organizations riven by major fault lines of factional and doctrinal division, both internally and in terms of external alliances and relations.

Social democratic political parties with strong external sponsors, such as the union movement, are examples of complex political arenas. Traditionally, these parties represented organized labor. However, in many countries (such as the United Kingdom and Australia), the labor movement is considerably less significant than it used to be, with most employees not being union members except in a few sectors. For those parties that had once relied on union-friendly policies, a new recipe for success needed to be found. New recipes have to be acceptable to the old sponsors, or else the parties need to find new sponsors. Britain's old-style Labour Party, before "New Labour" emerged from its ashes, would be a case in point. We can also think of examples from religious organizations. The Uniting Church in Australia, the Episcopalian Church in the United States, and the Anglican Church in the United Kingdom, as they struggle to develop doctrine that acknowledges the existence of homosexual clergy yet remain united, are also good illustrations. Political parties and churches split by doctrinal issues exemplify a general proposition: People in organizations that cannot manage their power relations, because they cleave around fundamentally opposed worldviews, will end up spending more time fighting each other than seeking to find common purpose against competitor organizations. Only very large organizations or those with no competition can survive sustained complex politics for long.

> **Political games are to be expected—they are neither aberrant nor deviant.**

Power and the politics of resistance

Resistance is a term that has long been a part of the vocabulary of students of organization. Coch and French (1948) noted that resistance to change is normal. Because power in organizations rarely if ever flows effortlessly as pure authority—because its legitimacy is often contested—power is typically not free of friction. And where there is friction, there must be resistance. To use these metaphors betrays the origins of the terms—they derive, of course, from physics. They are rather mechanical terms, as is so much of the vocabulary in organization and management theory. However, resistance need not be simply a question of physics—it can be more organic and dialectical. *Dialectics* refers to the contradiction between two conflicting forces, where each shapes the other, often against the pressure that is being exerted. A picture says more than a thousand words, as Image 5.5 illustrates.

Resistance is "a reactive process" whereby people embedded in power relations actively oppose initiatives enacted by others (Jermier, Knights, and Nord

Image 5.5   *The dialectics of nature: power and resistance*

1994: 90). Often, resistance has been researched in terms of industrial relations conflicts at work between management and workers, especially where the latter are collectively organized in unions (Clawson 1980). More recently, researchers have focused on subjectivities of resistance as these are constituted through memories of a fairer time or better work, perhaps, or through social organization, such as familial or local community networks, as well as solidaristic organization, such as trade unions (Clegg 1994; Knights 1990). A number of studies provide graphic examples of how resistance may be variably organized. In the next section, we highlight one study in particular because it demonstrates the ways in which power and resistance, culture and meaning, are densely interconnected.

Resistance by distance

Collinson (1994) presents a case study of a factory in northwest England in which the management had traditionally treated the workers as if they were commodities, easily hired and fired, who were marked by decidedly second-class employment in terms and conditions. The organization, recently taken over by an American firm, applied some current management ideas, such as a corporate culture campaign and a collective bonus scheme, in their dealings with the men—there were no women—on the shop floor. The workers resisted these moves because what management said symbolically did not tie in with what the workers experienced in day-to-day practice. The corporate culture campaign was resisted as "Yankee bullshit" and "propaganda." The bonus scheme made the workers more economically oriented toward work, more closely tied to the cash nexus than to a corporate culture. The workers, regarding themselves as objects of contempt by management, found an alternate system of values in the camaraderie of their masculinity that was expressed in hard, dirty shop-floor work. Securing themselves in this identity, they distanced themselves as much as possible from what, in terms of their values, was the culturally strange—and comparatively "soft"—foreign world of (Yankee) management. They resisted promotion from the shop floor as selling out to the other side. In fact, what they did was turn the world of work as seen from the heights of management on its head. They devalued the clean, white-collar world of the office in favor of the harder-edged and "blokey" masculinity of the shop floor as an authentic sphere of real knowledge grounded in experience rather than theory. Collinson termed this phenomenon "resistance through distance." The workers distanced themselves from management by asserting that it was "management's right to manage" and something they wanted no part of. They resisted through keeping their distance.

The use by management of collective bonus schemes meant that when faced with layoffs, the shop stewards in the union argued for wage cuts rather than layoffs, which many of the men, in need of the higher wages, resisted. So although the resistance strategies might have appeared to be based on a collective identity, it was one that was fragile and easily ruptured. It was also highly reactive; it resisted through reacting to the authority attempts of management. Like many studies of resistance, Collinson shows both how resistance creates space for employees in organizations and how those spaces serve to further secure their incorporation within the organizations. Resistance is a two-edged sword.

Resistance, whatever form it takes, is always *against* something. Organizationally, those resisted against usually seek to construct or construe the resistance that they encounter as illegitimate, as something outside authority. To the extent that initiatives and actions are given sanction by organizational authorities, then, by definition, resistance to them *must be* illegitimate. In cases in which whatever is being resisted is represented as being normal, rational, and desirable (e.g., "we need to change periodically to regain market share"), any opposition can easily be regarded as lacking legitimacy.

Resistance is undoubtedly part of politics. The definition of political activity offered by one of its foremost students is that it is "activity . . . undertaken to overcome some resistance or opposition" (Pfeffer 1981: 7). The vocabulary makes it clear: Politics are what you get when you don't get your own way. In other words, when there is opposition, there is politics—or, as we might as well say, the presence of politics points to the absence of tyranny, for if there were no opposition or resistance, there would be no politics. Looked at this way, organizational politics seem better than the alternative.

CRITICAL ISSUES: DOMINATION AND HEGEMONY

Hardy and Clegg (1999: 375) suggest that "organizational structures and systems are not neutral or apolitical but structurally sedimented phenomena. There is a history of struggles already embedded in the organization." The paradox of power seems to be that you have power only if you are in a superior position in the organization and are opposed in what you want to do by others who are at the same or a lower level; when you want to do something against the resistance of these others, it is termed *authority*. When they want to do something against superordinate will, it is considered *resistance*. Authority is seen as legitimate; resistance is seen as illegitimate. Organizational politics become defined as the unsanctioned or illegitimate use of power to achieve unsanctioned or illegitimate ends, as Mintzberg (1983a, 1984), Mayes and Allen (1977), Gandz and Murray (1980), and Enz (1988) all argue. From this perspective, organizational life reduces to a morality play about efficiency: Either members do what they are scripted to do in their formal organization roles in the terms that authorities determine for them, or, if they do not, they are behaving illegitimately. Being moral and being efficient become coterminous in a well-designed system.

Organizations should never be seen just as systems, as engineering that is more efficient when there is less resistance, in the analogies of physics. Organizations always have vested within them traces of the past, as something recurrent, shifting, taking on new meanings, shaping the future. In Weber's terms, organizations already incorporate a "structure of dominancy" in their functioning. The relations that they encompass are invariably saturated and imbued with power. It is distilled deep in the structure, culture, and history of the organization, which often "normalizes" power relations so that they hardly seem like power at all. One of the major strategies of normalization is to practice empowerment. Thus, much recent management theory has been written in praise of teamwork and against bureaucratic hierarchies, because it is believed that this is the way to minimize the expression of power. In the next section, we show that neither the presence of teams nor the absence of hierarchy means an end to power. First, we look at power structured through soft domination, where hierarchies seem to be blurred by project teams, and then consider the role power plays in teams.

Soft domination

The central tension in organizations, when viewed through a power lens, is between resistance and obedience (Courpasson 2002). On the whole, from the perspective of management control, the latter is a far more productive result of policies than the former. Excessive use of coercion and force invites resistance; therefore, power as a hard instrumentality, a presence as unsubtle as a billiard ball ricocheting around the table, will, on the whole, be declined in favor of more subtle mechanisms. One theorist who has explored such methods is Steven Lukes (1974), who built on debates in political science to analyze power not only in terms of its mechanics but also its underlying dimensions. The main insight was that power could be used to prevent conflict by shaping

> perceptions, cognitions, and preferences in such a way that [people] accept their role in the existing order of things, either because they can see or imagine no alternative to it, or because they view it as natural and unchangeable, or because they value it as divinely ordained and beneficial. (Lukes 1974: 24)

Power is able to achieve these effects to the extent that it is effectively subsumed through legitimation within an integrated system of cultural and normative assumptions. Given the integrated system of cultural and normative assumptions and an efficient organizational apparatus, goals can be achieved. Hence, analysis of power in organizations needs also to focus on the subtle mechanisms through which obedience is produced—soft domination. *Soft domination* is characterized by the administration of rules that give managerial discretion to managers while reinforcing the strength of centralized authorities, because those who are delegates know that their obligation is to act creatively within the systems of authority (Courpasson 2002). Authorities create legitimated rules reinforced by clear and credible threats to career, rewards, status, employment, and so on. What sustains senior management and limits organizational members, ultimately, is the political concentration of the power of control over the deployment of human resources in the hands of a minority combined with the regular use of credible sticks (e.g., formal warnings) and carrots (e.g., performance-related pay) deployed within clear rules. Soft domination is based on the appearance of equality in the organization among peers and the reality of a pervasive system of controls, chief among which are instrumentally legitimate techniques used by the entire management community, such as human resource management, audit, and holding managers accountable to plans. These are modern modes of making people responsible, of rendering them surveyable, and of exercising surveillance over them.

More often than not, these forms of accountability and surveillance become the basis for the games people play at work (Burawoy 1979). People conceive of the workplace as a game in which they are "survivors." There are many things to survive—for example, a performance appraisal, not losing face over a policy or procedural conflict, not being downsized and made redundant, and not getting a promotion. Above all, these people are skilled game players— they know the rites and the rules of the games inside out and constantly use the spaces that they can create from these to exercise whatever discretion they can produce and to rationalize that which they cannot.

Electronic surveillance

A number of writers, including Poster (1990), Lyon (1994), Bogard (1996), and Sewell (2002), see modern electronic forms of surveillance as replacing the apparatus of power laboriously constructed by bureaucracy. Extended electronic surveillance has been seen as the hallmark of high modernity, of a world in which surveillance is insidious, making the majority of people increasingly transparent to others who may not be transparent to them (Robins and Webster 1985).

Zuboff (1988) introduced the "Information Panopticon" as a key term. The *Information Panopticon* privileges organizational elites by making it possible to consolidate various sources of electronic information about the many who serve the organization (Robey 1981). Sewell (2002) argues that electronic surveillance supplements, rather than replaces, earlier forms of surveillance. Its basic thrust is to make people in organizations more accountable and less autonomous. However, it is often used in conjunction with policies whose avowed purpose is quite opposite to these intentions. Sewell concentrates on teamwork.

Teams operate with two dimensions of surveillance: vertical and horizontal. Vertical surveillance focuses on the aberrant: aberrant waste, time, quality, and so on. To define the aberrant, you must first define the normal, which is usually done by establishing performance norms on a statistical basis that enables the aberrant to be immediately transparent—it stands out as a deviation from the norm of time taken, quality produced, or waste accumulated. Electronic forms of monitoring of performance make the norms more transparent and are supported by peer review through horizontal surveillance. Although electronic and traditional forms of surveillance reinforce the vertical dimension, which seeks to make the subject of surveillance his or her own monitor, the horizontal dimension causes us to monitor each other. Panopticism explains only some vertical aspects of this group scrutiny (Hetrick and Boje 1992).

Empowerment?

Teamwork is not usually thought of as a mechanism of power, but recent theory has suggested that it is (Sewell 2002; Barker 2002). Indeed, as Sewell notes, teamwork is usually associated with the rhetoric of empowerment, trust, and enhanced discretion. Sometimes it is even referred to as "giving away" power. There is a flood of popular management books whose message is cast in terms of this normative rhetoric, as analysis by Barley and Kunda (1992) demonstrates. These books often espouse single-answer solutions for harried managers; TQM (total quality management), organizational learning, lean production, and BPR (business process reengineering) are among the recipes that Sewell notes. What all of these methods have in common, he suggests, is a reversal of the highly individualistic approach to the employee that earlier

Image 5.6   *The eye in the sky: an example of an Electronic (or Information)*
Panopticon

perspectives such as scientific management had championed. Rather than isolate, observe, and individually measure the times taken by individuals for doing standardized tasks and discouraging them from communicating with others while doing so, the new approach encourages communication and sociability. No longer are employees to be set competitively against each other; instead, they work together as members of teams that have been designed to cope better with more flexible manufacturing methods and to provide opportunities for more intelligent organization of work (Clarke and Clegg 1998), where there is greater distributed intelligence of systems and discretion. However, teamwork does not abolish politics but relies on what Barker (2002) terms "concertive control" as its horizontal mode of surveillance. The forms of power at work help create the types of subjects that work there (Foucault 1983; Knights and Vurdubakis 1994; Townley 1993, 1994).

Barker on concertive control

Barker begins his account with a brief snatch of interview data with an employee called Ronald, who is reported as saying that he is more closely watched under a new team-based work design than when he was closely supervised by a manager. The team is a stricter supervisor than his supervisor had been! Barker calls this situation one of "concertive control," something that occurs where there is "a substantial consensus about values, high-level coordination, and a degree of self-management by members or workers in an organization" (Barker 2002: 180).

Concertive control, argues Barker, is what occurs when organizations become post-bureaucratic, when they adopt decentralized, participative, and more democratic designs, a strategy that has long been promoted by more liberal management theorists such as Follett (1941) and Lewin (1951). Recently, the trickle of liberal management writing has become a flood as theorists increasingly have sought an alternative to bureaucratic models (see also pp. 61–64; 97–99; 120–122). What characterizes these arguments is a stress on a new age of post-bureaucratic liberation, in which control by formal rules and hierarchy is abandoned in favor of consensual and values-based action by organization members. Popular writers such as Kanter (1990), Peters (1988), and Drucker (1998) promote the benefits of "unimpeded, agile authority structures that grow out of a company's consensual, normative ideology, not from its system of formal rules" (Barker 2002: 183). The argument is that "cutting out bureaucratic offices and rules" will "flatten hierarchies, cut costs, boost productivity, and increase the speed with which they respond to the changing business worlds" (Barker 2002: 183). Employees collaborate to develop the means of their own control. The Panopticon sought to make each worker the governor of what they did at work, aware as they were of the supervisory gaze, and concertive control reinforces this awareness through the discipline of teams (see also pp. 168–171; 214–215).

Under the new forms of concertive control and soft domination, power is refined into ever more subtle techniques using instrumental means to make employees accountable and transparent. For example, there may be a vision statement that states, "We are a principled organization that values teamwork" (Barker 2002: 183). On this basis, team members agree that being principled means that they all arrive at work on time—and they ensure that they do, using norms that they have enacted from the agreed-upon value statement to structure the systems of their own control. Authority shifts from the hierarchy and formal rules to the team and socially created and generated rules.

One arena in which teamwork can be seen to great effect is in collaborations between national defense forces in peacekeeping and related operations.

Here the normal relations of command and hierarchy, which flow within the national military, have to be combined with collaboration across organizations, between different national defense forces.

Teamwork is now seen to have a much wider utility. It is not just a means of producing collaboration between distinct organizational units; it is also a way to enhance the effectiveness of members of the same organizational unit. One researcher who has looked closely at teams that have been designed to be self-managing is James Barker, himself an ex-military man and now a professor in the service of the U.S. Air Force Academy. He charts the shifts in management style from more hierarchical to self-managing teams; see Table 5.1.

One reason that many organizations are designed in terms of self-managing teams is that such teams are supposed to cut costs by laying off front-line supervisors and gaining productivity benefits from better motivated and more committed employees (Mumby and Stohl 1991; Orsburn, Moran, Musselwhite, and Zenger 1990; Wellins, Byham, and Wilson 1991). In Barker's case study of ISE Communications, he observed that a shift away from hierarchy and formal rules led to a tighter form of control based on peer surveillance. Empowered organizations not only provide new means for control, as Barker (2002) suggests, but also make opportunities for the everyday negotiations and games of power more difficult. It is more difficult to negotiate when the people that you work with, rather than a supervisor, impose the limits. It is much easier to steal

TABLE 5.1 Barker's self-managing teams

Hierarchical Management: Hierarchically Ordered Supervision	Team Management: Shift to Self-Management
The supervisor has precise supervisory responsibilities.	The supervisor is replaced by a team of 10 to 15 people, who take over the responsibilities of their former supervisor.
The supervisor gives instructions.	Self-managing employees gather and synthesize information, act on it, and take collective responsibility for their actions.
Management relies on formal rules and authority expressed in terms of disciplines that seek to reinforce this authority.	Management provides a value-based corporate vision that guides day-to-day actions by being a reference point from which employees infer appropriate action.
The supervisor checks that instructions have been followed.	The self-managing team guides its own work and coordinates with other areas of the company.
The supervisor ensures that each employee fulfills his or her job description.	The self-managing team is responsible for completing a specific well-defined job function for which all members are cross-trained. All members of the team have the authority and responsibility to make essential decisions, set work schedules, order materials, and coordinate with other teams.

some time from a supervisor or manager with whom you do not share any obvious interest, other than a necessity to work, than it is from colleagues. You all depend on each other—and that is the subtlety of concertive control. Everyone is empowered to speak—but with the same agreed-upon voice.

Organizational hegemony in the International Monetary Fund

Organizational hegemony occurs when one point of view is predominant. It is marked by a strong organizational culture and an absence of countervailing points of view, because almost everyone has come to accept the dominant views (Lukes 1974). The best way to guard against hegemony in organizations is to develop *polyphony*—exposure to and tolerance of many voices. Polyphonic organizations, theoretically, are incipiently democratic and deconstructive. In this section, we consider a case in which the absence of polyphony has been crucial for a very significant global organization.

Joseph Stiglitz (2002) provides an account of the International Monetary Fund (IMF). (Stiglitz, a Nobel Economics Prize winner and ex-World Bank economist, is someone both well enough placed to make a diagnosis and someone hardly likely to be dangerously radical in doing so.) The IMF is an organization that was established in the late stages of World War II with the express purpose of minimizing the harm from—and, if possible, preventing—global depressions. Its mandate was to maintain international liquidity through loans to economically distressed countries that had insufficient economic resources to stimulate aggregate economic demand domestically. It is a global organization funded by taxpayers around the world. Yet it is not responsible to them, nor does it have their views represented to it. Instead, it hears, represents, and reflects the views of national finance ministries and central bankers, over which one country—the United States—has effective veto in its deliberations. Its contemporary policies champion "market supremacy with ideological fervour . . . the IMF typically provides funds only if countries engage in policies like cutting deficits, raising taxes or raising interest rates that lead to a contraction of the economy" (Stiglitz 2002: 12–13). These policy positions were the outcome of a hard-fought battle in the IMF that occurred in the early 1980s, when it became dominated by free-market economists who were under the thrall of the fashionable prescriptions associated with the governments of President Ronald Reagan in the United States and Prime Minister Margaret Thatcher in the United Kingdom.

Stiglitz (2002: 15) argues that the IMF has functioned in what is sometimes called, after a medical metaphor, an "iatrogenic" manner—its policies have exacerbated the very problems that they were supposed to solve, rather as a surgical procedure might complicate an underlying condition it was designed to cure. Rather than contributing to global stability, they have made the international economy less stable, more crisis-ridden, and indebted countries poorer. Why and how has that been possible? Central to the argument is the absence of polyphony and the presence of homogeneity.

Stiglitz sees two main factors contributing to the absence of *polyphonic reason* (debate between opposing viewpoints): first, a problem of *governance,* and second, a problem of *representation.* Governance addresses the question of who decides. Commercial and financial interests from the wealthiest countries in the world dominate the IMF. Its policies reflect these interests—hence the market emphasis—because why would the suppliers of capital let the state do something that they believe markets cannot only do better but certainly more profitably? These suppliers are the dominant commercial and financial interests in the wealthiest countries. Institutions such as the IMF, as well as the World Bank and the World Trade Organization, intervene in the economic management of poorer countries. But those intervening are always representatives of the most-developed countries, are chosen by those developed countries behind closed doors, and do not necessarily have any experience of the developing world. As Stiglitz (2002: 19) says of these institutions, they are "not representative of the nations they serve."

Raising the problem of representation addresses the issue of who speaks for the countries in need of assistance. The answer is simple: "At the IMF it is the finance ministers and the central bank governors" who "typically are closely tied to the financial community; they come from financial firms, and after their period of government service, that is where they return" (Stiglitz 2002: 19). Such people "naturally see the world through the eyes of the financial community" in the advanced economies. It is not surprising that the IMF policies have been addressed more to the interests of commercial and financial power rather than those of poor peasants or hard-pressed local businessmen trying to pay off the taxes that the IMF imposes. Taxation without representation is what Stiglitz calls it. Classic political sociology suggests that when people are taxed without political representation, they resist through nonrepresentational means—they take to the streets, riot, and rebel. Ever since the WTO met in Seattle in 1999, the rebellions in the developing world have been echoed in the heartlands of the global institutions, as idealistic and impassioned opponents of the dominant consensus about globalization have rioted to try to have their alternative views broadcast (see also pp. 334; 464–465; esp. 474–481). In organizations designed to be more polyphonic through more inclusive governance and representation, there would be less need for illegitimate means of resistance.

THE FINE PRINT: THE EXTREMES OF POWER

We can bring polyphonic organization into sharper relief if we contrast it with its antithesis—organizations that are *total institutions,* those in which hegemony is reinforced by the totality of the organization's everyday practices. There are two extremes to power, which we can characterize as negative and positive. Whereas negative power is constraining, positive power is enabling. First, we take a look at some extremes of negative power and consider some of the ethical questions they raise. Then, we return to the question of polyphonic, positive power and of how you, as a manager, might manage in such an environment.

Total institutions

Organizations always place constraints on freedom of action, which people sometimes resist. However, a more important question about power in organizations is not why people sometimes resist but why, much of the time, they do not. Obedience, in fact, is a far more fundamental question than resistance. One way of researching the mechanism of obedience is to look at some extreme cases. The rationale for doing this is that in extreme cases, the normal tendencies of everyday organizational life are more obvious because they are more concentrated.

The Canadian sociologist Erving Goffman used anthropological research to investigate how authority was configured in extreme contexts. He chose extremes because the everyday mechanisms of authority and power were much more evident there than in the world of the corporate "organization man" (Whyte 1960). Goffman (1961) initiated the discussion of extreme organizations when he coined the term "total institution." *Total institutions* are organizations that contain the totality of the lives of those who are their members. As such, people within them are cut off from any wider society for a relatively long time, leading an enclosed and formally administered existence. In such contexts, the organization has more or less monopoly control of its members' everyday life. Goffman's argument is that total institutions demonstrate in heightened and condensed form the underlying organizational processes that can be found, albeit in much less extreme cases, in more normal organizations.

Total institutions are often parts of a broader apparatus, such as a prison or detention center. Total institutions do not just include organizations that make people inmates against their will, however. They can also include organizations founded on membership contracted on voluntary inclusion—for instance, a professional army, a boarding school, a residential college, or a religious retreat, such as a monastery or convent. Several types of organization can be a total institution:

- Places to put people that the state deems incapable of looking after themselves (these people, who vary historically and comparatively, have included the "feeble," the "lunatic," or the "disabled")
- Restrictive organizations that institutionalize people who pose a threat to others, such as people with communicable diseases of contagion who are legislatively contained in sanitaria for the duration of their disease

Image 5.7   *Lock them up and throw away the key?*

- Punitive organizations, such as prisons, gulags, concentration camps, reform schools, prisoner-of-war camps, or detention centers for asylum seekers
- Organizations dedicated to a specific work task, such as boarding schools, military barracks, and vessels at sea, or remote company towns
- Retreats from the world, such as monasteries, abbeys, convents, or growth and learning centers

What do these very different types of organizations have in common that make them total institutions?

- Each member's daily life is carried out in the *immediate presence* of a large number of others.
- The members are very *visible;* there is no place to hide from the surveillance of others.
- The members tend to be strictly *regimented.*

- Life in a total institution is governed by *strict, formal rational planning of time.* (Think of school bells for lesson endings and beginnings, factory whistles, timetables, schedules, and so on.)
- People are not free to choose how they spend their time; instead, it is *strictly prescribed* for them.
- Members lose a degree of autonomy because of an all-encompassing demand for *conformity to the authoritative interpretation of rules.*

The depiction of life in the U. S. Marines boot camp in the 1987 Stanley Kubrick film *Full Metal Jacket* is a good cinematic representation of one type of total institution. In the film, identities are stripped through organizational means: the arbitrary assignment of nicknames and numbers; the loss of personal characteristics, such as haircuts, under the Marine razor; total conformance is demanded with instructions that are almost always shouted at recruits, often at close range, sometimes associated with physical violence to the person so that they are intimidated into obedience; the person is "remade" through rigorous discipline and physical exercise; an esprit de corps, based on the new identity as Marines, is developed.

But what does *Full Metal Jacket* have to do with being a member of an organization that is not a total institution? If we accept Goffman's analysis, it becomes evident that the essential core of organization is power—organizations exert power over their members by making them do things that they would not otherwise do. Think about it; organization members may have to dress up in uncool uniforms, have haircuts that are not trendy, and pretend to be interested while doing stupid things. Of course, the uniforms can vary from an explicit uniform to one that is implicit: the black suits, white shirts, black ties of the earnest Mormon; the almost de rigueur pants suit and contrasting T-shirt of the corporate woman worldwide; or the pinstripe suit of London businessmen. Even the boys from a neighborhood skater gang have a dress code, and becoming a part of their gang means learning their ways of behaving, doing, and thinking, and often speaking (using certain slang words and listening to certain music).

If organizations necessarily exercise power over their members, what are the ethical implications of the ways in which they do so? A short trip into history can help answer this question by looking at one of the twentieth century's most extreme cases of systematic abuse of power and ethics on a large-scale, organizational basis.

The ethics of organizational obedience

Adolf Eichmann was one of Hitler's deputies, the Head of the Department for Jewish Affairs. He led the Reich's effort for the Final Solution, efficiently organizing the roundup and transportation of millions of Jews to their deaths at infamous camps such as Auschwitz, Treblinka, and Bergen-Belsen. After World

War II, Eichmann escaped capture and lived in Germany for five years before moving to Argentina, where he lived under an alias for another ten years. Israeli agents finally captured him in 1960, and Eichmann was tried for crimes against humanity. Eichmann's defense was that he was just a bureaucrat who had to obey because he was just following orders. (Hannah Arendt [1994] wrote an account of his trial, in which she coined the memorable phrase "the banality of evil" to register her interpretation of the events she reported, in which evil was delivered through mechanisms such as a punctual and efficient railway timetable.) Although Eichmann was subsequently found guilty and executed, his defense was important because it posed the question of the extent to which a person who is obedient to organizationally legitimate authority can be held accountable as an individual for his or her actions. In the context of an inquiry into the nature of the Holocaust, the renowned sociologist Zygmunt Bauman (1989) extensively addressed such questions.

Bauman's answer is interesting for management scholars; essentially, he notes how central aspects of organizations contribute to the ease with which organizational malfeasance can occur. At the heart of the moral question is the interpenetration of power and ethics. Why do ordinary people in organizations do morally bad things when asked to do so? What aspects of an organization make unquestioning obedience feasible? It has been suggested that three organizational attributes, at a minimum, make this phenomenon more probable (Kelman 1973):

- *When the highest authority sanctions the organizational action in question:* That a strong leader tells you to do things might be a good reason to actually do them, because he or she is the leader whose will is usually fulfilled. Eichmann's commitment to Hitler as a strong authority figure shaped his behavior.
- *When the actions that enact the organizational action in question are routinized:* Work in an organization is often repetitive. You see only a small part of the whole organizational chain when accomplishing your task; you cannot see where and how your task fits into the big picture, nor can you see its consequences. This setup is another way of cutting off ethical responsibility and organizational effects.
- *When those who are the victims of the action are dehumanized:* When ideological definitions and indoctrination convince organizational members that the victims are less than human, it creates distance between organizational members and people who are affected by its action. Representing victims as numbers rather than people also makes it easier to forget the ethical consequences of actions.

Techniques of power

When we master a technique, our skill has its own charm, aesthetics, and beauty, and we can take sheer delight in using it, irrespective of its moral effects:

Technical responsibility differs from moral responsibility in that it forgets that the action is a means to something other than itself . . . *the result is the irrelevance of moral standards for the technical success of the bureaucratic operation.* (Bauman 1989: 101[emphasis in original])

When technique is paramount, action becomes purely a question of technical power—the use of means to achieve given ends. For instance, as a master of logistics, Eichmann was enormously proud of his achievements in the complex scheduling of trains, camps, and death.

Organizational power that makes you technically accountable and responsible for results expressed in a purely quantitative form has two profound effects. First, it makes you *utterly transparent*—you either achieve your targets or you do not. Second, *it relieves you of moral indeterminacy*—if you are authorized to do something and given targets to achieve by superordinates' guiding strategies and plans, obedience surely is appropriate, and authority should be served.

Organization work is a ceaseless round of activity. Most organizational members are in the middle of organizational chains whose links are not always clear. People are not always aware of the consequences of what they do and do not do—after all, most of the time, they are just doing what they are told (shred those files, write those checks, dispatch those troops, maintain those train schedules). Divisions of labor in the complex chains enable us to keep a distance from effects; we can represent them in terms of intermediary forms of data (kill rates, efficiency statistics, and so on). Our labor moves minute cogs in a bureaucratic machine necessarily intermeshed with so many others that we are just one small element in the overall scheme of things. We don't even have to try to understand the totality. The system of which we are a part is responsible, not us.

Especially when actions are performed at a distance on people defined as administrative categories, the people are effectively *dehumanized* (Kelman 1973). The more dehumanized they are, the easier becomes the application of pure technique to their cases. When whatever is being worked on can be represented quantitatively, as a bottom-line calculation, it is so much easier to make rational decisions (cut costs, trim fat, speed throughput, increase efficiency, defeat the competition) without concern for the human, environmental, or social effects of these decisions.

"The department's strategy is to keep asylum seekers dehumanised"

In Australia, the Coalition government led by Prime Minister John Howard was reelected in 2002 on the back of a concerted campaign against asylum seekers, under the motto "We will choose who will come here." Australia had become a destination point for organized "people smugglers" operating from Indonesia who were seeking to land asylum seekers on Australian territory. A few thousand asylum seekers, mostly from the Middle East, who had arrived in Australian waters were rounded up and placed in detention centers, either in Australia or in neighboring and extremely impoverished Pacific Island states, such as Nauru. These countries were paid to place the asylum seekers in camps as part of the Australian government's "Pacific solution." At the same time, the government made it impossible for any asylum seeker to ever become a legitimate refugee by changing the laws. If asylum seekers had spent more than seven days in a country or countries other than the place that they had fled (including Australia), they were disqualified from application. Look on a map and work out how difficult it would be to get from the landlocked Middle East to Australia without spending some time in another country for seven days. Almost all asylum seekers would be ineligible based on that criterion.

Into this institutional environment came a number of unaccompanied male minors from the Hazara people of Afghanistan, who had been persecuted by the Taliban and conscripted to fight against the Northern Alliance because of their minority Shia Muslim faith. Many of their families sold their belongings to smuggle the boys out of Afghanistan to a safe haven; a number of the boys ended up in Australia. There, they were subject to bureaucratic processing. They were considered "illegal asylum-seekers" who could obtain only temporary visas for three years; they were not "real refugees" who had applied through the Australian High Commission for asylum. (There was no such way for the boys to contact this organization from Afghanistan, where it had no offices.) The boys who ended up in Brisbane were fortunate to find a small number of middle-class people with access to resources who wanted to assist them. They did so by helping the boys form a soccer club, which gave the asylum seekers an introduction to the everyday life of Australia. After a series of "good news stories" about the soccer club appeared in the local press and on TV, the federal government's Department of Family and Community Services contacted the soccer club mentors with the instruction that refugees under 18 came under departmental control and were not to talk to the media. As an ex–Immigration Department staff member said, "The department's strategy is to keep asylum seekers dehumanised. . . . That means not letting people see their faces or hear their voices" (Robson, 2002, p. 36). And what their soccer success had done was to "give them a voice, their own voice, and put their faces before millions of Australians via their TV sets" (Robson 2002, p. 36).

How ordinary people can use authority to do extraordinary things

Ordinary people do extraordinary things, as an experiment by Milgram (1971) shows. Milgram's research question was quite simple: He asked to what extent individuals are inclined to follow the commands of figures perceived to be in authority. His answer demonstrated that the kind of situation in which people are embedded determines, in part, how they will act. He designed an experiment in which white-coated scientists instructed ordinary people (whom we call the subjects) to do cruel and unusual things to other people (whom we call the participants) as part of an experiment in a laboratory. In a nutshell, the subjects were instructed to administer increasing levels of electric shocks to the participants as part of a behavioral learning program. They did so under a range of circumstances. When participants gave incorrect answers to test questions, they were to be administered a shock, with each one to be higher than the one before. (No shock was actually administered—the participants, unbeknownst to the subjects, were actually actors who performed the responses that, physiologically, would be the normal reaction to the levels of shock being administered.) When the subjects were face-to-face with the participants and told to administer the electric shock directly to their hands, using force if necessary, only 30% of the experimental subjects did so. When the subjects could still see the participants but used a control lever that administered the shock instead of having to force the hands of the participants onto the plates administering the shock, 40% did so. When the subjects could no longer see the participants but could only hear their distress as the current surged, 62.5% were able to apply the current. Moving the others out of earshot marginally improved the rate to 65%.

The more distance—both physically and psychologically—there was between the controllers and the controlled, the easier it seemed to be to do seemingly inhumane and cruel things. The closer the relation between the controller and the supervisor, and the more removed the subject, the easier it became to continue. Obedience flows more easily when the subjects of action are at a distance. When these subjects can be transformed into objects in the controller's mind, obedience flows even more easily.

Another factor facilitating the application of current was its incremental thresholds—once someone had committed to the action, each increase in the threshold was just a small step, just another slight increase in pain to be endured. It is not as if they started out to kill another person or cause them irretrievable injury. They just did what they were instructed to do, only they did a little bit more of it each time. Where such action should stop, once started, is not at all clear. And after someone has committed to the action, especially if others are complicit, what Milgram (1971) termed "situational obligations arise." In other words, people felt obliged to do what they were asked to do in a specific situation, which tended to override more general and abstract moral principles that they might also hold. In organizations, with complex divisions of labor, sequential action invariably makes us complicit with many others, in many interactions.

Milgram (1971) made one crucial change to the experiments to test out a further hypothesis: that plurality produces space for reflection and pause for consideration. In the experiments reported thus far, there was only one expert giving instructions. He introduced another expert and instructed them to disagree with each other about the command being given. The disagreement between authorities paralyzed the capacity for obedience of the research subjects—out of twenty subjects in this experiment, one refused to go further before the staged disagreement; eighteen broke off after it, and the remaining subject opted out just one stage further. *Polyphony*—the presence of competing and conflicting voices—increases the probability that people will think for themselves rather than just do what they are told. Thus, strong organizational cultures that suppress value difference are more likely to produce unreflective and sometimes inappropriate organizational action than more democratic and pluralistic settings.

This discussion leads us back to total institutions. It is in these, precisely, that we would least expect to find polyphony and difference. As Bauman (1989: 165) suggests, *"the readiness to act against one's own better judgement and against the voice of one's conscience is not just the function of authoritative command, but the result of exposure to a single-minded, unequivocal and monopolistic source of authority"* (emphasis in original). *Total institutions*—organizations that presume to exercise strong cultural control over their members, to the extent that they diminish pluralism—squeeze the space in which civility, reflection, and responsibility can thrive. As Bauman (1989: 166) urges, "The voice of individual moral conscience is best heard in the tumult of political and social discord."

Even in times and circumstances that are considered normal, you might find powerful total institutions at work, which the following case demonstrates. Again, the absence of polyphony is one of the preconditions for the establishment of total institutions. Haney, Banks, and Zimbardo (1973) designed an experiment that resonates with government practices that are accepted as normal and routine in many societies. The researchers divided a group of male American college students into two types of people: guards and inmates. They created a mock prison in a laboratory basement, using as subjects twenty-one healthy male undergraduate volunteers. Each person was to receive $15 a day for two weeks. Nine were randomly selected to be "prisoners," with the remainder designated as "guards" who were to supervise the prisoners in a rotating three-shift system. Each wore the symbolic garb of the role. Prisoners were given unflattering uniform clothing and tight caps to simulate shaven heads. Guards were put in a militaristic-type uniform and given L.A. cop sunglasses. Names were suppressed with norms of impersonality, and complex rules and penalties for their infraction were promulgated. Then the experiment began.

The experiment had to be aborted after less than a week. No sense of solidarity developed between the two groups, and almost all of their conversation centered on the roles assumed in the experiment. An escalatory chain of events occurred; the construed authority of the guards was enforced by the submissiveness of the prisoners, tempting the guards to further and increasingly illegitimate displays of the power that their authority allowed them to exercise, leading to further humiliation of the prisoners (Bauman 1989: 167). Bear in mind that the subjects were all normal, well-adjusted people before the experiment began but that after one week they were playing their roles with such conviction that the experiment had to be abandoned because of the real possibility of harm to the "prisoners."

Managing with positive power

One consequence of the insight that power is a normal feature of organizations is that managers must learn how to manage with power on a daily basis in ways that are enabling, genuinely empowering, and positive rather than merely constraining, smart but unethical, and largely negative. To be a good manager means knowing how and when to use what kind of power wisely to manage polyphony so that it is neither anarchic nor stifled. Modifying Pfeffer (1992) somewhat, we can note that there are seven steps to the effective use of power:

1. Decide what your goals should be and what you are trying to accomplish in consultation with direct stakeholders in your organization.
2. Diagnose patterns of dependence and interdependence; which individuals both inside and outside the organization are influential and important to achieving these goals?
3. What are the points of view of the important people likely to be? How will they feel about what you are trying to do?
4. What are the power bases of the important people? Which of them is the most influential in the decision?
5. What are your bases of power and influence? What bases of influence can you develop to gain more positive control over the situation?
6. Which of the various strategies and tactics for exercising power seem most appropriate and are likely to be effective, given the situation you confront?
7. Based on Steps 1 through 6, choose an ethical course of action to get something done.

When using power to manage others, always remember that those you are seeking to manage probably also will be trying to manage you with power, so the old adage "do unto others as you would have others do unto you" is worth recalling. Although you may think of their response as resistance, to do so presumes a value legitimacy that may not be justified on your part. They are trying to manage your management of power through their management of the power that they can enact in the situations in which they find themselves or that they can create. Power is nothing if not creative. Crucially, your managing with power means achieving common definition, a genuine accord, on which to base strategies, tactics, and actions. Positive uses of power make things happen that wouldn't otherwise have happened—not by stopping some things from occurring, but by bringing new things into creation, involving less force and more listening, working with, rather than against, others.

Managing with power does not always mean seeking to impose a specific meaning on an uncertain context because it entails arbitrary structuring of others' realities. In contrast, the alternative model is often seen as one where people advocate bottom-up decision making, seeking to listen to what others in

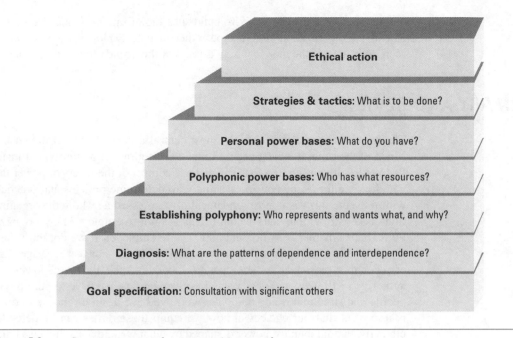

Ethical action

Strategies & tactics: What is to be done?

Personal power bases: What do you have?

Polyphonic power bases: Who has what resources?

Establishing polyphony: Who represents and wants what, and why?

Diagnosis: What are the patterns of dependence and interdependence?

Goal specification: Consultation with significant others

Figure 5.3   *Seven steps toward a more positive use of power*

the organization have to say. From *empowerment* (the giving of voice to those frequently unheard), organizations that use this model seek to enhance the overall systemic powers of the organization, to mobilize resources, and to get things done. This use of power frequently means giving way in the organization conversation, not claiming a special privilege because of title or experience, and not being selectively inattentive to others, but listening and attending to them.

The challenge for future power theory, as Pfeffer (1992: 340) suggests, is "to manage with power," where you recognize, diagnose, and respect the diversity of interests and seek to translate and enroll members within organizational courses of action, while at the same time listening to what others are saying, modifying your position accordingly, and choosing the appropriate strategies and tactics to accomplish whatever is chosen. Sometimes, after taking all that into consideration, it still means making others do what they would not otherwise have done, against their resistance. Power can be like that. Yet, it does not have to be so. Coercive power should be the refuge of last resort for the diplomatically challenged and structurally secure, not the hallmark of management's right to manage.

Organizations may listen or may not, may work with the creativity and diversity of people's identities or work against them. The politics of power can be based on active listening rather than assertive denial through the instrumentality and ritual of established power. To build such organizations—ones that seek to extend the organization conversation rather than to exploit its lapses—would seem to be one of the more pressing aspects of the agenda for future managers.

SUMMARY AND REVIEW

The pervasiveness of power is the most central aspect of organizational life. Much of the time, it is wrapped up in the velvet glove of authority, but inside that velvet glove is an iron fist. This fist has control of the levers of power that authority confers—the power, essentially, to determine policies and practices within the organization, most fundamentally expressed as whom the organization chooses to employ and whom it chooses not to employ. Many organizations shape whether we work and how we are employed if we do; thus, these types of organizations have power over most of our life chances as wage earners. For this reason, it is important to understand the limits of power and authority, resistance, and obedience. In organizations, we have to put up with people and situations while doing the work we have to do or choose to do. It is important that our choices in how we equip these duties can be defended ethically. Fundamentally, power is shaped by what we know and how we know what to do. Organizationally, it is easy for this knowledge to be applied questionably, which is why it is important that organizations always be polyphonic rather than totalitarian spaces. Being able to articulate organizational dissent should be a normal and essential bulwark of civil liberty.

ONE MORE TIME . . .

Getting the story straight

- Why is there more to understanding power than listing its most common bases?
- In what ways are organizations similar to power games?
- In what way is managing with power positive?
- Are power and resistance inseparable?

Thinking outside the box

- Who gets empowered through empowerment strategies?
- What common features do total institutions and (seemingly) normal organizations share?
- Where is the border between use and abuse of power in management?

ADDITIONAL RESOURCES

1. Many people have written about the topic of managing power in organizations, and finding just a few suggestions for further reading is hard. One place to start would be Steven Lukes' (1974) slim volume, *Power: A Radical View,* if only because of its brevity—fifty pages—as well as its elegance and lucidity.

2. If you find the previous resource interesting, you might want to try Stewart Clegg's (1989) *Frameworks of Power,* although it is not written for the introductory student.

3. The work of Michel Foucault is important and notoriously difficult. A good introduction is Phillip Barker's (1998) *Michel Foucault: An Introduction.*

4. Probably the most interesting case study of power in and around organizations in recent years is Bent Flyvbjerg's (1998) *Rationality and Power: Democracy in Practice,* researched in the arena of urban planning in the town of Aalborg in Denmark.

5. A good introduction from a managerial point of view is Jeffrey Pfeffer's (1992) *Managing With Power: Politics and Influence in Organizations.*

6. An example of the power of distance can be found in the novel *Atonement* by Ian McEwan (2002: 202), where a character involved in the British retreat to Dunkirk reflects on

   > the indifference with which men could lob shells into a landscape. Or empty their bomb bays over a sleeping cottage by a railway, without knowing or caring who was there. It was an industrial process. He had seen their own RA units at work, tightly knit groups, working all hours, proud of their discipline, drills, training, teamwork. They need never see the end result. . . .

7. We would like to recommend the definitive episode of *Yes, Prime Minister,* "The Key" (Lotterby 1986), in which Permanent Cabinet Secretary Sir Humphrey Appleby's authority is questioned and then undercut. The doors to government are literally closed to him as he makes a frantic attempt to retain his vanishing power. From this point on, Sir Humphrey never controls Prime Minister Hacker with the same effectiveness as he had in earlier episodes. His undoing is the result of gender politics, in the form of the prime minister's ruthlessly efficient female political adviser, Dorothy Wainwright, whom Sir Humphrey wishes to banish because she offers advice contrary to the interests of the Civil Service. Her office is moved to the outer reaches of Number 10 Downing Street. She fights to retain her place—opposite the men's toilets—from which vantage point she can see all the comings and goings of the cabinet as they meet to plot against the prime minister. The episode is a wonderful illustration of how different

resources can come into play in power games. We have heard it said that this episode was inspired by the fact that British Prime Minister Margaret Thatcher, who had an all-male cabinet, would only allow them to leave cabinet one at a time to use the bathroom to prevent them plotting against her—but this may well be an apocryphal tale.

8. The classic film about a total institution and organizational power is Milos Forman's (1975) *One Flew Over the Cuckoo's Nest*. McMurphy is a prisoner who has been assigned to a mental institution because of his persistent rebelliousness in prison. After he gets there, he is assigned to Nurse Ratched's ward, where a series of power games occur. The most memorable are the group therapy scenes, with Nurse Ratched practicing what she calls "therapy" on the group of patients. McMurphy (played by Jack Nicholson) sets out to undermine her domination of the ward. The ward is organized and controlled through a rigid set of rules and regulations, which McMurphy questions.

The contest of wills with the nurse is played out as a struggle, with McMurphy trying to win over the other inmates to a spontaneous and independent style of thinking rather than one stuck in the routines that the nurse reinforces because they make the ward more manageable. In the first of the two group therapy scenes, McMurphy butts in and tries to get the nurse to switch on the TV set so they can watch the World Series. This suggestion is put to the vote—she clearly disapproves, and her domination is such that only three inmates vote. During the next therapy session, Nurse Ratched determinedly presses one member with questions he doesn't want to answer. Another member proposes another vote about watching the second game of the World Series. McMurphy encourages the patients with the great lines, "I wanna see the hands. Come on. Which one of you nuts has got the guts?" Nine votes are cast in favor, and McMurphy senses victory—but Nurse Ratched changes the rules to defeat the proposal: "There are eighteen patients on this ward, Mr. McMurphy. And you have to have a majority to change ward policy. So you gentlemen can put your hands down now." McMurphy turns and gestures to the patients of the ward who are uninvolved in the therapy group, most of whom are seemingly in their own private worlds. "You're tryin' to tell me that you're gonna count these, these poor son-of-a-bitches, they don't know what we're talkin' about." Nurse Ratched replies: "Well, I have to disagree with you, Mr. McMurphy. These men are members of the ward just as you are." Nurse Ratched adjourns the meeting and closes the voting session. One of the outer group members not in the therapy session, a pivotal character called Chief, slowly raises his hand, so McMurphy says, "The Chief voted. Now will you please turn on the television set? The Nurse replies, "Mr. McMurphy, the meeting was adjourned and the vote was closed." "But the vote was 10 to 8. The Chief, he's got his hand up! Look!" "No, Mr. McMurphy. When the meeting was adjourned, the vote was 9 to 9." Democracy in action in organizations often involves the highly undemocratic manipulation of the numbers.

The film also illustrates the ways in which ordinary people can do quite extraordinary things as well after they have a uniform and are dealing not with people but with institutionally defined inmates: McMurphy ends up being lobotomized to "cure" him, although there is palpably nothing wrong with him other than a strong and stubborn streak of individualism and antiauthoritarianism.

9. We also suggest watching the 2001 German movie *Das Experiment*. It is very similar to the Haney, Banks, and Zimbardo (1973) experiment, which we described in this chapter. It shows, impressively, how the abuse of power can shape human relations and create a fatal dynamic. And it illustrates Lord Acton's dictum, with which we began the chapter, perfectly.

10. Organizations frequently enact routine deeds that, at the end of the functional chain of action, have appalling consequences. Have you seen the 1999 film *The Insider,* starring Russell Crowe? It is a good example of this point. Tobacco companies knew that their products were killing people, but they kept on making those products because the fact that people died was an externality of their business model, and it had no immediate causal consequences in terms of legal responsibility. Besides, people smoking made profits for the tobacco companies, and they needed to recruit new smokers to replace those who died, or they would lose market share.

In addition to these suggested additional resources, don't forget to look at what is also available on the Web site **www.ckmanagement.net,** including free PDF files of recent papers related to this chapter, which you can download; video interviews with famous academics talking about related themes; as well as many other resources, such as connections to interesting Web sites.

CHAPTER 6

MANAGING ORGANIZATIONAL BEHAVIOR

Personalities, Teams, Emotions

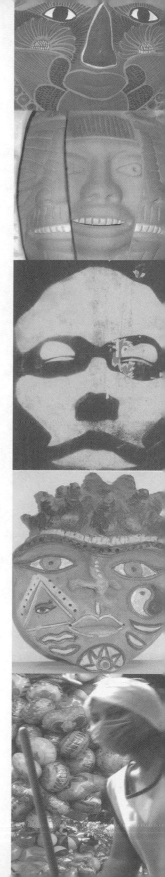

Objectives and learning outcomes

By the end of this chapter, you will be able to

- Appreciate the role that psychology plays in management theory and practice when applied to organizational behavior

- Understand the key concepts and principles of organizational behavior as they apply to managing people

- Understand and appreciate the opportunities and challenges of group work

- Identify the emerging trends in management theory

- Understand the limitations of management theory

Outline of the Chapter

Setting the Scene

Central Approaches and Main Theories
   Values: Managing Me, Myself, and I
   Personality
   Personality and Management
   Managing Us and Them: Working in Teams and Teams Working

Critical Issues: Toxic Handling

The Fine Print: Positive Psychology and Compassion

Summary and Review

One More Time . . .

Additional Resources

Before you get started . . .

Remember that, where psychology is concerned, as George Santayana once said, "Sanity is a madness put to good uses" (Santayana 1997–2004).

OUTLINE OF THE CHAPTER

A browse through any management section in most bookshops reveals a wide variety of self-help books that claim to make you a better manager. These books suggest that today's managers should be skilled in many areas other than core technical competencies—cost control, planning, rostering, and so on. Today, much of a manager's task requires an ability to deal with a full range of human relations issues—for example, the ability to motivate, mentor, and develop staff, inspire and transform organizations, communicate in culturally and spiritually diverse contexts, foster and build successful organizational culture, think in terms of being part of the global community, design and manage high-performance work teams, and provide stability and harmony in an increasingly complex, ambiguous, and uncertain environment. Managers today are expected to have some of the skills of a workplace psychologist, therapist, and counselor and, as such, need a basic understanding of psychological principles and theories to help them in the complex task of managing people.

Psychological properties can be analyzed at both an individual and a group level, both of which are critical to managing people at work. This chapter explains the basic psychological concepts and principles we believe are central for managing people in organizations. First, we take a close look at values because they are the fundamental building blocks for managing culture, diversity, and communication (all topics covered in detail in this book). You need to consider how our values are formed and how they can drive us throughout our working lives; how they bind us but also how they separate and isolate us; and how they can lead to conflict. Second, personality is clearly important because it is seen as the essence that makes each of us who we are, determines how we behave, and shapes how we feel. We ask, "Can we categorize people as types, or are each and every one of us unique individuals?" Third, we look at how working in groups can not only be rewarding but also how doing so can lead to major problems and issues. Finally, we close the chapter by looking at "positive psychology" and one of the topics it has brought into focus, organizational toxicity—a concept that has made an exciting contribution to organizational behavior.

SETTING THE SCENE

Psychology first explicitly emerged in Greece more than 2,500 years ago when philosophers tried to explain the nature of the self, the soul, and personality. The word *psychology* is derived from the Greek work *psyche,* meaning one's thoughts and feelings, and *ology,* which roughly translates to the quest for knowledge. Fundamentally, psychology is about answering the question, "Why are we the way we are?" We can all answer this question to a degree, but how we answer it depends upon our beliefs about human nature. Over the last 100 or so years, there has been a great deal of theory, research, and practice in psychology that addresses these questions. Our intention is to guide you to what you need to know.

In almost all fields of psychology, two main themes drive theory and research. The first theme centers on the *nature versus nurture* debate. At issue is whether we are who we are because of genetics and thus come preprogrammed into the world, such that how well you achieve in specific spheres depends on your *genetic dispositions*—your intelligence, dexterity, mathematical ability, reasoning, and so on. In other words, we are born with predispositions, such as personality, an ability to be a leader, or our intelligence. Others argue that we come into this world *tabula rasa*—that is, with a clean slate—and that we learn our personality, we learn to become leaders, and that we are heavily influenced by social contexts such as the socioeconomic status of our families, their culture, the environment in which we grow up, our schooling, and so on.

The opposing views of nature versus nurture frame much of what you will learn in the field of organizational behavior. Some theorists and researchers hold dearly to one or the other view. Others, however, prefer more moderate, integrative theories about what makes us who we are. Our view is that we are born with aspects of what constitutes us but that much of who we are is learned over time and that context has a profound impact on development. How you approach the question of nature and nurture greatly influences how you manage people and the assumptions you make about how they might, or might not, work.

An important theme that has emerged in organizational behavior theory and research suggests that nurture is overridden because of the fundamental drives that underpin human nature. Some arguments stress the "selfish gene" perspective: we are programmed for *competition* in a fundamental struggle to perpetuate our genes over those of others. Others stress that fitness and survival depend far more on the fact that we are social animals seeking affiliation and human relations; hence, we are more committed to *cooperation* than competition to ensure our survival as a species. Many management scholars and theorists use Darwinian theory to validate and substantiate their claims about human nature as being based in a competitive instinct and struggle. Evolutionary psychology has made substantial inroads into management research and theory such that it is now steeped in the Darwinian tradition of "survival of the fittest." Some of those who strongly believe in the survival of the fittest as a competitive concept are the first to claim a liver or a kidney transplant. In the ideal world of survival of the fittest, of course, such individuals would be left to die because they are simply not fit enough. Conversely, some of those who believe that the fittest survivors are those best able to cooperate are the first to complain when their taxes are raised to help support 16-year-old single parents.

Before Darwin published *On the Origin of Species by Means of Natural Selection, or the Preservation of Favoured Races in the Struggle for Life* in 1859, a work that explained his evolutionary view of biology, Adam Smith (1776/1961), a political economist and philosopher credited with being the father of capitalism, argued that progress and economic growth occurs because human behavior is based on self-interest, which is best served by the operation of free and unfettered markets in the supply of goods and services. For instance, if we as consumers want more leisure time and express a preference for this through our purchasing decisions in markets—maybe by buying vacations and appliances rather than saving—businesspeople who market vacations and innovations in labor-saving devices are rewarded. We buy and sell in markets that achieve balance between the supply and demand of goods such that, in the long term, efficiencies will prevail, and the price mechanism will maintain equilibrium. By being self-interested, we create demand preferences that markets emerge to meet; these markets benefit all of society because they create a self-regulating economic system.

Fundamental self-interest does not necessarily provide welfare or products or services that cannot be privately owned to generate income and so, the argument goes, government must become involved in providing such public goods. When another 16-year-old single parent has produced a baby and needs some support to sustain herself and her child, no business will assist her because there is no profit in giving resources away unless someone is paying you to do so. Hence, government typically provides social security and basic support. Of course, in doing so, in the long term, this is a subsidy to business in general because it enables the reproduction of another recruit to the next generation of workers and consumers. It is not surprising that social responsibility and economic, social, and environmental sustainability have long been perceived as the duty of government to regulate or a task for charity and other "do-gooders."

The views of Adam Smith have certainly been influential. Look at any newspaper story on corporate behavior to see parallels with notions of survival of the fittest, the centrality of self-interest, and the primal pursuit of economic wealth as the end of human activity. Today, this bundle of beliefs assumes that self-interested economic action is the only rational basis for human behavior. Hence, it is a small step to arguing that our rationalities are formed this way as a constitutive feature of our human nature. Using Darwin and Smith as authorities, some scholars such as Nicholson (2000) would argue that that competition is genetically a human predisposition.

Values are critical in how we perceive and interact. Your views on welfare provision, workplace redundancies, the provision of maternity or paternity leave, religious freedom in the workplace, taxation, and so many other issues are inextricably linked to your values, attitudes, and beliefs about the world, framing how you see it, interpret it, and operate within it. For this reason, our ability to understand our values as well as those of the people we work with and manage is one of the most important aspects of being a manager—both in managing ourselves and in managing others.

CENTRAL APPROACHES AND MAIN THEORIES

Values: Managing me, myself, and I

For many scholars, values can be thought of as the building blocks of culture (Howard 1988; 271–274; see also pp. 280-283). However, values can also be understood within the context of people management; to form, sustain, and improve relationships with people, or to motivate people, we must understand what is and what is not important to them. To a great extent, management is about managing people in a coordinated way to ensure that organizational outcomes are realized while also ensuring that one's own and others' values are met. Understanding values is a fundamental attribute for managing today. Moreover, we should also have an understanding and appreciation of how our values filter information and create knowledge, coloring the world we perceive as tinted lenses do. Not everyone sees things the same way. Although there are many theories and approaches to values, we look in detail at Shalom Schwartz's (1992) account of the role that universal values play at the personal level. We choose to highlight Schwartz for two reasons: first, because his work underpins much of the values research evident in organizational behavior today, yet his role is underemphasized; and second, his work is influential and well respected in psychology. In the next section, we provide you with the necessary background to values theory to help you start managing values.

Values

So what are values? *Values* are a person's or social group's consistent beliefs about something in which they have an emotional investment. Schwartz defines values as desirable goals, varying in importance, which serve as guiding principles in people's lives (Schwartz 1992, 1994). People are social animals living in a state of tension between values associated with their individuality and values associated with social conformance (Aronson 1960). Values can create tension because some that drive our behavior as individuals are not consistent with others that regulate our behavior socially.

For example, superstar football players earn more money in a week than most people earn in a lifetime. They have the means to have whatever—or whomever—they desire and to live a lavish lifestyle in competition with other fit, wealthy young men. Not surprisingly, these young men express both highly competitive and team-based values. Sometimes their competitive values as young men competing for success can clash with social norms. In addition, sometimes the team norms of sharing with your teammates may conflict with social norms respecting the individuality and privacy of others, particularly as one comes into contact with others from outside one's field who are, nonetheless, relatively overawed followers of it. A number of high-profile cases of

TABLE 6.1 Schwartz's universal values

Achievement	Conformity	Power	Self-direction	Tradition
Benevolence	Hedonism	Security	Stimulation	Universalism

sexual assault by professional sportsmen underscore this point. For instance, from a social values perspective, one might see young football players as overpaid, oversexed, and undereducated louts, whereas from an individual values perspective, they are supercompetitive and thus appropriately rewarded, but they have some problems adjusting to societal rather than team values.

Values have a personal component and a social component. Sometimes what we value as individuals might not be valued by society and vice versa—the interaction of personal and social values can result in tension because values are something people feel strongly about. Typically, individuals become very upset when they feel their values are threatened or compromised. In essence, this is where the role of a manager is most difficult—managing and sharing understanding about values, whether they are those of a coworker, a customer, a superior, or other organizations. Understanding values is critical in aligning organizational behavior and managing people. For example, if you were a football team manager, how would you manage the private lives of your players when they are lived in the public face of the paparazzi? Any desires the players have can be easily satisfied because they are so wealthy, so bored when not playing or training, and so ready for whatever action is going down.

Schwartz (1992) identifies some values as "trans-situational," meaning that, irrespective of the situation in which you find yourself, your values do not change; you take them with you wherever you go. For instance, if you value life and freedom above all else, and one day you see a march protesting about your country going to war, it is likely that you will join this march to protest. Another day, you may be at the football stadium watching your team win another amazing victory. At this time, your values for life and freedom may not be at the forefront of your thoughts, but does this mean that you no longer value life and freedom, or hold them any less important?

Values appear to have a strong motivational aspect to them. Rokeach (1968, 1973) argued that values guide our behaviors throughout life. Accordingly, Schwartz (1992) identified a number of motivational value types organized according to sets of associated values. He identified ten universal values that he believed all people and peoples would hold in common; see Table 6.1.

Some of these values are mutually exclusive, but most are what Schwartz calls "continuous," meaning that they overlap. Because values overlap, people behave or respond differently to certain things in life. Study each of the representations of Schwartz's value types in Table 6.2 for a moment, and look at their associated values:

TABLE 6.2   Schwartz's values by type and their associated meanings

Value Type	Description	Associated Values
ACHIEVEMENT	Valuing of personal success by demonstrating one's competence according to social standards	*Success* (Goal achievement)
		Capability (Competence, effectiveness, efficiency)
		Ambition (Hard work)
		Influence (The ability to influence people and events)
BENEVOLENCE	Preservation and enhancement of the welfare of people with whom one is in frequent personal contact	*Helpfulness* (Working for the welfare of others)
		Honesty (Genuineness, sincerity)
		Forgivingness (Willingness to pardon others)
		Loyalty (Faithful to friends, group)
		Responsibility (Dependable, reliable)
CONFORMITY	Restraint of actions, inclinations, and impulses that are likely to upset or harm others and that might violate social expectations or norms	*Politeness* (Courtesy, good manners)
		Obedience (Dutiful, meet obligations)
		Self-discipline (Self-restraint, resistance to temptation)
		Honoring parents and elders (Showing respect)
HEDONISM	Pleasure and sensuous gratification for oneself	*Pleasure* (Gratification of one's desires)
		Enjoyment in life (Enjoyment of food, sex)
POWER	One's social status and prestige, control, or dominance over people and resources	*Social power* (Control over others, dominance)
		Authority (The right to lead or command)
		Wealth (Material possessions, money)

Value Type	Description	Associated Values
SECURITY	Safety, harmony, and stability of society, of relationships, and of self	*Family security* (Safety for loved ones)
		National security (Protection from enemies)
		Social order (Stability of society)
		Cleanliness (Neatness, tidiness)
		Reciprocation of favors (Avoidance of indebtedness)
SELF-DIRECTION	Independent thought and action	*Creativity* (Uniqueness, imagination)
		Freedom (Freedom to think and act)
		Independence (Self dependence, self-reliance, self-sufficiency)
		Curiosity (Exploring)
		Choose own goals (Select own direction in life and be free to choose)
STIMULATION	Excitement, novelty, and challenge in life	*Daringness* (Risk taking)
		A varied life (Challenge, novelty, change)
		An exciting life (Stimulating experiences)
TRADITION	Respect, commitment, and acceptance of the customs and ideas that traditional culture or religion provides	*Humility* (Modesty, self-effacement)
		Acceptance of my portion in life (Submission to and acceptance of one's life's circumstances)
		Devotion (Hold to religious faith and belief)
		Respect for tradition (Preservation of time-honored customs)
		Moderate (Avoiding extremes of feeling or action)

(Continued)

TABLE 6.2 (Continued)

Value Type	Description	Associated Values
UNIVERSALISM	Understanding, appreciation, tolerance, and protection for the welfare of all people and for nature	*Broadminded* (Tolerant of different ideas and beliefs) *Wisdom* (A mature understanding of life) *Social justice* (Correcting injustice, care for the weak) *Equality* (Equal opportunity for all) *A world at peace* (Free of war and conflict) *A world of beauty* (Beauty of nature and the arts) *Unity with nature* (Fitting into nature) *Protecting the environment* (Preserving nature)

Source: Adapted from Schwartz (1992, 1996) and Rohan (2000)

Value priorities refer to the order of values in terms of their importance to us as individuals. Much research supports Schwartz's views of values and has shown that we all, more or less, have the same sets of values—irrespective of culture, gender, and religion (Schwartz 1996). However, we differ in the priorities we assign to our values (Rohan 2000). Using Schwartz's values, let's look at an example of how people might think and act according to their value priorities. Imagine two new students meeting in a first-year tutorial in management—let's call them Anne and Samantha. Anne's values rate highly on tradition, power, and conformance, but low on universalism, so she respects and upholds her cultural and religious traditions and believes they are dominant, and that people who violate or threaten such traditions should be converted to her views or should be punished. Like Anne, Samantha also highly rates values of tradition and conformance but, rather than having power as a priority, she views universalism as a higher-order value. Take a look at the associated values for power and universalism in Table 6.2; do you think that over time Samantha and Anne will find it difficult to get along? What do you think might happen after they start discussing issues important to them? Sure, they might agree that it's a nice sunny day, that Brad Pitt is a hunk, and that Jennifer Aniston's new Jimmy Choo shoes are to die for—but what about when they start discussing issues such as whether asylum seekers from different religious backgrounds should enter their country? This is where values are very important because we tend to prefer people who have the same value priorities as we do, and often we find it difficult to tolerate people with different value priorities. For this reason, there has been a lot of interest over the last decade in understanding values, especially in organizational settings (Sagiv and Schwartz 2002). We explore values in greater detail later (see also pp. 248–257), when we look at values in association with leadership, social responsibility, and sustainability.

Personality

Why do managers need to know about personality, and what is a personality, anyway? Management, above all, is about managing people. And people, unlike machines or numbers, have individual personalities. *Personality* refers to the stable patterns of behavior and internal states of mind that help explain a person's behavioral tendencies (Monte 1991). Most of us are already everyday theorists of personality—we make observations about people's actions and behaviors, and we categorize people accordingly, on an almost daily basis. Consider the following example. A group of friends go to the university bar every Friday night. One friend, Jo, is always joking and making people laugh; another friend, Sal, is quiet and reserved. Jo is a "fun" person, and people might say Jo is *extroverted.* Sal, however, is perceived as *introverted.* Their individual personalities influence how others react and behave in response to them, both in the bar and at work. In the workplace, depending on the task, Sal and Jo's different personalities have a profound effect on how those they work with perform their work and the quality of their working relationships. For this reason alone, the ability to manage diverse personalities is an important repertoire for a manager's set of skills. In addition to values, personality is important in understanding why and how humans behave, think, and feel as they do, and people's personalities can have a strong impact on what they choose to do and how they perform at work (George 1992). Think of yourself, for instance. How would you feel about being one against nature, fishing in the surf from a cliff face, confronting the elements, similar to the man in Image 6.1? Would this be you? What kind of personality with what kind of values is likely to enjoy this leisure activity? And if, as we suspect, the person fishing is a loner, what kinds of organizational and team roles would best suit this individual? These are some of the issues that organizational behavior explores.

In this section, we consider a handful of theories that have emerged from quite distinct backgrounds. The fascinating story of how personality has been theorized has many twists and turns. We look at four broad accounts: the trait, the sociocognitive, the psychoanalytical, and the humanist. Each approach views the subject matter of personality from a quite distinct perspective.

You are what you are: The trait approach

The trait approach develops from the perspective that personality is something that can be clearly identified, operationalized, and measured. *Traits* refer to a mixture of biological, psychological, and societal influences that

Image 6.1   *Team player or rugged individualist?*

characterize a person's thoughts and actions throughout their lives. The trait perspective became popular in the 1930s, when Allport and Odbert (1936) sought to identify all the traits that might describe people. To do this, they decided to look in a dictionary. (We have discussed this technique already; remember that the Aston School used it when they started to think about organization structure (see also pp. 128–131). They found about 18,000 words that could be used as descriptors, and subsequent psychologists have sought to reduce and condense this enormous list. The most popular approach is through factor analysis. *Factor analysis* involves taking all the words or traits that go together and categorizing them under a common factor.

Let's revisit Jo. Jo might be funny, friendly, easy to get along with, and might also enjoy experiencing new things and taking risks. Each of these traits reflects Jo's personality. Traits that cluster together are called a *factor*. In this example, the factor would be "extraversion."

By far the best-known trait theory using factorial analysis is McCrae and Costa's (1996) "Big Five" personality factors. The Big Five–personality factor approach has been found to be one of the most reliable trait-based approaches to personality measurement (Endler and Speer 1998). Almost every textbook on personality, organizational behavior, and management includes the Big Five, also sometimes referred to as the NEO-PI, and OCEAN. The five factors and their associated meanings are presented in Table 6.3.

TABLE 6.3 The Big Five personality factors

Factor	Description
Emotional stability	Emotional stability includes whether a person is calm vs. anxious, self-satisfied vs. self-pitying, secure vs. insecure, emotionally stable vs. emotionally unstable.
Extraversion	Extraversion refers to whether a person is sociable vs. reserved or assertive vs. timid.
Openness	Openness refers to a person's approach to life—whether they are independent vs. conforming, broad-minded vs. narrow-minded, creative vs. practical.
Agreeableness	Agreeableness refers to how people get along with others—whether they are warm-hearted vs. ruthless, trusting vs. distrusting, helpful vs. uncooperative.
Conscientiousness	Conscientiousness refers to high vs. low tolerance for risk, well-organized vs. disorganized, well-disciplined vs. impulsive.

Source: Adapted from McCrae and Costa (1996) and Costa and McCrae (1999)

You are what we think: The sociocognitive approach

The sociocognitive approach seeks to explain how learning, social behavior, and cognition compose and shape our personality. Its popularity started with the work of Alfred Bandura and his concept of "reciprocal determinism" (Bandura 1986). By *reciprocal determinism,* Bandura meant that our personality is a product of our behavior, our thoughts, and our feelings in interaction with our environment. For example, Samantha might come from a very quiet and reserved home. She has grown to like peace and quiet, and this has helped make up much of her personality. The fact that the bar is loud and crowded makes Sam uncomfortable, so she becomes quieter and more reserved. It is not that she is unsociable: Sam may be sociable and friendly at home but not in the bar because it is the wrong milieu for her personality.

One of the most appealing sociocognitive theories of personality is known as the *locus of control,* developed by Rotter (1966). To get a feeling for the locus of control approach, consider the following example. You are walking along the street and you trip. You look back at the spot where you tripped and notice there is a brick on the path. Do you say "Oh, I'm such an idiot because I didn't see that brick" or do you say, "Argh, what idiot put that brick there?" In one case, you internalize your behavior (it is your fault for falling over), and in the other you externalize (the reason you fell over is someone else's stupidity). In the former, we describe an internal locus of control, which refers to the belief that you control your own fate. In the latter, we describe an external locus of control, which is the perception that outside forces, or even chance, predominantly determine your fate—your fate is outside your control. Internals have a

Image 6.2   *Representing and revealing*

high level of achievement, they are much more independent, enjoy better psychological health, and have much better coping strategies (Myers 2001).

The locus of control has been shown to be very important in terms of how people behave in organizations (Spector 1982). Think of ways that an internal might behave compared to an external when you, as a manager, are trying to give someone feedback on a job they have not performed well. How might each type of person reflect on the information? How would you try to manage each of them differently? Would they mask or reveal what they feel?

You are what you don't know: The psychoanalytical approach

Unlike the trait-based and the sociocognitive approaches to personality, the psychoanalytical approach is typified by unconscious desires and defense

For Freud, absolutely nothing happens by accident.

mechanisms aimed at fighting pent-up sexual anxiety and the pervasive fear of death. Sigmund Freud is considered the father of the psychoanalytical approach to personality. Freud is a theorist who is one of the most loathed (by many psychologists and feminists) and, at the same time, one of the most admired (by many artists, writers, and psychiatrists). Certainly, Freud, along with figures such as Charles Darwin and Adam Smith, did much to define the ways in which we understand the nature of the reality that we experience today. Freud believed personality was made up of thoughts and actions emerging from what he called the *unconscious*. The unconscious surfaced in dreams and slips of the tongue, because it contains desires, thoughts, and feelings that were "unconscionable" and often repressed. For Freud, absolutely nothing happens by accident; an explanation was usually to be found hidden in the unconscious. It is deep in the unconscious that we store our troubled feelings and thoughts, and the mind keeps them hidden by working in a number of remarkable ways. According to Freud, there are three ways in which our mind is structured. First, the unconscious mind (the *id*) operates on the pleasure principle and is driven by desires like hunger, sex, and aggression. The *id* must be controlled, or it will be impossible to delay gratification. Second, there is the *ego,* which allows us to cope with our world based on the *reality principle* (the principle that, as we grow, we become aware of the real environment and the need to adapt to it). It recognizes desires and satiates them, but in ways that ensure minimal pain and destruction.

Image 6.3   *Fragmented self*

The *ego* is the "control room" of our personality. Third, there is the *superego*—our social and personal monitor, constantly judging our behavior, thoughts, and feelings, looking at how we should behave through the eyes of all those others around us who constitute our society. The superego and the id are usually in battle, so the ego must ensure that the two are reconciled—and, as we shall see, this is where all the trouble starts.

Freud (1935) believed personality development coincided with certain psychosexual stages. For example, at the oral stage (up to about one and a half years of age), a child is fixated with oral pleasures, such as sucking, gumming, and chewing, whereas at the anal stage (around one and a half to two and a half years of age), the child becomes fixated on the anal stage of development, focusing on anything to do with what comes out of the anus. Fart jokes work well with the anally fixated—think of the Terrence and Patrick characters from the cartoon *South Park*. From about 3 to 6 years, the child is in the phallic stage (you can see why feminists might dislike Freud given the "phallocentric" nature of his theory!) and gains arousal and pleasure from stimulation of the genital region. Then, from around age 6 until puberty, people go into a sort of hibernation—or what Freud calls *latency*—where everything lies dormant. Finally, individuals enter the genital phase as they hit puberty and start getting interested in sex.

Quite a lot of the language you hear today has its origins in Freudian theory based on the sexual stages of development—for example, the notion of a Freudian slip, an Oedipus complex, penis envy, fixation, repression, and many other concepts in everyday use. Table 6.4 provides a description of some of the concepts related to three of the psychosexual stages (oral, anal, and phallic).

Obviously, if this had been the entirety of Freud's view of the world, and it was an accurate depiction, most people would have a problem achieving anything. The anxiety, guilt, and fear we would constantly feel would be unbearable. However, in addition, Freud argued that there exists an intricate system of checks and balances that enable us to operate in our world—the defense mechanisms that allow us to reinterpret reality and to fool ourselves that everything is fine. There are a number of defense mechanisms; here, we look briefly at three: repression, reaction formation, and projection (adapted from Myers 2001: 494).

First, through *repression* we block all our incestual thoughts and feelings and try to present a smooth façade to the world. However, repression is an imperfect mechanism because some thoughts still slip out. Freud believed such thoughts would manifest themselves through symbolism or in slips of the tongue. For example, the fact that many missiles are designed in a shape similar to a penis suggests to some psychoanalysts that men create these weapons of mass destruction because of their repressed sexual feelings and aggression. Second, we use *reaction formation* to block our impulses and feelings by acting in ways opposite to them. One common social problem today is the violence that some young men perpetrate toward homosexuals (gay bashing). Freudians would argue that such young men are trying to cope with their homosexual thoughts and feelings by causing violence to the very people they fear they might be. Thus, being macho both enables them to repress any anxieties and to

TABLE 6.4   Freud's three stages of development

Stage	Description
Oral	If we are traumatized or disciplined during the oral phase, we become fixated at that stage. So an oral person becomes fixated with pleasures of the mouth, which can be quite sensual. They constantly place things in their mouths, tend to overeat, and possibly smoke. Orally fixated people tend to become artists. Or they can deny their overdependence on oral pleasures and tend to become aggressive to compensate—so maybe they end up as bouncer at a bar or a black belt in judo.
Anal	Being punished during the anal stage tends to make a person what Freud calls "anally retentive." Such people discover that they can control their parents by refusing to go to the toilet or by going to the toilet at inappropriate times and in inappropriate places. Such individuals are quite stringent, control oriented, and tend to choose a career in accounting or something similar. Or they might become anally expulsive—highly disorganized and messy.
Phallic	The phallic phase is where we start seeing some real problems. For example, based on the ancient Greek fable of Oedipus, who killed his father and married his mother, Freud believes males develop an Oedipus complex. Because mothers tend to clean up after children after they dump a load in their diapers, children get sexual gratification and arousal from maternal attention. Slowly, the male child develops sexual feelings for his mother and hatred for his father, who is perceived as a competitor for maternal affections. These feelings create intense anxiety and guilt in children, and they come to fear castration by their fathers. The only way to cope with such overwhelming feelings is to repress and hide all these fears deep down in the unconscious.

Source: Adapted from Hall and Lindzey (1957: 29–75)

demonstrate, by overcompensating, their own sense of the sexuality that they wish to project to the world. Third, *projection:* When we have feelings and thoughts that are threatening for us, we project them onto others. For example, a distrustful and incompetent office administrator may treat everyone who comes into their office with distrust and see them as incompetent. Such a person denies his or her own incompetence by projecting it onto others.

Although Freud produced one of the most interesting of personality theories, there is very little evidence to support his notions. Even so, there is no doubt that he has been, historically, one of the most influential psychological theorists and practitioners. His concepts have had considerable intellectual appeal and remain the most salient aspect of Freud's work. Still, Freud's theory takes a very negative view of humanity and overemphasizes sexual desire as the main motivator behind behavior and thought. Imagine reprimanding an employee by saying that he is fixated at the phallic stage of development and is acting the way he is because he wants to sleep with his mother and kill his father—that might not go down too well! Fortunately, there are other personality theories that approach the subject from a more positive view—the humanist approach.

Image 6.4   *Symbols on/of the self*

You are what you grow: The humanist approach

The humanist places our sense of self at the center of personality. The aim of the humanist is to ensure that humans realize personal growth and potential. The humanist tradition experienced its greatest growth in the 1960s as psychologists became increasingly critical of the reliance on objectivity in trait-based approaches to studying personality, where paper and pencil inventories and factor analysis substitute for more interpretive skills that the analysts might have. They were equally wary of Freud's overly negative orientation, with its view that our personalities are mainly based on suppression of deviant thoughts and incestual sexual desires. By far the best-known humanist psychologists are Carl Rogers (1967) and Abraham Maslow (1968) (see also pp. 250–254).

Most critical for Maslow and Rogers is the notion of how we express self-concept. When we try to answer the question "who am I?" the self-concept refers to our thoughts and feelings about ourselves. We view ourselves as being in the world in a number of ways. First, we have an actual self and an idealized self, and we strive to reduce the gap between the two by becoming as close to our idealized self as possible. When we act in ways consistent with our ideal self, we have a positive self-image. If we feel there are gaps between our ideal self and actual self, we have a negative self-image.

Carl Rogers approached personality from the perspective that we are all unique and fundamentally "good" people, all striving for what Maslow termed *self-actualization*. For Rogers, the key to positive self-image is the environment within which we grow because it provides three basic conditions enabling that growth:

- People must be *genuine, honest, and open* about their own feelings.
- People must be *accepting,* in that they value themselves and others. Even one's own failings should be seen with a positive regard, or what Rogers referred to as "Unconditional Positive Regard."
- The final important aspect for Rogers is empathy; *empathy* concerns how we communicate our feelings to the world and how we, in turn, share and reflect on these meanings. Empathy is very important in concepts like emotional intelligence (see also pp. 217–222; 496) and is an integral part of our ability to function in the social world.

Personality and management

Personality is clearly complex; although we all have one, it is by no means clear what it is or how it should best be conceived, and many very successful people are adept at masking the true nature of their personality. Rather like the graffiti mask in Image 6.5, they present a smooth but inscrutable front to the world. But if so much about personality is hidden or unclear, how are we supposed to use it as a tool to manage people? Perhaps the best thing to do is to take a few pointers from each theory. Try to identify the traits that those with whom you work exhibit, and try to adjust your expectations and behavior appropriately. Be sensitive to people's conceptions of the locus of control. Appreciate that some people will be more anal retentive in their dispositions than others, and try to deal with them in a way that takes this into account. Above all, try to be a practical humanist and facilitate human growth and potential.

Managing us and them:
Working in teams and teams working

At some stage in our working lives, almost every one of us will work as part of a team. It is therefore important for us to have a general understanding of teams their psychological properties, how they influence us, and how teams

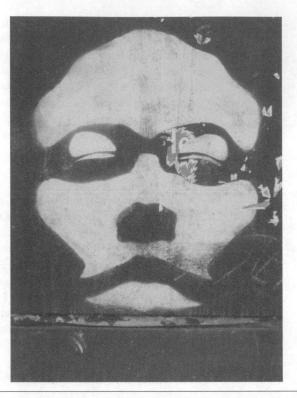

Image 6.5   *Graffiti mask*

Image 6.6   *A sunny disposition*

work. In Chapter 5, we saw how teams can be used to manage power. In this chapter, we consider broader aspects of teams. A *team* can be defined as two or more people psychologically contracted together to achieve a common organizational goal in which all individuals involved share at least some level of responsibility and accountability. We explore this definition in greater detail shortly. First, however, we want to point out that management academics like to distinguish between a team and a group, and in this chapter we sometimes use the terms interchangeably because early in the development of psychology, all teams were referred to as groups. Today, the differences between teams and groups are subtle but for some people remain important. A *group* can be defined as two or more people working toward a common goal, but there is no psychological contract between them; the outcomes are less dependent on all the members working together, and there is usually no shared responsibility and accountability for outcomes.

Let's look at an example. Jenny, Mary, Sarah, and Joanne all play for the Mount Pleasant Rangers—the local soccer team that has made it into the finals. Every day, the players get together and practice their shots at goal, their long and short passing, and their game plan. The coach also makes sure that the players imagine themselves winning, holding up the trophy after the game. She points out to her team how important it is that they understand each other's roles and positions, and stresses that even though some of them don't get along that well, they need to work together to achieve the all-important win. On finals day, people from all around Mount Pleasant leave their houses for the game. The traffic is bad; some people are driving on sidewalks, others are waiting for an hour or so for a bus, and some are walking. Obviously, these groups of people are all there for a common purpose—to get to the stadium to see their team play—but they are not bound by any psychological contract. If the people on the bus never get to the stadium, it does not affect the people who get there by walking or driving. In this example, the Mount Pleasant Rangers are a team, and the fans are a group.

Working in teams means we are quite dependent upon others in achieving outcomes. This interdependence among people in teams poses many challenges and opportunities to us as managers because it means increased saliency has to be given to managing issues such as personalities and values; coordinating behaviors; establishing direction, roles and responsibilities; and resolving conflict. For this reason, managing teams can be both the most rewarding part of a manager's job and the most frustrating. To help you better understand teams, we look at how group psychology came about, mainly in the form of group dynamics. We then consider how an individual can be affected by groups of people.

The story of teams: What, where, and why?

Earlier, we saw how management theory grew from different, and sometimes competing, traditions (see also pp. 5–10; 10–29). The human relations tradition partly evolved in reaction to Taylor's scientific management, and it

Image 6.7   *A group of workers or a team?*

was from the human relations approach that interest in teamwork enjoyed most of its growth and development. Groups are a critical party of the human relations philosophy, which includes notions such as the following: people want to be liked, respected, and wanted; management's role is to ensure that people feel like part of the team; all staff and teams should be involved in decision making and provide staff with at least some levels of self-direction; and management should clearly define objectives and expected outcomes, and seek input or buy-in from staff (Mayo 1946). Teams, for the human relations school, are critical, and there are many feel-good statements made about teams. Some influential theorists, researchers, and authors argue that many organizations have unreal expectations of teams; in fact, they say, it can take up to ten years for an organization to transform itself into one with effective teams (Greenberg and Baron 2003). Teamwork can be extremely difficult because it is so open to interpersonal psychological issues. Certain psychological properties of teams can attract and bind individuals, or they can orient people toward destructive behaviors, causing some managers to question the value of teams because they require substantial management time and resources.

The things that bind: Why we form groups

Why do we form groups? First, we consider safety in numbers. In evolutionary terms, forming groups rather than existing alone is a very important way that many animals ensure their survival. Ants and bees have very large, highly structured and organized societies, comprising many groups of worker ants or bees, queens, and armies. Small fish in the ocean and animals in the wild (such as the impala, buffalo, and zebra) all travel in large groups for safety. In the tradition of Charles Darwin, imagine yourself as an animal who knows that a predator might be waiting to make you their lunch. If there were a series of points on your journey where attack was more likely, your chances of surviving would be greater if you traveled in large numbers than if you were on your own—especially if you were fitter, smarter, and could run faster than the others. However, to say that we form groups simply to avoid getting killed is a bit too simplistic. Psychologically, being part of a group is critical to our survival in other very important ways.

Second, we form groups because of a sense of belongingness. If you pick up any psychological textbook and turn to the chapter on psychological disorders, you will notice one remarkable thing: All the disorders (regardless of their cause) are considered problems for individuals because they cannot function effectively as part of society. Being part of a group is necessary for healthy psychological development and identity. In their classic text, *The Social Psychology of Organizations,* Daniel Katz and Robert L. Kahn state the following:

> By being part of something beyond the physical self, the individual can achieve a sense of belongingness and can participate in accomplishments beyond individual powers. Moreover, affiliating with others can extend the ego in time as well as space, for individuals can see their contribution to the group as enduring over time even though they themselves may not survive. (Katz and Kahn 1978: 374)

Being part of a team is, therefore, important for our own psychological needs because it provides us with a sense of self beyond our physical life. We all belong to one form of group or another. A family, a group of friends, a work team, a student group, a union, a special interest group, a religious group, a nationality, and so on. We either feel like we belong or don't belong to those groups for myriad reasons. Take a few moments to think about the groups you feel you belong to or are a part of. You do not need to identify these groups to anyone unless you want to—just think about them. In the first column of Table 6.5, list the reasons why you feel included as part of these groups. After you complete that list, think about the groups that you feel you do not belong to or feel excluded from and, using the second column of the table, list the reasons why you feel like you do not belong.

TABLE 6.5   Feelings

I feel I *do* belong because . . .	I feel I *do not* belong because . . .

Now, with some friends, compare and contrast your answers. What do you notice about why people felt they did or not belong to each group? Can you see any common themes emerging? Are there any major differences?

With this little thought-exercise, you will notice that for almost all of us, whether we feel part of a team or not is based on whether we are made to feel we belong, whether our interests and values are similar, and whether we fit in. Organizationally, when thinking about teamwork, the manager must design a team that cultivates the feelings in column one and reduces the feelings in column two. By identifying, or not identifying, with certain teams, we are effectively creating a distinction between "us" and "them." Each of us is treated as either in or apart from the group. When part of a group, we, in turn, probably treat others in the same "us" and "them" terms.

Much research has shown that in organizational settings we tend to favor certain individuals when making decisions. This phenomenon, called the *in-group bias,* occurs when you favor members of your own group over others (Hogg 1996; Turner 1987). Over time, this strong identification to your group can lead to quite problematic relations, such as prejudice and distrust, and even hatred and anger, toward members of different out-groups (see Whitely 1999). Team cohesion and identification is important, but it can pose problems that make managing teams a complex art.

Social facilitation

Groups of people have a profound effect upon individual behavior. Social facilitation is a concept that is as old as the discipline of psychology itself. In the late 1800s, Norman Triplett observed that children fishing would wind in their reel much faster when other children were present (Myers 2001). This increase in performance in the presence of others is called *social facilitation* and is similar to the effect found in the Hawthorne studies discussed earlier in this book (see also pp. 25–28). However, almost always, social facilitation occurs on fairly simple tasks only, or on tasks a person is experienced in doing. If the task is complex or the person performing them is a novice, social facilitation produces performance that is actually worse in social settings than when the person works alone. Thus, how you introduce and train new team members needs careful consideration and thought. Also, people who can do something competently alone may not necessarily perform competently in the presence of others. Training and experience, therefore, can be a critical aspect to successful teamwork.

Conformance and obedience

In 1955, Solomon Asch, in a now-classic study that appeared in the journal *Scientific American,* reported on an interesting and simple experiment about how groups influence individuals. He had prearranged groups of five people who were seated in a room. Another individual, who had been recruited for the study, would arrive at the experiment to find this group already seated at the table. The individual was told that the group consisted of other people who were recruited for the experiment. What the individual did not know was that everyone in the group was a confederate of the experimenter. After the subject (who was the real focus of the experiment) sat down with the group, the experimenter began the study by telling the group that he would show them a standard line and a set of comparison lines (similar to the lines in Figure 6.1). The group had to decide which comparison line was identical to the standard line, and each person spoke in turn, with the individual who was the subject of the experiment being asked to speak last. The process was repeated a couple of times. On each occasion, the answer was obvious, but each person in the group would answer in a way that was clearly incorrect—for example, they would all say C is identical to the standard line. Now if you were the individual who was the real focus of the study, how do you think you would answer? You think you would say B, wouldn't you? Well, don't be so sure, because over the course of the experiment approximately one third of the individuals agreed with the group—even though all the information available showed that the answer was incorrect.

It should be made clear, however, that many times conformity is absolutely necessary. Imagine a workplace in which no one conformed to the rules and no one followed policy on decision making. Imagine the chaos; you would be in a workplace that looked a lot like the Wild West with its lawlessness, bandits, and outlaws. Even so, many people tend to follow or conform blindly to the group even when what the group is doing is clearly wrong. Conformity might help explain why so few people resist their organizations and why a group may tolerate or engage in unethical and socially irresponsible behaviors (see also pp. 181–183).

Groupthink

Similar to conformity, *groupthink* refers to the tendency of members of a group to seek and maintain harmony in a group, at the cost of ignoring or avoiding

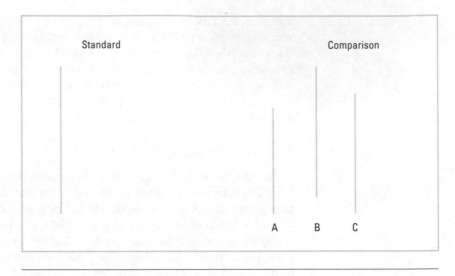

Figure 6.1   *Solomon Asch's experiment demonstrating conformity. Which line is identical to the standard line: A, B, or C?*

important decisions that may disrupt harmony. *Groupthink* is a term coined by Irving Janis, who was intrigued by how teams arrive at devastating decisions—even when the teams appear to be prestigious, well educated, or carefully selected (Janis 1982). Since Janis's study, many researchers have found that groupthink occurs across broad levels of an organization. Even when the team culture of a senior leadership team is made up of experts of equal power and status, it can become too strong. When this occurs, the team reinterprets information so that members can avoid any thinking that might disrupt the strong team culture, sometimes leading to a belief that, together, the team can overcome any obstacle faced (Clegg, Pitsis, Rura-Polley, and Marosszeky 2002).

By far one of the most famous cases of groupthink is Esser and Lindoerfer's (1989) analysis of the Challenger space disaster. On a freezing day in 1986, NASA engineers instructed key NASA administrators to abort the takeoff of the space shuttle Challenger because conditions were unsafe. NASA had a proud history of leading the space race, a very strong culture of invulnerability and success, cohesion and close personal contact. There was extreme pressure for this flight to succeed due to future funding issues, time pressures, and world expectations. After the instruction to abort, the engineers and other members of the NASA team involved in the launch finally gave what appears to be a unanimous decision to continue with the flight. It ended in tragedy, with the crew all being killed in an explosion shortly after takeoff. Tragically, groupthink can be so pervasive that even accidents such as the Challenger disaster have little effect on enacting change. In 2003, we saw similar events at NASA; the space shuttle Columbia broke up during its reentry into Earth's atmosphere, killing all aboard.

Social loafing

Social loafing—colloquially known as shirking, bludging, free riding, or laziness—is a phenomenon that we have all experienced. It refers to a situation in which members of a group exert less work effort than their peers. One of the reasons that people exert less effort in some group situations is that people feel less accountable for their behaviors when they know other people will pick up the slack (Harkins and Szymanski 1989). For instance, when everyone around you is applauding a performance, you don't need to do so demonstratively because your applause will neither add much nor be missed if it cannot be heard. But if everyone at a performance thought this way, what would happen? There are many reasons that people might appear to be social loafers in an organizational setting, such as lack of confidence, being poorly matched to the job, and having personal problems such as family relationship or health problems. However, although social loafing is an important issue,

> **In general, don't use teamwork for simple, routine, or meaningless tasks.**

especially for student teams doing an assignment, in a team at work it is quite unlikely that people will be able to socially loaf for a long period of time without other team members seeking to correct the situation. Theoretically, one would assume that social loafing would be much less likely to exist in work teams because, as we saw in Barker's (2002) work in Chapter 5, team pressures can be a powerful source of conformance. Even if social loafing does occur, it is easy to address by, for example, ensuring that team members have clear roles, responsibilities, and accountability. Also, you can ensure that there are clear goals set for individuals and the team, and that team and individual performance are measured. When team rewards are based on individual contributions, allow team members to decide how members will be punished for failure to perform. In general, don't use teamwork for simple, routine, or meaningless tasks or in situations in which the whole team is dependent on the performance of only one or two members. For example, many department stores use sales teams; however, in sales there are often one or two individuals that have the ability to close or complete the sales transactions. In such situations, a team is only a team by name. It is probably more effective to use individuals in competition with each other rather than a team that relies on cohesion and the equal input of many individuals.

CRITICAL ISSUES: TOXIC HANDLING

One certainty in life is that almost all of us must work for one reason or another, and for most of our lifetime. Some of us will be fortunate enough to work in jobs we love. Such jobs fill people with excitement and a sense of self-esteem, provide important social interaction, help build their sense of self-identity, and provide them with monetary and other forms of wealth. Unfortunately, for others this is less true—work can be a miserable, dangerous, unfulfilling, and even lethal place of existence. Recently, Peter Frost and Sandra Robinson (1999) systematically reflected on the impact and coping strategies that emerge from such situations in an influential article in the *Harvard Business Review*. They were concerned with how to address what happens when organizations do bad things to good people. The article begins by discussing the impact that a new CEO had when brought in by the corporate board of a public utility. According to Michael, an employee in the utility, the CEO was authoritarian and insensitive to the needs of others:

> He walked all over people. . . . He made fun of them; he intimidated them. He criticized work for no reason, and he changed his plans daily. Another project manager was hospitalised with ulcers and took early retirement. People throughout the organization felt scared and betrayed. Everyone was running around and whispering and the copy machine was going non-stop with resumes. No one was working. People could barely function. (Frost and Robinson 1999: 96)

However, as we soon learn, Michael was not just a passive observer of these bullying behaviors—he played a vital role in helping the organization and its members absorb and handle the stresses that were being created. Frost and Robinson termed these stresses "toxins" and noted that Michael became a "toxic handler" in the organization. According to Frost (2003: 3–4), *toxic handlers* are individuals within organizations " . . . who take on the emotional pain of others for the benefit of the whole system . . . like psychic sponges for a family or work system . . . they pick up all the toxicity in the system." The toxic handlers, therefore, play a very important role in organizations. Managers deal with toxic emotions at work every day in the role of toxic handlers, and can also be the source of toxicity. The following excerpt from Peter Frost's book *Toxic Emotions at Work*: *How Compassionate Managers Handle Pain and Conflict* provides a graphic sense of one particularly unpleasant way that a manager created toxic emotions at work:

> Ryan was a senior manager who kept two fishbowls in the office. In one were goldfish, in the other, a piranha. Ryan asked each of his staff to pick out the goldfish that was most like themselves (the spotted one, the one with deeper color, and so forth). Then, when Ryan was displeased with someone, he would ask that person to take his or her goldfish out of the bowl and feed it to the piranha. (Frost 2003: 35)

Think about the symbolism Ryan is trying to communicate. You are as insignificant as a fish, swimming around in the fishbowl, and as long as I like you and you do what I expect of you, you will survive. The minute you do otherwise, you cease to be a survivor and will be eaten alive by the piranha. You are dispensable and will remain only while you are useful. What kind of working environment might such behavior create and sustain? Employees might be productive, but the environment would be one based on fear and distrust. Many managers manage people in this way. They inadvertently, and sometimes purposefully, create toxic conditions at work by managing through fear and anger.

Frost characterizes the emotional pain that undermines hope and self-esteem in people at work as a toxin. To explain how managers create toxicity in the workplace, he identified seven deadly "INs" of toxic emotions (Frost 2003: 36). A brief description of these INs appears in Table 6.6.

Looking at these toxic emotions, we can see that in most organizations some level of toxicity is unavoidable. However, the skills of toxic handlers ultimately make toxic emotions at work either disastrous or enabling. Think about situations in your life in which you either have handled toxic emotions or caused them. How good are you at emotional recognition? What kind of emotions do you think are represented in Image 6.8?

TABLE 6.6   The seven deadly INs of toxic emotions

INs	Description
Intention	Managers who intentionally seek to cause others pain. They can be abusive and distrust staff. They manage through control, fear, and constant surveillance. They lead through punishment and fear.
Incompetence	Managers who lack the skills and abilities for effective people management. They may be excellent in technical skills but lack the necessary people skills. They are inconsistent in their decisions and lack integrity. Conversely, they may lack faith in their employees' abilities and skills, so they try to control every decision their employees make.
Infidelity	Managers who do not value the trust and confidence of their employees and who betray any discussion made in confidence. Or, such bosses may make promises (e.g., a promotion) and never deliver, and some may take the credit for other people's work.
Insensitivity	Managers may lack social intelligence. They have no idea, and don't care, how others feel. Such managers may also have no idea how others feel about them. They may be unable to regulate their own emotions and behave in inappropriate ways.
Intrusion	Managers who expect employees to forgo their own social or family lives for their work. They expect people to work long hours, weekends, and so on. They work long hours and expect everyone else to do the same—even if it is to the detriment of the person's family life.
Institutional forces	Toxicity can become embedded within the policies, procedures, and rules of the organization, especially when people are expected to act in ways antithetical to their own values and beliefs. Similarly, toxicity can be seen in organizations in employees that may not live by the organization's vision, mission, and policies. Imagine what it would be like to work in the police force and to blow the whistle on corruption when many of the police leaders are corrupt.
Inevitability	Some toxicity is inevitable and cannot be expected or controlled for—for example, death of a coworker, a change in the world economy, or a terrorist flying a plane into a building. Sometimes, managers must cause pain in the short term to ensure growth in the long term. Inevitable toxicity can become a problem only in terms of how it is handled and managed in the context of the preceding INs of toxicity.

Source: Adapted from Peter J. Frost (2003: 36–50)

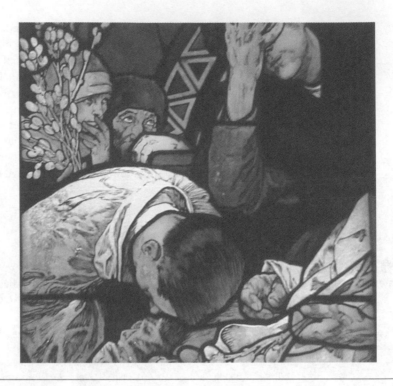

Image 6.8   *Emotions in a detail from a church window*

Here is a simple story from Tyrone that makes some of the points about toxic workplaces clear. Many of Frost's (2003) seven deadly INs are clearly evident in this case. When he was much younger, about 15 years old, Tyrone got a summer job in a café near his school. Two middle-aged brothers (whom we'll call Nick and John) ran the café in a very unethical way. Many of the staff, including Tyrone, were working illegally because Nick and John had not registered their staff with the tax department. Knowing that Tyrone and the others were young and inexperienced, Nick and John would have them work extremely long hours without breaks, did not pay pension and other compulsory contributions, never logged overtime, and did not provide appropriate training—after all, they had no training themselves (incompetence). If employees questioned these conditions, they were either ridiculed or fired (intention). One day, Tyrone cut his finger very badly while working. John took him to the hospital but instructed Tyrone to say it happened while Tyrone was visiting John at home and that if he said otherwise, he'd be fired (insensitivity). After about two weeks, Tyrone returned to the café, where he was told he was no longer needed. He received no severance pay nor the previous two weeks' pay. Six months later a number of former employees, including Tyrone, complained to the Industrial Relations Commission that they had been underpaid, unfairly dismissed, and exploited.

Image 6.9   *Masking against toxicity?*

Nick and John filed for bankruptcy, never paying a cent to anyone, and therefore got away with behaving in unethical ways (institutional).

Now try to think of—and jot down—a few scenarios in which you were either a toxic handler or you might have caused toxicity. They do not have to be work related. Thinking about your examples, which of the seven deadly INs of toxicity applied?

If organizations reward or are run by thugs, bullies, and the diplomatically challenged, expect toxicity to be pervasive.

Typically, toxic handlers fulfill vital but often formally unrecognized tasks for their organizations. Often, they burn out doing it. Think of them as filters that help remove the toxins that the organization or particular members in it can create. Although they may help to cleanse the organization, their doing so carries profound personal costs—they have to hear, share, and bear the misery and pain that the organization imposes on those it employs. Often, because the sources of the toxicity are people in formally authoritative and senior roles in the organization, there is little that they can actually do to rectify the situation. If organizations reward or are run by thugs, bullies, and the diplomatically challenged, expect toxicity to be pervasive. The best remedy is compassion, but this commodity is often a tender, precious, and vulnerable bloom, easily trampled by the foolhardy insensitivity of others, especially those in positions of formal authority.

THE FINE PRINT: POSITIVE PSYCHOLOGY AND COMPASSION

Psychology emerged from the study of the deviant and the abnormal but has become increasingly interested in more positive phenomena. Although the essence of positive psychology has been advocated since William James, the concept can be attributed to Martin E. P. Seligman and Mihaly Csikszentmihalyi (2000: 5), who describe that

> The field of positive psychology at the subjective level is about valued subjective experiences: well-being, contentment, and satisfaction (in the past); hope and optimism (for the future); and flow and happiness (in the present). At the individual level, it is about positive individual traits: the capacity for love and vocation, courage, interpersonal skill, aesthetic sensibility, perseverance, forgiveness, originality, future mindedness, spirituality, high talent, and wisdom. At the group level, it is about the civic virtues and the institutions that move individuals towards better citizenship: responsibility, nurturance, altruism, civility, moderation, tolerance, and work ethic.

In its simplest form, positive psychology is the study, research, and theorizing of the psychological bases for leading the best life possible through positive thinking, feelings, and behavior. In a management sense, positive psychology seeks to understand and to foster civic virtues, social responsibility, altruism, tolerance, happiness, and psychological well-being. Positive psychology, in the form of positive organizational behavior (POB), is growing and attracting attention in management theory, research, and practice. In essence, it is an overnight success that was one hundred years in the making. Historically, psychology predominantly concerned pathology and treatment of a variety of mental illness (Seligman and Csikszentmihalyi 2000). As such, its initial application to disciplines such as management also bound management psychology to pathology. Psychology centered on asking what was wrong so it could establish what could be right rather than asking what was right and how it could be made better. In regard to organizational toxicity, it asks how we might foster compassion.

There are a number of assumptions that might lead you to foster organizational compassion. You would start from the premise that the capacity to be compassionate and to express compassion is universal; it is not a property of any one type of person, religion, gender, or creed. Institutions such as work can facilitate or restrain the innate capacity to express compassion, as we saw in Chapter 5 when we looked at the Milgram (1971) experiments and the accounts of total institutions. The more we design our organizations as if they were like total institutions, the less surprised we should be if they are not compassionate places. Organizations magnify or depress the effects of individual compassion as they facilitate or retard efforts at its mobilization, or focus interpersonal and group relations on power and domination, competition and solitary survival, rather than coordination and cooperation. The more organizations commit resources to action premised on low trust of others and a greater need for surveillance and control, the more likely it is that they will foster a toxic environment in which people know that they are not trusted.

Management thinkers such as Frost, Dutton, Worline, and Wilson (2000) see compassion as a healing act both for those who participate in offering it as well as for those who receive it. Although compassion involves the capacity to feel empathy, it also requires you to take a stand, reach out, and help someone who is suffering, someone who is in pain. Even a small act such as listening can relieve suffering. Exercising compassion in organizations contributes to healing (the capacity to draw from inner resources to lessen suffering), human resilience (the capacity and rate of recovery from setbacks), and human attachment to the groups who express compassion. The effectiveness of compassionate organizing can be assessed by considering the scope, scale, speed, and customization of compassionate responses to the needs of individuals and groups who are suffering.

What can you do if you want to encourage compassionate rather than toxic management? Providing contexts in which communication is open and transparent is important because better quality and reliable knowledge reduces uncertainty about the security of jobs or of people's place in an organization. It is important that leaders use their status, visibility, and power to communicate what the organization is doing and why it is doing it. They should make available resources that enable work to be done and for employees to excel (see also pp. 243–245; 254–257). One way of using positive psychology to manage is to be a leader who is available rather than aloof, someone who can be seen and talked to easily. A leader's visibility and an employee's access to him or her help create a social relation within which people may develop a sense of security and safety. The easier it is to access managers and leaders and the more visible they are, the less chance of their being toxic either by intent, conceit, or carelessness.

The language that managers use is important; it needs to allow for the expression of pain and human suffering to allow the catharsis that must precede healing. The language of efficiency and effectiveness, of one best way and singular rationalities, may not have the same potential to heal and encourage compassion when people are hurting. Clearly, the organization culture is important here (see also pp. 267–275). Through affirming positive values in the culture, people can develop a shared sense of relatedness, purpose, and power, providing motives and resources for initiative and action. Mission statements that place value on people help develop this sense of community.

From a now-defunct University of Michigan Web page (University of Michigan Business School 2001) dedicated to "Leading in Trying Times," there are a number of examples of what compassionate leadership might be:

Windows of Hope: Family Relief Fund

David Emil, owner of Windows on the World; the restaurant's executive chef, Michael Lomonaco; Tom Valenti, Chef/Owner Ouest Restaurant; and Waldy Malouf, Chef/Owner, Beacon Restaurant, established "Windows of Hope" as a way to help the families of the people who died in the World Trade Center who worked in the food service profession. On October 11 participating restaurants around the world donated up to 10% of their proceeds to the fund. For more information, see the following Web site: www.WindowsofHope.org

Job Expo Held for Workers Displaced by Terror Attack

Many people who lost their jobs as a result of September 11 were given the opportunity to find a replacement at the Twin Towers Job Expo at Madison Square Garden. Numerous companies were involved offering 13,000 temporary and permanent jobs. "The expo was part of a joint effort between the city, the state and hundreds of private companies." As a result, more than 6,000 job seekers attended and more than 20,000 interviews were held. More than 4,300 prospective hires were made! Although some people were disappointed their search was not successful, another job fair will be held giving precedence to those who attended this one. For more information, see www.ny1.com/ny/Search/SubTopic/index.html?&contentintid=16583& search_result=1

Brooklyn Lures Displaced WTC Businesses

The Brooklyn Chamber of Commerce is trying to lure some of the former World Trade Center businesses across the Brooklyn Bridge. Since the events of September 11, the Brooklyn Chamber of Commerce has been lining up available office space in different neighborhoods across Brooklyn. "We put together about a million square feet of space for different types of businesses," said Kenneth Adams of the Brooklyn Chamber of Commerce. One construction firm, Two Trees, has offered an incentive for displaced business: "Move in here and get three months rent-free." The Chamber of Commerce is also offering equipment, supplies and office furniture that has been donated from people all over the country. A "skills bank" also is being put together in which volunteers have been asked to use their professional skills in any way they can, such as setting up Web sites or helping with paperwork. The city is showing outstanding leadership and compassion in helping companies get back on their feet. For more information, please see the following Web site: www.ny1.com/ny/Boroughs/SubTopic/index.html?topicintid=3&subtopicintid=9& contentintid=16373

SUMMARY AND REVIEW

Organizational behavior (OB) is a vast and complex field. It represents the cohabitation of psychology with management, and in this chapter we have barely scratched the surface. Our task has not been to provide you with a complete account of OB—there are other books that do that—but simply to suggest some ways in which psychology and its insights may be useful in understanding management and work. We have ranged over a broad canvass, nonetheless. We have addressed values, personality theory, and teamwork. We have looked at the new currents in organizational psychology, which stress positive organizational behavior, and visited the fascinating and important work of Peter Frost on toxic handlers. Finally, we have explored the importance of compassion in and for organizations.

ONE MORE TIME . . .

Getting the story straight

- How do the ways in which different people express universal values have an effect on how they might manage them?
- What are the four main approaches to understanding personality?
- Discuss some of the positive and negative aspects of teamwork in relation to groupthink.

Thinking outside the box

- What do toxic handlers do, and how do they do it?
- Why and how could positive psychology be used in management?

ADDITIONAL RESOURCES

1. Jerry B. Harvey's 1988 book, *The Abilene Paradox and Other Meditations on Management,* is a very good OB/management text. It covers a range of topics relevant to organizational behavior, some of which some textbooks ignore, and provides a sound basis for learning more about OB.
2. There are some excellent organizational behavior textbooks that we recommend for their clear writing, great examples, and discussion, including: Greenberg and Baron's (2003) *Behaviour in Organizations,* eighth edition, and George and Jones's (2001) *Understanding and Managing Organizational Behavior.* An excellent, well-thought-out textbook (but a

little outdated) is McShane and Von Glinow's (2000) *Organizational Behavior.*

3. If you are interested in psychology, a very well-written, easy-to-read text is Myers's (2001) *Psychology,* sixth edition. In addition, an excellent reference on positive psychology is Cameron, Dutton, and Quinn's (2003) "Foundations of Positive Organizational Scholarship." This text provides an excellent grounding and introduction to the work being done in positive psychology.

4. For more advanced students, an excellent resource is Buchanan and Huczynski's (2004) *Organizational Behaviour: An Introductory Text.* The textbook is comprehensive and very well written, from a European rather than North American perspective. The text is, however, quite heavy going, and some students find it a little hard to navigate and difficult to read. So we do not recommend it to students who are not particularly interested in organizational behavior or management education.

5. The books by the Russian novelist Fyodor Dostoyevsky brilliantly and playfully introduce you to the world of organizational behavior. *The House of the Dead* (1965), which describes his experience in a Siberian prison, is a detailed account of the many facets of organizational behavior. George Orwell's (1945) *Animal Farm* is also an excellent book to read, showing how people (represented metaphorically as animals) become corrupted through power and domination, and how groups create stereotypes and in-group/out-group mentalities.

6. There are many films that more or less intentionally demonstrate an organizational behavior perspective. A good starting point is the film (Radford 1984) that was made of George Orwell's (1949) *Nineteen Eighty-Four.* It demonstrates how anticipated behavior might be controlled in the workplace one day through one omniscient observer aided by the tools of an Information or Electronic Panopticon. It is worth watching just to think about how the technologies that have developed since Orwell wrote the novel have, in fact, been more subtle than those he imagined.

7. The classic prisoner of war film *The Great Escape* (Sturges 1963) and the war movie *Platoon* (Stone 1986) are relevant to teamwork.

8. Check out the Web site of the Academy of Management (AOM) at www.aomonline.org. It contains some excellent resources for students, and more than 25% of the AOM's membership is management students.

In addition to these suggested additional resources, don't forget to look at what is also available on the Web site **www.ckmanagement.net,** including free PDF files of recent papers related to this chapter, which you can download; video interviews with famous academics talking about related themes; as well as many other resources, such as connections to interesting Web sites.

CHAPTER 7

MANAGING LEADERSHIP

Motivation, Inspiration, Transformation

Objectives and learning outcomes

By the end of this chapter, you will be able to

- Define what is meant by leadership

- Identify the main approaches to leadership theory

- Understand the underlying assumptions in motivation theories and their relevance to leadership

- Appreciate the complexity in leading and motivating people

- Identify the emerging and alternative approaches to leadership

Before you get started ...

A little story from one of Tyrone's lectures:

When I was around 8 years of age, I would follow my mother out into the front garden of our house and, every so often, our little old lady neighbor, called Pearl, would peer over the fence. I remember my mother would ask old Pearl, "How are you today, Pearl?" and Pearl would usually answer in the same sad and tired voice, "I'm managing, love; I'm managing." Because I was from a non-English-speaking background, I took Pearl's notion of what "managing" meant literally. So as I grew up I always thought "managing" meant just coping, just doing the bare minimum to survive. Now, almost a quarter of a century later, I have come to realize that Pearl's notion of management is spot on. Most managers I see or talk to today are just managing, just coping, and they are one day, one decision, one missed deadline, or one miscommunicated sentence away from failure or a disaster.... A leader, therefore, might be someone who goes beyond just coping or just managing. The leader inspires, develops, and mentors people. Above all else, a leader is a humanist. We cannot afford our leaders to be anything else.

OUTLINE OF THE CHAPTER

At face value, leadership appears to be a simple domain of interest. Almost anyone can think of a leader and can provide a definition of leadership or make feel-good statements about what a leader does or should do. However, after you go past leadership at a superficial level, it is one of the most complex, problematic, and time-consuming domains of management and organization theory. As an experiment, go to your library Web page and access any database—such as Psychinfo, ABI inform, Sociofile—and type in *leader* or *leadership* as the keyword search term. You can also try google.com, alltheweb.com, or any other search engine. You will find several thousand hits for this keyword, and it would take more than a lifetime for any one person to read, review, and critique each and every one of these Web pages, articles, books, and book chapters.

Literally, to lead or to exercise leadership is to be ahead of the others, to take them forward where they might not necessarily want to go, to make them go where they need to be, and to motivate them so that they overcome any fears or qualms that they might have. Leadership has become an unnecessarily complex, confusing, and contradictory domain of interest. Attempting to present old and new leadership theories in one chapter is challenging. First, there are the differences of opinion in terms of what leadership is: Is leadership, as the *trait* theorists argue, a question of unique traits that people are born with, like their height, weight, intelligence, and personality? Or is leadership, as the *behaviorist* school argues, specific ways of behaving that either make you an effective or ineffective leader? Or is leadership *situational*, where different situations create different leaders? Or is leadership *contingent* upon the interactions between leaders and the led? Or is leadership a *socially constructed*

Image 7.1   *Leading—but where to?*

concept? Or is there no such thing as leadership per se, only what members of specific organizations take it to be?

In this chapter, we introduce you to the current and central approaches to leadership. Rather than going into each and every theory in depth, we look at the main approaches to leadership. The chapter is written with the assumption that you will one day go on to leadership roles rather than become academics who will specialize in leadership theory and research. Moreover, this text is aimed at first-year management students and, usually, leadership normally makes up only a small component of the semester. It is therefore unrealistic to expect you to digest all the theories on leadership available, which is a task better left to more advanced and specialized subjects or for postgraduate study. Rather, we believe it is more important for you to get a feel for the different approaches to leadership without going into each and every theory in depth. After we introduce the main approaches, we then explore some newer contributions to leadership. Because the task of leadership is often expressed as being able to motivate people to achieve outcomes that benefit the individual, the team, the organization, and, some would argue, more collective entities such as society, we think it is necessary to introduce you to the concept of motivation from the perspective of being a leader. We then look at substitutes to leadership and explore the possibility of life without leaders and the blurring of boundaries between leadership and followership. We close the chapter by discussing some positive psychological perspectives on leadership that argue that leadership should primarily be about inspiring and fostering positive change, corporate citizenry, and social, economic, and ecological sustainability.

SETTING THE SCENE

The Collins English Dictionary defines a leader as "a person who rules, guides, or inspires others" and the process of leading as "'to show the way by going with, or ahead . . . to serve as the means of reaching a place" (Hanks 1986: 476). Embedded within this definition is the notion that a leader: (a) leads people as a ruler; (b) inspires people as a motivator; and (c) facilitates or guides them as a mentor. Katz and Kahn (1978: 527–528) believed leadership is commonly viewed

> as the attribute of a position, as the characteristic of a person, and as a character of behavior. . . . Moreover, leadership is a relational concept implying two terms: The influencing agent and the persons influenced. . . . Leadership conceived of as an ability is a slippery concept, since it depends too much on properties of the situation and of the people to be "led."

Leadership may thus be seen as a product of one's position; as a set of personality traits; as a set of observable behaviors; as dependent upon the situation in which it is exercised; and as contingent upon how the leader and the people being led react and interact with each other. Obviously, leadership may be all of these many things, and so, not surprisingly, it is one of the most overtheorized, overresearched, and empirically messy areas of management and organizational theory.

Who am I?

To help students cope with the complexity of the topic of leadership, Tyrone always starts his leadership lectures with a guessing game called "Who am I?" The aim of the game is to help you think about the qualities and life events that make someone a leader and how no one theory or concept adequately accounts for leadership. Tyrone states a series of facts, such as those in the following list, and students consider the leadership qualities inherent in the facts and come up with an answer.

- I was regarded as a good *artist* and had a flair for sketching and watercolors yet I was rejected from a prestigious art school.
- I then joined the armed forces and was awarded a prestigious medal for *bravery,* yet some of my officers claimed I would never be a suitable leader of men.
- After the war, unhappy with how my country was being run and eager to prove my detractors wrong, I joined a small political party and became a great orator able to *inspire* others.
- At the time that my ideas became popular, my country was plagued by *poverty and economic recession.*
- I was soon imprisoned as a political agitator but it was in prison that I helped grow my political party, and I wrote one of the most influential books in history.
- After leaving prison, I was given charge of my political party, and we went from a handful of members to hundreds and thousands of followers—many of whom abandoned senior positions in opposition parties to join me because they could see I was committed to changing how things were done in my country forever and they wanted to *follow* me.
- I eventually became *leader* of my country and one of the most influential figures in history. Indeed, all around the world I continue to *inspire* many followers even though I am long since dead.
- Who am I?

Before you answer, think about the clues and consider the qualities—artistic, brave, ambitious. He was able to write books and change society from within a prison and to attract followers even from his opposition. Nelson Mandela did this—but it's not him. He inspired people in his country toward major change and to rise above harsh economic conditions. Mahatma Gandhi did this too, but it's not him either. So who is it?

Adolf Hitler. A man with horrific intentions who gained the power to implement appalling practices ultimately responsible for the murder of millions of people, who inspired hundreds of thousands to carry out his dirty work, including many unspeakable acts against humanity as well as the barbarism of total war.

The aim of the "Who am I?" game, above all, is to have you critically reflect on the term *leadership*. In each clue are fundamental aspects of the leadership concept: character, behavior, situation, and contingencies. Although we often see leadership as composed of factors that make us feel good, leaders are not always enlightened, humane, and oriented to personal growth; they are sometimes tyrants more concerned with their own egos than those of followers, adept at practicing domination, power, and delusional self-interest. Therefore, it is necessary to think beyond leadership as a simple construct and to reflect critically on what leadership might mean. Much of this reflection is evident in leadership theories such as the trait, behavioral, and situational, as well as many newer theories steeped in the positive psychological tradition.

Yet many students ask: "What's the point of all this theory? Who cares if leaders are born or made?" Our answer is that leadership theory is critical for our understanding of the role individuals can play in shaping society and its organizations. More importantly, *leaders can and do change society,* so it is imperative that they do so in a socially responsible and ethical way (see also pp. 29–31; 222–224; 477–478; 485–487). Only if we understand the theoretical underpinnings of those leadership perspectives in use by particular writers and leaders can we adequately reflect upon and answer appropriate questions about leadership. Moreover, the theory you subscribe to will underpin your own approach to leadership—after all, you may one day be a leader, and what you believe about leadership will influence your approach to what a leader is, what a leader does, and how he or she does it. Conversely, learning about different theories may cause you to reflect upon and to question your own beliefs. For example, for most of his undergraduate studies, Tyrone was a firm believer in the trait approach to leadership. Life seemed simple back then, but, after being subsequently exposed to many additional points of view, arguments, and ideas, he has found that aspects of all schools of leadership thought—but especially positive psychology—play an important role in his understanding of leadership. Stewart used to think that transformational leadership was just a card trick, but having been exposed to leadership that was decidedly ordinary, he is not so sure now. And Martin thinks that leadership is impossible without being extraordinarily creative—and that being creative, means, by definition, being able to transform the mundane into the extraordinary.

> **The clearest sign that a manager is doing an excellent job managing her team: she takes time off work and no one notices she is gone.**
>
> **—Anonymous**

CENTRAL APPROACHES AND MAIN THEORIES

Strolling through the leadership landscape

If we thought of the field of leadership theory as a landscaped garden, what might it look like as we stroll through? Most likely, it would be overgrown with many different plants, some exotic ones with beautiful flowers, and others just weeds. There would hardly be room to move, and many of the plants would be unidentifiable. Moreover, there would be people continuously seeding new plants without stopping to consider whether the garden can sustain them. Another way of making the same point would be to say that in leadership theory, you encounter a lot of rubbish, but what you think is rubbish depends on your preferences and outlook. Some might see merits and weaknesses in all the theories, and others may believe no one theory is adequate. Anyway, let's review the approaches, and you can decide whether any of it is rubbish in terms of your interests and projects.

Leadership as traits

For a long time, trait theorists believed that leadership was dependent upon certain physical features and personality characteristics. To investigate leadership, trait theorists would consider a wide range of demographic variables like age, gender, height, weight, and ethnicity, to name a few. They also looked at certain personality characteristics similar to those found in the trait approach to personality (see also pp. 201–203). Such key demographic and personality variables differentiate truly exceptional leaders from mere mortals, which is why trait theory has also been known as the "great person theory" (Barker 2001). According to House, Shane, and Herold (1996), the difference between those of us who emerge as outstanding leaders and those of us who are always destined to follow is an undying drive for achievement, honesty, and integrity, and an ability to share and to motivate people toward common goals. Such people have confidence in their own abilities as well as intelligence, business savvy, creativity, and an ability to adapt to ever-changing environments (also see Kirkpatrick and Locke 1991).

No doubt, many people strongly believe in the great person theory. In reality, there is little evidence to support the notion that leaders are born with special traits that nonleaders lack. However, let us assume for a minute that the great person theory of leadership is correct and that certain physical features and personality characteristics will make you a leader. If we believe this, many of us might as well stop reading this chapter now, for leadership can never be taught. In other words, teaching leadership helps only those with a predisposition toward leadership, and the rest of us should either pack up immediately or (considering that we believe leadership is innate), perhaps enroll in a course teaching us how to be better subordinates.

More importantly, it seems that many who argue for the great person approach often miss the point—that is, many characteristics they believe to be critical to successful leadership have been made important through social norms and culture. If we look at leadership in most organizations, leaders tend to be taller rather than shorter, and, more often than not, are male. After all, these theorists argue, because most leaders of major corporations are male, it must be an important trait in successful leadership. Also, most of them are also white, usually well educated in elite schools and institutions, and often from wealthy backgrounds. In fact, it makes a huge difference if you can choose your parents carefully! Of course, you can't, but it is clear that a major factor propelling leaders such as George W. Bush to their present positions of leadership is that their fathers had already founded dynasties on substantial fortunes. Sure, if you are nonwhite or female, you can still make it, but it will be much harder for you, and you will have to expend more energy on the leadership attributes you have available or can cultivate. The trait theory of leadership, despite its shortcomings, has played a critical role in the evolution of leadership theory and research. Whether you agree or disagree with it, many have used it to critique and to reflect upon what it means to be a leader.

To try to address the fact that many leadership traits that are assumed to be innate are actually based on norms and culture, newer theories have chosen to look at what leaders do rather than what traits they have. Some see leadership as situational or contingent upon many factors. Others see leadership as a socially constructed phenomenon—that is, what a leader is, and what a leader does, changes as society changes over time or as we move from one culture to another. Next, we visit these different perspectives of leadership, beginning with the behavioral school.

Leadership as behavior

The behavioral theory of leadership is not concerned with the traits or characteristics that make someone a successful leader; it is concerned only with observable behavior. Thus, for behaviorists, you either act like a leader or you do not. This is an important departure from trait theory because it implies that if we can observe how leaders act, we can codify and measure this behavior, find out ways to teach it, and help to develop future leaders. A critical concept that is common to all behavioral theories of leadership is the notion that there are two underlying behavioral structures that characterize leadership—an orientation toward the following:

- Interacting and relating to other human beings
- The task at hand, or the technical side of work

You will find these two behavioral orientations in just about every theory you read, even those outside the behavioral school. Their names may change, but, fundamentally, they refer to the same thing: employee centered/task centered; relationship behavior/task behavior; concern for people/concern for production; consideration/initiating structure; and so on.

The behavioral perspective

The most recognized behavioral approach to the study of leadership was developed by Blake and Mouton (1985) at the University of Texas. The approach was later expanded upon by Blake and McCanse (1991) and is referred to as the *leadership grid* or the *managerial grid* (see Figure 7.1).

In the managerial grid, leaders are ranked according to their performance on two basic dimensions, concern for production and concern for people. As the manager approaches the upper right-hand cell and becomes a team manager, this is regarded as the normatively best style of management. Two major types of leadership behavior are identified in this tradition of work: first, *consideration,* or the extent to which leaders take into consideration subordinates' feelings, needs, concerns, and ideas; and second, *initiating structure,* or the

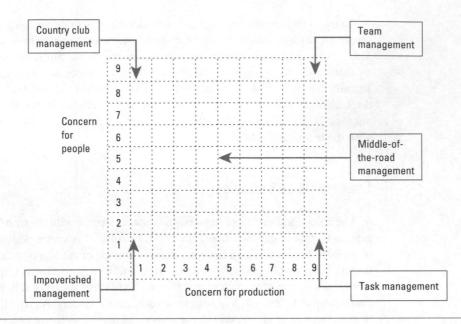

Figure 7.1   *The managerial grid*

Source: Adapted from Blake and Mouton's (1985) registered model

extent to which leaders are task oriented and more focused on ensuring that subordinates do what is required through autocratic direction, control, and surveillance. These two styles are independent of each other, so a leader can be high or low on initiating structure and high or low on consideration, and it was long held that superior leadership was characterized by being high-high on both dimensions. However, there is little research to support the notion that effective leaders are only those high on both initiating structure and consideration (see, for example, Nystrom 1978). As a result, researchers began to compare and to contrast effective and ineffective leaders.

According to Likert (1979), *employee-centered* leaders were more successful than *job-centered* leaders, mainly because job-centered leaders tended to be overly concerned with achieving efficiency, cost reduction, and deadlines rather than people's needs and goal achievement. However, common sense says that an overemphasis on people might compromise the completion of tasks and getting the job done, just as an overemphasis on tasks can alienate people and affect motivation and job satisfaction. It is therefore more likely that both dimensions are equally important, and this is the argument underlying the managerial grid. More a behavioral training tool than a leadership theory, the managerial grid emphasizes the need to develop a person's ability to manage both people and tasks. The grid is divided into two dimensions. On one axis is the *concern for production* and on the other axis is the *concern for people.* Depending on their responses to standardized questions, a person is rated by an accredited psychologist on both dimensions on a scale from 1 to 9 (or low to high). The ideal position is to be high on concern for production and concern for people (9,9), or what Blake and Mouton (1985) refer to as *team management.* However, very few if any ever score 9,9 on their first try, so leaders are helped to develop their concern for people and their concern for production skills so that they reach the ideal position on the grid. Leaders that score 1,1 are said to practice *impoverished management* because they lack both a concern for people and production, so their ability to manage will be quite poor. Other styles include *country club management* (1,9), where there is a high concern for people while the concern for production is forgotten or ignored, so people being happy and having fun is more important than getting the job done. (These styles can be seen in action in the British TV show *The Office,* if you have seen it.) Conversely, a person may be concerned with only production, or what Blake and Mouton call *task management* (9,1), and then there is *middle-of-the-road management* (5,5).

Thus far, we have looked at the behavioral and the trait approaches to leadership. However, both traditions have weaknesses:

- The behaviorist usually is interested only in observable behavior and ignores often-unobservable intentions. We can never know people's thoughts and intentions other than through social cues, and these can be masked behind observable behavior that, on face value, appears to be exemplary.
- If honesty and integrity are inherited traits necessary for elevation to leadership, then why do so many people reach leadership positions and attain enormous material wealth, power, influence, and control, only later to be revealed as crooks and charlatans who sometimes even use their "leadership" to try to avoid the wrath of the law?
- Why are the attributes that one group of people see as exemplary regarded as evil by others? For example, some compare Adolf Hitler, Benito Mussolini, Osama bin Laden, Saddam Hussein, and David Koresh to Satan, but they were presumably viewed as great leaders by their many followers—if not, then how did they attain such influential leadership positions?
- At what point does observable behavior tell us that people are no longer acting like leaders? After they murder people or corrupt organizations and steal millions of dollars? Were the bosses at Enron and WorldCom really the corporate heroes they were often lionized as being before their malfeasance became evident?

The managerial grid appears to suggest that all outstanding managers must have special skills in both the job and in people. Yet throughout history we have seen people reach the heights of leadership who are not always expert in tasks and others who are not always expert in managing people. Moreover, if you consider some of the people who have inspired you, we are sure that at least some of you will mention people who are no longer alive or people you have never met. It is a bit hard to manage people and tasks when you are dead or you never have face-to-face contact with your followers, so something else must make leaders be regarded as effective or ineffective besides merely what they do here and now.

The trait and behavioral approaches should not be totally discounted. Some situations, for example, call for high concern for people, whereas others call for high concern for production, and others call for both. However, leadership can also be thought of as being situational and contingent.

Situational and contingency theories

Some new(ish) approaches to leadership argue that leadership emerges out of the situation. The same person who may emerge as a leader in one situation may find him- or herself unable to cope, let alone lead, in a different situation. Anecdotally, there is some merit to the situational argument. For example, prior to the September 11 attack on New York City, the former mayor of New York, Rudolph Giuliani, was known mainly for his strong stance on crime in New York. He implemented a "three strikes and you're out" policy for repeat criminals. He had many critics, especially people who lived outside the New York area, who experienced escalating crime as a result of criminals moving away from the city. City crime rates were going down because the city was exporting rather than solving crime. Other than this policy, Mayor Giuliani had few things going for him. However, during the September 11 attacks, Mayor Giuliani took a strong leadership role—indeed, the moment made the man. The mayor's leadership was seen as so strong that he even eclipsed President George W. Bush, and the world watching the events that unfolded in New York could have easily been forgiven for believing that Mayor Giuliani was the leader of the United States. Realizing the effect a situation can have upon a leader's success and popularity, President Bush was also quick to try to leverage statesmanlike success out of the situation. He went from low legitimacy (because of the fiasco of the Florida vote recount during the presidential election) and relative political obscurity in the shadow of the charismatic Bill Clinton to record-high popularity ratings, at least until Americans began to question the reason the country went to war with Iraq and the high number of American casualties involved.

There are many situational and contingency theories of leadership. We list only a handful here to acquaint you with the main arguments that characterize these schools of leadership theory. However, if what you read here creates an appetite for more, consult a good organizational behavior or leadership text-book (such as those listed at the end of this chapter) to read about the many situational and contingency theories available, as well as other approaches to leadership.

We group together the situational and contingency approaches, even though some people like to separate the two. There are subtle differences between them, but we believe that these differences are not enough to make them distinct schools of thought. Underlying contingency theories is the notion that leadership is all about being able to adapt and be flexible to ever-changing situations and contexts. Contingency leadership theories have made one of the most important contributions to the evolution of leadership theory because leadership effectiveness is seen as being less dependent on innate traits or observable behavioral styles and more dependent on the context of leading, such as the nature of work, the internal working environment, and the external economic and social environment (Fiedler 1964). Two main contingency leadership theories are discussed here: House's (1971) path-goal theory and Hersey, Blanchard, and Johnson's (1996) situational leadership model.

Path-goal theory of leadership

Arguably the most studied and tested contingency theory is House's path-goal theory of leadership. According to Robert House (1971; see also House and Mitchell 1974), effective leaders motivate employees by helping them understand that their needs and expectations can be fulfilled through the performance of their jobs. The better an employee performs, the greater the need fulfillment. Moreover, the path-goal theory emphasizes that an ability and commitment to providing employees with the psychological and technical support, information, and other resources necessary to complete tasks is integral to the leader's effectiveness. The path-goal theory has been extended, developed, and refined, and it is probably one of the most influential leadership theories around (House 1996; Jermier 1996). The path-goal theory is more advanced and complex than any of the theories we have looked at thus far because it lists four leadership styles and a number of contingencies that lead to leadership effectiveness.

Table 7.1 lists and describes each of the four main leadership styles. However, you will notice that we have added networking and values-based leadership as two more issues that are currently emerging from House's (1996) and others' work (see, for example, Jermier 1996; O'Toole 1996:101–108). We believe these will be increasingly important additions to House's original work because they move the leadership theory away from solely being interested in person-to-person relations to include relationships on team and organizational levels. Who knows—maybe one day the model will add national and international concerns, such as sustainability, to the mix.

Depending on the situation, the effective leader adjusts and adapts his or her style and can use one or more styles as needed. However, the effectiveness of the leader ultimately depends upon two broad sets of contingencies. The first

TABLE 7.1 Path-goal leadership styles and descriptions

Style	Description
Directive	The directive leader clarifies goals, what must be done to achieve them, and the outcomes of achieving the goals. They use rewards, discipline, and punishment and are mostly task oriented.
Supportive	The supportive leader shows concern for the needs—especially psychological—and the aspirations of people at work. They provide a supportive and enjoyable working environment.
Participative	The participative leader actively seeks and encourages the input and involvement of staff in decision making and other work-related issues.
Achievement-oriented	The achievement-oriented leader, as the name suggests, expects from people the highest commitment to excellence both at a personal and an organizational level. This type of leader believes that work should be challenging and that people will strive toward achieving these goals by assuming responsibility.
Networking	The networking leader knows how to play the political power games to acquire resources, achieve goals, and to create and maintain positive relationships. (For more on power, see also pp. 203–204.)
Values-based	The values-based leader is skilled in creating, sharing, and inspiring vision, and in ensuring that the organization and its people are guided by that vision and the values related to that vision.

Source: Adapted from House (1996) and Jermier (1996)

concerns employee-relevant contingencies, such as the employee's competencies, knowledge, skills, experience, and even their personality, such as whether they have an internal or external locus of control (see also pp. 222–225). The second concerns environmental-relevant contingencies, such as the nature of teams and the structure and nature of the task, just to name a few.

So, for example, let's assume you have completed your college education, you have been working for a leading bank for the last five years, and, over time, you have finally reached the position of head of corporate services. Up to this point, you have managed very junior staff in positions low on task structure that required little if any teamwork. Experience has shown you that a directive leadership style works best in this situation. However, last week, you were promoted, and now you manage a team of 15 people who value a high level of control over their work and their environment (i.e., high internal locus of control). They all have several years of experience in the department, have taken several training courses on implementing change, and enjoy working as part of a cohesive team that shares leadership duties.

How well would your directive leadership style work in your new position? It would be safe to assume that you and your team would not operate effectively, and, over time, you would experience friction because your staff would see you as unnecessarily controlling and directive. Your options for change would be: change the nature of the work and the type of staff so that they support your directive leadership style, change your leadership style, or cruise into crisis! Ideally, if people could change their leadership style, many problems could be overcome. However, more often than not, people avoid changing themselves and seek to change others and their environments instead.

Situational leadership model

Hersey, Blanchard, and Johnson's (1996) Situational Leadership® Model is to contingency theory what the managerial grid is to behavioral theory: It is more a training and consulting tool than a theory per se. We say this mainly because there is close to no supporting research for the theory (Graeff 1997). Rather, the model's intellectual appeal resides in its emphasis on the subordinates' readiness and willingness to be led by others. As with path-goal theory, it is up to the leader to use the appropriate style after he or she has established what kind of people work for him or her. Figure 7.2 shows the four leadership roles—known as delegating (S4), participating (S3), selling (S2), and telling (S1)—together with the associated follower readiness (R4 through to R1). The most appropriate leadership style depends on the amount of emotional support followers require in conjunction with the amount of guidance that they require to do their jobs—in other words, the follower's readiness.

Where contingency approaches differ from the behavioral approach is in concentrating attention toward factors outside the actual person leading.

As you may be able to tell from the Situational Leadership® Model and other contingency theories, they depart from the trait perspective but share many elements of the behavioral approach. Where contingency approaches differ from the behavioral approach is in concentrating attention toward factors outside the actual person leading. Later, we discuss contingency-based views that argue that leaders may be substituted for processes, technology, policies, and can even be made obsolete in the workplace.

If a leader's performance is contingent upon factors outside his or her control, then there could be thousands of contingencies that affect leader performance. So where does one start the search for the contingent factors that might affect leadership performance? Moreover, you could argue that contingency theories have diluted the notion of leadership and have confused it with management. Obviously, there are changing and emergent contingencies: riskmanagement, especially focused on the management of terror and security; sustainable management, focused on the environment and the political ecology of the material inputs and outputs that the organization is involved with; and gender management, managing in a gender-specifically sensitive way. These are all relatively recent contingencies that leaders have to deal with today, but in each case they are the result of a changing political agenda. What counts as a contingency for management thus depends on what is made to count. And what is made to count depends in part on the changing institutional environment of regulation, opinion, and politics.

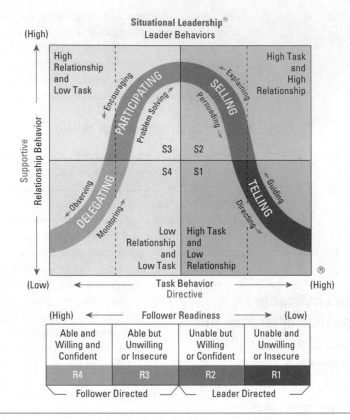

Figure 7.2   *Situational Leadership® Model*

Reading through the multitude of textbooks on management, you would be forgiven for thinking that "leadership" and "followership" are two distinct concepts: a leader is a person, whereas a follower is a person who does not ask why but only how; a leader says something, whereas a follower does that which is said. What tends to be underemphasized is that inherent in many of the perspectives of leadership is a lack of explanation about how exactly a good follower becomes a good leader and whether there actually is a difference between followers and leaders. Just because you are in a leadership position does not make you a leader any more than being in a subordinate position necessarily makes you subordinate. To become a leader in many fields, you are required to do your apprenticeship under a master, often for many years. So, might not good leadership also require an ability to be a good follower? More important, is there actually a difference between followers and leaders other than the labels attached? Perhaps leadership theorists and researchers should become more active in asking such questions. Such issues become pertinent when we look at leadership substitutes and

Might not good leadership also require an ability to be a good follower?

neutralizers, as well as the postmodern and dispersed leadership approaches, later in this chapter.

In addition, perhaps theorists should view films more often because the dramatic quality of a good script, expert direction, and brilliant acting can often bring leadership issues to the fore, as in *Master and Commander: The Far Side of the World* (Weir 2003), where the relationship of the master and commander with his followers is a vital ingredient to his leadership. In one of the finest films about leadership, *Lawrence of Arabia* (Lean 1962), T. E. Lawrence, a historical character, refuses the leadership position offered to him and exercises that leadership which he believes in inherently, from an ethical point of view. He is committed to the cause of the Bedouin with whom he associates rather than to the duplicitous policies of the British politicians and generals. Typically, in the Army, leadership is predicated on good followership, and it is the good follower who is given the opportunity to climb the ranks from private to corporal to sergeant, and so on. In this respect, Lawrence could be said not to have leadership qualities, despite the extraordinary charisma that attached to him and his evident success.

Everything old is new again: Transactional, transformational, and charismatic approaches

We now look at three relatively recent approaches to leadership that incorporate all the leadership theories we have discussed thus far. Although there are many newer leadership approaches, we look at the three main approaches that dominate almost all textbooks about leadership: the transformational, the transactional, and the charismatic. In the "Critical Issues, The Positive Psychology of Leadership" section later in this chapter, we visit some new leadership theories that have just emerged. The positive psychology approach emphasizes strengths of leadership and does not limit the definition of a leader to one special person in a million, but suggests, rather, that the strengths of leadership exist within all of us and are just waiting to be realized, fostered, and nurtured.

The leadership theories presented in this section, however, are still much more in line with the trait, behavioral, and contingency schools. From the perspective of some positive psychology views of leadership, neither Adolf Hitler nor many other political and organizational leaders would be viewed as positive leaders because they lack those humanist ideals that underpin positive psychology (see also pp. 222–225), whereas in the approaches presented here, Hitler and many other violent and brutal leaders could still be defined as leaders and listed along with Nelson Mandela, Mahatma Gandhi, and the Dalai Lama as examples of charismatic and other types of leaders.

Transactional leadership epitomizes the initiating structure, concern for production, and task-oriented themes of the behavioral leadership literature. *Transformational* leadership, as you probably could guess, epitomizes consideration and concern for people, and similar relations-oriented themes. You could probably define each of these leaders yourself just by looking at the words *transactional* and *transformational*. The terms appeared in James M. Burns' (1978) book on leadership but were popularized by Bernard M. Bass (1985, 1990). Charismatic leadership also appeared in Burns' text on leadership, but Robert J. House (1977) (remember path-goal theory) wrote about it also as, of course, did Weber (1978). See Table 7.2 for a breakdown of each leadership approach.

Transactional leadership is effectively what good management is all about: It's the paperwork, the budgeting, the scheduling, with a bit of psychological support and motivation of people thrown in for good measure. However, transactional leaders do not cope well with major change and are not adept at managing the change process. Charismatic leaders can create the impetus for change, but they can be volatile and inconsistent and can be blinded by their own vision. (Our "Who am I?" exercise earlier in this chapter shows that Hitler had many charismatic leadership qualities, but we do not think that you would want someone similar to Hitler as your boss.) Indeed, there are not many business leaders who would be classified as charismatic leaders; typically, such leaders tend to lead social or political movements rather than commercial organizations. They have sources of inspiration that seem to deal with more fundamental human values than just the end of achieving profit. They are also concerned with the purposes to which such resources may be put.

> **Charismatic leaders can create the impetus for change, but they can be volatile and inconsistent and can be blinded by their own vision.**

Finally, transformational leadership is an agent of change. Transformational leaders are the ideal people to have during major organizational change because they have the visionary component of the charismatic leader but also have staying power and provide energy and support throughout the change process. If the transformational leader has a weakness, it is that organizational life is not always about constant change, so the effectiveness of a transformational leader can be short-lived. After the change occurs, another type of leadership style might be more appropriate. The transactional leader may be more useful during periods of homeostasis, when you want things to run smoothly.

From the perspective of situational contingency argument, in some situations you need a transactional leader to hold the ship steady, at other times you need a charismatic leader to create a vision and inspire the need for change, and sometimes you need a transformational leader to foster and manage the change process through to completion. Still, there are risks: Transformational leaders may end up believing too literally in their own hype; they might really think they are the heroes that their strategies seem to position them as being, effortlessly changing minds, actions, and paradigms. The Stranglers had an appropriate response to this mindset back in 1977 when they wrote the song "No More Heroes." It had the wonderful refrain, "Whatever happened to all the heroes? All the Shakespearoes? They watched their Rome burn. Whatever happened to the heroes?" (Stranglers 1977). The point seems to be that writing epic sagas in

TABLE 7.2   The transactional, charismatic, and transformational approaches to leadership

Approach	Description
Transactional	Transactional leaders do all the necessary and critical management functions such as role clarification and task requirements, and they know how to allocate and provide rewards and punishments. They adhere to organizational policies, values, and vision and are strong on planning, budgeting, and meeting schedules.
Charismatic	Charismatic leaders are a bit more complex. They have a motivating effect upon people and are able to create grand visions about an idealized future. They are able to unify people toward that vision and to foster conditions of high trust.
Transformational	Transformational leaders inspire change and innovation. They are the opposite of transactional leaders because they deal mainly with abstract and intangible concepts like vision and change.

which you star as hero is easy, but making them happen in reality is a little harder, and ensuring happy endings for the triumphant hero is nearly impossible.

No more heroes?

A critical question and challenge to leadership theory and research is the question of whether *leadership* is a term or concept that actually exists. Will there come a time when leaders can be substituted, if not made obsolete from organizations? Some contingency theorists argue that such a time is here. Others, such as the postmodernists, turn the term leadership on its head, painting a picture of leaders as servants. So let's look at both these perspectives a little closer, starting with the contingency view of *leadership substitutes* and *neutralizers*. Before we visit these approaches a quick word: Leadership as a concept has come under constant bombardment—with statements like "Leadership is dead"—even from the contingency theorists. However, we should remember one thing: Many of these approaches, but especially contingency theory, fail to account for the fact that leaders can and do change the situation and the environment within which they operate—and they often do so intentionally. That is, leaders can sometimes control contingencies. In this way, they can actually use the contingent variable to control or to increase their effectiveness—and they do this in quite subtle and pervasive ways (see, for example, Clegg, Pitsis, Rura-Polley, and Marosszeky 2002).

Substitutes and neutralizers

Some contingency theorists, such as Kerr and Jermier (1978), argued long ago that situational variables could act as substitutes for leaders, thus rendering the leader irrelevant or useless. Let's look at two examples to help illustrate how such a theory works. Substitutes to leadership can be used irrespective of whether or not subordinates are self-motivated, well skilled, very professional, and have a high internal locus of control because a number of contingent variables can be used as substitutes for both task- and person-oriented leaders. Substitutes for leadership can be found in one's professional experience. If you are a professional or possess a high level of expertise, a leader might be redundant. Or, you might work as part of a self-managed work team (SMWT). In an SMWT, each team member might be involved in all decision making about rostering, goal setting, performance measurement and evaluation, setting of wages, and so on. There could be high levels of trust, shared responsibility, interdependence, and support. A leader, be it transactional or transformational, is not required. Conversely, even people with low professional affiliations, skill level, and autonomy can be managed without leaders through carefully designed jobs high in formalized, routinized procedures and with training for employees to be able to identify and to rectify simple breakdowns in routinized tasks—really, not much different from monkeys flying multimillion-dollar rockets into space for NASA. (For more in-depth discussions of substitutes for leadership, see Podsakoff, Niehoff, MacKenzie, and Williams 1993).

A related notion to substitutes for leadership is that of empowerment (see also pp. 170–172). As we saw in Chapter 5, empowerment is meant to be about addressing the power inequality inherent in subordination. We are subordinate because someone or something holds power over us. Empowerment, therefore, is about releasing the shackles placed on us by those who have power over us in the workplace. Employees are empowered when they are given control of organizational decision making, as well as many other aspects of their work life, and by the use of SMWTs. By empowering people, you are lowering their reliance on and need for leaders to rule over them and to be constantly monitoring them. Followers, through empowerment, start looking more like leaders.

However, what if you manage a small music store and you employ students who work on the weekends while studying law or medicine? They come to work because it's fun, they like listening to music, and many of their friends come in on the weekends. (Maybe you have read Nick Hornsby's (1995) novel *High Fidelity*—which was also made into a film (Frears 2000)—in which the sales staff are interested in only those customers who are as cool and knowledgeable as the sales staff think they themselves are.) Such people don't mind working in low-status jobs because one day they know they'll be wealthy doctors or lawyers. But although they're having fun, customers find they are extremely poor salespeople—they are rude and ignore customers in favor of their friends, and they take your business for granted. You know they do not need the job, and the unemployment rate is so low that people can walk in and out of low-skilled jobs like these. Because of all these contingencies, your ability to lead actually *neutralizes* your leadership ability. So rather then being able to substitute your leadership through contingent variables, your leadership becomes impotent. Obviously, neutralizers can be viewed in a more negative light than substitutes. Indeed, substitutes can be very useful tools of empowerment and can free up your time for other duties, whereas neutralizers cancel out the benefit or effectiveness a leader might have.

As the boundaries between leaders and followers continue to blur, the focus on "the leader" by the more traditional theories highlighted earlier in this chapter become increasingly problematic. When leadership skills and responsibilities are dispersed or shared throughout an organization through empowerment, or leadership is substituted or neutralized, an emphasis is placed upon the process of leadership and not upon the attributes or style of a unique person or set of persons—the "leaders." In short, *dispersed leadership theories*—theories that move leadership away from an individual person—may imply that leadership is something that many people can do, and actually do, and is therefore not a fruitful basis upon which to differentiate people at work. Furthermore, viewing leadership as a process suggests that the leader/follower relationship is no longer of central importance to the study of leadership (see, for example, Gordon 2002). As the dispersed approaches to leadership continue to gain interest and validity, such a view suggests that the boundaries that once differentiated "the leader" from "the follower" are becoming very gray—a follower is a leader is a follower is a leader, and so on, ad infinitum. This has opened the door to postmodern (see also pp. 55–56; 60–61) concepts, so it is appropriate to review at least one postmodern perspective on leadership—that of Boje and Dennehey (1999).

Leaders as servants and the postmodern condition

Postmodernism stresses the role of discursively negotiated, shared, and conflicting conceptions in arriving at a common sense of things, such that the role of language becomes central to the settlement of what is true and false, "and all our attempts to discover truth should be seen for what they are—forms of discourse" (Parker 1992: 3). Thus, in this perspective, leadership becomes equated not with some essence outside of its discussions, to which these discussions refer. Instead, leadership is seen as existing only in the ways in which it is talked into being, both practically and in theory. Therefore, postmodernist leadership is whatever people do when they talk in ways that people recognize as leadership.

Postmodernism, then, further blurs the boundaries of how we understand and make sense of leadership. Indeed, it turns leadership on its head and presents a very novel conception of leadership that stresses that leaders are servants of the types of leadership that others recognize as leadership in discourse about what characterizes leadership. Let us go through the ABC's of Boje and Dennehey's (1999) approach, in which each letter in the word SERVANT is given a special significance, to get some of the flavor of the postmodern approach from their analysis.

- S is for *servant*. The leader is the servant to the network. Leaders serve people and the people, in turn, serve customers. For a long time in the past, leadership was about differentiating oneself so that a leader would be different from a follower. In a postmodern perspective on leadership, leaders seek to rid the world of such differentiation; the leader articulates the servant conceptions of what the leader should be. Think of the CEO who dresses down and on Fridays works on the shop floor with the other workers.

- E is for *empowers*. The leader empowers participation in social and economic democracy.
- R is for *recounter of stories*. The leader tells stories about the organization's history, heroes, and future.
- V represents being *visionary*. Leaders without vision, the reasoning goes, offer nothing, and people's hopes perish. At their best, visionary leaders should articulate a clear concept of what it is that followers already are committed to and believe in.
- A is for being *androgynous*. Androgyny means no gender; the leader must be able to speak in both male and female voices (no, not like Michael Jackson).
- N is for *networker*. The leader manages the transformation and configuration of the diverse network of teams spanning suppliers to customers.
- T is for *team builder*. The leader mobilizes, leads, and dispatches a web of autonomous teams.

Boje and Dennehey provide a description and comparison of premodern, modern, and postmodern leaders, as shown in Table 7.3. Their approach is novel and creative but take a closer look at the table. Can you see any parallels with transformational, transactional, and charismatic leadership? Also, can you see some link to behavioral and contingency theory? Note how Boje and Dennehey conceive leadership almost from the perspective of a behavioral style. Moreover, if leadership transforms through time, something must be accounting for that transformation from master to servant; are time and place the contingent factors? Or is it the case that the nature and expectations of those of us who were once led are changing as we access education, gain instant information through the Internet, and use the new technologies to receive greater exposure to contrasting views of political, social, and economic current affairs? So, is postmodern leadership theory merely an expanded contingency theory, where the ultimate substitute for leadership is the follower? What a postmodern thought!

> **Motivation is necessary whether you are to lead yourself, lead others, or be led by others.**

Leaders as motivators

There is not a single theory or approach to leadership that fails to recognize that a fundamental quality of leaders—irrespective of whether leadership is innate, learned, situational, or whatever—is an ability to inspire and motivate people. Motivation is necessary whether you are to lead yourself, lead others, or to be led by others. Even the postmodern approach of Boje and Dennehey (1999), which we discussed previously, incorporates the traditional motivational

TABLE 7.3   Premodern, modern, and postmodern leadership

Premodern Leaders	Modern Leaders	Postmodern Leaders
Leader as Master	**Leader as Panoptic**	**Leader as Servant**
Master. Head of the work institution. Owner of the slaves, serfs, and tools.	**Panoptic.** Leader does the gaze on everyone, Big Brother style. Bentham's principle of the Panopticon is central here: power should be visible and unverifiable (see also pp. 15–18).	**Servant.** The leader is the servant to the network. Leaders serve people who, in turn, serve customers. Differentiates self from the people.
Authoritarian. Enforces unquestioning obedience through authoritarian rule over subordinates.	**Authoritarian.** Final evaluator of performance and quality.	**Empowers.** The leader empowers participation in social and economic democracy.
Slave driver. A leader oversees the work of others. A real taskmaster.	**Network of penal mechanisms.** Penal mechanisms are little courts for the investigation, monitoring, and correction of incorrect behavior and then the application of punishments and rewards to sustain normalcy and reinforce leader's power.	**Recounter of stories.** Tells the stories of company history, heroes, and futures.
Tyrant. Sovereign and oppressive control over other people.		**Visionary.** Without vision, we perish.
Elite. Leaders are regarded as the finest or most privileged class and usually are drawn from such classes.	**Organizational.** Lots of divisions, layers, specialties, and cubbyholes to cellularize people. Pyramid. Leader sits at the top of the pyramid.	**Androgynous.** Male and female voices.
Ruler. Leaders govern and rule over other people.	**Top.** The head boss, the top of the hill, and the highest-ranking person.	**Networker.** Manage the transformation and configuration of the diverse network of teams spanning suppliers to customers.
	Inspector. In charge of surveillance, inspection, and rating of everyone else. Centralist. All information and decision flows up to the center and back down to the periphery.	**Team builder.** Mobilize, lead, and detach a web-work of autonomous teams.

Source: Adapted from Boje and Dennehey (1999)

and inspirational aspects of leadership. It is therefore important to visit briefly some approaches to motivation and see how they are relevant to you as a leader. We discuss two key approaches to motivation—the process and content theories—and two key motivation concepts—intrinsic versus extrinsic motivation.

Rather than talking about individual motivation theories, we explore the assumptions behind the theories and how such approaches might specifically relate to leadership. This section is not, therefore, nor does it pretend to be, a section on motivation theory—you can refer to the reading list at the end of this chapter for some excellent resources on motivation. We do not provide you with enough detail and information here to design jobs or to produce incentive schemes that will motivate people. Rather, we introduce and discuss some basic assumptions underlying motivation concepts with the objective that it will help you to reflect critically upon what motivation means for you as a future leader and will help you think about and reflect upon the concept of motivation and how it is presented to you, without context or reference to the fundamental ideals that make up motivation theories.

Today, motivation is about ensuring that people behave in the organization's best interest (Rousseau 1996)—even if it is not in one's own interest. There has been a clear shift away from motivation theory's original objective, which was first and foremost about the psychological well-being and esteem of individuals, not how much harder we can make them work. For many centuries, philosophers have contemplated why we do the things we do. For instance, in the eighteenth century, Adam Smith (1776/1961) held the simple view that we are motivated purely by self-interest. Adam Smith believed that self-interest was a central concept leading to the wealth of nations. As people set up companies to become wealthy, they created jobs, which provided income to people and tax revenue to government, which would be spent on health, education, security, and so on. For Smith, this would even lead to innovation and technological change; because people would want more leisure time, they would innovate and change machinery to free up time for socializing. However, the perspective is seriously flawed because it cynically assumes that all action is motivated only by self-interest. Other philosophers such as John Stuart Mill (1962) suggest that we value only what is useful to us. Therefore, if other people cannot be useful, we will not value them.

More contemporary approaches to motivation address the satiation of needs—we all need food, love, shelter, and safety, for instance. When you do not have these things, you are "pushed" to go out searching for them. There are many negative consequences if we do not satiate our needs—for example, starvation, loneliness, illness, injury, or death. In organizational behavior, theories that focus on needs are known as *content theories* of motivation because they refer to those "contents" within us that drive or push us. One of the most famous (as well as one of the most misappropriated and underrepresented) content theories of motivation is Maslow's (1970) hierarchy of needs theory. According to Maslow, there is a hierarchy of needs; as we meet the needs within each tier of the hierarchy, we can move on to meet the next level of needs. The hierarchy begins with typical physiological needs, such as the need to satiate hunger and thirst; second in the hierarchy are safety needs, such as shelter and security; third are the needs to belong, love, and be loved; fourth are esteem needs that are met by professional or other achievements, respect, and recognition. At the top of the hierarchy is the self-actualization need, or the need to live the happiest and most fulfilled life possible, the achievement of which usually requires us to realize our fullest potential.

The self-actualization component of Maslow's theory was its most critical part because it was embedded in his philosophy of life. Yet, if you look at almost any organizational behavior textbook, you will find fleeting mentions of Maslow's theory as an early and outdated theory of motivation, criticized because it assumes that motivation is hierarchical. Such thin criticisms and representations of Maslow's life work ignore his notion of *eupsychian management* (Maslow 1965). Maslow coined the term "euspsychia" for his vision of utopia, which, he argued, society should aspire to; with this vision, he attempted to refocus attention on motivation back to psychological well-being. Maslow believed we could promote, support, and maintain psychological well-being at work by basing the structure of society and its organizations upon virtues, which, in turn, would filter into the broader society and the community. He saw leadership in organizations as integral in helping people self-actualize. Yet, if you look at Maslow's hierarchy of needs theory in any organization behavior textbook, it will not tell you that Maslow was driven to try to understand why some self-actualized people were what he called "fully functioning" and how to capture and foster such positive virtues in society at large.

There is a tension in Maslow's work between self-actualization as a natural human condition, open to all, and the premise that some are more likely to achieve self-actualization than others, and that some will never do so. This tension can first be seen in his early work on primates (Maslow 1933), where he observed that some chimpanzees are instinctually and naturally superior and dominant over others. Buss (1979: 50) sees the same tension manifesting itself in Maslow's account of human society in terms of "democracy and elitism— between the non-actualized masses and the actualized few." The tension was most evident when Maslow's reflections shifted from individuals to societies. Maslow argued in his diaries that

> Democracy of Western sort is OK for rich & well organized, educated society & capitalism can then work fairly well. For people with lower basic needs satisfied, higher needs emerge & we can talk about freedom for self-fulfillment, autonomy, encouragement of growth, humanitarianism, justice, democracy etc . . . . There is now a hierarchy of societies paralleling the hierarchy of basic needs. (Herman 1995: 272)

Nonetheless, despite these evident tensions between democratic and elitist impulses, the idea of self-actualization is, in principle, appealing. According to Payne (2000), many of Maslow's principles have entered our working lives, such as an emphasis on the concerns with quality of working life, total quality management, empowerment, and self-managing work teams. In essence, fifty years ago, Maslow theorized and mused about issues that still dominate much of leadership education and theory today. If people have to worry about where their next meal will come from, or where to sleep, or whether they have family support, how can they realize their full potential? The fundamentals of Maslow's arguments remain humanist despite their grounding in the early work that he conducted on primates. Maslow's work, which has been widely influential, revolved around a tension between elitism and democracy, a tension which was also constitutive of the society in which he lived and developed his thinking: the United States.

Content theories do not sufficiently explain why people are motivated to behave in certain ways. To answer such questions, we need to consider what processes are involved in motivation. Some argue that the process is one of expecting that behaving in a certain way will realize certain outcomes. Proponents of this view assume that you are more likely to behave in such ways if: (a) your effort leads to your expected level of performance, (b) your level of performance get the results you expect, and (c) you value such outcomes. Such assumptions are typical of expectancy theories of motivation (see, for example, Georgopoulos, Mahoney, and Jones 1957).

To make the point about expectancy theory clear, let's assume that you take your management final exam after having missed classes all semester, fallen behind on your reading, and having rarely studied. In rational terms, you would expect that lack of study would lead to failing the exam, and you find that you do actually fail. You thus learn that effort influences performance, and performance, in turn, influences outcomes. Let's also assume the reason you have missed your studies is that your rap crew or rock band is becoming increasingly popular, so you have decided to concentrate your efforts there; you value the result in your management class much less than a successful rap or rock career.

Another process theory, equity theory, extends the expectancy argument by adding that we also compare our inputs and outcomes to other people's inputs and outcomes (see Adams 1963; Mowday 1991). Equity theory—or social exchange theory—is by far one of the most dynamic and influential process theories. As an example, let's say that your rock band has been playing for ten years now but has never garnered the recognition and rewards you believe you deserve, even while others become pop stars overnight through *American Idol,* or one of its many clones globally, such as *Australian Idol.* You compare your effort, performance, and outcome to theirs and realize that the world is damn unfair. You believe that your inputs—your skills, experience, time, and effort—were well above those of the idol star, yet she is rewarded with fame, wealth, and a recording contract, whereas you end up playing at a roadside diner on Saturday nights. If only you had studied for that management exam. You give up being a musician in disgust and start your own music store, managing medical and law students who really don't need the job, money, or hassles, living out the alienated *High Fidelity* lifestyle.

Unlike many of the process theories, equity theory does not assume a rational process. If it did, we would expend effort when we think it will lead to an outcome that we value, and we would not expend effort when it leads to outcomes that we do not value. The theory acknowledges that sometimes our motives are hidden or subconscious (Adams 1963). Why do people murder? Why do some leaders hide unethical and corrupt behaviors? Why do some people avoid effort? Why do some people put themselves in danger for other people? Why do some of us stay in a job or a relationship that make us unhappy, sometimes for many years? Human behavior is not always a rational and linear process. Often we find ourselves doing the very things that do not make us happy, and we, in turn, expect those working for us, or with us, to

TABLE 7.4 Examples of intrinsic and extrinsic motivation

Intrinsic	Extrinsic
Behavior motivated by intrinsic factors such as self-expression, interest, and enjoyment.	Behavior motivated by extrinsic factors such as the promise of reward or threat of punishment.
Motivated to finish reading because you are interested.	Motivated to finish reading to meet a deadline.
Working because you find the job stimulating and enjoyable.	Working because you need the money.
Changing jobs because you want the challenge.	Changing jobs because you are certain you will be fired.
Motivated to work in difficult jobs that challenge you.	Motivated to work in difficult jobs to get the pay raise.
Study to improve yourself.	Study to get a high-paying job.

Source: Adapted from Deci and Ryan (1987); Myers (2001: 451–452); Ryan and Deci (2000)

suffer the same existence. Perhaps a more fruitful way of thinking about motivation is to think about *extrinsic* and *intrinsic* motivation. Table 7.4 lists descriptions and some examples of intrinsic and extrinsic motivation.

Obviously, you could think of more examples, but you should get the idea by now that *intrinsic motivation* refers to those internal states that drive us toward behaviors that directly meet self-actualization and belongingness needs. On the other hand, *extrinsic motivation* refers to those internal states that drive us toward behaviors that directly meet esteem needs. Theoretically, the two types of motivation are not mutually exclusive; however, notice that we used the word "directly" in the previous sentence. In other words, sometimes money is important, even for an intrinsically motivated person, but it can be simply a means to an end—for example, to save enough money to realize your life dream of starting your own little restaurant. So, as a leader you have to know whether people—including yourself—are extrinsically or intrinsically motivated and not assume that all people are always intrinsically or extrinsically motivated by the same things. Moreover, much research suggests that the overuse of extrinsic motivation can kill or thwart intrinsic motivation (Deci and Ryan 1985, 1987).

Ryan and Deci (2000: 70) argue that "no single phenomenon reflects the positive potential of human nature as much as intrinsic motivation, the inherent tendency to seek out novelty and challenges, to extend and exercise one's capacities, to explore and to learn." Intrinsically motivated people tend to parallel Maslow's concept of self-actualization and its associated higher positive self-regard and positive psychological health. Thus, Maslow's eupsychian managers would be conversant with intrinsic motivation. Imagine a wonderful world in which leaders manage and motivate people with an emphasis on self-actualization and the realization of intrinsic desires, and in which, in turn, organizations foster and promote self-actualization. Is this the hopeless dream of a handful of "do-gooder" psychologists and dead rock stars—such as John Lennon, who wrote the song "Imagine" (Lennon 1971) and who once said that all the great leaders (like Martin Luther King, Jr., John F. Kennedy, and Mahatma Gandhi) end up shot, and was himself later assassinated? These days, are we over the hope of such days?

According to positive psychology, we should not abandon hope. We can imagine that a better world of leadership need not be unachievable.

CRITICAL ISSUES: THE POSITIVE PSYCHOLOGY OF LEADERSHIP

To be a leader is a huge moral responsibility because executive leadership can easily overwhelm reason. Hitler was able to lead men and women and influence them so strongly that they committed horrific acts. Indeed, his ability to read and use the situational contingencies, his vision, and his drive all came together, and he nearly achieved his ultimate goal. Because many researchers

Image 7.2   *John Lennon: singer, writer, peace activist. Born October 9, 1940; assassinated December 8, 1980. (Here depicted with his wife, artist Yoko Ono.)*

Image 7.3   *Mohandas K. (Mahatma) Gandhi commemorated*

wanted to figure out how this type of blind loyalty to an evil leader could be avoided in the future, a large body of work is emerging that emphasizes and distinguishes leadership by behaviors and *cognition*s (or ways of thinking). Such approaches have emerged out of the traditions of positive psychology (see also pp. 222–225) and places virtues such as strength of character, wisdom, authenticity, and humanity before all else.

As we saw from the work of Milgram (1971), these values are extremely important (see also pp. 181–183). Milgram was intrigued as to why people would follow some leaders to the point where they would engage in atrocious behavior. As a person of Jewish ancestry and as a social psychologist, Milgram was especially interested in why Germans, and many others, blindly followed the Nazi quest to exterminate all Jews. How could leaders have so much power and influence over people? Was there something specific about those Germans that made them obey the Nazi leader's orders? Or could any one of us become violent, murderous, blind followers given the right conditions? As Milgram so eloquently noted a few years after his original study was published, ordinary people, simply doing their jobs, and without any particular hostility on their part, can become agents in a terrible destructive process. Moreover, even when the destructive effects of their work become patently clear, and they are asked to carry out actions incompatible with fundamental standards of morality, relatively few people have the resources needed to resist authority. A variety of inhibitions against disobeying authority come into play and successfully keep the person in his place. Sitting back in one's armchair, it is easy to condemn the actions of the obedient subjects. But those who condemn the subjects measure them against the standard of their own ability to formulate high-minded moral prescriptions. That is hardly a fair standard. Many of the subjects, at the level of stated opinion, feel quite as strongly as any of us about the moral requirement of refraining from action against a helpless victim. They, too, in general terms know what ought to be done and can state their values when the occasion arises. This has little, if anything, to do with their actual behavior under the pressure of circumstances. (Milgram 1974: 4–5)

Luthans and Avolio's (2003) concept of the *authentic* leader differs from the type of leader encountered in Nazi Germany and the Milgram experiment. Their *Authentic Leadership Development* exemplifies many of the qualities espoused by positive psychology. According to Luthans and Avolio (2003: 242–243), authentic leaders are transparent. Their intentions seamlessly link espoused values, actions, and behaviors. Authentic leaders have the qualities of transformational leaders but also work on moral and ethical grounds; possess great self-awareness, integrity, confidence, and self-control; are positive and optimistic; are resilient (bouncing back from adversity); and are future oriented. They inspire, transform, mentor, and develop. The authentic leader might be the perfectly designed leader to achieve Maslow's eupsychian philosophy that we discussed earlier. Indeed, for many of his generation, John Lennon, with his commitment to peace, seemed to be such a leader, capable of taking his celebrity and parlaying it into consciousness-raising about profound and not just entertainment values. In this respect, Lennon was that unlikely iconic phenomenon: an authentic leader, writer, and musician.

Of course, the authentic leader is an ideal, and many criticize the approach by arguing that no one on this earth can behave in an exemplary way all the time—they say that this is just a utopian view of the world. Lennon's (1971) "Imagine," for instance, is sometimes cynically dismissed as an easy song for a multimillionaire to have written; it imagines a world without possessions where all the people live in peace. Others might argue that yes, authentic leaders lead by using morals and ethics, but the question remains: whose morality and whose ethics?

The authentic leader, by definition, should be able to realize when she or he makes a mistake or inadvertently does wrong and, unlike many, will take responsibility, accept accountability, and seek to amend the situation. In addition, a very important aspect of the model is that authentic leadership occurs within a context in which leaders are able to empathize with subordinates and to reflect cultural, moral, and ethical standards in their approach to management, so the authentic leader is not only a way of being and a way of seeing but is also situational.

A closely related approach to leadership, but one that is currently more of a theory than a tested model, is *leadership wisdom* (Dunphy and Pitsis 2003). As with Luthans, Luthans, Hodgetts, and Luthans (2002), the authors argue that leaders of the future will need to take stock of principles and concepts typified by positive psychology—but especially the notions of ecology, ecosystems, biospheres, diversity, and community. Leaders of the future will be authentic and will realize how interconnected everything is in the world. Our organizations are not free enterprises meant to consume all resources to produce products for all consumers. Rather, organizations are made up of you and me, our families, friends, and even our enemies, and what they do has an impact on all of us, both now and in the future. Leadership is about principles of social, economic, and ecological sustainability and ethical responsibility (see also pp. 29–32; 478–481). Sustainability is not about keeping things the same; it still involves change and development, but it is about transforming society toward positive behavior and cognition by avoiding overconsumption; addressing inequality; and using intelligent business methods, long-term vision and planning, and future mindedness.

Imagine a world in which our leaders at least try to live by such guidelines and values, and in which our organizations operate upon principles raised by Luthans and Avolio (2003) and Dunphy and Pitsis (2003). This type of world would mean that many of the ways we do things at work today would have to change forever. This is a big challenge, but it is one that more and more people seem to believe in.

THE FINE PRINT: LEADERSHIP FRAMING AND REFRAMING

To finish this chapter, we want to introduce you to an innovative approach designed to help leaders make sense of their world—that of framing and reframing introduced by Lee G. Bolman and Terrence E. Deal (2003). According to the authors, frames can be thought of as

> windows, maps, tools, lenses, orientations and perspectives . . . a set of ideas or assumptions you carry in your head. It helps you understand and negotiate a particular "territory." The territory isn't necessarily defined by geography. It could be a sport, an art form, an academic subject, or anything else you care about . . . . Like maps, frames are both windows on a territory and tools for navigation. Every tool has distinctive strengths and limitations. The right tool makes a job easier, but the wrong one just gets in the way. (2003: 12–13)

In its simplest form, their theory suggests that we use frames to view and to make sense of the world. Obviously, many phenomena—such as genetics, when and where we were born, education, upbringing, experience, and culture—are influential in framing how we think and behave and seek to make sense of the world. Bolman and Deal (2003) developed four basic frames that they believe all people, regardless of culture and inheritance, use as points of reference in making sense of the world. They termed these frames the *structural,* the *human resources,* the *political* (or power), and the *symbolic* (or culture). See Table 7.5 for metaphors that describe organizations from each perspective and for characteristics of leaders who view their domain through different frames.

The beauty of Bolman and Deal's (2003) approach is that it shows that leadership has as much to do with how we perceive it as how leaders behave. Moreover, how a leader behaves is a function of how he or she views the world. If the structural frame dominates, her focus is on ensuring that the job gets done, through task design, clear and defined procedures, and lines of authority and control. On the other hand, if she views the world from the human resources frame, she is more interested in meeting people's needs and wants, and believes work should be about fulfillment.

Of course, regardless of the frame a leader normally functions in, for some situations, the structural frame might be critical. For example, imagine that you are an executive chef with a team of six employees and that you have a function with 600 people that all need to be served at the same time, with many different entrees and courses. The perspective from the structural frame provides us with key elements of organizing and leading in such situations. However, if we concentrate solely on the structural frame, we open ourselves to "blind spots"—it could be just as important to consider the human resources frame, too. Does the team of chefs get along? Is the team made up of the right people who fit together? Are they all motivated and happy in their jobs? Do they take pride in their work? Such issues can be as important and, in some cases, more important than getting the structural issues right. So sometimes we need to consider issues from multiple frames. Bolman and Deal refer to this as *reframing*—using multiple frames to examine and make sense of a situation or an event to develop a holistic approach to organizing.

Finally, to help leaders understand which style of leadership works best under which frame, Bolman and Deal (2003) describe the approach and process the leader might use if she or he is to be effective—or ineffective. In Table 7.6, you can see that leaders working under a structural frame might think a lot about analyzing problems and opportunities, view themselves as architects of organizing and designing work and processes, and avoid petty and obsessive attention to every single bit of detail that might require high levels of surveillance and control. The human resources frame requires a leader who empowers change through mentoring and support but who must still possess strong qualities; this leader must avoid always asking staff to solve the problem themselves—that is, ignoring problems and challenges not for reasons of empowerment but because of a desire to avoid responsibility. In the political frame, the leader takes on the role of advocate and negotiator to establish, develop, and maintain important networks of relationships, but political leaders can easily resort to thuggery, deceitfulness, manipulation, and force,

TABLE 7.5 Bolman and Deal's four frames

Frames	Characteristics of the Frame
Structural	Sense is made through metaphors of the organization as a machine or a factory, because an organization, like a machine, has parts that must follow a set process, be managed, and be controlled. When a part of the machine breaks down, the whole machine stops; therefore, focus is on ensuring that the machine keeps running.
	Leaders who view the world from this frame are primarily concerned with goals and objectives. They believe all problem solving and decision making can be approached in a rational way. Efficiency comes through specialization and division of labor. Emphasis is on strong coordination and control to ensure that the job gets done. All change is considered from a structural perspective. Formal top-down authority and motivation is linked to performance and is usually extrinsic. Leadership tends to be autocratic, task oriented, and transactional.
Human Resources	Sense is made through metaphors of the organization as a family because people need people, love, caring, and affiliation.
	Leaders who view the world from this frame are primarily concerned about Maslow's self-actualization needs. Human resources policies dominate these organizations because of the strong belief that how you treat people in the organization determines how they work. Therefore, the organization incorporates many personal and organizational development policies within its HR department. Emphasis is on the use of teams and participative management. Intrinsic motivation dominates, and the leader's goals are to empower, mentor, and inspire people. Such leaders tend to be transformational and high in concern for people.
Political	Sense is made through metaphors of the organization as a jungle or a political arena full of conflict over resources, power struggles, and self-interests.
	Leaders who view the world from this frame are expert political players. They emphasize that organizational effectiveness is about access and control over resources and power over people. Ultimately, the aim is not to reduce conflict; instead, the emphasis is on power, influence, and political strategy. The leader is an expert in establishing coalitions and networks of power to address power imbalance or inequality. The leader is like a politician and seeks to set agendas, gain votes, and be an expert in negotiating and bargaining.
Symbolic	Sense is made through metaphors of the organization as a temple full of symbolism and cultural artifacts, rituals, storytelling, and values.
	Leaders who view the world in this frame see symbolism as integral to organizational life and seek to build strong organizational culture through norms and symbolism, such as dress, corporate logos, vision, and mission. Critical to the leader is the need to create meaning and to establish beliefs systems and a faith that symbolize the organizations culture. Emphasis is on sense making, diversity, identity, and organizational commitment. These leaders lead by example, not by command and control.

Source: Adapted from Bolman and Deal (2003: 44–298)

TABLE 7.6   Reframing leadership

Frame	Leadership is effective when the:		Leadership is ineffective when the:	
	Leader is	*Leadership process* is	*Leader* is	*Leadership process* is
Structural	Analyst, architect	Analysis, design	Petty tyrant	Management by detail and fiat
Human Resources	Catalyst, servant	Support, empowerment	Weakling, pushover	Abdication
Political	Advocate, negotiator	Advocacy, coalition building	Con artist, thug	Manipulation, fraud
Symbolic	Prophet, poet	Inspiration, framing experience	Fanatic, fool	Mirage, smoke and mirrors

Source: Adapted from Bolman and Deal (2003: 349)

and thus abuse the authority attached to their position. Finally, the symbolic frame requires leaders who view themselves as prophets or poets willing to inspire and to create meaning and sense making within organizational life. Of course, such leaders can go too far and become cult leaders or fanatics, or, of course, they can look foolish.

Bolman and Deal (2003) present an interesting way of looking at leadership and organizations by focusing on frames and how they provide us with a point of reference for viewing the world. However, all frames have their weaknesses, so a powerful tool for leaders is to be able to reframe problems and issues.

SUMMARY AND REVIEW

What leaders do and what leaders say have profound effects upon the world. Leaders influence others and can make life fulfilling, enriched, and empowered. Although some leaders provide others with the tools to become leaders themselves, other leaders abuse their power, authority, and trust to achieve and to realize their vision and mission of how they think society ought to be. In this chapter, we have seen that leadership is an extremely complex and value-laden domain of theory and research. Is a leader, as the trait theory suggests, made up of inherent characteristics? The literature does not support such an argument. Behavioral theory sought to refocus leadership away from traits to how a person behaves—that is, one's behavior makes one a leader or not. Yet even the behaviorist could see that this was not the entire story, so theorists determined that situational/contingent factors were influential in determining what made leaders and, more important, what made them effective. Leaders were then conceptualized as charismatic and transformational, with an ability to envision, to inspire, and to implement change. Others may be transactional in that they know how to be exemplary managers.

Some contingency theorists argued that the situational factors are so strong that contingencies could be used as substitutes for leadership, and some others could even argue that leadership is null and void. The dispersed and postmodern approaches to leadership attempted to turn leadership around. The leader has changed over time, from premodern to modern to postmodern. The postmodern leader is a SERVANT.

No matter which leadership theory we look at, motivation appears to be a critical concept. Leaders must be motivated, but they must also motivate others by inspiring, envisioning, and empowering. We tied motivation into Maslow's hierarchy of needs—but from quite a different perspective from that of most other textbooks—by focusing on eupsychian management. We then discussed the importance of intrinsic and extrinsic motivation as a way of understanding motivation and leadership. In light of Maslow, and from the perspective of positive psychology, we discussed what our roles and responsibilities might be as members of the human race and related this discussion to the positive psychological traditions of leadership, including the authentic leader and leadership virtues. Finally, we completed this chapter by looking at reframing—a novel and refreshing approach to how leaders make sense of their world and a way in which they can improve their understanding and sense making.

ONE MORE TIME . . .

Getting the story straight

- To be a leader, you must have followers. Is this a true statement? Think about the statement in relation to the main leadership theories raised in this chapter.
- How practical is it to argue that leadership can be substituted or neutralized? Can we create leadership substitutes or neutralizers in any industry or organization? Why or why not?
- Why is it important to understand motivation? What differences are there in what motivates people? How might you account for such differences when leading people in organizations?

Thinking outside the box

- Choose two perspectives or theories of leadership—the one you liked best and the one you liked least. Compare your choices with those of your peers and try to find out why you and your peers chose those theories or approaches. What was it about the theories that you liked or disliked? What were their strengths and weaknesses? Take note of how and why you and your peers differed or agreed.

- Do you agree that if you pay people enough money they will do anything you want them to do—that everyone has a price?
- As an exercise, cut out a newspaper article that illustrates an organizational problem and try to consider all the issues involved from each of Bolman and Deal's (2003) frames. Which frame was the dominant frame used in this organization? How does looking at the problem through each of the frames add to our understanding of it? When you reframe the problem, what issues and possible solutions emerge?

ADDITIONAL RESOURCES

1. There are many excellent resources on leadership. Two interesting approaches to leadership that paint a picture of the importance and influence of leadership upon organizations are Goleman, Boyatzis, and McKee's (2002) *The New Leaders: Transforming the Art of Leadership Into the Science of Results* and Kouzes and Posner's (1995) *The Leadership Challenge: How to Keep Getting Extraordinary Things Done in Organizations.*

2. Another excellent recent source is Hartog and Koopman's (2001) "Leadership in Organizations," in the *Handbook of Industrial & Organizational Psychology.*

3. There are many good movies on leadership and motivation. One such movie is *Glengarry Glen Ross* (Foley 1992), a film about a small organization made up of a dysfunctional sales team and a leader who (at the surface level) seems overly concerned about people. When the organization hires a management consultant to motivate the team, the consultant makes it clear that the organization is not a place for relationships with statements like, "You want a friend? Buy a dog." He also stresses that motivation in the organization is extrinsic only; those who fail to reach high sales targets get second prize—but there is no second prize except unemployment.

4. Other films about leadership and inspiration include "heroic quest" movies such as *Gladiator* (Scott 2000) and *Master and Commander: The Far Side of the World,* as well as the *The Lord of the Rings* (Jackson 2001–2003) trilogy. It is interesting to compare this form of account with that used by chief executives in their memoirs—they seem to be as seduced by the genre of the heroic quest as an archetype as are filmmakers.

In addition to these suggested additional resources, don't forget to look at what is also available on the Web site **www.ckmanagement.net,** including free PDF files of recent papers related to this chapter, which you can download; video interviews with famous academics talking about related themes; as well as many other resources, such as connections to interesting Web sites.

CHAPTER 8

MANAGING CULTURES
Values, Practice, Manipulation

Objectives and learning outcomes

By the end of this chapter, you will be able to

- Understand the central ideas of organization culture and why they are considered important for management

- Discuss some of the major studies of organization culture

- Explain some of the limits to the management of culture

- Discuss the ethically problematic side of corporate culture programs

Before you get started . . .

"Unfortunately, it takes just a bit longer for organizational members to change their organization than it takes the organization to change its members."

—Joschka Fischer, German Foreign Minister

OUTLINE OF THE CHAPTER

Designing an appropriate organization structure had long been the major concern of organization theorists and consultants. In the 1980s, this central concern changed markedly as a result of the publication of Peters and Waterman's *In Search of Excellence: Lessons From America's Best-Run Companies* (1982), which propelled culture to center stage in corporate analysis, resulting in related research that we'll refer to later in this chapter as *excellence studies*. The message was simple: Great companies have excellent cultures. Excellent cultures deliver outstanding financial success. What makes a culture excellent are core values and presuppositions that are widely shared and acted on. Books—such as *In Search of Excellence,* as well as others—such as *Corporate Cultures: The Rites and Rituals of Corporate Life* (Deal and Kennedy 1982) and *Organizational Culture and Leadership* (Schein 1997)—helped make culture a popular and acceptable topic in business. Excellence studies stressed how a pattern of learned and shared basic assumptions framed organization members' perceptions, thoughts, and feelings. Put simply, culture encompassed the following questions: How were things done in particular organizations? What was acceptable behavior? What norms were imparted to new members? What norms were members expected to use to solve problems of external adaptation and internal integration, and which ones did they actually use? Theorists presumed that if you forged a strong culture that incorporated all organization members in shared beliefs and commitments, everything else—good morale, performance, and results—should follow. Having such a widely shared and integrative culture in organizations is often viewed as a panacea for management and an algorithm for corporate success.

Current approaches argue that organizational culture tends to be more fragmentary than unitary; there may not necessarily be a dominant culture because the nature of culture is contingent on a wide range of identities, including those deriving from social markers such as occupation, region, class, ethnicity, gender, and so on. In a specific organization, several cultures can be embedded and flourish locally under conditions that are highly variable for their patterning and formation. Put simply, for advocates of these approaches, *organization culture* is a term that includes many organizational subcultures.

All approaches, whether fragmented or homogenous, understand that culture encompasses the extremely important patterns that shape organizational realities. Understanding an organization means understanding its culture.

SETTING THE SCENE

What do you think of when you hear the word *culture?* Beethoven, Picasso, Shakespeare's *Hamlet,* and Tchaikovsky's *Swan Lake,* or Eminem's rhymes, Damien Hirst's dead animals, Harry Potter novels, and *The Lord of the Rings* movies (Jackson 2001–2003)? Well, of course, these are all *culture*—not just because of where they are performed or exhibited but because they are resources that some people use and relate to in their everyday lives. Although culture includes the formally approved pieces that are a part of the established order of that which is deemed to be tasteful, culture is not just "high art"; it also includes the pop and the transient. In fact, everything that is constructed according to some underlying rule, even if the rule is one of randomness, is a part of our culture, no matter if it is gangsta rap, Shakespearean sonnets, or the ancient Chinese book/oracle, *I Ching.*

Of course, art objects, paintings, popular music, and poetry are not the only things that are constituted according to rules—so are societies and organizations. All societies have rules about who can do what to whom and under what circumstances, or what you can and cannot wear on particular occasions, or what people (particularly, people of what age and gender) are allowed access to specific places and under what circumstances. Perhaps most obviously, given that we all need to eat to live, it is interesting to consider the rules that surround food. All societies have rules about what is edible and what is not. How do *you* feel about chicken's feet, a delicacy in Hong Kong; Witchety grubs, an Australian Koori treat; dog, a perennial favorite in Korea and some other parts of Asia; rats, sometimes on the menu in China; or cow's intestines (tripe) popular both in the North of England and in many other parts of Europe?

Of course, culture also includes lacrosse, surfing, soccer, drag racing, crocheting, chess, cookery, dating and mating rituals, ways of giving birth and dying, and just about anything that is patterned in any way. Matters of religious or other structured belief systems are organizationally reinforced and sometimes policed. Many rules are organizationally located; each major sport has an organized body that is the custodian of its rules and appeals. The Royal and Ancient Golf Club of St. Andrews, custodian of the game of golf, is probably the best known of these internationally.

Organizations such as The Royal and Ancient Golf Club of St. Andrews have elaborate rules about membership and members' duties, as well as the rules of the game that they enforce. Sometimes the rules of a sport may be much more informal, as is the case with skateboarders. But just because there is no formal body does not mean that skaters do not have a fairly organized sense about the rules of the game they play. The two parts of Image 8.2 show an informal skate competition in Paris that was set up on a bridge closed to traffic. The apparatus was composed of found materials (notably street barriers, which the participants picked up on the street as they sped to the venue on their skates). All the participants understand the rules: The aim, as can be seen

Image 8.1   *Golf at St. Andrews*

from the pictures, was to clear an obstacle set as high as possible, as stylishly as possible.

Sports make the metaphor of rules clear. All organizations have rules—and not just the ones that are formally committed to paper or proclaimed by officials in public. The culture of an organization consists of many small acts of obedience and transgression that informally define the myriad rules that constitute behavior in and of the organization. At issue in discussions of organization culture is the extent to which these rules form patterns that are coherent and integrated, conflicting and cloven, or fragmented and inchoate.

CENTRAL APPROACHES AND MAIN THEORIES

The concept of culture(s)

Culture is a concept with its own complex history that stretches back long before organization theorists began to study it. For instance, if you look at Image 8.3, some of you who have visited the Tower of London may recognize it as Traitor's Gate—the place where traitors, having been transported by

Image 8.2   *Skaters*

Image 8.2 (Continued)

Image 8.3   *Traitor's Gate*

barge up the River Thames, entered the tower to await their execution (or, if they were lucky, imprisonment). Traitor's Gate stands as a stark reminder of what the consequences of breaking the organizational culture rules might be in an organization ruled by an absolute authority, such as the Tudor Monarchy of Henry VIII. For different reasons of cultural offense, many of the king's courtiers and two of his wives—Anne Boleyn and Catherine Howard—saw that gate close behind them. Few organizations today have this power of absolute authority (although occasionally you might read about CEOs who imagine that their organizations' cultures were constructed as if they were such absolute rulers). Modern CEOs cannot be absolutist rulers because they do not have the powers of an absolutist monarch. Nonetheless, their organizations are just as full of complex culture as any Tudor court.

Although organization theorists were relative latecomers to the consideration of culture, they discovered it quite early in the development of the field. Parker (2000b: 128) notes perceptively that F. W. Taylor sought to create a single utilitarian culture to minimize employee resistance and to maximize productivity—and, of course, to increase profits. However, Taylor (1911) did not have an explicit analytical focus on culture. The earliest that culture was specifically studied was when Roethlisberger and Dickson (1939) realized that the most significant variables governing the output at the Hawthorne plant appeared to be not physical but social (see also pp. 25–28). As Mouzelis (1967: 99) pointed out, such factors defined the "culture of the group."

Since the late 1940s, managers have had available the use of various types of expert knowledge (psycho-technological and managerial) to manage culture by translating comprehensible prescriptions into regular actions (Kono and Clegg 1998; Mayo 1946). Increasingly, managers sought to regulate workers by attending to their thoughts and emotions (Albrow 1997) as well as by securing compliance through shaping workers' attitudes and sentiments (Senge 1990). Take, for instance, the personnel counseling program of human relations (see Baritz 1960 and Friedman 1955). Here, organization culture was conceptualized in such a way that it should cater to the welfare of subordinates. However, such conceptions differ greatly from the techniques that later promoted the entrepreneurial self in the excellence literature.

Views that link an organization's culture with its performance seek to shape managers' and employees' understandings in a common and coherent direction (Kotter and Heskett 1992). The theoretical assumption that organizations should be conceptualized as having a central objective to which internal action will necessarily be subordinated is called *functionalism* and is rooted in a concern with explanations of social order, consensus, social integration, solidarity, need satisfaction, and the status quo (Burrell and Morgan 1979). The principal orientation of functionalism is to provide rational explanations of the current organization of social affairs. Knowledge should be put to use to provide practical solutions to pressing problems. Functionalism is committed to a philosophy of social engineering as a basis for social change and emphasizes the importance of order, equilibrium, and stability and the ways in which these can be maintained.

The earliest approaches to organizational culture actually used a term from the psychological literature, *organizational climate,* which, as Schein (2002) argues, was a precursor to the concept of organizational culture. As Neal Ashkenasy (2003) demonstrates, these roots are pervasive in discussions of organizational culture. However, as previously noted, the phenomenon of culture predated by many years the emergence of a concept that explicitly addressed it. A number of substantial accounts offer insights into the ways that management and organization theorists have developed the concept of culture (Alvesson 1993a; Parker 2000a; Schein 2002), its fashions (Anthony 1994; Ten Bos 2000), and its treatment in the practitioner and academic arenas (Barley, Meyer, and Gash 1988). The development of the concept by various authors has resulted in considerable debate about what is the essence of culture (Martin and Frost 1996). Although some writers have seen culture as the great unifier in organizations, others have seen it as the great divider.

Levels of culture

Edgar Schein (1997) defines culture as the deep, basic assumptions and beliefs that are shared by organizational members. Culture is not displayed on

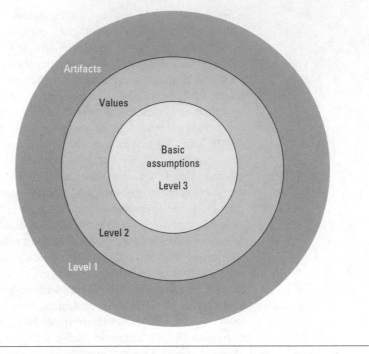

Figure 8.1   *Schein's three levels of culture, represented as a dartboard*

the surface; instead, it is hidden and often unconscious. It represents the taken-for-granted way an organization perceives its environment and itself. To get a better understanding of the different components of culture in organizations, Schein differentiates between three levels of culture.

Level 1 represents artifacts, including visible organizational features such as the physical structure of buildings and their architecture, uniforms, and interior design. This level is easily observable but does not reveal everything about an organization's culture. For instance, the rich and powerful have often used architecture to impress the less fortunate with the magnificence of their wealth. The ways in which these artifacts of power are manifested vary enormously from society to society: see Image 8.4.

Level 2 refers to values. They represent a nonvisible facet of culture that encompasses the norms and beliefs that employees express when they discuss organizational issues. A mission statement or a commitment to equal employment opportunities is part of this level.

The deepest culture—the basic assumptions hidden beneath artifacts and expressed values—is found in level 3. This bull's eye in the dartboard of culture is the most important level. It includes the basic assumptions that shape organizational members' worldviews, beliefs, and norms, which guide their behavior without being explicitly expressed. It is the most influential

Image 8.4   *Artifacts of culture as power*

level because it works surreptitiously and shapes decision-making processes almost invisibly. It is hard to observe and even harder to change. Nonetheless, it is the level that carries the most potential for transformation. (Notice the Freudian influence on these conceptions of culture in terms of unconsciousness and hidden depths (see also pp. 204–208.).

Kent Pearson conducted an illuminating study that showed how culture makes a difference, organizationally, in different ways of using the same setting (Pearson 1982a, 1982b). Kent, a New Zealand sports sociologist, conducted an instructive comparison of two sports, comparing two organizations of young people who used a common set of resources. One sport was surfing, the other surf lifesaving.

Australian surfies (or board riders) and members of the Surf Lifesaving Association of Australia both used the same resources—the surf and the beach—but defined and used these resources in almost diametrically opposed ways and had very different organization cultures. Surfies were long haired, casual, small-group oriented, bohemian, used their boards to go with the flow of the surf, preferred to smoke marijuana for recreation, expressed themselves individualistically, and were hedonistic. Surf lifesavers were short haired, disciplined, organization oriented, more conventional, sought to master the surf by rowing or swimming through it with a belt and reel to perfect rescues, drank beer at their gatherings, were highly organized in a form of quasimilitary drill, and were public spirited.

In the 1980s (when this study was conducted), the surfies and the surf lifesavers often disliked each other intensely and contested each other's use of the beach and the surf. In addition, as young men tend to do, they exhibited their masculinity in rival competitions for young women who also used the beach. (The 1979 novel *Puberty Blues,* by Gabrielle Carey and Kathy Lette, provides a feminist critique of the masculine worldview of surfie culture.) These differences were expressed through cultures that were diametrically opposed. Each culture was strongly integrative, cohesive, and coherent and was expressed in a contested and rival relation to the other culture.

We can better understand the contrast by using the frame of Schein's (2002) three levels of culture. For surfies, the main artifacts were their surfboards and board shorts. In contrast, surf lifesavers' major artifact was their standard uniform of Speedos (a tight-fitting, small bathing suit, usually worn in such a way that the buttocks are unclothed, which allows better adhesion when rowing through the surf in wooden longboats), with small caps tightly fixed to their heads with chin strings. It is a fairly macho look.

Of course, artifacts tell us something about the cultures of the two groups, but not as much as their values and basic assumptions do. Surfies value individualism and hedonism, whereas surf lifesavers value rules and order. However, the biggest difference may be found on the level of their basic assumptions; surfers seek to be at one with nature, whereas surf lifesavers want to master it. These basic assumptions profoundly influence their actions.

Strong cultures?

Tom Peters and Robert Waterman (1982), two consultants from McKinsey & Company (the multinational consulting firm) with links to Stanford's Graduate School of Business, offered an account of culture that was based on an instrumental view of the relation between managerial practice and management knowledge. They promoted the concept that culture is strong and unifying. Few management books have been as popular as Peters and Waterman's *In Search of Excellence*. Published in 1982, it has sold many millions of copies worldwide. Its charm is apparent; it is packed with anecdotes, lively stories, and lists. According to Peters and Waterman, top management's job was to show leadership through culture building by making values clear, transmitting them widely, reinforcing them in practice, and backing them up. Formal policies, informal stories, rituals as well as rules, and constantly practicing what you preach should ensure a strong culture. Effective cultures were also unambiguous, unitary, harmonious, and managerially integrative. On the other hand, pluralistic cultures that accommodated dissent and conflict were regarded as dysfunctional and were a sure sign that the culture was unproductive. Strong leadership that articulated clear values should overcome opposition.

Top managers embraced these arguments, as did many scholars who produced studies on the keys to excellence in organizations (e.g., Deal and Kennedy 1982; Kanter 1984, 1990; Pascale and Athos 1981). They argued that improvements in productivity and quality would be the results when corporate cultures systematically align individuals with formal organizational goals. Culture was understood as the glue that should hold organizational objectives and individual needs together.

The research on corporate cultures used as data stories about top leadership that circulated widely in the organization. These tales captured something special and unique about the organization and often showed the exemplary qualities of the leadership in some way. For instance, when British Airways reviewed its service quality in first-class cabins, the airline held a top executive retreat at which the managers were surprised to find that their comfortable hotel beds had disappeared and had been replaced by aircraft seats! The point was that the executives were being made to experience the results of their past investment decisions. Phenomena such as myths and legends became important objects for research. The culture became identified with everything from common behavioral patterns to espoused new corporate values that senior management wished to inculcate (Schein 2002).

Capturing culture empirically

Some researchers argue that we can measure an organization's culture and its effects on performance (see Gordon and DiTomaso 1992). One prominent researcher along these lines is Ashkenasy (2003), for whom values are the core component of organizational cultures. He says that conceptions of organization culture are more reliable when they can be measured rather than just described and argues that the concept of a value system allows you to do this.

Cultural homogeneity?

The writer best known for having measured organization culture in terms of values studied only one organization—but he studied it in over 40 countries! It is now widely known that the unidentified organization that Hofstede (1980) reported on in his book *Culture's Consequences*: *International Differences in Work-Related Values* was the multinational company IBM. Because the available data on more than 75,000 employees worldwide could be classified in terms of the different national operations of IBM, Hofstede argued that any systematic variation in the patterning of the value systems must arise not from the organizational culture—which he held constant because he studied just one company—but from systematic differences in national cultures that were reflected in the national organization of the firm. Indeed, Hofstede claimed that, through careful analysis of the data, he could identify four universal pattern variables for value systems: the degree of masculinity-femininity of a culture; the degree of power distance in a culture; the degree of uncertainty avoidance in a culture; and the degree of individualism or collectivism in a culture. On this basis, he categorized the cultures that he studied as belonging to a number of distinct taxonomic categories. He arrived at the national patterns by averaging the means of the distribution of the data collected on individuals in terms of the national samples. Consistent patterns were established in terms of national variation—variation according to the means, which were, of course, statistical devices for representing the sum of individual variance. The upshot would be similar to saying that the average Dutch person is taller than the average Chinese person; the statement accepts that the average is a summary device. The average tells you nothing about what any particular Dutch or Chinese person's height may be any more than it informs you about the values he or she holds. An average of values, although it is economical, is about as meaningful as an average of height.

To accept the Hofstede position on the reality of value systems requires some heroic assumptions, many of which are also implicit in organization studies that seek to measure values within the organization rather than the nation. First, it assumes the cultural homogeneity of nations—that lines on a map inscribe a unitary, patterned, and consistent common culture. In the vast majority of cases in the contemporary world, this is hardly feasible. Not all nations are as polyglot as Australia, a multicultural country of mass immigration from almost everywhere in the world, but there are few singularly ethnically, linguistically, and culturally homogeneous countries among the major nations in the world today. Indeed, one of the countries that Hofstede (1980) treated as a unitary cultural space in his study, Yugoslavia, no longer exists as such—precisely because it was not a unitary cultural space in the first place, as indicated by the horrors of the "ethnic cleansing" and associated mass murders in the early 1990s that were its major contribution to world affairs. How realistic would it be to assume cultural homogeneity in the face of so much counterfactual evidence? Indeed, in many countries, modern identities are much more likely to be plural than singular, as shown in hybrid, hyphenated identities such as Anglo-Indian, Viet-Australian, and so on. Thus, if a nation cannot be considered to be unitary, how can the organization that draws on its citizens be called homogeneous? Won't the diversity that the organization's members display in their everyday life be reflected as diversity in the organization as well?

You could argue that it is precisely because organizations are able to pick and choose who joins them—through human resource management practices, for example—that they may be said to have cultures. In other words, they select people to fit the culture. Contrary to this viewpoint, however, many organizations have been riven by bitter internal conflicts, even when professionally managed, which make the idea of their having only one culture seem questionable. So, to counter the view that organizations *have a* culture, is the perspective that organizations *are* cultures (Smircich 2002). Another possibility is that organizations might *have cultures* and that the plurality, or degree of integration of these cultures, might be measurable. For instance, Kono and Clegg (1998) discuss Japanese organizations as being more-or-less stagnant or vitalized cultures in which the assumption is made that cultures will be characterized by different patterns of distribution of data on values, decision making, and behavior.

Various studies demonstrate that organizations are often unstable and characterized by conflict (Calás and McGuire 1990; Gregory 1983; Martin 1992; Meyerson 1991; Riley 1983). Organizations may have members who share strong values about basic beliefs with some, but not all, of the other members of the organization. There will be cliques and cabals, relatively separate lunch networks, and distinct coffee circles. When these groups are sufficiently clearly articulated in terms of cultures, we refer to them as *subcultures,* which are occupational and professional groups that reflect different interests, tastes, and habits; such subcultures develop alongside whatever may be the formally acknowledged organizational culture (Gagliardi 1990). Subcultures coexist with other cultures and can become dominant if they can unify adherents through the use of resources, symbols, and other forms of meaning (Clarke, Hall, Jefferson, and Roberts 1987). If a subculture reflects a cohesive group and defends plausible ideas, it may become dominant and legitimate (Gagliardi 1990). If it challenges legitimate values, it becomes a *counterculture.* Countercultures engage in oppositional political activities (De Certeau 1988; Scott 1990).

Martin's (1992) view is that cultures are always simultaneously somewhat integrated, somewhat differentiated, and somewhat fragmented. An organizational culture might be *integrated* when it reflects a wide consensus, *differentiated* when it is confined to separate subcultures, or *fragmented* when there is little consensus and the situation is essentially ambiguous. Although Martin suggests that these conditions can be found simultaneously at *a given time,* they also provide a framework for depicting changes in organizational culture *over time,* such as we saw in Gouldner's (1954) study of a gypsum plant (see also pp. 89–91). We could easily describe the study's events in terms of a shift from an integrated culture of community to one that became differentiated and then fragmented by the unexpected strike action.

From any perspective that sees organization culture as more akin to fluid processes than stable value systems, measuring culture would be meaningless. We can understand its fluent and changing nature better through ethnographic case studies. Chan (2003: 313) argues that the "treatment of culture as a fixed, unitary, bounded entity has to give way to a sense of fluidity and permeability." He suggests that earlier studies of organizations as essentially "negotiated orders" (Strauss, Schatzman, Ehrlich, Bucher, and Sabshin 1963) show the way research should be done. Rather than seeing the organization as a fixed pattern, we should instead look at the ways that the members of the organization use its resources (including conceptions of its values and culture) constantly to negotiate the sense of what it is that they are doing in and as an organization. Culture thus becomes an emergent property of the ceaseless round of negotiation, whose stability or fluidity cannot be settled a priori but has to be looked at as an empirical matter. In this view, the members of the organization create culture from the mundane, everyday aspects of their work and often use the managerially approved dominant culture as a resource in doing so, but not always in ways that would be approved within its rhetoric (Linstead and Grafton-Small 2002).

CRITICAL ISSUES: UNPICKING STRONG CULTURES

For *anthropologists* (people who are trained to study cultures), the enthusiasm for unitary cultures as a source of excellence in organizations might have been surprising. Usually, it is societies whose belief systems are in trouble that seek to reemphasize symbols and rituals to stress that there are unitary beliefs (Alvesson and Berg 1992). In doing so, their elites are making a conscious effort to impose value consensus. An example from twentieth–century history is the post–Prague Spring Soviet-backed Husak regime in Czechoslovakia (as it then existed), which was imposed by Soviet tanks in 1968 along with martial law and the fall of the Dubcek government. The new policy of the Husak government was actually termed "normalization"!

Highly developed value integration may be seen as a way of emphasizing underlying basic assumptions—especially when they are under threat. Anthropologically oriented organization researchers are attuned to the politics of symbolic action (Smircich 2002). Sometimes, from this perspective, one implication is that people might, on occasion, mean more than they say. It would not be surprising if this were the case; the world of organizations usually includes different types of actors, opinions, and conceptions of culture that quite often come into conflict with each other. Organizations are arenas within which many things might happen that put a big smile on top management's faces, but there is also much going on that will just as surely wipe them off.

From this perspective, organizations with friendly public images are revealed to have elaborate facades. For example, Van Maanen (1991) revealed Disneyland at that time was not the fun place its marketing promoted; instead, it was an environment with many stressed-out workers, often-obnoxious customers, and generally hassled supervisors, all seeking an advantage over others, and using organization resources to do so. Despite this reality, in the "smile factory" (as Van Maanen calls it), a strong corporate culture sought to make sure that every employee behaved according to Disney's philosophy. Uniforms, education through the University of Disneyland, and an employee handbook embodied this spirit. However, the stressed-out staff found its own way of dealing with the masses of visitors. For especially nasty customers, employees developed informal mechanisms to discipline them. For instance, the "seatbelt squeeze" on amusement rides was but a "small token of appreciation given to a deviant customer consisting of the rapid cinching-up of a required seatbelt such that the passenger is doubled-over at the point of departure and left gasping for the duration of the trip" (Van Maanen 1991: 71). Or bothersome pairs could be separated into different units so that they had to enjoy a ride without each other (the so-called "break-up-the-party" gambit; Van Maanen 1991: 72). These and many other unofficial and informal rules and practices were learned and developed on-the-job and formed a part of the culture of Disneyland. Probably not quite what Walt had in mind, though! (For more on Walt Disney's personality, see Boje 2002.)

According to researchers who are more critical of formal organization culture, top-management views of culture on their own are not important because culture is far more than what they think it is. Culture is not just the formally approved ways of doing things; it is also the sly games, informal rules, and deviant subcultures of lower-level employees against supervisors and supervisors against lower-level employees, women against men and men against women, and creative against management types as well as management types against creatives (Burawoy 1979; Rosen 2002; Young 1989).

Like prisms, organizations have many facets that are seen and refracted through different perspectives. Rather like a kaleidoscope, what you see is patterned in different ways. Strong-culture researchers hold the kaleidoscope fixed firmly in a managerial view. In doing this, they distort the complex nature of reality by simplifying it. Their interest is in an organization's top managers, not the gofers, wage slaves, and drones. Hence, rather than report anthropologically on all of the complex realities, these researchers concentrate only on top managers' accounts of their leadership, judgment, and values.

Such researchers, including Peters and Waterman, have a nice story to tell: Superior performance is the outcome of excellent culture. Subsequent researchers supported (Denison 1990) this idea. However, as critics are not too unkind to point out, many of the so-called excellent companies had in fact become far less successful within eighteen months of *In Search of Excellence* (Peters and Waterman 1982) being published. The change in their circumstances did not slow the rollout of the rhetoric of excellence in management-speak, however. It proliferated rapidly. Soon, nearly every manager and wannabe manager could be heard talking about how important searching for excellence was, and many management consultants were only too happy to help design a culture to make this happen.

Integration and differentiation perspectives

Not everyone in organizations or in the management and organization literature was entirely happy with this enthusiasm for strong cultures. Organizationally, if, for whatever reasons, you felt unable to bond with the cultural values being stressed, you were likely to feel some degree of unease. For instance, many women in organizations felt excluded from strong cultures that were implicitly masculinist. If work was to become even more of a boy's club as a result of it having a strong culture, these women were not going to be happy with this outcome. Linda Smircich and Joanne Martin, both major American feminist organization theorists, know a thing or two about dominant (masculine) cultures—and about how to resist them. And what they saw in the strong culture literature raised their feminist hackles; they thought that it seemed to privilege an exclusive club to which leaders could aspire—but the implicit message was that they could succeed only if they were male. Knowing what it was like to be a female in a world dominated by men, they tried to create a theoretical space within which to make sense of why resistance to dominant masculine culture projects might occur—and not just as a result of poor socialization. They argued that if resistance was an attribute of insufficient socialization, the culture literature was ideological in the extreme. If you opposed the dominant culture, you were automatically a deviant and needed more socialization and training. There was no space from which it might be legitimate and justified to resist. It sounded like Mayo for moderns!

Smircich (2002) began with methodological criticisms. She was particularly critical of the smash-and-grab approach to research of the functionalist accounts of culture. Its data was often based on survey findings, with little deep knowledge gained from ethnography and the use of anthropological methods (for example, living in and mingling intimately with the community being researched). One consequence was that the studies of excellence often ended up being panegyrics to the espoused values of the top management rather than a study of the values actually in practice. Thus, these excellent

> **Many women in organizations felt excluded from strong cultures that were implicitly masculinist.**

cultures were more often than not managerial wishes, the fulfillment of which was empirically questionable because the ethnographically rich data that might address this issue had often not been collected.

Martin (1992) became particularly concerned with the lack of concordance between researchers from two different perspectives using different methodologies. In the perspective that she classified as "integration research," the a priori assumptions were that culture was the vehicle of integration for organizations; consequently, that was what was researched. In the perspective that she called "differentiation research," the assumption was that more than one culture was more likely to be the norm; thus, researchers started with a predisposition to see plural cultures rooted in different experiences within organizations. The integration researchers were not the only practitioners of smash-and-grab and quick-and-cheap survey methods; some of the ethnographers were integration researchers (Barley 1986). The research field became quite contested as accusations flew in the publications and lecture halls. Integration theorists, it was said, practiced tautology. They defined *culture* as a phenomenon that was consistent and clear, including in their evidence only manifestations of it that accorded with this definition, thus excising all the plural and nonintegrative aspects of the culture. They did so through defining *culture* in strong culture terms as

> organization wide agreement with values espoused by top management, but their sampling procedures were seldom either random or stratified to include all levels of the hierarchy. Instead, integration studies tended to study those cultural members who were particularly articulate informants, or those who were most likely to have views similar to top managers . . . . Unfortunately integration studies seldom hesitated to generalize from such limited subject samples to the culture of the whole organization. (Martin and Frost 1996: 608)

When decisions were not as overtly biased as the quote suggests, they were often made to exclude any data that seemed to suggest a weak or fragmented culture as an inconsequential margin to the central cultural values. Martin and Frost (1996: 608) are scathing:

> Not surprisingly, the portraits of culture that emerged from these research designs were entirely consistent with integrationist theoretical preconceptions: each "strong" culture was a monolith where every manifestation reinforced the values of top management, employees complied with managerial directives, and preferences were assumed to share these values, and there was, apparently, only one interpretation of the meaning of events shared by all. These studies were designed so integration research would find what it was looking for.

 Of course, much the same could be said—and was—about the differentiation perspective. The integration theorists argued that if you went looking long enough and hard enough for subcultures, you would be sure to find them. This was especially the case, the critics continued, if the research consisted of "focused, non-random samples of lower level employees" and if the process involved "ignoring (or not searching for) evidence of values shared on an organization-wide basis"

(Martin and Frost 1996: 608). They went on to say that, if properly conducted with appropriate skill, even ethnographers could come to see that deep fundamental values might be shared by a majority of organization members (Schein 1997).

Predictably, with such disagreement between researchers surfacing in the public arena, the idea that culture might be a quick fix for corporate ills became harder to market. The committed ethnographic researchers were never very interested in the market, anyway. They saw themselves as more akin to anthropologists who practiced long-term participant observation and brought tales from the field to the public arena (Van Maanen 1988).

Although functionalists argued for the values of strong cultures, their critics saw those dominant cultures as unitarist because they privileged the views of managers of the organization to subordinate and incorporate other members (Willmott 2002). Without such privileging, one would instead see that these other members, if not totally disorganized by the ruling culture, would usually share a subculture or even subcultures. Subcultures cleave on the status attributes of the workforce (such as ethnicity, gender, class and skill) or on spatial markers (such as where they work and the conditions under which that work is performed). Sometimes, there may be a well-organized counterculture centered on the union and reinforced by a strong sense of community among coworkers. Often this is the case among those who do blue-collar, dangerous work, including dockers, miners, and construction workers.

One of the strongest critiques of the dominant orthodoxy that strong cultures are good cultures came in a scathing article by a British academic, Hugh Willmott (2002), who drew inspiration from George Orwell's (1949) most celebrated book, *1984,* to make sense of corporate culture programs. In the book, Orwell imagined Oceania, a totalitarian state set in the future. It maintained coercive control through, among other things, making the official parlance of Oceania *Newspeak,* a perversion of the English language. Although Newspeak is based on English, all contentious political words are removed, and, more generally, the vocabulary is much reduced. The purpose of the language is to limit that which can be said and thought. The ultimate aim of Newspeak is to produce a mode of communication that requires no thought on the part of the speakers. This ideal is achieved, in part, through the use of abbreviations that serve to conceal the true meanings of terms. For instance, the Oceania Ministry of Law and Order, where torture occurs, is known as Miniluv. One of the important features of Newspeak is *doublethink,* which refers to the capacity to hold mutually contradictory views at the same time.

So what does the dystopian fiction of a writer who has been dead for half a century have to do with corporate culture? Willmott (2002) argues that Orwell can help us understand what he characterizes as the dark side of the corporate culture project. Willmott contends that corporate culture is best regarded as a form of Newspeak in which culture is represented as that which can make us free—it is a gift to be bestowed on organization members through cultural design. Moreover, he regards the language of corporate culture programs as a means of controlling the choices and identities open to employees. He continues the

Orwellian analogy by suggesting that the world of corporate culture is plagued by doublethink, in which the values of community and autonomy can be simultaneously celebrated and contradicted. Like the Party member in Orwell's Oceania, the well-socialized, self-disciplined corporate employee is "expected to have no private emotions and no respite from enthusiasm. . . . The speculations which might possibly induce a sceptical or rebellious attitude are killed in advance by his early-acquired inner discipline" (Orwell 1949: 220). Under the guise of giving more autonomy to the individual than would be the case in organizations governed by bureaucratic rules, corporate culture threatens to promote a new, hypermodern neoauthoritarianism. Willmott finds this potentially more insidious and sinister than bureaucracy was, with its clear formal rules and limits, because it leaves no space for an autonomous professional ethos. Everything must be subordinated to the greater good of the corporate culture. Only within its frame can organization members find freedom and value.

Fragmentation perspective

Chan (2003) suggests that culture should be thought of as a verb rather than a noun, as a way of accounting for what has been done in and around an organization, as a way of making sense of what has been experienced. Thought of in this way, culture is far harder to engineer than the strong-culture perspective suggests. Rather than being just a matter of replacing one set of normative assumptions with an alternate set, producing yet another mission and vision statement, culture consists of loosely negotiated, tacit ways of making sense that are embedded in specific situations in the organization rather than an all-enveloping structure that somehow contains all who are members. Being a member doesn't necessarily mean accepting the formal rhetoric of an organization. Taking a salary doesn't mean a suspension of judgment or critical faculties. Possessing a business card doesn't mean subscribing to everything done in the organization's name. Moreover, empirical coherence need not be reflected in the views of those who hold these positions and cards, as empirical case studies have shown (Knights and Murray 1994). Every person regulates his or her own position within the cultural spaces created for and around him or her. Because culture is overwhelmingly situational, the culture is usually quite fragmentary, forming around certain emergent issues and then dissolving. Often, managers take different sides on these issues and are thus divided among themselves.

These views are known as the *fragmentation perspective*. This approach shares very little with the normative integration theorists, who argue for the benefits of a strong culture, and the differentiation proponents, who say that a strong culture equals a dominant culture, and a dominant culture is one that subordinates differentiated subcultures. The fragmentation perspective is

> **Being a member doesn't necessarily mean accepting the formal rhetoric of an organization.**

suspicious of the desire to make culture clear. According to the fragmentation view, culture is neither clearly consistent nor clearly contested. The picture is more likely to be one that represents contradictory and confusing cultures battling for the soul of the organization as well as those of its employees. Individuals are more likely to exist in a state of competing cultural interpellations, where they are constantly under competing pressures to identify themselves and their organization with rival conceptions of an appropriate cultural

Culture does not make us free, only confused.

identity. In such a situation, "consensus is transient and issue specific, producing short-lived affinities among individuals that are quickly replaced by a different pattern of affinities, as a different issue draws the attention of cultural members" (Martin and Frost 1996: 609, citing the work of Kreiner and Schultz 1993 on emergent culture in R&D networks as an example). Culture does not make us free, only confused. Culture is not about a clear, sharp image of corporate and individual identity; it is about ambiguity. Confusion is normal; asking questions about clarity is not. Culture is an artifact of the methods used to investigate it and the assumptions that make such an investigation possible. Realistically, if you can't define culture clearly, and the people whose culture it is supposed to be don't know what it is, it can hardly be the cure for corporate ills.

Fragmentation studies report a world in which ambiguity provides a protective shroud from the meaninglessness of everyday organizational life. Meyerson (1991) discovered in her study of social workers that "ambiguity pervaded an occupation whose practitioners had to operate in a world where the objectives of social work were unclear, the means to these goals were not specified, and sometimes it wasn't even clear when an intervention had been successful or even what success in this context might have meant" (Martin and Frost 1996: 609). Cynics might say that this is not surprising, given that the example is social work, an area that is usually underresourced and that is one in which people have to deal with the many complex problems of often severely dysfunctional clients. However, there are studies of other cultural contexts, which are certainly not resource poor and that have a premium on clarity and detail, in which fragmentary cultures were normal. For example, Weick (1991) discusses a case involving air-traffic controllers in which normal fragmentation produced tragic effects. They were working at Tenerife airport one foggy night as two jumbo jets maneuvered in their air space. Pilots, controllers, and cockpit crews struggled to communicate but failed. The barriers of status and task assignment, not to mention the more general problems of languages spoken, all conspired to produce an organization culture that was mired in fatal ambiguity. The two jets collided, and hundreds of lives were lost in the atmospheric and the cultural fog.

Strong cultures, homogeneity, and disaster

When a foggy day met a fragmented culture in the airspace of the Tenerife airport, a disastrous impact occurred. But it would be mistaken to assume that a strong, unambiguous culture is necessarily a safe place, with no disaster lurking. The idea of a strong, coherent culture can be potentially just as dangerous and unethical in organizational practice. As research on the demise of England's Barings Bank has shown (Stein 2000), too much consensus and homogeneity in an organization can easily lead to blind spots that can be fatal. Barings was the world's first merchant bank, but its proud tradition ceased suddenly in 1995 when it collapsed because of the activities of a 27-year-old trader in its Singapore office, Nick Leeson. Of course, one could blame Leeson personally for the disaster because he was acting unethically (trading speculatively without telling anyone what he was doing, and covering up his tracks as he did so), but this would not explain why Barings collapsed. Rather, it collapsed because he was able to do these things due to a lethal mix of elements in its organization culture. As Stein (2000: 1227) argues, "Barings' problem (is located) squarely with the institution rather than with Leeson (. . .) the conditions for Leeson's fraud were set in place substantially prior to his arrival at Barings." They were deeply embedded in the culture of Barings as an organization.

Barings was a very conservative and established bank that recruited its board members from the English aristocracy. Indeed, previous generations of Barings had been governor general in colonial Egypt and Kenya. It was the Bank of the British Monarch's Queen Mother. In the 1980s, the British government deregulated the banking industry. One consequence was that banks faced more challenges in a more turbulent environment than they had previously. Barings decided to employ a risk taker who was expected to make sense of the new situation: Nick Leeson. Nick was known as a maverick, someone who told stories about himself that were not always exactly true, as well as someone who liked to drink and gamble. At its worst, these predilections occasionally resulted in unseemly behavior; as Stein (2000: 1219) writes, "in a drunken stupor one night, Leeson had exposed his buttocks to several local women in a bar." In short, he was not the publicly acceptable face that young men drawn from the English aristocracy would have preferred to present (not that male members of the English aristocracy have not been known to appreciate, on occasion, the fine sight of a young man's naked and quivering buttocks!). But the bank's management agreed that they needed someone different than they were used to hiring if they were to master the challenges ahead. Barings promoted Leeson, and soon he was trading in Singapore with the bank's money—and lost it. Normally, there are many control mechanisms in place that should ensure that an individual employee can't lose all the companies' assets by gambling on the stock market (in the case of Barings, it was 860 million UK pounds!). But Barings management ignored all the signs that Leeson was losing the bank's money. The organization culture at Barings was strongly homogeneous among the gentlemen of the top-management team, which made them blind to seeing what was really going on in the accounts that Leeson managed for Barings. Moreover, their bonuses depended on his gains as he reported them. They had hired an entrepreneurial type of person, and they left him to do the job, with very hands-off control because, in the past, class and breeding had made strong discipline by management unnecessary. As the Bank of

England subsequently reported, there was no clear explanation as to why Barings management did not question why the bank should be apparently lending more than 300 million pounds to its clients to trade on the Singapore Exchange when it had only collected 31 million pounds from clients for those trades. Barings had a strong culture—one in which no one dared to point out that all was not quite what it might seem—which had disastrous outcomes. Leeson described the culture as one in which employees never asked questions because they did not want to appear ignorant. The dominant unofficial culture was one of no questions, despite whatever may have been maintained officially.

Officially unofficial strong cultures

As the case of Barings shows, we should not assume that a dominant culture is always the official one. In some organizations, such as various police services or firms such as Enron and WorldCom, a dominant culture of corruption has become widespread. Although such cultures are not "officially official," their proliferation suggests that formal tolerance enabled them to flourish and to become established as the local norm. To illustrate this point, we refer to a study of hospitals and the way that they dealt with terminally ill patients; it shows that there was a well-established "officially unofficial" culture that shaped the organization's treatment of those of its "members"—i.e., patients— who departed the organization by dying.

David Sudnow's (1967) *Passing On: The Sociology of Dying* compares the culture of two hospitals, one private and one public. One characteristic of both was that most deaths in the hospitals seemed to occur in the mornings. Although Sudnow initially could not figure out why this was the case, he eventually discovered that when death occurred on the night shift, the staff would try not to recognize the fact because of the attendant duties associated with it. Dead bodies are a bureaucratic nightmare; heaps of paperwork and a lot of physical and cleanup work are associated with them. Thus, the shift culture regarded dead bodies as a nuisance best left for the new morning shift to attend to. Hence, deaths peak in the morning, when the new shift clocks on and has to register, statistically, the fact of death.

THE FINE PRINT: REFLECTING ON CULTURE'S PRACTICE

A short genealogy of culture

The idea that organizations with good leaders will have a strong culture is a view that is at least 2,000 years old. In the Bible, you can find accounts of the "good shepherd," whose goodness resided in tending his flock. For many management writers, leaders should be good shepherds. In this view, managers are perceived to use culture to secure consent to their projects.

Actually, given its etymology, the pastoral conception of culture and its subsequent articulation as a political concept is not as strange as it might initially appear. The influential cultural theorist Raymond Williams (1976) constructed an etymology of culture that examined divergent contexts and meanings in the applications of the concept, and it is interesting to follow the traces of the concept in his account. According to Williams, the term *culture* emerged in the sixteenth century in English (and other European languages) as a process that denoted the tending or rearing of crops and animals. The word developed by the eighteenth century into an independent noun referring to a general process or to the *product* of such a process. The sense of tending of the natural growth of crops and plants was extended to the sense of a process of human development. As the term evolved further, it began to accentuate more directly the sense of human tending and its specificities. Thompson (1990) points out that in both English and French, the uses of the words *culture* and *civilization* overlapped; *culture* began to be used as a synonym for the word *civilization,* which was derived from the Latin word *civilis,* meaning of or belonging to citizens. The term *civilization* was used in English and in French in the late eighteenth century to describe a movement toward refinement and away from barbarism and savagery (see Elias 1994; Van Iterson, Mastenbroek, Newton, and Smith 2002). Both culture and civilization were used increasingly to describe a general and progressive process of human development in the mind, faculties, manner, and comportment through education and training; the process led to people becoming *cultivated* or *civilized* (Thompson 1990: 124). At the same time, the word *culture* was used to refer to that which gave the civilized and cultivated a superior form of resource usually available to the more privileged members of society; today, we might refer to this aspect as *high culture*. In addition to Thompson (1990), Bauman (1987) also pointed out culture's connection with a public discourse of social control that emerged in the late eighteenth century. Thus, the contemporary usage of organization culture as a term denoting the processes whereby the politics of consent are accomplished in organizations is one that is well founded. It simply represents the extension of a political project from the organization of the state to organizations in the market.

Pastoral culture

Bauman's (1987, 1992) idea of culture echoes the shepherding notion of pastoral power, from the Christian tradition, focused on efficient management. Under Christian tradition, people were taught to submit themselves to a whole gamut of apparatuses of self-examination and ascetic renunciation of the world, as well as practices of confession, guidance, and observance. McNay (1994) points out that, under Christianity, the relation between the shepherd (or the king or the leader) and his flock underwent a subtle transformation from a relation of obedience to one of dependence. Culture was thought of as being similar to a farmer cultivating his plants "to ennoble the seeds and enrich the crop" (Bauman 1992: 8). Culture as human tending conjures up the metaphor of a gardener weeding out unruly crops or the gamekeeper ferreting out rats and rabbits from burrows to eliminate those rivals who might also reap or harvest the game. The good gamekeeper, farmer, and shepherd were closely related in that all were good managers. Weber (1976) recognized this explicitly at the outset of modern organization studies when he described the battle that the Protestant ethic fought with other rationalities to replace the rhythms of a rural and Catholic past of holy days, saint's days, name days, with a more disciplined regime of a rational management of time (see also Hassard 1996; Thompson 1968). The Protestant ethic overlaid and rationalized previous traditions of the local past that were less selective in their reproduction (see also p. 9).

In contemporary multicultural and secular societies, as religious norms decline in importance, such pastoral management plays a diminished role. Yet, the tending of the organizational crop of current and prospective employees and their cultivation in organizationally approved ways does not disappear. Hence, in the world of public-sector and private-sector organizations, what had previously been the pastoral role increasingly falls to senior managers. You could say that the pastoral role has been secularized. The contemporary manager, rather like a gamekeeper, tends an organizational arena wherein his employees may be vicariously treated as the crop—that which is to be cultivated. Or, if you were a cynic, most of us are like sheep, and there is certainly some suggestion of the tendency to blindly follow in strongly normative views of culture.

Culture's history in practice

In the earliest days of the new factory organizations of the nineteenth century, contemporary observers observed that the "manufacturing population . . . new in its habits of thoughts and action" was "formed by the circumstances of its condition, with little instruction, and less guidance from external sources" (Thompson 1968: 209). Andrew Ure (1835), in one of the earliest systematic texts on management, *The Philosophy of Manufactures,* called for mill owners to organize their "moral machinery" on principles that were as sound as those that organized the mechanical works in their factories. During the nineteenth century, as recorded by Thompson (1968) and Weber (1976), owners and managers sought workers who were instructed and guided spiritually by religious, often Protestant, ethics. Sometimes, as Spybey (1984) recounts, the moral machinery was supported by a social organization of the built environment that facilitated its surveillance, much as the Panopticon provided (see also pp. 43–44). However, by at least the early twentieth century, other forms of instruction were superseding the support of the external moral machinery lodged in Protestantism.

Gutman's (1977) research on the International Harvester Corporation clearly demonstrates this shift. In the first decades of the twentieth century, the philanthropic managers at Harvester were teaching new Polish laborers—Catholic and untutored in English—the rudiments of both English and their organization culture through factory-sponsored language lessons, including the following:

I hear the whistle.
I hear the five-minute whistle.
I must hurry.
It is time to go into the shop.
I take my check from the gate board and hang it on the department board.
I change my clothes and get ready to work.
The starting whistle blows.
I eat my lunch.
It is forbidden to eat until then.
The whistle blows five minutes before starting time.
I get ready to work.
I work until the whistle blows to quit.
I leave my place nice and clean.
I put all my clothes in the locker.
I must go home. (International Harvester Corporation circa 1913)

The lessons taught a language and a culture. It was a culture that stressed timeliness, discipline, and cleanliness, all of which were designed to overcome any tendencies to recalcitrance that Polish peasants in American factories might display in the face of arduous and demanding work. Culture was about turning aliens into Americans. It was a project that was instrumental and hegemonic (which, as a view of how organization culture works, is characteristic of much of the critical literature—for relevant examples, see Ackroyd and Crowdy 1990; Burawoy 1979). Hegemonic projects are clearly evident in the case of the Polish workers, and, from a critical perspective, remain characteristic of contemporary culture projects.

How do the practice and theory of organization culture relate?

The science behind culture and its application

The basic assumptions behind *In Search of Excellence* (Peters and Waterman 1982) and the work it influenced did not emerge in an a priori way from a practitioner agenda separate from and uninfluenced by an academic agenda. The excellence studies shaped the world of practice through involvement of the authors with McKinsey & Company, the multinational consulting firm (Colville, Waterman, and Weick 1999). Peters and Waterman's (1982) work translated ideas from quite subtle and complex organizational theories to apply them to practical exigencies. The origins of these theories were the sensemaking perspective of Karl Weick (1969, 1979, 1995). As Colville, Waterman, and Weick (1999: 135) state, these origins were reflected in *In Search of Excellence* through the insights that "fundamentally . . . meanings matter" and that "mundaneity is more scarce than people realize" (Colville, Waterman, and Weick 1999: 136). *In Search of Excellence* (1982) was not simply a publication "offering advice for addressing pragmatic problems thought to be relevant to managers, consultants, and other individuals who work in or with organizations" (Barley, Meyer, and Gash 1988: 34). Peters and Waterman (1982) produced a work that translated unfashionable and highly abstract organization theory into a form that a wider audience was able to appreciate (Colville, Waterman, and Weick 1999).

Practicing managers need to find solutions to new problems every ten minutes or so (Mintzberg 1973). Not surprisingly, they have little time for other than the most local, contextual, and bounded working knowledge. In such a situation, the excellence studies make perfect sense because they provided generic solutions that seemed to be capable of being applied to many problems that could be now reclassified as culture issues. The great strength of the culture perspective was that it seemed to promise the dissolution of all that friction and resistance that managers know they often produce routinely, as a normal part of their work. Cultural practices enable managing to happen by binding entities together, and sometimes there is friction. Managing creates a nexus of peoples, ideas, materials, and technologies that can act semiautonomously in pursuit of strategies. Culture is the shorthand term that captures the ways in which people are able to make sense of their managing and being managed. Modern managing involves the creative destruction of existing recipes and practices embedded in cultures. Such managing means disorganizing and deconstructing past routines, retaining some while changing others. Culture is always in process, never static.

In Search of Excellence (Peters and Waterman 1982) was a huge commercial success. However, there was considerable skepticism among more theoretical and critical academics as to its truth value. Some judged it as too one-dimensional, too focused on culture as just one aspect of organization life. Others saw it as too focused on the stories of top managers, with some considering it as almost crude propaganda for the managerial elite and their views of the way culture should be. But millions read it. So the important question to ask is not whether the book was true—a correct representation of what organization culture is really like—but, instead, to ask what effect it was having upon management, and management practice, given the book's popularity. For some writers, such as Donaldson (1992) and Hilmer and Donaldson (1996), management is a science, and only knowledge validated by proper scientific method should be taught. If we are to redesign organizations in terms of their cultures, we had better be sure that we were not just responding to a fad. *In Search of Excellence,* with its mixture of exhortation, normative prescription, and organization storytelling, does not measure up to the proper conduct of science. Therefore, Donaldson and others would argue that the major effect of the book would be to mislead managers about culture. Managers would be wrongfully seduced by a simplistic and scientifically inaccurate account of organizations. One could draw parallels between management and medical practice, in each of which there is a strong lobby for evidence-based knowledge. However, some critics argue that too many doctors are dispensing prescriptions based on what they learned in medical school twenty or thirty years ago rather than on the basis of the best science available now. The significant difference between the management and medical situations is that all doctors practicing medicine have to undergo training in a medical school whose curriculum is under a degree of professional control. However, there is no similar universally accepted form of professional regulation of managers. Anyone can be a manager, and no regulatory body controls the qualifications you must have to be a manager. Medicine has a regulatory body, but even so, one cannot assume that doctors will make evidence-based judgments; what chance do we have, then, that managers will make rational, evidence-based decisions? Moreover, there is no body that can strike them off the register of licensed practitioners if, as a result of their reading habits, they apply knowledge gleaned from popular—if misleading and scientifically inappropriate—books to their everyday practice.

The culture of management

Of course, the more often that managers are informed by well-conducted empirical research—not only when it comes to culture, but all areas of management—the less likely they are to make errors of judgment based on matters of misunderstanding or because they do not know the empirical relation between different scientific constructs. But bear in mind the point made by Mintzberg (1973): Managers change tack every ten minutes or so. Managers are more likely to steer with intuitive judgments than scientific ones because managing means doing many things under tight pressure rather than having leisurely opportunities to consult the latest research. Doubtless, it would be a better world if all managers were rationalists that sifted evidence scientifically before they made decisions, but most of what we know about decision making suggests that this is not the case (see also pp. 56–61). In addition, the world of management theory and the world of management practice inhabit different rationalities. In the former are academics seeking to do research that will be published in the most prestigious peer-reviewed journals, and they often work on projects for many years to reach this goal. In the latter dwell the harried ten-minute managers.

What Donaldson (1992) wants managers to do, armed with information from management science, and what managers actually do are significantly different. There is a great deal of anecdotal evidence suggesting that managers—even very important ones—are not necessarily as rational as they might seem to be. Our favorite example is one of the most popular of U.S. presidents, Ronald Reagan. A former actor, Reagan consulted the scripts of films that he knew, such as *Star Wars* (Lucas 1977), when communicating the sense that he made of the world that he sought to manage. Meanwhile, his wife, Nancy, consulted her astrologer. Don't laugh; the predictions of astrologers or *feng shui* practitioners, for example, are at least as important as those of econometricians or management consultants for many significant economic actors in some economies, such as Hong Kong—and are sometimes as effective. Some other managers, trained in business schools, may seek to apply some models that they dimly remember from their MBA, when they were taught that a culture of "excellence" was the way to go. They thus replicate lessons from their youth, repeatedly, even though the truths of that time may have become the errors of today. Still others manage their organization culture by thinking of the most recent columns they read in the press or that last book they bought at the airport on a business trip, or how their mother or father brought them up, or how a winning sports team is managed. Managers in various contexts have different relevancies guiding their culture managing, and not all are guided by management theories.

Sometimes managers and academicians speak the same language and may be said to play coincidental language games; however, more often they do not. One of the rare instances of commonality happened with the excellence studies: There was a high degree of consensual grammar across academic and practitioner concerns for a short period of time. If excellence is useful to managers in managing, perhaps researchers should research how they use it empirically rather than tell them that they are wrong to do so (Astley and Zammuto 1992). Whereas Donaldson (1992) and Beyer (1992) saw the role of organization science as the proper source of management practice, Astley and Zammuto (1992) regarded management practice as an autonomous sphere. If managers think that a unitary culture will be less troublesome and more supportive of their projects, that is what they will apply, as a kind of recipe of knowledge. For a while, *In Search of Excellence* seemed like a good recipe.

The trouble with recipes is that if everybody cooks according to the same script, the lack of variety becomes bland and boring, and there is no innovation in the diet. The lack of innovation applies not only to the competition between organizations but also to organizations in which everyone subscribes to the same culture, enacting the same realities. The more recipes we have to work from, from different approaches, the more skilled we will be in blending experience and ingredients, theory and practice, management and managing. Thus, we would argue for polyphony in preference to strong cultures. We would tell managers that they are better with pluralism, better with dissonance, because it offers more space for innovation. If everyone agrees on the direction being steered and the underlying values, such a situation is foolish if they are wrong and their common agreement does not enable them to see the dangers ahead. The Titanic was not just a ship; it serves as a metaphor for all those who are secure in the belief that they are unsinkable.

Academics and their students should be the skeptics—those who are prepared to suggest that the recipe may not necessarily be all that it is cracked up to be. Sometimes skeptics might suggest alternate recipes, whereas other times they might ask whether you really want to use *that* recipe if you want to achieve *that* outcome. Sometimes, they scoff at the recipe. We think that management academics, at their best, should be like jesters in the feudal court: able to speak out about organizational power without suffering adverse consequences. Some of them are well-paid people, engaged in secure positions, with a privileged access to potentially influential people—their students. As such, they should not be afraid of speaking or writing in ways that represent views that, to paraphrase the economist J. K. Galbraith (1969), challenge the conventional wisdom. Saying what is popular is no guarantee of probity. Like many other management academics, we have seen classes of MBA students seduced and delighted by corporate heroes, only to find those lionized for what they do today sometimes become tomorrow's corporate villains. We should not be afraid to challenge conventional wisdom.

Making up culture

Much contemporary organizational culture discourse represents a desire by management to enlist workers' cooperation, compliance, and commitment to create an esprit de corps with which to limit human recalcitrance at work (Barker 1998). The rhetoric of control, coupled with a new vocabulary of teamwork, quality, flexibility, and learning organizations, constitutes culture management projects that seek to create culture as a mechanism of soft domination (see also pp. 168–172).

The managerially most relevant genre of culture writings increasingly came to focus on the ways in which organization cultures make up or manufacture subjects (Casey 1995; Jacques 1996) with a specificity that benchmarked strategies for cultural change (Du Gay 2000b). At the furthest point, what such thinking about the relation of organization members and organization culture sought to construct were "designer employees" (Casey 1995)—people made up in such a way that they were organizationally most functional. The ultimate designer employee is depicted in a Cathay Pacific recruitment advertisement from 1997. He or she is a specific category of organizational subject imbued with an obvious, natural or acquired demeanor, comportment, and specifications:

> Who am I?
> I travel the world but I'm not a tourist.
> I serve 5-star cuisine but I'm not a chef.
> I walk the aisle but I'm not a fashion model.
> I care for people but I am not a nurse.
> And I do it all from the heart.
> Who am I?
> I am . . .
> . . . a flight attendant with Cathay Pacific and you could be one too! (Cathay Pacific Airways 1997)

Management practitioners seek to use culture and control to frame employee subjectivity. We see this most readily in some post-excellence accounts of quality management, such as the Six-Sigma movement popular in Japan and much of East Asia (Kono and Clegg 2001). Principles such as *seiri* (putting-in-order), *seiton* (arrange properly), *seiketsu* (cleanliness), *seiso* (cleaning), and *shitsuke* (good behavior), seen in many plants of Japanese corporations, seek not only to govern the workplace but also the comportment of employees in the workplace (March 1996). Organizational culture prescribes norm-defined management techniques and habit-inducing routines that culminate in a new consciousness and a new set of beliefs and values that promise a new personhood, a new subjectivity, and even a new embodiment. Think of highly designed conceptions of organization culture that frame what it means to be an organization member, such as those associated with the advertisement for Cathay Pacific that we saw previously. The employee has to work from the heart; this is the course that is designed for her.

For Casey (1995), a designer culture has the following characteristics. First, people in this culture have individual enthusiasm that is manifested in the values of dedication, loyalty, self-sacrifice, and passion. These values translate into the use of the correct language forms, engagement in appropriate interpersonal interactions, and service in long hours at work. Second, there is a strong customer focus, where customers are not just the end users but are also employees and other significant stakeholders. Third, discourse is characterized by a language of team and family. Finally, there is public display of the designer culture. Designer cultures are the outcome of highly developed culture programs conducted under the auspices of an integrative focus. Often, they are associated with management programs such as total quality management (TQM), where the idea that the customer is king is institutionalized as a mantra that "family" of employees, all oriented to customer service, repeat.

Of course, the family metaphor is highly suspect, as we should recognize. Not all families are a haven from a heartless world; some are awful places, with institutionalized abuse, violence, and cruelty that are hard to escape. But an idealized notion of family is the one that is at work in these designer cultures, never the one that takes the sad facts of the family law courts as its empirical compass. Actually, when families are involved, the compass is not empirical; rather, it is deeply normative, deeply patriarchal, and deeply exploitative. Although we cannot choose our families, we can, in principle, choose our organizations. Therefore, we can choose to escape a perverse organization and go elsewhere, but membership in many families does not allow such choice. We suspect that most of you would prefer being exploited by an organization that you can leave easily rather than being held captive in a family (or a family business) that is relatively inescapable. Family bonds are much harder to escape than an employment contract, so here is our advice: Beware of employers claiming family ties or suggesting that the organization in which you work is like a family!

The texts of culture

Culture is less like a family and more like a text, according to some recent accounts (e.g., Chan 2003). What does this mean? Well, at the simplest level, the way we come to know organization cultures is through textual accounts. All of these accounts are either literal texts or discourses that are text-like. These texts might be those of researchers or consultants, or they may be managers' artifacts, such as reports. They could even be the texts of everyday life embedded in the discourses of people at work. These carefully constructed textual artifacts, say some contemporary theorists, mirror the practices that they address. Social realities in organizations are much like texts as well. They consist of actors attached to various accounts and stories with which they seek to enroll and influence others who are trying to influence them at the same time. There are official accounts, but there are also unofficial and downright

All texts of culture suppress, silence, and marginalize some elements of discursive reality.

scurrilous accounts as well, and only a fool would ever believe just the official story. All of these stories circulate as either literal texts or discourses that are text-like. Such stories are all social constructions whose social constructionists are positioned within them—on whom the texts reflect, and who reflect on the texts—in various ways. They are elaborate constructs fabricated out of the bricolage that organizations provide for cultural construction rather more than literal representations of a reality that somehow stands outside and independent of those accounts that talk it into being. Hence, excellence is not so much a phenomenon as a variety of perspectives of seeing and talking in which phenomena of various shades of excellence come into view. Fragmentation in culture is not its clearly defining feature but the hallmark of a certain way of capturing a certain reality. Social realities are always already textual—the words and deeds of the subjects concerned—before they are reworked into the texts of culture. All texts of culture suppress, silence, and marginalize some elements of discursive reality that some other account of the same underlying texts might instead privilege.

The view that organizations should be thought of as complex cultures which can be read in fragments, like incomplete and multifaceted texts, has become widely associated with postmodernist accounts of culture. Rather than join what Martin and Frost (1996) call the culture war games, postmodern theorists seek to demonstrate the strategies that make moves in these games possible and the reflexive edge of thinking about those debates that occupy center stage (Clegg and Kornberger 2003). Typical postmodern accounts include reflexive analysis by analysts of their ordering of the data that constitutes what they take to be the culture, and sometimes it also includes the voices of research subjects, which are usually omitted by others (Jeffcut 1994; Clegg and Hardy 1996). Methodologically, postmodern analysis seeks to deconstruct the assumptions that undergird particular accounts of culture and to show that the account is an artifact of these assumptions (Smircich 2002).

SUMMARY AND REVIEW

The notion that we can make others do what we want them to do by persuading them to want to do it is one that has a long pedigree. It eventually became formalized as an integrative view of organization culture, spurred by the remarkable commercial success of *In Search of Excellence* (Peters and Waterman 1982). But this perspective, even though it is the most popular, is not the only well-developed view of organization culture. Other views see strong cultures as the problem, not the solution, and think of them as dominant rather than empowering. More recently, ethnographers have suggested that it may be quite normal for some organizations to have neither a strong nor a dominant culture. On the contrary, culture may be characterized by fragmentation. Finally, postmodern theorists suggest that all representations of culture are characterized by such a complex intertextuality—the texts of the subjects, the texts of the organization, and the texts of the authors—that they are better thought of as occasions for further analysis than as in any sense a definitive account of what really happens. Managers who are familiar with postmodern thought are at least less likely to be duped into believing that culture is a panacea and might be more sophisticated in the ways that they seek to understand and possibly to use it.

ONE MORE TIME . . .

Getting the story straight

- What are the three levels of culture, and how do they operate?
- What are the management arguments for a strong culture?
- What is the difference between seeing a culture as strong or dominant?
- What are the differences between integration, differentiation, and fragmentation accounts of culture?
- Why might the kaleidoscope of culture shift cyclically?
- What would postmodernists make of organization culture?

Thinking outside the box

- In what ways are contemporary managers the pastoralists of the modern age?
- Should management academics prescribe organizational cultures?
- How useful is the construct of national cultures?
- If culture is a multilevel concept, how easy is it to design?
- Can culture be managed, or is it just something that is there?

ADDITIONAL RESOURCES

1. Probably the best way to come to terms with organization culture is to consult some exemplary studies of it. Peters and Waterman's (1982) *In Search of Excellence: Lessons from America's Best-Run Companies* is the obvious point to start.
2. From a more anthropological and ethnographic perspective, Martin, Knopoff, and Beckman's (1988) study, "An Alternative to Bureaucratic

Impersonality and Emotional Labor: Bounded Emotionality at The Body Shop," is of considerable interest because it demonstrates how the distinctive culture of the The Body Shop, a cosmetics chain, produces highly committed employees. Many of you have probably been in a Body Shop at some time; now you can read all about what it means in terms of an integrationist organization culture. Another easily accessible and good narrative account can be found in John Van Maanen's (1991) *The Smile Factory.* He provides an entertaining account of the corporate culture at Disneyland.

3. An excellent account of organization culture from a detailed ethnographic perspective is Dorinne Kondo's (1990) *Crafting Selves,* which does a really nice job of unpicking the integration illusions often attached to Japanese organization culture.

4. Films often provide a detailed insight into organization cultures. Think of the stress on family values as an integration metaphor in *The Godfather* (Coppola 1972, 1974, 1990) movies or the emphasis on the sources of gender differentiation in the otherwise seemingly integrated "organization man" world of the movie *Down With Love* (Reed 2003) or the *Legally Blonde* movies (Luketic 2001; Herman-Wurmfeld 2003).

5. Interesting examples of strong organizational cultures and their effects are provided by military/war movies, especially *A Few Good Men* (Reiner 1992), starring Jack Nicholson, Demi Moore, and Tom Cruise.

6. Perhaps one of the most interesting movies ever made about organization culture is one based on a true story: *Colonel Redl* (Szabo and Dobai 1985). Colonel Redl is an outsider in the Austro-Hungarian court at the turn of the nineteenth century. He is part Jewish, part Catholic, part Ukrainian, part Hungarian, and gay. Within this sociopolitical context, he does not fit anywhere into the culture. He manages to pass himself off as a member of the dominant culture; however, he ends up being blackmailed and disgraced, and the culture leaves him with only one organizational option, which occupies the closing reels of the film.

7. There is also a film of the Barings Bank disaster caused by Nick Leeson, *Rogue Trader* (Deardon 1999). This makes particularly interesting viewing, if seen in conjunction with the classic business movie *Wall Street* (Stone 1987), as an illustration of an organization culture premised on absolute selfishness and ruthlessness.

In addition to these suggested additional resources, don't forget to look at what is also available on the Web site **www.ckmanagement.net,** including free PDF files of recent papers related to this chapter, which you can download; video interviews with famous academics talking about related themes; as well as many other resources, such as connections to interesting Web sites.

CHAPTER 9

MANAGING COMMUNICATIONS

Identity, Sensemaking, Polyphony

Objectives and learning outcomes

By the end of this chapter, you will be able to

- Explain the different basic concepts of communication

- Understand the importance of communication processes at different levels

- Appreciate the different levels of, and audiences for, communication in organizations

- Discuss the benefits and shortcomings of different communications approaches

Outline of the Chapter

Setting the Scene

Central Approaches and Main Theories

    Theories of Communication

    Levels of Communication

    Organizational Communications and Organizational Design

    Audiences

    Communication as Marketing

    Communication as Branding

Critical Issues: Communication at Work

    Creating the Expressive Organization

    Managing with Words?

    Power and Communication

The Fine Print: Communication as Deconstruction and Translation

Summary and Review

One More Time . . .

Additional Resources

Before you get started . . .

Philosophize, or sing, with the Beatles:
"There's nothing you can do that can't be done.
Nothing you can sing that can't be sung.
Nothing you can say but you can learn how to play the game.
It's easy."

Lennon and McCartney (1967), "All You Need Is Love"

OUTLINE OF THE CHAPTER

Organizations are first and foremost communicating entities; they are composed of people who are able to speak to each other and who want to speak to others. They have products to sell, news to distribute, clients to reach. Plans, change programs, and strategies all need to be communicated. Gossip, PR strategies, informal chats and jokes, as well as marketing campaigns, branding exercises, and Web sites all communicate what an organization is all about. If you have a great business idea and a really smart plan with which to realize it but no one knows, you will not achieve anything. You need to communicate your ideas to others. Some might be closer, such as partners or managers, whereas others may be farther away from you. For instance, you might need a bank to lend you money to kick off your project and help you through cash flow problems, or you might have to convince an investor to finance your project or recruit reliable suppliers to ensure the quality of your product. No wonder that one of the earliest treatises in organizational communication was Dale Carnegie's (1944) multimillion-dollar-selling *How to Win Friends and Influence People*. In short, communication is the circuitry that connects all organizational activities together. It's a game that we all learn to play.

SETTING THE SCENE

Fascination with communication reaches back to the ancient Greek philosophers, who emphasized the importance of rhetoric as a distinct discipline. Aristotle analyzed the role and power of rhetoric in public speeches and events. Following this tradition, it was "studies of propaganda and the flow of information and mass media effects (in the first half of the twentieth century) that would lay the foundations of what is now commonly thought of as the beginning of a communication science" (Bodrow and More 1992: 7). The old study of rhetoric transformed into that of opinion making, propaganda, and the strategic use of information to ensure or create "suitable" common sense.

Whereas these studies understood communication as a direct cause-effect relation, as an act in which information is passed from a sender to a receiver, in the 1950s the emerging discipline of cybernetics changed the field dramatically. The concept of feedback made it clear that communication was not only a one-way effort from a sender to a receiver but a reciprocal undertaking. A sends some information (message) to B, this information is transported through channels (media) that might affect and change it. The message does not simply inform B but might change his or her behavior. B's change in behavior is noticed (received) by A, influencing future action. Put simply, communication is an interactive circle that involves sender and receiver, messages, media, and feedback loops.

Early communications research used cybernetics to focus on the relationship between superior and subordinate in terms of flows of information, their impact on efficiency, and the possible distortion of communication as it moved up and down various channels in the organizational hierarchy (Bodrow and More 1992). Nowadays, communication is understood not just as merely passing on information but as an active way of creating, shaping, and maintaining relationships and enacting shared values, common cultures, agreed goals, and means for their achievement.

Normally, different disciplines within management try to explore the relations between organizations and the diverse groups created, maintained, and nurtured through distinct patterns of communication. These disciplines are marketing (customers), public relations (shareholders and stakeholders such as local communities or environmentalists), and human relations (internal staff). Bypassing this division of labor, we synthesize aspects of each discipline in this chapter to produce insight into the fascinating ways in which organizations communicate.

CENTRAL APPROACHES AND MAIN THEORIES

Theories of communication

Organizations can be seen as multiheaded hydra, the mythical beast of Greek mythology, with many mouths speaking to different internal and external audiences. Of course, with many mouths speaking simultaneously, it is sometimes difficult to gain agreement, understand what is being said, or to remain consistently "on message." Organizations often have these problems. Communication from one organization is contradicted by a message from one of its other organs. Usually, information is communicated in terms of stories—about what the organization has done, is doing, and will do. Of course, the giant hydra does not live in a vacuum, where no other messages circulate. Instead, the environment is full of other stories: someone's got it in for the organization; they're planting stories in the press. Maybe the unions are agitating, or employees are gossiping and the markets chatter about the stories that circulate as the hydra tries to chill out the stories it doesn't like or want.

Different theories try to map this terrain. In *organizational behavior* (OB) theory, the flow of instructions from the top to the bottom of an organization is supposed to ensure that employees do what management decides they should do. Within an OB perspective, there are several different emphases (Frank and Brownell 1989). First, there is a cultural emphasis, in which communicating produces and shares common meanings and interpretations (see also pp. 271–275). Theorists who stress the primacy of human relations emphasize the importance of communication for a climate of openness, trust, commitment, and collaboration (see also pp. 25–28). Those who view organizational behavior from a power perspective understand communication as a medium through which conflicts and struggles will be played out as a means to influence and recruit others to preferred views and interests (Frank and Brownell 1989). They do not assume that your preferences and those of others will necessarily align; in fact, they are more inclined to think they will not (see also pp. 283–284).

A recent school of analysis is referred to as *discourse theory.* From this perspective, discursive communication (including writing, speaking, etc.) informs our actions and decision-making processes. For instance, the discourse of human resource management allows you to ask certain questions, make assumptions about employees, and so on, that are entirely different from those that would be triggered by Frederick Taylor's scientific management (see pp. 18–20; 24–28). Thus, discourse is constitutive of the object one is talking about. Morgan (1985) writes of "images of organizations": If you think of organizations as machines, instead of cultures, or as living organisms, for example, it makes a big difference when you try to understand them and act on that understanding. Thus, discourse significantly shapes and powerfully constructs organizational reality.

Analysis of organization discourse suggests that it is the language employed in the communication occurring in organizations that shapes organizational reality. Gordon Shaw, formerly executive director of planning and international business within 3M, describes the importance of discourse in organization by using the concept of storytelling: "Storytelling is the single most powerful form of human communication. Stories allow a person to feel and see information, as well as factually understand it. The events come alive for the listeners so that they 'see' with you and become physically and mentally involved in the story. Storytelling allows you to create a shared vision of the future. . . . The potential leverage in conceptualising, communicating, and motivating through the use of strategic stories (both inside and outside the enterprise) will define superior management in the future" (Shaw 2000: 194). Corporate stories differentiate a company from its competitors (just as your personal story—your history—distinguishes you from anybody else) and create a shared sense of community and belonging among internal and external audiences. As organizational boundaries blur more and more, external and internal are concepts that lose their descriptive importance. Looking at communication, this becomes obvious; employees also read external messages intended for stakeholders, and internal communication shapes how employees represent the organization to outsiders (Cheney and Christensen 2001). Everything an organization does communicates meaning, both verbally and nonverbally. It is not only glossy brochures that tell you what an organization stands for but also, much more important, the actual behavior of its management and employees.

"One cannot not communicate."

The well-known saying that "one cannot not communicate" means that even noninteraction is a form of interaction. Think of your mom who is angry with you because you did not spend time with her on Mother's Day and therefore will not speak to you. This noncommunication expresses something more than words. Also, think of that text message you never wrote to your boyfriend about something else that you did other than be with him. That can bring you trouble. When the girl you dated the other day does not answer your calls, she is also communicating something. It is almost impossible not to communicate. What is true of people is also true of organizations, which communicate even when they think they don't. And they communicate all the time, sometimes explicitly, sometimes implicitly. Consider the messages communicated by the essentially similar signs shown on the next page. What do they suggest to you about the organization that each represents?

Levels of communication

A conventional way of making sense of communication in organizations is to begin by distinguishing the different levels of communication. Communication can be analyzed by looking at the level of personal and social involvement. Littlejohn (1989) differentiates between four levels of communication, shown in Figure 9.1.

Whereas the first three types of communication are mainly situated in an interpersonal context (face-to-face, with exceptions such as a phone call or e-mail), the fourth type is mediated through channels of mass communication (again, there are exceptions, such as "word of mouth"). Dyadic communication occurs between an employee and manager; small group and team communication happens in meetings, brainstorming sessions, and workshops; and finally, mass communication is at work in marketing and PR campaigns. Wherever it occurs, through whatever modes, organizational communication is a culturally driven process of sensemaking. People communicate to make sense for themselves and others; sometimes they communicate to mislead, other times they do so to be understood clearly. No wonder there is ample opportunity for messages to become mixed and for the wrong audience to receive or interpret an incorrect message (Watzlawick, Beavin, and Jackson 1967).

Image 9.1   *Representing mass transit*

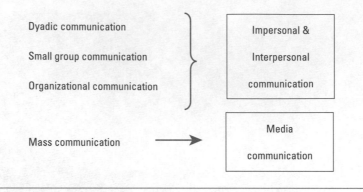

Figure 9.1   *Levels of communication*

Source: After Littlejohn (1989)

Dyadic communication: interpersonal

You communicate interpersonally with others when you talk with them about something or other. When the manager from production and the newcomer in the marketing department go for lunch together, or meet while smoking outside the building, they might build some understanding of each other's task that will be helpful when their company launches its next product. Sure, they may be doing other things, such as flirting, chatting about sport, or fashion, but they are also getting to know each other's work.

Interpersonal communication is based on interdependence, where each person's behavior is a consequence of the other's. Such behavior can be expressed both verbally and nonverbally and have either a formally framed or informal character. A selection interview, for instance, is a formally framed organizational procedure, whereas a chat over lunch may be informal.

Every communication has an informational aspect and simultaneously tells you something about the relationship of the people involved. The manager saying to his subordinate "You have until Monday to write this report" or "Would it be possible to have your report by Monday" communicates almost the same information, but the two sentences define the relationship quite differently. Communication always has a metacommunication aspect, and organization managers should be well aware of this—the way the message is projected and received is as important as the content it contains.

Communication involves multiple meanings and interpretations, distortions and omissions, pathologies and paradoxes. It is not so much the smooth processing of information but rather the complex, interactive emergence of knowledge, meaning, and narratives that drive communication. And in this process, the transitions are neither additive nor linear; what you learn now may change everything you thought you knew before or will know in the future. This theme is often played out in movies such as *Sliding Doors,* a film that

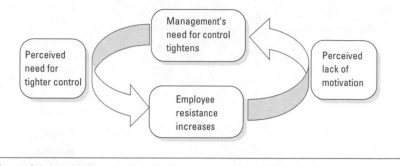

Figure 9.2   *Vicious circles at work*

showed how an accident can change the whole foundation of a relationship and a life.

Communication comprises a series of interactions seen differently by the participants. For instance, a leader with a need for control can generate resistance from employees. If the leader responds with tighter control, this is likely to generate further resistance, which may be interpreted as a lack of motivation. But the increased control produces even more resistance and less motivation! Of course, we encountered this previously in Chapter 5 when we discussed Gouldner's analysis of vicious circles. When a vicious circle is in play, it is quite tricky to resolve. Both parties have good reason for their behavior. They are part of the same interaction, but they differ fundamentally in punctuating what is happening. Whereas the subordinate might argue that she or he is demotivated *because* of a lack of trust, the superior might stress that *due* to a lack of motivation only strictly enforced controls can guarantee a minimum of engagement. Both parties are weaving the same story, participating in the same dialogue, but punctuate it differently and thus create different realities in which causes and effects are reversed. The amplification of misunderstanding escalates in such circumstances. According to Karl Weick (1979), organizations consist of processes that he calls a double interact. Weick defines the double interact as an *act* followed by a *response* that leads to a *reaction* changing the initial act followed by a response, in an ongoing loop.

The earlier example demonstrated the double impact, using the example of a manager who tells his employee that the employee must increase productivity and quality and will be monitored more closely in the future (act). Demotivated through this lack of trust, the employee responds by taking more sick days and taking less care of quality standards (response). The manager understands this behavior as proof of the necessity to tighten the control mechanism and reacts by increasing pressure on the employee (readjusted action), which leads to a drop in employee motivation, resulting in even more sick days and poorer quality! It is important to see that this vicious circle is played out in daily communication. As you already know by now, such fatal dynamics result from the complexity of communication processes (Watzlawick, Beavin, and Jackson

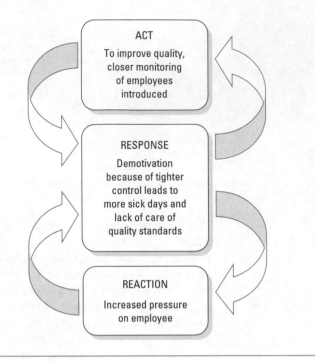

Figure 9.3   *The double interact*

Source: After Karl Weick (1979)

1967). The difference in punctuation, especially, makes such a vicious circle enduring and hard to change.

Dyadic communication: Impersonal

Dyadic communication is usually interpersonal but it need not be. Think of a call center that is, by definition, an interface between customer and organization. When it puts you on hold and bombards you with uninteresting new offers while you are waiting, it is communicating how the organization that you are seeking to gain information from takes care of customer needs. Directing you through a complicated number system to the "right" person, call centers assume that digital communication is the appropriate level of involvement. However, it is not an appropriate frame for establishing a metalevel of communication. Put simply, companies miss out on the chance to express and actively shape their relationship with their clients when they restrict themselves to such forms of communication. Also, the relationship is purely complementary: If the customer has a problem, the call center resolves it as long as it is a standard problem—one for which they have a standard solution. But, as we will see shortly, organizations can learn a great deal from their customers about what they want, how they actually use their products, and what improvements they wish. A more dialogical style would involve customers and create a stronger relationship, triggering interactivity, connectivity, and creativity (see also pp. 388–398).

Small group communication

Group-level dynamics differ from those in dyadic communication. Think of a team with nine members. Communication is not only face-to-face, but roles are established, subgroups formed, and a different dynamic is created. A group is formed by dynamics beyond the influence of its individual members. The culture, as well as the quality of problem solving within a group, depends on the interaction between its members. Group pressures influence their members' ways of thinking as the phenomenon of groupthink demonstrates (Littlejohn 1983: 237).

Groupthink

Groupthink occurs when a group of people used to working together end up thinking the same way (see also pp. 215–216). There are six negative impacts of groupthink: (1) groups limit the discussion of alternatives to only a few and do not consider the whole range of possible solutions, (2) those options favored by the majority are often taken without being revisited, (3) the group does not reexamine disfavored alternatives, (4) expert opinions are generally not valued more, (5) groups are highly selective in collecting and valuing information, and (6) once a decision is made, the group is so confident that it does not think of alternatives for Plan B scenarios.

Groupthink is often marked by several symptoms. Groups have an illusion of invulnerability; they undertake joint efforts to (post) rationalize the actions they undertake; they tend to see themselves as inherently moral; persons outside the group are branded not only as outsiders but also as less worthy in some ways—they are stupid or bad, for instance; self-appointed mind guards protect the group; and finally, the group exercises self-censorship, which both ensures uniformity and homogeneity. Thus, the negative outcomes of groupthink are enacted, reinforced, and exercised in communication. Taken that organizations rely more and more on teamwork, these tendencies to groupthink are frightening. They indicate that organizations actively have to manage communication in teams if they are to overcome these problems.

Shared meanings

Organizational communication comprises a series of recurring communication patterns that occur throughout the entire organization. Weick (1979) has a rather formal way of talking about this. He says that organizing is a consensually validated grammar used to reduce equivocality by means of what organization members constitute as sensible interlocking behaviors. Now, this is all rather a mouthful, but what we think he means is the following: Communication takes place on the basis of shared understandings and implicit rules, which function almost as if they were a grammar. They produce predictable communication patterns, which organization members use to try to reduce the time spent worrying about the huge amount of things they don't know in order to make their tasks more manageable by focusing on the predictable. That is, they seek to reduce equivocality. The way they do this is through developing shared routines with others in the organization. These shared routines produce the interlocked behavior expressed in and through the double interacts.

Placing an emphasis on consensual validation helps you understand that shared meanings form one fundamental aspect of organizations. These shared meanings are "agreements concerning what is real and what is illusory" (Weick 1979: 62). But meanings are not always shared. Think of organizations where the newly merged partners turn out to be sharing the same bed but not the same dreams. The merger between two companies that appeared synergistic but shared totally different cultures, styles of communication, and ways of making sense—such as the Time Warner/AOL merger or Citibank and Travelers—are cases in point.

All organizational reality is constituted and constructed through communication *and* miscommunication. Although formal communication programs try to facilitate shared meaning, there will always be stories, myths, and gossip circulating as well. It is important not to assume that organizations are some privileged space of shared meaning— even though they may strive hard to achieve this, there are often countervailing tendencies.

> **All organizational reality is constituted and constructed through communication *and* miscommunication.**

Besides this internally focused communication, organizations also constantly talk to their environments and diverse stakeholders (such as suppliers, network partners, investors, etc.). Basically, organizations communicate their identity, their values, and their reason for being to these audiences. Corporations seek to express a sense of what they are and, in doing so, they build strong relationships with key stakeholders. Mass communication is one (preferred) way of achieving this.

Mass communication

Since Marshall McLuhan (1964) coined the phrase the "global village," the importance, power, and influence of mass communication has constantly increased. In contrast to the three other levels of communication, mass communication is defined by four characteristics: (1) it is communication to a large, anonymous, and heterogeneous audience, (2) it is primarily one-way communication, meaning that feedback from the audience is restricted, (3) it is transmitted through different channels that work fast, and (4) the sender is usually a big organization rather than individuals (Littlejohn 1983). Billboard

Image 9.2   *Commercial mass communication from nineteenth-century Paris*

advertisements were an early form of commercial mass communication but by no means the earliest or the most pervasive in Western experience.

One of the earliest forms of explicit mass communication developed in the Christian church. In an age when literacy was not widespread, the church controlled the most powerful means of mass communication. Because the majority of the church's congregational members were nonliterate, they were able to relate to iconic symbols much more easily than to sophisticated literary sources such as the Bible, which, prior to the development of the Gutenberg press and mechanically reproduced pages, was not available outside of religious centers anyway. The church realized this, and, as well as through the words spoken by priests to the masses as they interpreted the Bible and papal edicts, it communicated through religious art as its central representational form. Religious art provided opportunities for uplifting as well as spectacular and frightening visions. Its depictions of cherubs, seraphims, and angels as well as huge amounts of pain, burning, institutionalized torture, execution, and individual torment made both the otherworldly and the grotesque seem part of normal everyday life (Robb 1999: 247–248, citing Mereu 1979). It was no accident that these representational devices of "[n]ailed hands, rolling eyes, exposed breasts, floating veils, bleeding wounds and cherubs' heads on wings" (Robb 1999: 326) were strongly opposed by the Protestant reformers of the north, more attuned to an educated and literate population than a peasantry whose imagination's energies were, as Robb (1999: 3) says, channeled into the runnels of Catholic doctrine by these images. The most sophisticated representational forms were the paintings and stained-glass windows of religious art, still to be seen in the churches and cathedrals of Europe. However, much more numerous and available to the populace at a local level, in their homes and everyday observances, far from the cathedrals and churches, were representations of Christ on the cross and the Virgin Mary, objects that could as easily fill a niche in the home as play a role in a procession. These were the core icons and, as such, examples of one of the earliest and best developed forms of mass communication. These symbols played an important function. In Weick's (1969) terms, we might say that they helped to reduce equivocality about belief.

Image 9.3   *Established forms of implicit mass communication*

Image 9.4   *The real representing the wooden: a Virgin of Guadeloupe procession in Oaxaca, Mexico*

Pieces of inert wood, when appropriately rendered and painted, could become holy icons, calling forth attendant rituals and behaviors. Of course, it is not only in the Christian religion that such iconography occurs. Buddha also has the same iconic powers.

Conversely, the same rituals could be used to make people appear as if they were wooden representations, as in the religious procession shown in Image 9.4. The Virgin in this tableau is a young woman, representing the famous Virgin of Guadeloupe, who, according to the story, manifested herself to a poor Indian at Tepeyac, a hill northwest of Mexico City, in 1531. Yearly, an estimated 10 million visit her Basilica, making her Mexico City home the most popular Marian shrine in the world and the most visited Catholic church in the world next to the Vatican. Around the time of her manifestation, in the second week in December, poor people from the countryside can be seen in processions in their hometowns and villages while millions more can be seen either traveling by pickup, bus, or bike, perhaps running, walking, or even crawling some of the way, to the Basilica in Mexico City, bearing representations of the Virgin. It is a potent example of the power of mass communication.

Where there are so many believers, there are opportunities for markets. Ancient holy symbols can be fully integrated into modern commerce by offering retail choice of which cross to choose, examples of which can be seen in Image 9.5.

Although the church was particularly effective at mass communication when there were few other organizations offering competing messages, today most large organizations have marketing and PR departments or agencies that seek to find appropriate channels to help them reach relevant audiences and get their

Image 9.5   *Which cross to bear?*

message across. Advertisements on TV, billboards, Web sites, and newspapers remain organizations' preferred ways to tell the rest of the world who they are and what they have to offer. However, mass advertisement can be costly and, as specialists argue, ineffective and inefficient. Other means of mass communication are therefore explored, including sponsorship of events (like Hugo Boss sponsoring Porsche or Volvo in the round-the-world yacht race) or the opening of concept stores (such as Diesel). Through these channels, companies can frame their message differently and communicate it more authentically. However, an original template for almost all forms of highly effective mass communication remains the church, with its simple and powerful icons.

Organizational communications and organizational design

In a large and strictly hierarchically organized company, it is unlikely that the CEO will speak to people from the bottom, or that people from the bottom will be able to communicate their ideas directly to top management. Also, it is hard for different departments that are not directly linked to each other to interact. Put simply, the organization design decides who communicates with whom directly. The more specialization, formalization, and centralization, the more restricted is communication (see also pp. 99–101; 395–400).

Devices such as open-space offices, shared photocopiers where people intermingle and chat, and corporate events where the usual hierarchy is dismissed (usually when everybody is a little drunk and people may forget themselves, taking risks that only become evident when the hierarchy reinstates itself) are all means of triggering internal flow communication and ensuring the necessary exchange that is inhibited by the formal structure. To undo these structures is the necessary precondition of rich communication processes. Following Bodrow and More (1992), these have four major functions:

1. *Informative function:* Communication transports information about facts and figures that are the basis for informed action. Thus, communication generates action.
2. *Systemic function:* Communication is the glue between organizational members. It establishes efficiencies for social interaction.
3. *Literal function:* Communication does not merely transport facts from sender to receiver but also connotes meaning and sense. In fact, communication is sensemaking.
4. *Figurative function:* Communication links an organization to its wider environment. It represents an organization's identity, its mission, and its purpose. Simply, it legitimizes an organization.

Communication conveys all organizational attempts, including verbal and nonverbal, as well as formal and informal, to create an organization's most powerful point of differentiation—its identity. Whether they want to or not, organizations communicate all the time. Job advertisements, recruitment processes, the annual salary negotiation, logos, statements of the spokesperson, products, and outlets—all these processes and more tangible manifestations of organizations actually communicate the organization's core values and reflect its identity (see also pp. 319–334).

Christensen and Cheney (2000) argue that the distinction between different communication disciplines such as marketing, public relations, and advertising is no longer easy to draw. Public relations functions were once specialized in their focus on an organization's contact with the public, whereas marketing tried to manage relations with customers. But when Shell, for instance, tried to sink the Brent Spar oil platform in the North Sea, it was the public who reacted quickly, loudly, and impulsively. Unfortunately, this public was simultaneously its customers, so who should have reacted for Shell—the public relations or the marketing department? As we can see, the difference gets blurred. Both functions manage an organization's communication with its environment, seeking to get relevant information from the environment and respond to it adequately. In addition, well-informed and briefed employees can serve as employee-ambassadors spreading the message an organization seeks to promote. General Motors, for instance, integrated internal and external communication in the 1980s as it relied on its employees (who received both commercials on TV at home and memos at the workplace) to promote the emphasis on safety (Christensen and Cheney 2000: 248).

Audiences

Communication is not just sending messages; it also involves receiving them, and different audiences are involved in the reception of meaning—which may not always be that intended. Three main audiences receive organizational communication: internal audiences (employees) targeted through intraorganizational communication; other organizations (partners, suppliers, etc.), who receive interorganizational communication; and the wider society (markets, society, press, etc.).

Intraorganizational communication

Communication can be downward, upward, or horizontal, and comprises both formal and informal messages. Downward communication means the flow of communication from superior to subordinate. Such communication has several functions. It instructs employees, provides them with goals, explains how they can achieve them, gives feedback concerning their performance, and seeks to build commitment. Upward communication means the flow of communication from subordinates to superiors. It includes employees' feedback concerning rules, strategies, implementations, and so on. Employees often know most about customers, services, and products, as they are in daily contact with them. Naturally, management lacks this knowledge, even though it forms the basis for strategic decision making. So to be good strategists at the macrolevel, they need to be good communicators at the microlevel. A study conducted by MIT focused on the difference between Japanese and American ways of producing cars, and it revealed that Japanese employees were more actively involved in the definition and refinement of car manufacturing process improvements (Womack, Jones, and Roos 1990). U.S. industry, however, was still mainly organized according to concepts derived from Taylor, making such communications difficult. This difference in the management of communication was one of the determinants of the success of Japanese corporations during the 1980s. Finally, horizontal communication describes communication that takes place between different departments. Marketing, for instance, might need to know planned product innovation for the next few years in order to align their campaign with the long-term image.

A good deal of managerial work involves providing information and facilitating communication (Mintzberg 1973). Managers spent most of their time gathering information from other people, by talking, listening, and negotiating in meetings, by informal conversation, and through other media. Peters and Waterman (1982) took this idea one step further and defined a leadership style called "management by walking around." In essence, the manager must not only be seen around the place but also must be seen to be aware of what is going on and acting on it.

An example of the power and importance of such intraorganizational communication is given by Ginger Graham, CEO of a $300 million U.S. company. Newly appointed, she found it in denial of the real roots of its recent failures. She wrote a plea for open and honest communication within the company (Graham 2002). And she started to practice what she preached when, at an annual meeting, instead of saying the usual friendly things, she said, "I've always heard about what a wonderful company ACS is, but frankly, that's not what I see." After saying straightforwardly what everyone knew but nobody openly dared to admit, there was a huge relief in the audience and among employees that—finally—someone from top management could see and address the hot issues. What Graham did from this moment on was, in her own words, to "create a culture that would allow everyone in the company to feel free to tell the truth, from top managers to the people on the loading dock. Only by arming ourselves with the truth, I felt, by owning up to it, and by acting according to it, could deep-rooted problems be identified, understood, and ultimately solved" (Graham 2002: 43).

An atmosphere of openness and honesty can be a trigger for change. All communication is important internally, even when it is addressed externally. For instance, branding and marketing communication is usually directed toward the environment, but it also affects employees. Colin Mitchell (2002) argues for the importance of "selling the brand inside"; when done, it creates a powerful link between the services you sell and the employees who actually sell it. If employees don't know what an organization is promising its clients, how can they live up to what is being preached? In fact, it becomes important that external and internal marketing are connected. All internally focused information is important externally: If the markets get negative reports from within a company, it will be reflected in their valuation of the firm. Mitchell (2002) provides an instance of a financial services institution that announced it was shifting from being a financial retailer to becoming a financial adviser. A year and a marketing budget later, nothing had happened. Customers did not feel that the announced shift had occurred and still seemed to see the institution in retail terms. The reason was simply that employees were not convinced by the new strategy. Marketing had targeted only customers and forgotten that there was an important internal market to convince—its own employees.

Interorganizational communication for collaboration

Interorganizational collaboration and networks have become increasingly important for organizations. Like humans, organizations build relationships that sometimes end up happily ever after but other times end in acrimony. Oliver (1990: 104) distinguished six reasons why organizations might collaborate with other organizations:

1. *Necessity:* Collaboration might be based on the fact that an organization is working together with another organization in order to meet legal or regulatory requirements.
2. *Asymmetry:* Collaboration can be driven by the wish to control relevant environments. A clothes manufacturer might work closely together with its suppliers in order to exercise control and power over them.
3. *Reciprocity:* The interests of two organizations might be better pursued when they join forces and form an alliance from which both benefit, such as occurs in a trade association.
4. *Efficiency:* Obviously, this motivation to collaborate is based on the idea of improving organizational performance through collaboration.
5. *Stability:* Organizations might collaborate in order to maintain a level of stability otherwise unreachable.
6. *Legitimacy:* Organizations seek collaboration in order to legitimize their own business. Shell, for instance, works together with Greenpeace, which obviously helps them to produce the image of a caring and responsible company.

For the growth of networks, mutual trust and consensus is decisive. This can only be achieved by communication. Two organizations working together need lots of coordination, cooperation, and bargaining, which sometimes inevitably produce conflict and coercion, all of which will be played out in communication and noncommunication (Irwin and More 1994).

Successful networks rely on managed communication in which two roles are especially important. First, the boundary spanner: She or he represents and communicates an organization's goals in and to its environments and acquires information from the outside, which is necessary for the organization. The second figure is the interlocker: She or he basically is a member of two organizations and knows things that the boundary spanner, as an outsider, would not hear or understand (rumors, gossip) (see also pp. 354–360).

Communication with stakeholders

Organizations use different distribution channels (TV, print, radio, Internet, and specially organized events) to communicate what they offer. As products and services become more and more refined and simultaneously more similar and exchangeable, organizations seek unique ways to position themselves in the marketplace. Public relations, marketing communication, reputation management, and branding are the organizational means for differentiation. They communicate what an organization stands for—not only promoting its products but also its core values and its identity.

As products and services change quickly, and the difference between original and generic products increasingly blurs (think of the cola market with all its cheap generic brands), companies try to establish a unique identity, which they create through communication, including mission statements, corporate design (business cards, stationery, etc.), retail outlets, logos, and other activities, such as sponsorship. The soft drink producer Red Bull, for instance, the biggest global energy drink manufacturer, selling more than a billion cans a year, promotes its soft drink heavily through promoting extreme sports events (www.redbull.com). The goal is to establish an image of the organization that goes beyond the characteristics of its products. Rather, the products should be promoted through this image.

Consider the example of Nike. People buy Nike shoes not only because of their qualities but also because of the fitness aesthetic these products promote, the lifestyle people associate with them, and the hardly tangible but tremendously valuable identity that Nike provides to their customers; that is, if Shaq O'Neal or Michael Jordan uses Nike, wouldn't you want to as well? There is, however, a dark side to the Nike story—a story not of excellence but of exploitation, of sweated labor, and maggots in the canteen food. Sometimes what is communicated corporately is not what is communicated organizationally. The short version of the story, as reported by David Boje on his Web site, is as follows.

> While consumers and sports-spectators associate Nike with fast and powerful athletes, it's no surprise that not everyone associated with the company is a Marion Jones or Tiger Woods. In fact, some Nike factory workers find everyday activities, let alone sports, to be daunting challenges. When you work sixty hours a week making sneakers in an Asian or Latin America factory and your friends disappear when they ask for a raise, it is not so easy to be a sports-spectator. Two prime examples: At Kukdong, Nike's partner factory in Mexico, women . . . asked for fair wages, no worms in their food, and their own union. These women were physically beaten and given bruises and black eyes for asking for basic human rights you and I take for granted. It's a familiar story: young girls set out on a magical journey of adventure, seduced by Nike partner ads for better jobs, only to find that things they value most are living without terror.

Communication as marketing

Because it is a well-developed discipline in its own right, people in marketing wouldn't necessarily agree that their subject is a part of organizational communication. However, the core activity of marketing—promoting products, services, and, by extension, an organization's identity—is, in fact, a communication exercise. The shortest definition of marketing is meeting customer needs profitably. Behind these words, however, lurks a complex task and libraries filled with research. EasyJet, for instance, discovered people were willing to fly more cheaply by doing without on-board service. The Body Shop found cosmetics produced in an ethically and environmentally responsible and sustainable way, which were not animal tested, met a broad-based consumer need. Once identified, such needs become the starting point for strategy making (see also pp. 408–444). The initial steps are accomplished inside a company by a few strategic minds. The next step is to communicate this strategy to customers and stakeholders. This means making people understand why you offer what you offer and why they should buy your services or products. You have to communicate your unique selling proposition to potential customers. Marketing is all about this communication. Optimal communication develops in six steps (Kotler 2000: 552):

1. Identifying target audience
2. Defining communication objectives
3. Designing the message
4. Selecting communication channels
5. Deciding on the communication channel
6. Measuring the communication process's results.

Marketing is one part of organizational communication. It includes advertising, sales promotion, public relations, personal selling, and direct marketing. Typically, it communicates through communication and distribution channels used to display the products (the strongest message of organizations in areas such as retail) and selling channels (e.g., banks that facilitate transactions). The marketing mix is the combination of marketing tools an organization uses to accomplish its goals. McCarthy (see Kotler 2000) differentiated between four main categories: products, price, promotion, and place. These form the tool kit for both marketing and communication tools. As the marketing guru Philip Kotler (2000: 550) suggests,

> Company communication goes beyond the specific communication platforms. . . . The product's styling and price, the package's shape and color, the salesperson's manner and dress, the place's décor, the company's stationery—all communicate something to the buyers. Every brand contact delivers something, an impression that can strengthen or weaken a customer's view of the company. The whole marketing mix must be integrated to deliver a consistent message and strategic positioning.

The concept of integrated marketing becomes more and more important as organizations become increasingly customer oriented and less product focused. For instance, cheap airfares, friendly staff, no delays, and clean cabins describe a service designed around customer needs. But in order to deliver on these, you have to integrate finance, human resources, cleaning staff, and airport management. The task is to make sure that the whole organization, including its suppliers and network partners, deliver and communicate the services offered.

Marketing research is often more reactive than proactive. Akio Morita, founder of Sony, says Sony doesn't serve markets—it creates them. The Walkman, for instance, would have probably never been produced if Sony had done ordinary market research. A product that is new and innovative surprises the customer and creates new needs rather than satisfies old needs. Like every analysis, market research explains past behavior and, at best, captures current realities, but extrapolating future trends from the present can be dangerously misleading. The Walkman or Post-it notes are perfect examples of things no one needed, for the simple reason that people did not know how to use them or realize the many roles they could play in everyday life.

Contemporary marketing works closely with clients, trying to work out what their needs are and offering solutions. Strong links need to be created between the customer and the company. Customers are less manipulated and more involved, communicating and sharing knowledge. Marketing is, after all, nothing other than the establishment of a relationship between the organization and its clients (McKenna 1991: 68). Communication is what nurtures this relationship, expressing the value of your services and products, the experience they create, and ultimately the company's character.

Instead of communicating the benefits of a certain product in a market crowded with similar messages, organizations increasingly try to build a strong, lasting, and powerful image in the minds of their potential customers. This allows organizations to decouple their products from their image and establish themselves as a strong brand. For instance, although you might not know what clothes Benetton currently sells, you certainly know what Benetton means in terms of its ethical engagement. Benetton is a brand.

Communication as branding

Olins (2000) and Hatch and Schultz (2001) identified several reasons why branding is so influential and a key to success. First, brands make choice easier. You probably know the feeling of standing in front of a packed supermarket shelf and being completely overloaded by the information and choices you face. Market economies create choices that are paralyzing when you are confronted by many interchangeable products with slight variations in packaging and product information. Powerful brands shortcut the need for you to make comparisons, thus making choice easy—if somewhat redundant.

Second, brands bring consistency and continuity to your consumer life. Third, brands help us to make up our own identity and provide us with devices to tell others who we are (or at least, what we try to be). Just think of clothes. Wearing a Hugo Boss or Chanel suit, sunglasses designed by Porsche, and a

Rolex instantly says a great deal about who you want to be taken to be. The same goes for street-level fashions and design; they provide a source of identity construction. However, the icons can be quite different. For instance, see if you can identify in Image 9.6 some of the images being marketed in the selection of T-shirts hanging in the market and imagine the kind of identity construction that would accompany wearing them.

Fourth, corporate brands reduce costs. Instead of marketing every single product separately, promoting the brand saves money. Take Sony. Regardless of whether it's a TV, a stereo, or a game, people associate quality with this brand name.

In companies purchased as a result of a merger or acquisition, it is difficult to impose new identities and retain customers happily attached to old brands. When firms invest in risky businesses and fail, the negative image can badly influence the brand and core business. This seems to have

Image 9.6   *Faces on T-shirts*

happened with the Australian AMP company, which made some disastrous takeovers when it was first demutualized in the late 1990s. Finally, having a strong brand means being vulnerable; people look extremely closely at what Nike or Shell are doing, and due to their visibility, any negative message about them travels quickly through newspapers or Web sites. At best, brands become universal signs, such as Coca-Cola, the world's most recognizable brand.

Branding expresses what and who an organization is. It is not just a matter of cosmetics—where stylish packaging promotes a product whose real costs are a fraction of the asking price, or packaging old ideas in new boxes—but a way of communicating the substance of the company. Think of Absolut Vodka. Their image as a company that is young, sophisticated, and chic does not derive from their product, but rather their products are incubated by their style. Vodka is vodka, one might say, but Absolut managed to transform its product into a unique, recognizable, and successful brand, as an icon that inspires people. It is witty, droll, iconoclastic, and cool. Icons, as Douglas Holt (2003) argues, are encapsulated myths that bring products alive. Nike, for instance, is not just in the business of selling sneakers—which are merely a vehicle for a story—because its products embody the myth of individual achievement through perseverance. In this game, products are but one way to tell the corporate myth and to provide a story that customers appreciate.

Image 9.7   *Coca-Cola's registered trademark, Mexico City*

Image 9.8   *Do you want a Coke with that?*

Successful branding involves customers and creates a relationship between them and the company—often without using mass media. The Body Shop is an excellent example of such branding. Anita Roddick, founder and CEO, created a strong brand identity around the notion of a profit-with-principles philosophy. The company protests against animal testing, helps third world countries, supports the women's movement, to name but a few of its many activities (Joachimsthaler and Aaker 1997). These express the company's values clearly and consistently and simultaneously motivate staff members. Benetton, on the other hand, got into trouble with its brand strategy. When Benetton started advertising using images of HIV-positive people on its billboards and picked up similar hot issues, it doubtless created brand awareness, but it failed to link this awareness back to its business—selling clothes. Rather, it alienated both target market and retailers (Joachimsthaler and Aaker 1997).

Branding is about interacting with the public and communicating your organization, its values, and its contribution to society. Benetton, apart from launching campaigns that made it one of the most recognized (but also most contested) companies worldwide, also feature a magazine called *Color* dedicated to issues such as slavery, prisons, and refugees. *Color* is translated into many languages and sold in over sixty countries. It analyzes topics and makes people aware of marginalized problems. Doing so, Benetton positions itself not just as a clothes manufacturer but also as a highly socially responsible organization that is concerned with social issues.

CRITICAL ISSUES: COMMUNICATION AT WORK

Given the variety of approaches, channels, audiences, and levels of communication, it is critical for organizations to coordinate their communication activities. One way of managing the multiheaded hydra is explored through the concept of the expressive organization.

Creating the expressive organization

In an outstanding contribution to organization theory and management practice, Majken Schultz, Mary Jo Hatch, and Mogens Holten Larsen (2000) defined the concept of the "expressive organization." Communication is a vital part of every organizational activity, and the concept of the expressive organization takes this into account. In a nutshell, this concept captures different levels of organizational expressions and their impact on processes such as strategy making, HR, marketing, and others. The key task of an expressive organization is to communicate its identity to its internal and external audiences. It integrates the levels of communication and the different audiences and aligns corporate communication accordingly. Think of churches and other places of worship. Their windows are designed not to communicate light, to be translucent, but instead, to inspire the faithful through beauty and religious messages.

If a company manages to communicate an identity associated with values such as being innovative, fresh, and creative, it will attract top-level employees and simultaneously motivate its staff members. It will also attract new customers and build strong ties to existing customers. Furthermore, it will be easier for such a company to get financial investors on board as well as build strong relations to key suppliers.

In an increasingly competitive environment, advertising and branding will not be sufficient tools to differentiate yourself from your competitors. More and more, organizations will compete on the basis of what they are and their ability to express a core identity and values. Managing symbolic and emotional capital through communication thus becomes a core business of management. Even the symbol of manufacturing and production that invented the assembly line, Ford, announced a shift in its orientation toward, and understanding of, its core business. As one of its executives stated, "The manufacture of cars will be a declining part of Ford's business. They will concentrate in the future on design, branding, marketing, sales and service operation" (quoted in Olins 2000: 51). Ford's move from tangible cars to more intangible assets implies that understanding communication is its prime task. Taken that different brands such as Skoda, VW, Audi, and Seat all belong to the same company and share a body platform with each other, it makes it obvious that the difference between these products is not so much the physical characteristics of the car but more the different look, feel, and intangible values associated with them. Thus, managing

Image 9.9   *Church window*

a car manufacturer means, more and more, managing meaning. And this management of meanings relies heavily on communication.

It is important to understand that an organization expresses itself through various activities: its employees' behavior, its physical design (including uniforms, retail outlets, buildings, etc.), its corporate identity (logo, Web page, etc.), its advertisement, its strategic intent, its involvement in community activities, and so on. Put simply, everything speaks. Organizations always communicate and cannot avoid doing so. Thus, the expressive organization focuses on the communications that constantly (consciously or not) enact any organization.

As Hatch and Schultz (2001) argue elsewhere, in order to compete successfully with its competitors, an organization has to create a strong corporate identity reflected in the corporate brand. Such an expressive organization aligns three major organizational features that are normally separately analyzed: vision (strategy), culture (employees), and image (brand). In order to align these "strategic stars," the authors suggest analyzing the three possible gaps between them:

1. The vision-culture gap emerges when management moves away from its employees, developing a vision that is not shared, understood, or supported by the rest of the organization. The vision does not inspire the whole organization sufficiently.
2. The image-culture gap derives from a misalignment between employees' behavior and expressed image. The company does not practice what it preaches.
3. The image-vision gap results from a conflict between an organization's vision and the environment's image of the organization. If management wants the company to go in a direction in which its customers and other stakeholders are not going, the best strategic plan is in vain and will eventually fail.

The key to success is to analyze the gaps and, through careful research, close them by understanding the stakeholders' point(s) of view and needs, the employees' perspective, and the strategic intent of top-management.

Listening

Communication for an expressive organization starts not with speaking but with listening. As Carl R. Rogers (1991) found in his experience as a psychotherapist in counseling, the main obstacle to communication is people's tendency to evaluate. This phenomenon can be overcome by strengthening another skill—listening. Especially when people talk about emotionally charged issues, they stick to their own frame of reference and forget to understand the other's point of view. But as Rogers suggests, change can only be accomplished by understanding *with* someone, not by understanding *about* someone. A simple technique can help you grasp this: Before you start to argue with people, summarize their points so accurately that they agree and are satisfied. This means you have actually fully understood what they want to say.

Managing with words?

Understanding the power of communication and language enables you to utilize words to manage organizations. Take the example of employees. As a manager, you might refer to them generically as employees, but you could also call specific people, on different occasions or in different contexts, "hands," "human resources," "team players," "stars," "deadbeats," "losers" (or the equivalent Australian expression, "drongos"), and so on. Different metaphors not only affect people differently but also trigger different thoughts. Resources can be exploited and developed, whereas hands are only utilized and, symbolically, come independent of minds, brains, and bodies. By using different metaphors and communicating through them, managers create different realities (see also pp. 408–444).

Through telling stories, organizational members shape the organization. Deal and Kennedy (1982) identify three roles that stories play in organizations. First, they anchor the present in the past. They locate an organization's history and its background, which makes it possible for people to understand the current situation. Second, they maintain cohesiveness. By sharing the same stories, they provide members with a sense of community and common values. Finally, they explain why things are the way they are. Stories explain a good deal of the practices and behavior that are displayed in organizational life. To this we might add also that they define normalcy and its range; they locate the deviant both as extraordinarily good as well as extraordinarily bad.

If communication is constitutive for processes of organizing, if language is the everyday means through which organizations make sense, plan, negotiate, and make decisions, change can be enacted through different languages. The simple example used above demonstrates this quite easily. Thinking and talking of your employees as "hands" (as Taylor did) means dismissing a wide range of potential opportunities. Using the metaphor of human resources opens a whole world of potential management opportunities in which people treated as resources cannot only be exploited but also developed and used more or less efficiently. This new language of managing people differentiates between different skills, learning, and development potential, which you could not even see or manage while using the term *hands* for employees. Put simply, a shift in language, a new metaphor, a new communication can trigger organizational change and development. Of course, just as the notion of being a hand has its downside, so does the notion of a person as a resource. People can be used up, exploited, and worn out as resources. We need to think strategically about our communication strategies, metaphors, and language—in the expressive organization they are tightly coupled.

An example drawn from the Navistar Company illustrates the linkage of communication to strategy (Argenti and Forman 2000). John Horne, CEO of the heavy truck manufacturer Navistar, joined it in 1993 and found the organization in a less than ideal situation. Key stakeholders (employees, unions, senior management, the financial community, media) had lost trust in the company, and the overall situation was not very pleasant. Horne decided that the way to change this was through bringing his employees on board (again)—and this happened through a well-developed communication initiative.

The first step was to visit the plants in order to engage all employees in a discussion of how to beat competition. Soon this became a formal management task, and every month, a member of senior management visited a plant. At meetings that involved some thirty workers, who talked to their colleagues about their needs beforehand, they spoke about the good things and things that could be improved. After the meeting, management published a report that included their answers to the issues raised. Furthermore, assembly-plant workers were invited to visit the headquarters and discuss workers' needs with the decision makers informally and directly. Such communication practice develops joint processes of strategy making and implementing, where workers and mangers learned mutually from each other (see also pp. 29–31; 184–186; 354–359; 395).

Second, Horne started a survey of employees focusing on their specific work situations. The results of the survey were published, and an action plan was developed, including deadlines and deliverables, involving, especially, union leaders, making them participants in the change process. Through these efforts and a couple of related exercises (such as a PR campaign, introduction of leadership conferences to improve leadership, etc.), Horne brought Navistar back on the road to success. He started communication processes with different audiences. Through creating a shared communicative basis, the organization enacted a common future in and through these communications (see Argenti and Forman 2000).

Power and communication

Every way of managing involves power. Communication is no exception; it is never a neutral device to express reality. In fact, it creates reality. It is a powerful means to establish and reinforce organizational reality. Bordow and More (1992) suggest three steps (that we extend with two additional steps) for managers to manage communication actively. First, managers should realize that in managing with power in and through communication, they are, essentially, managing values (see also pp. 196–201). Whether they prioritize tight budgetary management and low risk-taking or are prepared to invest in opportunities for innovation with a high risk of failure, they are communicating the values that dominate the organization. It is absolutely important that these values are internally consistent and adhered to across the board; otherwise, their dissonance breeds cynicism and alienation. Once the values are in the frame, then managers need to consider agenda setting. This means ensuring that people talk about the right things. You take leadership in selecting the topic of communication. Whatever happens, it is important that people talk about and make sense of events relating to issues you raise. If sales decrease, there are many ways of tackling this problem. You could train the sales team, drop prices, increase quality or services around the product, promote it better, produce more cheaply, or change the market, for instance. It is important to isolate one or two topics that are then employed to discuss and make sense of events. Make sure not only that people talk about the issue but also that the right people talk about it. Create networks of people who are key players that have knowledge, contacts, ideas, energy, and power to change things. These key players should gather and form a temporary network that discusses the problem and elaborates possible solutions.

Such a network might involve people from all levels of the hierarchy, with different backgrounds and personalities. In developing solutions to problems the organization faces, make sure that you manage the dissemination such that the information is communicated throughout the organization and to key stakeholders outside the organization. There are many ways of disseminating ideas: announcing them in speeches, broadcasting them via an intranet or the organizational newspaper, or publishing a glossy report. These top-down strategies can be supplemented by bottom-up tactics—such as gossip or informal conversation with key players within the wider audience that will communicate your message to their audience. Do not rely purely on formal, authoritative messages, but seek to find informal ways of communicating the message. It is best to model the message symbolically in values that are not only espoused but also evident in practice (see also pp. 257–260).

The following story illustrates modeling the message. Thomas Watson Jr., chairman of the board of IBM, was challenged by a supervisor, described as "[a] twenty-two-year-old bride weighing ninety pounds whose husband had been sent overseas and who, in consequence, had been given a job until his return." The young woman, Lucille Burger, was obliged to make certain that people entering security areas wore the correct clear identification. Surrounded by his usual entourage of white-shirted men, Watson approached the doorway to an area where she was on guard, wearing not a green badge, which alone permitted entrance at her door, but an orange badge acceptable elsewhere in the plant. "I was trembling in my uniform, which was far too big," she recalled. "It hid my shakes, but not my voice. 'I am sorry,' I said to him. I knew who he was alright. 'You cannot enter. Your admittance is not recognized.' That's what we were supposed to say." The men accompanying Watson were stricken; the moment held unpredictable possibilities. "Don't you know who he is?" someone hissed. Watson raised his hand for silence, while one of the party strode off and returned with the appropriate badge. (Peters and Waterman 1982, quoted in Mumby 1987: 121)

The story makes clear that regardless of power and the status within the organizational hierarchy, all members have to obey the rules equally strictly. Both Watson and the supervisor set an example of correct behavior: Watson by organizing the right badge and the supervisor by acting strictly according to the rules. But the story also functions as a reference point for organizational members (especially for newcomers who do not yet know how the organization works in reality) and has some more subtle meaning. As the story demonstrates, everybody at IBM has to accept the rules equally. What the story does not say, however, is that these rules are established by management and people like Watson and not by the supervisor.

Mumby (1987) argues that the story has several hidden meanings that powerfully influence organizational reality. If Watson was really just another employee who has to follow rules, the story would not be worth retelling. Simultaneously, Watson is introduced as an "ordinary" employee who can be spoken to much as any other member of the organization, but at the same time he appears as a godlike figure in the story. Just look at the description of the two actors. The supervisor is described as "twenty-two-year-old bride weighing ninety pounds whose husband had been sent overseas"; her clothes don't fit her, and she is nervously facing Watson. Although the story paints a poor picture of her, only working because her husband is overseas, Watson appears almost mythical, surrounded as if by the kind of entourage that normally accompanies a king. Whereas the supervisor speaks, Watson, again godlike, does not speak at all—other people speak for him. And even at the point in the story when he might have spoken, he simply raises his hand and things happen (Mumby 1987). Using this ostensibly innocent story as an example, you can see communication at work. It tells organizational members how they have to behave (follow rules strictly) and simultaneously it promotes and reinforces organizational power relations (Watson as a godlike figure, Burger as a woman who struggles with her job).

Speaking generally, communication is more powerful when it uses images instead of words and concepts. Looking at how leaders spark people through communication, a team of researchers analyzed the communication style of U.S. presidents and the inspiration felt by citizens (Roche 2001). The result was impressive. Presidents who were described as charismatic and great used image-based words to communicate their vision. They painted verbal pictures that truly inspired their fellow citizen. John F. Kennedy said in his inaugural address, "Together let us explore the stars, conquer the desert, eradicate disease, tap the ocean depths, and encourage the arts and commerce." Compare this with Jimmy Carter's address in which he said, "Let our recent mistakes bring a resurgent commitment to the basic principles of our nation, for we know that if we despise our own government, we have no future." Whereas Kennedy used lively pictures, Carter used abstract concepts that seem to remain empty and fail to create commitment. Put simply, image-based communication is much more powerful than conceptually driven language. Instead of talking just about sustainability, managers should talk about how we stay in touch with our children and nature.

Effective and powerful managers create feedback loops. It will be decisive that you know what other people think about your initiatives, because exercising power without learning how it is being received is to head for a fall. Scanning the environment thus becomes a vital task. Messages might be ambiguous or difficult to understand, which makes it necessary to find out how they actually are understood. This involves all levels—from employees to stakeholders and clients. Again, this challenges the organizational structure to provide channels where this communication can happen. Prerogative has its privileges, because managerial communication does not merely reflect reality but also seeks to constitute it. An example from sport that you can find in Karl Weick's book (1979) illustrates this humorously: "The story goes that three umpires disagreed about the task of calling balls and strikes. The first one said, 'I calls them as they is.' The second one said, 'I calls them as I sees them.'

The third and cleverest umpire said, 'They ain't nothin' till I calls them.'" As the third umpire argues, balls and strikes do not exist independently of judgment; rather, they become real only when they are pronounced as such. But most managers are involved in games that are far more complicated than baseball and have far more ambiguous and inherently problematic rules, and under these circumstances it would be a foolish manager who believed his or her own pronouncements without first securing feedback.

Securing feedback is especially important where a particular set of unanticipated consequences can arise. Major changes in management and organizations are not only disseminated in and through words but only come to life when people adopt the newly provided vocabulary and redescribe their experiences using this new language, such as total quality management (TQM). Through using a new language, they create and enact a new reality. You have to pay attention to the paradoxes lurking in communication, however. For instance, to tell people to "be spontaneous!" represents a catch-22 that makes it impossible for them to behave truly spontaneously. If they do, they obey your suggestion and simply aren't spontaneous. Some types of pronouncements are referred to as self-fulfilling prophecies; they convey communication that causes what they announce to happen. Think of the stock market. If everyone believes that the economy will go down, each person will be careful with their investment, which actually causes what they have been afraid of. Or if you're scared that you will fail an exam, this fear might inhibit you from functioning as well as normal and you may fail because of your fear.

THE FINE PRINT: COMMUNICATION AS DECONSTRUCTION AND TRANSLATION

In a metaphor often used by writers and artists, organizations may be said to be similar to the Tower of Babel, imperfect and diverse buildings, the product of people speaking many tongues. Different cultures and subcultures, each having their own voice, enacted messy organization reality. Instead of forcing all people to speak one language, homogenizing the organization in monotonic communication, which would lead ultimately to the death of creativity (see also pp. 380–403), management must take on the tasks of deconstruction and translation.

Usually, in most organizations, there is a persistent plurality of different linguistic constructions that shape organizational reality. Boje (2002) has a metaphor for understanding organizations that makes use of *Tamaraland,* a theatrical production. *Tamaraland* is a play in which different acts take place simultaneously in different rooms, which the audience is free to move between. What a member of the audience encounters, as well as the sense they make of it, will vary markedly according to the route they take around the rooms. The production makes notions of what it is to be a member of the audience

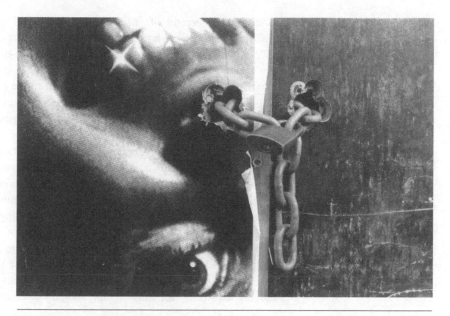

Image 9.10   *Who knows why she's smiling?*

problematic. More important, however, the play disrupts notions of linearity, especially through the way in which the audience may have infinite experiences of the play by virtue of the order in which they have entered particular rooms. For Boje, *Tamaraland,* as multiplicities of meaning, outcome, and experience, is a projection of contemporary organizations. His suggestion is that although organizations may well be scripted through missions, strategies, and so forth, there are too many directors (i.e., finance, marketing, human resources) for only one script to be followed.

Boje suggests that we regard organizations as a metatheater, as a multiplicity of simultaneous/discontinuous dramas, whose sense you make as you go along. Multiple people make multiple senses, and as you will see in Chapter 12, successful processes of strategy making listen democratically to voices normally silenced. People from the periphery (newcomers and outsiders) will think more creatively because they are "exposed to ideas and developments that do not conform to the company's orthodoxies" (Hamel 1996: 77). Thus, rather than provide strong leadership that silences dissent, organizations should use the polyphony they have available in their narratives. "Narratives," as Mumby (1987: 113) suggests, "provide members with accounts of the process of organizing. Such accounts potentially legitimate dominant forms of organizational reality, and lead to discursive closure in the sense of restricting the interpretations and meanings that can be attached to organizational activity." Thus, narratives are not only devices of sensemaking but also a "politically motivated production of a certain way of perceiving the world" (Mumby 1987: 114). 3M fundamentally changed how to write business plans and the process of strategy making. Instead of coming up with a bullet-point-to-do list, 3M people create a story that explains the new idea and how it should come alive. This narrative approach creates commitment and excitement in the entire organization.

To the extent that they enact and reinforce a certain image of an organization that can influence its members almost subliminally, beneath the threshold of their awareness, those narratives that provide the matrix for normal organizational talk, action, and decision making can be potentially productive or counterproductive, functional or dysfunctional. If the images are monotonic, have been conceived remotely, and imposed downward onto organization members, there is more probability of a lesser sense of ownership, commitment, and responsibility, because few opportunities for participating in meaning making or sharing have been created. By contrast, seeking to manage organizations polyphonically means engaging in discursive practices circumscribed by the processes of *deconstructing* existing language games and *translating* between different language games. Thus, deconstructing these narratives provides a means of understanding and changing the stories that guide organizational sensemaking.

Deconstruction

Experienced managers appreciate that it is through narratives and stories that organizations are constituted, guiding the lives within and speaking to the identities they constitute. Organization constantly talks itself into existence; we make sense of its experience through narratives and stories. Practically, deconstruction is a means that allows one to question these sensemaking activities, to analyze the language games that shape reality, and to open up space for different concepts and perceptions. Managers who want to change the direction of an organization have to know how to reposition old ways of doing things so that the sense of their being natural and normal that members and publics share is changed, or deconstructed. Deconstruction provokes curiosity with regard to alternative versions of how things might be. It opens up possible realities and gives birth to real possibilities. It sensitizes us to those concepts that frame the realm of the imaginable and to those stories that structure the flow of our experience. Deconstruction questions the taken-for-granted, the seemingly self-evident and natural, in order to uncover its history.

Experienced managers appreciate that it is through narratives and stories that organizations are constituted.

Deconstruction demonstrates how the world is accomplished linguistically and its status quo maintained discursively. Even more important, it provides the space for things to be different. As organizations are powerfully constituted and constantly enacted through languages, deconstruction is thus the precondition of change; it melts all necessities and shows that they were established at a particular moment in history. If deconstruction is managed effectively, then reconstruction can take place in its wake.

Translation

Organizations that seek to change direction have to translate their new direction to significant others, such as customers, suppliers, and employees, and often they have to establish a new identity. They must translate a new sense of what they are to these others. Translation is always a form of improvisation, a movement from the known and established to the new and yet unknown. Like improvisation, translation helps us linguistically to maintain the images of order and control that are central to organizational theory and to simultaneously introduce images of innovation and autonomy (Weick and Westley 1996). Translation is concerned with understanding the other. In short, translating is a constructive way of managing polyphonic organizations. Translation is a form of mediation between different and contradicting language games and their ways of seeing and the realities they constitute.

Accepting the polyphony of organization as normal has important ethical implications. Managing the polyphonic organization means listening carefully to the voices of others and mediating between different language games. There can never be something like a perfect translation—it is always only a provisional way of coming to terms with the otherness of languages. Instead of seeking one's own ideas in others' words, polyphony forces one to focus on the difference, and ultimately triggers understanding and listening.

Speaking managerially, polyphonic organization has many advantages. Arguably, employees will be more empowered, motivated, and committed. The organization can position itself differently and realize a competitive advantage through reputation management by marketing itself as democratic, open, and multicultural (see Schultz et al. 2000). The diversity of voices and perspectives unleashes creativity and innovative potential beyond conformity (see Hamel 1996, offering the example of strategy making). Drawing on a wider range of perspectives and heterogeneous resources can improve decision-making processes (Fenwick and Neal 2001; Glover et al. 2002). Finally, a polyphonic organization is less standardized and hierarchical, which provides the necessary flexibility to cope in a fast-changing environment.

SUMMARY AND REVIEW

Organizational communication is absolutely central to managing. It ranges across many approaches to analysis, as we have seen. You need to know some organizational behavior, marketing, public relations, and much else besides to fully grasp the significance of communication. Bringing it all together is the recently developed concept of the expressive organization, which is an important development for understanding the way that contemporary organizations are developing into largely communicative entities that subcontract almost everything other than control over the central brand. It is this path that major corporate organizations such as Nike and Zara follow.

Managing communication means managing with power. Typically, power has been thought of in negative terms, but as seen in Chapter 5, it need not be. In the context of managing communication, the positive aspects of power are particularly evident. Communication, involving speaking, listening, and meaning making from and across many different identities, necessarily involves polyphony. Managing polyphony requires a subtle management of power to deconstruct and translate rather than to impose monotonic meaning, singular cultures, and one-way communication organized in a top-down authoritative model (see also pp. 51–52).

ONE MORE TIME . . .

Getting the story right

- What are the main approaches to communication theory?
- How do organizations communicate through marketing and branding?
- What are vicious circles and how do they happen?
- What are the main media for organization communication?

Thinking outside the box

- What needs to be aligned in an expressive organization?
- Do words socially construct organization realities?
- What is the power of silence in the IBM story?
- How would you manage in a polyphonic organization?

ADDITIONAL RESOURCES

1. It's probably just as well that you be familiar with some of the popular accounts of the importance of organizational communication—as they have been so influential—and none has been more influential than Dale Carnegie's (1944) *How to Win Friends and Influence People.*
2. A classic text for understanding the mass media of communication is Marshall McLuhan's (1964) *Understanding Media.* It would be interesting to take his ideas about what constitutes "hot" and "cool" media and apply them to some of the media that have developed since he wrote.
3. In terms of critical perspectives on communication, including the nature of organizational communication as gendered discourse, the volume

edited by Steven R. Corman and Marshall Scott Poole (2000) called *Perspectives on Organizational Communication: Finding Common Ground* is a useful, if advanced, text.

4. The most innovative contribution in this area in recent years is *The Expressive Organization: Linking Identity, Reputation and the Corporate Brand,* edited by Majken Schultz, Mary Jo Hatch, and Mogens Holten Larsen (2000).

5. The classic film about organizational communication is the superb early Francis Ford Coppola film *The Conversation.* The context of *The Conversation* (1974) was Watergate and the fascination with the Nixon tapes and Nixon's surveillance tactics on his colleagues as well as his enemies. We see it as an organizational allegory on the centrality and difficulty of really understanding communication when the message is opaque, the intent mysterious, and the effects can be deadly. It is also an allegory on how we can use communication strategies to conceal rather than reveal.

6. We started the chapter with a line from the Beatles' "All You Need Is Love," originally written by John Lennon and Paul McCartney and performed by the Beatles and some friends for a BBC segment of the world's first global TV broadcast on June 25, 1967, of a program called *Our World.* Thus, we could have used the lyric just as easily to illustrate globalization—it was the only memorable moment of the world's first global television transmission. Nonetheless, it is a perfect exercise in organizational communication, as the brief from the BBC was to make the song simple and accessible enough so that people all over the world would be able to understand it. It could, just as easily, be used as an illustration of the postmodern, of course: John Lennon's ironical chanting of "She loves you, yeah, yeah, yeah" as the song fades away is an instance of reflexivity as he is making reference to one of the Beatles early hits. The song is available on a number of compilations, including the *Beatles 1* (1993: Apple CDP 7243 5 29325 2 8) and *Magical Mystery Tour: The Beatles* (1967: Parlophone PCTC 255).

In addition to these suggested additional resources, don't forget to look at what is also available on the Web site **www.ckmanagement.net,** including free PDF files of recent papers related to this chapter, which you can download; video interviews with famous academics talking about related themes; as well as many other resources, such as connections to interesting Web sites.

PART III
MANAGING CHANGE

CHAPTER 10

MANAGING KNOWLEDGE AND LEARNING

Communities, Collaboration, Boundaries

Objectives and learning outcomes

By the end of this chapter, you will be able to

- Explain the basic assumptions of knowledge management and learning

- Understand the importance of these assumptions for organizations

- Analyze different approaches to these assumptions

- Examine the benefits and shortcomings of these approaches

- Understand the challenge that learning and managing knowledge poses for management

- Discuss organizational practices that have the potential to trigger learning

Before you get started . . .

Remember the old proverb, "A little learning is a dangerous thing." But what does it mean—that too little learning is dangerous or that "ignorance is bliss"? Would you want to work in an ignorant organization or one that knew that it didn't know what it didn't know, and tried to do something about it? Remember, Socrates was declared the wisest man in Athens because he knew what it was not to know!

OUTLINE OF THE CHAPTER

In 1988, Arie De Geus, senior manager at Royal Dutch/Shell, wrote a paper in which he stated "the only competitive advantage the company of the future will have is its managers' ability to learn faster than their competitors." (1988: 74). Since then, knowledge management and organizational learning have become two of the buzzwords of our age. Not only should students and adults learn from time to time, but whole organizations and even societies are supposed to learn constantly. Lifelong learning seems to be the most valuable asset in an age in which information is everything and knowledge is the key to success. According to management guru Peter Senge and his colleagues (Senge et al. 1999), the distinctive feature of successful companies is their ability to learn. Companies like General Electric, Coca-Cola, and Shell use learning concepts in their organization and claim that they are the key to success. Knowledge seems to be the most important strategic asset of many organizations, including large consultancies such as BCG (Boston Consulting Group) or Accenture; what they offer is knowledge, from which they make heaps of money, despite the fact that what they are selling is an intangible product.

Management theorists differentiate between knowledge management and organizational learning in most accounts. However, for us, knowledge and learning are closely interlinked concepts, or two sides of the same coin. Whereas knowledge management focuses on the actual creation, dissemination, and transformation of knowledge, learning involves change in the existing state of knowledge. Thus, we could argue that knowledge management focuses on the existing resources within an organization, and learning focuses on the dynamic development of these resources.

SETTING THE SCENE

The concepts of learning and knowledge management have many parents, as Mark Easterby-Smith (1997) pointed out. Two distinct streams—one from psychology and one from more technical approaches to management information—come together in this literature. The older tradition of information management emerged from library studies because, once upon a time, if you sought knowledge, it could most readily be found in books and libraries. In the past, some

Image 10.1   *The library of Monasterio de Santa Ane'ka, in Prague*

libraries, especially when books were not yet in widespread mass production, were major centers of power because they contained not only the knowledge that was power but were often organizationally located in major political centers of religious or state rule. In the medieval world, clerics were the major repository of literacy—the key to knowledge and thus power. Image 10.1 shows an outstanding library in the Monasterio de Santa Ane'ka, in Prague.

What was scarce and zealously guarded in medieval society is now freely available. Knowledge in the modern world is everywhere; it is no longer under strict control by monastic authorities. Books are just one medium used to process and store technical information; information processing now includes databases and the Internet as well. There are many places where we can acquire and learn different approaches to knowledge. Today, you are more likely to find out what you need to know from a laptop than a book. When you begin to investigate the ways in which management researchers have addressed knowledge, some distinctly different approaches are discernible. Psychologically oriented researchers focused on different learning styles: how knowledge is acquired, how people learn, and how knowledge is transferred. Sociologists looked at learning from the more general perspective of social structures and interaction, emphasizing the influence of power, politics, and ideologies. From the 1980s, with the rise of a cultural perspective on management, the importance of norms, values, and rituals is more obvious. However, knowledge really sprang into prominence when change management became linked with management learning. In particular, Peter Senge's bestseller, *The Fifth Discipline* (1990), made knowledge a hot topic. We live in a knowledge society, in which information is paradoxically both the most valuable resource and one that constantly overloads us to such an extent that we neglect its richness and depth. In such a world, the management of this knowledge and its development—i.e., learning—becomes one of the most important concepts in management and organization theory.

CENTRAL APPROACHES AND MAIN THEORIES

Knowledge management

Knowledge management is the process of managing knowledge to meet existing and future needs, and to exploit present knowledge to develop opportunities for further knowledge (see Von Stamm 2003). Put simply, it is all about know-how and know-why. We investigate, first, where know-how might come from, and then we consider the types of knowledge that might be the sources of know-how (what we have referred to as *know-why*).

Sources of knowledge

Knowledge can take many different forms and can derive from many sources: figures, information, written instructions, stories, rumors, gossip, beliefs, and so on. Think about where people at work—in particular, decision makers—get their knowledge. In the modern world, much of what people know comes from formal bodies of knowledge, especially science. Universities educate tomorrow's managers and, through imparting information about management research, these educational institutions seek to provide knowledge about how current issues might be resolved. Unfortunately, this process is not the only way knowledge is translated into practice (see also pp. 289–291). Liz Fulop and William Rifkin (1999) argue that the following three particularly influential sources of knowledge are far more important than scientific treatises and management:

- *Learning by doing:* The complexity and variety of managerial tasks make it hard to formalize what managers do when they manage (see also pp. 316–319). Thus, to obtain most of their knowledge, they learn when they are actually in the middle of managing. Common sense tells them how to react and what to do in certain situations. Such action-oriented behavior is not always the best, however. Consider how often things get broken when you learn while you do, compared to an approach where you think before you do, and then learn. The classic example of the difficulties of learning while doing is the story of the Apollo 13 space mission, which introduced the phrase "Houston, we have a problem" to the wider world. Here the mission, seemingly routine, was underway, when the crew and ground-based flight command had to learn and improvise their way from disaster to triumph.

- *Hearing stories:* Managers learn what their job is all about through stories that are told in the organization. Stories are good formats because they relate the core of an experience (and take the freedom to embellish it a little to make it more interesting). Accounts of how a tricky problem was solved, an important deadline was met, or a disobedient employee was disciplined communicate the message of how things are done in the organization. Regardless of whether these stories are true or not, they form a template for managers' own experiences and help them make narrative sense of messy situations.

- *Being exposed to popular accounts:* Fulop and Rifkin (1999) refer to stories that are printed and communicated through management seminars as exemplary cases drawn from a great organization culture. These accounts often tell how great CEOs managed to turn around large organizations and how their practices can be applied by almost everybody, everywhere, anytime. These popular accounts, sometimes communicated through the quality popular business press (such as *Harvard Business Review*) as well as the general media, provide a clear focus on how to do things, summarizing them in case studies. Equipped with the success story of how other managers developed outstanding practice and gained standing ovations, it is intended that manager readers will be impressed.

Types of knowledge

Ironically, what we know about the concept of knowledge is limited. Michael Polanyi (1962, 1983) came up with a distinction that still dominates debate. His basic idea was that we know more than we can tell. Although this may sound paradoxical, it is not. Think of the example of riding a bicycle; you might be able to do it, but you cannot describe this complex process in all its aspects and facets. Another example would be the rules of grammar; you must be using them to communicate clearly, but you probably couldn't spell out the set of rules that you were using at any particular time. Thus, Polanyi differentiated between *tacit knowledge,* the knowledge you actually use when you do things, and *explicit knowledge,* which is the knowledge you can consciously talk about and reflect on.

Ikujiro Nonaka (1991) and his colleague Takeuchi (Nonaka and Takeuchi 1995) adapted the notion of tacit knowledge for management theory and practice. For Nonaka and Takeuchi, *explicit knowledge* is the formalized, accessible knowledge that can be consciously thought, communicated, and shared. *Tacit knowledge,* on the other hand, consists of personal beliefs, values, and perspectives that individuals take for granted; they are not easily accessible

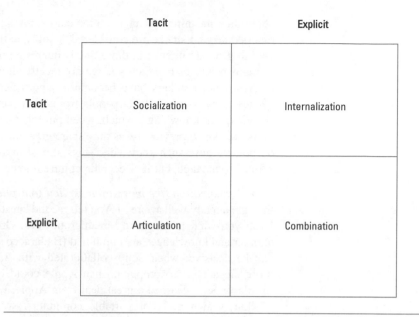

	Tacit	Explicit
Tacit	Socialization	Internalization
Explicit	Articulation	Combination

Figure 10.1   *Nonaka's tacit and explicit knowledge dimensions*

and thus are hard to communicate. Tacit knowledge is a personal cognitive map that helps you navigate—consciously or not—through routines, practices, and processes. Organizationally, it enables you to fill in the gaps between what is formally stipulated and what you actually do.

The difference between the two types of knowledge is easy to understand when you look at artificial intelligence programs. For example, the information needed to play chess is highly explicit knowledge that you can program into a computer; indeed, the computer can calculate faster than a human brain what would be the best move in any given situation. On the other hand, if you instruct a computer to make small talk, it cannot do so; the rules for what you are supposed to say, when you are supposed to laugh (even if it is just to be kind), or when something is meant to be ironic, cynical, or offensive are deeply embedded social behaviors that are almost impossible to turn into explicit knowledge. If you ask a friend why he or she behaved in a certain way during a conversation, and the friend says, "Well, simply because that is what you do," then you know that your friend is referring to tacit, not explicit, knowledge.

Nonaka (1991) differentiates between four basic patterns of knowledge creation, as shown in Figure 10.1. Looking back at the fourfold table that he creates, we can see that, as the grid suggests, there are four major movements during which knowledge is created:

- *Socialization (the move from tacit to tacit):* People learn codes of conduct and rules of behavior implicitly from other people without ever thinking about their meaning. Teenagers often start smoking because they tacitly learn that people who smoke are considered "cool" and that smoking is an effective way to generate interest in those one is interested in by offering them a light. In many countries in which you are not legally allowed to smoke inside (such as Australia), smokers have become a superb network of tacit knowledge, because they routinely meet people from other parts of the organization and share explicit knowledge, which, when put together, often says more than the parts they knew previously, as they share cigarettes in a way that nonsmokers do not. Because such knowledge stays almost invisible, it is hard for organizations to manage, but it affects the culture immensely.

- *Combination (the move from explicit to explicit):* People combine ideas they are already well aware of. You tell me the latest news in microbiology, and I tell you what is happening in microphysics. One organization allies with another and knowledges are combined (Badaracco 1991). Such a combination can be decisive; when Sony collaborated with Apple, they produced much more elegant microcomputers than Apple could have achieved on its own. Similarly, Sony learned a great deal from Apple, which led to the production of Sony's own away of portable computers, such as the VAIO (see also pp. 385–392).

- *Internalization (the move from explicit to tacit):* Things that you learned once become a pattern in your repertoire; you begin to take them for granted, and you forget that you learned them in the first place. If you start working in a new job in a different country, you might at first wonder why things are done the way they are done, but after a while you accept them as a social fact of that society. For example, Americans, used to two weeks annual leave might find the European or Antipodean custom of a fully-paid month off at the height of summer, a strange ritual. They might wonder how these companies can afford such largesse when the top U.S. companies do not. One consequence of these different leave patterns is that, unlike Americans, Europeans or Antipodeans are more likely to travel extensively beyond their national boundaries and to have a greater comparative experience of everyday life in other places. In fact, such knowledge can be a source of innovative advantage: think of how great restaurants can introduce recipes and ingredients that their chefs have experienced while travelling, for instance, rather than just being stuck in the familiar routines.

- *Articulation (the move from tacit to explicit):* Through articulating and sharing within the organization, new knowledge becomes accessible and part of official processes. An obvious example of such learning is formal training programs for new members of organizations—such as how to make a new dish or design a new feature in a product.

In the last decade, management theorists have increasingly found that tacit knowledge contributes significantly to innovation processes (see also pp. 396–398). Thus, it is very important for management to know how to organize and manage tacit knowledge, and how to transform elements of tacit knowledge into organizationally explicit knowledge—an idea that marks the birth of the concept of knowledge management.

No wonder management tries to dip into the pot of tacit knowledge; whereas explicit knowledge encompasses all you can talk about, tacit knowledge is a much deeper and richer source, and knowledge management is the instrument that is supposed to allow managers to savor this rich stew. Developing this resource and aligning it effectively with change became the domain of what is known as *organizational learning*.

Organizational learning

Obviously, talking about learning touches on a rather broad field: for example, you can learn to drive a car, you can learn a mathematical formula by heart, you can learn how to play the drums, and so on. Each of these processes requires different skills, timing, and involvement. Although learning something by heart goes rather quickly (and is in fact forgotten quickly because it involves repetition and lodges in short-term memory), learning to play an instrument can take years and requires that you have *talent* (an inherent potential which you either have or do not). Learning to drive a car is an entirely different kind of process from the others; it involves not only cognitive but also complex bodily skills. To be a proficient driver, your feet must touch the clutch and accelerator, your hands must act according to what you see and the information you are processing (about the road conditions, traffic, and so on), and you must factor in your experience of similar situations.

In the past, managers valued only what was explicit, codified, and routine, but gradually throughout the systematic development of management they began to realize that organizational learning—similar to the skills mentioned in the previous paragraph—involves far more than meets the eye. Whereas Taylor (1911) sought to establish the one best way to do things as management's way, elsewhere, especially in Japan, the emphasis shifted to one of continuous improvement (Kono and Clegg 1998). The premise was that it was not only managers who should know what was happening–other members of the organization might also know—and might even be able to think of better ways of doing things. The organization could learn from the tacit knowledge, shortcuts, experience, and improvements introduced by its members. If all of these were captured and implemented then they could be a powerful source of competitive advantage. That management might not, a priori, know best, was a significant retreat from the position of scientific management.

Taylor's (1911) scientific management was basically an attempt to find out what workers were actually doing when they were doing their job so that it could be codified and used as evidence against them. Before Taylor, managers set the agenda and the objectives on what was to be done, but they did not know how workers actually achieved what they did. Taylor wanted to change this situation; the lack of knowledge on management's side made it hard for managers to tell realistically how much time workers should take to do a certain task. Moreover, when problems suddenly occurred, management could not react because it lacked the know-how of workers. Taylor set out to change this state of affairs, trying to get the knowledge out of the workers' heads and into management's prescriptions to make it an accessible and objective phenomenon for managerial manipulation. Taylor was convinced knowledge was power and managers should own it; more contemporary managers, exposed to the philosophies of continuous improvement and quality management might agree with the sentiment but not have the same expectation of monopoly rights. Knowledge can be generated anywhere in the organization if the organization is prepared to learn from it.

Can organizations learn?

Although you might agree that learning is an important concept for individuals and even for classes, can entire organizations learn? Isn't it only the members who learn how to do things, or the different strata within the organization that are provided with or denied different opportunities for learning? Think of old and established organizations, such as the Catholic Church. Its liturgy has changed entirely over the centuries, but the organization goes on, seemingly forever. In the Church as well as in secular organizations, what persists are the routines, practices, and stories that embody and enact the organization's individual character. The specific character of an organization is formed through its routines, processes, practices, and stories—put simply, those cultural facets—that constitute where organizational knowledge is "stored." To change organization culture—the store of knowledge—organizations must both relinquish old habits and learn new ways (see also pp. 267–271).

Knowledge as a barrier to learning

The biggest enemy of learning (besides the usual suspects, such as lack of interest) is, ironically, knowledge itself. Whenever we assume that we know something, this implies that we can stop learning about it. In fact, often we think that when we know we don't have to learn any more. We know how to ride that bike, drive that car, or chant that liturgy.

The biggest enemy of learning (besides the usual suspects, such as lack of interest) is, ironically, knowledge itself.

We do not know how to know otherwise. Large corporations often seem to suffer from this phenomenon, more widely known either as *ignorance* or *arrogance*. Starbuck (1983) offers a good example: Facit, the assumed name of an organization in the 1960s that produced better mechanical calculators at lower costs than any other company in the world, failed exactly because it thought it knew what to do:

The engineers within Facit itself concentrated on technologies having clear relevance for mechanical calculators, and Facit understood these technologies well. Top, middle and lower managers agreed about how a mechanical-calculator factory should look and operate, what mechanical-calculator customers wanted, what was key to success, and what was unimportant or silly. . . . No resources were wasted gathering irrelevant information or analyzing tangential issues. Costs were low, service fast, glitches rare, understanding high, expertise great! . . . Relying on the company's information-gathering programs, the top managers surmised that Facit's mechanical-calculator customers would switch to electronics very slowly because they liked mechanical calculators. Of course, Facit had no programs for gathering information from people who were buying electronic calculators. (Starbuck 1983: 92)

Facit's problem was exactly that it already knew a lot, which made learning more seem like a waste of time. However, after the market and technology had changed, it was already too late to learn the lessons that the competition had learned already. Facit failed because it knew too much about what it did and had insufficient knowledge about competitors, technologies, and customers.

Learning as adaptation

Levitt and March (1988) as well as Chris Argyris and Donald Schön (1978) tackled the kinds of problems that led to Facit's failure when they thought about how organizations can learn and change. Their theories still provide the template for most accounts of organizational learning, so we explore them in detail. Levitt and March (1988) understand learning as a process of adapting to the environment an organization is dealing with. Organizations turn past experiences into routines and learn in this way. Learning is played out as adaptation to environmental changes; think of new technologies that force organizations to explore the new possibilities they make possible. Speaking generally, such learning processes increase an organization's competence and thus are beneficial. However, Levitt and March identified what they call the "competency trap." It occurs when an organization does something well and learns more about it until it becomes such an expert organization that it does not see the limits of its achievements. It cannot change in response to the changes in its environment because it has become so focused on doing things its way, even when it becomes evident that the old routines are no longer working. Many ancient civilizations have gone down this path and disappeared because they got caught up in their routines and ways of doing things to such an extent that, even when their habits proved to be dysfunctional, they could not imagine different ways of organizing themselves. The impressive ruins of the ancient Mayan civilization, which flourished in the Yucatan peninsula from about A.D. 250 to 900, are the silent remainder of such decay. The civilization's structure was complex—that much archaeologists have been able to glean—but they do not know exactly what led to its eclipse, although they suspect it probably involved extreme warfare.

It is not only ancient civilizations that can lose their way, as the example of the more recent corporate failure of Facit demonstrates. Although Facit learned

Image 10.2   *Vestiges of an ancient civilization with a highly organized structure, in the Mexican Chiapas highlands*

to build the best calculators in the world, it failed because it relied on its competencies. It did not know what it did not know. What it did not know was that electronic innovations were outflanking the knowledge basis of what it was that they knew so well. In common parlance, they were about to expire, and the future would consign their technology to the junkyard. It was this phenomenon that Argyris and Schön (1978) tackled from an interorganizational perspective when they distinguished between single and double loop learning—which sounds a bit knotty but is not difficult to grasp.

Single and double loop learning

Argyris and Schön (1978) were among the first researchers to focus on the phenomenon of organizational learning. In contrast to Levitt and March (1988), they researched organizationally internal preconditions and implications of learning processes. To understand ways of learning, they differentiated between two types of learning: single loop learning and double loop learning (or learning I and II). *Single loop learning* means, basically, optimizing skills, refining abilities, and acquiring knowledge necessary to achieve resolution of a problem that requires solving. For instance, if you attend a training seminar

Single loop learning involves learning the competencies necessary to play a certain game successfully, whereas double loop learning requires thinking and learning about what is the most valuable game to play.

where you learn to use PowerPoint and related programs, you will obviously learn something (even if you only learn that you don't want to learn how to use PowerPoint because it is too predictable, limited, and boring and stifles your great and sophisticated ideas). Such learning happens within a given frame of reference: The parameters are given and clearly defined, and the learning experience focuses on how to optimize (or maximize or increase) your capacity within this frame.

Double loop learning is a bit more complex; this type of learning actually means changing the frame of reference that normally guides behavior. Double loop learning is not the acquisition of knowledge that you need to accomplish a given task; rather, it involves rethinking the task and considering whether its accomplishment is beneficial or not. Managers in a weekend seminar discussion of the company's mission and core values could be engaged in double loop learning processes when they redefine the market for their products or the products themselves. To put it metaphorically, single loop learning involves learning the competencies necessary to play a certain game successfully, whereas double loop learning requires thinking and learning about what is the most valuable game to play. Single loop learning concerns acting according to the rules of a certain game; in contrast, double loop learning involves learning what the actual rules of the extant game are and how they could be changed to make another game. Single loop learning focuses on optimizing problem-solving behavior in a given context, whereas double loop learning challenges the core assumptions, beliefs, and values that frame the context. In the words of Argyris and Schön,

> When the error detected and corrected permits the organization to carry on its present policies or achieve its presents objectives, then that error-and-correction process is *single-loop* learning. Single-loop learning is like a thermostat that learns when it is too hot or too cold and turns the heat on or off. The thermostat can perform this task because it can receive information (the temperature of the room) and take corrective action. *Double-loop* learning occurs when error is detected and corrected in ways that involve the modification of an organization's underlying norms, policies and objectives. (Argyris and Schön 1978: 2)

For organizations, these distinctions have important implications. Whereas single loop learning is important to improve performance incrementally, double loop learning questions the business an organization is in, its culture, and its strategic vision. Double loop learning represents an ability to reflect on the single loop learning processes and to understand when fundamental change is required.

To make these concepts more concrete, think of the example of Nike (see also p. 319). When Nike learned how to produce shoes more cheaply through outsourcing to Asia or learned to improve the quality of its shoes by engaging athletes in their design, it was engaged in a single loop learning process. But when Nike, thinking that its shoes were completely overengineered for everyday use, stripped the design out of them, it began a process of double loop learning. The result of Nike's action was that customers no longer wanted to buy the shoes because they no longer embodied the Nike spirit. Customers wanted to wear the shoes their idols wore. In facing and resolving this challenge, Nike was engaged in a double loop learning process. In such a situation, Nike had to find out which business it was in, what its mission was, and what its core value proposition was. Learning that normal customers loved overengineered sports shoes because such shoes communicated something that customers could not get anywhere else fundamentally changed Nike's understanding of its identity and how the company should do and be what its identity entailed (Hatch and Schultz 2001).

CRITICAL ISSUES: DRIVING FORCES BEHIND KNOWLEDGE AND LEARNING

In summary of the chapter so far, we can understand organizational learning as being "best applied to organizations which are able regularly to monitor and reflect on the assumptions by which they operate, so that they can quickly learn about themselves and their working environment, and change . . ." (Gabriel, Fineman, and Sims 2000: 323). As we saw with Levitt and March's (1988) and Argyris and Schön's (1978) analyses, learning is about self-reflection that triggers insights into organizational routines, beliefs, and values. After these facets of an organization are understood, they are open to being changed—theoretically. But how is such learning actually accomplished, and what are the driving forces behind learning? In this section, we focus on two major arenas that drive learning: communities of practice and collaborations. Whereas the first concept focuses on learning within an organization, the second explores the learning that occurs when organizations collaborate.

Learning in and through communities of practice

With his concept of "communities of practice," Etienne Wenger (1998, 2002), a consultant and researcher, understands learning as a process deeply embedded in what he calls "social learning systems." He argues that learning does not happen in the individual mind, departmental routines, or organizations; rather, learning is a process that occurs in social learning systems. Consider your own experience as a student of management; of course, learning takes place (we hope!) while you are reading the lines we have written. But, equally important, you learn in the classroom when interacting with colleagues and teachers. Perhaps you might talk to a friend who is working, or think of the experiences you had in casual jobs you took during summer vacation, or maybe you already have a job—these are the resources that you use to make sense of what you hear. Or maybe you watch movies or read newspapers and link what you see and read back to what you are learning in the higher-education context. When you speak to a friend who decided to study law instead of management, maybe you try to explain why you enjoy studying management and why it is important. Combined, it is all these interactions that make up what Wenger calls a "social learning system." When such a system is established, it often blurs the boundaries of single organizational contexts. It creates learning alliances (between a university and an organization, perhaps), regional clusters (maybe a group of organizations in a high-tech industry, such as in Silicon Valley), and global networks (think of all those Linux users, unknown to each other, who, through cyberspace, are making the Linux system ever more robust and challenging the dark side of Microsoft). Learning often takes place through the almost imperceptible networks that bind us together with others, both inside and outside the organizations in which we work. Translucent and like a spider's web, the objective of networks is to capture knowledge.

For organizations, Wenger's (1998, 2002) ideas have important implications; learning does not occur in isolated activities such as training weekends or

Image 10.3   *The web of knowledge*

know-how seminars offered every six months. Rather, it happens within the normal contexts that span organizational boundaries and processes and that bring many different activities together. As Wenger puts it, what triggers learning is the interplay between the competence that an individual's institutional environment represents and an individual's own experience.

Communities

Wenger's (1998, 2002) notion of "communities of practice" captures the interplay that is embedded in social learning systems. Regardless of whether you look at a group of students who work together on a project, the R&D (research and development) team of an organization, or a street gang, they are all communities of practice because they are the social building blocks of learning systems. It is within these communities that we define what counts as competence, whether it involves designing a successful project answer, developing breakthrough innovations, or orchestrating a drive-by shooting. Of course, the moral consequences differ; whereas deferring to legitimate authorities might be an important competence in an R&D department (although not necessarily—for instance, where "skunk works"—entrepreneurially conceived, informal, and illegitimate projects that are pursued in moments of non-routine—are launched behind the back of authorities), in a street gang it would not be one of the competencies required, where the moral authority of the gang leader would be likely to be greater than that of legitimate authority external to the gang, such as the criminal law system. In contrast, whereas dressing in a particular way, taking the "right" drugs, and generally being "tough" might be important artifacts of the street gang, they are less likely to be highly regarded in an R&D department—although there may well be significant stylistic differences between R&D and finance members, for instance. In both cases, each community of practice defines what constitutes competencies. According to Wenger (2002), these competencies are defined by three elements:

- *Sense of joint enterprise:* Members need to understand and share what their particular community is about and how they can contribute to their community. Put simply, if you work for the International Monetary Fund and think that it is a force for autonomous models of development, you might be surprised when you find out how the organization actually operates, and you probably won't remain employed for very long (see also pp. 174–175).
- *Relationships of mutuality:* Communities are built and sustained through interaction between their members. Through interaction with each other, they establish relationships of mutuality. To be a member, you must be trusted as a member of this community. Put simply, if you are a member of a street gang, or want to pass for one (like the cop in *The Fast and the*

Furious [Cohen 2001]), you have to be prepared to live outside the law that everyone else follows.

- *Shared repertoire:* Over time, communities of practice produce a common history. They establish a shared repertoire of stories, languages, artifacts, routines, rituals, processes—put simply, a culture (see also pp. 267–271). Being a member of a community means having access to this repertoire and the knowledge of how to use it accordingly. Think of the scene in the movie *Gladiator* (Scott 2000) in which the character Maximus, played by Russell Crowe, finally gains the acceptance of his peers by behaving, fighting, and talking like a gladiator.

The social learning system encompasses many smaller communities of practice. These communities, equipped with a sense of joint enterprise, relationships of mutuality, and a shared repertoire, are the building blocks of learning. Obviously, these building blocks are not good per se—just think of the shared repertoire of stories that can often be organizationally quite scathing. Shared understanding and trust is the basis for communicating about change; but, as we have seen—theoretically, with Argyris and Schön (1978), and practically, with the example of Facit—these shared assumptions can lead to homogeneity, blindness, and groupthink (see also pp. 215–216; 309).

Boundaries

Communities of practice must interact with other communities, which shifts the focus to the boundaries around communities. On one hand, boundaries are important because they trigger the establishment of a community. However, on the other hand, they need to be spanned and transgressed to facilitate the flow of information. The boundaries around communities of practice are less clearly defined than organizational boundaries. For instance, a community of practice can involve not only parts of an organization but also an important supplier who works closely with the organization. Thus, these communities can evolve across organizational boundaries and can include nonorganizational members. Boundary-spanning activity is important because it offers unique and rich learning opportunities. Being confronted with an outsider's perspective or challenged by someone with a different social and cultural background can trigger new insights. The clash between what you take for granted and what someone else might see in a different light can become the starting point of an innovative and creative process (see also pp. 379–381).

Wenger (2002) argues that communities of practice can become hostage to their own history, and an outsider or newcomer might challenge the repertoire that makes them inert and reactive (see also p. 433). Managing the boundaries of interaction between the communities of practice that form a social learning system is thus an important managerial task. As Wenger (2002) suggests, there are three ways of managing boundaries—through people, artifacts, and interaction:

- *People:* People can act as brokers between communities of practice and span their boundaries. Think of a woman who is a board member of an organization and who also works as senior manager in another company. She lives in two worlds simultaneously and can infuse one community of practice with knowledge from the other. By doing so, she creates learning opportunities for both. Of course, brokers run the danger of being marginalized, overlooked, and becoming invisible in communities because they do not exclusively and fully belong to only one community. Thus, managing their needs, expectations, and experiences is an important task. Sometimes organizations explicitly seek such members—for instance, when they want to have *interlocking directors* (people who already hold a directorship in another company and can bring to bear their experience from that firm and industry to a different type of organization).

- *Artifacts:* Objects such as tools, documents, models, discourses, and processes can act as boundary spanners as well. The discourse of postmodernism in the 1990s and the language of engineering in the first decade of the twentieth century functioned as a bridge between different communities such as architects, managers, and academics. Put more mundanely, think of a bar in which people from different backgrounds meet and chat. In this case, a bar's preferred beer brand, the type of music it plays, or the sports it broadcasts can function as a broker between different groups. As another example, some groups—such as surfies, skaters, or homeboys—might be linked to each other through their preference for specific clothes and fashion items. In this case, a common interest of all three groups in Nike products—even though they might use them quite differently—creates a potential bridge that could minimize the gaps between them.

- *Interaction:* Interaction can be a direct boundary-spanning activity because it exposes the beliefs and perspectives of one community to another. Think of an exchange program between your university and a university in another country; through the exchange program, you are exposed to another culture. By comparing your own culture to the other one, you might learn new perspectives and change established ideas. Organizationally, this interaction happens between customers and sales staff; sales persons that form one community of practice talk to the community of users about their products and services, and complaints from customers are used to improve existing services and products or even to develop completely new ideas (see also pp. 385–392).

In complex interdisciplinary project teams, such as the collaboration between Swatch and Mercedes that resulted in the Smart Car, different communities of practice combine and challenge the knowledge and competencies of the others. When this is done well, it provides a rich learning opportunity for organizations, given that they accept that they cannot fully own or control these processes. As Wenger (2002) notes, organizations can participate in such opportunities, leverage them, and learn in and from them. However, they cannot be managed through the limited means of traditional management, which focuses on control, predictability, and power. We will come back to this issue in a few pages when we discuss the paradox of organizational learning.

Learning in and through collaborations

Not much more than a decade ago, many companies were not too keen on working together collaboratively. They were scared that their competitors could gain access to the scarce resources they owned and would run off with the fruits of the valuable learning they had acquired over the years. Growth was to be achieved through mergers and acquisitions rather than through networking and collaborating. Today, however, everything is negotiable.

Negotiating alliances and collaborations have become new ways of growing and expanding. Take the example of the airline industry: Instead of competing and pushing each other out of the market, there are two major alliances: One World and Star Alliance. Through a clever network, the companies in each alliance build on their respective strengths and compensate for each other's

Image 10.4   *Everything's negotiable*

weaknesses. Without each airline having to fly to every destination in the world, the alliances are able to offer flights just about everywhere through their networks. And through a smart reward system (frequent flyer points), they retain customers and create loyalty.

Collaborations can trigger knowledge creation and organizational learning when organizations work closely together with suppliers, retailers, customers, universities, or consultants. Or they might focus on collaboration internally among different divisions, teams, and experts. The electronics company Philips and the sportswear giant Nike, for instance, announced in March 2002 that they were collaborating (see Von Stamm 2003: 164). The rationale behind the deal was simple. Nike, is a world leader in marketing, sports, innovation, and material technology, Philips is a leading innovator in the field of "wearable electronics" technologies and has considerable knowledge about consumers and digital technology. Thus, their collaboration brings together different expertise and should enable them to combine and transform their knowledge into new products. It is important that both companies learn from each other and, through broadening their knowledge base, trigger innovation and change (see also pp. 383–395).

From a learning perspective, collaboration is an important means to access new knowledge and transfer skills that an organization lacks. Moreover, facing the challenge of creating more and more complex products, it is hard for any organization to stay at the cutting edge in every single detail. Just think of the automobile industry; almost every part of a new car is a complex mini-project in itself, from the stereo system to the computer-controlled engine, the light aluminum subframe, and even the tires. Thus, car companies are forced to work closely with their suppliers and, in collaboration, they learn from each other. Obviously, this is a dangerous game because no one wants to give away too much information or divulge secret knowledge that competitors could use. However, without trusting and sharing, collaborations are hard to keep alive. As in every learning situation, a collaboration needs an open and relaxed environment in which ideas can grow and spread.

Drawing on extensive research, Tidd, Bessant, and Pavitt (2001) identified three major issues that determine successful learning through collaboration. First, an organization must have the intent to learn through collaboration. Instead of trying to steal its partner's assets, it needs to see the opportunity to learn mutually. Second, it requires transparency. If cultural barriers block the flow of knowledge between companies, or if one partner refuses openness, learning cannot take place. Also, if the knowledge is more tacit than explicit, it will be harder for a partner organization to acquire it. Finally, absorptiveness, referring to the capacity to actually learn, is important.

Some organizations simply seem incapable of absorbing learning. For example, think of the poem *The Charge of the Light Brigade,* in which cavalry were mowed down in an absolutely predictable carnage, as Alfred Lord Tennyson (1870) wrote so memorably:

Half a league, half a league,
Half a league onward,
All in the valley of Death
Rode the six hundred.
"Forward, the Light Brigade!
Charge for the guns," he said;
Into the valley of Death
Rode the six hundred.

"Forward, the Light Brigade!"
Was there a man dismayed?
Not though the soldier knew
Some one had blundered:
Theirs not to make reply,
Theirs not to reason why,
Theirs but to do and die:
Into the valley of Death
Rode the six hundred.

Cannon to right of them,
Cannon to left of them,
Cannon in front of them,
Volleyed and thundered;
Stormed at with shot and shell,
Boldly they rode and well;
Into the jaws of Death,
Into the mouth of Hell
Rode the six hundred.

Flashed all their sabres bare,
Flashed as they turned in air,

Sabring the gunners there,
Charging an army, while
All the world wondered:
Plunged in the battery-smoke,
Right through the
   line they broke:
Cossack and Russian
Reeled from the sabre-stroke,
Shattered and sundered.
Then they rode back, but not
Not the six hundred.

Cannon to right of them,
Cannon to left of them,
Cannon behind them,
Volleyed and thundered:
Stormed at with shot
   and shell,
While horse and hero fell,
They that had fought so well
Came through the jaws of Death
Back from the mouth of Hell,
All that was left of them,
Left of six hundred.

When can their glory fade?
O the wild charge they made!
All the world wondered.
Honour the charge they made!
Honour the Light Brigade,
Noble six hundred!

Management that sees in mistakes only the negative is likely to block organizational learning processes.

The six hundred were noble, but they were doomed by codes of honor and chivalry belonging to an age when cannons did not cut a swath through cavalry. Never has an inability to learn organizationally been captured so poetically.

Poetry apart, when armies fail, generals are usually blamed. Failure and blame are not usually organizational strangers. Organizations usually need a scapegoat to blame when a failure occurs. However, learning often happens through a trial-and-error process in which mistakes and failure provide the richest source of learning. Management that sees in mistakes only the negative is likely to block organizational learning processes because it excludes mistakes from its agenda and brands as "losers" those people who make mistakes. Even generals can learn from their defeats.

What lessons should we learn?

It is not always clear what we should learn from a certain experience. Although we share the same experience, we might disagree completely on the consequences of the event. Take the terrorist attacks on America on September 11, 2001. What happened is clear, but the learning that different people and factions draw from this event could not vary more fundamentally. Whereas some suggest fighting fire with fire, others argue that doing so will simply lead to more of the same problems. The action of one party is the occasion for reaction from the other party, and what one side identifies as cause is seen by the other as effect. Thus, learning is based on the interpretation of a particular situation, and this is always contested terrain.

THE FINE PRINT: ORGANIZATIONAL LEARNING AS OXYMORON?

The paradox of organizational learning

In mainstream texts on learning and knowledge management, learning is depicted as an easy process for organizations. Next to organizational behavior, organizational development, or organizational change, organizational learning is a topic in its own right, an attribute that makes the descriptions of organizations a bit more colorful and textbooks a bit thicker. Karl Weick and Frances Westley (1999) would not necessarily agree with this dominant view; rather, they challenge the concept of organizational learning in its fundamentals, arguing that the term *organizational learning* is, in fact, an oxymoron. Just like the members of the British royal family, organization and learning are things that don't seem to fit together well. As Weick and Westley argue, learning and organizing are "essentially antithetical processes, which means the phrase 'organizational learning' qualifies as oxymoron" (Weick and Westley 1999: 190). Organizing is all about ordering and controlling—or, as the authors put it, about decreasing variety—whereas learning is about disorganizing and increasing variety. If learning is about exploring new terrain and understanding the unknown, and organizing is about exploiting routines and the already known, organizational learning would be a paradox (see also pp. 67–73). Weick and Westley suggest not that we should simply forget the concept but that we should be careful that in using it, we make sense of its ambivalence. They understand learning as a process that is possible only in those spaces where order is juxtaposed with disorder. Put simply, learning happens when the old and the new clash and create a tension (see also pp. 379–381).

As we saw with Jim March (2002) in Chapter 3, learning happens somewhere between organizations exploring what they don't know and exploiting what they do know (see also pp. 99–101). Or, to put it another way, profound learning happens when single loop learning (exploitation, evolution, adaptation, and habit) intersects with double loop learning (exploration, revolution, and thinking outside the box) (Weick and Westley, 1999: 195). To make their ideas a bit more tangible, Weick and Westley (1999) analyze three ways of exploring the space in between the old and the new by using the metaphors of humor, improvisation, and small wins as moments of learning.

- *Humor:* Jokes and funny situations provide opportunities for learning because they play with the meanings we normally associate with specific words and deeds, turning them upside down. Almost every joke pulls together things that are normally separated and, in doing so, creates a surprising element that makes us laugh. In addition, the normal social order is suspended for a moment when we are telling a joke; you might say "just joking . . ." when you are telling a joke and you say something that might be true but that is not socially acceptable. (Remember, in the ancient feudal kingdoms, the only one allowed to tell the truth was the fool or the jester!) Finally, humor happens spontaneously; it cannot be planned or forecasted. The funniest situations happen out of the blue. Humor carries the flexibility and richness of quick and creative response to the environment and represents a way of exploring the space between order and disorder in which learning happens.

- *Improvisation:* Improvisation is another concept of learning that deals productively with the tension between learning and organizing. Actors and jazz musicians improvise, and so do employees; rather then sending people to seminars where they learn things they cannot apply back in the organization, learning on the job—improvisation—encourages people to play around with everyday patterns and to change them slightly, not necessarily radically, but in situ. Improvisation is always based on an interplay between past, present, and future; by carefully listening and changing past rhythms, something new emerges. Also, errors play an important role within improvisation. To enable learning and development, errors are tolerated and used as starting points for future improvisation. Finally, improvisational learning is a team event, not a one-person show. It relies on the feedback of others, their feelings (rather than their rational capacity alone), and their contribution to change.

- *Small wins:* Small wins, according to Weick and Westley (1999), are not the big revolutionary changes promised by consultants or management gurus but the learning opportunities that happen when you *almost* do business as usual. The researchers give the example of feminists, who sought to change laws and regulations, which turned out to be quite a successful learning strategy. However, while working to achieve their overriding goal of equality for women, the feminists scored a small win by showing that language itself was deeply gendered (chair*man,* post*man,* and so on). This seemingly small win had a big impact, making our society learn much more about the ways in which gender is deeply embedded in how we normally do what we do and become who we are. Thus, small wins might look small, but their effect can be quite big. Again, they are moments of learning because they juxtapose order (common language) and a sense of disorder (new language), creating the space in which learning happens.

Learning, unlearning, nonlearning?

As we have seen, learning is a process that is in tension with the core processes of managing and organizing. Because learning happens only when there is some freedom to experiment with actions and ideas, it challenges management practices that focus on order, predictability, and control. Given this problematic relationship between learning and organizing, you might wonder whether learning is always good for organizations. If learning challenges organizations, why should they learn at all? This is exactly the question that Brunsson (1998) asks in a thought-provoking and ironic paper introducing the idea of the nonlearning organization. He argues that nonlearning organizations are healthier than learning ones, which is an idea directly in opposition to the commonly accepted view that there is a positive relationship between learning and organizational performance. In fact, most scholars and management gurus argue that learning leads to greater efficiency and better performance. The learning organization seems to improve itself continuously through learning.

Brunsson (1998) looks at public-sector organizations and wonders whether their nonlearning is simply pathological (something bad) or whether their persistence with routines (their nonlearning) is something more fundamentally positive. He starts by suggesting that if learning is as extremely positive as theorists suggest, nonlearning must be dysfunctional and negative for organizations. To find out more about this hypothesis, he looks at what are often regarded as notoriously unlearning organizations—those in the public sector. Analyzing the public budgeting process in Scandinavian and other countries, he found that, when faced with challenges or problems, such as incomplete information and an insecure future, Scandinavian budgeting organizations repeat the same behavior over and over again—they ask for better reports from their employees and partners. However, the reports are never complete enough to capture what is not known and cannot be predicted. Nonetheless, reports are supposed to capture information and to make predictions. Consequently, they do so, but they do a poor, incomplete job. The reports do not improve, which leads to the same behavior again—the complaints about the bad quality of reports and the request for better reports next time. The same circle is reproduced every time, and, instead of getting better reports, these organizations simply repeat what they have said already. In short, budget agencies do not seem to learn anything from past problems and just repeat the behavior they have displayed in the past. They are nonlearning organizations that confront insurmountable problems with tired routines that cannot be refreshed. Hence, they work on the basis of the information and skills they have available, always knowing that they will never be sufficient. Still, the reports, though they are poor, serve a function: They can always blame bad reports when surprises are encountered.

Instead of following the mainstream argument (learning is good, and therefore nonlearning must be bad), Brunsson (1998) turns the order upside down and argues that nonlearning can result in the following unexpected benefits for the organization:

- *Tolerance of contradictions:* When learning organizations face contradictions, challenges, or problems in their environments, they have to adjust either their behavior or their objectives. They have to act consistently over time and constantly align their behavior with their objectives. Nonlearning organizations, on the other hand, are much more flexible. If they face an environment in which contradictions and uncertainties are the norm rather than the exception, they can still operate normally. The budget agencies, for instance, were confronted with unsatisfactory reports and asked for better reports next time. However, despite the incomplete reports, they accomplished their tasks. Nonlearning organizations manage contradictions well because they accomplish what they have to do, even though they hope that things will be better next time.

- *Organizational discretion:* Nonlearning organizations are capable of benefiting from the gap between talk, action, and decision (see also pp. 61–67). Although they kept asking for better reports, they did their job based on the same unsatisfactory reports that they had always received. Facing this situation, a learning organization would probably become unsatisfied, and its employees would be frustrated enough to seek better sources of information, whereas the nonlearning organization is able to differentiate between what they would like to have (better reports) and what they actually have (incomplete reports). Again, this makes the nonlearning organization flexible, and it provides a certain kind of freedom—they can be realistic in their task accomplishment and remain idealistic about the future.

In light of these positive aspects of nonlearning, Brunsson argues that the nonlearning organization is in fact an emancipated organization. Learning organizations have to change, adjust, and align all the time, whereas nonlearning organizations can deal with contradictions, inconsistent demands, and gaps between ideal worlds and actual reality. They are emancipated because they can disregard the (ostensible) need for change that drives learning organizations.

The power of learning

Knowledge management and scientific management

Knowledge management practitioners like to think of themselves as conceptually new and innovative. They are the bold face of the new consulting, the chief information officers of the new millennium. However, the focus of knowledge management is quite old; transforming tacit knowledge from employees into explicit knowledge that is owned by the company was the driving force behind Taylor's (1911) idea of scientific management (see also pp. 18–22). Taylor disliked the fact that the workers knew more about the actual process than he or their managers did. Workers could tell stories about why things are the way they are, and others had to accept these stories. Management lacked any better, alternative knowledge because they did not have a basic understanding of the tasks that the workers did. Without such objective knowledge, how could they manage effectively? Taylor's (1911) initiative in getting the knowledge out of workers' heads and making it an object of managerial manipulation in Bethlehem Steel was a harsh way of transforming tacit into explicit knowledge. It sought to destroy the craft basis of existing know-how from the situation in prior generations, where knowledge and status were coterminous—that is, one did not become a master without having acquired the knowledge of a journeyman and apprentice—so this separation of power and knowledge was unthinkable (see also pp. 5–10).

Lifelong learning equals lifelong examinations

In organizational terms, we have already talked about Taylor's (1911) approach and the way he empowered management: He simply gained knowledge that had been the workers' domain. Scientific management changed the power relations, made the worker an object of study, formalized the worker's task, and made any worker exchangeable with another. The difference between Taylor's scientific management and modern knowledge management is that Taylor thought you have to codify knowledge only once, whereas knowledge management realizes that you can never stop learning or codifying—it is a lifelong process.

Given the enthusiasm for the concept of lifelong learning, it is interesting to consider one of Foucault's (1979) core arguments that shows the dark side of lifelong learning—that lifelong learning might very well imply lifelong examination. Foucault focused especially on the examination as a common practice integrating knowledge and power. Once, the integration was institutionally fairly specific: It occurred mostly at school and university. Thus, Western societies that praise continuous learning are simultaneously paving the path of lifelong learning with exams that assess the learners, given the centrality of performance measurement to contemporary management culture. As you know from your own experience, exams are powerful instruments that shape your behavior and, by extension, your personality. Or think of the assessment centers that are widely used tools of human resource management. They are almost perfect examples of the knowledge/power link because they have the power to assess someone (using their knowledge dimension) and change him or her (using their power dimension).

For Foucault, the examination is such a powerful tool because it combines both a hierarchical observation and a normalizing judgment. There are two functions of examinations. First, they make individuals visible (who is clever, who is not?) and allow the supervisor to categorize them. Exams enable supervisors to find out who are their potential stars and who is the deadwood. Second, examinations make it possible to judge people and to compare them with each other. Think of your class: You and your classmates might have different strengths and skills that are not easily comparable. The exam ignores all these individual differences and judges everybody by the same template; it normalizes people as it ignores their differences and subjects them all to the same metric. The process of scrutiny transforms ordinary individuals into cases who are obliged to compete with each other in the expression of a unique individuality.

Foucault analyzes three mechanisms that form the heart of the examination:

- *Visibility:* During examinations, the learning subjects are fully visible, whereas the examiners are almost absent. We saw this power at work at the Panopticon; transforming the individual into an object that is visible and that can be assessed ensures discipline.
- *Individuality:* Examinations transform a group of people into individuals by means of homogenization of individual features. Exams establish a hierarchy within a group and put each individual in his or her place within the hierarchy.
- *Case:* Exams transform individual characters into cases that are documented and objectified. Every individual has a history in this system that can be compared to others. Individual development can be assessed and, if necessary, corrected.

Examinations combine the hierarchical surveillance of people with the normalizing judgment of the supervisor: It makes individuals visible, transforms each into a case, and renders them open to powerful intervention. A society that understands itself as continuously learning must see its shadow as well in a series of powerful examinations that both constitute and mark the individual life.

That exams are powerful can be seen in the fact that they are highly ritualized in almost every society. And they are not just confined to schools and universities but can even be the basis for popular entertainment. Consider other forms of examination (and more broadly, judgment) that can be seen in popular TV shows such as *American Idol* or *Big Brother,* where people are constantly watched and assessed by an audience that is completely invisible to the people on the show.

SUMMARY AND REVIEW

Organizations cannot avoid learning, but that is no guarantee that what they will learn will benefit them. Organization theorists interested in knowledge management seek to ensure that organizations learn the appropriate lessons and retain what is good while avoiding or discarding what is bad. That seems pretty straightforward, but, as this chapter has repeatedly suggested, the process is not quite as simple as it seems. Sometimes, nonlearning organizations may have an advantage over learning organizations. Learning organizations can place their members under a fearsome audit and sap their vitality; they can also codify what is unimportant and inconsequential while missing that which is profound because it is so deeply embedded in the normal ways of doing things. These issues often come to haunt organizations that downsize; thinking that they have routinized and learned everything that they need to know from their members, organizations find out too late that downsizing results in not only live bodies walking out the door but also the departure of some deeply embedded and important knowledge that managers didn't know would be missed because they didn't know what they had until they lost it. Still, as the chapter has covered, there are many ways of seeking to ensure that knowledge is managed appropriately. However, we have to consider the deeply subversive thought that perhaps knowledge that is genuinely important can rarely be managed explicitly because it is so often cast into darkness by the reason that prevails.

ONE MORE TIME . . .

Getting the story straight

- What does Nonaka think is the most important knowledge to manage and why?
- What kind of learning must organizations do to survive?
- What differentiates single loop learning from double loop learning?

Thinking outside the box

- What do communities of practice do in terms of learning?
- Why should organizations collaborate across boundaries?
- Why might the term *organizational learning* be an oxymoron?

ADDITIONAL RESOURCES

1. Absolutely essential is the formative work of Nonaka and Takeuchi (1995), although it is a good idea to look at the source material in Polanyi (1962). The concept of tacit knowledge as Polanyi develops it is not quite as easily tamed and domesticated by management as these Japanese authors suggest.

2. The missing dimension from most treatments of knowledge management is the way that knowledge always implicates power and is always implicated in power. The classic text is Foucault's (1979) *Discipline and Punish,* especially the graphic opening pages, in which he contrasts a gruesome execution with the rules of a model prison established in France just sixty years later. To the former belongs a fearsome vengeance, to the latter a reforming zeal—but neither vengeance on the body nor zeal toward the mind of the criminal is a practice of knowledge that we can easily understand unless we consider the regimes of power associated with them.

3. In terms of films, *Terminator 3: Rise of the Machines* (Mostow 2003), comes to mind. In this movie, a machine, played by Arnold Schwarzenegger, knows what the future holds for the hero and heroine, and he has to ensure that they meet their fate. If only organizations were able to have such prescience!

4. *The Right Stuff* (Kaufman 1983), about the NASA space program, is a good resource for organizational learning. The movie is based on Tom Wolfe's bestselling 1979 book of the same name. The film dramatically depicts the way that an organization—in this case, NASA—learned and did not learn. In a similar vein, the film of *Apollo 13* (Howard 1995) is also required viewing.

5. We also suggest watching *Bowling for Columbine* (Moore 2002), which is an absolutely surreal journey through American society. The movie explores why and how American gun culture emerged and is learned anew with each generation.

In addition to these suggested additional resources, don't forget to look at what is also available on the Web site **www.ckmanagement.net,** including free PDF files of recent papers related to this chapter, which you can download; video interviews with famous academics talking about related themes; as well as many other resources, such as connections to interesting Web sites.

CHAPTER 11

MANAGING INNOVATION AND CHANGE

Creativity, Chaos, Foolishness

Objectives and learning outcomes

By the end of this chapter, you will be able to

- Explain the basic assumptions of innovation strategies

- Grasp the role of change in organizations

- Understand the role of creativity in business

- Analyze different approaches to change and creativity

- Discuss the benefits and shortcomings of these approaches

- Appreciate these approaches' challenges for management

- Discuss organizational practices that trigger (potentially) innovation and change

Before you get started . . .

Sing along with a little verse from Bob Dylan (1963):
The line it is drawn, the curse it is cast, the slow one now will later be fast.
As the present now will later be past, the order is rapidly fadin'.
And the first one now will later be last, for the times they are a-changin'.

OUTLINE OF THE CHAPTER

When did you last do something for the first time? Ask many organization managers this question, and the answer would probably be that it was quite a long time ago because, like bad habits, organizations are hard to change. Changing processes, practices, routines, products, or services and coming up with new ones is neither easy nor always enjoyable; doing something new can be quite painful and difficult. Thus, organizations tend to stick to the format they are used to and the things they already know. In this case, change means adapting incrementally (step by step). If they just do as before, but increase output, they will neither facilitate change nor trigger innovation. When they change they do things differently; when they innovate they do things in a new way or produce new things.

Innovative change is important for organizations. Speaking organizationally, innovation (either of practice or of products) leads to change that allows a company to position itself differently from its competitors. It does things differently (practices) or it offers different things (products/services). Either way, it establishes itself strategically in the market. The competitive advantages of organizations are built on this core concept (see also pp. 417–424). Because innovation and change are interrelated (see Tidd, Bessant, and Pavitt 2001), we have put them together in this chapter.

SETTING THE SCENE

When we think of innovation, it is customary to make the following distinction: A company can change the products and services it offers (*product innovation*), or it can change the way it delivers them (*process innovation*). Let's use a concrete example. Henry Ford, founder of the Ford Motor Company and the assembly line, was one of the greatest inventors in the history of management, according to Wren and Greenwood (1998: 41). However, his way to success was anything but smooth. Born in 1863 as the son of a farmer in Michigan, he fiddled around with engines on his father's farm. In those days, cars were seen as a curiosity, and the majority of people did not believe that they would have a bright future; most cars were based on experiments with electric- or steam-powered engines. In fact, there were not many cars around in 1900; of the 4,192 cars that were built in 1900, not even 1,000 were gasoline powered. After the failure of his first business venture, Ford raised more money and developed his models N and T, which became big successes. In 1908, he sold more than 10,000 cars. Ford's assembly line, the idea for which he got from the methods used for butchering steer in the Chicago slaughterhouses, was a process innovation that made changes in management style, production, marketing, and strategy possible. The assembly line innovation allowed for massive growth. In 1909, Ford produced 13,840 cars; seven years later, in 1916, the company produced 585,388 cars! Simultaneously, the cost of producing each car decreased from $950 in 1909 to $360 in 1916. The Ford success story illustrates impressively how technology innovation (engine), change in payment of employees ($5 per day for workers, which was a lot of money back then), and production (assembly line) all led to something new and revolutionary. However, at the beginning, he was struggling with the common sense notions of his time, and probably not many of his contemporaries would have had much trust or confidence in his adventures. For example, his high wages were called "industrial suicide" and "socialism" by Ford's critics. The $5-a-day wage that Ford introduced was not necessary; it didn't flow from the assembly line, but improvements in production occurred as a result of this innovation. Even great innovators can be outflanked, of course. In those early days, when the Model T Ford was dominant, Ford offered cars in black only and, by the 1920s, was losing market share to General Motors and Chrysler, who offered color.

To use a more up-to-date example of how change and innovation are interlinked, think about the technological innovation of the Motion Picture Experts Group level three protocol. If you think you've never heard of it, maybe you know it better as MP3. It allows you to compress large music files and transfer them fast through the Internet. This product innovation is changing an entire industry and forcing it to rethink its business practices of handling music—recording, distributing, and so on. The success of Napster (see Tidd et al. 2001), and now Kazaa (www.kazaa.com/us/index.htm), is the story of an industry whose business model is under technological siege.

CENTRAL APPROACHES AND MAIN THEORIES

Arguments about change have not altered much in the last few thousand years. The history of change and innovation is arguably as old as mankind. Heraclitus, the ancient Greek philosopher, promoted the idea of change by arguing that you can never step into the same river twice because, basically, he did not believe in the possibility of stable relations and things, likening experience to the constant flow of water. His philosophical opponent, Parmenides, was suspicious of Heraclitus's exaggeration, and so, in response, he exaggerated by stating that nothing ever changes (Craig 2000).

Today, some scientists still argue that change is the exception and stability is the norm, whereas others support a process-based view in which almost everything is in flux and transformation. Speaking generally, there are four types of change that can be separated analytically: life cycle, dialectical (struggle-based), evolutionary, and teleological (vision-based) (Van de Ven and Poole 1995). Life cycle change can be thought of in terms of stages of maturation and growth or aging. Dialectical changes occur through the interplay, tensions, and contradictions of social relations, such as being engaged in specific communities of practice. Evolutionary changes, such as developing sustainability strategies to deal with environmental regulations, are essentially adaptive. Finally, teleological change is driven by strategic vision, such as when a city government aims to host a future Olympics and creates an organization to oversee the bid.

Some writers see innovation as very specifically concerning science and R&D (research and development), whereas others view it as part of a broader picture. Nelson and Rosenberg (1993) suggest restricting the concept of innovation solely to new knowledge or new combinations of existing knowledge of technical innovations as measured outputs. Others suggest inclusion of organizational, institutional, and social innovation (see Edquist 2000). This chapter follows the broader conception of innovation as a social process.

The history of innovation in management and organization theory can be delineated in three steps (Clark 2003): from after World War II up to the 1980s; the 1980s; and the last decade or so. During the post–World War II era up to the 1980s, innovation was conceptualized in terms of technological progress. Advances in technology (new machines, refined technologies, or new products such as the Concorde airplane) were created as a result of national investments in big science—expensive, prestigious mega-projects—undertaken by major research centers. Organizations had to adapt incrementally to the changes that the stream of modern technologies produced if they were to keep up with their competitors. Hence, developments in technology were seen as the driving force behind organizational change, a view that can be characterized as "technological determinism" (Clark 2003), where technologies are seen to change autonomously and have necessary causal consequences.

Between 1980 and 1990, the emphasis shifted from technology as the driving force toward a conception of technology and organization as interactive systems. The success of Japanese companies in the 1980s showed that technological innovation and change were deeply embedded and, in fact, depended on a national, cultural, and social context. By analyzing the innovation process, researchers found that forces beyond management's rational planning tools (and, hence, beyond their control) shaped the process significantly. Suppliers, users, and employees translated change processes and innovation into their own context and made sense of it in ways that confused management. The notion of the rationally developed and executed plan as the core device of change and innovation began to be questioned, which ultimately challenged notions of predictability and control.

In the last decade or so, managers and theorists have started to recognize that the driving force behind innovation is not always the same. Whereas in the past, changes in the environment have been viewed as responsible for change and innovation, lately two considerations have been highlighted: the roles of different stakeholders, especially customers; and the fact that innovation does not happen in a vacuum. An infrastructure is required to provide a platform for innovation to grow. There are many levels to this infrastructure, including scientific knowledge, institutional norms, competent human resources, curious financial investors, educated consumers, and stable legal, political, and economical cornerstones. These parameters of innovation can only be controlled by an organization to a limited extent because most of them are out of an organization's reach. Think of a biotechnology company that experiments with genetically modified food. It needs not only highly trained staff from universities but also relies heavily on public opinion and the favorable resolution of legal and ethical issues that dominate the debate. None of these are implicit in the science or the organization of innovation, yet they are fundamental to its eventual success.

Planned change

Recall Taylor's (1911) concept of scientific management, which we encountered in Chapter 1. Based on an empirical analysis, Taylor argued for a complete reorganization of the entire shop floor base of the enterprise. Taylor's change initiatives were built upon two principles that have been remarkably resilient: (a) that change is accomplished through rational plans developed, implemented, and monitored by management, and (b) that these change programs are put in place to minimize future changes. Put simply, the promise is that if you adapt change ideas (from scientific management, for instance) and change your organization accordingly, you'll never need to change again. This approach views change as something that is unfortunately necessary; change is undesirable because it is an interruption to the natural state of organizations, which is a stable equilibrium. The expectation is that stability will be interrupted by short periods of change, forced upon an organization either by technological progress or by new organizational processes. In any case, the environment induces change externally, and the organization has to adapt as quickly as possible to achieve equilibrium again. Business as usual is the ideal, with everything else being a disturbance.

Kurt Lewin (1951) packaged this philosophy of change theoretically. In his model of change, he identified three steps that are involved in changing organizations and people. First, you have to unfreeze the current state of affairs; second, you move things to where you want them to be; third, after you've succeeded, you refreeze again. This simple chain of unfreeze, move, refreeze became the template for most change programs. Some differ in terms of how many steps they assign to each phase, but few question the underlying rationale and logic of Lewin's model (see Cummings 2002: 265). In each case, change is a linear input to output process initiated either by top management or by the environment (consultants, for example).

A typical example of such a rational approach to change is business process reengineering (BPR), which was developed, disseminated, and successfully marketed by Hammer and Champy (1993). BPR encompasses a radical rethinking and redesigning of core organizational activities to achieve higher efficiency and performance. It is based on two simple assumptions. First, BPR analyzes organizational activities step by step so it can develop suggestions for improvements (such as time saving, cost cutting, and so on) on a micro level and reassemble the whole process in the most efficient way. Second, it redesigns the entire organization in accordance to these findings without paying attention to its past history or its cultural and social context. If you think this sounds a lot like the Taylorist approach to scientific management that we met in Chapter 1, you would be correct. Even the name gives it away as an engineering rationality. However, the engineering is not very robust—roughly 70% of the change initiatives made as BPR fail, which explains why BPR has been less successful in colonizing the change market than its proponents had hoped.

Theories of processual change

Most contemporary approaches to the analysis of organizational change reject the approaches of Lewin and those he influenced. The root metaphor of unfreezing/freezing is profoundly problematic because organizations are always in motion; they never respond solely to singular design imperatives but usually emerge from many pressures and directions, even though management change agents may be able to exercise a steering capacity (Buchanan and Badham 1999).

The processual perspective emerged out of the work of a number of writers, but there is no doubt that it was Pettigrew who had the single greatest impact. His magnum opus, *Awakening Giant: Continuity and Change in ICI* (1985), was a careful case study that challenged many of the dominant assumptions about how organizations change. The plans of change agents equipped with formal schemas were not reflected in what actually occurred. Instead, change appeared to be both incremental and evolutionary, as well as being punctuated by revolutionary and radically discontinuous periods. He saw "change and continuity, process and structure" as "inextricably linked" (Pettigrew 1985: 24). Rather than stages of change being observed, processes could be seen changing in patterns produced by the interplay between the contextual variables of history, culture, and political processes (Pettigrew 1990). In addition, exogenous environmental variables also played a role. Different rationalities were in flux as rhetorical strategies and political positions competed in the organizational arena with significant resource-based implications. The distribution of who got what depended on which rationalities were triumphant or trounced.

ICI (Imperial Chemical Industries) unleashed political energies that were both positive and defensive when, undergoing a crisis in its traditional way of organizing, it made the decision to change its organization structure and processes, treating the sense of crisis as a strategic opportunity rather than just a threat. A large organization such as ICI often initiates major programs of change, but there are also changes introduced by snipers and ambushes as well as those that are planned; symbols are used to advance change as much as to retard it, and rumors about boardroom maneuverings and executive succession, both in the organization and the wider business community, are rife. Organizational change is not unlike a long and contested campaign in which successfully positioning and maintaining the dominant myths and symbols is of vital importance. And it is the task of leadership to achieve such positioning (see also pp. 243–245). In doing so, as Buchanan and Badham (1999: 231) remind us, management is a contact sport, one in which "if you don't want to get bruised, don't play." In the game of organizational change, it is directed and strategic change that retains the central focus, so there is little room for gifted amateurs, although many participants may well try to press sectional or local advantages in the opportunities that widespread change presents.

Taking Pettigrew (1997) as our cue, what does the process perspective require for a theory of organizational change? It has a strong emphasis on process and temporality rather than seeing change as a sequence of linear events that occur and are then frozen. Change is viewed as multilinear and multivariable, where many changes occur simultaneously as the effect of many different variables. Anyone seeking to change organizations must exhibit mastery of power and politics. Managers usually seek to manage as if these entities were rational, even when rationality is a mere façade or veneer for mobilizing resources, allies, and opponents in a political struggle for change.

The process is cyclical; major programs of change point in directions that top managers have defined—using the results of previous change projects to do so. However, a direction is not a destination, and where the change projects actually lead depends on the contextual processes within which, as well as the here-and-now from which, they are being seen. Of course, there may be more than one here-and-now at work; a long-term strategy for large-scale radical change may be unveiled to the organization members and stakeholders as a necessary reactive change to changed markets or as a small-scale incremental change made necessary as a part of continuous adjustment. Meanwhile, the strategic plans for the coming campaign are known and shared among a secretive and select few. The opposite scenario is just as likely; changes may be opposed because their implications are thought, from the position of the unions or a specific department, to be much more radical than they actually are. Organization change can be thought of as a dynamic process in which management seeks to steer meanings. We can conceptualize the directions that

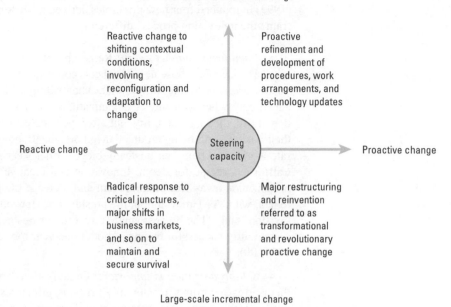

Figure 11.1   *The capstan steering change model*

Source: Adapted from Dawson (2003: 23)

it might steer in terms of a yachting metaphor: the capstan of change, a device by which strategic managers seek to exert great power by traction.

Innovation and change at the edge of chaos

Current approaches to innovation do not place much onus on rational planning and accountability. Instead, they stress the politics of innovation and the balance that is necessary between freedom and the responsibility required for autonomous and disciplined creativity. Change cannot be prescribed through one-best-way or prescriptive practices but instead there are many different ways of achieving innovative outcomes. In fact, innovation sometimes happens while management is busy making other plans.

Chaos

Some writers suggest that, rather than planning and order being the normal conditions for organizations, management needs to become accustomed to chaos. Innovation challenges established management practices and beliefs, especially planning and controlling functions. Richard T. Pascale (1999) introduced four new principles derived from complexity theory that can frame the innovation process differently:

- *Equilibrium equals death:* Remember when you first learned to ride a bike? The idea that those narrow wheels could stay balanced might have struck you as crazy until you learned that, when riding a bicycle, you can stay balanced only when you move. Organizations are not that different; as long as they move, they gain stability, but after they cease to move, they do not retain their balance, and being an unbalanced organization in the fast-moving corporate world (like being an unsteady bicycle rider steering through fast-moving traffic) is a recipe for death. Innovation and creative breakthroughs push an organization away from equilibrium and increase the necessary variety it has to deal with. As Tim Mannon, the president of Hewlett Packard's (HP) printer division, said, "The biggest single threat to our business today is staying with a previously successful business model one year too long" (quoted in Pascale 1999: 90).

- *Self-organization is important:* Organizations are capable of organizing themselves according to internally evolving principles. In managing complex unforeseeable tasks or events such as disasters, people organize themselves, and an order evolves that is not imposed by a mastermind. Instead of acting according to a purposefully designed plan, people interact spontaneously, and patterns of collaboration emerge. From the perspective of the innovation process, this means that management should give up fantasies of control. That the future can be extrapolated only on the basis of the past is an illusion. Innovation, by definition, is a break with the past if it is to be radical. If it is not radical, it will only be incremental change within, rather than change of, a paradigm (Clarke and Clegg 1998). Thus, plans are an imperfect, hindering means of coordinating action; organizations must rely on improvisation and self-organizing forces if they want to achieve radical innovation.

- *Complex tasks need more complex problem-solving processes:* To maintain a complex system, many apparently chaotic and unstable processes work together. Think of a high-wire performer for whom many small, ostensibly chaotic movements maintain balance on the high wire. The same goes for innovation; lots of trial-and-error steps may finally come into balance and lead to successful innovation. During the initial process of innovation, a chaotic patchwork of actions and outcomes seems to prevail, whereas in the final stages, more orderly patterns emerge. We know what sense we make only after we have made it. As Weick (1995) says, all sensemaking—even that projected into the future—has a retrospective quality about it. The fact that we did not achieve a certain plan by the due date turns into a great step in the innovation process because it helped us realize that we were doing the wrong thing, going in a foolish direction. Without some foolishness, we would never find our way to what we can later determine is wisdom. All the mistakes on the way can be represented retrospectively as learning that will eventually be rewarded in the final successful innovation outcome (see also pp. 345–354).

- *Complex organizations can only be disturbed, not directed:* Small causes might have huge effects, and vice versa. In a complex organizational environment, changing one pattern might transform the entire company. In innovation processes, calculations about invested resources and predicted outcome are meaningless because what innovation will produce may simply not be calculable. Think of ideas that were truly new, such as the telephone, the Internet, or simple things such as Post-it notes; their potential for changing organizational practices and consumer behavior could not be forecast simply because no one could imagine the impact they would make on everyday life. Thus, all that can be done is to make sure that the system does not come too close to equilibrium, that it keeps on moving, experiencing new ideas as opportunities and not as threats.

We are a long way from engineering rationality with this approach. These four principles conceptualize innovation and change in a way that is radically different from the rational approach outlined previously in this chapter. They take into account the limited capacity of management to order and to prescribe, and argue for a more complex, chaotic, and emergent understanding of the process of innovation. Innovation that is supposed to lead to truly new outcomes and change cannot be detailed, prescriptively, in advance. For example, the Millennium Wheel in London is now the most visited attraction in the city; it was initially intended only as a temporary exhibit.

The changing innovation agenda

At the Minnesota Innovation Research Program, started in 1983 with the goal of analyzing processes of innovation, more than fourteen research teams conducted a longitudinal study of service, product, technology, and program innovation from concept development to implementation. This huge research effort resulted in the book *The Innovation Journey* by Van de Ven, Polley, Garud, and Venkataraman (1999). It describes the journey from an initial idea to its development and realization. What the authors found, however, did not confirm mainstream opinion that innovation is a stage-wise, linear, clear-cut process of trial-and-error learning that unfolds in a stable environment. Rather, innovation is a more complex adventure that is inherently uncertain and far from equilibrium. At the same time, they were critical of conceptions of innovation that see it as a random process or as merely an accidental event that is fundamentally unplanned, unpredictable, and unmanageable. Such an approach, they suggest, implies that you should somehow "turn the organization off to invent and develop innovations, and turn it

Innovation is a political game that means enrolling others to your interests and translating their dreams into your projects.

Image 11.1   *Millennium Wheel*

TABLE 11.1 Shifting agendas of change

Old Agenda	New Agenda
• Dichotomy between epochal/normal innovation	• Emergence/discontinuities as normal
• Minimize context	• Context dependency
• Stable characteristics	• Emergent hybrids
• Best practice	• Best practices
• Center-periphery model	• Network/interactive models
• Supplier domination of change agenda	• Stakeholder/customer involvement
• Power obscured, processes apolitical	• Contested terrain, politics of innovation uppermost

Source: Adapted from Clark (2003)

on to implement and diffuse innovations when they emerge" (Van de Ven et al. 1999: 5). Such a view leaves no option for managing innovation; instead, it suggests that "innovation management" is an oxymoron and that innovation happens not because, but in spite, of management.

Change cannot be prescribed through one-best-way practices; instead, you need to see that there are many different ways of achieving innovative outcomes. Following Clark's "new agenda," innovation and change are framed differently—they happen emergently rather than being planned, and they depend on contextual factors such as organizational culture, societal resources, and national programs of innovation. There are usually multiple ways leading to innovation and multiple partners involved in innovation. Innovation is a political game that means enrolling others to your interests and translating their dreams into your projects. Finally, it must involve the creative minds of the users. Innovation cannot be done through habit, by custom, or according to tradition.

CRITICAL ISSUES: MANAGING CHANGE AND INNOVATION?

We wish to fly in the face of the conventional wisdom concerning the management of innovation, best represented by the view of Peter Drucker, who defines innovation and change as the "specific tool of entrepreneurs, the means by which they exploit change as an opportunity for a different business or service. It is capable of being presented, as a discipline, capable of being learned, capable of being practiced" (Drucker, quoted in Tidd et al. 2001: 38). There are several key features in this definition: (a) innovation is a tool, an entrepreneurial tool; (b) it should be exploited; and (c) it is a discipline that can be learned and practiced. But there is also much that is missed: (a) the probability of resistance and (b) the likelihood of organizational politics shaping the unfolding innovation process as much as any rational plan. Innovation will always be a blend of rational planning and anticipation, and unanticipated as well as predictable political actions. Thus, innovation changes organizational power relations: "Accomplishing innovation and change in organizations requires more than the ability to solve technical or analytical problems. Innovation almost invariably threatens the status quo, and consequently, innovation is an inherently political activity" (Pfeffer 1992: 7).

Managing the politics of change and innovation

Innovation is enacted in the inherently political arena of organizational micro-politics. As Van de Ven and his colleagues (1999: 65) found, "managers cannot control innovation success, only its odds. This principle implies that a fundamental change is needed in the control philosophy of conventional management practices." At its core, innovation is a journey into the unknown and thus is inherently unpredictable and uncontrollable. Most change initiatives fail (recall those BPR programs with a failure rate of more than two thirds) not because the ideas or concepts were not refined or smart enough but because the actual implementation was not understood and executed properly. Thus, as Larry Hirschhorn (2002) discusses in the *Harvard Business Review,* change can be conceptualized as consisting of three different, though closely inter-linked, initiatives. First, there will be a political campaign, which should create strong and lasting support for the desired change (see also pp. 162–165). A second initiative will be a communication campaign, ensuring that all major stakeholders understand and share the idea of change and are committed to the principles and consequences behind it (see also pp. 327–329). Finally, there will be a rationally planned campaign that makes sure that the human and material resources necessary for a successful change are available. Without paying attention to these political implications, innovative ideas cannot be turned into actionable and tangible outcomes.

Hirschhorn's focus is intraorganizational, which makes sense managerially because the organizational arena is the one most subject to managerial control. However, innovation is not something that occurs just within the firm, because the firm itself is embedded within a broader innovation system.

Recent studies of innovation demonstrate the interdependence of economic, political, social, and cultural factors. Some of these factors are external to the organizations involved, as a part of the broad institutional setting, whereas others are internal, such as those that Hirschhorn focuses on. The relative degree of success enjoyed by organizations and networks of organizations in nations and regions in the global knowledge-based economy depends on the effective management of these factors. Therefore, there is a need to better understand the complex interdependencies between internal firm dynamics around the innovation process and the broader institutional settings in which the firms operate.

Institutional settings have been identified in terms of local contexts that interact with the system of innovation—including networks of organizations in the public and private sectors—to initiate, import, modify, and diffuse new technologies. The concept of the system of innovation shifts the focus from an isolated firm so that it may be seen as part of a network of organizations embedded within specific contexts. The type of context may be identified not only at a regional or a local level but may also include deliberately constructed virtual networks that seek to eclipse contextual specificity.

Innovating through significant stakeholders

There are many driving forces and many stakeholders behind innovation. In the last decade or so, managers and theorists started to recognize that the driving

Image 11.2   *A network in nature*

force behind innovation is not always the same. Whereas in the past, changes in the environment have been held responsible for change and innovation, more recently, the roles of different stakeholders, especially customers, have been highlighted.

Market-technology linkages

The process of bringing innovation from conception through design and implementation is referred to as "market-technology linking" (Burgelman 1983). Innovative Japanese organizations have been recognized for completing this process particularly well (Kono and Clegg 1998, 2001). *Market-technology linking* involves integrating the firm's unique competencies with customer needs, market structure, and technologies, together with their manufacturing, sales, and distribution capabilities. Various techniques have been used for success, such as cultivating "lead users" (Von Hippel 1986) and developing empathetic design where multidisciplinary team members work with potential users to create innovative product features (Leonard-Barton 1991).

Market-technology linkages embody a tension between outside markets and the firm's technologies. Multifunctional project teams are an attempt to deal with tensions that arise when the necessary technology may exist in a division whereas the essential resources for market knowledge may be elsewhere, such as in sales or marketing. Organizations have to relate innovative proposals to resources not necessarily involved in the innovation process. Incorporating competencies that are not necessarily a part of the innovation team can create a potential tension between *control* and *innovation*. Many complex organizations concentrate best on what they can control through routines and standard operating procedures. However, concentration on control minimizes learning from innovation by filtering out new information, reinforcing past routines, and focusing on foreseeable and manageable issues. It also tends to reinforce existing circuits of power within the firm, based on existing resource control (Clegg 1989; Pfeffer and Salancik 1978), thus reinforcing conventional sensemaking (Weick 1995). Innovation may require organizations to rethink their business in ways that operational controls do not easily allow (Workman 1993). Managers tend to remain fixed on solutions to yesterday's problems rather than finding tomorrow's solutions. However, the following subsections give examples of how to do better.

Customer scenarios

So-called "customer scenarios" (Seybold 2001) map the needs of different customers and use them as input for new ideas. This approach harnesses both rational planned initiatives (technologically driven change) as well as creative and lateral thinking. Let's look at how this actually works. Tesco, a U.K.-based supermarket chain with 19 billion pounds of revenue yearly, decided to let its customers do the innovative thinking when the company started Tesco

Direct in 2001 as an on-line shopping window. Most Internet grocers assumed that on-line shopping would attract customers because it would be a way for customers to save time because they could avoid being physically present in the supermarket. However, these grocers failed in their venture. Tesco Direct listened to its customers and found out that they actually loved shopping in stores, seeing new and fresh products. In other words, shopping was not a chore that they wanted to avoid. Tesco Direct also found out that, when customers purchased on-line to save time, they wanted to do so from the grocery stores where they usually shopped rather than from some remote location they did not know. Thus, Tesco Direct changed its on-line service and came up with an innovative system that both made Tesco Direct successful and the customers happy. Customers shop on-line from their own store, the one with which they are familiar, where they have confidence in the fresh quality of the produce. Tesco Direct then changed its organization to center on this innovative concept and came up with a whole set of new practices: The in-store order pickers employed by Tesco for the Internet shoppers have special shopping carts with on-line displays. The display shows them their route through the market, including data on peak traffic areas (such as the fresh bread section between 8.30 a.m. and 9 a.m.). As the order picker walks down the aisle, the display tells him or her which product to pick. After it is dropped into the shopping cart, it is automatically scanned. If a product is not available, the display suggests a similar product, which was recently bought by the specific customer whose order is being met. These innovative concepts were triggered by listening to and observing the customer closely and imagining how technology could deliver what they wanted. These concepts were then refined by changing routines and practices. The system now has 750,000 customers who place 60,000 weekly orders on-line, generating revenues of more than 5 million pounds.

It pays to empower your customers so that they can do the innovative thinking for you because they might know what they want, and what they do not

It pays to empower your customers so that they can do the innovative thinking for you.

want, better than do experts in a remote lab. But there is more to be learned from the Tesco Direct story. Innovation and change are just one side of the same coin, and creativity is closely linked to technological possibilities. The source of creativity and innovative concepts is not captured within the company but found in the community. Creative customers use products that are built for a specific purpose in different ways. Think of skateboarders who redefine urban landscapes and use seemingly stable things such as pathways, park benches, or railings as ramps to perform their magic; they simply use well-known things in a different way, and this is how they bring new practices into the world. The phenomenon of skate culture, clothes, and shoes has spun off from the popularity of skateboarding. It is the customers' use and interpretation of products that creates innovation in such cases. (See the case of Nike pp. 353–354).

Innovating through employees

Of course, innovation does not happen only from the outside in; often, creative companies employ creative people to come up with new ideas. However, the practices needed to manage creative staff differ fundamentally from traditional management practices. Chris Bangle, global chief of design for BMW in Munich, manages creative staff; his job is to mediate between financial and technological constraints and innovative and creative design ideas. Thus, he has to balance creativity and the commercial side of BMW. He suggests three main leadership tasks to trigger innovation and simultaneously achieve commercial goals (Bangle 2001). First, because innovators are usually not accountants, the logic of commerce often sounds odd to them. On the other hand, finance departments often understand the latest innovation as a fancy of the design team and regard it as a cost rather than an investment in a valuable asset. Bangle decided to protect his creative resources and make sure that they could work without being interrupted by people who did not understand what they were doing. In this way, innovative products could emerge—regardless of whether they were financially feasible or not. At BMW, Bangle sent his design team away from their normal work environment so that they could develop their ideas without being interrupted by criticism: "To make certain that no one could possibly trample on the seeds they were planting, I instructed the group to keep their whereabouts a secret—even from me" (Bangle 2001: 50). In such safe spaces, away from business-as-usual constraints, creativity and innovation is born.

> **Organizations must manage the tension between freedom and responsibility to balance commitment with accountability.**

Similar to the findings of Van de Ven and his colleagues (1999), Bangle views the type of innovation process a company uses as a crucial component in its success. Shifting the focus from design (innovation) to engineering (implementation) too quickly kills creativity. Therefore, designers must have the space and the time to play around with ideas and act outside the usual constraints. By protecting the process of innovation, managers are kept from overstepping creative boundaries. To make sure that creative people don't fool around forever, deadlines are imposed to ensure that playfulness and exploration find an end rather than becoming an end. These deadlines also assure managers and engineers that these processes, which to them may appear to be uncontrollable, will result in tangible outcomes.

Managing innovation requires extraordinary communication skills (see also pp. 332–335). Both sides must understand each other's language; innovators must understand corporate requirements, budgets, and deadlines, whereas managers must let go and trust in the people involved in a process with unknown output. The art of managing innovation is to bridge this gap and create a mutual understanding. As Bangle (2001) concludes, business and creativity are not the same, but they can be directed toward the same ends. Think of the Post-it notes that the guy at 3M developed against the orders of his boss.

Image 11.3   *Bridging the gap*

His boss could not see the value in this tool because he could not relate to it at all. The same goes for the chairman of IBM when he claimed five decades ago that there was a world market for only about five PCs. Again, he simply did not understand the new concept because he could not relate to it. Or think of groundbreaking artists; how many of them had the same fate as Van Gogh, who died poor and lonely, because everybody thought his art was nothing but madness? Years later, we know better.

Innovation is much more demanding than is routine. Routine can be managed mechanistically, whereas innovation needs to be managed organically. Mechanism requires only routine action (Burns and Stalker 1961). Organic structures require members to enact not only innovation but also to make sense of the plurality of organization and network members that may be involved in many indeterminate aspects of innovation. Organicism implies commitment of psychic energy and attention. It embodies the tension between responsibility and freedom. In innovation, people have to be free to follow the lead of the TV series *Star Trek,* going boldly where no one has gone before, but they also have to be organizationally responsible in terms of timelines, budgets, and goals. Organizations tend to be much better at framing these responsibilities than they are at empowering creativity. Organizations must manage the tension between freedom and responsibility to balance commitment with accountability.

Innovating through collaborators

Collaboration between organizations is usually temporary but often produces long-lasting relationships because it usually involves cooperative and competitive strategies that are both strategically determined and emergent. Collaboration has intended purposes but its emergent benefits may be more important. Collaborations are dialectical systems, and their stability is determined by balancing multiple tensions within systems of accountability (Das and Teng 2000). Certain large-scale, complex, project-based tasks are rarely completed by a single organization; instead, they involve many project partners, each of which brings specialized skills and competencies to the task at hand, such as constructing a tunnel.

The global economy is marked by the increasing importance of knowledge and creativity, which, paradoxically, places a premium on innovation facilitated by proximity. Although the modern economy is global, it is also resolutely regional; Silicon Valley is the best example. Innovative capabilities are frequently sustained through sharing of a common knowledge base, interaction through common institutions, and proximal location. Local, socially embedded institutions play an important role in supporting innovation (Leonard and Sensiper 1998). Organizations that are able to relate to one another in a proximate geographical or regional space seem better able to collaborate.

Collaborations link people and knowledge, simultaneously tying them to multiple external contacts. Knowledge circulates through internal and external networks at various levels. Achieving sustainable competitive advantage means being faster and better at innovation, which often comes down to being better

Image 11.4 *Groen Hart Tunnel, the Netherlands*

Image 11.5   *Networks make strong structures*

connected and having more effective collaborations. Swann, Newell, Scarbrough, and Hislop (1999) suggest that what is important is how networks interact with knowledge: what knowledge, who has it, and how it can be accessed. National and regional institutions—such as universities and research centers, as well as firms, government policies, and programs—frame regional innovation capabilities (Bartholomew 1998; Dodgson 2000: 25–26) because they define the availability and quality of the *what, who,* and *how* of innovation and its knowledge networks.

Failure is the norm for approximately 50% of innovation projects, according to research by Cozijnsen, Vrakkin, and Van Izerloo (2000). Hence, feedback on failure is essential to achieve successful innovation because it revises present understandings and shifts stakeholder projections. Because innovation is highly complex, uncertain, and creative, regular feedback is essential (Romme 2002). Indeed, the success of feedback processes may be related to the frequent failure of the projects being managed (Morin 1984).

Mapping innovation

Although innovation challenges management's urge for planning and controlling, it is not a purely random process. Van de Ven et al. (1999) delineated a road map to innovation that encompasses major steps on your way toward the new. It is neither a how-to-do list nor a first-class ticket, but it does offer a rough outline of the complex, ambiguous, and dynamic terrain from where discovery and creation emerge. According to Van de Ven et al., the innovation journey can be differentiated in three main periods: initiation, development, and implementation. These periods are covered in the following subsections.

The initiation period

Innovations are usually initiated through a gestation period of several years in which apparently coincidental events happen that, looking back, set the stage for innovation. This period levels the playing ground for innovation to emerge. Then, internal or external shocks (such as a new manager, a loss in market share, and so on) trigger concentrated efforts to initiate innovation. These shocks lead to a concentration of attention from diverse stakeholders. Plans are developed to gain resources internally and to create legitimacy externally. However, these plans are marketing tools more than project descriptions (see also pp. 319–321).

The development period

As soon as development begins, the initial idea splits up into multiple ideas that proceed in different directions. Because it is unclear which path will be

Image 11.6   *Exploring, journeying*

paved with gold and glamour, innovators have to explore many of them only to find out that they were not glittering highways. Innovations also depend on other innovations—think of innovations in the mobile phone industry that are highly dependent on developments in other fields. In this stage, setbacks and mistakes are common as unexpected changes erode the basic assumption the innovation was built on. Also, criteria to assess the achievements of the project differ between resource controllers and innovation managers. People who are committed to the idea tend to see progress and new opportunities where external agents see only hesitation and dead ends. Moreover, staff changes frequently occur in the development period. Motivation and euphoria are often high at the beginning, whereas setbacks and mistakes breed more and more frustration and closure toward the end of the innovation journey.

Top managers and powerful key stakeholders (such as investors) act in contrasting ways and serve as checks and balances on each other. It is at this stage that network building with other organizations is necessary, and top management should be involved in this process to gain political support, which can sometimes lead to unintended consequences. A partner today may well be a competitor tomorrow. Close and successful partnerships may lead to groupthink (see also pp. 215–216; 309). In addition, drivers of the innovation project are often engaged with external stakeholders (such as competitors, state authorities, and so on) to generate an infrastructure that supports (rather than undermines) their innovation, creating the paradoxical danger of simultaneous cooperation and competition.

To innovate means to build multifunctional communities of practice (Wenger 2002), where the disparate views of various and often incoherent disciplinary knowledges can be integrated and the politics managed (see also pp. 354–359). In addition, project responsibility has to be maintained in terms of emergent criteria that allow for both exploratory and exploitative learning. Techniques such as phase reviews and budgetary accountability help achieve project milestones that assist exploitative learning. *Exploratory learning* involves a critical tension between strategic emergence and strategic determination because top-down plans do not easily allow new opportunities for learning to emerge. Bottom-up emergence does not easily allow innovation to be integrated and incrementally cumulated (see also p. 99).

Project teams have been found to punctuate projects through a midterm transition in which progress is reviewed and a new sense of urgency and a new agenda created, suggesting that surprise and interruption are devices that can be used to raise levels of arousal or tension (Gersick 1988, 1989, 1994). This behavior is an instance of a periodic, consciously generated sense of crisis used to interrupt inertia (Kim 1998). The alternation between inertia and crisis can be seen as a means for a system to remain in a state of continuous change, neither settling into equilibrium (equating with low tension or emotional closure) nor falling into chaos (equating with high tension) (Brown and Eisenhardt 1997). Management evaluation requires great subtlety if it is to capture these elements of the innovation process. It is rare to incorporate all the organizational competencies that successful appraisal of innovation requires in the initiation period.

The implementation period

The implementation and adoption of the innovation are achieved by integrating the new with that which is old, established, and already known, fostering a fit within a local context and situation. Politically, the radically new and different will probably not be embraced by everybody because people have committed time and emotions to the status quo. Evolution and integration, not revolution and transformation, seem to be the keys to success.

Finally, innovations reach their goal—they are either released or dumped as top management and investors assess whether the innovation was a failure or a success. However, the criteria against which management assesses the innovation are often inappropriately loaded in terms of short-term financial indicators. Thus, it is important to focus on monitoring and evaluating the innovation process. This process challenges usual management evaluation, which rarely incorporates all the organizational competencies that successful appraisal of innovation requires. Management generally involves abstract and generalized calculations. With such calculations, it is difficult to capture novelty and uniqueness. Standard budgets, deadlines, and reporting protocols can all sabotage innovative efforts. Members can be transferred or let go, and crucial tacit learning can be lost from the innovation process. Formalization can be demanded and the critical detail missed. Managing innovation successfully means that organizations must manage the tension between determination and emergence to link innovation with the firm's resources and strategy.

Being innovative or producing innovations is not automatically useful or profitable. Rather, usefulness can be assessed only at the end of the innovation journey, and what the destination seems to be is always subject to redefinition and renegotiation as the journey unfolds because during the journey the criteria of judgment change.

Leading the innovation journey

Managing innovations requires leadership skills and involvement from the top of an organization. As Van de Ven et al. (1999) established, many managers are usually involved in innovation processes, shifting among four roles: sponsors, mentors, critics, and leaders. Each understands and acts from different perspectives, providing a checks-and-balances function. Their decision making is influenced by the pragmatics of innovation more than by long-term strategic orientations. For simple and trivial tasks, a hierarchical power and leadership structure might be appropriate, but for the complex and ambiguous innovation journey, it would be highly inappropriate: "Directing the innovation journey calls for a pluralistic power structure of leadership that incorporates the requisite variety of diverse perspectives necessary to make uncertain and ambiguous innovation decisions" (Van de Ven et al. 1999: 15). Thus, leadership in innovation processes differs from business-as-usual management tasks. Given the ambiguous nature of the innovation journey, we should recognize that it is highly unlikely that the innovation process will be smooth, rationally unfolding, and bereft of politics and contestation. On the contrary, the production of consensus and a single strategic intent unifying the heterogeneous opportunities of innovation would seem to be rather more a part of the problem than the solution (see also pp. 438–443).

THE FINE PRINT: CREATIVITY, FOOLISHNESS, AND FASHION

The innovator's dilemma

In his influential book, Clayton M. Christensen (1997) analyzed why successful organizations (such as Apple, IBM, and Xerox) sometimes fail when they face change and innovation. Describing this failure as the *innovator's dilemma,* his provocative thesis is that not poor but good management is the reason.

> Precisely *because* these firms listened to their customers, invested aggressively in new technologies that would provide their customers more and better products of the sort they wanted, and because they carefully studied market trends and systematically allocated investment capital to innovations that promised the best returns, they lost their position of leadership. (Christensen 1997: xii)

Christensen regards good management as the reason for failure, which he explains in the following way. Disruptive technologies are the key to innovation. However, most technologies are *sustaining technologies,* meaning that they improve the performance of existing products rather than replace them. Disruptive technologies, on the other hand, result in worse product performance (at least in the short term) for existing products. Compared to established products, new disruptive technologies often perform at a lower level of perfection. For instance, top-end decks, tone arms, and immaculate quality vinyl beat early CDs hands down for tonal warmth and resonance, but CDs did not scratch as easily and were easier to use, played more music, and were portable. The CDs had characteristics valued by markets: They were smaller, and they were also easier and more convenient to use. Another example of disruptive technologies was the off-road motorbike manufactured by Honda and Kawasaki. Compared to sleek BMW and Harley Davidson machines, these models were primitive, but they could go places that the big bikes, with their smooth finish, could not. The desktop computer was a disruptive technology relative to the mainframe computers developed by IBM. The problem for established companies is that they generally do not invest in disruptive technologies because they are simpler and cheaper and thus promise less profit, or they develop in fringe markets that are not important to big players and, after the market is big enough to create serious profits, it may be too costly or too late to join. Often, the established firm's best customers do not want, and cannot use, the new, disruptive technologies, and the potential customers of the new technology are unknown. Proven marketing tools and planning skills do not necessarily work under these conditions.

Being foolish and creative

It should be clear by this point in the chapter that innovation and change cannot be entirely planned and will not unfold in predictable and controllable ways. These facts might be scary and challenging for the world of management, which is used to control (see also pp. 50–52). As the senior vice president of research and development at 3M puts it,

> innovation . . . is anything but orderly. . . . We are managing in chaos, and this is the right way to manage if you want innovation. It's been said that the competition never knows what we are going to come up with next. The fact is, neither do we. (Van de Ven et al. 1999: 181)

Image 11.7   *Creative tile work*

This practical statement is echoed, and somehow anticipated, by James March (1988), one of the most thought-provoking minds in the field of management and organization theory. In his playful paper "The Technology of Foolishness," he criticizes two major building blocks of commonsense thinking that are both closely linked to the concept of rationality (see also pp. 55–61). First, he tackles the idea of preexisting purposes that inform our action generally and change initiatives especially, and second, he questions the principle of consistency that should link our purposes, decisions, and actions so that they are aligned. March says that innovation happens not because of but despite these two principles; the problem is that goals are not given beforehand but are developed in context and are thus subject to change. He argues that sometimes we have to do things for which we have no good reasons to come up with a new objective.

Think of the team at Sony who came up with the idea of the Walkman. At the beginning, the Sony team did not have the image of a portable little music playing gadget in their minds; rather, they bounced ideas around without having a clear purpose (Du Gay, Hall, Janes, Mackay, and Negus 1997). It was exactly this freedom, this lack of clear-cut objectives, that made it possible to come up with something innovative.

The call for consistent rational behavior is counterintuitive when it comes to innovation. March (1988) juxtaposes playfulness with rationality and argues that playfulness unleashes creativity and innovation because it emphasizes improvisation, trial and error, and the general openness to try out new things (see also pp. 364–365). The urge for consistency would not allow us to act in different, maybe even contradictory, ways because this course of action seems to be irrational and hence undesired. As March (1988: 262) argues, "we need to find some ways of helping individuals and organizations to experiment with doing things for which they have no good reason, to be playful with the conception of themselves." He delineates this as the technology of foolishness, an approach that "might help . . . in a small way to develop the unusual combinations of attitudes and behaviours that describe the interesting people, interesting organizations, and interesting societies of the world" (March 1988: 265).

In summary, March (1988) suggests that a narrowly defined rationality that is obsessed with order and control might be counterproductive when it comes to the question of innovation, change, and creativity. Rather, he suggests that a technology of foolishness that allows us to do playful things for which we have no good reasons might be more appropriate to explore new terrain. This technology of foolishness happened at 3M, where a chemist discovered the not overly sticky adhesive that formed the basis of the Post-it note. Playfully exploring where new ideas lead, without a purpose in mind, can lead to great outcomes; at 3M, management learned this lesson, and asks employees to devote 15% of their time to working on things they fancy.

Paradox of innovation and change

To paraphrase the Greek philosopher Plato (1968), innovation is a paradoxical concept; if things are really new and innovative, we would not understand them at all because they would embody a radical break with all we know. What we usually call new is not really new—it will resemble phenomena we are used to. Take a new car; is it new because of its styling and engineering? Doesn't it resemble all the other cars so much that it is hardly justified to speak about innovation in this case? Thus, the paradox is that the new is either already known and established, but disguised in new clothes, or, if it is really new, it is unrecognizable and beyond the ken of our understanding. The perfect example is the invention of the telephone. Alexander Bell presented his idea to senior managers at Western Union. They listened patiently to him, and, after a couple of days, Bell got a letter from them, saying "after careful consideration of your invention, which is a very interesting novelty, we have come to the conclusion that it has no commercial possibilities . . . we see no future for an electrical toy . . . ." Obviously, the guys at Western Union were not exactly right; after four years, there were more than 50,000 phones in the United States, and after 20 years, there were 5 million, and the patent became the single most valuable patent in history (see Tidd et al. 2001). Innovation requires the creativity of foolishness to stick with an idea beyond the stage where most people would dismiss it entirely.

How to kill creativity

It is hard to tell how one can actually nurture creativity, but it is quite clear how one can kill it quickly. We have compiled with the help of others' research a practical guide for managers who want to avoid innovation and creativity (Amabile 1998; Kanter 1984: 204; Morgan 1989: 54; Ordiorne 1981: 79). Think of it as ten easy steps for sustaining routines to the point that they will eventually destroy your organization:

1. Always pretend to know more than anybody around you. Especially be suspicious when people from below come up with ideas. You know better!
2. Police your employees by every procedural means that you can devise. Insist that they stick to the rules of good old bureaucracy and fill in many forms that need to be signed by almost every senior manager in the organization.
3. Run daily checks on the progress of everyone's work. Be critical (they love it!), and withhold positive feedback, which would only encourage them to do things that are potentially dangerous.
4. Make sure that creative staff do a lot of technical and detailed work. Make sure that they do their own bookkeeping, and count everything you can count as often as possible.
5. Create boundaries between decision makers, technical staff, and creative minds. Make sure that they speak different languages.
6. Never talk to employees on a personal level, except for annual meetings at which you praise your social and communicative leadership skills.
7. Be the exclusive spokesperson for every new idea, regardless of whether it is your own or not.
8. Embrace new ideas when you talk, but don't do anything about them.
9. When the proposed idea is too radical, you can always argue that no one has done it before and that there might be reasons for this.
10. When the proposed idea is not radical enough, just say that the idea isn't really new and that someone else already did it.

Of course, this list is far from being complete; there are many small practices that can be built into organizational routines that may help you effectively avoid unnecessary creativity, such as organizing endless meetings in which you discuss and rehash every new idea without actually developing them; sticking to the protocols of ways that have been successful in doing things so far; throwing lots of detailed questions on the table (cash flow in the next couple of weeks, uncertainties in your business environment, and so on); insisting that everything needs to be planned carefully before steps of action can be taken; nurturing the not-invented-here syndrome . . . the list is endless, sadly. Although the vast majority of organizations seem to follow the ten rules, some more creative organizations try to work with a structure that actually triggers innovation and change.

Usefulness?

Innovation is meant to be something good and useful per se. However, what is useful and what is not is seen only at the end of the innovation journey; it cannot be assessed at the beginning. As Van de Ven et al. (1999: 11) suggest,

> the usefulness of an idea can only be determined after the innovation process is completed and implemented. In this sense, it is not possible to determine whether work on new ideas will turn out to be "innovations" or "mistakes" until a summary evaluation occurs after the innovation journey is completed.

Or, to put it more philosophically, according to Nietzsche,

> Indeed, we have not any organ at all for *knowing*, or for "truth": we "know" (or believe, or fancy) just as much as may be *of use* in the interest of the human herd, the species; and even what is here called "usefulness" is ultimately only a belief, a fancy, and perhaps *the most fatal stupidity by which we shall one day be ruined.* (Nietzsche 1974: 301 [emphasis in original])

Karl Weick (1979) puts it more bluntly when he advises us to stamp out utility.

Similar to the innovator's dilemma, this question of usefulness forms quite a big challenge to ordinary management thinking. The whole task of management seems to be ordering, planning, and calculating; usefulness seems to be the benchmark of everything managers do—if it is useful for growth, it is good, and, if not, it should be abandoned. However, innovation challenges this thinking and thus questions the underlying core fundamentals of management theory. Innovation brings up the possibility of monstrous creations—strange and threatening phenomena not previously seen. As the French philosopher Jacques Derrida (1995) suggests:

> A future that would not be monstrous would not be a future; it would already be a predictable, calculable, and programmable tomorrow. All experience open to the future is prepared or prepares itself to welcome the monstrous. All of history has shown that each time an event has been produced, for example in philosophy or in poetry, it took the form of the unacceptable, or even of the intolerable, of the incomprehensible, that is, of a certain monstrosity.

Think of new products and processes in the history of management; they were monstrous to the extent that they seemed to be unacceptable and incomprehensible for their time. Thus, truly innovative undertakings always have something monstrous about them, something that scares and frightens many people.

Creative structures?

The creative process can be illustrated by using the example of Frank Heart, one of the key team members in the group that invented the computers at the heart of the Internet. He remembers how the members of the group worked together:

> Everyone knew everything that was going on, and there was very little structure.... There were people who specifically saw their role as software, and they knew a lot about hardware anyway; and the hardware people all could program. (quoted in Brown and Duguid 2001: 93)

These highly creative people were working in a relatively small team, driven by highly motivated people, built around self-organizing and flexible principles. Creativity, because it is the ability to combine previously unrelated dimensions of experience, flourishes in such an environment. However, this communication-intensive practice challenges companies when they start to grow; professional management structures are put in place to manage new ideas—their design, development, sales, marketing, and so forth. Brown and Duguid (2001: 94) observe that "once separated, groups develop their own vocabularies; organizational discourse sounds like the Tower of Babel." At Xerox, for instance, what had been intuitive to scientists turned out to be unintelligible to the engineers who were supposed to transform the idea into a marketable product. As each group told its tales, "the scientists dismissed the engineers as copier-obsessed 'toner heads,' whereas the engineers found the scientists arrogant and unrealistic" (Brown and Duguid 2001: 94). Thus, as the researchers go on to say, one of the greatest challenges that innovative companies face is the step from initial innovation to sustainable growth, a challenge that can be managed only by carefully balancing structure and creativity. Creativity without structure tends to grow out of touch with reality, whereas structure without creativity results in a loss of innovation. This conundrum brings us back to the exploration/exploitation dialectics that we discussed in Chapter 3 when we considered Jim March's (2002) views on future organization forms.

One strategy to overcome this problem is to use structures as shelters—that is, to create literal and nonpejorative sheltered workshops in which innovation can occur undisturbed by routine. Establishing safe "playgrounds" in which innovators can explore without being constrained by a business-as-usual philosophy can help to create new ideas and trigger innovation. The risk, however, is that sheltered workshops can become ivory towers. Disseminating and integrating new knowledge into everyday organizational structures and practices from remote eyries seems to be almost impossible.

Turning creative ideas into successful products takes more than business-as-usual concepts; the process must combine elements of structure with elements of process by building project teams that include both R&D people and process improvers, together with end-user representatives and those who will have manufacturing and delivery responsibilities for the design that is implemented. There is no point in having a great design that cannot be made, improved, sold, or used. Thus, creativity becomes a major asset in the conceptualization of innovation and change. The ability to think outside the box, however, is something organizations find hard because their efforts are focused on order, control, and predictability. Ralph Stacey (1999: 75) argues that creativity is linked to instability:

> Organizations with the potential for creativity are those which are tensed by the presence of efficient formal hierarchical systems that are continually being subverted by informal network systems in which political and learning activity takes place. Creative systems are systems in tension and the price paid for creative potential is an unknowable long-term future.

A good example of how creativity can be harnessed in a business environment (and turned into money) is St. Luke's, a young London-based design and ad agency. It includes on its client list some big names, such as British Telecom and The Body Shop. St. Luke's is an organization that succeeds in the creative industry through carefully managing a key paradox: How do you push employees to their limits and provide a safe and flourishing environment for them at the same time?

The *Harvard Business Review* (Coutu 2000: 143) recently called St. Luke's "the most frightening company on earth." The unique structure of the company enables it to master the paradox; it is entirely owned by its employees and, as the founder, Andy Law, says, they are Star Trekkers:

> Our employees must take nothing for granted; they must peel away all the levels of their personalities to become who they really are. That's frightening. It's terrifying to have no pretences about yourself, yet that's what gives you the psychological resources to question all the rules. . . . What accounts for our creativity is that we constantly go deeper into ourselves than other people do. (Coutu 2000: 145).

The whole company keeps moving constantly. For instance, it just opened an office in Stockholm:

> Why Stockholm? We didn't analyse the market to see whether there was an opportunity there. But we analysed ourselves and saw that we needed a bigger canvas for people to experiment on, and we needed a more diverse group of employees to produce more creative work. So we are going to Stockholm to set the creative process on fire by doing some intercultural experimentation. We are going to learn from people who were taught to think differently than we were and whose culture requires them to communicate in a different way. We are mixing the creative gene pool. (Coutu 2000: 146)

In their work practice, people at St. Luke's do unusual things as well. They intentionally destabilize the workplace to keep habit at arm's length. If you were an employee there, when you started working in the morning you would not know where you would be sitting, and your contract and actual job might change without any notice. At St. Luke's, everything is in constant flux, which keeps the employees creative. St. Luke's practices are similar to the essence of jazz improvisation. For example, when Miles Davis formed his various quintets, he liked to keep them underrehearsed so that they would not lapse into routine. When he recorded his bestselling album *Kind of Blue* (Davis 1959), he

> **Just imagine a company that went with every fashion; it would never be able to form a unique character.**

took the musicians into the studio with no rehearsal, no charts, and just told them to play the tunes that he had prepared loose arrangements for. Recently, this kind of improvisation has been held up as a model for how creative organizations should operate, and St. Luke's seems to have learned these lessons well (Barrett 2002; Kamoche, Cunha, and Cunha 2002). St. Luke's might prove to be the exception to the rule that businesses are boring and the opposite of creative. Thus, this approach, much like the movement from chaos that we considered earlier, challenges the assumptions of the innovation-as-technology and the change-as-rationally-planned schools of thought. However, as we have seen, innovation does not rely on chaos; structures can help maintain the balance between routine and random.

Fashion

If being monstrous is a hallmark of innovation, how do we separate the truly innovative monstrosities from ones that are merely fashionable? Companies such as St. Luke's might be trendy, but what if they were a mere fashion? Recently, management scholars have put emphasis on the role of fashion in the dissemination and application of new ideas and practices. As Abrahamson (1996) argues, fashions are set by gurus and adopted quickly by consultants and the media. They are nicely packaged collective beliefs sold and communicated through highly symbolic labels such as business process reengineering (BPR) or lean management. Using a highly seductive rhetoric, these fashions promise simple solutions to complex problems. The power of these fashions derives less from their actual message (for instance, as we said previously, BPR is in many ways a restatement of Taylor's [1911] scientific management) than from the symbolic power they unleash. Managers and companies who do not adopt the latest trends are supposed to be inert, reactive, and past-oriented instead of dynamic, proactive, and future-oriented. Thus, fashions create considerable pressure on organizations. The problem, however, is that fashions offer lots of rhetoric but little substance. Although they claim to be innovative solutions, they are superficial one-best-way recipes that ignore the complexity of the actual situation. The task for management lies in the tricky job of differentiating mere fashion from true innovation. Just imagine a company that went with every fashion; it would have to change every couple of years, and it would never be able to form a unique character. Instead of learning, it would change its practices like fashion victims change their clothes.

Anyway, who said change is good?

A common story goes like this: Management (equipped with expensive consultancy reports) recognizes the dark clouds on the horizon and changes the organization so that it does not have to go through the storm. The employees, trapped in their day-to-day routine and inertia, don't, can't, or won't see the upcoming danger, so they resist the managerial change initiative. Then, change has to be forced upon the organization for the sake of its survival. Thus, change and resistance are closely related phenomena. Obviously, lots of change programs (tricked up with sexy formulas such as TQM [total quality management], BPR, and so on) are simple downsizing and cost-cutting tools. That the employees organize resistance as soon as they understand the underlying rationale of the program seems pretty reasonable. However, paradoxically, improvements in their interests in terms of a change in what are seemingly miserable conditions can also be a contested terrain. In a study of how English working-class lads got working-class jobs, Paul Willis (1977) demonstrated that some jobs were prized in terms of the degree of dirt, hard labor, and working-class masculine authenticity that they offered those who do them. Like Collinson's (1994) workers, whom we met in Chapter 5, there are many people for whom resistance to change is not just negative but also a positive affirmation of something that they value—something that, from a management perspective, might seem odd.

SUMMARY AND REVIEW

It is doubtful if change and innovation can be successfully and continuously achieved in a planned, rational manner. As Peter Clark (2003: 137) argues, most innovation in organizations occurs through alterations to the population of organizations. Firms that do not innovate die, and new firms will replace them. Change and innovation happen through replacement, mergers, or acquisition of organizations more than through the reorganization of companies.

Innovation is one of the biggest topics in contemporary management because it is so important to achieve and so hard to do well. In this chapter, we suggested some of the reasons why this goal is difficult to realize. Rather than view innovation, creativity, and change as a rationally planned process, we concentrated on the emergent, processual, and political aspects of technology. Central to this process are what we have identified as the key tensions of innovation in organizations, which center on making innovations happen in terms of the organization changes and creativity that is required. It is for this reason that we have linked creativity and change with innovation; as we have said, you can easily change organization design and not be very creative or innovative—the whole point of institutional theory, which we discussed in Chapter 2. However, it is difficult to be really innovative and not change.

ONE MORE TIME . . .

Getting the story straight

- What are the assumptions behind planned change?
- Why is change a process?
- Why does innovation occur between chaos and order?

Thinking outside the box

- How do politics frame change processes?
- Who are the main stakeholders in change, and how do they shape the processes?
- What does the innovation journey look like?
- What is the innovator's dilemma?
- How do foolishness, fashion, and structure shape change?

ADDITIONAL RESOURCES

1. There are so many books about innovation, change, and creativity that it is rather hard to know where to begin, but we shall keep it brief. A good sourcebook on change is the text by Cynthia Hardy (1995), *Managing Strategic Action: Mobilizing Change: Concepts, Readings, and Cases.* It is especially useful because it looks at not just success stories but some failures as well. A good starting point for innovation is Christensen's book (1997), *The Innovator's Dilemma: When New Technologies Cause Great Firms to Fail,* or the more narrative account by Wren and Greenwood (1998), *Management Innovators: The People and Ideas That Shaped Modern Business,* which tells stories about inventive managers.

2. Jim March's (1988) paper, "The Technology of Foolishness," is a must read.

3. The best article on the politics of innovation is the rather demanding but extremely excellent article by Peter Frost and Carolyn Egri (2002), "The Political Process of Innovation."

4. There are many useful films on the topic of innovation, change, and creativity. Perhaps the best is *Apollo 13* (Howard 1995), especially its emphasis on the creative processes that brought the astronauts of the Apollo mission back, even in the midst of chaotic problems. It illustrates organizational learning as improvisation in action.

5. As an example of how *not* to innovate, consider the film *Titanic* (Cameron 1997), about an innovation that failed because of some of the assumptions of the designers about basic aspects of the ship and the environment in which it operated.

In addition to these suggested additional resources, don't forget to look at what is also available on the Web site **www.ckmanagement.net,** including free PDF files of recent papers related to this chapter, which you can download; video interviews with famous academics talking about related themes; as well as many other resources, such as connections to interesting Web sites.

CHAPTER 12

MANAGING STRATEGY

Competition, Games, Differences

Objectives and learning outcomes

By the end of this chapter, you will be able to

- Explain the basic assumptions of strategic planning

- Understand the process of strategic planning

- Be aware of the main contemporary schools

- Discuss their benefits and shortcomings

- Understand the challenges of strategic management

- Grasp the ethical, gendered, and power relations implicit in all strategies

Before you get started . . .

Some strategic advice:
What does a squirrel do in the summer? It buries nuts.
Why? Well, in wintertime it'll have something to eat and won't die.
So, collecting nuts in the summer is worthwhile work.
Every task you do at work, think, Would a squirrel do that?
Think squirrels.
Think nuts.

OUTLINE OF THE CHAPTER

Strategy is everywhere—soccer teams have strategies, as do political parties, and, more personally, people have strategies for making themselves available when they desire to create an interest in someone—and they usually have strategies for rebuttal. And, of course, organizations have strategies—or they are supposed to. In management and organization theory, the contemporary focus on strategy reflects significant changes in the corporate environment that have occurred in recent decades. Although many organizations read the discourse of strategy back into their ancient history, strategy has an interesting duality. Strategy can be traced back to time immemorial, but as a conscious management discourse it is a relatively recent phenomenon (with, of course, a grand teleology now invented for it!). Although in the past organizations might have pursued strategies, they were not articulated through the contemporary discourse of strategy, a discourse that, at its strongest, developed around issues of competition. Wherever similar products are sold in the same market, there will be competition. Competition leads to firms developing a competitive strategy. If there were no competition, there would be no need for strategy. Where there is only a monopoly provider, then the monopolist is able to sell or distribute whatever quality of goods they wish without regard for strategy, because if people want what they provide, they have to accept what is offered. Competition immediately changes the picture.

SETTING THE SCENE

In a corporate environment that has become increasingly dynamic and complex, strategy is management's response to turbulence. Strategy is supposed to lead an organization through changes and shifts to secure its future growth and sustainable success. Without a clear strategy, organizations will drift much as might a small yacht, disabled, without sails or rudder, on a storm-tossed sea. No steering capacity will be evident. Thus it is hardly surprising that strategic management is increasingly understood as *the* task of top management. To be able to say "I set strategy" has great cachet. It marks out the top managers from the also-rans. Yet, as Richard Whittington said almost ten years ago, the average book on strategic planning is pretty cheap. So, how come, if the secrets of strategic management are so cheaply and easily available, many organizations fail to develop successful strategies? Is there something wrong with the literature—or maybe even the concept itself? Introducing the main approaches to strategy as well as critical issues will help you to find out yourself!

Strategy and warfare

The concept has a long history, derived from military and competitive operations. One of the earliest writers to make extensive use of strategic analysis was the fifteenth-century Florentine political theorist, Niccolò Machiavelli. His book *The Prince* (1981) is a veritable manual of strategic advice for a wealthy corporate family of his day, the Medici. The advice was more akin to guerrilla strategy, to what one might term a war of maneuver rather than a war of position. However, it used strategic and tactical metaphors without being an explicit war manual.

Machiavelli has not been as influential as a more recent writer, Carl von Clausewitz (1968), a Prussian who wrote explicitly on war in the early nineteenth century. As Clausewitz (1968: 165) suggests in his book *On War,* strategy "forms the plan of the war, and to this end it links together the series of acts which are to lead to the final decision, that is to say, it makes the plans for the separate campaigns and regulates the combats to be fought in each." And this simple insight has been at the heart of much of the strategy that has been taught in business schools. Facing competition has been seen to be analogous to facing an enemy in warfare.

The metaphors of war are pervasive. Even a reflective practitioner of strategy, such as Henry Mintzberg, understands strategic positioning as "consisting of a *launching* device, representing an organization, that sends *projectiles,* namely products and services, at a landscape of *targets,* meaning markets, faced with *rivals,* or competition, in the hope of attaining *fit*" (1998: 93). The sources of inspiration could hardly be clearer: Strategy, like war, is clearly a very masculine activity—a point we return to in our conclusions to this chapter.

Obviously, strategy is more complex than it first appears to be. It is not just the extension of the arts of war to the seductions of commerce, the challenges of public service, or the altruism of voluntary organization. Admittedly, all of these sectors of organizations may be said to require strategies if they are to secure their aims and objectives, but what model of strategy to follow—this is the question. To make it easier to answer this question, we have reviewed all the main approaches and then produced a synthesis of the field with which you can guide yourself in future strategic action.

CENTRAL APPROACHES AND MAIN THEORIES

Strategic differentiation

The arenas in which competitive strategy occurs usually involve quality or performance of product, cost and price, sales promotion and service, and strength of sales channels. Typically these four arenas for strategic differentiation lead to distinct organizational strategies. But not always—see Image 12.1!

Where firms do have a sense of themselves as being involved in a competitive environment, they will need to pose a number of basic strategic questions:

1. *Product differentiation:* Companies such as Coca-Cola or Nike invest a great deal of time and money to brand their products and position them uniquely at the marketplace. Any competitor will struggle with the distinctiveness and the uniqueness these products represent in the (potential) client's eyes.
2. *Market segmentation:* Due to demographic factors (age, income, etc.), socioeconomic factors (social class, etc.), geographic factors (climate, regional culture, etc.), and psychological factors (lifestyle, etc.), different customers have different needs. Segmenting the market into competitively relevant groups allows you to tailor products and their marketing to one precise group of (potential) customers.
3. *Price policy and cost leadership:* House brands in supermarkets build on this strategy. Offering comparable products for a cheaper price is a simple but successful strategy—as long as you operate according to the economics of scale, which means increase the quantity of the product so that the cost per unit decreases.
4. *Construction of entry and mobility barriers:* This strategy is basically a strategy to prevent competition (and thus strategy) in the first place. If (potential) competitors fear that it would be a difficult undertaking to enter a market, they might leave you alone in your niche. If you build space shuttles, you are in such a highly specialized and complex market that it is not likely that a new competitor will pop up surprisingly.

Although the centrality of these four points would be unlikely to be disputed today, they were not quite so evident when strategy first emerged as an area of academic concern. The reason for this was that the earliest school to emerge with an interest in strategy was one that had a strong economic history focus; it sought to establish why the companies that had succeeded in the twentieth century had been able to do so, and what their evolutionary path had been.

Image 12.1   *No strategy to speak of*

Strategy and structure: The Chandler School

Strategy drives structure

Chandler focused attention on the strategic plan driving, dominating, and determining organizational structure. Reflecting on strategies became an inevitable means to success (Chandler 1962: 15). Chandler's story is quite simple. Changes in the environment created a need for new strategies. As new strategies were developed, they required a new organizational structure to house them. Thus strategy, driven by changes in the environment, should drive the organization.

Chandler looked at how, in the United States, nineteenth-century preindustrial, small-scale, family-owned, and rudimentarily managed enterprises were transformed into large-scale, impersonally owned and bureaucratically managed multidivisional structures in the twentieth century. Until the advent of the continental railway system in America, business organizations remained typically small, usually under the control of merchants. The first change was due to the enormous geographic diversity of the railways. To manage their

Image 12.2   *Once upon a time in the West: the Santa Fe Railroad, Diablo Canyon*

geographic spread, they developed military models of bureaucracy and a modern "multiunit" corporate form. The markets that the railways opened up caused the second change. The possibilities of a mass market could now be entertained. The railroads made accessing the market easier; they also played a third role, causing property speculation to occur around railheads, thus creating new concentrated markets, a theme explored to great dramatic effect in the classic 1969 Sergio Leone film, *Once Upon a Time in the West.*

The railroads allowed firms to grow by opening up a continental market that replaced hitherto local markets. Chandler argued that as businesses enlarged, they found it more efficient to incorporate the multiple services previously bought from commission agents on the market, such as the purchase of raw materials, debt financing, marketing, and distribution. Administrative coordination began to replace market exchanges as the major mechanism of control because it was technically a more efficient way of doing *a greater volume* of business. Productivity and profits were higher and costs were lower where the fragmentation of markets was replaced with rudimentary bureaucratization of organization.

The end of the nineteenth century saw a wave of both horizontal, diversification mergers and vertical mergers that incorporated suppliers, marketing outlets, and so on (see also pp. 5–10). The upshot of these was that what had been distinct family businesses were reconstituted under one center of organizational control. Past family owners were often retained as more or less independent managers in the new organizations (Edwards 1979: 18), fulfilling contracts with labor they hired and organized. Organizations grew as a strategic response to the failure of markets in those situations where contracts tended to be longer rather than shorter term, where the environment was more, rather than less certain, and where the barriers to entry for new agents were high. Implicitly, these barriers were frequently organizational in that they concerned the capacity to hire labor, raise credit, and secure supplies. Hence, modern organizational forms were a necessary strategic adjustment to market conditions.

The strategic planning school

Strategy is rational planning

In Chandler's model, strategy is the result of smart decisions that achieve a fit between strategy and structure. If early strategy was largely a question of individuals being smart, by the latter half of the twentieth century, smart individuals had smart machines to assist them further. For as long as strategy had to function with the resources of the human mind, it remained limited to what its strategic thinkers could process. Of course, computers—to the extent that they can deal with binary representations of data—can handle far more data than a strategic thinker, and do so far faster. So computer technology gave hope to planners that one day they would be able to analyze past data to determine the future probabilities for an organization. Strategy was a matter of long-range planning and rational decision making, extrapolating from the past to plan the future.

The most important contribution to the planning school was Igor Ansoff's book *Corporate Strategy* (1965). Ansoff identified three different levels of action: the administrative, the operational, and the strategic action level. Whereas the first level (administrative) concerned the direct production processes, the second level (operational) focused on the maximization of efficiency of the first-level processes. The realm of strategic action is directed toward an organization's relation with its environment; forecasting changes in the environment, planning adequate responses, and controlling the organization's correct realization of these plans should be top management's task. The rational planning model has a strong influence in areas such as project management in the construction industry. Image 12.3, from the Dutch leg of a giant EU rail and tunnel construction project, demonstrates this rational planning in action. With major projects, it is absolutely imperative that the many separate elements meet seamlessly.

Ansoff's influence is echoed in modern management thinking, which understands those at the top as the strategic thinkers of an organization, seeing their task as defining the big picture, steering the organization with a strong grasp, whereas the lower levels of hierarchy realize and implement what they have been told but which they could never see—because they lack the capacity for strategic vision.

The design school

Strategy is analyzing

Simultaneously with the planning school there emerged the design school, an approach that analyzed organizations in terms of strengths, weaknesses,

Image 12.3   *The importance of accuracy in constructing the future*

(Continues)

Image 12.3 (Continued)

opportunities, and threats (SWOT). The first two concepts focus on an organization's internal condition, and the latter two analyze its environment. The core strategic assumption concerns the identification of opportunities that an organization can exploit better than its competitors. From this point of view, strategic management audits the environment carefully for opportunities and threats and looks internally for strengths and weaknesses. Once the strengths and weaknesses have been elaborated and the opportunities and threats have been identified, then appropriate strategies can be developed. Due to its simplicity and straightforwardness, this approach became widely recognized in the field and is still in frequent use today (Learned et al. 1969).

The positioning school

Strategy means positioning oneself in a competitive environment

The positioning school was strongly shaped and influenced by Michael Porter's *Competitive Strategy: Techniques for Analyzing Industries and Competitors* (1980), authored by probably the most influential figure in the strategy pantheon. As the subtitle of his book indicates, Porter focused on the structure of industries and their impact on strategies. Unlike the design school, Porter developed analytical tools to understand more differentiated environments and provided a more refined way of understanding and managing strategy. Porter elaborated that the determinants of an organization's profit can be summarized through his Five Forces Model.

Porter argues that the profitability of an organization depends on the bargaining power it exercises in negotiating prices with suppliers and customers. Logically, a strong bargaining position means that an organization pays (relative to its competitors) less to its suppliers and is capable of selling at a higher price to customers. The economic structure of the market—represented in the five forces—determines the bargaining power of enterprises. For example, in a market with low barriers to entry, the threat of newly competing rivals is high only when the level of profitability in this industry is high as well. Thus, a strategy for a company in an industry with a high threat of new entrants might

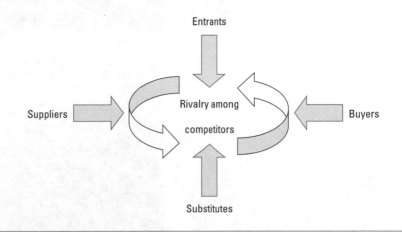

Figure 12.1   *Porter's Five Forces Model*

be to choose the strategy of "limit pricing," meaning that it will keep its profit low in order to avoid attracting competitors.

According to Porter, the threat of substitutes also influences the bargaining power of companies. Whereas companies that offer similar or identical products or services are rivals (e.g., two ski resorts), substitution means products or services that are not in direct competition but have nonetheless an important impact (a holiday provider offering attractive packages to spend winter holidays under palm trees in the Caribbean Islands). Strategic management, in Porter's sense, means navigating through the web of opportunities and threats framed by external competitive forces.

The value chain

In 1985, Porter came up with a second major contribution to the field of strategic management, *Competitive Advantage: Creating and Sustaining Superior Performance,* which shifted attention toward internal dimensions of strategic management. Porter again embedded strategy within the market forces characteristic of an industry. It was here that he developed the concept of the value chain to analyze processes of production or delivery of services. Although an industry is characterized by the process of transforming resources and/or raw materials into final products or services, the concept of the industry value chain analyzes the steps in this process that actually add value to these services and products. The added value is the difference between cost of production and the revenues realized in the marketplace. That

Image 12.4   *Condoms with cabbage?*

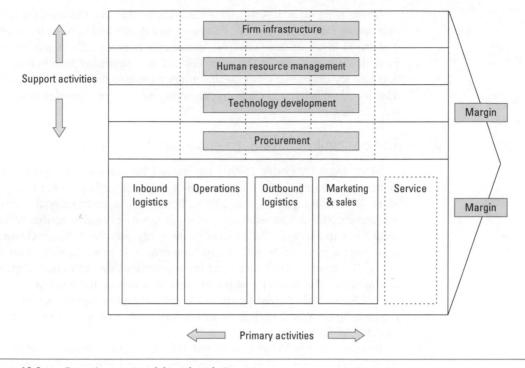

Figure 12.2   *Porter's concept of the value chain*

sounds more awkward than it actually is. Think of a preferred restaurant that serves the most enjoyable food. It transforms fresh produce into great meals. However, the value it adds consists of the skills of the chef, the friendliness of the waiter, and the overall ambience—in short, the added value is that which exceeds the value of the sum of the parts. Sometimes the value added is quite surprising!

As you see in Figure 12.2, there are several primary activities (from inbound logistics to services) that describe the chain of production. Porter also includes support activities that keep the primary activities going. Analytically, the model investigates the value-specific parts of an organization added to its services or products.

What does the value chain concept add to our example of the restaurant? Through analyzing the value chain, the manager might find out that it is worth spending more time and money on buying better quality food if, as a result, the restaurant could increase its prices and its turnover. In order to spend more time and money on shopping, management might decide to cancel the pianist who currently plays in the restaurant each night, having decided, through some basic market research, that guests came not because but in spite of her. Thus, she did not add any value to the chain and, subsequently, is terminated.

Outsourcing often flows from a value chain analysis. Outsourcing means eliminating parts of the production system that do not add value to the product and can be better or more cheaply contracted ("outsourced") to another company that is a specialist in this area. For instance, instead of having their own accountancy department, companies might outsource the tasks to specialists. They can do it better and cheaper, preserving more value, than if it were internally organized.

The competitive advantage of nations: Porter's diamond

More recently, Porter (1990) has turned his attention to questions of competitive strategy at the national level. Commissioned by former U.S. president Ronald Reagan in the 1980s, Porter led a multinational team of researchers who conducted a comprehensive study of twelve nations to learn what leads to success. The genesis of the study was the U.S. government's increasing disquiet at the rise of Japanese economic power, which, inter alia, saw U.S. consumer electronics and car companies lose out to their Japanese competitors. The loss of competitiveness was especially traumatic, as the United States had enjoyed unparalleled cultural and economic dominance in the post–World War II period. Some commentators referred to this as the age of Pax Americana.

Reagan's brief to Porter was to search for the elixir of success and find out what had gone wrong. How could America be competitive once again? Porter started out by rephrasing the question, arguing that talking in terms of national competitiveness is a problematic activity, as it is an exercise that conflates and aggregates different sectors and regions. Simply put, for instance, in the 1970s and 1980s, Britain lost competitiveness in a number of sectors, such as car production and consumer electronics; in others—confectionary, financial services, and military arms—it retained competitiveness. Taking the point more literally, at the time of the U.K.'s economic nadir, container loads of Hobnobs (an English biscuit) were being routinely exported to Japan!

Porter not only stresses the importance of the sector but also concentrates attention on the region. For instance, in a relatively small country such as Britain, there are stark differences between different regions. Porter's study looked at twenty sectors, across twelve nations at three points in time. His research question was whether the home base of a firm matters. Porter suggests that the home base—where your organization starts out—is of critical importance. The implication of this is that a firm such as Benetton, a very Italian story, could not have succeeded in the same way had it started up elsewhere. Equally, think how particular genres of music have been so tightly associated with particular cities. What is it about Manchester in England that has led so many bands—Joy Division, The Smiths, Stone Roses, Happy Mondays, and Oasis, to name a few—to emerge from there? Or what was it about Seattle that led to it being the home base for the

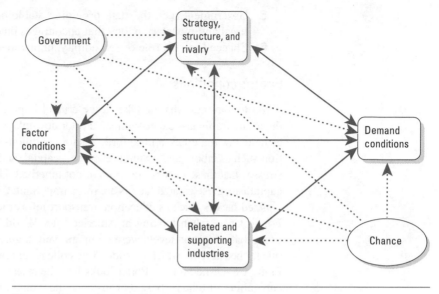

Figure 12.3   *Porter's diamond*

enormously successful grunge scene? Why have countries such as France and Germany been so lamentably poor at producing competent pop and rock music? Why is it that so much moviemaking takes place in Hollywood, Bollywood, or Hong Kong? These examples make Porter's point precisely: Home base matters.

In exploring Porter's diamond, our position is that it is a useful framework to think with, but you should not accept it without qualification. Moreover, such is the power of Porter's brand—governments employ him, corporate executives listen to him, students study him—that his nostrums can become self-fulfilling. Having sounded that caveat, let us explore Porter's diamond. The diamond is a constellation of four primary components (strategy, structure, and rivalry; demand conditions; factor conditions, and related and supporting industries) and two secondary components (chance and government).

Attributes of a nation comprising Porter's diamond,

1. Factor conditions (i.e., the nation's position in factors of production, such as skilled labor and infrastructure)
2. Demand conditions (i.e., sophisticated customers in home market)
3. Related and supporting industries
4. Firm strategy, structure, and rivalry (i.e., conditions for organization of companies and the nature of domestic rivalry)

5. Government (i.e., the state providing stable economic conditions with fiscal and monetary policy that encourages enterprise)
6. Chance (i.e., the role of serendipity, unintended consequences)

Factor conditions

Porter outlines what he takes to be crucial important factor conditions. In a departure from classical economics, Porter downplays natural endowments such as land, raw materials, and so forth. Factor conditions refer to factors of production such as labor, land, natural resources, capital, and infrastructure, but Porter stresses that these factors are *created*, not inherited. He argues that in advanced capitalism, these created factors are more important. Created factors include specialized factors, such as education, transport infrastructure, and health services. For instance, when looking at America after World War II, Porter makes the point that education levels were comparatively high. This was in no small part due to the G.I. Bill, which provided free college tuition for those who had served in the U.S. armed forces. Porter looks into the research and knowledge creating capabilities of a home base. For instance, he would regard institutes that generate specific knowledge (such as the Australian Institute of Sports) as being means that can lead to a home base being relatively more competitive. Many New World wine producers have specific wine research institutes creating knowledge that in turn can be fed back into the innovation process.

Porter argues that a lack of resources can actually help countries to become competitive because abundance generates waste, whereas scarcity generates an innovative mind-set. Countries that have scarce resources are forced to innovate to overcome their shortage; Japan is the most often cited example of a country with no natural resources. Equally, the Netherlands is a world leader in the production of tomatoes and flowers—although its climate is hardly suited to either pursuit, with much being grown under glass. It did have preeminence in the tulip market in the seventeenth century when the tulip market was a national obsession and an inflationary bubble, rather like the dot-com market before the 2001 crash. Its competitive advantage in flowers dates from this period (see Moggach 2000, whose novel, *Tulip Fever,* is an evocative and romantic rendering of that period in history).

Demand

Porter argues that a sophisticated domestic market is an important element in producing competitiveness. When the market demands high quality, the close proximity to demanding consumers requires successful firms to be smarter and more innovative. Customers that will complain and not be afraid to switch their loyalties if service is unsatisfactory help make better products and processes. Some have argued that this has been a particular problem in some cultures—such as Britain—where people tend not to make a fuss or complain. This would probably do much to explain the relatively poor levels of service, experienced, for instance, in restaurants and hotels. Indeed it has been noted (Clark 2000; Whipp and Clark 1986) that one of the real problems that Rover (the British car company) faced was that people did not complain when their new car had several minor problems. Rather than complain, many British customers would simply do the repairs themselves. It was a lack of assertiveness that cost Rover dearly as it tried to establish itself on the world stage. For instance, in a market such as Australia, buying a British car became widely regarded as a passport to rapid depreciation and unreliable performance. A good friend would counsel against it.

When a nation's discriminating values spread to other countries, then local firms will become competitive in the global market. One example is the Australian wine industry, which has become the preferred provider of wine in many key European markets, beating the French at their own game, due to offering quality, innovation, and value. Equally, consider the consumer electronics market, which has been dominated by the Japanese for the past few decades. In the 1970s, the bigger the stereo, generally the better it was likely to be. Any self-respecting '70s student had speakers that covered a whole wall—the better to listen to Pink Floyd or Led Zeppelin. By comparison, contemporary stereos are tiny. These changes have been driven by consumer demand in Japan. Japan is a densely populated country with serious shortages of space for real estate. The corollary of this is that it serves to fuel demand for smaller products. Thus, the innovations made in consumer electronics, which saw products become ever smaller, arose from the Japanese predilection for "smaller is better." This was combined with a very active consumer market, one that bought new products such as cameras, stereos, and Walkmans with great regularity. The key for Porter is, therefore, the extent to which home demand shapes or, at least, reflects world demand.

Clustering

Strongly related and supporting industries are important to the competitiveness of firms, including supplier and related industries. Think of subnational areas such as Milan for fashion goods or Silicon Valley for software. Clustering close to competitors enables easier knowledge diffusion and a pool of more knowledgeable employees, such that consumers associate a region with a product and high quality and, therefore, it gains some market power.

Keen domestic competition leads to more sophisticated consumers who come to expect upgrading and innovation.

Domestic capital markets affect firm strategies; some markets have a long-run outlook whereas others are short-run focused. Countries with a short-run outlook (like the United States) tend to be more competitive in industries with short-term investment cycles, such as the computer industry. Countries with a long-run outlook will tend to be more competitive in industries where investment is long term, such as the pharmaceutical industry in Switzerland. A country will be competitive in an industry whose key personnel hold positions that are considered prestigious and intense competition spurs innovation. Domestic rivalry for final goods stimulates the emergence of an industry that provides specialized intermediate goods. Keen domestic competition leads to more sophisticated consumers who come to expect upgrading and innovation. Thus, the diamond promotes clustering.

When there is a large industry presence in an area, it will increase the supply of specific factors, such as workers with industry-specific training, since they will tend to get higher returns and have more chances of better employment. At the same time, upstream firms that supply intermediate inputs will invest there to save on transport costs, tariffs, interfirm communication costs, and inventories. Downstream firms who use the industry product as an input will also invest in the area, causing additional savings. Related industries that use similar inputs or whose goods are purchased by the same set of customers will also invest, triggering subsequent rounds of investment and virtuous growth cycles. Finally, governments influence all four of Porter's determinants through a variety of actions such as subsidies to firms, either directly (money) or indirectly (through infrastructure); through tax regimes; through raising industry standards; and by educational policies that affect the skill level of workers.

It is really important not to neglect the role of the state. For instance, in the United States, how can one ignore the role the state plays in the massive military industrial complex? If we look at some of the most innovative regions, such as Huntsville, Alabama, then the U.S. Missile and Space Programs were the mother of the considerable invention that occurred, fueled by federal funding on a grand scale.

Scenario planning

Strategy isn't calculating but playing with futures

Scenario planning arose, indirectly, out of a war. In 1973, the second Arab-Israeli war occurred, when the Israeli armed forces blitzkrieged across neighboring territories to defeat the Arab forces massed against them. The Arab response was swift and potent. The Organization of Petroleum Exporting States (OPEC) immediately started to raise the price of crude oil through an effective cartel, which, by the later 1970s, had a substantial effect on crude oil prices. As demand collapsed in the face of the escalating prices of crude oil, the subsequent "oil crisis" had a major impact on Western oil companies. In the past, their future strategies had always been based on an extrapolation from past trends. Demand was predicted to grow quite evenly with population growth, growth in auto use and GDP, and other easily extrapolatable measures. But these extrapolations assumed that the environmental conditions characterizing the past were going to be much the same in the future. There was an assumption of continuity—rather than of the radical discontinuity that the OPEC cartel produced.

All oil companies were hard hit equally, but one responded in a way that dealt effectively with the new world of strategic planning—a world where the past did not simply extrapolate into the future. That company was Royal Dutch Shell, where, under the inspired leadership of Pierre Wack, the Shell approach of scenario planning was born. Essentially, this consisted of trying to envisage what the best and worst case scenarios for the future might be and what sorts of factors might be critical in dealing with them. In practical terms, the scenarios could be constructed from strategic conversations held with the senior executive team of the organization, using some simple questions as the trigger. Armed with a range of scenarios, and a range of strategic responses to deal with them, organizations could be more fleet-footed and nimble in responding to their environments than if they just assumed that the future was an extrapolation from the past. Books such as Ringland's (1998, 2002) helped these ideas become widely adopted.

Scanning the environment

Scenario planners begin by inquiring into four environmental factors that they see as framing an organization's future:

1. Social dynamics, including quantitative, demographic issues (e.g., increased immigration and visible minorities, the aging of the baby boomers and next-generation successors to Generation Xers), and softer issues of values, lifestyle, demand, or political energy (the way that the war on terror seems to entail more surveillance and less autonomy)
2. Economic issues, including macroeconomic trends and forces shaping the economy as a whole, microeconomics (e.g., competition between small, innovator companies), and unique resource-based internal forces (e.g., employee training)
3. Technological issues, including direct (e.g., updating and innovating technologies or software), enabling (e.g., autonomous banking), and indirect (e.g., increased need for security experts) issues
4. Political issues, including regulatory issues, such as the likely framing of future policies as more or less neoeconomically liberal in key areas such as health, education, and transport

Essentially, scenario planners seek to build up a composite answer to a series of questions, answers to which will frame the imaginable boundaries for future action.

. . . and more questions . . .

The actual questions that scenario planners will use vary, creatively, from case to case as they explore each case's specificities, but typically, they seek insight into the areas detailed in Table 12.1.

TABLE 12.1   Scenario-planning questions

Themes	Questions	Rationale
The vital issues	*Would you identify what you see as the critical issues for the future?* [When the conversation slows, continue with the following comment] *Suppose I had full foreknowledge of the outcome as a genuine clairvoyant. What else would you wish to know?* [Strategic drivers]	Here, the scenario planner is searching for data on where an industry or organization is going; what events might influence it and force the organization to change.
A favorable outcome	*If things were to turn out really well for the organization, being optimistic but realistic, talk about what you see as a desirable outcome.* [Questions that really matter; positive scenario factors]	Here, the scenario planner is searching for data on what really might make the organization successful.
An unfavorable outcome	*If things went really badly, what would be the key factors that you would need to manage to try to prevent this from happening?* [Questions that really matter: negative scenario factors]	Here, the scenario planner seeks out information on what threatens the organization, what is putting it at risk.
Internal systems	[Where culture, structure or processes will need to change:] *What do you think the organization would have to do to achieve the desired future?* [Preferable actions]	With, these questions the scenario researcher is trying to find out what the organization member knows about what it will have to do.
Lessons from past successes and failures	*Looking back, what would you identify as the significant events that have produced the current situation?* [Critical pathways]	Here, the analyst is seeking to identify what the key drivers have been for the construction of the present reality.
Decisions that have to be faced	*Looking forward, what would you see as the priority actions that should be carried out soon?* [Strategic priorities.]	With this question, the scenario researcher seeks to isolate those factors necessary for the change scenario to be implemented.
If you were responsible	*If all constraints were removed and you could direct what is done, what more would you wish to include?* [The "epitaph" question]	Here, the scenario planner thinks beyond the constraints of business as usual and explores the future.

Source: Adapted from Ringland (1998)

These questions, which were developed initially at Shell by Gareth Price of the St. Andrews' Institute of Management and recorded in print in Ringland (1998: 87–88), are used to frame a series of interviews with the top management team and any other members of the organization that they think appropriate.

Crafting answers

All the data will be recorded so that the scenario planners can work on it, pulling out generic themes rather than isolated individual contributions. In this process, the data become a mirror on the organization and its themes rather than something generated by particular individuals. The themes become the focus for discussion with the management team at a subsequent meeting. Working with the members at that meeting, the scenario planners will identify critical uncertainties and what members think should be done about them.

The key factors then form the basis for different scenarios. These scenarios describe how the driving forces might plausibly behave, based on the assumption of the predetermined elements and critical uncertainties. For example, in the recording industry, three scenarios might be created, depending on the degree of proliferation of Web sites like Kaaza. In Scenario 1, a large number of music lovers spend their time downloading music and get out of the habit of buying CDs. Scenario 2 is the opposite: People become more oriented to buying CDs because downloading does not offer any added value or absolutely superb reproduction. But there is also a third possible scenario—faster growth for the recording industry, because more people spend their time with a variety of music, including the Internet, which mutually reinforces the demand for each type of consumable. Driving forces, predetermined elements, and critical uncertainties structure the exploration of the future.

To create the scenario stories, the planner leads the members of the organization to determine which of the driving forces are most important. What is most uncertain and what seems inevitable? The idea is to develop narratives that best capture the dynamics of the situation. Once the scenarios have been developed in some detail—usually about three—then it is time to identify what decisions need to be made. If a decision works for only one of several scenarios, then it is risky. The question that should be discussed by management is how the strategy should be adapted to make it more robust if the desired scenario doesn't occur as predicted. As soon as the different scenarios have been defined, then a few indicators should be selected with which to monitor emergent strategy. If the scenarios have been carefully developed, they will identify and translate movements on some key indicators into an orderly set of implications, rather like a game of chess where the opponents are constantly seeking to outmaneuver the other player's potential moves—just as their opponents are doing to them.

The most important difference between rational approaches to strategic planning and scenario planning is the idea that the past does not progress linearly into the future. Rather, as the example of the oil crisis indicates, environments develop surprisingly, quickly, and dynamically. A purely rational and analytical planning process is thus an inadequate means of managing strategically. Scenario planning, on the other hand, points toward a more complex and more refined way of developing strategies. Challenging taken-for-granted assumptions and questioning the status quo provides an organization with the flexibility it needs to master turbulent environments.

Image 12.5 *Which move next?*

The resource-based view of the firm

Strategy is driven by what you are able to do and have

Developed originally from the influential economics perspective of Edith Penrose (1959), the resource-based view of the firm concentrates on the resources and capabilities controlled by a firm and how they can be used to develop strategy. Against the industry school of Porter, the resource-based view of the firm suggests that it is not industry but firm factors that are vital. Resources come in four types: financial (such as equity capital and loans), physical (plant, equipment, and land), human (the experience, knowledge, and training of employees), and organizational (trust, which we have previously referred to as embeddedness). Two basic assumptions are implicit in the resource-based view of the firm: that resources and capabilities can vary significantly across firms (the assumption of firm heterogeneity) in a stable way (the assumption of resource immobility). The specificity of the distribution of these resources can become unique sources of competitive advantage. (You will notice some similarities here to strategic contingencies and resource dependence theory; see also pp. 159–161.)

When resources are the basis for competitive advantage, they must be

- Valuable in enabling the firm to exploit opportunities and counter threats
- Rare among competitor organizations

- Costly to imitate
- Without close substitutes

In a sense, the resource-based view of the firm is the flip side of institutional theory as we encountered it in Chapter 2. It seeks to identify those things that organizations have that cannot easily be the basis for copying, because it would be too costly to do so or they cannot access them. The resources that confer the advantage might arise for any number of reasons. For instance, many students interested in golf choose to attend the University of St. Andrews because of the town's association with the home of golf. Nowadays, while Prince William, an heir to the British monarchy, is studying there, it has become very fashionable with female students—especially from overseas. The lure of a dashing young prince is quite a drawing card! Sometimes the reason why the organization enjoys its unique advantage is difficult to unravel from the casual mix of possible factors—there is a causal ambiguity that can become a strategic factor. Finally, the sources of advantage may be complex and somewhat intangible, such as an "excellent" culture, in Peters and Waterman's (1982) terms.

The emergence school

Strategy's paradoxes

Rational planning was increasingly questioned as an approach to strategy by a school of thought that can be described as the emergence school. Basically, this refreshing school focuses on the social and human dynamics that make strategy a powerful organizational tool. Its theorists included Cohen, March, and Olsen (1972), Lindblom (1959), and Weick (1979). What they have in common is that they are all influenced by the work of the Nobel Economics Prize winner Herbert A. Simon on decision making (see also pp. 55–61). Simon's essential insight was that when we make decisions, we never do so under conditions of perfect rationality—we always do so in conditions of more or less uncertainty and knowledge. Rather than being utterly rational optimizers, weighing every known fact and interpretation, waiting for all the evidence to be available, we operate in a "boundedly rational" way.

Bounded rationality

The notion of bounded rationality is meant to capture the way in which organizational decisions are actually made; evidence is searched for, usually through channels of information that are known in advance. The evidence weighed is by no means exhaustive, but it is usually thorough in terms of the familiar ways of making sense that the organization and its decision makers use. Hence, rather than seeking optimization—in an economic model of the rational consumer under conditions of perfect competition—organizations typically seek to "satisfice"—a term that Simon created to capture the process of drawing on limited but familiar channels of information to arrive at the most satisfactory decision with regard to the evidence available.

Garbage can

We can see how these assumptions are worked out by reference to the garbage can model, in which organizations can be viewed as collections of choices looking for problems, issues, and feelings looking for decision situations in which they might be aired, solutions looking for issues to which they might be an answer, and decision makers looking for work. In this model it is assumed that structures influence outcomes of decisions by affecting the time pattern of the arrival of problems, choices, solutions, and decision makers, determining the allocation of organizational and individual energy and establishing linkages among the various streams of resources.

Sensemaking

Karl Weick (1979) uses an anecdote that describes this school of strategic thinking quite well, because it stresses the virtues of resources being available at a specific point in time as well as opportunism in their use. As the story goes, a group of soldiers became lost in the bitterly cold and snowy Alps. Unfortunately, they didn't have any compasses or proper maps that could help them find their way out. By coincidence, one of them found an old map in one of his pockets. Although the map didn't represent the terrain too well, after a few wrong turns they found their way. As they returned to their camp and showed the life-saving map to their colleagues, one of them noticed that it wasn't a map from the Alps at all but from the Pyrenees. Turned strategically, the moral of this story is quite appealing: Strategies, like maps, are means of orientation, but not in a simple way that maps tell you, literally, where you are and how you should go to get where you want to be. Like the map in the story, strategies can assure people and give them confidence as well as make them think about future directions and ways of arriving there. Strategy does not give you an accurate and true picture of where you are—but it helps you to orientate yourself. It is a social construction of reality, constructing a terrain it ostensibly mirrors.

> **Strategy motivates and animates an organization—it represents an organization's dreams and, in scenario planning, a way of overcoming its worst nightmares.**

According to Karl Weick (1979), strategic planning has many important functions, although they are different from what one might assume. As Ambrose Bierce said, to plan is to "bother about the best method of accomplishing an accidental result" (quoted in Weick 1979: 10–11). First, it brings people together and makes them think about where they are and where they want to go. It is simply a way of addressing the future—speaking about missions and visions, hopes and fears, opportunities and threats. Strategy motivates and animates an organization—it represents an organization's dreams and, in scenario planning, a way of overcoming its worst nightmares.

Think of a high-tech company that announces its vision in big words—being the world's leading innovator in its market. Regardless of whether this is realistic or not, this statement might capture the attention of young, ambitious, and highly motivated scientists who hope to realize their ambitions in this company and so get hired. As a result, the company might really become an innovative enterprise. In this case, the strategic intent was realized because it was announced. The strategic goal was accomplished not because of a major planning effort but because of smart communication, which talked the plan into reality. This is what is referred to as self-fulfilling prophecy: The communicated plan is realized because it is communicated (see also p. 332).

CRITICAL ISSUES: PUTTING STRATEGIC THINKING TO WORK

Applying strategy

Do things differently or do different things

Porter (1996) shows in his seminal contribution "What Is Strategy?" that it is important to understand the difference between operational effectiveness and strategy. Operational effectiveness means performing similar activities better than competing companies Doubtless, operational effectiveness is necessary for success, but it is not enough, as it can easily be imitated. The more they benchmark, the more they look alike (see also pp. 53–55).

Strategy, on the other hand, is about being different or doing things in a different way. Porter (1996) uses the example of the airline industry to illustrate this point. Southwest Airlines, for instance, specialized in offering short-haul and low-cost services between middle-sized U.S. cities and smaller airports in large cities. Through a number of strategic decisions, the airline differentiated itself from its competitors. Southwest Airlines did not offer meals, did not assign seats, had no premium service class, no interline baggage checking or automated ticketing. Because it offered this no-frills service, the airline was able to have shorter turnaround times at the gates, which meant its planes flew longer hours, providing for more frequent takeoffs with less staff. Southwest Airlines performs a different activity from traditional airlines, who potentially offer flights to all major airports, provide business and first class service, coordinate schedules for passengers who change planes, as well as transfer their baggage. It is the way in which the firm has evolved to avoid this mixture of activities that allows it to position itself strategically. Now it has became a strategic model for many airlines elsewhere, such as EasyJet and Ryanair in Europe, which copied and added to the basic recipe that Southwest Airlines innovated.

The three cornerstones: Purpose, difference, value

Three requirements are needed to develop an effective strategy: a well-articulated, stable purpose, establishing a difference with regard to one's competitors, and developing insights about how to create more value than other companies (Porter 1996). Organizations usually say that they aim to be successful, better than their competitors, in a word—excellent. These are common statements of *purpose* (check the Web sites of some companies that you know of and see what their statement of purpose is). How many companies ever aim to be ordinary, to be indistinctive? Almost all organizations and businesses have some version of excellence as their universal objective. Even permanently failing organizations claim to seek excellence. For instance, organizations that rarely achieve their purposes, such as state correctional services and prisons, still maintain targets—commitment to rehabilitation of the offender—that in the vast majority of cases they rarely reach.

Such general statements offer little guidance for strategy making. In fact, the purpose must circumscribe the raison d'être of the business. Take The Body Shop. Its business is dedicated "to the pursuit of social and environmental change" (The Body Shop 2004). Have you shopped there recently? What do

Strategy has to establish a difference.

you see? Soaps, cosmetics, shampoos, bath oils, and other perfumed products. How can soap help achieve social and environmental change? The Body Shop creates profits out of making cosmetics, which it produces without hurting animals or harming the environment. This purpose informs their business strategies and has enabled the firm to turn a relatively indistinct line of business—cheap and cheerful cosmetics and consumer soap and skin care products—into a distinctly positioned "ecologically conscious" brand. Everyone feels good about not hurting cuddly little animals, such as rabbits, or not harming the environment. When you shop at The Body Shop, you not only buy soap but righteousness as well. That is their strategic positioning.

Let's stay with The Body Shop. Its vision is "[t]o courageously ensure that our business is ecologically sustainable: meeting the needs of the present without compromising the future" (The Body Shop 2004). It has a clear purpose and establishes a series of *differences* that distinguish it from its competitors. This is a positioning that, for its customers, makes a difference. Just renaming or repackaging of already established products would not be sufficient. There must be a clear differentiation between a company's products or services and its competitor's. Consequently, The Body Shop is able to call itself "a company with a difference."

Strategy has to establish a difference: to perform different activities or to perform familiar activities differently—this is the key. By merely imitating competitors, a company might strive for operational effectiveness, but as we have seen, this is not sufficient for success.

Strategy has to answer the question, What value does the business add to its customers? Do the chosen purpose and the differences that enact it really add anything valuable to potential customers? For instance, Southwest Airlines added value by selling cheap tickets. Although they offer no meals, which could be seen as providing less value than other airlines, this enabled them to offer other services perceived as more valuable by some customers. Also, it doesn't really matter: U.S. air terminals are choked with fast-food outlets so customers can sate themselves on familiar food prior to or after their flight anyway.

The Body Shop offers ecological products at a fair price, and it is relatively easy for it to communicate the value it provides to its customers. It obviously is not enough just to define a purpose (like creating a mousetrap that kills mice instantly without letting them suffer) and establish a difference compared to competitors (who produce only ordinary but much cheaper mousetraps). The value that such a mousetrap would add is, for most potential customers, ambiguous. Only when all three points—purpose, difference, value—are considered and addressed sufficiently will a strategy be of use for business.

Strategy as revolution

Unusual times require unusual strategies, suggests Gary Hamel (1996), saying that "strategy is revolution; everything else is tactics." What matters is being unique, different, and revolutionary, overturning the industrial order, being "industry revolutionaries" (Hamel 1996). (Perhaps it was this enthusiasm for revolution that led Hamel to endorse the Enron approach to business before its dark side became evident?) There are ten principles of "revolutionary" strategy according to Hamel:

1. *Strategic planning may be planning, but it isn't strategic.* Planning is a rational process that resembles programming, whereas strategizing is about discovering and playfully exploring the potentials for revolution.
2. *Strategy making must be subversive.* Strategy must question the taken-for-granted and the conventions that inform yesterday's business and competitor's actions. Anita Roddick (2000), founder of The Body Shop, is on record as saying that she watches where the cosmetic industry is going and then heads in the opposite direction.
3. *The bottleneck is at the top of the bottle.* Normally, senior managers define strategy. The normal organizational hierarchy is based on experience, but in fast-changing environments, successful past experience can become the obstacle to tomorrow's success. Thus, it has to be supplemented with a hierarchy of imagination, which might be inversely distributed compared to the formal hierarchy.
4. *Revolutionaries exist in every company.* It is a fallacy to believe that top management is pro-change, whereas employees always resist. Every organization has its revolutionaries who do not sit in the front row—but they have the ability to provide fresh insights. If they don't challenge the company from the inside, they will challenge it from without in the marketplace.

5. *Change is not the problem, engagement is.* Too often *change* is a word for routine attempts to restructure a business. However, it is more important to engage people, especially revolutionaries, in a discourse about the future and create commitment.

6. *Strategy making must be democratic.* Instead of being a form of intellectual incest among top managers who have known each other for years and are culturally rather uniform, strategy making must be flexible. It should include young people, outsiders, and people from the margins, as they develop views that are normally unseen and unheard. They don't conform to an organization's orthodoxy and thus can provide truly revolutionary insights.

7. *Anyone can be a strategy activist.* Revolutionaries are never on the top of a hierarchy—they are spread throughout the entire organization. Giving them a voice and providing them with space to speak means transforming their anarchistic potential into activist energy.

8. *Perspective is worth fifty IQ points.* It's not easy to make people smarter, but one can provide new glasses through which the world looks different. Change of perspective leads to shifts in the things that an organization sees, which, implicitly, makes new opportunities visible.

9. *Top-down and bottom-up are not the alternatives.* It is not either-or but a question of organizing communication between people who have responsibility and expertise and people who have fantasy and engagement.

10. *You cannot see the end from the beginning.* Open-ended strategy-making processes lead to surprises. The new cannot be judged on the premises of the old because it follows different rules. Moreover, a really open process leads to a future that cannot be predicted as it unfolds because people explore new avenues.

Judo or sumo?

In an intriguing metaphor that blends war, games, and rationality, Yoffie and Cusumano (1999) define strategy as a fluid process informed by the martial art of judo, an art distinguished through three principles: rapid movement, flexibility, and leverage. What the judo strategist tries to avoid is a sumo match. The battle between Netscape and Microsoft explains these principles. The Netscape Navigator 1.0 was released in December 1994. One year later, Netscape was worth $7 billion. With its 700 employees and $80 million in sales, it outperformed Microsoft (17,000 employees, $6 billion in sales). Netscape moved quickly and surprisingly to uncontested terrain, as judo experts should, to avoid head-to-head conflicts. Netscape offered its browser via the Internet using a novel pricing strategy: "free but not free" was the slogan, which meant that it cost officially $39.90 but that it was free for nonprofit use. Lacking normal distribution channels, Netscape used the Internet to distribute and test its product.

Judo strategy tells us to act flexibly and avoid direct confrontation with a superior force—a lesson that Netscape did not learn very well. In December 1995, Bill Gates announced that Microsoft would "embrace and extend" the Internet across its product range. Netscape countered and tried to beat Microsoft on its terrain instead of focusing on its weaknesses. While they were fighting about distribution channels, Netscape lost deal after deal because it simply did not have the money and the leverage that Microsoft offered through bundling the browser with its Office product. In judo you use the weight and the strategy of your opponents against them: the latest version of Microsoft's Internet Explorer only worked with the most recent operating system. Although Netscape knew that they simply could not compete with Microsoft, which delivered a free browser with every computer sold, it relied upon the fact that there were lots of older systems that were not supported by the latest Microsoft technology.

Strategy as process

The Prisoner's Dilemma

That strategy is always a political game of high stakes, and great uncertainty, is demonstrated by Rapoport and Chammah's (1965) illustration of a paradox that two strategically thinking players must resolve. The Prisoner's Dilemma unfolds as follows. Two prisoners are interrogated independently of each other. If both keep quiet, they will both get a sentence of two years. If one of them confesses, that prisoner will get off free whereas the accomplice will get five years. But if both confess, each will get four years. The dilemma is, What is the best strategy for each prisoner? If they could trust each other and both keep quiet, they would get away with two years each. But if one keeps quiet and the other one confesses, one will get off free and the other one will get five years. If they both confess, they both will get four years. Best for both would be to keep quiet. Neither knows the other's strategy. Thus, their own strategic decision-making remains a paradoxical enterprise that cannot be resolved analytically (see Morgan 1989: 84).

The Prisoner's Dilemma is much wider in application than it might at first appear to be. It applies, actually, in any situation when the other party against whom one is formulating strategy is also formulating a strategy against you. If neither of the two sides really knows what the other is doing and each is trying to outguess and out-strategize the other, they can quickly find themselves in a Prisoner's Dilemma. What looks like a great strategy in the light of the information that you have available to you may not seem so smart at all if you knew what the other knew and was doing with it.

Therefore, strategy is more a process than a state. From this perspective, there have recently been attempts to redefine static views into process-based perspectives on strategy and strategy making. The process-based view of strategy making "refers to how the collective system called organization establishes, and when necessary changes, its basic orientation. Strategy-making also takes up the complex issue of collective intention—how an organization composed of many people makes up *its* mind, so to speak" (Mintzberg 1989: 25). For instance, when top management, enclosed in boardrooms and detached from corporate everyday life, works out a seemingly perfect strategy, major problems can occur when employees have to bring this strategy into existence on a day-to-day basis. Moreover, serious concerns can be raised as to whether top management knows enough and has the necessary information to make a sound decision concerning its possibilities and impossibilities. Employees might know much more about customer needs, business operations, practices, and how to improve them than a detached management.

The process of strategy making

As Mintzberg (1990) pointed out, high complexity and fast rates of change require emergent strategies, whereas a top-down strategy-making process is most suitable for relatively stable situations characterized by low complexity. In turbulent environments (high uncertainty), the process of defining a strategy becomes a messy and experimental process driven from the bottom-up.

Take the example of the two fast-food chains McDonald's and Wimpy in the United Kingdom (see Campbell and Alexander 1997). Managers at Wimpy noticed that McDonald's restaurants were much cleaner, and since cleanliness is a decisive factor in the fast-food business, they tried to make their restaurants cleaner. Failing to raise the standard without spending lots of money, managers at Wimpy scrutinized how McDonald's standards were achieved. They found out that it was the attitude of staff, using their downtime to clean the restaurant, that was important. So what was the strategy of McDonald's? Did they spend money and time to create a corporate culture that would lead to highly motivated staff? Or did they decide to create especially clean restaurants and build a corporate culture program around it? Or did they find out that they had already motivated staff and that it would be easy to turn this into an advantage? Was cleanliness a purpose or rather an (unintended) effect of other objectives, like developing a strong corporate culture? At any rate, the distinction between preplanned objective and emergent results gets blurry. This is why the process of strategy making has to be both top-down and bottom-up. First, valuable insights for strategy formulation may reside in the head of the employees who implement strategy as much as in the heads of those who think (they think) it. Second, the implementation and the emerging shortcomings and insights can be the basis for tomorrow's strategy. In fact, implementation becomes a part of the strategy formulation process.

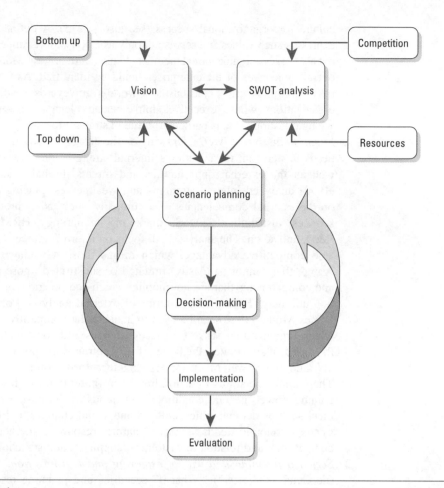

Figure 12.4   *Integrating strategy*

Synthesizing strategy

We have developed a seven-step model that integrates the most important developments in the field and serves as a basis for strategy analysis.

1. *Defining vision and mission.* Drawing on the entrepreneurial school, at the beginning of the strategy-making process, organizations should formulate a vision explaining and reflecting on why they do what they do and why they do it exactly the way they do it. A mission statement provides, in principle, a source of motivation for all organizational members, and it should function as a general guideline for decisions at all levels. The seminal contributions of Peters and Waterman (1982) and Deal and Kennedy (1982) stressed the importance of shared values and a strong

culture for organizational success (see also p. 275). A defined mission expresses such values and serves not only as a constant reminder of these but also sparks organizational members to give of their best. Moreover, the overall objectives of the enterprise should be identified. As Christensen (1997) reminds us, "[T]he business world's graveyards are filled with organizations whose executives implemented elegant answers to the wrong question. That is particularly true in strategy formulation."

2. *Situation analysis (SWOT).* Drawing on the design school, management needs to audit an organization's internal strengths and weaknesses as well as the external opportunities and threats. Prahalad and Hamel (1990) analyzed internal strengths and weaknesses, placing emphasis on the internal competencies of a company, such as its products and services, distribution network, marketing, technology, HRM, culture, R&D, and so on. The analyses will focus on internal sources of sustainable competitive advantage, which means those advantages that are scarce, that cannot be (easily) imitated or substituted, those resources and competencies that are not mobile, which can position an organization uniquely (Foss 1997). In terms of external analysis, Porter's Five Forces Model (1980) can be used to analyze the competitive arenas in which organizations strive for success. Forces and constraints, such as the threat of substitutes, the threat of new entrants, the power of suppliers, and the power of customers, together form competitive rivalry. These affect the ability to realize higher profitability through strong bargaining power, general conditions and trends in the business environment such as demographics, cultural and social changes, politics, legal trends, economic trends, access to natural resources, the activities of competitors, and relation to customers, suppliers, and stakeholders.

3. *Scenario planning is a way of exploring and learning from the future* (de Geus 1988, 1997). "What if" scenarios and planning responses to them prove very effective learning tools, best described as a form of game playing. Scenario planning develops a wide range of possible futures that question the taken-for-granted and the established frames of imagination. An example that we touched on previously was Shell Oil Company, which, after the 1973 oil crisis, became the market leader and the most profitable company in its business. Shell was better prepared for the crisis than its competitors, since Shell used scenario planning that did not just extrapolate from past events but also included worst-case scenarios—such as happened during the oil crisis—whereas its competitors were not prepared; their rationality had been bounded by past expectations and extrapolations, premised on stable, continuous growth, and investment.

4. *The planning school provides the tools for organizations to create a portfolio of plans.* These vary in terms of the scale of plans (global or local), the level of management involved, and the time horizon. Such a portfolio involves a hierarchy of plans coordinating an organization's activities on different levels, ranging from its broad role in society, to its products and

their marketing, and to sales forecasts. The organization seeks to translate and apply the generic plan to all levels. Such detailed planning allocates resources, tasks, and responsibilities in order to achieve the defined goal. It bridges the gap between strategy formulation and its implementation.

5. *Decision making, muddling through, and garbage can approaches enable you to take intended and unintended effects of strategy into account and be aware of the human side of strategic planning.* Think of the unintended effects that strategies can have. They can be advertising tools, means of creating a secure future, and hence sheltering an organization from rough reality, absorbing angst and uncertainty. They are a game in which every move forces the other players also to move, which might lead to a dynamic situation—but one that it not controllable. Looking at these dark sides of strategic planning will certainly make you more aware rather than subsequently being surprised about why things went the way they did.

6. *Implementation.* In most approaches, it is taken for granted that the formulated strategy will be implemented. However, many organizational stakeholders will influence and change strategy during its implementation. Strategy making and its implementation is a powerful process that has to deal with the different interests, values, and expectations of different stakeholders.

7. *Evaluation.* Finally, to ensure accurate implementation of designed strategies, it is necessary to monitor their realization. Depending on the targeted outcome, many different parameters can be evaluated, such as market share, profit, customer satisfaction, and environmental impact. Such evaluation can be seen as a constant feedback loop generating information that feeds back on Steps 1 and 2 of the strategic management model.

THE FINE PRINT: NARRATING STRATEGY . . . AND HYPOCRISY, RATIONALITY, AND ETHICS

Narrating strategy: Act before you plan!

Heinrich von Kleist (1997) presents a witty and instructive story that allows you to playfully and practically to understand what emergent strategies consist of. In his narrative, Kleist highlights the mutually constitutive interplay between thinking and speaking, or turned strategically, planning and doing. Notice that he emphasizes the importance of this process when trying to explore new and innovative ways:

If there is something you wish to know and by meditation you cannot find it, my advice to you, my ingenious friend, is: speak about it with the first acquaintance you encounter. He does not need to be especially perspicacious, nor do I mean that you should ask his opinion, not at all. On the contrary, you should yourself tell him at once what it is you wish to know. I see astonishment in your face. I hear you reply that when you were young you were advised only to speak of things you already understood. . . . But because I do have some dim conception at the outset, one distantly related to what I am looking for, if I boldly make a start with that, my mind, even as my speech proceeds, under the necessity of finding an end for that beginning, will shape my first confused idea into complete clarity so that, to my amazement, understanding is arrived at as the sentence ends. I put in a few unarticulated sounds, dwell lengthily on the conjunctions, perhaps make use of apposition where it is not necessary and have recourse to other ticks which will spin out my speech, all to gain time for the fabrication of my idea in the workshop of the mind. (Kleist 1997: 405–406)

All the ostensibly useless, unproductive, noneffective circumstances that seem to hinder the unfolding of thoughts are, perhaps, the precondition for their coming into being. Translated into our context, management and the organization—strategy and structure, function and form—supplement and complement each other, fluctuating and oscillating, deferring and transforming each other, generating a space within which creativity and innovation emerge. Instead of distinguishing between planning and action and imposing a hierarchical relation upon them, we rely on the "activity of people who are thrown into the *middle* of things and play their way out by *thinking while doing*" (Weick and Westley 1996: 453; italics added).

Strategy as big talk

Rather than see visions, mission statements, and strategies as just the rational frame for rational action wisely controlled by those who know more and better, because they have more information at their fingertips, another way of seeing them would be as fashionable gimmicks in the world of management. Barry and Elmes (1997: 430) suggest, ironically that "strategy must rank as one of the most prominent, influential, and costly stories told in organizations." Sometimes strategy provides a good cover-up story; it deflects attention away from ethically questionable actions or paradoxes. For instance, pretentious vision statements can be quite helpful. Nils Brunsson (1995) suggests the "principle of distance" with which you can see the positive effect of making master plans and grand strategies as managerial activity:

[The] main principle should not be "management by walking around" (Peters and Waterman 1982) but rather "management by walking away" (or perhaps "by going abroad"). Distance between management and actors (and action) reduces the risk of management being controlled by the actors, and makes it easier for management to maintain inconsistency between talk, decisions and action. Distance also reduces the risk of management obstructing action by involving its own conflicts and its problem orientation or its own rationality in the action, thus undermining its force. . . . An organizational management that keeps its distance from action and from the concrete conditions of action acquires instead excellent opportunities for thinking big. It can generate and establish lofty principles, unrealistic goals and beautiful visions, which can become associated with the organization. This production of high morality is important in showing the organization's good intentions to the rest of the world. (Brunsson 1995: 138, 140)

Gendering strategy

Irrespective of its substantive paradoxes or ethical ellipses, you may see another highly problematic dimension of strategic management to be its gendering effects. Strategy is a game that reinforces the dominant masculine character of organizations. As we have already seen, the connection between military and (strategic) management is obvious and omnipresent. Through this connection, the masculine and martial character of management becomes apparent. In this martial model, strategy and masculine characteristics (such as striving for dominance and power through a competitive war model) are inextricably interlinked. Remember Henry Mintzberg's description of strategic positioning as a *launching* device that sends *projectiles* at a landscape of *targets* (markets) faced with *rivals?* Mintzberg's thinking is inspired by war metaphors, in which the organization is a phallocentric vehicle of managerial combat-machinery. It is a part of the armory of big boys' toys, you could say. In this concept, instrumental rationality and masculinity are inextricably intertwined and form, implicitly, the basis for the continuing gendering of strategic management.

Clear strategies in an unclear world?

Strategists typically take their goals as clear, unambiguous, and given. However, in reality, goals are shifting and changing over time. Think about the U.S. response to 9/11. First, the goal was to destroy the terrorist network; after defeating the Taliban in Afghanistan, an axis of evil became the new main target of the George W. Bush administration; then the new threat of weapons of mass destruction was identified in Iraq; rapidly, the new objective became disarming Iraq, which eventually changed to capturing Saddam Hussein and bringing freedom and liberty to the Iraqi people; subsequently, the goal became neutralizing those terrorists, insurgents, and nonfreedom-loving citizens still operative in Iraq despite the "regime change" that had occurred. Notice that these changes in goals occurred within less then one and one-half years, and that these changing goals required completely different strategies to be realized. Also, notice that the strategic objectives were not necessarily abandoned because they had been achieved—often they were abandoned because they had not been achieved.

Predictable futures?

Mainstream strategic thinking sees external threats and opportunities as predictable. The history of management tells a different story: "I think there is a world market for about five computers," said Thomas Watson, IBM chairman, in 1943, whereas Kenneth H. Olson (president of the Digital Equipment Corporation) said, even as late as 1977, "There is no reason for any individual to have a computer in their home" (cited in Ahl 1984: 209). Not that these people were not smart enough, but from their point of view, they simply could not see and predict the electronic revolution that was about to happen. Similarly, internal strengths and weaknesses are hard to identify. Is it a weakness to have playful employees who experiment with little papers and adhesives that do not stick (although they were told not to)? Well, when Post-it is the result, the apparent weakness turns into strength.

Strategy as top-down approaches

Mostly, strategy is something that is developed in the corporate headquarters, far from daily organizational life. Management makes strategies that the organization has to enact accordingly: "The notion that strategy is something that should happen way up there, far removed from the details of running an organization on a daily basis, is one of the great fallacies of conventional management. And it explains a good many of the most dramatic failures in business and public policy today" (Mintzberg 1989: 31). The so-called implementation problems are a direct result of this division of labor in which management thinks lower employees should realize their ideas. This model, widely practiced since Taylor, not only demotivates the workforce but cannot deal with rapid changes. Furthermore, it is problematic to assume that managers at the top get all the information necessary to plan strategically, as they are remote from daily routines, processes, and customers. Finally, companies are often organizationally incapable of carrying out the sophisticated strategies managers have developed. "Over the past 20 years, strategic thinking has far outdistanced organizational capabilities" (Bartlett and Ghoshal 1998: 187).

Rational strategies?

Nowhere else in management is rationality as deeply embedded as it is in strategic planning. March suggested supplementing managerial rationality with a "technology of foolishness," which is more likely to help detect interesting goals (see also p. 397). He argues that every rational process of (strategic) decision making assumes the preexistence of a set of stable and consistent goals. March suggests that goals may sometimes change in interesting and, as he terms it, "foolish" ways. Understanding that these goals change begs the question, How can we find new and interesting goals? Enter foolishness: "Individuals and organizations need ways of doing things for which they have no good reason. Not always. Not usually. But sometimes. They need to act before they think" (March 1988: 259). Kleist and March meet at this point. In order to find new goals, one has playfully to explore and exploit circumstances and different avenues that do not lead anywhere—at the first glance. "Playfulness," according to March, "is the deliberate, temporary relaxation of rules in order to explore the possibilities of alternative rules. . . . Playfulness allows experimentation. At the same time, it acknowledges reason. . . . A strict insistence on purpose, consistency, and rationality limits our ability to find new purposes. Play relaxes that insistence to allow us to act 'unintelligently' or 'irrationally,' 'foolishly' to explore alternative ideas of possible purposes" (March 1988: 261). Again, think of Post-it notes one more time.

. . . and ethics?

Where goals are predetermined, such that they just have to be implemented, important ethical issues can arise. The Nazi regime, for instance, developed powerful and deadly efficient strategies to accomplish their goal of an Aryan Third Reich. Although the strategy might have been functional and efficient, the outcomes it produced were absolutely inhuman. The process had already been set in a direction that was evil. When strategy making takes the goal as pregiven and sees its major challenge to be realizing them as efficiently as possible, ethical issues can become apparent.

Humanity and ethics are often not considered together in strategic approaches. Nike, for instance, maximizes its profits through outsourcing production to third world countries. The unethical results of this strategy are that they employ workers who, by the standards of most of their customers, are poorly paid and oppressed. Moreover, some of them are under the age of fourteen and work in sweatshops. Of course, in the third world countries in which they work, there might be considerable competition for these jobs. But the cost of the labor used in production hardly compares to the millions that Nike spends on marketing its products, especially through promotional tie-ups with leading sportspeople such as Tiger Woods or Cathy Freeman. Speared by these inequities, a critical audience picked up these practices of Nike and protested against Nike management, successfully lobbying them to change strategies. Nike's strategy was successful in terms of business goals, but as the goals were achieved in ways that liberals in the developed countries could question, the strategy turned out to be counterproductive in marketing terms.

> A young woman working in a factory sweatshop for a few dollars a day looks like exploitation. Indeed, it is, but in the third world, it is exploitation that might mean the difference between starvation and survival for her family, despite the humiliations and beatings that might sometimes accompany its earning.

Of course, ethical issues are rarely as clear cut; the picture is much harder to calibrate from the perspective of the third world workers themselves. Yes, they are exploited in global terms, and the work is demanding and detailed. But in terms of comparable wages in their domestic economies, they are privileged. A young woman working in a factory sweatshop for a few dollars a day looks like exploitation. Indeed, it is, but in the third world, it is exploitation that might mean the difference between starvation and survival for her family, despite the humiliations and beatings that might sometimes accompany its earning.

SUMMARY AND REVIEW

Strategy runs the whole gamut from rational to whimsical approaches, thinking of March's "technology of foolishness." In this chapter, we have covered the range of approaches to strategy. With our concern for multiple rather than singular rationalities and attention to the politics of rationality, we are most sympathetic to the process and emergence approaches because they seem to us best able to capture the complexity. In addition, again unlike many writers on strategy, we have been at pains to point out that there are always ethical and political issues associated with the choice of strategies. Conceptualizing strategy as a game enables one to understand it as a dynamic and complex process in which every move from one party provokes a reaction from the other that influences it again. Strategy is neither planning nor fighting but interacting that sometimes brawls, lies, cheats, fights, and plays. The emergence school and the concept of scenario planning emphasize this aspect most strongly. Strategy is not just about rationally analyzing what's going on, nor is it simply survival of the fittest, but a complex web of moves. Some are made to lead others astray, some to cheat and to fool, and others to disguise reality or to talk fiction into facts. Emphasis should be put on the processes by which strategy is played out. And there is no shortage of strategy professors to help management, all competing for fame in the guru market (Boyett and Boyett 1998). The competition is intense—as you would expect it to be for people who make strategy their business. Porter is presently the top strategy guru, with Mintzberg pushing up from the ranks. Ansoff has had his day, and Chandler is old hat. That's strategy for you—a dynamic and competitive market.

ONE MORE TIME . . .

Getting the story straight

- According to Chandler, what is the relation between strategy and structure?
- What is the relation between strategic and other levels in the planning school?
- What does SWOT stand for?
- What are Porter's main contributions to the field of strategy?
- How does producing scenarios differ from producing plans?
- What do the terms *bounded rationality, garbage can,* and *sensemaking* mean?

Thinking outside the box

- What are the three cornerstones of strategy?
- What do judo, sumo, and revolution have to do with strategy?
- What is the Prisoner's Dilemma?
- How might good strategy mix up with bad ethics?

ADDITIONAL RESOURCES

1. Currently, the best book on strategy, combining a holistic and critical understanding of the issue, is Stephen Cummings's (2002) *Recreating Strategy*. It is a comprehensive, well-written book on the past, present, and a bit about the future of strategic thinking in management and organization theory. It contains a nice introductory chapter, good case studies, and not so easily understandable trips into the ancient Greek world.

2. Also, we would encourage you to have a look at Mintzberg's countless contributions to the development of the field, especially his 1994 book *The Rise and Fall of Strategic Management* and Mintzberg, Ahlstrand, and Lampe's *Strategy Safari: A Guided Tour Through the Wilds of Strategic Management* (1998).

3. An extremely rich source for further studies is the *Handbook of Strategy and Management* (2002), edited by Andrew Pettigrew, Howard Thomas, and Richard Whittington. It contains more than twenty papers and many more useful links for further reading.

4. In terms of films, think of *The Lord of the Rings* trilogy or the initial *Star Wars* trilogy. These films are all about strategy, with heroes, villains, and quests—just like real-life corporations!

5. To get a grasp of the enormous changes wrought by the railroads, which Chandler stresses, you should watch the 1969 cinematic masterpiece by Sergio Leone, *Once Upon a Time in the West*. It is, without doubt, the greatest western movie ever made. The movie is a farewell to the old world of the West, nostalgic for the loss of the frontier while also being a record of the new breed of person, the businessman, who will dominate now that the frontier is disappearing and the old West dying. The plot of the film centers on the railroad creating the continental market, urban spaces, and long-distance connections that are Chandler's focus. It also has one of the best opening sequences of any movie made.

In addition to these suggested additional resources, don't forget to look at what is also available on the Web site **www.ckmanagement.net,** including free PDF files of recent papers related to this chapter, which you can download; video interviews with famous academics talking about related themes; as well as many other resources, such as connections to interesting Web sites.

CHAPTER 13

MANAGING GLOBALIZATION

Global Flows, Winners and Losers, Local Specialization

Objectives and learning outcomes

By the end of this chapter, you will be able to

- Understand debates around, and dynamics of, globalization

- Discuss their impact on organizations

- Identify some key strategic issues involved in managing in a global economy

- Identify who are the winners and losers from globalization—and why

Before you get started . . .

What some presidents of the United States have said:

"Globalization, as defined by rich people like us, is a very nice thing. . . . [Y]ou are talking about the Internet, you are talking about cell phones, you are talking about computers. This doesn't affect two-thirds of the people of the world."

President Jimmy Carter (n.d.), as an ex-president

"If you look at the facts of the last 30 years, hundreds of millions of people have had their economic prospects advanced on every continent because they have finally been able to find a way to express their creativity in positive terms, and produce goods and services that could be purchased around the borders of their nation."

President Bill Clinton (1999)

OUTLINE OF THE CHAPTER

We live in a global world. What this implies is that anywhere/anything is potentially or actually linked to anywhere/anything else in the management of commerce, government, aid, or other globally exchanged goods and services. Thus, globalization is vitally important both in terms of the factors making this connectedness possible and the consequences flowing from it. Globalization, as the enveloping context, provides the big picture within which the rest of the book should be situated. Whereas the Cold War, the world wars, or the Age of Empires shaped previous generations of organizations, the contemporary scene is shaped by globalization. As the chapter highlights, globalization is multifaceted, almost holographic in the dazzling array of images that it conjures. Just as plentiful are debates about its meaning. In this chapter, we capture some of these debates and represent them in terms of a flowing, mingling, interpenetrating, and overlapping of experiences and stories from differing cultures, peoples, and places. Globalization involves flows between four key phenomena linked by circuits of organizational production and consumption: nation-states, the world system, our selves, and humankind. We use these categories to generate debate around some key themes, focusing our discussion, eventually, on the winners and losers from globalization.

SETTING THE SCENE

Since the time of the earliest civilizations, trade across frontiers and regions has occurred. Economy and society involving exchange of raw materials, animals, and crops, semifinished and finished goods, services, money, ideas, and people has existed since the dawn of civilization (Diamond 1997). For several hundred years from the sixteenth century onward, trade between European state systems and their colonial offshoots defined international trade. Such trade involved the world's major trading companies, organized religions, and local chiefs and merchants. Often it comprised plunder and looting, dealing in slaves as well as precious and rare commodities. Only later, with the advent of industrialization, did it involve more mundane commodities spreading globally, often replacing indigenous products, propelled by the artillery of cheap prices. Some of the earliest struggles against globalization, as it was experienced in terms of political colonialization, used usurped domestic commodities symbolically in their struggle: Gandhi's domestic cotton spinning wheel, for instance, recalling the village craft displaced by the Lancashire textile industry.

Once national markets were relatively well established, business became organized in what some theorists refer to as "organized capitalism" (Lash and Urry 1987). Essentially, this meant that national firms with strong identities in their domestic markets would move to capture non-national markets, based on this expertise. The impact of this trade was significant. In Florianopolis, a regional city and state capital of Santa Catarina, in the far south of Brazil, Stewart has seen a "Huddersfield" store, called this because it sold woolen textiles. Such stores are named after the town in Yorkshire, England, that was a center of wool textile manufacturing. More generally, anywhere in Australia and New Zealand, as well as in Brazil and elsewhere in Latin America, you can walk into the "Manchester" section of a department store and buy cotton goods there, or go to a separate Manchester shop. Retailing inexorably linked nationally specific places with particular types of products. These products not only captured markets but also the language.

Intercontinental markets have been around for nearly 150 years. They are the result of the extensive laying of submarine telegraph cables from the 1860s onward, making possible virtually instant trade across thousands of miles. Bond markets also became closely interconnected, and large-scale international lending—both portfolio and direct investment—grew rapidly during the latter half of the nineteenth century (Hirst and Thompson 1996). Foreign direct investment (FDI) grew so rapidly that in 1913 it amounted to over 9% of world output (Bairoch and Kozul-Wright 1996: 10).

By the early years of the twentieth century, significant transnational activity was established, characterized by the transfer of resources, especially capital and to a lesser extent labor, from one national economy to another. The process was uneven. In many countries the patterns of imperial preference in trade meant that semiperipheral economies in the world system did not compete directly with core countries in manufacturing finished goods but instead concentrated on primary production for the global market that the core countries structured. For instance, much of Central America fell under the sway of the United Fruit Company, which dominated the trade in bananas and other tropical fruit to the U.S. market.

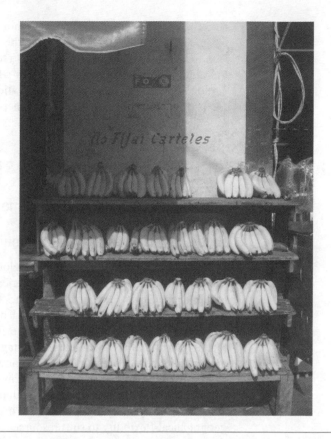

Image 13.1   *Bananas*

When finished goods were required, the core countries could provide them. In the 1920s, the Sydney Harbour Bridge was fabricated bit by bit, piece by piece, in the northeast of England and shipped halfway around the world to be constructed. Only after the emergence of a national economic industrial capacity during World War II, when the old patterns were disrupted, did Australia fully develop industrial capabilities. In the past, typically, where national firms expanded into other markets, this involved the creation of other country production capacities through direct subsidiaries, acquisitions, or various types of cooperation (commercial, financial, technological, and industrial). This is how the car industry spread globally to countries such as Mexico, Brazil, and South Africa. Today, international ventures are commonplace, and transnational corporations (firms with a global national presence) have become the major forces driving globalization, opening up global production and markets.

Globalization is everywhere today—and, so it seems, is resistance to it. No longer characterized by Gandhi's principles of nonviolent resistance, from the streets of Seattle to those of Venice, from Cancun to London, wherever there is a meeting of global agencies such as the World Trade Organization, there are sure to be protestors. The protests take to the streets to create media scapes for the nightly news: They try to publicize what are seen as the costs of globalization. Hence, no account of globalization would be complete that did not focus on the losers as well as the winners, that did not look at resistance to globalization as well as its mechanisms.

CENTRAL APPROACHES AND MAIN THEORIES

Introduction to globalization in management

Globalization as an economic phenomenon

When management writers refer to globalization as a process, they tend to focus mostly on European, North American, and Japanese trade, investment, and financial flows. Globalization is marked by the integration of deregulating markets and technology and facilitated by telecommunications and ease of transport. International activities enable firms to enter new markets, exploit technological and organizational advantages, as well as reduce business costs and risks. These organizations are known as transnationals because they extend beyond national space in their routine activities. Transnational organizations have significant control over both production and consumption in more than one country. They dominate world trade. In principle, they have sufficient geographical flexibility to shift resources and operations between global locations. In practice it may be a bit more difficult. There is a plurality of transnational corporations, which neither dominate national industrial sectors in all markets nor operate without regard for more or less sovereign states. The power of transnationals can easily be overestimated. Only a small number of transnational corporations are truly global, and not all transnational corporations are necessarily large, in conventional definitions of that term. Global patterns differ markedly according to the national origin of the firms. New supplies and sources of transnational corporations evolve as the world economy evolves, so that we now have emergent markets transnational corporations in newly industrializing countries.

Strategies of globalization

Business history suggests that organizations learn in tandem with technological changes (Chandler 1993). In *Scale and Scope,* Chandler (1990) argues that the evolution of the global corporation is the final stage in the transformation of industries in search of economies of scale, economies of scope, and national differences in the availability and cost of productive resources. It is economic rationality, coupled with changing technologies, that drives globalization

(Chandler 1993). In many industries, economies of scale are such that volumes exceeded the sales levels individual companies could achieve in all but the largest countries, forcing them to become international or perish. The minimum efficient level for capital-intensive plants is 80% to 90% of capacity in contrast to labor-intensive industries. The costs and profits of capital-intensive industries are determined by plant utilization and throughput, rather than by the simple amount produced.

Less capital-intensive industries are not as affected by scale economies. But opportunities exist for scope economies through worldwide communication and transportation networks. Trading companies handling the products of many companies can achieve greater volume and lower unit cost. With changes in technology and markets came requirements for access to new resources as lower factor costs. Cheap labor may be important, but not as much as one might think. It is misleading to assume that the search for cheaper labor in itself is the central driving force of the increasing internationalization of many industries. In most industries there are more important factors than labor costs, including access to markets, technology, and other resources. Increasingly, industry requires more highly skilled labor, and the possession of relevant skills is more immediately important than the price of labor. A focus on globalization that sees it in terms of economies of scale and scope, or the search for cheap labor, or in terms of the business strategies of transnational corporations is not necessarily wrong. But it is limited, as we shall see.

Defining globalization

Goran Therborn (2000a: 154) defines contemporary globalization in terms that we think are useful: "tendencies to a worldwide reach, impact, or connectedness of social phenomena or to a world-encompassing awareness among social actors." He goes on to say:

> "Globalization" is the most immediate legacy to the new century of the social sciences of the outgoing 20th century. Basically it is a concern of the second half of the 1990s. . . . In the major dictionaries of English, French, Spanish and German of the 1980s the word is not listed. In Arabic at least four different words render the notion. Whereas in Japanese business the word goes back to the 1980s, it entered academic Chinese only in the mid-1990s. The Social Science Citation Index records only a few occurrences of "globalization" in the 1980s but shows its soaring popularity from 1992 onwards, which accelerated in the last years of the past century. . . . In comparison with the preoccupations of the social sciences 100 years earlier, the current overriding interest in globalization means two things. First of all, a substitution of *the global* for *the universal;* second, a substitution of *space* for *time*. (Therborn 2000b: 149)

First, let us consider the triumph of the global over the universal. That the global is being substituted for the universal means that whereas in the past we might have regarded the most developed nations and their organizations as heralding the universal form of the future, now we are more inclined to think that dominant organizations globally need not necessarily tell us anything about the future. They advise us only about the present and the past, times when they were able to command the economic heights. But today, the commanding economic heights are easily lost. Twenty years ago, among the world's major firms were companies such as Pan Am, and TWA—both major players in the archetypically global business of airlines. Today, none exist. Past dominance is no guarantee of future success.

Second, we concentrate on the dominance of space rather than time in what follows. Space remains important precisely for the reasons that Porter was seen to have outlined in the previous chapter (see also pp. 417–424). The home base is significant as are the clusters of activity that we find in particular locales such as Silicon Valley. The ultimate contradiction of the Internet revolution is that although firms could be located anywhere in cyberspace, they still seem to cluster together in global cities such as New York, London, and Sydney (Castells 2001). Moreover, on the average in the Organization for Economic Development and Cooperation (OECD) economies, about 36% to 40% of what is spent in the economy is spent by the national state, in terms of defense, health, education, and so on, and these sorts of expenditures tend to be well grounded in national capabilities and concentrated in national space.

> **Space is superseding time because, in a world of trade in symbolic images such as software, currencies, and other forms of representation, time is no longer an issue.**

Space is superseding time because, in a world of trade in symbolic images such as software, currencies, and other forms of representation, time is no longer an issue. If you have trading facilities in the right time zones, for instance, you can trade twenty-four hours a day, moving money, or other "signs" of commerce, symbolically, across the globe, from London to New York to Tokyo to Sydney to London. There is an increasing separation of the "real" economy of production and its simulacra in the "symbol economy" of financial flows and transactions. A new international division of labor compresses and fragments both space and distance in such a way that not only production but also various business service industries become distributed in unlikely places. Global currencies facilitate trade across the world: MBAs become global warriors in the new world order. New divisions restructure geographic space. In principle, anywhere is virtually immediately accessible by information and communication technologies. In practice, most national capitals can be reached within twenty-four hours of air travel.

Third, globalization does not mean that we now live in a "borderless world" (Ohmae 1990) in which nation-states are of diminished significance. Some national governments, notably the United States, play an extraordinarily strong and unilateral role in the global *political* economy, as the recent war and occupation of Iraq demonstrate. To the extent that the world is becoming *economically* global, it is a world dominated by U.S., Japanese and Southeast Asian, Western European, and allied interests. Technological, economic, and cultural integration is developing within and between these three regions and is evident

Image 13.2   *Above the clouds*

in the patterns of international trade and investment flows. Interfirm strategic alliances are heavily concentrated among companies from these countries. It is here that scientific power, technological supremacy, economic dominance, and cultural hegemony are concentrated (Petrella 1996: 77).

A model of global flows

The characteristics of contemporary globalization include the internationalization of financial markets and corporate strategies, the diffusion of technology and related R&D and knowledge worldwide, as well as the emergence of global media. These help transform consumption patterns into cultural products through worldwide consumer markets. A global political economy, its social and ecological impact, as well as critical responses to it, is now reported widely (Therborn 2000b), if largely still with a focus skewed by Western interests. Although the focus on globalization has been dominated by discussion of global business interests, it is apparent that social identities, just as much as business, are now being organized through a system of global flows, as represented in Figure 13.1.

People only develop a sense of self in relation to others. For most of human history, these others were framed by what was available at the local, often village, level. Today, even the most remote villager can see themselves against the mirror that the media projects into their communities. Everything

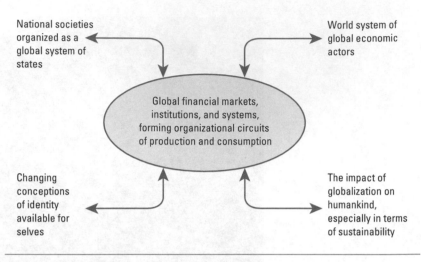

Figure 13.1   *Global flows and social identities*

relational flows through space: what it means to be human, what it means to be a member of a society, what it means to be a part of a society within a world system of states. All of these are infinitely expandable once the security of village perimeters are breached. Each one of us has to consider ourselves in relation to those others that flow through and colonize the spaces we are in. Two of these flows are of particular importance. First, the global flows of money, knowledge, people, and politics: the material flows of the global world. Second, the invisible flows: trade in the export of cultural consciousness and changing conceptions of the self. It is the latter that always pose the fundamental question of identity: Where and how in the world do I fit in—or who and what am I?

Global flows of money, knowledge, people, and politics

It is a familiar comment that the economic scale of the largest of giant corporations now exceeds the gross domestic product of most countries. International financial flows and foreign currency exchanges now dwarf the value of international trade in goods. Financial services are fundamental to the operation of every aspect of the economic system. Each element of the production chain depends upon necessary levels of finance to keep it in operation (Dicken 1992: 358). If you were to look at the relative size and value of some well-known countries and companies compared in terms of the value of the GDP and sales, you might be surprised. The fourth-largest entity, Euronext, is equal to the combined single stock market of France, the Netherlands, Belgium, and Portugal. Although most of the listed entities are in the United States, not all are. It is also a dynamic list with a number of new entrants. Of

TABLE 13.1 The world's 100 largest economic entities

Rank	Economic Entities: National Stock Markets and Publicly Listed Companies in Terms of Turnover[a]	Position $U.S. Billions	Rank in 2002
1	U.S.A.	13,778	1
2	JAPAN	2,750	2
3	U.K.	1,936	4
4	**Euronext (Europe)**	**1,936**	**4**
5	GERMANY	979	5
6	CANADA	855	7
7	HONG KONG	680	9
8	SWITZERLAND	677	6
9	SPAIN	653	10
10	ITALY	584	8
11	AUSTRALIA	566	11
12	CHINA	484	—
13	TAIWAN	356	13
14	**General Electric (U.S.)**	**308**	**14**
15	SWEDEN	298	20
16	**Microsoft (U.S.)**	**294**	**12**
17	SOUTH KOREA	287	17
18	INDIA	274	—
19	**Pfizer (U.S.)**	**264**	**18**
20	**Exxon Mobil (U.S.)**	**624**	**15**
21	SOUTH AFRICA	256	22
22	**Citigroup Inc (U.S.)**	**247**	**19**
23	**Wal-Mart (U.S.)**	**229**	**16**
24	**Intel (U.S.)**	**204**	**32**
25	BRAZIL	203	29
26	**BP (Europe)**	**181**	**24**
27	FINLAND	171	26
28	**AIG (U.S.)**	**169**	**23**
29	**Vodaphone (Europe)**	169	28
30	MALAYSIA	165	30
31	**Cisco (U.S.)**	**164**	**35**
32	**IBM (U.S.)**	**160**	**25**
33	**Johnson & Johnson**	**150**	**21**

(Continued)

TABLE 13.1 (Continued)

Rank	Economic Entities: National Stock Markets and Publicly Listed Companies in Terms of Turnover[a]	Position $U.S. Billions	Rank in 2002
34	**HSBC (Europe)**	149	39
35	SINGAPORE	142	41
36	**GlaxoSmithKL (Europe)**	137	31
37	**Berkshire Hathaway (U.S.)**	128	37
38	**Procter & Gamble (U.S.)**	127	34
39	**Coca-Cola (U.S.)**	122	33
40	**Bank of America (U.S.)**	118	38
41	MEXICO	118	45
42	**Toyota (Japan)**	116	45
43	DENMARK	114	50
44	**TotalFinalElf (Europe)**	112	46
45	**Altria (U.S.)**	110	42
46	**NTTnDoCoMo (Japan)**	109	—
47	**Royal Dutch (Europe)**	107	44
48	**Merck (U.S.)**	100	27
49	**Wells Fargo (U.S.)**	99	48
50	**Nestle (Europe)**	99	55
51	GREECE	98	61
52	THAILAND	95	—
53	**Verizon (U.S.)**	94	36
54	**Telecomm Italia (Europe)**	91	75
55	**Chevron Texaco (U.S.)**	90	54
56	**PetroChina (China)**	89	—
57	NORWAY	88	65
58	**Dell Computer (U.S.)**	67	62
59	**Royal Bank of Scotland (Europe)**	85	60
60	**UPS (U.S.)**	84	56
61	**SBC Comm (U.S.)**	83	43
62	**AstraZeneca (Europe)**	82	76
63	CHILE	81	90
64	**TimeWarner (U.S.)**	81	63
65	**PepsiCo (U.S.)**	80	43
66	**Nokia (Europe)**	79	49

Rank	Economic Entities: National Stock Markets and Publicly Listed Companies in Terms of Turnover[a]	Position $U.S. Billions	Rank in 2002
67	Eli Lillly (U.S.)	79	52
68	Amgen (U.S.)	79	64
69	Home Depot (U.S.)	79	83
70	IRELAND	77	73
71	Viacom (U.S.)	76	51
72	Nippon T&T (Japan)	76	78
73	Eni (Europe)	75	70
74	Deutsche Telkom (Europe)	74	72
75	J. P. Morgan Chase (U.S.)	74	80
76	Abbott Labs (U.S.)	73	71
77	Telefonica (Europe)	73	82
78	Comcast (U.S.)	72	67
79	Fannie Mae (U.S.)	72	57
80	USB (Europe)	72	74
81	Shell Trading (Europe)	71	66
82	Roche (Europe)	70	68
83	Hewlett Packard (U.S.)	69	69
84	Oracle (U.S.)	68	58
85	ISRAEL	68	—
86	3M (U.S.)	66	89
87	France Telcom (Europe)	63	—
88	Morgan Stanley (U.S.)	62	93
89	American Express (U.S.)	62	84
90	Wachovia (U.S.)	60	81
91	China Mobile (Hong Kong)	60	100
92	Barclays (Europe)	59	100
93	Medtronic (U.S.)	58	77
94	Wyeth (U.S.)	57	—
95	BHP-Billiton (Australia)	57	—
96	USBancorp (U.S.)	57	98
97	Samsung Group (South Korea)	56	95
98	Banco Santander (Europe)	55	—
99	Kraft Foods (U.S.)	55	59
100	L'Oreal (Europe)	54	85

Note: a Merging data from the International Federation of Stock Markets and the Yahoo! Finance Stockscreener, cross-referenced against the Financial Times's FT Global 500, reported in Sheehan (2004).

course, there are other ways of assessing the relevant data that might throw up a different set of rankings, but the important point is that the rank order demonstrates clearly the significance of the listed entities: There are 28 countries and 72 listed public companies in the top 100.

What is notable is the potential that corporations have to shape policy within nation-states. There are two effects of this. In the host nations, it remains the case that politicians have to be mindful of the adage that what is good for national champions is good for the national state. In countries that are competing with one another for foreign direct investment from these global entities, then, in a process more akin to a beauty contest than any economic planning model, less developed nations will sometimes compete against each other in terms of tax incentives, grants, and other inducements to attract firms to their country. Within countries, regional policies operate similarly to try and bring investment to particular regions. Of course, these corporations are not entirely footloose and fancy-free; often they are deeply embedded within specific locales, perhaps because of a specific infrastructure, suppliers, or university research centers. However, there are a lot more firms than countries in the world. UNCTAD (the United Nations Centre on Transnational Corporations) estimates that there are 60,000 transnational corporations globally (UNCTAD 2001). Because states are spatially fixed, they are immobile compared to firms, and so their governments have to struggle with the policy implications of globalization; they cannot decamp or disengage. Most of these global corporations are domiciled in relatively few countries. Firms from Japan and the United States dominate the list of Global 500 firms. There are twice as many U.S. firms (nearly 200) as Japanese (about 100). Germany, Britain, and France each have nearly half as many as Japan, with numbers distributed around forty. After these few countries, most other countries hardly rate, with the exception of Switzerland, Italy, South Korea, and Canada, who each have about ten such firms, and there are a small handful of firms from the remaining OECD countries as well as one or two from China, Taiwan, Venezuela, and some other industrialized economies (Bergesen and Sonnett 2001).

Global financial markets, institutions, and systems

The impact and contribution of global financial institutions on the processes of globalization are extremely significant. Institutions such as the IMF, according to ex-World Bank economist Stiglitz (2002), have had a deleterious developmental effect by patterning development on a limited number of assumptions and models. Such institutions have a convergent effect in patterning globalization. However, as he makes clear, we have to counter this patterning with that encouraged by other related institutions, such as the World Bank, which in recent years have sought to encourage development based on local initiatives and resources, not just those deemed appropriate in terms of hegemonic models. Equally, it is important to note that recent years have witnessed the rise of well-organized antiglobalization campaigns. The upshot of such activity is that protestors target the meetings of the finance ministers of the developed world. Seattle, Prague, and so on have been the locations for the disruption of the financial establishment.

The liberalization of the financial system that took place in the 1980s, accelerating through the 1990s, together with the digital revolution in information technology (IT), led to the widespread use of new financial instruments, such as junk bonds, leveraged buyouts, and currency speculation, which became de rigeur as finance capital took on a hyperreal quality. One consequence of globalization, Harvey (1992: 194) suggests, is that the financial system has achieved an unprecedented degree of autonomy from real production, becoming dominated by an economy of signs representing capital flows rather than an economy of things. What globalizes an economy of signs are the instantaneous representational possibilities afforded by new communications technology (Harvey 1992). The rapid spread of IT systems links markets globally such that, for instance, differentials in interest rates between states can lead to rapid, almost instant transfers and movement of large volumes of capital, sometimes with speculative effect, as currency traders take a punt on short-term futures markets for the currency in question.

The global integration of financial markets collapses time, creating instantaneous financial transactions in loans, securities, and other innovative financial instruments while the deregulation and internationalization of financial markets creates a new competitive spatial environment (Harvey 1992: 161) in which globally integrated financial markets increase the speed and accuracy of information flows and the rapidity and directness of transactions.

The increasing coordination of the world's financial system emerged to some degree at the expense of the power of nation-states to control capital flows and hence fiscal and monetary policy. At times, when confidence in a national currency is tested, it is evident that the definition of a weaker nation-state is that it can no longer hold the line. Britain, for instance, is a country with a history of foreign exchange crises. In 1992, it left the European Monetary System following its inability to hold its exchange rate. "Black Wednesday," as it was called, cost the British government billions of pounds, much of which went straight into the bank account of George Soros, a celebrated player on global money markets. Instantaneous financial trading means that shocks felt in one market are communicated immediately around the world's markets.

Dot-com boom and bust

Perhaps the most striking example in recent years of the globally speculative basis of much of the financial system as a global economy of signs occurred during the dot-com boom. In the late 1990s and up until the middle of 2000, one of the most remarkable share booms in history took place.

Amazon.com, the on-line book retailer, was worth $30 billion at the height of the boom, which made it worth far more than many established manufacturing multinationals. In itself this is perhaps unremarkable, until one considers the circumstances of the Amazon.com story. In 1999, the organization lost $700 million and in 2000 was losing some $100 million a month. The collapse in the share price in Amazon was mirrored throughout the dot-com sector as many shares became, quite literally, worthless. The investment public was for a short time mesmerized by the notion that huge sums of money could be made from Internet sites that purported to sell goods and services. What followed was a hyperreal boom in which the mantra of the new economy was accompanied by images of trendy young people becoming millionaires with apparent ease. When the public woke up to the idea that most of these companies had few customers, huge running costs, and very little income, the crash ensued. Like every other bubble in history, the dot-com boom was ultimately unsustainable. Perhaps if the dot-commers had been more familiar with economic history or had taken the time to read more novels, they might have been less captivated with illusory numbers and might have realized that, just like tulip fever, dot-com fever would burn out (Moggach 2000).

Global strategic alliances

Outside the economy of signs represented in dot-com fever, a major mechanism of global integration occurs through frequent collaborations and strategic alliances. Alliances are essentially an intermediate strategic device, and part of a web that includes many other transactions. Yoshino and Rangan (1995: 17) define alliances as "cooperation between two or more independent firms involving shared control and continuing contributions by all partners." They identify the major strategic objectives of alliances as maximizing value, enhancing learning, protecting core competencies, and maintaining flexibility. "The more a company becomes globalized, the more it is likely to lose its own identity within a tangle of companies, alliances and markets," suggests Petrella (1996: 76). Particularly in industries where there is a dominant worldwide market leader, strategic alliances and networks allow coalitions of smaller partners to compete against the leading companies rather than each other.

Strategic alliances help transfer technology across borders. Access to new markets is facilitated by using the complementary resources of local firms, including distribution channels, and product range extensions. Alliances allow partners to leverage their specific capabilities and save costs of duplication (see also pp. 359–361). Strategic alliances are a way of focusing investments, efforts, and attention only on those tasks that a company does well, as we discussed when we looked at the value chain (see also pp. 418–420). All other activities can be outsourced either through alliances or subcontracting. Another way of looking at virtual companies, alliances, and joint ventures is as the outsourcing of risk, allowing organizations at arm's length from the parent companies to take risks more freely, something that the parent organizations wish to avoid.

Mergers and acquisitions

The consulting company Pricewaterhousecooper concludes that about 70% of mergers and acquisitions are destined to fail and destroy value rather than make it (Feldman and Spratt 1999). Being big and being global is no surefire success recipe, despite whatever the financial institutions—whose profits come from brokering these deals—might say. Going global seems to open firms to challenges and risks rather than global dominance and easy profits. Interfirm alliance through merger and acquisition is risky because it carries the cost of strategic and organizational complexity. As we have seen in Chapter 8, managing organization culture is not straightforward, and this is especially the case where the organization is the result of a merger between two or more quite distinct cultures.

Transnational space?

Transnational activity is not easily managed precisely because it transcends so many spaces. It involves negotiation with different states, suppliers, interest groups, contractors, customers, and so on, which adds to the burden of senior managerial complexity. For instance, different mentalities and business institutions will be located in different countries: U.K. and U.S. companies are stock-price-oriented, whereas, in contrast, Japanese, Dutch, and Swiss companies are less sensitive to stock prices. Indeed, there has been much debate on the role that the city and financial institutions play in Anglo-American organizations. Critics such as Will Hutton (1995) argue that the primacy of finance creates an atmosphere in which a short-term orientation prevails, as companies aim to satisfy shareholders, who can easily sell their stock. He contends that this stifles innovation and makes for capricious organizations. In contrast, he notes that ownership of German and Japanese companies, with stable and major bank investments, enables them to plan for the medium and long term. Around half of all cross-border strategic alliances terminate within seven years. Often, where one or other of the partners purchases the alliance, then its termination does not necessarily mean failure—but it does suggest that their management at a distance might tax managerial capabilities.

Globalization of knowledge

Globalization is driven by the strategic responses of firms as they exploit market opportunities and adapt to changes in their technological and institutional environment, and attempt to steer these changes to their advantage. The most important competitive force in the global economy is the capacity for innovation, a thesis powerfully illustrated by Michael Porter (1990) in *The Competitive Advantage of Nations* (see also pp. 420–424). Porter correlates the advance of knowledge, achievement in innovation, and national competitive advantage. In his search for a new paradigm of national competitive advantage, Porter starts from the premise that competition is dynamic and evolving, whereas traditional thinking had a static view on cost efficiency due to factor or scale advantages. But static efficiency is always being overcome by the rate of progress in the change in products, marketing, new production processes, and new markets. Firms gain competitive advantage by changing the constraints within which they and their competitors operate. The crucial issue for firms, and nations, is how they "improve the quality of the factors, raise the productivity with which they are utilised, and create new ones" (Porter 1990: 21). The capacity to successfully innovate on a worldwide basis becomes the key competency of leading international companies (see also pp. 373–374). It frequently leads to substantive injustices as employees' knowledge in one part of the world is used to deliver cheaper and more efficient manufacturing in another part of the world and then their jobs being scrapped (Clegg 1999).

Global intellectual property

Market imperfections and high transaction costs provide an incentive for firms to internalize firm-specific knowledge and expertise. In addition, another incentive is to protect intellectual property rights within the firm. Intellectual property is information that derives its intrinsic value from creative ideas. It is also information with a commercial value that can be realized through its sale on the market. Intellectual property rights are bestowed on owners of ideas, inventions, and creative expression that have the status of property. Like tangible property, they give owners the right to exclude others from access to or use of their property. What protects intellectual property rights are national laws centered on specific legislative spaces and environments.

Intellectual property rights are probably most easily understood through the example of music. (Music is an interesting metaphor to keep in mind because once it flows through the Internet in an immediate digital way, the central issue becomes how it is that corporations are able to retain their central nodal point in its distribution and channel profit from the transactions.) You have probably downloaded or swapped some MP3 files from the Web to your digital player or iPOD. If so, be careful: You could be legally breaching the intellectual property rights held in that music by the artists, composers, and record company. When you buy a CD, you are paying in part for the intellectual property rights embedded in it. Some elements of royalty will flow to the artists, the composers, as well as the record company. When you download from the Web, then these rights are not waived and may be breached. Legally, you may be stealing these rights from those who have a legal entitlement to see them protected.

The harsh reality of national law, as a spatially based phenomenon, coming into tension with the possibilities of digital technology, was brought home to three Sydney students who pleaded guilty to sixty-eight copyright infringement charges in November 2003. The trio had set up an MP3/WMA Land Web site that was uncovered by music piracy investigations and police action. Using digital technologies, as you will realize, it is very easy to breach such rights—but even though it is digitally easy, it is still legally injudicious. Although digitalization drives globalization, making intellectual property easily available anywhere in the world, national laws limit it.

Global corporations and neoliberal economic rationality

Kenneth Ohmae (1990), an opponent of the thesis that national, state-based spaces are still significant, insists that the nation-state is now a dysfunctional unit defining no meaningful flows of economic activity—which sounds like a social democrat's nightmare and a neoliberal's dream rather than an accurate picture of most states in the world today. Not that the supporters of neoliberalism in the economic sphere are lonely voices; indeed, in many ways they comprise a new orthodoxy. It is economic rationality as neoliberalism defines it—the triumph of markets over politics. Efficiency has become a universal value. What it means in a global world is that capital should move freely, anywhere. (People, however, are another matter. Border protection is a term more often used in connection with policing people movements rather than the flow of money in or out of a national space.) Firms should be rent seekers, searching the globe for competitive advantage, according to this scenario of restless corporations. Ordinary people are expected to accommodate to the new global world order, one in which states no longer protect citizens through delivering citizenship rights so much as structure markets in which they can compete efficiently.

Against the rhetoric of liberalization, we must counter the reality of transnationals as, by definition, somewhat disembedded in their international operations and realize that this disembeddedness can sometimes cost them dearly. They get things wrong, precisely because they do not really know the contexts in which they operate in a deep and embedded way. When Mitsubishi managers in America managed in their customary ways, they did not expect to be landed with a lawsuit for sexual harassment of female employees and for breaches of the equal employment opportunity laws—but they were. Transnational companies are huge and complex organizations to manage, less gazelles than dinosaurs, and open to many sources of pressure, tension, and contradiction in their global operations.

Not the least pressure under which transnational corporations operate is the countervailing tendency of states to try and secure national spaces to their advantage.

A fundamental tension exists between national governments and transnational companies. Transnationals want unrestricted access to resources and markets throughout the world and freedom to integrate manufacturing to other operations across national boundaries, as well as an unimpeded right to try to coordinate and control all aspects of the company on a worldwide basis. Thus, governance of the corporation, especially as a taxable entity, can frequently cut across the government of the territories in which it operates, especially as a taxing authority (Bartlett and Ghoshal 1995: 119). For instance, Will Hutton (1995) discusses the tax avoidance schemes of numerous multinational firms, a theme also explored in an article by Nick Mathiason (2003). He reveals that Newscorp Investments, Rupert Murdoch's main U.K. holding group, paid no corporation tax throughout the 1990s. The issue of Murdoch's taxes are addressed by the Australian Broadcasting Corporation, pointing to the way in which much of Newscorp's profits flow through to countries with low-tax regimes, such as the Dutch Antilles, the Cayman Islands, and Hong Kong (*Australian Broadcasting Corporation News* 1998). Such a strategy has led to huge reductions in the amount of corporation tax paid. There is no suggestion that any of this activity is illegal—quite the contrary—but it does attest to the difficulties that governments face when dealing with multinationals. Some flows are, as we have remarked, easier to police and more front-page newsworthy than others.

Not the least pressure under which transnational corporations operate is the countervailing tendency of states to try to secure national spaces to their advantage. In a world where traditional protectionism increasingly seems not to be an option (other than for the most powerful players such as the European Union—agriculture—and the United States—steel as well as agriculture), states have to make a choice between the prospects of free trade with associated costs, or developing the conditions for managed trade. Many countries join trade blocs, such as NAFTA or the European Union, while building a regulatory environment within which they offer incentives for economic growth through institutional arrangements that protect national economies from international economic disorder (Tyson 1992).

Governments face demands from business to make their economies more competitive. To do so they often seek to lighten the regulatory frameworks and eliminate unnecessary government expenditures. It is difficult to reconcile extensive social programs for health, education, and retirement with these demands. At risk, as governments seem increasingly to have realized, are those many fibers of a civil society, its "social capital," that enable a market economy to operate efficiently; markets work best when they are socially embedded rather than disembedded. If you—as a consumer rather than a citizen—must learn to rely on yourself to fund your education, health, and retirement, rather than the state, then many vital economic development functions will be abrogated as state managers cede control to transnational corporations less able to exercise strategic control. Moreover, turning citizens into consumers may only be good for business in the short term—while they have effective demand. If they lose it, as in Argentina in the crises that have dogged the economy since its meltdown in 2001 but which were long prefigured, then no one benefits and everyone loses. Transnational corporations represent important external sources of investment, technology, and knowledge for national and regional governments. These may further national priorities, including regional development, employment creation, import substitution, and export promotion, but they will only do so within explicit policy frames that state managers set. The failure of state managers in this respect might explain, in part, why students increasingly have to pay for their own education when the companies that might hire them in the future are not always making their contributions through the tax system.

Government priorities to develop prosperous national competitive economies demand tax receipts that transnationals, as rational economic actors, will seek to minimize in the interest of their major stakeholders, the shareholders. Governments conceive of capturing global competitiveness within the national economy while transnational organizations think of global competitiveness globally. (We shall see that, in terms of the global system, if it is economically more rational to move call center jobs to India, then even when the company is 50% owned by the government on behalf of the taxpayers, it is not surprising that it will move jobs offshore—whatever the embarrassment to the government may be. The case in point is Telstra, the national Telco in Australia.) The rationalities of government and commerce differ greatly. The transnational company has a bottom line to which it can reduce costs and benefits, whereas governments have a far more complex and ambiguous set of life-chances to deal with. They have to manage changing definitions of what constitute "citizenship rights," such as taxpayer-funded provisions of big-ticket items like health and education, or else they have to manage to persuade people who once saw themselves primarily as citizens to become consumers in markets that transnational corporations are only too keen to enter.

Governments seek to prevent the use of "screwdriver plants" to evade trade restrictions through simple assembly of products essentially manufactured overseas, because, as well as relatively small tax receipts, these plants offer low-skilled employment, with little local value added, minimal new technology, and few multiplier effects. Governments have learned that very often, as soon as the grants and subsidies come to an end, the transnational seeks a new state offering a fresh bounty. The corollary of such experiences is that governments increasingly apply investment regulations that define specific levels of local content, technology transfer, and a variety of other conditions in an effort to make transnational companies increase the extent of their local activities.

Transnationals expect states to cover the costs of basic infrastructure. These include things such as funding of basic and high-risk research, universities and vocational training systems, promotion and funding of the dissemination of scientific and technical information and technology transfer, as well as economic and physical security and a communications infrastructure, such as up-to-date and high-speed international rail links.

In addition, companies often expect states to provide tax incentives for investment in industrial R&D and technological innovations, as well as guarantees that

Image 13.3   *Trains*

national enterprises from the given country have a stable home base. Privileged access to the domestic market via public contracts (defense, telecommunications, health, transport, education, and social services) is also often required. Transnational firms also expect appropriate industrial policies, particularly for those in the high technology strategic sectors (defense, telecommunications, and data processing). With respect to these sectors, it was in 1960 that U.S. President Dwight Eisenhower noted that American military spending was greater than the income of all American corporations. In addition, he observed that relations between corporations and the military were now increasingly seamlessly interwoven with five-star generals serving as consultants to such companies immediately on retirement. He termed this the rise of a military industrial complex, a term that passed into the lexicon of American political analysis. The relationship between the state and the defense industry is crucial for the U.S. economy. Eisenhower regarded this as having grave implications for democracy. As noted, an important feature of the military industrial complex is the extent to which large corporations rely upon government contracts. (The web page devoted to the military industrial complex at www.cdi.org/issues/usmi/complex is well worth checking for current information and debate.) Such policies protect designated sectors of the domestic market from international competition, as well as support and assist (through regulatory, commercial, diplomatic, and political means) local companies in their efforts to survive in international markets, issues addressed by Charles Perrow (1972) in his seminal study of *The Radical Attack on Business.*

The expectation that states will support business is often represented in terms of capital mobility and its logic. That is, if the local state does not provide the required sweeteners, mobile capitalism will simply exit the scene and set up where the benefits sought can be ensured. The thesis is overstated, because in terms of the important criteria of share of assets, ownership, management, employment, and the location of R&D, home bases remain important. Very few firms are genuinely transnational in these respects (Weiss 1997: 10, citing Hu 1992). With Petrella (1996) and Weiss (1997) we can conclude that states can adapt and innovate around their specific national institutional frameworks.

Government actions often work well for transnationals. For instance, downsizing of the state often produces new commercial opportunities in fields such as defense contracting and telecommunications. Nonetheless, most of the social and economic programs of national governments, even though they have been subject to severe efficiency drives and a transformation in management, resources, and methods of delivery, are still in existence. Even after the great waves of privatization that have swept the world, nation-states remain in charge of essential parts of their sovereignty, such as legislation and the formation of national economic policy. Globalization is itself in part a consequence of adaptations and innovations by firms to state capacities in these areas.

Global jobs

There is no doubt that globalization spreads certain universal values and attachments through its world of global consumer products and brands. Rolex, Chivas Regal, and Porsche spell success in just about every language. All young global symbolic analysts, whether working on the semiotics of money, films, or words, would recognize such symmetry. From Reich's (1991) perspective, these people are the research scientists, new professional engineers, public relations executives, investment bankers, lawyers, real estate developers, and creative accountants; management, financial, tax, energy, armaments, agricultural, and architectural consultants; management information and organization development specialists; strategic planners, corporate headhunters, and systems analysts as well as advertising executives, marketing strategists, art directors, architects, cinematographers, film editors, production designers, publishers, writers and editors, journalists, musicians, television and film producers, and even a few global university professors. Symbolic analysis manipulates symbols to solve, identify, and broker problems. It simplifies reality into abstract images by rearranging, juggling, experimenting, communicating, and transforming these images, using analytic tools, such as mathematical algorithms, legal arguments, financial analysis, scientific principles, or psychological insights that persuade, amuse, induce, deduce, or somehow or other address conceptual

> **Creative cities act as magnets for talent, offering lifestyle and recreational attractions that draw the creative class to live there.**

puzzles (Reich 1991). They are the creative class who populate creative cities (Florida 2000).

To what degree are these symbolic analysts or knowledge workers, comprising the creative class, different from those who have gone before? What marks out their professional identity? Management analysts, such as Mats Alvesson (1993b; Alvesson and Karreman 2001), have argued that what marks such work as different are its linguistic and symbolic accomplishment in circumstances of high ambiguity and uncertainty. In such circumstances, there is not one correct answer; instead, there are a number of competing, plausible alternatives. It places the persuasive abilities of the knowledge worker to the fore, comprising both their image intensity (the suit they wear, the briefcase they carry, the sleekness of their PowerPoint presentation) and the persuasiveness of their rhetoric (the robustness of their argument, their vocabulary, their accent). These workers are global, working for Big 4 firms or their small boutique equivalents. They regularly move between the great commercial capitals of the world, creating genuinely international corporate elites. Such transience, perhaps, fostersnetworking skills and alters sensibilities around risk, two other important characteristics of the symbolic analysts. In summary, they are the stressed-out but well-remunerated shifters and shapers of money, meanings, and markets, doing deals, making business, moving from project to project (Garrick and Clegg 2001).

The evidence of these jobs suggests that, despite attention to the issues of wages and associated cost of taxes raised by journalists and politicians, transnational companies do not, by and large, invest their main facilities where wages and taxes are the lowest. If they did, the theory of comparative costs would work far better than it does. The reasons are self-evident: Wages are often a minor cost factor; greater transaction costs are associated with the presence or absence of densely embedded networks for business in particular locales, such as the world cities of New York, London, Paris, and Tokyo, which are likely to remain so. Creative cities act as magnets for talent, offering lifestyle and recreational attractions that draw the creative class to live there. In addition, domestic linkages institutionally frame businesses in embedded relationships with universities, financial institutions, government institutions, and so on. Government-business relations typically have an exclusive rather than open character, and can be an important component in building national competitive advantage (Porter 1990), which then attracts globally skilled knowledge workers.

The international flow of expert migrant professional and knowledge workers helps create a global labor market in a growing number of occupations, not only those that are glamorous. Supporting the cars, shopping, apartments, and travel of these wealthy symbolic analysts is all the dirty work done by those who cook, wash, and clean up, who pack and sell convenience foods, who park and service cars, who tend and care for appearance: the face workers, nail workers, and hair workers—the necessary body maintenance to keep all the wealthy and beautiful people sweet. In global cities such as Hong Kong and Singapore, you can see street-level globalization in the form of the mainly Filipina and

Sri Lankan female domestic workers who congregate in the public spaces of the central business district on Sunday, their day of rest. The rest of the week it is more likely to be thronged with global businesspeople while the maids, chauffers, and other domestic servants make global households run smoothly.

In addition, there is a shadow labor force of workers in the symbolic sphere—but workers who are tightly scripted, operating in unambiguous and simple environments, unlike their symbolic analyst counterpoints. Outside the confines of the corporate glitterati and the symbolic analyst elite there is a category of disaggregated work quintessentially associated with globalization: that of call centers. Enabled by developments in technology, call centers were ushered into existence in the 1990s, the idea being particularly attractive to corporations, as it allowed them to downsize parts of the organization and establish call centers in relatively deprived areas where wage rates were lower and the workforce more pliable. The growth of information technology allowed for the increasing codification of knowledge, reducing the need for physical contact between producers and consumers, of which call centers are the perfect example—they can be located anywhere. Work is cheapened by routinization of existing tasks; reengineered tasks can then be moved to places where wages are cheaper. The transaction costs associated are not great: satellites and computers can ensure virtual linkage. The blueprint is clear: rationalize parts of the organization; introduce jobs at just over minium wage in deprived, postindustrial parts of the country or another country; institute a system of surveillance aimed at maximizing efficiency.

By 2002, 3% of the U.S. workforce and 1.3% of the European workforce were making a living from working in call centers, otherwise termed "factories of the future." To put a more concrete number on this, in 2002 there were 650,000 call center workers in 3,300 call centers in the United Kingdom (ContactBabel 2002). A good deal was written about the repetitive nature of the work, the exacting management controls, and the sheer amount that operatives were expected to do. The last few years have seen call centers go global, as it were. Increasingly, corporations are shifting their operations out of relatively poor areas of developed countries into the developing world. For instance, BT, the telecoms corporation, is cutting back its U.K. call centers in favor of opening up operations in Delhi and Bangalore. Once call centers are established, they are estimated to be considerably cheaper to run in India than in the United Kingdom. For instance, in 2003, a British call center worker typically earned 13,000–14,000 pounds a year; in India a worker doing a similar job made 1,200. The move to India is continuing apace, to the extent that a recent report by Mark Tran (2003) in *The Guardian* suggests that by 2008 there will be around 100,000 call center jobs created by British companies alone. The Philippines, the Czech Republic, and South Africa are also among the nations attempting to make inroads into the call center industry, to a sufficient extent that the industry forms an important pillar of each nation's economic policy.

In terms of globalization, there are also "grunge jobs" (Jones 2003: 256). Jones sees grunge jobs as essentially bifurcated. First there are the semiskilled workers who work in the lower reaches of the supply chains established by the global giants, which Castells (2000) estimated at about 35% of the jobs in the U.S. economy. It is a contingent, easily dismissible, and reemployable mass of people who can be used and laid off to absorb transaction costs and cushion demand for the core transnational companies globally. When these transnational companies react to signs of economic distress, then it is these subcontract workers in the supply chain who bear the pain first, buffering the core company employees. These workers are low skill, add little value, and are easily disposable, but at least they may have social insurance and do work in the formal economy.

The second element in the composition of the grunge economy comprises an underclass of workers who are often illegal immigrants working sporadically in extreme conditions outside the formally regulated labor market: think of sweatshops in the garment industry, for instance. As you sit reading this book, you are probably wearing clothes (possibly designer clothes) that have been manufactured in the developing world. What are the conditions like for those producing the clothes that you are now wearing? As Jones (2003) reports, there is research from Deloitte & Touche (1998) that suggests that informal sector activity ranges from 40% in the Greek economy, through to 8% to 10% of the British economy. States often encourage the informal sector as an arena from which street-level and taxable entrepreneurs might develop in enterprises other than the marketing of drugs, prostitutes, and the proceeds of crime (Deloitte & Touche 1998; Sassen 1998).

In the United States, with its porous land borders, wealthy middle-class people in major cities live off the backs of such migrant, often illegal, labor. Victor Villaseñor's (1992) book *Rain of Gold* tells a moving story. He writes of a Mexican American friend who swam the Rio Grande five times before he became a hybrid, and of another who lived and raised a family in New York City for seventeen years. When he first came, he told him, it was difficult to adapt because there were no shops selling the ingredients of Mexican cooking, no chilies, tomatillos, or masa harina. Now those items can be bought five minutes from his New York home. Even in cities such as Melbourne or Manchester, far from Mexico, it is possible to buy these things. The globalization of languages, food, and cuisines, together with the spread of places of worship, is a good index of globalization, because wherever people move, they take their everyday material cultures with them, and their language, religion, and food are the most evident manifestations of such culture.

Of course, transnationals also employ people indirectly through global supply chains. Transnational corporations often get bad press for their subcontracting practices in the third world. For instance, writers such as Naomi Klein (2001) are extremely critical of the role that transnationals play in the developing world. Her argument is that transnationals behave irresponsibly by employing subcontractors who pay low wages, have poor working conditions, and potentially abusive environments. She singles out the famous companies

Image 13.4   *Commerce at the street level*

whose brands are known the world over. In a campaign by Oxfam—the nongovernmental organization—Nike has been taken to task over these issues. One thing that such campaigning activity has delivered is assurance from Nike that such concerns have been addressed, which for many is a contestable point. On balance, it is fair to say that they may be positive agents of change. It is clear that, they have the potential to create stable, long-term jobs with decent pay and conditions. Those that do not will be subject to campaigns throughout the Western world. Thus, potentially, they deliver better jobs and better wages in many economies. In addition, they set standards that local industry has to aspire to in both labor and industry practice. If there really were "no logos," it would be much harder to police these standards, as there would be no brand differentia offering opportunities for discrimination between the choice of one T-shirt or another. We would expect that in such a situation, price signals would be even more sovereign and would exercise still stronger downward pressure on local wages and conditions in the third world. Fair logos rather than no logos might be better policy. Subcontract manufacturing jobs also create higher export earnings domestically, which potentially enhance the tax base of national governments. We say "potentially" because often these companies are quite sophisticated in moving tax losses around their global operations and using transfer pricing of internally traded goods to minimize liabilities where they will attract the highest regimes of tax.

The employees in the sweatshops of the third world are in some respects fortunate; it all depends on the point of comparison. They have jobs; they are not hustling on the street, selling gum to standing motorists, shoe shines to seated customers in restaurants on the street, or their bodies to whoever wants to buy their services. In the cities of the third world and in the ghettoes of the first world, many people on the mean streets of the barrios and favelas, desperate and poor, are in this underclass position. For them any organizational employment would be a step up the ladder of opportunity. It seems perverse, in these circumstances, for Western liberals to oppose the opportunities that they actually get on the basis of standards never applied to life lived on the streets. Of course, as we shall see shortly, there are only too many unscrupulous contractors (and sometimes their powerful friends in government) who are only too prepared to use the threat of a life that can too easily be nasty, brutish, poor, and short as an unsubtle alternative to conditions that are barely better and certainly offensive to liberal opinion.

Global flows of cultural consciousnesses

More complex notions of personal identity emerge as a result of globalization, attendant upon revolutions in gender, sexual, ethnic, and racial mores having an impact on hitherto more restricted societies. The interpenetration of culture and economy produces not only social change and tension but also new micromarkets. These markets are for branded goods and services premised on the differentiation of cultural identities based on the possession of positional goods: things whose value is wholly culturally defined by who has them and who does not. The drivers for this differentiation occurred first within sophisticated societies, whose market niches were increasingly distributed by global corporations, and were then spread through the global reach of mass media of communication. Watch the advertisements between CNN news stories to get the picture. If the proposition that globalizing strategies form a singular rationality were true, the homogenization of taste and consumption would inevitably lead to standardization of products, manufacturing, marketing, and trade. Such a saturation of markets, with a few common products gaining enormous profit, is manifested in McDonaldization (see also pp. 108–110). You might think that with so much homogenizing pressure, the world and its peoples are becoming more one-dimensional, less complex and differentiated, and more alike. However, standardization has its limits, and there are important cultural, political, and economic forces for local differentiation that have emerged powerfully in recent years to question the logic of globalization.

The differentiation of identity opens up new opportunities for market differentiation. Not all questions of identity can be resolved through markets, however. Old questions of identity reemerge in the global era, partially as a consequence of the breakup of state socialist hegemony, principally in the former U.S.S.R. and the Balkans, but also through the assertion of religious identities founded in Islam, Hinduism, and sometimes, as in East Timor, Catholicism. These issues frame the global world of consciousness within which today's international managers operate and which they must navigate.

Global consciousness?

Most major social theorists of the past, such as Karl Marx (1976) and Talcott Parsons (1966), agreed on one thing: The future would be much more homogenous than its past and the trajectory of future development would be toward convergence rather than divergence. We are now living in the future that they foresaw, but do we live in a moment of global convergence? On the contrary, suggest a number of influential analyses. Partly inspired by a broader debate about culture, a number of writers have suggested that the strengths of indigenously embedded ways of doing things need reevaluation (Yeung 2000). The interest in indigenous peoples is not just restricted to liberals interested in different philosophies of the world. Some pharmaceutical transnationals, seeking to develop new drugs to deliver more growth, higher earnings, and profits, are taking a keen interest in indigenous peoples. Their interest is in patenting their DNA, in case they should contain genetic secrets that can help treat contemporary Western diseases. In some respects, such reappraisal often attaches itself to postmodern themes which seek an expressive identity in the unique and special qualities of peoples who remain in some respects premodern (Clegg 1989). Convergence may neither be necessary nor desirable. Individual identities, it is realized, differ greatly across national societies as well as within them. Culture is increasingly seen as critical and convergence is seen as less likely and less productive than divergence.

The spread of the mass media, especially television, means that in principle, almost everyone can be instantaneously exposed to the same images. However, the world is becoming less a "global village" and more a "global market," in which privileged commodities for sale are often based on hybridization, created from the intermingling of peoples and items from different cultures. Once more, music is a good example, with the huge growth in the world music market from the 1990s, when, encouraged by the example of Jamaican reggae superstar Bob Marley, third world musicians became global stars in the new niche market. But to do so they had to move through the circuits of power of the global recording companies, such as BMG, Sony, and so on. Maybe now, in the days of MP3 and iPod, this will no longer be the case. As we have discussed, music flows digitally and seamlessly in the global economy.

It could be argued that intersubjective experience has become global today through exposure to international media reporting. However, what such reporting means may be highly variable. While there may be no one who cannot recall the images of the planes ripping into the World Trade Center, the images mean very different things for different political actors in different parts of the world. The consequences of global exposure are profound. States wage war preemptively against concepts, such as "terror," attached to socioreligious movements in a world where states are no longer the only organizations controlling use of the means of violence. In the nineteenth century, as a sign of global power, Europeans could shell the coastline of the African jungle in a vain assertion of their technological superiority (read Joseph Conrad's [1970] *Heart of Darkness*). Today, America and its allies can bomb anywhere on the planet as a sign of their global reach while adversaries in the war on terror can cause carnage through lower-tech but no less fearsome weapons. We are informed in ceaseless detail about the latest "victories" and "advances" in this war from Al-Jazeera and CNN—although the detail of what is a victory or a defeat may vary with what you watch and where you watch it. The emergence of global communication gives rise to a global consciousness that is hotly contested. The freedoms offered by a market-based culture can be seen as residing anywhere on a continuum from seductively glamorous to threateningly dangerous—depending on the presuppositions that one starts with. Not all religions, ideologies, or belief systems want the liberation that a consumer society offers their members.

Globalization exacerbates tensions between local senses of self, of who you are, and who you could be. And these are not free-floating signifiers of equal weight in dreamtime stories that imagine futures now rather than pasts lost, but are stories that lodge in different forms of consciousness. Some are encoded in the lore of the elders, the wisdom of the tribe, whereas others present themselves through the news on the airwaves, the sights and sounds that come down the tube, the transmissions through the satellites, optical cables, and microwaves. The local is now truly global.

Some global significations channel more global imagination than others. We have already mentioned CNN, but it is not the only global media entity. The Murdoch Newscorp satellite now spreads its footprint over almost all of Europe, North America, and the Asian region. Certainly, there is considerable fixity to the messages that the media transmit, but recalling the error with which McLuhan (1964) started the whole globalization debate, there is also considerable diversity in the way in which the messages are interpreted, instantiated, and used. That forms of production and distribution are fixed in a technological form does not mean closure in forms of cultural consumption. Murdoch discovered this when he found that his analysis that the digital age meant the end of dictatorship was a message received extremely coolly in Beijing. His subsequent ditching of the BBC from his satellite broadband, for unfriendly reporting, helped appease sensibilities somewhat, as have critical remarks about the Dalai Lama and the decision not to print Chris Patten's (1998) book based on his experiences as the last Hong Kong governor, as well as the diplomatic efforts of Chinese-born Wendy Deng, who is also Mrs. Rupert Murdoch.

Global rights?

Globalization in the cultural sphere has meant the global proliferation of norms of individualized values, originally of Western origin, in terms of a discourse of "rights" (Markoff 1996). Such discourse is not unproblematic. It meets considerable opposition from religious, political, ethnic, sexual, and other rationalities tied to the specificities of local practices, but it does provide a framework and set of terms through which resistance to these might be organized. One theorist who has realized this is Barber (1996), who has popularized the idea that the world is set on a collision between McWorld and Jihad, where convergence in the form of primarily U.S. business interests meets stubborn and deep-seated sources of local resistance, embedded in religious worldviews. From this perspective, the trajectory of convergence produces a globalization of culture, technologies, and markets against which local forms of retribalization, through Jihad, will react.

Perhaps the clearest expression of the emergence of a discourse of global rights occurs in relation to the status of women. Moghadam (1999: 368), for instance, suggests that

> the singular achievement of globalization is the proliferation of women's movements at the local level, the emergence of transnational feminist networks working at the global level, and the adoption of international conventions such as the *Convention on the Elimination of All Forms of Discrimination against Women* and the *Beijing Declaration and Platform for Action of the Fourth Conference on Women.*

Such doctrines are clear expressions of a global discourse of rights applying to just over a half of humankind. However, at the same time as these rights documents are issued globally, other aspects of globalization have contradictory effects. In many ways, suggests Moghadam (1999: 376), working-class and poor urban women have been the "shock absorbers" of neoliberal economic policies. Structural adjustment policies that increase prices, eliminate subsidies, diminish social services, and increase fees for essentials hitherto provided by the state place women at greater risk of ill health and poverty. However, to the extent that transnationals enter into employment in these regions, then they represent unparalleled opportunities for employment outside of either the informal sector of dubious work and conditions or outside domestic service—opportunities that are often accompanied by education programs, as governments seek to equip their human capital with the upgradeable skills that will attract further investment.

> **Real economies root themselves in places; simulacra are free-floating signifiers that invest in signs that translate only randomly into decisions that affect the lives and deaths of people in real economies remote from the centers of financial flows.**

Purser, Park, and Montuori (1995) suggest that if we focus only on the economic dimension, considered in relation only to those selves whose profits are served by corporate power, anthropocentrism will result. The global constituents of the environment, including other selves, humankind, and the natural environment, will suffer, particularly where there is a high degree of separation of simulacra from the real economy. Real economies root themselves in places; simulacra are free-floating signifiers that invest in signs that translate only randomly into decisions that affect the lives and deaths of people in real economies remote from the centers of financial flows.

The subjects who are adversely affected by the experience of globalization are not only human. Some subjects cannot articulate discursively the momentous changes occurring in their constitution. We think of whales, seals, or "mad" cows whose rights to be ruminants have been violated by organized agri-industry and have had to be reasserted by government policies, as well as other species that have been the subject of organized campaigns to represent or save them in some way. Animal rights are now well established (Singer 1976).

The ecosystem as a whole is now often ascribed rights and interests, in the name of sustainability. Other entities incapable of interest representation, such as fetuses, those who are on life-support systems, and so on, are also ascribed rights. All of these are represented as global subjects with assigned rights and interests that some organizations violate, others ignore, and a few choose to represent (Meyer 2000: 239). It matters not whether a cow is British or French in an economy where meat, sperm, livestock, and meat-derived products, such as gelatin and cosmetic additives, trade globally. Greenpeace, as an organization for expressing a standardized moral consciousness that can mobilize activists anywhere, can represent Canadian seals as easily as those that are Russian and, through global media, can act its way into the global consciousness. Local species can become global icons.

CRITICAL ISSUES: WINNERS AND LOSERS IN GLOBALIZATION

Newscorp and some other global media companies such as CNN are undoubtedly winners from globalization—but there are also losers. Some of these losers are the organizational behemoths created in response to the opportunities for global action that the digital world presents, companies that simply overreached their corporate governance and integrative capabilities. A case in point, staying in the media space, would be the Time Warner/AOL merger, which created an overvalued corporate entity with a difficult blend of organizational cultures (see also pp. 267–271). Indeed, ungovernable entities that are too complex culturally, organizationally, and financially could be seen as one aspect of the collateral damage that globalization has sustained on the ranks of business. But these are neither the primary nor the most desperate casualties.

The primary casualties of globalization appear to be low-skilled grunge workers in traditional manufacturing countries who either lose their jobs as they slip overseas or experience a painful slide in their wage rates as employers strive to reduce costs.

The primary casualties of globalization appear to be low-skilled grunge workers in traditional manufacturing countries who either lose their jobs as they slip overseas or experience a painful slide in their wage rates as employers strive to reduce costs. Particularly vulnerable are the relatively unskilled and undereducated, especially in labor market systems that do not develop very active and interventionist labor market policies. Wood (1994) reckons that trade with developing countries is the prime suspect for the increase in inequality *within* industrial countries. He estimates that it has reduced the demand for low-skilled workers in rich economies by more than a fifth. Against this, however, you must balance the fact that most jobs are still in spatially discrete and nontradeable sectors. A wharfie in Australia cannot easily relocate to become a longshoreman in the United States. And even for the 16% of U.S. workers who make their living in manufacturing, the overlap of production with low-wage countries is relatively small. Their main competitors in most sectors are workers in other high-wage countries, as is true of most OECD states.

It should also be noted that global capital markets provide poor countries with better access to capital and thus to transferable technology. For instance, Sri Lanka is a poor country—but it has some of the most technologically sophisticated jersey textile plants in the world, such as JerseyLanka, staffed by technology and management graduates from Sri Lankan universities, trained by British, Australian, and South African expatriates. When Stewart visited there in 2002, the plant was gearing up for global production, producing knitted jersey destined for manufacture by contractors fulfilling orders for Marks & Spencers.

The main beneficiaries of globalization are undoubtedly the employees of the transnational companies and those symbolic analyst professionals who service these companies: lawyers, researchers, consultants, IT experts, and so on. Meyer (2000: 240–241) is unequivocal that those who organize scientific and professional activity on a global scale are the real winners. Professional associations represent such people; international knowledge businesses, universities, and research laboratories employ such people, as do international governmental associations and agencies. These are the people at home in airport lounges, with frequent flyer programs and portable computers as global talismans of their universality. The winners also include not just those whom Meyer identifies as being able to make universalistic claims about rights, science, or any other form of expert knowledge, as well as the digital content providers, but also include those who are experts in various global sports, representing sponsors such as Nike, Adidas, and other transnational sports companies whose brands are ubiquitous, as well as the global entertainers, the J.Lo's and Kylies. Global brands and those whom they sustain are unequivocal winners from globalization (see also pp. 321–324).

With the emergence of global brands, international outsourcing, and supply chains, there is a natural tendency for the market leader to get further ahead, causing a monopolistic concentration of business (Arthur 1996). Real dangers attach to winning when the losers are excluded and abandoned to their situation. The winners can come together and increasingly integrate with one another. Where such processes occur within societies, serious consequences may result in terms of increased poverty, unemployment, alienation, and crime. But the consequences are of a higher order of magnitude when the processes of exclusion and alienation involve countries and whole regions of the world. The share of world trade in manufactured goods of the 102 poorest countries of the world is falling as the share of the developed world increases. There is a delinking of the less from the more developed world, particularly in Africa. The core of an increasingly globally integrated world economy excludes those countries from the margins. For instance, the World Bank *Poverty Report* (2001) highlights that "[o]f the world's 6 billion people, 2.8 billion live on less than $2 a day and 1.2 billion on less than $1 a day. Eight out of every 100 infants do not live to see their fifth birthday. Nine of every 100 boys and 14 of every 100 girls who reach school age do not attend school." One can only speculate on the political consequences of such a new global division; they are unlikely to be integrative for the world system as a whole (Petrella 1996: 80–81).

The cultural implications of economic analysis remain somewhat underdeveloped. Attitudes toward the overwhelming political and economic forces for globalization range from enthusiastic integration, to determined isolation, and from a belief that the free market will resolve all resulting tensions, to a commitment for comprehensive political regulation. "New Right" politicians are against globalization; it brings people they don't want to their nation, it threatens them with ideas they don't like, and while it sells them lots of cheap goods that they can afford, it does so at the cost of vulnerable jobs in previously protected parts of the domestic economy—the heartland of their political support. They see globalization as fragmenting national identities. Those under threat demand to be protected from its adverse effects. Ethnically distinct identities (those who do not share what extremists constitute as national identity, usually because of skin color or religion, or both) are denounced and marginalized as denying the majority of "ordinary people" their rights to economic surplus, relief, jobs, housing, or whatever.

The New Right sometimes meets the Old Left in the shadows cast by politics. We also find S11 anarchists, agreeing, in Sklair's (1999: 158) words, that "globalization is often seen in terms of impersonal forces wreaking havoc on the lives of ordinary and defenceless people and communities." As he goes on to say, it "is not coincidental that interest in globalization over the last two decades has been accompanied by an upsurge in what has come to be known as New Social Movements (NSM) research" (Sklair 1998; Spybey 1996). NSM theorists argue for the importance of identity politics (of gender, sexuality, ethnicity, age, community, and belief systems) in the global era. S11 are a perfect example of this—and their strategies are based on global tactics. They do not seek to build effective conventional political alliances and positions, but use the tools of globalization, such as the Internet, to create activist happenings as spectacular media events whenever the leading global players meet internationally. But if you are against a concept such as globalization, which seeks to capture a broad array of social detail, which bits of it are you most against? And what is the alternative to globalization? Is it protectionism? Of course, there is an argument that sometimes protectionism, especially where it preserves unique intellectual/cultural property, such as national cinema or television, is necessary if the juggernaut of cheap U.S. mass-produced and McDonaldized products is not to eliminate cultural differences.

> The main beneficiaries of globalization are undoubtedly the employees of the transnational companies and those symbolic analyst professionals who service these companies: lawyers, researchers, consultants, IT experts, and so on.

And in the world at large, the effects of globalization can be seen through studying the GNPs of the world of nations in the postwar eras. Those that have been phenomenally successful in lifting themselves up those tables have, by and large, engaged, and been engaged with, the world globally. The states that have not been engaged or have remained disengaged have remained poor and the real losers from globalization.

THE FINE PRINT: LOCAL SPECIALIZATION IN A GLOBAL WORLD

A paradoxical consequence of increasing globalization is the concentration of clusters of world-class expertise in specialist industries in different local economies around the world. The significant local dimension of the globalization phenomenon consists of regional economies built upon interlinked networks of relations among firms, universities, and other institutions in their local environment (see OECD 1996; Storper and Scott 1993). Early specialization is reinforced by the growth of similar firms and institutions to create highly competitive industrial and service clusters.

The OECD (1996: 52) explains the rationale for the local concentration of specialist industry in terms of the advantages of being in the same location as similar firms, specialized suppliers and contractors, as well as knowledgeable customers (see also pp. 417–424). In addition, these locations tend to provide a good technological infrastructure and specialist research institutions, as well as a highly skilled labor force, where specialization within firms enables extensive outsourcing (vertical disintegration) and encourages similar new firms to be set up in the location (horizontal disintegration). For instance, Lash and Urry (1994) discuss the importance of local concentration in the making of movies, and a number of U.K. authors have described the networks and clusters associated with "Motorsport Valley"—a small area north of London that accounts for most of the automotive innovation associated with Formula 1 motor racing (Tallman et al. 2004).

Local geographic concentrations of three broad groups of industrial and service activities have been noted. First are highly competitive traditional, labor-intensive industries, which are highly concentrated, including textiles and clothing in Italy. Second are high-technology industries that often cluster around new activities, such as biotechnology in San Francisco, semiconductors in Silicon Valley, scientific instruments in Cambridge (U.K.), and musical instruments in Hamamatsu (Japan). Third, services, notably financial and business services, such as advertising, films, fashion design, and R&D activities, concentrated in a few big global cities such as Los Angeles, Tokyo, London, Paris, Sydney, and Shanghai. Globalization increases the competitiveness of these local economies by attracting international firms with their own specific advantages and enhancing established sourcing and supply relations. Local firms individually may respond to heightened competition through improving their innovative performance. Innovation may be extended through developing greater interactions between firms, suppliers, users, production support facilities, and educational and other institutions in local innovation systems. Local firms, particularly if they are highly specialized, will cooperate with international firms seeking complementary resources in the specialized assets of small firms.

Some writers, following Robertson (1992), such as Clarke and Clegg (1998), Helvacioglu (2000), and Ritzer (2004), have referred to the phenomenon of the interpenetration of the global in the local and vice versa, as "glocalization." However, it is not only in areas of straightforward global business, such as manufacturing, that locality can become a source of competitive advantage; it can also be built from marginalized and stigmatized local cultures. Think of hip-hop, now the dominant popular music trend globally. It emerged from the ghetto culture of alienated black youth in the big cities of the United States. But it is not the artistry of Wu-Tang Clan and others that we address here to make the point. Instead, we want to fly you down to Salvador, Bahia, where it's carnival time.

Going from the cultural margins to the global market

In 1990, when Stewart first visited an area called Pelhourino in the old Brazilian city of Salvador, Bahia, it was almost completely derelict, with over thirty buildings a year collapsing. The dereliction was occurring despite its having been placed on the World Heritage Registry of UNESCO in 1984, after an initial report on the district in the 1960s. By 1994 the picture had been reversed totally. The whole district was served by sewers, repaired, refurbished, and repainted in vibrant pinks, blues, and yellows on the colonial stucco that fronted the buildings. Salvador became the second most visited tourist spot in Brazil. Just four years previously, it was only the eighth most visited. Many bars, restaurants, museums, arts and crafts shops, workshops, cultural troupes, and schools occupy space that previously had been virtually ungovernable and nontaxable.

The initiative for cultural revitalization was taken by the state government in 1991 to commit the funds necessary to save Pelhourino before it was too late. As Caetano Veloso (1994: 83) points out, one contributory factor to this decision was the organizational basis provided by cultural resistance. Non-Brazilian audiences may have a glimpse of this resistance through *The Rhythm of the Saints,* a best-selling record released by Paul Simon in 1990. The opening track introduced a new sound to many ears—recorded in Pelhourino Square, Salvador, Bahia, in Brazil—the sounds of a troupe of drummers called Grupo Olodum. They play a martial, insistent, hypnotically rhythmic beat, percussive and shuffling, behind a typical Paul Simon lyric, "The Obvious Child."

Olodum were founded on April 25, 1979. Olodum means the God of Gods or the Supreme God in Yorubá. Although music fans may know Olodum as a band, they are, in fact, much more than that. They are a social and a cultural movement. Inspired by the profound example of Bob Marley for black consciousness, they began as a movement of cultural resistance, of the outcast, the dispossessed, and the despised, drawn from the ranks of those who lived in Pelhourino. While the music was inspired in part from the reggae music of Marley and Bahiano traditions of *tropicalismo,* it also drew nourishment from the surrounding culture of syncretic religion, the blend of African animism and Catholic rite that is institutionalized as the church in Bahia.

Samba is the music of the people brought from Africa as slaves to work the sugar plantations in Brazil. Forced to adopt the religion of their oppressors, the people infused it with a parallel system of beliefs, deities, and saints, in the Macumba, which preserved and recreated the animism of traditional belief systems in Africa. Olodum built on this heritage, taking it further to create an imagined community (Anderson 1982) through its imagery of Africa, especially in the recreation of the Ashanti rhythms of Ghanaian music. Moreover, it had a particular liminal or in-between, borderline, space in which to develop— the traditions of Bahiano *carnaval.* Carnival, derived from the Latin *carnelevāmen,* has common characteristics wherever we encounter it: theatricality;

Image 13.5   *Representing Olodum*

being, however briefly, what ordinarily you are not; a zone and a space in which one can try out various masks, sometimes literally, sometimes more metaphorically, as identities that define sensibility. Traditionally, carnival reversed social orders and sanctioned transgression—a space of release prior to Lent, a space of pleasure prior to a period of denial.

In Bahia, since about 1950, carnival has been synonymous with the *trios eléctricos.* The *trios* are a spectacular procession of articulated trucks, with musicians and dancers on top of a revolving platform, itself built over a massive bank of speakers, flanking each side of the truck. The amplification is loud, the music pulsating, the costumes colorful, and the dancing marvelous. The *trios* are today predominantly the voice of the Afro-blocos, the black version of the *escola de samba,* that, starting historically with the Filhos de Ghandy, first imagined, and thus created, a space in the Latin carnival in which black people could parade with dignity and without fear.

Through the cultural innovations associated with *carnaval,* Salvador changed from a space that was declining and dangerous to one that was entrepreneurial. Salvador provides an object lesson in how cultural innovation can seed and produce a global industry, even in the least likely circumstances. The vision that Olodum developed transformed the dereliction of what had been *the* architectural heritage of the Americas. The *blocos* aesthetic interest in projecting a positive image of Africa, and of black identity of, for, and to the dispossessed, created not only a counter-hegemonic project that became, in its own space, hegemonic, but one that also became a space for a cultural entrepreneurship that *The Rhythm of the Saints* broadcast globally.

The local project of cultural hegemony, plus the resources that the state government brought to the restoration of Pelhourino, produced a conjuncture that mirrors almost exactly that which Lash and Urry (1994: 216–217) propose as the scenario of a successful postmodern, consumption, and tourist-based place-image. Thus, even in the heart of grunge, there are opportunities for business—as, to take another, related example, the entrepreneurs and performers of gangsta rap know only too well.

Bahia is linked to the global diaspora from Africa, (the exodus, "Movement of Jah People"; see Marley 1977), the most significant forced migration of people that the global world has ever seen. And it is now part of the global tourism and music industries. Europeans and Americans may have thought that they were colonizing Africa and Africans when they shipped black bodies around the world for profit, but they were also culturally cross-pollinating. In contemporary times, at least in the global trade in popular music, it is the descendants of these Africans who have successfully colonized the world that Europe founded and represents. But in so many other ways, they, together with those others who remain excluded from the postmodern global world, are locked out in symbolic oppositions.

Workers' resistance outside of global markets

As remarked a few pages previously, there are too many unscrupulous contractors (and sometimes their powerful friends in government) only too prepared to use the threat of a life that can too easily be nasty, brutish, poor, and short as an unsubtle alternative to conditions that are barely better and certainly offensive to liberal opinion. Under such circumstances, it would be normal to expect workers to resist global projects that work against the interests of those employed therein. We encountered one Mexican example of these in Puebla, in the Korean-managed *maquiladora* in which Nike products were being manufactured (see also p. 319). There is another Mexican example, which we display here. It is a case of indigenous people from the state of Oaxaca who are pitted against transnational agribusiness. They are struggling not only over sustainable agriculture but also for a way of life under threat from the actions of both state and transnational business. The irony is that the struggle is over a crop that is indigenous to the region of Oaxaca, over which the giant U.S. transnational Monsanto now claims intellectual property rights.

CIPO-RFM and the globalization of maize

On the morning of October 15, 2003, sixteen paramilitaries attacked a meeting in the village of Santa Maria de Yaviche (Oaxaca, Mexico), which was being held by CIPO-RFM (Consejo Indígena Popular de Oaxaca-Ricardo Flores Magon). One participant was killed by paramilitaries and eight others were seriously wounded. None of the participants of the meeting were armed. Paramilitaries had attacked the CIPO-RFM earlier and the group had suffered from other kinds of persecution. The CIPO-RFM has been active in the campaign against globalization because of their traditional role as maize farmers. The people of Oaxaca call themselves "people of maize," and were the originators of corn as a crop. A spokesperson for CIPO-RFM explains, "Our ancient varieties are being destroyed by GM corn coming in from the U.S., cheaper than we can produce." Last year, university researchers discovered that between 20% and 60% of traditional maize varieties of crops in CIPO-RFM's community were contaminated with modified genes from imported Monsanto gene-patented corn. These indigenous peoples are struggling for respect for their rights, battling against imprisonments, kidnappings, torture, and attacks allegedly supported by officials in the state government. Image 13.6 depicts some signs of their resistance. (See Ainger 2003 for more details.)

Although many injustices have occurred to indigenous peoples, globally, the situation may be changing with the latest developments in globalization "because the indigenous is now part of a larger inversion of Western cosmology," a part of a world we have lost, "a voice of Wisdom, a way of life in tune with nature, a culture in harmony, a *gemeinschaft*" (Friedman 1999: 390). As the example of the resistance of the people of Oaxaca might suggest, a terrible irony may attach to these views: Either you stay primitive, poor, and pure or become involved in the global economy and be exploited. Indigenes can either conform to a role in some kind of protected "natural" theme park or, with the patina of existential exoticism that the development of "creole" cultures offers, show positive new sources of hybridity—perhaps as cynics might say of Olodum. However, there is a third way that the contributions of the researchers associated with the Odyssey Group (see Little and Grieco 2004) suggest. New forms of communication based on the Internet offer opportunities for local and indigenous communities to meet the global market and benefit from it on their own terms. As Diawara (2000) stresses (in a discussion of Western agencies and their work in the Malian Sahara), there is a need for researchers and managers to try to work with, and integrate, local knowledge and culture with expert knowledge—not to oppose them as mutually impermeable spheres, a point also made by Flyvbjerg (2001) in his conclusions.

Image 13.6   *Resisting globalization*

SUMMARY AND REVIEW

Our everyday life is global. Wherever we live, we cannot escape globalization. Next time you go to the shopping mall, take a look at the people around you—in fact, take a look at yourself and what you are wearing. There are no frontiers to fashion. We are all the result of globalization resulting from the movement of people as they seek new opportunities, markets, lives, resources, land, and so on. In essence, organizations do the very same thing for the very same reasons. Sometimes it is to access new markets, and other times it is to access cheaper resources, while sometimes it is both. However, with globalization come many problems and opportunities. It is no coincidence today that there are many organizations opposed to globalization—ironically, many of them gaining in popularity as they themselves become global. Increasingly, those who are learning to become managers today will have to manage in a global world and be skilled and well versed in both the challenges and opportunities that come about through globalization—whether they prefer to or not.

In this chapter we have identified the major areas of concern with which such managers will have to grapple. These include managing the intersection of national societies and all their tacit assumptions, with an increasingly systemic, patterned, and interconnected world. You will also have to manage the impact of these systemic processes on yourself and those with whom you work and whom you employ, globally. Finally, you will have to manage the impact of your global activities and those of the organization that employs you, on the fate of humankind in general.

In some circles, it is fashionable to shrug and simply deny that management has any responsibility to any other humans, apart from shareholders. Such an idea is a ridiculous and deeply irresponsible fiction. There is no simple, disembedded global rationality, focused only on accounting fictions, that a manager can apply, as if it were a powerful talisman, ritual, or incantation. There is no special method to inure you against, and insure your organization from, the perils that occur when an irresistible force, such as globalization, meets an old immovable object, like a deeply embedded local reality with its own ways of being, thinking, and feeling. Globalization means singular strategic visions colliding with a world composed of many local realities, interrupting and contaminating the purity of vision with the obdurate, messy rationalities within which we all work—including even the visionaries.

Ultimately, the only vision that matters is the futures that are imagined and ushered into being, which we are then obliged to serve. Better beware the futures that we imagine because being a global manager today entails moral as well as personal responsibilities, ethical as well as financial obligations, power as well as pleasure, a commitment to the production of better lives, not just the consumption and spewing out of goods and services. Globalization, at its best, would mean that all of us cannot prosper from being rapacious to any of us; to harm, damage, and blight any of us in the name of some of us is a crime against all. We are in this life together, on one fragile planet, one globe, one people, the human race, and we should try to manage on that basis, where oneness is not just the dominant ideology of the dominant power, nor something produced only in the name of those dominant nations with the most voracious and unsustainable global appetites. Sustainability matters because, simply, once used up, nonrenewed resources are gone.

> God gave Noah the rainbow sign.
> No more water, the fire next time!
>
> —Afro-American spiritual

If globalization ends up meaning that the vast majority need to be glad for any crumbs that fall their way, then, as James Baldwin (1995) wrote of the lamentable state of black-white relations in the United States during the civil rights struggle in 1963, without justice it will be "the fire next time!" Forty years later, the inequities analyzed then are apparent globally. Baldwin sought enlightenment, to exist with dignity and courage in cruel and unjust times, to build a better future; he also realized that when the struggle fails to produce justice, the flames will not be quenched but fanned, and the fire next time will forge resistance to injustice rather than purify balm with which to appease manifest wrongs. Overwhelming power now reinforces an unsustainable global maldistribution of resources as "the fate of our times" (Weber 1976), just as surely as it does nationally. It is institutionalized in the hands of the world's wealthiest companies and states, in marketplaces shadowed by those "merchants and thieves, hungry for power" (Dylan 1978) whose names the daily news recounts. They change with the times but their crimes and misdemeanours recite the familiar litany of avarice, stupidity, and global opportunism that are so familiar. The order may shift; the guards will change, but our duty remains clear. "So let us not talk falsely now, the hour is getting late" (Dylan 1968).

Indeed, it may already be later than we think . . .

ONE MORE TIME . . .

Getting the story straight

- What is globalization?
- Who are the major global actors?
- What are the different kinds of global jobs?
- How does globalization shape human consciousnesses?

Thinking outside the box

- Who are the winners and who are the losers from globalization?
- What is the best way to level the playing field?

- Why is it not a paradox to say that the global is always local?
- How can the local become global?
- What do local protagonists need to do?

ADDITIONAL RESOURCES

1. The BBC Radio Reith Lectures of 1999 by Anthony Giddens, published as *Runaway World: How Globalization is Reshaping our Lives* (2000), is a clear and useful sociological introduction to globalization as a broad phenomenon.

2. Thomas Friedman's (1999) *The Lexus and the Olive Tree* is one of the very best sources on globalization—and beautifully written, as befits a *New York Times* correspondent.

3. The debate between Barbara Parker (2003) and Marc Jones (2003) in *Debating Organizations* (Westwood and Clegg 2003) is worthwhile for those deeply interested in the topic. For others it might be a bit heavy.

4. Probably the most useful source is the World Wide Web. Try typing in "globalization" and you will come up with heaps of stuff. Also, look up the various antiglobalization sites such as www.GlobalEnvision.org and www.csis-scrs.gc.ca/eng/miscdocs/200008_e.html.

5. In terms of films, there are a number of good documentaries, such as *Gap and Nike: No Sweat?* It is a BBC Panorama production, focusing on Nike and Gap, both of whom claim that they have strict codes of conduct for manufacturing. They claim that they do not use sweatshops or child labor. They say they routinely "monitor" their factories, to make sure their codes are followed. But when the BBC's Panorama team visited Cambodia, they found severe breaches of these codes within days. By talking with workers and using hidden cameras, they show how one factory, used by both Gap and Nike, has sweatshop conditions and employs children. All the workers interviewed were working seven days a week, often up to sixteen hours a day, and some of the employees were children as young as twelve. After these findings, Panorama went back to speak with Gap and Nike, to hear what they had to say. They also show how U.S. companies can use foreign sweatshops and still claim that the goods are made in the United States. See the Global Exchange Fair Trade Store at http://globalexchange.org/tapes.html. (Global Exchange Fair Trade Store 2004). You might also want to look at www.caa.org.au/campaigns/nike (Oxfam 2004).

6. More commercially, there is the recent 2003 Stephen Frears film, *Dirty Pretty Things,* which dramatizes life in the grunge jobs that illegal immigrants fill in any global city, in this case, London.

7. In terms of music, you should listen to the CD *Rhythm of the Saints* by Paul Simon, and for Olodum, their official home page, in Portuguese, is at www.olodum.com.br. Olodum have made many excellent CDs. In particular, we recommend *Best of Olodum* (1997) and *Olodum Vidafilhos do sol* (1994).

8. One citation from Bob Dylan (1968) comes from the song "All Along the Watchtower," originally released on the album *John Wesley Harding* but subsequently recorded by many others, including Jimi Hendrix and Neil Young, as well as being available on various Dylan compilations. The other Dylan (1978) citation comes from "The Changing of the Guard," a song that is not as well known, which may be found on the 1978 album *Street Legal.* We started the book with a piece of prose quoted from this source, so there is a pleasing circularity in finishing with it.

In addition to these suggested additional resources, don't forget to look at what is also available on the Web site **www.ckmanagement.net,** including free PDF files of recent papers related to this chapter, which you can download; video interviews with famous academics talking about related themes; as well as many other resources, such as connections to interesting Web sites.

Image 13.7   *Sunrise*

GLOSSARY

Note: Words in italics denote other glossary entries.

acquisition   The process of purchasing ownership in some entity that was previously independent of the purchasing body.

adhocracy   A type of *organization design* that is not consciously structured but just develops spontaneously, in an ad hoc manner—hence, adhocracy.

authority   Authority is the legitimate use of *power.* Power is legitimate when a person in a position does something according to the rules that define what someone in such a position is permitted to do. Authority attaches to the person in the position but is derived from the position itself, not the person. If the person chooses to act in an unauthorized way, that person may lose the authority that he or she has.

bounded rationality   Bounded *rationality* refers to decision making under conditions of uncertainty. Lacking complete *knowledge* about the parameters of that which is to be decided, the decision makers work within the bounds of their *rationality*—the limited search options that are an effect of individual psychology, *knowledge, networks,* and so on.

BPR   Stands for business process reengineering. Business processes are the standard tasks and organizational routines characteristic of the way a firm or organization does whatever it does. Reengineering refers to the redesign of the work that these tasks accomplish to cut out superfluous layers of coordination and control as well as redundant systems. The downside of BPR is that often elements that no one realizes are crucial can be reengineered out of existence. It is only when the tacit *knowledge* associated with them is gone, or when their latent rather than manifest role becomes evident in its absence, that their significance is realized—but it is often too late at that stage. BPR is strongly derivative of *scientific management* in its style of thinking.

bureaucracy   A bureaucracy is a form of *organization design* defined by a number of characteristics, including a rational career structure as a set of formal relations among positions, arranged in a hierarchy of ascending *authority,* with rights, responsibilities, and entitlements attached according to the place of the position in the hierarchy. In bureaucracy, action is supposed to be procedurally based on formal rules. When bureaucracies are classified as being of the rational-legal type, they are supposed to apply values and principles universally, without favor or prejudice.

capital   Capital is an abstract concept that might take many material forms. Traditionally, it was thought of purely in economic terms, as wealth invested in an asset with the intention of it delivering a return to the owner of that asset. As such, capital implies complex sets of relations of ownership and control of the asset and employment in its service. More recently, it has become common to talk of other abstract conceptions of capital as an asset: intellectual capital or social capital. The former would be *knowledge* that is worth something, that can earn its owner a return on the investments made in acquiring it. The most obvious example would be where one has intellectual property rights to benefit from a specific innovation or invention. Social capital refers to whom you know rather than what you own or what you know; social capital is the set of relations and *knowledge* embedded in those relations that you are able to mobilize.

capitalism   An economy and society based on the private ownership of property (*capital*) and the pursuit of profit through market-oriented action aimed at the realization of a surplus value greater than that extended in the creation of whatever goods and services are distributed, using formally free labor that is bought and sold in the labor market.

centralization   Centralization is the process whereby the roles and positions that exist in an *organization design* are associated with each other through a series of relations traced to a common central position or set of positions of command and control. Some organizations are much more centralized than others; those with only a single center of command and control that all matters of decision have to flow through are the most centralized. Typically, *bureaucracies* are thought of as being highly centralized.

charismatic leader   A leadership type that emphasizes the articulation of a vision and mission that promises a better life. Sometimes such leaders develop a cult following.

classical management theory   This type of theory is usually associated with first-generation management thinkers such as F. W. Taylor and Henri Fayol. The theory usually concentrates on the formal properties of *organization design* and is prescriptive in intent, seeking to establish the one best way of doing things.

coercive isomorphism   Coercive *isomorphism* occurs when some powerful *institution* obliges organizations in its domain, on threat of coercion, to comply with certain practices and designs. Think of the law; it obliges all organizations over a certain size to have equal employment opportunity practices. The managers may not want to provide equal opportunity, but they are obliged to do so under threat of legal penalty.

coercive power   The ability to get others do something that they would not ordinarily do, against their resistance.

collaboration   Collaboration is typically designed either to advance a shared vision or to resolve a conflict. It usually results in either an exchange of information or a joint agreement or commitment to action between two or more parties, such as organizations.

collectivism   Collectivism refers to a situation in which decisions and priorities are processed through a sense of what is good for the wider collective—such as a family, society, or organization—rather than the solitary individual.

communication   The process of exchanging information between two or more people or entities. Organizational communication is what occurs when an organization seeks to communicate a sense of itself to various audiences. These audiences may be employees, customers, investors, and so on.

configuration   The pattern of structured formal relations between conceptually designated elements in an *organization design,* such as *centralization, formalization,* and *routinization.*

contingency   A possible event, occurrence, or factor that, theoretically, management will probably have to deal with as a part of its normal repertoire of behaviors. Common contingencies are conceived of as technology, size, and environment.

control   The attempt to subordinate autonomous sources of action, such as those attaching to individual preferences, to some other set of superordinate preferences.

cooperative   A type of organization in which the members have democratic rights of control vested in them. Essentially, it is a member-based organization whose control, ultimately, is in the hands of the active voting members.

culture   The pattern of shared meanings and understandings passed down through language, symbols, and artifacts.

cybernetics   The theoretical study of communication and control processes in biological, mechanical, and electronic systems, especially the comparison of these processes with similar characteristics in organizations conceived as open systems.

decentralization   The opposite of *centralization.* Organizations often seek to decentralize when they feel that their systems and processes are becoming too slow because too much decision making, even on small and inconsequential matters, is being referred to the center. Often, organizations with low levels of trust are highly centralized because a decentralized decision structure requires that you trust those who are delegated to decide.

division of labor   A term often used in connection with Adam Smith's famous *An Enquiry into the Nature and Causes of the Wealth of Nations* (1961). In this book, Smith observed that when a complex task was *routinized* and divided up into constituent but simplified elements that different people became specialists in mastering, productivity was far greater than when each person sought to master all aspects of the same task. Thus, people working under the conditions of a division of labor could manufacture far more than the same number of people who did every task themselves. Smith used the example of pin making.

dyad   A relation defined as having two parts.

embeddedness   The realization that economic relations can never be grasped purely in terms of their economic *rationality* but need to be seen as organically situated within specific features of social settings. For instance, in the garment industry, much of the manufacturing may take place though loosely coupled *supply chains* of organizations whose members share a neighborhood and ethnicity. The economic action that ensues is embedded in these social relations.

emotional intelligence   The ability to understand oneself and others. It includes the ability to read people's emotions and to practice empathy while at the same time handling one's own emotions.

empowerment   Giving someone more *power* than he or she had previously. Transferring *power* to the individual by promoting self-regulating and self-motivating behavior through innovative human resource policies and practices, such as self-managing work teams, enhanced individual autonomy, and so on. Usually, it gives someone more opportunities for initiative and decision than he or she had previously by increasing individual autonomy to be able to act and diminishing external control of individual actions.

equity   An ownership stake in an asset.

equivocality   A state of being equivocal or uncertain about the nature of those things with which one is dealing. Karl Weick defines the central task of managers in organizations as being able to reduce the amount of equivocality that they and the organization have to deal with. In other words, managers are supposed to make things more, not less, certain.

ethnography   An approach to research that attempts to understand social phenomena, such as organizational life, as it happens and in its own terms. It involves in-depth interviews, participant observation, and detailed case study, and generally approaches research from the point of view of understanding what the subjects themselves think. It starts from the premise that meanings and understandings are socially constructed. (Compare with *positivism*.)

explicit knowledge   Explicit *knowledge* is elaborated and usually recorded in such a way that others can easily learn it.

extrinsic motivation Motivation factors that "pull" people toward certain behaviors to achieve an external reward. Examples include a performance-based bonus or a monetary reward.

feudalism An economy and society based on the private ownership of landed estates. The estates use indentured or bonded labor that is tied through obligations and responsibilities to create surplus product for appropriation by the estate owner.

formalization Refers to the phenomenon whereby roles, rights, and responsibilities attaching to positions in an *organization design* are defined formally. A high degree of formalization implies that there are many formal rules and regulations surrounding these positions; in contrast, a low degree of formalization describes a situation in which individuals in the positions have a high degree of relative autonomy in being able to define how they should do what they do, and indeed, what they choose to do.

functionalism An approach to analysis that assumes that phenomena exist to fulfill some function or other. Functionalism is often criticized for being conservative because, ipso facto, it assumes that what exists serves some purpose, therefore must be useful, and need not be replaced or revised. It is closely aligned to the "if it ain't broke, don't fix it" school of thinking.

globalization The process whereby the world becomes more interconnected and the fates of those people and organizations in it become more intertwined. In business terms, globalization means business without frontiers, crossing national boundaries, and dealing with the world, not just the home base.

global village The idea that we are all residents of Planet Earth, interconnected with everyone else, and that modern media of mass *communication* enable us to be instantly aware of events on the other side of the world. We are capable of global consciousness as we grieve with victims of natural disasters or celebrate with sports teams in competitions thousands of miles away.

group A socially cohesive set of individuals bound by the social or organizational relations that define them. These groups may be informal, and thus socially defined (say, the boys in R&D—research and development), or they may be formally defined in terms of the organization's definitions (say, the engineers in Maintenance).

groupthink The tendency for *groups* to become overly cohesive units—so cohesive that the individuals begin to think as one and no longer question or criticize decisions or ideas on their merits. It is an extreme type of *group* formation.

hegemony A state of ideological conformance said to have been imposed on a subordinated *group* of people because of the concepts through which they think—concepts that do not enable them to assert a point of view that reflects a better understanding of their interests and the situation they are in. These interests are assumed to be objective. In other words, it is assumed that, as workers, women, or whatever category of social identity one focuses on, there are some real interests that, if members of that *group* could see things clearly, they would articulate. The problem is that the definitions of these interests are always affected by the theory of implicit interests involved. Thus, feminists see gender, Marxists class, and so on.

horizontal structure   The relations between people, organizational units, or organizations that are at the same level of hierarchy. In organizations, an example of horizontal structure could be collegial relations; in relations between organizations, it might be relations within a *network*.

ideal type   Not a reference to something that is normatively ideal but to an ideational type that serves as a mental model that can be widely shared and used because analysts agree that it captures some essential features of a phenomenon. The ideal type does not correspond to reality but seeks to condense essential features of it in the model so that one can better recognize its real characteristics when it is met.

identity   A concept that cannot be defined easily, other than to say that identity refers to the way a person constructs, interprets, and understands who he or she is in relation to others in his or her life world. Identity may be more or less stable, more or less fragmented, more or less problematic, and more or less secure. The personal identities that we emphasize in one space may be very different from those that we emphasize in another. Thus, the identity that we develop and project at work may be very different from that which we project when clubbing or playing a sport. We have multiple identities. Corporate organizations often strive to shape our identities in ways that reflect their conception of the corporate image. In addition, they often seek to present a coherent corporate identity to the world.

ideology   An ideology is a coherent set of beliefs, attitudes, and opinions. The meaning is often pejorative, with a contrast drawn between ideology and science.

individualism   A context in which the individual is more highly prized than any other social entity such as the *group,* organization, or other collective definition. The opposite of *collectivism.*

institution   A recurrent patterned form of activity that fulfills basic functions for a society. Examples include political institutions, economic institutions, educational institutions, and so on. Institutions define basic arenas in which organizations operate: government, banks, schools, and so on.

institutional theory   A theory that proposes that organizations have the structures that they do largely for cultural reasons. Some designs and practices become regarded, for whatever reasons, as highly esteemed, as displaying high "cultural *capital.*" Through one or more of three specific mechanisms (coercive, mimetic, or normative *isomorphism*), the template becomes widely adopted. It may be so adopted as a result of *isomorphism.*

internal contracts   Sometimes referred to as "inside contracts," these describe a situation in which the owners of *capital* contract with an overseer to deliver a certain agreed amount of production using resources, plant, and equipment provided by the *capital* owner, and the internal contractor attends to the daily management of the labor hired to deliver the contract.

intrinsic motivation   Motivation factors that "push" people toward certain behaviors to appease some internal state—for example, a person completing a task because that person feels happy when he or she is seen as competent and reliable.

isomorphism   A term derived from biology, referring to a similarity in form of organisms of different ancestry. In organization and management theory, isomorphism is usually used in the context of *institutional theory* to refer to a situation in which *organization designs* and practices in different organizations are nonetheless similar.

knowledge   That which is a part of the stock of ideas, meanings, and more-or-less explicit understandings and explanations of how phenomena of interest actually work or are structured or designed and relate to other phenomena.

knowledge management   *Knowledge* management is management of the stocks of *knowledge* and information that compose the collective assets of an organization in order to deliver value to that organization. It is closely related to the distinction between *explicit knowledge* and *tacit knowledge.* Organizations may be said to contain a great deal of *tacit knowledge,* which, if it could be made more explicit, would add to the formal capabilities of the organization and be something that could be managed to deliver value to the organization in general rather than being merely useful to those who know it implicitly.

labor process   The social relations that people enter into when they are employed as well as the work that they actually do and the conditions under which it is done.

leadership   The process of motivating, inspiring, mentoring, and aligning people to organizational objectives while at the same time ensuring that the organization adapts, enacts, and interacts with its environment.

learning   Acquiring *knowledge* and capabilities in addition to those already known. Usually thought of as something that individuals do, it is often associated with specific *institutions,* such as a school or a university. However, recently there has been a shift of emphasis to informal and work-based learning that occurs outside these specific institutional areas and in employing organizations.

legitimization   The process whereby certain sorts of action and actors in social settings such as organizations become imbued with legitimacy—that is, that they exhibit a sense of propriety, are correct, and according to rule, whether these are formal or more informal.

limited liability   The incorporation of a company as a legal entity, limiting the liability of those who invest in it such that their personal fortunes are dealt with as legally separate from their investments in the asset.

locus of control   A view that people's personality differs depending on how people perceive their role in what happens to them throughout life. High "internals" believe they play a major role in what happens to them, whereas high "externals" believe that most of what happens to them is outside their control.

management   The process of communicating, coordinating, and accomplishing action in the pursuit of organizational objectives while managing relationships with stakeholders, technologies, and other artifacts, both within as well as between organizations.

managerialism   The belief in management as a means capable of solving any problem; an elevation of the idea of management as a means for solving any and every situation in such a way that the purpose or means of its application is overshadowed by a concern with its technical efficiency. Managerialism elevates the necessity of *management* into an *ideology* of the modern world.

merger   What happens when two independent entities become one—they merge.

mimetic isomorphism   In simple language, mimetic *isomorphism* means the process of copying. *Organization designs* and practices that are seen to be successful are copied because they are associated with success.

modernism   A way of seeing the world that is born from *modernity*. Originally, the term was developed in architecture to capture a revolt against overembellishment in design and a preference for functional architecture. In management and organization theory, modernism represents the same espousal of functionalist values and a preference for the economy and efficiency of forms of argument that rely heavily on an explicit espousal of scientific values, usually conceived in terms of positivism.

modernity   A term used by historians to represent stages in history—i.e., premodern, modern, and postmodern. Modernity refers to the time from the industrial revolution until the end of the twentieth century. Organizationally, it is characterized by *bureaucracy* and *formalization*. (See also the definitions of *modernism* and *postmodernism*.)

motivation   The psychological forces within each person that drive their behavior toward the pursuit of their implicit or explicit goals, and how hard and how long they work to attain those goals. Motivation used to be concerned with how people can achieve optimal psychological well-being, but now it is more about how managers can ensure that people do the job required efficiently and effectively.

network A set of relations that connect a multiplicity of independent agents, usually organizations or individuals, in a structure characterized by relations among the parts that make up the network. The relations may be more or less linear—one-to-another—or they be more complex, interconnecting many agents with many others.

networking At its simplest, networking is accomplished when people make sure that their business cards are widely distributed. What networking entails is collaboration between different people or agencies such as organizations. Often, independent organizations join together with others to form a *network* in which the other organizations have complementary skills so that together they can do something that neither alone would be able to manage.

new organization forms *Organization designs* for structure that seek to be nonbureaucratic—indeed are often anti-*bureaucratic*—stressing flat structures rather than tall hierarchies, multiskilled capabilities rather than a rigid division of labor, informality rather than a high degree of formality.

normative Normative order or behavior is action that is strongly shaped by social norms—the informal forms of regulation that make action socially recognizable as being of a certain type. What is normative depends on the context in which the action in question is situated. For instance, normatively appropriate action at a very relaxed party would probably not be normatively appropriate behavior in a formal office setting.

normative isomorphism Normative *isomorphism* occurs when an organization's members are normatively predisposed, perhaps through a long period of professional training and socialization, to favor certain sorts of design and practices. The widespread use of the partnership form by law and other professional firms is a case in point.

operationalize Turning abstract concepts into measurable, clearly defined constructs by specifying certain operations for the collection of data that are presumed to represent accurately the characteristics of the concepts.

organizational learning In many respects, organizational learning is similar to individual learning. The idea is that organizations learn when the *knowledge* that their members have is explicitly known and codified by the organization. Organizations should seek to make as much of what their members do as explicit as possible. If members leave, the *explicit knowledge* that they developed in their jobs stays. This learning may be single loop or double loop learning. Single loop learning means learning to do what they already do better; double loop learning involves doing different things *and* doing them differently.

organization design   The designated formal structure of the organization as a system of roles, responsibilities, and decision making.

outsourcing   Outsourcing involves contracting the provision of certain services to a third-party specialist service provider rather than seeking to deliver the service from within one's own organization. Usually, outsourcing is entered into to save costs and to deliver efficiencies and productivity benefits. By not concentrating on services and tasks that are peripheral to the main business, an organization can better focus on those things it needs to do well while leaving the peripheral tasks to organizations that specialize in the delivery of those services. Often, areas such as human resource management, catering, information technology, and equipment and facilities maintenance are outsourced.

panopticism   The capacity to be all seeing. It was an attribute of the architectural structure known as a Panopticon, designed by Jeremy Bentham in the eighteenth century. What was most significant about the Panopticon, and what gave it its panopticism, was the fact that those under surveillance did not know when they were being watched, but were aware that they were potentially always under surveillance. Thus, panopticism was not just an external attribute of the design; it became also a disposition of those under its sway. Panopticism means being aware that one may be being observed but never being sure whether one is actually being watched at that moment.

paradigm   A coherent set of assumptions, concepts, values, and practices that constitute a way of viewing reality for the community that shares them, especially in an intellectual discipline, in which the views are widely shared as a result of training and induction into the methods of the discipline. In more mature disciplines, there is usually a single dominant or normal paradigm, whereas less developed disciplines are characterized by a plurality of paradigms because there is a lack of shared agreement on what the discipline entails.

positivism   A view of *knowledge* that privileges a conception of science focused on explanation more than understanding, where explanation is best served by specifying formal causal relations between abstract concepts conceived as variables.

postmodernism   In management, postmodernism is often associated with nonquantitative and narrative approaches to research. These often stress the importance of organizational stories as small narratives but defer the choice of taking sides in determining which of these is really true. Instead, it explores the stories and other narrative accounts as discourses, looking at what makes them possible and asking what their effects are.

postmodernity   An era characterized by *postmodern* styles and values, one that comes after *modernity*.

power   The ability of an actor, such as a person or a collective of people—say, an organization—to shape, frame, and direct the actions of others, even against the resistance of those other parties. At its most mechanical, it means forcing others to do things against their will; however, power can be far more positive and less mechanical when it shapes and frames what others want to do—seemingly of their own volition.

prime function   The main activity engaged in.

rationality   Action that is produced according to some rule; action that is not random or unpatterned.

remuneration   The agreed-upon benefits paid to a staff member for a specified level of services and effort expended in any given job.

routinization   The development of routines for action so that it becomes regular and predictable in its parameters and consequences.

rule tropism   A term introduced by Robert Merton. The origins of the term "tropism" are in medicine, where it refers to an involuntary orienting response, a positive or negative reaction to a stimulus. In management, the stimuli are rules, and the response is one in which the existence of the rules in a bureaucracy immediately and involuntarily, as a learned response, structures actions within the organization.

scientific management   The Taylorist principle that there is one best way to organize work and organization, according to a science of management based upon principles of *standardization* and *routinization* decided by authoritative experts.

self-actualization   The optimal psychological state of fulfillment, in which one is actualizing one's full potentialities. This includes acceptance of the self, others, and one's feelings.

social Darwinism   The principle that human behavior should follow the evolutionary principles found in all other animals, such as survival of the fittest.

socialization   The gradual process of learning that occurs as a result of existing and operating in social settings. A person is socialized through *institutions* such as the family, church, and schooling. During the socialization process, one learns what is and is not acceptable or valued in that social setting.

span of control   The number of people reporting to a position in a hierarchy is the span of control of that position.

specialization   The skill formation that occurs when labor is divided and defined into smaller specific tasks rather than being seen as a general task that anyone might do.

stakeholders   Key individuals or *groups* of individuals with vested interests or "stakes" in a given decision or project. The stakeholder can be a direct or an indirect stakeholder. A direct stakeholder is a customer, supplier, a government body, or anyone else formally linked to the organization(s). An indirect stakeholder is a member of the community who is not directly involved in the organization(s) but who is affected by its behavior, such as a resident in its immediate community.

standardization   The prescription of constant and nonvariant ways of doing things.

state   The entity that claims a legitimate monopoly of the means of violence and taxation in a given territory.

strategizing   The process whereby rational future planning is created and implemented, with an emphasis on the processes and work involved in devising and implementing these plans.

subculture   A culture that defines a particular cohort within a wider organization.

supply chain   A *network* of organizations that collaborate to deliver a product or service to an end-user or market.

sustainability   Literally, ensuring that resources are renewed. A sustainable use of resources would leave the world short of nothing that was depleted in any process—that resource would be renewed—and would ensure that nothing deleterious to the world's natural systems resulted from whatever processes were being undertaken. The concept is often tied to the espousal of "green" values, which are becoming increasingly mainstream in the wake of the Kyoto Treaty and the realization that sustainable production is equivalent to more efficient production. Inputs that are not wasted and processes that do not provide outputs that have to be scrapped are both ecologically and economically rational. Waste is irrational and inefficient.

system   A system involves a stable set of relationships between inputs, transformation processes, and outputs. Outputs often have a feedback function on processes. A closed system is effectively sealed off from its environment and the influences that it brings to bear; an example is a laboratory that contains a vacuum chamber. An open system is open to its environment and the influences from it; an example is a thermostat regulating a boiler or air conditioner as temperatures fluctuate. It is often said that the classical *scientific management* conceptions of thinkers such as Taylor and Fayol were closed system models; later *contingency* theorists, who were open to environmental influences, are known as open system theorists. The underlying metaphor is that organizations are similar to self-regulating machines or biological entities.

tacit knowledge   Tacit *knowledge* is the *knowledge* that we have but may not be able to explicitly articulate. An example is the *knowledge* required to ride a bike.

team   Two or more individuals interdependently linked to the achievement of mutually agreed goals and bound together via a psychological and/or legal contract.

technocracy   An overwhelming belief in the viability of the technological fix—that is, that technology can solve all problems and resolve any issues.

technocratic rationalization   Closely related to *managerialism,* technocratic rationalization is based on the belief that technology can simplify and solve—that is, rationalize—everything. Thus, all phenomena can be rationalized—that is, simplified and made more efficient by the application of technology. These views are often disparagingly referred to as a commitment to the "technological fix"—a preparedness to commit substantially to technologies while not being ready to invest as much in nontechnological, often people-related aspects of a problem. Technological rationalization today is often associated with the implementation of information technologies. Millions can be spent on their application, and then the people who work with them are blamed when the systems do not work properly in situ—often because the sociotechnical aspects of the people/technology relations have not been considered properly.

top-down management   This notion refers to the idea that all organizational decision making and strategic communication should travel from the top of an organization (from leaders) down to subordinates. In contrast, bottom-up management seeks to build assent to actions before their implementation rather than seeking to overcome resistance to them in the process of implementation. Top-down management is often thought to characterize bureaucracy, but whether a bureaucracy is top-down in its style seems to be culturally contingent. In Japan, many corporate organizations are thought of as learning bureaucracies, and these tend to be characterized by bottom-up styles of decision making.

total institution   A typology of organizations in which all the examples of organizations collected under a certain rubric share the essential feature of controlling almost the totality of the individual member's day-to-day life. Boarding schools, barracks, prisons, and asylums can be categorized as total institutions.

TQM   TQM stands for total quality management. TQM has been an important management method that seeks to make managers realize that they are always responsible to a customer, whether he or she is a final customer, in the sense of being a purchaser, or someone who is an internal customer. An internal customer receives what is done or produced in his or her or another organization as an input for further work. Customer sovereignty is privileged in TQM, so all systems and processes should be designed to ensure maximum customer satisfaction. Usually, this goal is achieved by producing processes and systems that minimize variations in the quality of whatever is being processed. Sometimes the goal is reached by producing "zero defects," the idea being that waste minimization, and getting it right the first time, saves money and time.

transactional leader   A type of leadership that emphasizes the relationship between task and performance. An emphasis is placed on how jobs are done, how they are linked to goals and outcomes, and ensuring that the right resources are available to accomplish tasks.

transformational leader   A type of leadership that emphasizes change or transformations in organizations by aligning people to the organization's vision and mission, and communicating them to employees to inspire them.

transnationals   Sometimes known as multinational corporations, these firms operate across national frontiers—they are, literally, transnational. The acronyms TNC (transnational corporation) or MNC (multinational corporation) are sometimes used.

typologies   Using the method of *ideal types* to make complex realities more abstract and less concrete so that essentially similar features can be emphasized for comparative purposes.

value   Value is a complex term; at one level, it is simply the price of a thing, but at another, it is a term that implies that value is being added in and through the processes of production, such that the value of something should exceed its costs of production—its price. The term is often used in classical political economy in this way: to imply that the costs of production, in the form of wages, must create a surplus value over and above the actual costs incurred; otherwise there would be no profit.

value chain   The *value* chain refers to the elaborate transformations that goods and services undergo on their way to market. Think of a clipping of wool sheared from a sheep's back. The farmer is at one end of the *value* chain, selling the wool in international auctions for the best price. At the other end are designers such as Giorgio Armani, who use fine woolen suiting to make their fashions. *Value* is added as the wool is woven and fashioned into the suiting; however, the real added *value* comes with the application of the Armani design. Thus, Armani is at the high *value* added end of the value chain, whereas the grower is at the low end. The commodity used in this example, wool, undergoes many transformations on its way from the sheep's back to the catwalk, and most of the *value* is added nearer the catwalk than the sheep.

value priorities   The notion that we rank our *values*. Those values given higher priority are stronger in guiding our behavior across situations than those we value less.

values Principles held by people that they deem to be important in guiding their behavior. The clearest examples of values are the injunctions of the great religions, such as "Thou shalt not kill." Often, firms mimic religions by having statements of "Our Values," rather like a corporate form of the Ten Commandments or the Koran.

variable A characteristic distributed across an entire population or sample of that population that will vary in the extent to which it is displayed. For instance, a student class varies in terms of the variables of height, weight, and so on. Such variables are defined by certain measures, such as inches, kilos, and so on.

vertical structure A hierarchical structure of relations, either within an organization, among organizations in a *supply chain,* or some other interorganizational relation. Often, a vertical structure is contrasted with other possible structures, such as a *network* or *horizontal structure.*

BIBLIOGRAPHY

Abrahamson, E. (1996) "Management Fashion," *Academy of Management Review* 21: 254–285.

Abrahamson, E. (1997) "The Emergence and Prevalence of Employee Management Rhetorics: The Effects of Long Waves, Labour Unions, and Turnover, 1875 to 1992," *Academy of Management Journal* 40:3, 491–533.

Ackroyd, S., and Crowdy, P. (1990) "Can Culture Be Managed? Working with 'Raw' Material: The Case of the English Slaughtermen," *Personnel Review* 19:5, 3–13.

Acton, J. (1972) "Letter to Mandell Creighton, April 5, 1887," pp. 335–336 in G. Himmelfarb (Ed.), *Essays on Freedom and Power,* Gloucester, MA: P. Smith.

Adams, J. S. (1963) "Towards an Understanding of Inequity," *Journal of Abnormal and Social Psychology* 67: 422–436.

Ahl, D. (1984) in Christopher Cerf and Victor Navasky (Eds.), *The Experts Speak,* New York: Pantheon.

Ahuja, M. K., and Carley, K. M. (1999) "Network Structure in Virtual Organization," *Organization Science* 10:6, 741–757.

Ainger, K. (2003) *The Fence at Kilometre Zero.* Retrieved from www.newint.org/features/cancun/index2.htm.

Albrow, M. (1970) *Bureaucracy,* London: Pall Mall.

Albrow, M. (1997) *Do Organizations Have Feelings?* London: Routledge.

Aldrich, H. (2002) "Technology and Organizational Structure: A Reexamination of the Findings of the Aston Group," pp. 344–366 in S. R. Clegg (Ed.), *Central Currents in Organization Studies I: Frameworks and Applications, Volume 2,* London: Sage; originally published in *Administrative Science Quarterly* (1971) 17: 26–42.

Allmendinger, J., and Hackman, J. R. (2002) "Organizations in Changing Environments: The Case of East German Symphony Orchestras," pp. 217–252 in S. R. Clegg (Ed.), *Central Currents in Organization Studies I: Frameworks and Applications, Volume 3,* London: Sage; originally published in *Administrative Science Quarterly* (1996) 41: 337–369.

Allport, G. W., and Odbert, H. S. (1936) "Trait Names: A Psycholexical Study," *Psychological Monographs* 47 (1, Whole No. 211).

Altman, R. (Director) (2001) *Gosford Park* [Motion picture]. United States: USA Films.

Alvesson, M. (1993a) *Cultural Perspectives on Organizations,* Cambridge: Cambridge University Press.

Alvesson, M. (1993b) "Organizations as Rhetoric: Knowledge Intensive Firms and the Struggle with Ambiguity," *Journal of Management Studies* 30:6, 997–1015.

Alvesson, M., and Berg, P. O. (1992) *Corporate Culture and Organizational Symbolism,* Berlin: de Gruyter.

Alvesson, M., and Karreman, D. (2001) "Odd Couple: Making Sense of the Curious Concept of Knowledge Management," *Journal of Management Studies* 38:7, 995–1018.

Amabile, T. (1998) "How to Kill Creativity," *Harvard Business Review* September-October: 77–87.

Anderson, B. (1982) *Imagined Communities: Reflections on the Origins and Spread of Nationalism,* London: Verso.

Ansoff, I. H. (1965) *Corporate Strategy: An Analytic Approach to Business Policy for Growth and Expansion,* New York: McGraw-Hill.

Anthony, P. (1994) *Managing Culture,* Buckingham, UK: Open University Press.

Anthony, P. D. (1977) *The Ideology of Work,* London: Tavistock.

Arendt, H. (1994) *Eichmann in Jerusalem: A Report on the Banality of Evil,* New York: Penguin.

Argenti, P., and Forman, J. (2000) "The Communication Advantage: A Constituency-Focused Approach to Formulating and Implementing Strategy," pp. 233–245 in M. Schultz, M. Hatch, and M. Larsen (Eds.), *The Expressive Organization: Linking Identity, Reputation, and the Corporate Brand,* Oxford: Oxford University Press.

Argyris, C. (1960) *Understanding Organizational Behaviour,* London: Tavistock.

Argyris, C., and Schön, D. (1978) *Organizational Learning: A Theory of Action Perspective,* Reading, MA: Addison-Wesley.

Aronson, E. (1960) *The Social Animal,* San Francisco: W. H. Freeman.

Arthur, B. (1996) "Increasing Returns and the Two Worlds of Business," *Harvard Business Review,* Reprint 96401.

Asch, S. (1955) "Opinions and Social Pressure," *Scientific American* 193: 31–35.

Ashkenasy, N. (2003) "The Case for Culture," pp. 300–310 in R. Westwood and S. R. Clegg (Eds.), *Debating Organizations: Point-Counterpoint in Organization Studies,* London: Blackwell.

Astley, G., and Zammuto, R. F. (1992) "Organization Science: Managers and Language Games," *Organization Science* 3:3, 443–460.

Australian Broadcasting Corporation News (1998) *Not Shaken, Not Stirred: Murdoch, Multinationals and Tax.* Retrieved from www.abc.net.au/news/features/tax/page3.htm.

Babbage, C. (1971) *On the Economy of Machinery and Manufactures,* New York: Kelley.

Badaracco, J. L. (1991) *The Knowledge Link: How Firms Compete Through Strategic Alliances,* Boston: Harvard Business School Press.

Bairoch, P., and Kozul-Wright, R. (1996) "Globalization Myths: Some Historical Reflections on Integration, Industrialization and Growth in the World Economy," *UNCTAD* Discussion Paper 113.

Baldwin, J. (1995) *The Fire Next Time,* New York: Random House.

Bandura, A. (1986) *Social Foundations of Thought and Action: A Social-Cognitive Theory,* Englewood Cliffs, NJ: Prentice Hall.

Bangle, C. (2001) "The Ultimate Creative Machine: How BMW Turns Art Into Profit," *Harvard Business Review* January: 47–55.

Barber, B. (1996) *Jihad vs. McWorld,* New York: Ballantine.

Baritz, L. (1960) *The Servants of Power: A History of the Use of Social Science in American Industry,* Westport, CT: Greenwood Press.

Barker, J. (2002) "Tightening the Iron Cage: Concertive Control in Self-Managing Teams," pp. 180–210 in S. R. Clegg (Ed.), *Central Currents in Organization*

Studies II: Contemporary Trends, Volume 5, London: Sage; originally published in *Administrative Science Quarterly* (1993) 38: 408–437.

Barker, P. (1998) *Michel Foucault: An Introduction,* Edinburgh, UK: Edinburgh University Press.

Barker, R. A. (2001) "The Nature of Leadership," *Human Relations* 54: 469–494.

Barley, S. (1986) "Technology as an Occasion for Structuring Evidence From Observations of CT Scanners and the Social Order of Radiology Departments," *Administrative Science Quarterly* 31: 78–109.

Barley, S., and Kunda, G. (1992) "Design and Devotion: Surges of Rational and Normative Ideals of Control in Managerial Discourse," *Administrative Science Quarterly* 37: 363–399.

Barley, S., Meyer, G., and Gash, D. (1988) "Cultures of Cultures: Academics, Practitioners and the Pragmatics of Normative Control," *Administrative Science Quarterly* 33: 24–60.

Barnard, C. (1936) *The Functions of the Executive,* Cambridge, MA: Harvard University Press.

Barrett, F. J. (2002) "Creativity and Improvisation in Jazz and Organizations: Implications for Organization Learning," pp. 138–165 in K. Kamoche, M. P. Cunha, and D. V. J. Cunha (Eds.), *Organizational Improvisation,* London: Routledge.

Barry, D., and Elmes, M. (1997) "Strategy Retold: Toward a Narrative View of Strategic Discourse," *Academy of Management Review* 22:2, 429–452.

Bartholomew, S. (1998) "National Systems of Biotechnology Innovation: Complex Interdependence in the Global System," *Journal of International Business* 2: 241–266.

Bartlett, C., and Ghoshal, S. (1995) "Changing the Role of Top Management: Beyond Systems to People," *Harvard Business Review* May-June.

Bartlett, C. A., and Ghoshal, S. (1998) *Transnational Management,* New York: McGraw-Hill.

Barton, B. F., and Barton, M. S. (1993) "Modes of Power in Technical and Professional Visuals," *Journal of Business and Technical Education* 7:1, 138–162.

Bass, B. M. (1985) "Leadership: Good, Better, Best," *Organizational Dynamics* 13: 26–40.

Bass, B. M. (1990) *Bass & Stogdill's Handbook of Leadership: Theory, Research, and Managerial Applications,* 3rd ed. New York: Free Press.

Bauman, Z. (1987) *Legislators and Interpreters,* Cambridge: Polity.

Bauman, Z. (1989) *Modernity and the Holocaust,* Cambridge: Polity.

Bauman, Z. (1992) *Intimations of Postmodernity,* London: Routledge.

Benfari, R. C., Wilkinson, H. E., and Orth, C. D. (1986) "The Effective Use of Power," *Business Horizons* 29:3, 12–16.

Bennis, W. G., Berkowitz, N., Affinito, M., and Malone, M. (1958) "Authority, Power and the Ability to Influence," *Human Relations* 11: 143–156.

Berger, P., and Luckmann, T. (1967) *The Social Construction of Reality: A Treatise in the Sociology of Knowledge,* Harmondsworth, UK: Penguin.

Bergesen, A. J., and Sonnett, J. (2001) "The Global 500: Mapping the World Economy at Century's End," *American Behavioral Scientist* 44:10, 1602–1615.

Berle, A. A., and Means, G. C. (1932) *The Modern Corporation and Private Property,* New York: Harcourt, Brace & World.

Bertaux, D., and Bertaux-Wiame, I. (1981) "Artisanal Bakery in France: How It Lives and Why It Survives," pp. 121–154 in F. Bechofer and B. Elliot (Eds.), *The Petite Bourgeoisie: Comparative Studies of the Uneasy Stratum,* London: Macmillan.

Beyer, J. M. (1992) "Metaphors, Misunderstandings and Mischief: A Commentary," *Organization Science* 3:3, 467–500.

Biggart, N. W., and Hamilton, G. G. (1992) "On the Limits of a Firm-Based Theory to Explain Business Networks: The Western Bias of Neoclassical Economics," pp. 471–490 in N. Nohria and R. Eccles (Eds.), *Networks and Organizations: Structure, Form and Action,* Boston: Harvard Business School Press.

Bittner, E. (2002) "The Concept of Organization," pp. 76–87 in S. R. Clegg (Ed.), *Central Currents in Organization Studies I: Frameworks and Applications, Volume 2,* London: Sage; originally published in *Social Research* (1965) 32: 239–255.

Black, J. A., and Edwards, S. (2000) "Emergence of Virtual or Network Organizations: Fad or Feature," *Journal of Organization Change Management* 13:6, 567–576.

Blake, R. R., and McCanse, A. A. (1991) *Leadership Dilemmas—Grid Solution,* Houston: Gulf.

Blake, R. R., and Mouton, J. S. (1985) *The Managerial Grid III,* Houston: Gulf.

Blau, P. (1964) *Exchange and Power in Social Life,* New York: Wiley.

Blau, P. M. (1955) *The Dynamics of Bureaucracy,* Chicago: University of Chicago Press.

Blau, P. M. (2002) "A Formal Theory of Differentiation in Organizations," pp. 276–298 in S. R. Clegg (Ed.), *Central Currents in Organization Studies I: Frameworks and Applications, Volume 2,* London: Sage; originally published in *American Sociological Review* (1970) 35: 201–218.

Blau, P. M., and Schoenherr, R. (1971) *The Structure of Organizations,* New York: Basic Books.

Blau, P. M., and Scott, W. (1963) *Formal Organizations: A Comparative Approach,* London: Routledge & Kegan Paul.

Bodrow, A., and More, E. (1992) *Managing Organizational Communication,* Melbourne: Longman.

The Body Shop (2004) *Mission Statement.* Retrieved from www.thebodyshop.com/web/tb_sgl/about_reason.jsp.

Bogard, W. (1996) *The Simulation of Surveillance: Hypercontrol in Telematic Societies,* Cambridge: Cambridge University Press.

Boje, D. M. (2002) "Stories of the Storytelling Organization: A Postmodern Analysis of Disney as 'Tamara-Land,'" pp. 29–66 in S. R. Clegg (Ed.), *Central Currents in Organization Studies II: Contemporary Trends, Volume 7,* London: Sage; originally published in *Academy of Management Journal* (1995) 38: 997–1035.

Boje, D. M., and Dennehey, R. (1999) *Managing in the Postmodern World,* Dubuque, IA: Kendall-Hunt. Also available at http://cbae.nmsu.edu/~dboje/pages/CHAP5LEA.html.

Boje, D. M., and Rosile, G. A. (2001) "Where's the Power in Empowerment? Answers from Follett and Clegg," *Journal of Applied Behavioral Science* 37:1, 90–117.

Bolman, L. G., and Deal, T. E. (2003) *Reframing Organizations: Artistry, Choice and Leadership,* San Francisco: Jossey-Bass.

Bordow, A., and Moore, E. (1991) *Managing Organizational Communication,* Melbourne: Longman.

Bourke, H. (1982) "Industrial Unrest as Social Pathology: The Australian Writings of Elton Mayo," *Historical Studies* 217–233.

Boyett, J. H., and Boyett, J. T. (1998) *The Guru Guide: The Best Ideas of the Top Management Thinkers,* New York: Wiley.

Boyle, D. (Director) (1995) *Trainspotting* [Motion picture]. United Kingdom: Miramax.

Braverman, H. (1974) *Labor and Monopoly Capital,* New York: Monthly Review Press.

Brown, J., and Duguid, P. (2001) "Creativity Versus Structure: A Useful Tension," *Sloan Management Review* 42:4, 93–94.

Brown, S. L., and Eisenhardt, K. (1997) "The Art of Continuous Change: Linking Complexity Theory and Time-Paced Evolution in Relentlessly Shifting Organizations," *Administrative Science Quarterly* 42:1, 1–34.

Brunsson, N. (1995) "Managing Organizational Disorder," pp. 73–87 in M. Warglien and M. Massimo (Eds.), *The Logic of Organizational Disorder,* Berlin: de Gruyter.

Brunsson, N. (1998) "Non-Learning Organizations," *Scandinavian Journal of Management* 14:4, 421–432.

Buchanan, D., and Badham, R. (1999) *Power, Politics and Organizational Change: Winning the Turf Game,* London: Sage.

Buchanan, D., and Huczynski, A. (2004) *Organizational Behaviour: An Introductory Text,* 5th ed., London: Prentice Hall.

Burawoy, M. (1979) *Manufacturing Consent: Changes in the Labor Process Under Monopoly Capitalism,* Chicago: University of Chicago Press.

Burgelman, R. (1983) "A Process Model of Internal Corporate Venturing in the Diversified Major Firm," *Organizational Science Quarterly* 28: 223–244.

Burnham, J. (1942) *The Managerial Revolution,* Bloomington: Indiana University Press.

Burns, J. M. (1978) *Leadership,* New York: Harper & Row.

Burns, T., and Stalker, G. M. (1961) *The Management of Innovation,* London: Tavistock.

Burrell, G., and Morgan, G. (1979) *Sociological Paradigms and Organizational Analysis,* London: Heinemann.

Burris, B. H. (1993) *Technocracy at Work,* Albany: State University of New York Press.

Buss, A. (1979) "Humanistic Psychology as Liberal Ideology: The Socio-Historical Roots of Maslow's Theory of Self-Actualization," *Journal of Humanistic Psychology* 19:3, 43–55.

Calás, M. B., and McGuire, J. B. (1990) "Organizations as Networks of Power and Symbolism," pp. 95–113 in B. Barry (Ed.), *Organizational Symbolism,* Berlin: de Gruyter.

Calás, M. B., and Smircich, L. (1996) "Not Ahead of Her Time: Reflections on Mary Parker Follett as a Prophet of Management," *Organization* 3:1, 147–152.

Cameron, J. (Director) (1997) *Titanic* [Motion picture]. United States: Paramount.

Cameron, K. S., Dutton, J. E., and Quinn, R. E. (2003) "Foundations of Positive Organizational Scholarship," pp. 3–12 in K. S. Cameron, J. E. Dutton, and R. E. Quinn (Eds.), *Positive Organizational Scholarship: Foundations of a New Discipline,* San Francisco: Berrett-Koehler.

Campbell, A., and Alexander, M. (1997) "What's Wrong With Strategy?," *Harvard Business Review,* November-December: 42–50.

Campbell, F. (Producer) *Gap and Nike: No Sweat?* [Television broadcast]. United Kingdom: BBC.

Carey, A. (2002) "The Hawthorne Studies: A Radical Criticism," pp. 314–322 in S. R. Clegg (Ed.), *Central Currents in Organization Studies I: Frameworks and Applications, Volume 1,* London: Sage; originally published in *American Sociological Review* (1967) 32: 403–416.

Carey, G., and Lette, K. (1979) *Puberty Blues,* Carlton, Victoria, Australia: McPhee Gribble.

Carnegie, D. (1994) *How to Win Friends and Influence People: How to Stop Worrying and Start Living,* London: Chancellor.

Carter, J. (n.d.) Study World. *Quotes from Author Jimmy Carter.* Retrieved from www.studyworld.com/newsite/Quotes/quotebyauthor.asp?ln=Carter&fn=Jimmy.

Casey, C. (1995) *Work, Self and Society: After Industrialism,* London: Routledge.

Castells, M. (2000) *The Information Age: Economy, Society and Culture. Volume 1: The Rise of Network Society,* 2nd ed., London: Blackwell.

Castells, M. (2001) *The Internet Galaxy: Reflections on the Internet, Business, and Society,* New York: Oxford University Press.

Cathay Pacific Airways (1997) *Recruitment and Corporate Socialization Program Statement,* Hong Kong: Author.

Cattell, R. B. (1946) *Description and Measurement of Personality,* Yonkers-on-Hudson, NY: World Book.

Chan, A. (2003) "Instantiative Versus Entitative Culture: The Case for Culture as Process," pp. 311–320 in R. Westwood and S. R. Clegg (Eds.), *Debating Organizations: Point-Counterpoint in Organization Studies,* Oxford: Blackwell.

Chandler, A. D. (1962) *Strategy and Structure: Chapters in the History of the American Industrial Enterprise,* Cambridge, MA: MIT Press.

Chandler, A. D. (1990) *Scale and Scope,* Cambridge, MA: Harvard University Press.

Chandler, A. D., Jr. (1993) "Learning and Technological Change: The Perspective From Business History," pp. 24–39 in R. Thomson (Ed.), *Learning and Technological Change,* New York: St. Martins.

Chaplin, C. (Director) (1936) *Modern Times* [Motion picture]. United States: Kino International.

Cheney, G., and Christensen, L. T. (2001) "Organizational Identity: Linkages Between Internal and External Communication." pp. 231–270 in F. M. Jablin and L. L. Putnam (Eds.), *New Handbook of Organizational Communication,* Thousand Oaks, CA: Sage.

Child, J. (2002) "Organizational Structure, Environment and Performance: The Role of Strategic Choice," pp. 323–343 in S. R. Clegg (Ed.), *Central Currents in Organization Studies I: Frameworks and Applications, Volume 2,* London: Sage; originally published in *Sociology* (1972) 6: 1–21.

Child, J., and Kieser, A. (1979) "Organization and Managerial Roles in British and West German Companies: An Examination of the Culture-Free Thesis," pp. 251–271 in C. J. Lammers and D. J. Hickson (Eds.), *Organizations Alike and Unalike: International and Inter-Institutional Studies in the Sociology of Organizations,* London: Routledge & Kegan Paul.

Christensen, C. (1997) *The Innovator's Dilemma: When New Technologies Cause Great Firms to Fail,* Boston: Harvard Business School Press.

Christensen, L., and Cheney, G. (2000) "Self-Absorption and Self-Seduction in the Corporate Identity Game," pp. 246–270 in M. Schultz, M. Hatch, and M. Larsen (Eds.), *The Expressive Organization: Linking Identity, Reputation, and the Corporate Brand,* Oxford and New York: Oxford University Press.

Clark, P. (2000) *Organisations in Action: Competition Between Contexts,* London: Routledge.

Clark, P. (2003) *Organizational Innovations,* London: Sage.

Clarke, J., and Newman, J. (1997) *The Managerial State: Power, Politics and Ideology in the Remaking of the Welfare State,* London: Sage.

Clarke, T., and Clegg, S. R. (1998) *Changing Paradigms: The Transformation of Management for the 21st Century,* London: Collins.

Clawson, D. (1980) *Bureaucracy and the Labor Process: The Transformation of U.S. Industry 1860–1920,* New York: Monthly Review Press.

Clegg, S. R. (1979) *The Theory of Power and Organization,* London: Routledge & Kegan Paul.

Clegg, S. R. (1981) "Organization and Control," *Administrative Science Quarterly* 26:4, 545–562.

Clegg, S. R. (1989) *Frameworks of Power,* London: Sage.

Clegg, S. R. (1990) *Modern Organizations: Organization Studies in the Postmodern World,* London: Sage.

Clegg, S. R. (1994) "Power and the Resistant Subject," in J. Jermier, D. Knights, and W. R. Nord (Eds.), *Resistance and Power in Organizations: Agency, Subjectivity and the Labor Process,* London: Routledge.

Clegg, S. R. (1995) "Weber and Foucault: Social Theory for the Study of Organizations," *Organization* 1:1, 149–178.

Clegg, S. R. (1999) "Globalizing the Intelligent Organization: Learning Organizations, Smart Workers (Not So) Clever Countries and the Sociological Imagination," *Management Learning* 30:3, 259–280.

Clegg, S. R., Boreham, P., and Dow, G. (1986) *Class, Politics and the Economy,* London: Routledge & Kegan Paul.

Clegg, S. R., and Dunkerley, D. (1980) *Organization, Class and Control,* London: Routledge & Kegan Paul.

Clegg, S. R., and Hardy, C. (1996) "Representations," pp. 676–708 in S. R. Clegg, C. Hardy, and W. R. Nord (Eds.), *Handbook of Organization Studies,* London: Sage.

Clegg, S. R., and Kono, T. (2002) "Trends in Japanese Management: An Overview of Embedded Continuities and Disembedded Discontinuities," *Asia Pacific Journal of Management* 19:2 & 3, 269–285.

Clegg, S. R., and Kornberger, M. (2003) "Modernism, Postmodernism, Management and Organization Theory," pp. 57–89 in Ed Locke (Ed.), *Postmodernism in Organizational Thought: Pros, Cons and the Alternative,* Amsterdam: Elsevier.

Clegg, S. R., Pitsis, T. S., Rura-Polley, T., and Marosszeky, M. (2002) "Governmentality Matters: Building an Alliance Culture for Interorganizational Collaboration," *Organization Studies* 23:3, 317–337.

Clinton, B. (1999) *Remarks by the President on Foreign Policy.* Retrieved from http://globalization.about.com/blforpol.htm.

Coch, L., and French, J. R. P. (1948) "Overcoming Resistance to Change," *Human Relations* 1: 512–532.

Cockett, R. (1995) *Thinking the Unthinkable: Think Tanks and the Economic Counter-Revolution, 1931–1983,* London: HarperCollins.

Cocteau, J. (1988). *Die Schwierigkeit, zu sein,* Frankfurt: Fischer.

Cohen, M. D., March, J. G., and Olsen, J. P. (1972) "The Garbage Can Model of Organizational Choice," *Administrative Science Quarterly* 17:1, 1–25.

Cohen, R. (Director) (2001) *The Fast and the Furious* [Motion picture]. United States: Universal.

Collinson, D. (1994) "Strategies of Resistance: Power, Knowledge and Subjectivity in the Workplace," pp. 25–68 in J. Jermier, D. Knights, and W. R. Nord (Eds.), *Resistance and Power in Organizations: Agency, Subjectivity and the Labor Process,* London: Routledge.

Collinson, D. L. (1992) *Managing the Shopfloor: Subjectivity, Masculinity and Workplace Culture,* Berlin: de Gruyter.

Colville, I., Waterman, R., and Weick, K. (1999) "Organizing and the Search for Excellence: Making Sense of the Times in Theory and Practice," *Organization* 6: 1, 129–148.

Conrad, J. (1970) *Heart of Darkness and Other Stories,* with an introduction by Bruce Harkness, Boston: Houghton Mifflin.

ContactBabel (2002) *UK Contact Centre Report.* Retrieved from www.contactbabel.com/uk2002report.html.

Cooke, B. (2003) "The Denial of Slavery in Management Studies," *Journal of Management Studies* 40:8, 1895–1918.

Coppola, F. F. (Director) (1972, 1974, 1990) *The Godfather: Parts I, II, and III* [Motion pictures]. United States: Paramount.

Coppola, F. F. (Director) (1974) *The Conversation* [Motion picture]. United States: Paramount.

Corman, S. R., and Poole, M. S. (2000) *Perspectives on Organizational Communication: Finding Common Ground,* New York: Guilford.

Costa, P. T., Jr., and McCrae, R. R. (1999) *NEO Personality Inventory: Revised (NEO PI-R).* Retrieved from Psychological Assessment Resources, Inc. at www.parinc.com/products_search.cfm?Search=General.

Courpasson, D. (2002) "Managerial Strategies of Domination: Power in Soft Bureaucracies," pp. 324–345 in S. R. Clegg (Ed.), *Central Currents in Organization Studies II: Contemporary Trends, Volume 5,* London: Sage; originally published in *Organization Studies* (2000) 21: 141–161.

Coutu, D. (2000) "Creating the Most Frightening Company on Earth: An Interview with Andy Law of St. Luke's," *Harvard Business Review* September-October: 143–150.

Cozijnsen, A. J., Vrakkin, W. J., and Van Izerloo, M. (2000) "Success and Failure of 50 Innovation Projects in Dutch Companies," *European Journal of Innovation Management* 3:3, 150–159.

Craig, E. (2000) *Concise Routledge Encyclopedia of Philosophy,* London: Routledge.

Crozier, M. (1964) *The Bureaucratic Phenomenon,* London: Tavistock.

Crozier, M. (1976) "Comparing Structure and Comparing Games," pp. 193–207 in G. Hofstede and M. S. Kassem (Eds.), *European Contributions to Organization Theory,* Assen, Netherlands: Van Gorcum.

Crozier, M., and Friedberg, E. (1980) *Actors and Systems: The Politics of Collective Action,* translated by Arthur Goldhammer, Chicago: University of Chicago Press.

Cummings, S. (2002) *Recreating Strategy,* London: Sage.

Cyert, R. M., and March, J. G. (1963) *A Behavioral Theory of the Firm,* Englewood Cliffs, NJ: Prentice Hall.

Daft, R., and Lewin, A. Y. (1993) "Where Are the Theories for the 'New' Organizational Forms? An Editorial Essay," *Organization Science* 4: i–iv.

Dandeker, C. (1990) *Surveillance, Power and Modernity: Bureaucracy and Discipline from 1700 to the Present Day,* Cambridge: Polity.

Darwin, C. (1859) *On the Origin of Species by Means of Natural Selection, or the Preservation of Favoured Races in the Struggle for Life,* London: John Murray.

Das, T. K., and Teng, B. S. (2000) "Instabilities of Strategic Alliances: An Internal Tensions Perspective." *Organization Science* 11:1, 77–101.

Davidow, W. H., and Malone, M. A. (1992) *The Virtual Corporation: Structuring and Revitalizing the Corporation for the 21st Century,* New York: HarperCollins.

Davies, N. (1998) *Europe: A History,* New York: Harper Perennial.

Davis, M. (1959) *Kind of Blue* [Record album]. New York: Columbia.

Dawson, P. (2003) *Reshaping Change: A Processual Perspective,* London: Routledge.

Deal, T. E., and Kennedy, A. A. (1982) *Corporate Cultures: The Rites and Rituals of Corporate Life,* Reading, MA: Addison-Wesley.

Deardon, J. (Director) (1999) *Rogue Trader* [Motion picture]. United Kingdom: Newmarket Capitol, Granada Film Productions.

De Certeau, M. (1988) *The Practice of Everyday Life,* London: University of California Press.

Deci, E. L., and Ryan, R. M. (1985) *Intrinsic Motivation and Self-Determination in Human Behavior,* New York: Journal Plenum.

Deci, E. L., and Ryan, R. M. (1987) "The Support of Autonomy and the Control of Behavior," *Journal of Personality and Social Psychology* 53: 1024–1037.

De Geus, A. (1988) "Planning as Learning," *Harvard Business Review* March-April: 70–74.

De Geus, A. (1997) *The Living Company: Growth, Learning and Longevity in Business,* London: Nicholas Brealey.

Degreene, K. B. (1988) "Long-Wave Cycles of Sociotechnical Change and Innovation: A Macropsychological Perspective," *Journal of Occupational Psychology* 61:1, 7–23.

Deloitte and Touche (1998) *Informal Economic Activities in the EU,* Brussels: European Commission.

Den Hartog, D. N., and Koopman, P. L. (2001) "Leadership in Organizations," pp. 166–187 in N. Anderson, D. S. Ones, H. Kepir Sinangil, and C. Viswesvaran (Eds.), *Handbook of Industrial, Work & Organizational Psychology,* London: Sage.

Denison, D. (1990) *Corporate Culture and Organizational Effectiveness,* New York: John Wiley.

Derrida, J. (1995) *Points-Interviews 1974–1994,* Stanford, CA: Stanford University Press.

De Sanctis, G., and Monge, P. (1999) "Communication Processes for Virtual Organizations," *Organization Science* 10;6, 693–703.

De Vet, J. (1993) "Globalization and Local and Regional Competitiveness," *STI Review,* No. 13, Paris: Organization for Economic Co-operation and Development.

Diamond, J. M. (1997) *Guns, Germs, and Steel: The Fates of Human Societies,* New York: Norton.

Diawara, M. (2000) "Globalization, Development Politics and Local Knowledge," *International Sociology* 15:2, 361–372.

Dicken, P. (1992) *Global Shift: The Internationalization of Economic Activity,* London: Macmillan.

Dickens, C. (1982) *Little Dorrit,* edited with an introduction and notes by H. P. Sucksmith, Oxford: Oxford University Press.

DiMaggio, P., and Powell, W. W. (2002) "The Iron Cage Revisited: Institutional Isomorphism and Collective Rationality in Organizational Fields," pp. 324–362 in S. R. Clegg (Ed.), *Central Currents in Organization Studies I: Frameworks and Applications, Volume 3,* London: Sage; originally published in *American Journal of Sociology* (1983) 48: 147–160.

Dodgson, M. (2000) *The Management of Technological Innovation: An International and Strategic Approach,* Oxford: Oxford University Press.

Donaldson, L. (1992) "The Weick Stuff: Managing Beyond Games," *Organization Science* 3:3, 461–466.

Donaldson, L. (1996) "The Normal Science of Structural Contingency Theory," pp. 57–76 in S. R. Clegg, C. Hardy, and W. R. Nord (Eds.), *Handbook of Organization Studies,* London: Sage.

Donaldson, L. (1999) *Performance-Driven Organizational Change: The Organizational Portfolio,* London: Sage.

Donaldson, L. (2002) "Strategy and Structural Adjustment to Regain Fit and Performance: In Defence of Contingency Theory," pp. 379–389 in S. R. Clegg (Ed.), *Central Currents in Organization Studies I: Frameworks and Applications, Volume 2,* London: Sage; originally published in *Journal of Management Studies* (1987) 24: 1–24.

Donaldson, L. (2003) "Position Statement for Positivism," pp. 116–128 in R. Westwood and S. Clegg (Eds.), *Debating Organizations: Point-Counterpoint in Organization Studies,* Oxford: Blackwell.

Dostoyevsky, F. M. (1965) *The House of the Dead,* translated by Jessie Coulson, Oxford: Oxford University Press.

Drucker, P. (1998) *Management Challenges for the 21st Century,* Oxford: Butterworth-Heinemann.

Du Gay, P. (2000a) "Enterprise and Its Futures: A Response to Fournier and Grey," *Organization* 7:1, 165–183.

Du Gay, P. (2000b) *In Praise of Bureaucracy,* London: Sage.

Du Gay, P., Hall, S., Janes, L., Mackay, H., and Negus, K. (1997) *Doing Cultural Studies: Story of the Sony Walkman,* London: Sage.

Dunford, R. (1988) "Scientific Management in Australia: A Discussion Paper," *Labour and Industry* 1:3, 505–515.

Dunphy, D., Griffiths, A., Beneviste, J., and Sutton, P. (2000) *Sustainability: Corporate Challenge for the 21st Century,* Sydney: Allen & Unwin.

Dunphy, D., and Pitsis, T. S. (2003) "Leadership Wisdom," in C. Barker and R. Coye (Eds.), *The Seven Heavenly Virtues of Leadership,* Melbourne: McGraw-Hill.

Dylan, B. (1964) "The Times They Are a Changin." 'On *The Times They Are a Changin* [Record album].' United States: CBS.

Dylan, B. (1968) "All Along the Watchtower." On *John Wesley Harding* [Record album]. [Lyric copyright held by B. Feldman & Co.] United States: CBS.

Dylan, B. (1978) "The Changing of the Guard." On *Street Legal* [Record album]. [Copyright 1978 Special Rider Music] United States: CBS.

Easterby-Smith, M. (1997) "Disciplines of Organizational Learning: Contributions and Critiques," *Human Relations* 50:9, 1085–1113.

Eco, U. (1994) *The Name of the Rose,* translated by W. Weaver, New York: Harcourt Brace Jovanovich.

Edelman, M. (1964) *The Symbolic Uses of Politics,* Champaign: University of Illinois Press.

Edelman, M. (1971) *Political Language,* London: Academic Press.

Edquist, C. (2000) "Systems of Innovation Approaches: Their Emergence and Characteristics," pp. 3–37 in C. Edquist and M. McKelvey (Eds.), *Systems of Innovation: Growth, Competitiveness and Employment, Volume 1,* Cheltenham: Elgar.

Edwards, R. (1979) *Contested Terrain: The Transformation of the Workplace in the Twentieth Century,* New York: Basic Books.

Egelhoff, W. G. (1982) "Strategy and Structure in Multinational Corporations: An Information-Processing Approach," *Administrative Science Quarterly* 27:3, 435–458.

Elias, N. (1994) *The Civilizing Process: The History of Manners and State Formation and Civilization,* Oxford: Blackwell.

Emerson, R. M. (1962) "Power-Dependence Relations," *American Sociological Review* 27:1, 31–41.

Endler, N. S., and Speer, R. L. (1998) "Personality Psychology: Research Trends for 1993–1995," *Journal of Personality* 66: 621–629.

Enz, C. A. (1988) "The Role of Value Congruity in Interorganizational Power," *Administrative Science Quarterly* 33: 284–304.

Esser, J. K., and Lindoerfer, J. S. (1989) "Groupthink and the Space Shuttle Challenger Accident: Toward a Quantitative Case Analysis," *Journal of Behavioral Decision Making* 2:1, 167–177.

Etzioni, A. (1961) *A Comparative Analysis of Complex Organizations: On Power, Involvement, and Their Correlates,* New York: Free Press.

Fairtlough, G. (1994) *Creative Compartments: A Design for Future Organizations,* London: Adamantine Press.

Fayol, H. (1949) *General and Industrial Management,* London: Pittman.

Feldman, M. L., and Spratt, M. F. (1999) *Five Frogs on a Log: A CEO's Field Guide to Accelerating the Transition in Mergers, Acquisitions, and Gut Wrenching Change,* New York: HarperCollins.

Fenton, E. M., and Pettigrew, A. (2000) "Theoretical Perspectives on New Forms of Organizing," pp. 1–46 in A. M. Pettigrew and E. M. Fenton (Eds.), *The Innovating Organization,* London: Sage.

Fenwick, G., and Neal, D. (2001) "Effect of Gender Composition on Group Performance," *Gender, Work and Organization* 8:2, 205–225.

Fiedler, F. E. (1964) *A Theory of Leadership Effectiveness,* New York: McGraw-Hill.

Fligstein, N. (2002) "The Spread of the Multidivisional Form Among Large Firms, 1919–1979," pp. 343–364 in S. R. Clegg (Ed.), *Central Currents in Organization Studies I: Frameworks and Applications, Volume 4,* London: Sage; originally published in *American Sociological Review* 50:3, 377–391.

Florida, R. (2000) *The Rise of the Creative Class: And How It's Transforming Work, Leisure, Community and Everyday Life,* New York: Basic Books.

Flyvbjerg, B. (1998) *Rationality and Power: Democracy in Practice,* Chicago: University of Chicago Press.

Flyvbjerg, B. (2001) *Making Social Science Matter: Why Social Inquiry Fails and How It Can Succeed Again,* Cambridge: Cambridge University Press.

Foley, J. (Director) (1992) *Glengarry Glen Ross* [Motion picture]. United States: New Line.

Follett, M. P. (1918) *The New State: Group Organization, the Solution for Popular Government,* New York: Longman, Green.

Follett, M. P. (1924) *Creative Experience,* New York: Longman, Green.

Follett, M. P. (1941) *Dynamic Administration: The Collected Papers of Mary Parker Follett,* edited by H. C. Metcalf and L. Urwick, New York: Harper & Bros.

Forman, M. (Director) (1975) *One Flew Over the Cuckoo's Nest* [Motion picture]. United States: United Artists.

Foss, N. (Ed.) (1997) *Resources, Firms and Strategies: A Reader in the Resource-Based Perspective,* Oxford: Oxford University Press.

Foucault, M. (1979) *Discipline and Punish,* Harmondsworth: Penguin.

Foucault, M. (1983) "The Subject and Power: Afterword," pp. 208–226 in H. Dreyfus and P. Rabinow (Eds.), *Michel Foucault: Beyond Structuralism and Hermeneutics,* Brighton: Harvester.

Fox, A. (1974) *Beyond Contract: Work, Power and Trust Relations,* London: Faber & Faber.

Fox, E. M. (1968) "Mary Parker Follett: The Enduring Contribution," *Public Administration Review* 28:6, 520–529.

Frank, A., and Brownell, J. (1989) *Organizational Communication and Behaviour: Communicating to Improve Performance,* New York: Dryden.

Frears, S. (Director) (2000) *High Fidelity* [Motion picture]. United States: Buena Vista.

Frears, S. (Director) (2003) *Dirty Pretty Things* [Motion picture]. United States: Miramax.

French, J. P. R., and Raven, B. (1968) "The Bases of Social Power," pp. 150–167 in D. Cartwright and A. Zander (Eds.), *Group Dynamics,* New York: Harper & Row.

Freud, S. (1935) *A General Introduction to Psychoanalysis,* New York: Carlton House.

Friedman, A. (1977) "Responsible Autonomy Versus Direct Control Over the Labour Process," *Capital and Class* 1: 43–57.

Friedman, A. (1990) "Managerial Strategies, Activities, Techniques and Technology: Towards a Complex Theory of the Labour Process," in D. Knights and H. Willmott (Eds.), *Labour Process Theory,* London: Macmillan.

Friedman, G. (1955) *Industrial Society: The Emergence of the Human Problems of Automation,* New York: Free Press.

Friedman, T. (1999) *The Lexus and the Olive Tree,* London: HarperCollins.

Frost, P., Dutton, J., Worline, M., and Wilson, A. (2000) "Narratives of Compassion in Organizations," pp. 25–45 in S. Fineman (Ed.), *Emotion in Organizations,* London: Sage.

Frost, P., and Egri, C. (2002) "The Political Process of Innovation," pp. 103–161 in S. R. Clegg (Ed.), *Central Currents in Organization Studies II: Contemporary Trends, Volume 5,* London: Sage; originally published in *Research in Organizational Behaviour* (1991) 13: 229–295.

Frost, P. J. (2003) *Toxic Emotions at Work: How Compassionate Managers Handle Pain and Conflict,* Cambridge, MA: Harvard Business School Press.

Frost, P. J., and Robinson, S. L. (1999) "The Toxic Handler: Organizational Hero and Casualty," *Harvard Business Review* July-August: 96–106.

Fulk, J., and DeSanctis, G. (2002) "Electronic Communication and Changing Organization Forms," pp. 278–289 in S. R. Clegg (Ed.), *Central Currents in Organization Studies II: Contemporary Trends, Volume 2,* London: Sage; originally published in *Organization Science* (1995) 6: 337–349.

Fulop, L., and Rifkin, W. (1999) "Management Knowledge and Learning," pp. 14–47 in L. Fulop and S. Linstead (Eds.), *Management: A Critical Text,* South Yarra, Victoria, Australia: Macmillan.

Gabriel, Y., Fineman, S., and Sims, D. (2000) *Organizing and Organizations,* London: Sage.

Gagliardi, P. (1990) "Artifacts as Pathways and Remains of Organizational Life," pp. 3–38 in P. Gagliardi (Ed.), *Symbols and Artifacts: Views of the Corporate Landscape,* Berlin: de Gruyter.

Galbraith, J. K. (1969) *The Affluent Society,* Boston: Houghton Mifflin.

Gallery of the Open Frontier (2003) Lincoln: University of Nebraska Press E-editions.

Gambetta, D. (Ed.) (1988) *Trust: Making and Breaking Co-operative Relations,* Oxford: Blackwell.

Gandz, J., and Murray, V. V. (1980) "The Experience of Workplace Politics," *Academy of Management Journal* 23:2, 237–251.

Garrick, J., and Clegg, S. R. (2001) "Stressed-Out Knowledge Workers in Performative Times: A Postmodern Take on Project-Based Learning," *Management Learning* 32:1, 119–134.

George, J., and Jones, G. (2001) *Understanding and Managing Organizational Behavior,* Englewood Cliffs, NJ: Prentice Hall.

George, J. M. (1992) "The Role of Personality in Organizational Life: Issues and Evidence," *Journal of Management* 18:2, 185–213.

Georgopoulos, B. S., Mahoney, G. M., and Jones, N. W. (1957) "A Path Goal Approach to Productivity" *Journal of Applied Psychology* 41: 345–353.

Gersick, C. J. G. (1988) "Time and Transition in Work Teams: Toward a New Model of Group Development," *Academy of Management Journal* 31:1, 9–41.

Gersick, C. J. G. (1989) "Marking Time: Predictable Transitions in Task Groups," *Academy of Management Journal* 32:2, 274–309.

Gersick, C. J. G. (1994) "Pacing Strategic Change: The Case of a New Venture," *Academy of Management Journal* 37:1, 9–45.

Ghoshal, S., and Bartlett, C. A. (1997) *The Individualized Corporation: A Fundamentally New Approach to Management: Great Companies Are Defined by Purpose, Process, and People,* New York: HarperBusiness.

Giddens, A. (2000) *Runaway World: How Globalization Is Reshaping Our Lives,* London: Routledge.

Gilliam, T. (Director) (1985) *Brazil* [Motion picture]. United Kingdom: Universal.

Global Exchange Fair Trade Store (2004). *Documentary Films.* Retrieved from http://store.globalexchange.org/tapes.html.

Glover, S., Bumpus, M., Sharp, G., and Munchus, G. (2002) "Gender Differences in Ethical Decision Making," *Women in Management Review* 17:5, 217–227.

Goffman, E. (1961) *Asylums,* Harmondsworth, UK: Penguin.

Goldman, S. L., Nagel, R. N., and Preiss, K. (1995) *Agile Competitors and Virtual Organizations: Strategies for Enriching the Customer,* New York: Van Nostrand Reinhold.

Goleman, D., Boyatzis, R., and McKee, A. (2002) *The New Leaders: Transforming the Art of Leadership Into the Science of Results,* London: Time-Warner.

Gordon, G., and DiTomaso, N. (1992) "Predicting Corporate Performance From Organizational Culture," *Journal of Management Studies* 29:6, 783–798.

Gordon, R. D. (2002) "Conceptualizing Leadership With Respect to Its Historical-Contextual Antecedents to Power," *Leadership Quarterly* 13: 151–167.

Gouldner, A. W. (1954) *Patterns of Industrial Bureaucracy,* New York: Free Press.

Gouldner, A. W. (2002) "Metaphysical Pathos and the Theory of Bureaucracy," pp. 367–379 in S. R. Clegg (Ed.), *Central Currents in Organization Studies I: Frameworks and Applications, Volume 1,* London: Sage; originally published in *American Political Science Review* (1955) 49: 495–507.

Graeff, C. L. (1997) "Evolution of Situational Leadership Theory: A Critical Review," *Leadership Quarterly* 8: 153–170.

Graham, G. (2002) "If You Want Honesty, Break Some Rules," *Harvard Business Review* April: 42–47.

Graham, P. (Ed.) (1995) *Mary Parker Follet—Prophet of Management: A Celebration of Writings From the 1920s,* Boston: Harvard Business School Press Classic.

Granovetter, M. (2002) "Economic Action and Social Structure: The Problem of Embeddedness," pp. 363–389 in S. R. Clegg (Ed.), *Central Currents in Organization Studies I: Frameworks and Applications, Volume 3,* London: Sage; originally published in *American Journal of Sociology* 93: 481–510.

Greenberg, J., and Baron, R. A. (2003) *Behavior in Organizations,* 8th ed., Englewood Cliffs, NJ: Prentice Hall.

Greenwood, R., and Hinings, C. R. (2002) "Understanding Radical Organizational Change: Bringing Together the Old and the New Institutionalism," pp. 120–150 in S. R. Clegg (Ed.), *Central Currents in Organization Studies I: Frameworks and Applications, Volume 4,* London: Sage; previously published in *Academy of Management Review* 21: 1022–1054.

Gregory, K. L. (1983) "Native-View Paradigms: Multiple Cultures and Culture Conflicts in Organizations," *Administrative Science Quarterly* 28: 359–376.

Gutman, H. (1977) *Work, Culture and Society in Industrializing America,* New York: Vintage.

Halbak, C. (1950) *With Faith in Their Hearts 1925–1950,* Buffalo, NY: Author.

Hall, C. S., and Lindzey, G. (1957) *Theories of Personality,* London: Wiley.

Hall, R. H., Haas, J. E., and Johnson, N. J. (1966) "An Examination of the Blau-Scott and Etzioni Typologies," *Administrative Science Quarterly* 12: 118–139.

Hamel, G. (1996) "Strategy as Revolution," *Harvard Business Review* July-August: 69–82.

Hammer, M., and Champy, J. (1993) *Reengineering the Corporation: A Manifesto for Business Revolution,* New York: HarperBusiness.

Handy, C. (1993) *Understanding Organizations,* London: Penguin.

Haney, C., Banks, C., and Zimbardo, P. (1973) "Interpersonal Dynamics in a Simulated Prison," *International Journal of Criminology and Psychology* 1: 69–97.

Hanks, P. (Ed.) (1986) *Collins Dictionary of the English Language: An Extensive Coverage of Contemporary International and Australian English,* Sydney: Collins.

Hardy, C. (1995) *Managing Strategic Action: Mobilizing Change: Concepts, Readings, and Cases,* London: Sage.

Hardy, C., and Clegg, S. R. (1999) "Some Dare Call It Power," pp. 368–387 in S. R. Clegg and C. Hardy (Eds.), *Studying Organizations: Theory and Method,* London: Sage.

Harkins, S. G., and Szymanski, K. (1989) "Social Loafing and Group Evaluation," *Journal of Personality and Social Psychology* 56:3, 934–941.

Harvey, D. (1992) *The Condition of Postmodernity,* Oxford: Blackwell.

Harvey, J. B. (1988) *The Abilene Paradox and Other Meditations on Management,* Lexington, MA: Lexington Books.

Hassard, J. (1996) "Images of Time in Work and Organization," pp. 581–598 in S. R. Clegg, C. Hardy, and W. Nord (Eds.), *Handbook of Organization Studies,* London: Sage.

Hatch, M., and Schultz, M. (2001) "Are the Strategic Stars Aligned for Your Corporate Brand?," *Harvard Business Review* February: 129–134.

Havemann, H. A. (1993) "Ghost of Managers Past: Managerial Succession and Organizational Mortality," *Academy of Management Journal* 36:4, 864–881.

Heckscher, C. (1994) "Defining the Post-Bureaucratic Type," pp. 14–62 in C. Heckscher and A. Donellon (Eds.), *The Post-Bureaucratic Organization: New Perspectives on Organizational Change,* Thousand Oaks, CA: Sage.

Hedlund, G. (1986) "The Hypermodern MNC: A Heterarchy?," *Human Resource Management* 25:1, 9–35.

Helvacioglu, B. (2000) "Globalization in the Neighbourhood: From the Nation-State to Bilkent Centre," *International Sociology* 15:2, 326–342.

Henderson, L. J., and Mayo, E. (2002) "The Effects of Social Environment," pp. 299–313 in S. R. Clegg (Ed.), *Central Currents in Organization Studies I: Frameworks and Applications, Volume 2,* London: Sage; originally published in *Journal of Industrial Hygiene and Technology* 18: 7–27.

Herman, E. (1995) *The Romance of American Psychology,* Berkeley: University of California Press.

Herman-Wurmfeld, C. (Director) (2003) *Legally Blonde 2* [Motion picture]. United States: MGM.

Hersey, P., Blanchard, K. H., and Johnson, D. (1996) *Management of Organizational Behavior: Utilizing Human Resources,* 7th ed., Upper Saddle River, NJ: Prentice Hall.

Hetrick, W. P., and Boje, H. R. (1992) "Postmodernity, Organisation and Hyperchange," *Journal of Organizational Change Management,* 5:1, 5–8.

Heyl, B. S. (2002) "The Harvard 'Pareto Circle,'" pp. 3–23 in S. R. Clegg (Ed.), *Central Currents in Organization Studies II: Contemporary Trends, Volume 2,* London: Sage; originally published in *Journal of the History of the Behavioural Sciences* (1968) 4: 316–334.

Hickson, D. J. (2002) "A Convergence in Organization Theory," pp. 380–389 in S. R. Clegg (Ed.), *Central Currents in Organization Studies II: Contemporary Trends Volume I: Contemporary Trends,* London: Sage; originally published in *Administrative Science Quarterly* 11: 224–237.

Hickson, D. J., Butler, R. J., Cray, D., Mallory, G. R., and Wilson, D. C. (1986) *Top Decisions: Strategic Decision-Making in Organizations,* San Francisco: Jossey-Bass.

Hickson, D. J., Hinings, C. R., Lee, C. A., Schneck, R. E., and Pennings, J. M. (2002) "A Strategic Contingencies Theory of Intra-Organizational Power," pp. 3–19 in S. R. Clegg (Ed.), *Central Currents in Organization Studies II: Contemporary Trends, Volume 5,* London: Sage; originally published in *Administrative Science Quarterly* (1971) 16: 216–229.

Hickson, D. J., Hinings, C. R., McMillan, C. J., and Schwitter, J. P. (1974) "The Culture-Free Context of Organization Structure: A Tri-National Comparison," *Sociology* 8: 59–80.

Hickson, D. J., McMillan, C. J., Azumi, K., and Horvath, D. (1979) "Grounds for Comparative Organization Theory: Quicksands or Hard Core?" pp. 25–41 in C. J. Lammers and D. J. Hickson (Eds.), *Organizations Alike and Unlike: International and Inter-Institutional Studies in the Sociology of Organizations,* London: Routledge & Kegan Paul.

Hilmer, F. G., and Donaldson, L. (1996) *Management Redeemed: Debunking the Fads that Undermine Corporate Performance,* New York: Free Press.

Hinings, C., Hickson, D., Pennings, J., and Schneck, R. (1974) "Structural Conditions of Intraorganizational Power," *Administrative Science Quarterly* 19:1, 22–44.

Hirschbiegel, O. (Director) (2001) *Das Experiment* [Motion picture]. Germany: Samuel Goldwyn.

Hirschhorn, L. (2002) "Campaigning for Change," *Harvard Business Review* July: 98–104.

Hirst, P., and Thompson, G. (1996) *Globalization in Question: The International Economy and the Possibilities of Governance,* Cambridge UK: Polity.

Hobsbawm, E. (1975) *The Age of Capital 1848–1875,* London: Weidenfeld & Nicholson.

Hofstede, G. (1980) *Culture's Consequences: International Differences in Work-Related Values,* London: Sage.

Hogan, D. (1978) "Education and the Making of the Chicago Working Class, 1880–1930," *Historical Education Quarterly* 18: 227–270.

Hogg, M. A. (1996) "Intragroup Processes, Group Structure and Social Identity," pp 65–93 in W. Robinson (Ed.), *Social Groups and Identities: Developing the Legacy of Henri Tajfel,* Oxford: Butterworth.

Holt, D. B. (2003) "What Becomes an Icon Most?" *Harvard Business Review* March: 43–49.

Hornsby, N. (1995) *High Fidelity,* London: Riverhead.

House, R. J. (1971) "A Path-Goal Theory of Leadership Effectiveness," *Administrative Science Quarterly* 16: 321–338.

House, R. J. (1977) "A 1976 Theory of Charismatic Leadership," pp. 189–207 in J. G. Hunt and L. L. Larson (Eds.), *Leadership: The Cutting Edge,* Carbondale: Southern Illinois University Press.

House, R. J. (1996) "Path-Goal Theory of Leadership: Lessons, Legacy, and a Reformulated Theory," *Leadership Quarterly* 7: 323–352.

House, R. J., and Mitchell, T. R. (1974) "Path-Goal Theory of Leadership," *Journal of Contemporary Business* 4: 81–97.

House, R. J., Shane, S. A., and Herold, D. M. (1996) "Rumors of the Death of Dispositional Are Vastly Exaggerated," *Academy of Management Review* 21: 203–224.

Howard, G. S. (1988) "On Putting the Person Back Into Psychological Research, pp. 207–214 in D. M. Deluca (Ed.), *Essays on Perceiving Nature: How the Humanities, Arts, and Sciences View Our World,* Honolulu: University of Hawaii Press.

Howard, R. (Director) (1995) *Apollo 13* [Motion picture]. United States: Universal.

Howitt, P. (Director) (1998) *Sliding Doors* [Motion picture]. United States: Miramax.

Hu, Y.-S. (1992) "Global or Stateless Corporations Are National Firms With International Operations," *California Management Review* Winter.

Hutton, W. (1995) *The State We're In,* London: Vintage.

International Harvester Corporation. (c. 1913) *A Brochure to Teach Polish Common Laborers the English Language,* United States: Author.

Irwin, H., and More, E. (1994) *Managing Corporate Communication,* St. Leonards, UK: Allen & Unwin.

Jackson, P. (Director) (2001–2003) *The Lord of the Rings* trilogy [Motion pictures]. United States, New Zealand: New Line.

Jacques, R. (1996) *Manufacturing the Employee: Management Knowledge from the 19th to 21st Century,* London: Sage.

Janis, I. L. (1982) *Groupthink,* Boston: Houghton Mifflin.

Jeffcut, P. (1994) "From Interpretation to Representation in Organizational Analysis: Postmodernism, Ethnography and Organisational Symbolism," *Organization Studies* 15:2, 241–274.

Jefremovas, V. (2002) *Brickyards to Graveyards: From Production to Genocide in Rwanda,* Albany: State University of New York Press.

Jermier, J., Knights, D., and Nord, W. R. (Eds.) (1994) *Resistance and Power in Organizations: Agency, Subjectivity and the Labor Process,* London: Routledge.

Jermier, J. M. (1996) "The Path-Goal Theory of Leadership: A Subtextual Analysis," *Leadership Quarterly* 7: 311–316.

Joachimsthaler, E., and Aaker, D. (1997) "Building Brands Without Mass Media," *Harvard Business Review* January-February: 39–50.

Jones, D. (Director) (1992) *The Trial* [Motion picture]. United Kingdom: Angelika.

Jones, M. (2003) "Globalization and the Organization(s) of Exclusion in Advanced Capitalism," pp. 252–270 in R. Westwood and S. R. Clegg (Eds.), *Debating Organizations: Point-Counterpoint in Organization Studies,* Oxford: Blackwell.

Joyce, J. (1977) *Portrait of the Artist as a Young Man,* St. Albans, UK: Triad.

Kafka, F. (1956) *The Trial,* London: Secker & Warburg.

Kamoche, K., Cunha, M. P. E., and Cunha, D. V. J. (Eds.) (2002) *Organizational Improvisation,* London: Routledge.

Kanter, R. M. (1984) *The Change Masters: Corporate Entrepreneurs at Work,* Sydney: Allen & Unwin.

Kanter, R. M. (1990) *When Giants Learn to Dance,* London: Unwin Hyman.

Katz, D., and Kahn, R. L. (1978) *The Social Psychology of Organizations,* 2nd ed., New York: John Wiley & Sons.

Kaufman, P. (Director) (1968) *The Right Stuff* [Motion picture]. United States: Warner Bros.

Keiser, A. (2002) "From Asceticism to Administration of Wealth: Mediaeval Monasteries and the Pitfalls of Rationalization," pp. 120–140 in S. R. Clegg (Ed.), *Central Currents in Organization Studies I: Frameworks and Applications, Volume 1,* London: Sage; originally published in *Organization Studies* (1987) 8: 103–124.

Kelman, H. C. (1973) "Violence Without Moral Restraint," *Journal of Social Issues* 29:4, 25–61.

Kerr, S., and Jermier, J. M. (1978) "Substitutes for Leadership: Their Meaning and Measurement," *Organizational Behavior and Human Performance* 22: 375–403.

Kim, L. (1998) "Crisis Construction and Organisational Learning: Capability Building in Catching-Up at Hyundai Motor," *Organization Science* 9:4, 506–521.

Kirkpatrick, S. A., and Locke, E. A. (1991) "Leadership: Do Traits Matter?" *Academy of Management Executive* 5: 48–60.

Klein, N. (2001) *No Space, No Choice, No Jobs, No Logo: Taking Aim at the Brand Bullies,* New York: Picador.

Kleist, H. v. (1997) "On the Gradual Production of Thoughts Whilst Speaking," pp. 405–409 in *Selected Writings,* London: J. M. Dent.

Knights, D. (1990) "Subjectivity, Power and the Labor Process," in D. Knights and H. Willmott (Eds.), *Labour Process Theory,* London: Macmillan.

Knights, D., and Murray, F. (1994) *Managers Divided: Organization Politics and Information Technology Management,* Chichester, UK: Wiley.

Knights, D., and Vurdubakis, T. (1994) "Foucault, Power and All That," in J. Jermier, D. Knights, and W. Nord (Eds.), *Resistance and Power in Organizations,* London: Routledge.

Knights, D., and Willmott, H. (Eds.) (1986) *Gender and the Labour Process,* Aldershot, UK: Gower.

Knights, D., and Willmott, H. (Eds.) (1988) *New Technology and the Labour Process,* London: Macmillan.

Knights, D., and Willmott, H. (1989) "Power and Subjectivity at Work: From Degradation to Subjugation in the Labour Process," *Sociology* 23:4, 535–558.

Knights, D., Willmott, H., and Collinson, D. (Eds.) (1988) *Job Redesign,* Aldershot, UK: Gower.

Kondo, D. K. (1990) *Crafting Selves: Power, Gender, and Discourses of Identity in a Japanese Workplace,* Chicago: University of Chicago Press.

Kondratieff, N. D. (1935) "The Long Waves in Economic Life," *Review of Economic Statistics* 17:6, 105–115.

Kuno, T,, and Clegg, S. R. (1998) *Transformations of Corporate Culture: Experiences of Japanese Enterprises,* Berlin and New York: de Gruyter.

Kono, T., and Clegg, S. R. (2001) *Trends in Japanese Management,* London: Palgrave.

Kotler, P. (2000) *Marketing Management,* Upper Saddle River, NJ: Prentice Hall.

Kotter, J., and Heskett, J. (1992) *Corporate Culture and Performance,* New York: Free Press.

Kouzes, J. M., and Posner, B. Z. (1995) *The Leadership Challenge: How to Keep Getting Extraordinary Things Done in Organizations,* San Francisco: Jossey-Bass.

Kramer, R. M. (2003) "The Virtues of Prudent Trust," pp. 341–355 in R. Westwood and S. R. Clegg (Eds.), *Debating Organizations: Point-Counterpoint in Organization Studies,* Oxford: Blackwell.

Kreiner, K., and Schultz, M. (1993) "Informal Collaboration in R&D: The Formation of Networks Across Organizations," *Organization Studies* 14: 189–209.

Kubrick, S. (Director) (1987) *Full Metal Jacket* [Motion picture]. United States: Warner Bros.

Lash, S., and Urry, J. (1987) *The End of Organized Capitalism,* London: Sage.

Lash, S., and Urry, J. (1994) *Economies of Signs and Space,* London: Sage.

Lean, D. (Director) (1962) *Lawrence of Arabia* [Motion picture]. United States: Columbia.

Learned, E., Christensen, C., Andrews, K., and Guth, W. (1969) *Business Policy: Text and Cases,* Homewood, IL: Irwin.

Lennon, J. (1971) "Imagine." On *Imagine* [Record album]. United States: Apple/ Northern Songs.

Lennon, J., and McCartney, P. (1967) "All You Need Is Love." On *Magical Mystery Tour: The Beatles* [Record album]. United States: Apple/Northern Songs.

Leonard, D., and Sensiper, S. (1998) "The Role of Tacit Knowledge in Group Innovation," *California Management Review* 40: 3.

Leonard-Barton, D. (1991) "Implementation as Mutual Adaptation of Technology and Organization," *Research Policy* 17: 251–267.

Leone, S. (1969) (Director) *Once Upon a Time in the West* [Motion picture]. United States, Italy: Paramount.

Levitt, B., and March, J. (1988) "Organizational Learning," *Annual Review of Sociology* 319–340.

Lewin, A. Y., Long, C. P., and Carroll, T. N. (2002) "The Coevolution of New Organizational Forms," pp. 323–347 in S. R. Clegg (Ed.), *Central Currents in Organization Studies II: Contemporary Trends: Volume 8,* London: Sage; originally published in *Organization Science* 10: 535–550.

Lewin, K. (1951) *Field Theory in Social Science: Selected Theoretical Papers,* London: Tavistock.

Likert, R. (1979) "From Production- and Employee-Centeredness to Systems 1–4," *Journal of Management* 5:2, 147–156.

Lindblom, E. (1959) "The Science of 'Muddling Through,'" *Public Administration Review* 19:2, 79–88.

Linstead, S., and Grafton-Small, R. (2002) "On Reading Organizational Culture," pp. 227–250 in S. R. Clegg (Ed.), *Central Currents in Organization Studies II: Contemporary Trends, Volume 7,* London: Sage; originally published in *Organization Studies* 13: 331–355.

Little, S., and Grieco, M. (2004) "Electronic Stepping Stones: A Mosaic Metaphor for the Production and Redistribution of Skill in Electronic Mode," Chapter 11 in S. R. Clegg and M. Kornberger (Eds.), *Space, Management and Organization Theory,* Amsterdam: Benjamins.

Littlejohn, S. (1983) *Theories of Human Communication,* 2nd ed. Belmont, CA: Wadsworth.

Littlejohn, S. (1989) *Theories of Human Communication,* Belmont, CA: Wadsworth.

Littler, C. (1982) *The Development of the Labour Process in Capitalist Societies,* London: Heinemann.

Locke, R. R. (1984) *The End of the Practical Man: Entrepreneurship and Practical Education in Germany, France and Great Britain,* London: JAI.

Lotterby, S. (Producer) (1986) *The Key* [Television series episode]. In S. Lotterby (Producer), *Yes, Prime Minister* [Television series]. United Kingdom: BBC.

Lucas, G. (Director) (1977–2002) *Star Wars* trilogy [Motion pictures]. United States: 20th Century Fox.

Lukes, S. (1974) *Power: A Radical View,* London: Macmillan.

Luketic, R. (Director) (2001) *Legally Blonde* [Motion picture]. United States: MGM/United Artists.

Luthans, F., and Avolio, B. (2003) "Authentic Leadership Development," pp. 241–258 in K. S. Cameron, J. E. Dutton, and R. E. Quinn (Eds.), *Positive Organizational Scholarship: Foundations of a New Discipline,* San Francisco: Berrett-Koehler.

Luthans, F., Luthans, K. W., Hodgetts, R. M., and Luthans, B. C. (2002) "Positive Approach to Leadership (PAL): Implication's for Today's Organizations," *Journal of Leadership Studies* 8: 3–20.

Lyon, D. (1994) *The Electronic Eye: The Rise of Surveillance Society,* Cambridge, UK: Polity.

Machiavelli, N. (1981) *The Prince,* Harmondsworth, UK: Penguin.

Maier, C. S. (1970) "Between Taylorism and Technocracy: European Ideologies and the Vision of Industrial Productivity in the 1920s," *Journal of Contemporary History* 5: 27–61.

Malone, T. W., Yates, J., and Benjamin, R. I. (1987) "Electronic Markets and Electronic Hierarchies," *Communications of the ACM* 30: 6.

Mann, M. (Director) (1999) *The Insider* [Motion picture]. United States: Touchstone.

March, J. G. (1988) "The Technology of Foolishness," pp. 253–265 in J. G. March (Ed.), *Decisions and Organizations,* Oxford: Blackwell.

March, J. G. (2002) "The Future, Disposable Organizations and the Rigidities of Imagination," pp. 266–277 in S. R. Clegg (Ed.), *Central Currents in Organization Studies II: Contemporary Trends, Volume 8,* London: Sage; originally published in *Organization* (1995) 2: 427–434.

March, J. G., and Olsen, J. (1976) *Ambiguity and Choice in Organizations,* Bergen: Universitetsforlaget.

March, J. G., and Simon, H. A. (1958) *Organizations,* New York: Wiley.

March, R. M. (1996) *Reading the Japanese Mind: The Realities Behind Their Thoughts and Actions,* Tokyo: Kodansha International.

Markoff, J. (1996) *Waves of Democracy: Social Movements and Political Change,* Thousand Oaks, CA: Pine Forge.

Marley, B. (1977) *Exodus* [Record album]. United Kingdom: Island.

Martin, J. (1992) *Culture in Organizations: Three Perspectives,* New York: Oxford University Press.

Martin, J., and Frost, P. (1996) "The Organizational Culture War Games: A Struggle for Intellectual Dominance," pp. 599–621 in S. R. Clegg, C. Hardy, and W. Nord (Eds.), *Handbook of Organization Studies,* London: Sage.

Martin, J., Knopoff, K., and Beckman, C. (1988) "An Alternative to Bureaucratic Impersonality and Emotional Labor: Bounded Emotionality at The Body Shop," *Administrative Science Quarterly* 43: 429–469.

Marx, K. (1959) *Capital, Volume 3,* Moscow: Progress.

Marx, K. (1976) *Capital, Volume 1,* London: NLB/Penguin.

Maslow, A. (1933) "Food Preferences of Primates," *Journal of Comparative Psychology* 16: 187–197.

Maslow, A. (1965) *Eupsychian Management: A Journal,* Homewood, IL: Irwin.

Maslow, A. (1968) *Toward a Psychology of Being,* Princeton, NJ: Van Nostrand.

Maslow, A. (1970) *Motivation and Personality,* New York: Harper & Row.

Mathiason, N. (2003) "Corporate Tax Avoidance Is Costing Us All Billions," *The Observer* June 29.

Maurice, M., and Sorge, A. (2002) *Embedding Organizations,* Amsterdam: Benjamins.

Mayes, B. T., and Allen, R. W. (1977) "Towards a Definition of Organizational Politics," *Academy of Management Review* 2: 674–678.

Mayo, E. (1919) *Democracy and Freedom,* Workers' Educational Series No. 1, Melbourne: Macmillan.

Mayo, E. (1922) "Industrial Unrest and 'Nervous Breakdowns,'" *Industrial Australian and Mining Standard* 63–64.

Mayo, E. (1946) *The Human Problems of an Industrial Civilization,* Cambridge, MA: Harvard University Press.

Mayo, E. (1985) *The Psychology of Pierre Janet,* Westport, CT: Greenwood.

McCrae, R. R., and Costa, P. T., Jr. (1996) "Toward a New Generation of Personality Theories: Theoretical Contexts for the Five-Factor Model," pp. 51–87 in J. S. Wiggins (Ed.), *The Five-Factor Model of Personality: Theoretical Perspectives,* New York: Guilford.

McEwan, I. (2002) *Atonement,* Toronto: Vintage Canada.

McGregor, D. (1960) *The Human Side of Enterprise,* New York: McGraw-Hill.

McKenna, R. (1991) "Marketing Is Everything," *Harvard Business Review,* January–February: 65–79.

McKinlay, A., and Starkey, K. (1997) *Foucault, Management and Organization Theory: From Panopticon to Technologies of Self,* London: Sage.

McLuhan, M. (1964) *Understanding Media: The Extensions of Man,* New York: McGraw-Hill.

McNay, L. (1994) *Foucault: A Critical Introduction,* Cambridge, UK: Polity.

McShane, S. L., and Von Glinow, M. A. (2000) *Organizational Behavior,* Boston: McGraw-Hill.

Meiksins, P. F. (2002) "Scientific Management and Class Relations," pp. 192–221 in S. R. Clegg (Ed.), *Central Currents in Organization Studies I: Frameworks and Applications, Volume I,* London: Sage; originally published in *Theory and Society* (1984) 13: 177–209.

Mereu, I. (1979) *Storia dell'intoleranz in Europa,* Milan: Bompiani.

Merton, R. K. (2002) "Bureaucratic Structure and Personality," pp. 357–366 in S. R. Clegg (Ed.), *Central Currents in Organization Studies I: Frameworks and Applications, Volume 1,* London: Sage; originally published in *Social Forces* 18: 560–568.

Meyer, J. W. (2000) "Globalization: Sources and Effects on National States and Societies," *International Sociology* 15:2, 233–248.

Meyer, J. W., and Rowan, B. (2002) "Institutionalised Organizations: Formal Structures as Myth and Ceremony," pp. 253–273 in S. R. Clegg (Ed.), *Central Currents in Organization Studies I: Frameworks and Applications, Volume 3,* London: Sage; originally published in *American Journal of Sociology* (1977–1978) 83: 340–363.

Meyerson, D. (1991) "'Normal' Ambiguity? A Glimpse of an Occupational Culture," pp. 131–144 in P. Frost, L. Moore, C. Louis, C. Lundberg, and J. Martin (Eds.), *Reframing Organizational Culture,* Newbury Park, CA: Sage.

Miles, R. E., Snow, C. C., Matthews J. A., and Coleman, H. J. (1997) "Organizing in the Knowledge Area: Anticipating the Cellular Form," *Academy of Management Executive* 11:4, 7–20.

Milgram, S. (1971) *The Individual in a Social World,* Reading, MA: Addison-Wesley.

Milgram, S. (1974) *Obedience to Authority,* New York: Harper-Collins.

Mill, J. S. (1962) *Utilitarianism: On Liberty—Essay on Bentham, Together With Writings of Jeremy Bentham and John Austin,* edited with an introduction by Mary Warnock, London: Collins.

Miller, P., and O'Leary, T. (2002) "Hierarchies and American Ideals, 1900–1940," pp. 192–221 in S. R. Clegg (Ed.), *Central Currents in Organization Studies I: Frameworks and Applications, Volume I,* London: Sage; originally published in *Academy of Management Review* (1989) 14: 250–265.

Mills, A. J. (1996) "Corporate Image, Gendered Subjects and the Company Newsletter: The Changing Face of British Airways," pp. 191–211 in G. Palmer and S. Clegg (Eds.), *Constituting Management: Markets, Meanings and Identities,* Berlin: de Gruyter.

Mills, C. W. (2002) "Situated Actions and Vocabularies of Motive," pp. 183–192 in S. R. Clegg (Ed.), *Central Currents in Organization Studies II: Contemporary Trends, Volume 6,* London: Sage; originally published in *American Sociological Review* 5: 904–913.

Mindlin, S. E., and Aldrich, H. (2002) "Interorganizational Dependence: A Review of the Concept and Reexamination of the Findings of the Aston Group," pp. 367–378 in S. R. Clegg (Ed.), *Central Currents in Organization Studies I: Frameworks and Applications, Volume 2,* London: Sage; originally published in *Administrative Science Quarterly* (1975) 20: 382–392.

Mintzberg, H. (1973) *The Nature of Managerial Work,* New York: Harper & Row.

Mintzberg, H. (1981) "Organizational Design, Fashion or Fit?" *Harvard Business Review* 59:1, 103–116.

Mintzberg, H. (1983a) *Power In and Around Organizations,* Englewood Cliffs, NJ: Prentice Hall.

Mintzberg, H. (1983b) *Structure in Fives: Designing Effective Organizations,* Englewood Cliffs, NJ: Prentice Hall.

Mintzberg, H. (1984) "Power and Organizational Life Cycles," *Academy of Management Review* 9:2, 207–224.

Mintzberg, H. (1989) *Mintzberg on Management: Inside Our Strange World of Organizations,* New York: Free Press.

Mintzberg, H. (1990) "The Design School: Reconsidering the Basic Premises of Strategic Management," *Strategic Management Journal* 11: 171–195.

Mintzberg, H. (1994) *The Rise and Fall of Strategic Management,* New York: Prentice Hall.

Mintzberg, H. (1998) "Five P's for Strategy," pp. 10–17 in H. Mintzberg and B. Quinn (Eds.), *Readings in the Strategic Process,* Englewood Cliffs, NJ: Prentice Hall.

Mintzberg, H. (2002) "The Organization as a Political Arena," pp. 50–69 in S. R. Clegg (Ed.), *Central Currents in Organization Studies II: Contemporary Trends, Volume 5,*

London: Sage; originally published in *International Studies of Management and Organizations* (1975) 1: 78–87; 20: 382–392.

Mintzberg, H., Ahlstrand, B., and Lampe, J. (1998) *Strategy Safari: A Guided Tour Through the Wilds of Strategic Management,* New York: Free Press.

Mitchell, C. (2002) "Selling the Brand Inside," *Harvard Business Review* January: 99–105.

Moggach, D. (2000) *Tulip Fever,* New York: Random House.

Moghadam, V. M. (1999) "Gender and Globalization: Female Labour and Women's Mobilization," *Journal of World-Systems Research* 5:2, 367–388.

Monte, C. F. (1991) *Beneath the Mask: An Introduction to Theories of Personality,* Fort Worth, TX: Holt, Rinehart & Winston.

Moore, M. (Director) (2002) *Bowling for Columbine* [Motion picture]. United States: United Artists.

Morgan, G. (1985) *Images of Organizations,* London: Sage.

Morgan, G. (1989) *Creative Organization Theory: A Resource Book,* London: Sage.

Morgan, S. L. (2003) "China's Encounter With Scientific Management in the 1920–30s." Paper presented in the panel *The Genesis of Modern Management in China,* The Business History Conference and the European Business History Association Joint Meeting on the Theme of Regions, Nations and Globalization, Lowell, MA, June 26–28. Available at www.thebhc.org/annmeet/morgan.pdf.

Morin, E. (1984) "El error de subestimar el error," pp. 273–289 in E. Morin, *Ciencia con Consciencia,* Barcelona: Anthropos.

Mostow, J. (Director) (2003) *Terminator 3: Rise of the Machines* [Motion picture]. United States: Warner Bros.

Mouzelis, N. (1967) *Organization and Bureaucracy,* London: Routledge & Kegan Paul.

Mowday, R. T. (1991) "Equity Theory Predictions of Behavior in Organizations," in R. M. Steers and L. W. Porter (Eds.), *Motivation and Work Behavior,* New York: McGraw-Hill.

Mumby, D. (1987) "The Political Function of the Narrative in Organizations," *Communication Monograph* 54: 113–127.

Mumby, D. K., and Stohl, C. (1991) "Power and Discourse in Organizational Studies: Absence and the Dialectic of Control," *Discourse and Society* 2: 313–332.

Myers, D. G. (2001) *Psychology,* 6th ed., New York: Woth.

Nelson, R. R., and Rosenberg, N. (1993) "Technical Innovation and National Systems," in R. R. Nelson (Ed.), *National Systems of Innovation: A Comparative Analysis,* Oxford: Oxford University Press.

Niccol, A. (Director) (1997) *Gattaca* [Motion picture]. United States: Columbia.

Nicholson, N. (2000) *Executive Instinct: Managing the Human Animal in the Information Age,* New York: Crown Business Books.

Nietzsche, F. (1974) *The Joyful Wisdom,* New York: Gordon Press.

Nohria, N., and Ghohsal, S. (1997) *The Differentiated Network: Organizing Multinational Corporations for Value Creation,* San Francisco: Jossey-Bass.

Nonaka, I. (1991) *The Knowledge-Creating Company,* Boston: Harvard Business School Press.

Nonaka, I., and Takeuchi, H. (1995) *The Knowledge-Creating Company: How Japanese Companies Create the Dynamics of Innovation,* Oxford: Oxford University Press.

Nystrom, P. C. (1978) "Managers and the High-High Leader Behavior Myth," *Academy of Management Journal* 19: 325–331.

O'Connor, E. S. (1999) "The Politics of Management Thought: A Case Study of Harvard Business School and the Human Relations School," *Academy of Management Review* 24:1, 117–131.

O'Connor, E. S. (2002) "Minding the Workers: The Meaning of 'Human' and 'Human Relations' in Elton Mayo," pp. 333–356 in S. R. Clegg (Ed.), *Central Currents in Organization Studies I: Frameworks and Applications, Volume 1,* London: Sage; originally published in *Organization* (1999) 6: 223–246.

The Odyssey Group (2004) Retrieved from www.geocities.com/the_odyssey_group/index.html.

Ohmae, K. (1990) *The Borderless World,* London: Collins.

Olins, W. (2000) "How Brands Are Taking Over the Corporation," pp. 51–65 in M. Schultz, M. Hatch, and M. Larsen (Eds.), *The Expressive Organization: Linking Identity, Reputation, and the Corporate Brand,* Oxford and New York: Oxford University Press.

Oliver, C. (1990) "Determinants of Interorganizational Relationships," *Academy of Management Review* 15:2, 241–265.

Olodum (1997) *Best of Olodum* [Record album]. Brazil: Conti, GEL Continental Records.

Olodum (2002) *Olodum Pela Vidafilhos do sol* [Record album]. Brazil: Continental Warner Music Brasil.

Olodum (2004) Official Web site. Retrieved from www.olodum.com.br.

Ordiorne, G. (1981) *The Change Resisters,* Englewood Cliffs, NJ: Prentice Hall.

Organization for Economic Co-operation and Development (OECD) (1996) *Globalization of Industry: Overview and Sector Reports,* Paris: Author.

Orsburn, J. D., Moran, L., Musselwhite, E., and Zenger, J. H. (1990) *Self-Directed Work Teams: The New American Challenge,* Homewood, IL: Irwin.

Orwell, G. (1945) *Animal Farm,* Harmondsworth, UK: Penguin.

Orwell, G. (1949) *Nineteen Eighty-Four: A Novel,* Harmondsworth, UK: Penguin.

O'Toole, J. (1996) *Leading Change: The Argument for Values-Based Leadership,* New York: Ballantine Books.

Ouchi, W. G. (1980) "Markets, Bureaucracies and Clans," *Administrative Science Quarterly* 25: 129–141.

Oxfam (2004). Oxfam Community Aid Abroad. *The NikeWatch Campai.* Retrieved from www.caa.org.au/campaigns/nike.

Palmer, I., and Dunford, R. (2001) "Design and Form: Organizational," pp. 3535–3538 in N. J. Smelser and P. B. Bates (Eds.), *International Encyclopaedia of the Social and Behavioral Sciences,* Oxford: Elsevier.

Parker, B. (2003) "The Disorganization of Inclusion: Globalization as Process," pp. 234–251 in R. Westwood and S. R. Clegg (Eds.), *Debating Organizations: Point-Counterpoint in Organization Studies,* Oxford: Blackwell.

Parker, M. (1992) "Post-Modern Organizations or Postmodern Organization Theory?" *Organization Studies* 13:1, 1–17.

Parker, M. (2000a) *Organizational Culture and Identity: Unity and Division at Work,* London: Sage.

Parker, M. (2000b) "The Sociology of Organizations and the Organization of Sociology: Some Reflections on the Making of a Division of Labour," *Sociological Review* 48:1, 124–146.

Parkinson, C. N. (1957) *Parkinson's Law,* Boston: Houghton Mifflin.

Parsons, A., P.A. (2003) *Guardian Unlimited.* Retrieved from www.guardian.co.uk/gallery/image/0,8543,-11304207079,00.html.

Parsons, T. (1966) *Societies: Evolutionary and Comparative Perspectives,* Englewood Cliffs, NJ: Prentice Hall.

Pascale, R. (1999) "Surfing the Edge of Chaos," *Sloan Management Review* 40:3, 83–94.

Pascale, R., and Athos, A. (1981) *The Art of Japanese Management,* New York: Warner.

Patten, C. (1998) *East and West: The Last Governor of Hong Kong on Power, Freedom and the Future,* London: Macmillan.

Payne, R. L. (2000) "Eupsychian Management and the Millennium," *Journal of Managerial Psychology* 15:3, 219–226.

Pearson, K. (1982a) "Surfies and Clubbies," *Australian and New Zealand Journal of Sociology* 18:1, 5–16.

Pearson, K. (1982b) "Surfing: Conflict, Stereotypes and Masculinity," *Australian and New Zealand Journal of Sociology* 18:2, 117–136.

Pennings, J. M. (2002) "Structural Contingency Theory: A Reappraisal," pp. 3–41 in S. R. Clegg (Ed.), *Central Currents in Organization Studies I: Frameworks and Applications, Volume 3,* London: Sage; originally published in *Research in Organizational Behaviour* (1992) 14: 267–309.

Penrose, E. (1959) *The Theory of the Growth of the Firm,* Oxford: Basil Blackwell.

Perrow, C. (1972) *The Radical Attack on Business,* New York: Harcourt Brace.

Perrow, C. (2002) "A Framework for the Comparative Analysis of Organizations," pp. 197–215 in S. R. Clegg (Ed.), *Central Currents in Organization Studies I: Frameworks and Applications, Volume 2,* London: Sage; originally published in *American Sociological Review* (1967) 32: 194–208.

Peters, T. (1988) *Thriving on Chaos: Handbook for a Management Revolution,* New York: Knopf.

Peters, T. (1994) *The Pursuit of Wow! Every Person's Guide to Topsy Turvey Times,* New York: Random House.

Peters, T., and Waterman, R. (1982) *In Search of Excellence: Lessons From America's Best-Run Companies,* Sydney: Harper & Row.

Petrella, R. (1996) "Globalization and Internationalization: The Dynamics of the Emerging World Order," in R. Boyer and D. Drache (Eds.), *States Against Markets: The Limits of Globalization,* London: Routledge.

Pettigrew, A. (1973) *The Politics of Organizational Decision-Making,* London: Tavistock.

Pettigrew, A. (1985) *Awakening Giant: Continuity and Change in ICI,* Oxford: Blackwell.

Pettigrew, A. (1990) "Longitudinal Field Research on Change: Theory and Practice," *Organization Science* 1:3, 267–292.

Pettigrew, A. (1997) "What Is Processual Analysis?" *Scandinavian Journal of Management* 13:4, 337–348.

Pettigrew, A. (2002) "Strategy Formulation as a Political Process," pp. 43–49 in S. R. Clegg (Ed.), *Central Currents in Organization Studies II: Contemporary Trends, Volume 5,* London: Sage; originally published in *International Studies of Management and Organization* (1977) 1: 78–87.

Pettigrew, A. (2003) *Innovative Forms of Organizing,* London: Sage.

Pettigrew, A. M., and Fenton, E. M. (2000) *The Innovating Organization,* London: Sage.

Pettigrew, A., Ferlie, E., and McKee, L. (1992) *Shaping Strategic Change: Making Change in Large Organizations: The Case of the National Health Service,* London: Sage.

Pettigrew, A., Massini, S., and Numagami, T. (2002) "Innovative Forms of Organizing in Europe and Japan," pp. 323–347 in S. R. Clegg (Ed.), *Central Currents in Organization Studies II: Contemporary Trends, Volume 8,* London: Sage; originally published in *European Management Journal* (2000) 18: 259–273.

Pettigrew, A., Thomas, H., and Whittington, R. (Eds.) (2002) *Handbook of Strategy and Management,* London: Sage.

Petty, B. (1976) *Bruce Petty's Australia—and How It Works,* Melbourne: Penguin.

Pfeffer, J. (1981) *Power in Organizations,* Marshfield, MA: Pitman.

Pfeffer, J. (1992) *Managing With Power: Politics and Influence in Organizations,* Cambridge, MA: Harvard Business School Press.

Pfeffer, J., and Salancik, G. (1978) *The External Control of Organizations: A Resource Dependence Perspective,* New York: Harper & Row.

Pfeffer, J., and Salancik, G. (2002) "The Bases and Uses of Power in Organizational Decision Making: The Case of a University," pp. 21–42 in S. R. Clegg (Ed.), *Central Currents in Organization Studies II: Contemporary Trends, Volume 5,* London: Sage; originally published in *Administrative Science Quarterly* (1974) 19: 453–473.

Plato (1968) *The Republic,* translated, with notes and an interpretive essay, by Allan Bloom, New York: Basic Books.

Podsakoff, P. M., Niehoff, B. P., MacKenzie, S. B., and Williams, M. L. (1993) "Do Substitutes for Leadership Really Substitute for Leadership? An Empirical Examination of Kerr and Jermier's Situational Leadership Model," *Organizational Behavior and Human Decision Processes* 54: 1–44.

Polanyi, M. (1962) *Personal Knowledge: Towards A Post-Critical Philosophy,* Chicago: University of Chicago Press.

Polanyi, M. (1983) *The Tacit Dimension,* Gloucester, MA: Peter Smith.

Pollard, S. (1965) *The Genesis of Modern Management: A Study of the Industrial Revolution in Great Britain,* London: Edward Arnold.

Porter, M. (1980) *Competitive Strategy: Techniques for Analyzing Industries and Competitors,* New York: Free Press.

Porter, M. (1985) *Competitive Advantage: Creating and Sustaining Superior Performance,* New York: Free Press.

Porter, M. (1990) *The Competitive Advantage of Nations,* Basingstoke, UK: Macmillan.

Porter, M. (1996) "What Is Strategy?" *Harvard Business Review* November-December: 61–78.

Poster, M. (1990) *The Mode of Information: Poststructuralism and Social Context,* Cambridge: Polity.

Powell, W. W. (1990) "Neither Market nor Hierarchy: Network Forms of Organization," *Research in Organizational Behaviour* 12: 259–336.

Powell, W. W. (2002) "Hybrid Organizational Arrangements: New Form or Transitional Development?" pp. 309–328 in S. R. Clegg (Ed.), *Central Currents in Organization Studies I: Frameworks and Applications, Volume I,* London: Sage; originally published in *California Management Review* 30: 67–87.

Prahalad, C., and Hamel, G. (1990) "The Core Competence of the Corporation," *Harvard Business Review* May-June: 94–103.

Pugh, D. S., and Hickson, D. J. (1976) *Organizational Structure in Its Context: The Aston Programme 1,* London: Saxon House.

Pugh, D. S., and Hickson, D. J. (1997) *Writers on Organizations,* Harmondsworth, UK: Penguin.

Pugh, D. S., Hickson, D. J., and Hinings, C. R. (1971) *Writers on Organizations,* Harmondsworth, UK: Penguin.

Purser, R. E., Park, C., and Montuori, A. (1995) "Limits to Anthropocentrism: Towards an Ecocentric Organization Paradigm?" *Academy of Management Review* 20:4, 1053–1089.

Radford, M. (Director) (1984) *Nineteen Eighty-Four* [Motion picture]. United States: Polygram Video.

Ramsay, H. (1977) "Cycles of Control: Workers Participation in Sociological and Historical Perspective," *Sociology* 11:3, 481–506.

Ransom, S., and Stewart, J. (1994) *Management for the Public Domain: Enabling the Learning Society,* New York: St. Martins.

Rapoport, A., and Chammah, M. (1965) *Prisoner's Dilemma,* Ann Arbor: University of Michigan Press.

Reed, P. (Director) (2003) *Down With Love* [Motion picture]. United States: 20th Century Fox.

Reich, R. B. (1991) *The Work of Nations,* Vintage Books: New York.

Reiner, R. (Director) (1992) *A Few Good Men* [Motion picture]. United States: Columbia.

Riley, P. (1983) "A Structurationist Account of Political Cultures," *Administrative Science Quarterly* 28: 414–437.

Ringland, G. (1998) *Scenario Planning: Managing for the Future,* Chichester, UK: Wiley.

Ringland, G. (2002) *Scenarios in Business,* London: John Wiley.

Ritzer, G. (1993) *The McDonaldization of Society,* Newbury Park, CA: Pine Forge.

Ritzer, G. (2004) *The Globalization of Nothing,* Thousand Oaks, CA: Pine Forge.

Robb, P. (1999) *M,* Sydney: Duffy & Snellgrove.

Robertson, R. (1992) *Globalization: Social Theory and Social Culture,* London: Sage.

Robey, D. (1981) "Computer Information Systems and Organization Structure," *Communications of the ACM* 24: 679–687.

Robins, K., and Webster, F. (1985) "'Revolutions of the Fixed Wheel': Information Technology and Social Taylorism," pp. 36–63 in P. Drummond and R. Paterson (Eds.), *Television in Transition: Papers From the First International Television Studies Conference,* London: British Film Institute.

Robson, F. (2002) "Playing Away," *Sydney Morning Herald Good Weekend,* February 15: 36–40.

Roche, E. (2001) "Words for the Wise," *Harvard Business Review* January: 26–27.

Rockart, J. F., and Short, J. E. (1991) "The Networked Organization and the Management of Interdependence," in M. S. Scott Morton (Ed.), *The Corporation of the 1990s: Information Technology and Organizational Transformation,* Oxford: Oxford University Press.

Roddick, A. (2000). *Business as Unusual,* London: Thorsons.

Roethlisberger, F. J., and Dickson, W. J. (1939) *Management and the Worker,* Cambridge, MA: Harvard University Press.

Rogers, C. (1967) *On Becoming a Person: A Therapist's View of Psychotherapy,* London: Constable.

Rogers, C. (1991) "Barriers and Gateways to Communication," *Harvard Business Review* November-December: 105–111.

Rohan, M. J. (2000) "A Rose by Any Name? The Values Construct," *Personality and Social Psychology Review* 4: 255–277.

Rokeach, M. R. (1968) *Beliefs, Attitudes and Values,* San Francisco: Jossey-Bass.

Rokeach, M. R. (1973) *The Nature of Human Values,* New York: Free Press.

Romme, A. G. L. (2002) "Domination, Self-Determination and Circular Organizing," pp. 273–303 in S. R. Clegg (Ed.), *Central Currents in Organization Studies II: Contemporary Trends, Volume 5,* London: Sage; originally published in *Organization Studies* 20: 801–831.

Rose, M. (1975) *Industrial Behaviour: Theoretical Developments Since Taylor,* London: Allen Lane.

Rosen, M. (2002) "Breakfast at Spiro's: Dramaturgy and Dominance," pp. 334–352 in S. R. Clegg (Ed.), *Central Currents in Organization Studies II: Contemporary Trends, Volume 7,* London: Sage; originally published in *Journal of Management* (1985) 11: 31–48.

Rotter, J. B. (1966) "Generalised Expectancies for Internal vs. External Control of Reinforcement" *Psychological Monographs* 80: 1–28.

Rousseau, D. M. (1996) "Changing the Deal While Keeping People," *Academy of Management Executive* 10: 50–56.

Rubery, J. (1978) "Structured Labour Markets, Worker Organisation and Low Pay," *Cambridge Journal of Economics* 2: 17–36.

Ryan, R. M., and Deci, E. L. (2000) "Self-Determination Theory and the Facilitation of Intrinsic Motivation, Social Development, and Well Being," *American Psychologist* 55: 68–78.

Sagiv, L., and Schwartz, S. H. (2002) "National Values and Organizational Practices," in N. M. Ashkenasy, C. P. M. Wilderom, and M. F. Peterson (Eds.), *The Handbook of Organizational Culture and Climate,* London: Sage.

Sanchez, E., and Myrick, D. (Directors) (1999) *The Blair Witch Project* [Motion picture]. United States: Artisan Entertainment.

Santayana, G. (1997–2004) *The Elements and Functions of Poetry* [part of Online Poetry Classroom Web site]. Retrieved April 17, 2004, from www.onlinepoetry-classroom.org/poems/Prose.cfm?prmID210.

Sassen, S. (1998) *Globalization and Its Discontents,* New York: New Press.

Schein, E. (1997) *Organizational Culture and Leadership,* San Francisco: Jossey-Bass.

Schein, E. (2002) "Organizational Culture," pp. 196–205 in S. R. Clegg (Ed.), *Central Currents in Organization Studies II: Contemporary Trends, Volume 7,* London: Sage; originally published in *American Psychologist* (1990) 45: 109–119.

Schultz, M., Hatch, M. J., and Larsen, M. H. (Eds.) (2000) *The Expressive Organization: Linking Identity, Reputation and the Corporate Brand,* Oxford: Oxford University Press.

Schumpeter, J. S. (1934) *The Theory of Economic Development: An Enquiry Into Profits, Capital, Credit, Interest and the Business Cycle,* translated from the German by Redvers Opie, Cambridge, MA: Harvard University Press.

Schwartz, S. (1992) "Universals in the Content and Structure of Values: Theoretical Advances and Empirical Tests in 20 Countries," pp. 1–65 in M. P. Zanna (Ed.), *Advances in Experimental Social Psychology, Volume 24,* San Diego, CA: Academic Press.

Schwartz, S. (1994) "Are There Universal Aspects in the Structure and Contents of Human Values?" *Journal of Social Issues* 50: 1–18.

Schwartz, S. (1996) "Value Priorities and Behavior: Applying a Theory of Integrated Value Systems," pp. 1–24 in C. Seligman, J. M. Olson, and M. P. Zanna (Eds.), *The Ontario Symposium: The Psychology of Values, Volume 8,* Mahwah, NJ: Erlbaum.

Scott, J. C. (1990) *Domination and the Arts of Resistance: Hidden Transcripts,* New Haven, CT: Yale University Press.

Scott, R. (Director) (1982) *Blade Runner* [Motion picture]. United States: Warner Bros.

Scott, R. (Director) (2000) *Gladiator* [Motion picture]. United States: Dreamworks SKG.

Scott, W. R. (2002) "The Adolescence of Institutional Theory," pp. 390–410 in S. R. Clegg (Ed.), *Central Currents in Organization Studies I: Frameworks and Applications, Volume 4,* London: Sage; previously published in *Administrative Science Quarterly* 32: 493–511.

Seligman, M. E. P., and Csikszentmihalyi, M. (2000) "Positive Psychology: An Introduction," *American Psychologist* 55: 5–14.

Selznick, P. (1943) "An Approach to a Theory of Bureaucracy," *American Sociological Review* 8:47–54.

Selznick, P. (1949) *TVA and the Grass Roots: A Study in the Sociology of Formal Organization,* Berkeley: University of California Press.

Senge, P. (1990) *The Fifth Discipline: The Art and Practice of the Learning Organization,* New York: Doubleday.

Sewell, G. (2002) "The Discipline of Teams: The Control of Team-Based Industrial Work Through Electronic and Peer Surveillance," pp. 211–245 in S. R. Clegg (Ed.), *Central Currents in Organization Studies II: Contemporary Trends, Volume 5,* London: Sage; originally published in *Administrative Science Quarterly* (1998) 43: 397–428.

Seybold, P. (2001) "Get Inside the Lives of Your Customers," *Harvard Business Review* May: 81–89.

Shaw, G. (2000) "Planning and Communicating Using Stories," pp. 182–195 in M. Schultz, M. Hatch, and M. Larsen (Eds.), *The Expressive Organization: Linking Identity, Reputation, and the Corporate Brand,* Oxford and New York: Oxford University Press.

Sheehan, P. (2004) "A Rising Force in Capital and Culture," *Sydney Morning Herald Good Weekend,* January 3–4: 21.

Shenhav, Y. (1999) *Manufacturing Rationality: The Engineering Foundations of the Managerial Revolution,* Oxford: Oxford University Press.

Sievers, B. (2003) "Fool'd With Hope, Men Favour the Deceit, or, Can We Trust in Trust?" pp. 356–367 in R. Westwood and S. R. Clegg (Eds.), *Debating Organizations: Point-Counterpoint in Organization Studies,* Oxford: Blackwell.

Simon, P. (1990) *The Rhythm of the Saints* [CD]. United States: Warner Bros. Records.

Singer, P. (1976) *Animal Liberation: A New Ethics for Our Treatment of Animals,* London: Cape.

Sklair, L. (1998) "Social Movements and Global Capitalism," in F. Jameson and M. Miyoshi (Eds.), *Cultures of Globalization,* Durham, NC: Duke University Press.

Sklair, L. (1999) "Competing Conceptions of Globalization," *Journal of World-Systems Research* 5:2, 143–162.

Smircich, L. (2002) "Concepts of Culture and Organizational Analysis," pp. 152–174 in S. R. Clegg (Ed.), *Central Currents in Organization Studies II: Contemporary Trends, Volume 7,* London: Sage; originally published in *Administrative Science Quarterly* (1983) 28: 393–413.

Smith, A. (1961) *An Enquiry Into the Nature and Causes of the Wealth of Nations,* Indianapolis, IN: Bobbs-Merrill [Original work published 1776].

Spector, P. (1982) "Behaviour in Organizations as a Function of Employee's Locus of Control," *Psychological Bulletin* 91: 482–497.

Spybey, T. (1984) "Traditional and Professional Frames of Meaning for Managers," *Sociology* 18:4, 550–562.

Spybey, T. (1996) *Globalization and World Society*, Cambridge: Polity.

Stacey, R. (1999) "Creative Organizations: The Relevance of Chaos and Psychodynamic Systems," pp. 61–88 in R. Purser and A. Montuori (Eds.), *Social Creativity*, Cresskill, NJ: Hampton.

Starbuck, W. (1983) "Organizations as Action Generators," *American Sociological Review* 48: 91–102.

Stark, D. (2002) "Class Struggle and the Transformation of the Labour Process: A Relational Approach," pp. 84–119 in S. R. Clegg (Ed.), *Central Currents in Organization Studies I: Frameworks and Applications, Volume 1*, London: Sage; originally published in *Theory and Society* (1980) 9: 89–130.

Stein, M. (2000) "The Risk Taker as Shadow: A Psychoanalytic View of the Collapse of Barings Bank," *Journal of Management Studies* 37:8, 1215–1230.

Stiglitz, J. (2002) *Globalization and Its Discontents*, Victoria, British Columbia: Allen Lane, Penguin.

Stone, O. (Director) (1986) *Platoon* [Motion picture]. United States: Orion.

Stone, O. (Director) (1987) *Wall Street* [Motion picture]. United States: Fox.

Storper, M., and Scott, A. J. (1993) *The Wealth of Regions: Market Forces and Policy Imperatives in Local and Global Context*, Lewis Centre for Regional Policy Studies, Working Paper No. 7, Los Angeles: University of California Press.

Stranglers (1977) "No More Heroes." On *No More Heroes* [Record album], London: United Artists Records Limited.

Strauss, A., Schatzman, L., Ehrlich, D., Bucher, R., and Sabshin, M. (1963) "The Hospital and Its Negotiated Order," in E. Friedmann (Ed.), *The Hospital in Modern Society*, New York: Macmillan.

Sturges, J. (Director) (1963) *The Great Escape* [Motion picture]. United States: United Artists.

Sudnow, D. (1967) *Passing On: The Sociology of Dying*, Englewood Cliffs, NJ: Prentice Hall.

Swann, J., Newell, S., Scarbrough, H., and Hislop, D. (1999) "Knowledge Management and Innovation: Networks and Networking," *Journal of Knowledge Management* 3:4, 262–275.

Szabo, I., and Dobai, P. (Directors) (1984) *Colonel Redl* [Motion picture]. United States: Orion Classics.

Tallman, S., Jenkins, M., Henry, N., and Pinch, S. (2004). "Knowledge Clusters and Competitive Advantage," *Academy of Management Review*.

Tannenbaum, A. S. (1968) *Control in Organizations*, New York: McGraw-Hill.

Tarantino, Q. (Director) (1994) *Pulp Fiction* [Motion picture]. United States: Miramax.

Taylor, F. W. (1895) *A Piece Rate System*, New York: McGraw-Hill.

Taylor, F. W. (1967) *Principles of Scientific Management*, New York: Harper. (Original work published 1911)

Taylor, F. W. (1995) "Report of a Lecture by and Questions Put to Mr. F. W. Taylor: A Transcript," *Journal of Management History* 1:1, 8–32.

Ten Bos, R. (2000) *Fashion and Utopia in Management Thinking*, Amsterdam: Benjamins.

Tennyson, A. L. (1870). *Poems of Alfred Tennyson*, Boston: J. E. Tilton.

Therborn, G. (2000a) "Globalizations: Dimensions, Historical Waves, Regional Effects, Normative Governance," *International Sociology*, 15:2, 151–179.

Therborn, G. (2000b) "Introduction: From the Universal to the Global," *International Sociology* 15: 2, 149–150.

Thompson, E. P. (1965) *The Making of the English Working Class*, Harmondsworth, UK: Penguin.

Thompson, E. P. (1968) *The Making of the English Working Class,* Harmondsworth, UK: Penguin.

Thompson, J. B. (1990) *Ideology and Modern Culture,* Cambridge, UK: Polity.

Thompson, J. D. (1956) "Authority and Power in Identical Organisations," *American Journal of Sociology* 62: 290–301.

Thompson, J. D. (1967) *Organizations in Action: Social Science Bases of Administrative Theory,* New York: McGraw-Hill.

Thompson, P., and McHugh, D. (1995) *Work Organisations: A Critical Introduction,* 2nd ed., Houndmills, UK: Macmillan.

Tidd, J., Bessant, J., and Pavitt, K. (2001) *Managing Innovation: Integrating Technological, Market and Organizational Change,* Chichester, UK: Wiley.

Townley, B. (1993) "Foucault, Power/Knowledge and Its Relevance for Human Resource Management," *Academy of Management Review* 18:3, 518–545.

Townley, B. (1994) *Reframing Human Resource Management: Power, Ethics and the Subject at Work,* London: Sage.

Trahair, R. (1984) *The Human Temper: The Life and Work of Elton Mayo,* New Brunswick: Transaction Books.

Trahair, R. (2001) "George Elton Mayo," *Biographical Dictionary of Management,* Thoemmes Press. Retrieved from www.thoemmes.com.

Tran, M. (2003) "BT Confirms Plans for Indian Call Centres," *The Guardian* March 7.

Tribe, K. (1975) "Capitalism and Industrialization," *Intervention* 5: 23–27.

Turner, J. C. (1987) *Rediscovering the Social Group: A Self-Categorization Theory,* New York: Basil Blackwell.

Tyson, L. (1992) *Who's Bashing Whom? Trade Conflict in High Technology Industries,* Washington, DC: Institute for International Economics.

University of Michigan Business School (2001) *Leading in Trying Times.* Retrieved October 1, 2003, from www.bus.umich.edu/FacultyResearch/Research/TryingTimes.

Ure, A. (1835) *The Philosophy of Manufactures,* London: Charles Knight.

Urwick, L. F. (1947) *The Elements of Administration,* London: Pitman.

Van de Ven, A., Polley, D., Garud, R., and Venkataraman, S. (1999) *The Innovation Journey,* Oxford: Oxford University Press.

Van de Ven, A., and Poole, M. (1995) "Explaining Development and Change in Organizations," *Academy of Management Review* 20:3, 510–540.

Van Iterson, A., Mastenbroek, W., Newton, T., and Smith, D. (2002) *The Civilized Organization: Norbert Elias and the Future of Organization Studies,* Amsterdam: Benjamins.

Van Maanen, J. (1988) *Tales of the Field: On Writing Ethnography,* Chicago: Chicago Guides to Writing, Editing, and Publishing.

Van Maanen, J. (1991) "The Smile Factory: Work at Disneyland," pp. 58–76 in P. Frost, L. Moore, M. Louis, C. Lundberg, and J. Martin (Eds.), *Reframing Organizational Culture,* Newbury Park, CA: Sage.

Veloso, C. (1994) "Cateano Veloso Erudito: Fragmentos de Entrevista Coletiva á Imprensa Para Gideon Rosa," pp. 82–84 in N. Cerqueira (Ed.), *Pelhourino Centro Histórico de Salvador-Bahia: A Grande Restaurada,* Salvador: Fundação Culturaldo Estado da Bahia.

Villaseñor, V. (1992) *Rain of Gold,* New York: Delta.

Volberda, H. W. (2002) "Toward the Flexible Form: How to Remain Vital in Hypercompetitive Environments" pp. 298–322 in S. R. Clegg (Ed.), *Central Currents in Organization Studies II: Contemporary Studies, Volume 8,* London: Sage; originally published in *Organization Science* (1998) 7: 359–374.

Von Clausewitz, Carl (1968) *On War,* edited and with an introduction by A. Rapoport, Baltimore: Penguin.

Von Hippel, E. (1986) "Lead Users: A Source of Novel Product Concepts," *Management Science* 32: 791–805.

Von Stamm, B. (2003) *Managing Innovation, Creativity and Design,* Chichester, UK: Wiley.

Watzlawick, P., Beavin, J., and Jackson, D. (1967) *Pragmatics of Human Communication: A Study of Interactional Patterns, Pathologies, and Paradoxes,* New York: W. W. Norton.

Weber, M. (1947) *The Theory of Social and Economic Organization,* translated by T. Parsons and A. M. Henderson, with an introduction by T. Parsons, New York: Free Press.

Weber, M. (1948) *From Max Weber: Essays in Sociology,* translated, edited, and with an introduction by H. H. Gerth and C. W. Mills, London: Routledge & Kegan Paul.

Weber, M. (1976) *The Protestant Ethic and the Spirit of Capitalism,* London: Allen & Unwin.

Weber, M. (1978) *Economy and Society: An Outline of Interpretative Sociology,* Berkeley: University of California Press.

Weick, K. E. (1969) *The Social Psychology of Organizing,* 1st ed., Reading, MA: Addison-Wesley.

Weick, K. E. (1979) *The Social Psychology of Organising,* 2nd ed., Reading, MA: Addison-Wesley.

Weick, K. E. (1991) "The Vulnerable System: An Analysis of the Teneriffe Air Disaster," pp. 117–130 in P. Frost, L. Moore, C. Louis, C. Lundberg, and J. Martin (Eds.), *Reframing Organizational Culture,* Newbury Park, CA: Sage.

Weick, K. E. (1995) *Sensemaking in Organizations,* Thousand Oaks, CA: Sage.

Weick, K. E., and Westley, F. (1996) "Organizational Learning: Affirming an Oxymoron," pp. 440–458 in S. R. Clegg, C. Hardy, and W. R. Nord (Eds.), *The Handbook of Organization Studies,* London: Sage.

Weick, K. E., and Westley, F. (1999) "Organizational Learning: Affirming an Oxymoron," pp. 190–208 in S. R. Clegg, C. Hardy, and W. R. Nord (Eds.), *Managing Organizations,* London: Sage.

Weir, P. (Director) (2003) *Master and Commander: The Far Side of the World* [Motion picture]. United States: 20th Century Fox.

Weiss, B. (1981) *American Education and the European Immigrant,* Urbana: University of Illinois Press.

Weiss, L. (1997) "Globalization and the Myth of the Powerless State," *New Left Review* 225: 3–27.

Wellins, R. S., Byham, W. C., and Wilson, J. M. (1991) *Empowered Teams: Creating Self-Directed Works Groups That Improve Quality, Productivity and Participation,* San Francisco: Jossey-Bass.

Wenger, E. (1998) *Communities of Practice: Learning, Meaning and Identity,* New York: Cambridge University Press.

Wenger, E. (2002) "Communities of Practice and Social Learning Systems, pp. 29–48 in S. R. Clegg (Ed.), *Central Currents in Organization Studies II: Contemporary Trends, Volume 8,* London: Sage; originally published in *Organization* 7: 225–246.

Whipp, R., and Clark, P. (1986) *Innovation and the Auto Industry: Product, Process, and Work Organization,* New York: St. Martins.

Whitely, B. E. (1999) "Right Wing Authoritarianism, Social Dominance Orientation, and Prejudice," *Journal of Personality and Social Psychology* 77: 126–134.

Whyte, W. (1960) *The Organization Man,* Harmondsworth, UK: Penguin.

Williams, R. (1976) *Key Words: A Vocabulary of Culture and Society,* London: Fontana.

Williamson, O. E. (1985) *The Economic Institutions of Capitalism: Firms, Markets, Relational Contracting,* New York: Free Press.

Willis, P. (1977) *Learning to Labour: How Working Class Kids Get Working Class Jobs,* Farnborough, UK: Saxon House.

Willmott, H. (2002) "Strength Is Ignorance; Slavery Is Freedom: Managing Culture in Modern Organizations," in S. R. Clegg (Ed.), *Central Currents in Organization Studies II: Contemporary Trends, Volume 7,* London: Sage; originally published in *Journal of Management Studies* 30: 515–582.

Wolfe, T. (1979). *The Right Stuff,* New York: Farrar, Straus, & Giroux.

Womack, J. P., Jones, D. T., and Roos, D. (1990) *The Machine That Changed the World,* New York: Rawson/Macmillan.

Wood, A. (1994) *North-South Trade, Employment and Inequality,* Oxford: Clarendon.

Woodward, J. (1965) *Industrial Organizations: Theory and Practice,* London: Oxford University Press.

Workman, J. (1993) "Marketing's Limited Role in New Product Development in One Computer Systems Firm," *Journal of Marketing Research* 30: 405–421.

World Bank (2001) *Poverty Report.* Retrieved from www.worldbank.org/poverty/wdrpoverty/index.htm.

Wrege, D. (1995) "F. W. Taylor's Lecture on Management, 4th June 1907: An Introduction," *Journal of Management History* 1:1, 4–7.

Wren, D., and Greenwood, R. (1998) *Management Innovators: The People and Ideas That Shaped Modern Business,* New York: Oxford University Press.

Yeung, H. W.-C. (2000) "Economic Globalization, Crisis and the Emergence of Chinese Business Communities in Southeast Asia," *International Sociology* 15:2, 266–287.

Yoffie, D., and Cusumano, M. (1999) "Judo Strategy," *Harvard Business Review* January-February: 77–83.

Yoshino, M. Y., and Rangan, U. S. (1995) *Strategic Alliances: An Entrepreneurial Approach to Globalization,* Boston: Harvard Business School Press.

Young, E. (1989) "On the Naming of the Rose: Interests and Multiple Meanings as Elements of Organizational Culture," *Organization Studies* 10: 187–206.

Zuboff, S. (1988) *In the Age of the Smart Machine,* New York: Basic Books.

INDEX

CREDITS

The authors and publisher gratefully acknowledge the following sources for granting permission to reproduce the works or portions of works reprinted herein.

"The Changing of the Guards," written by Bob Dylan, copyright © 1978 Special Rider Music. All rights reserved. International copyright secured. Reprinted by permission.

Image 1.4. From Barton, B.F., & Barton, M.S., "Modes of Power in Technical and Professional Visuals," in *The Journal of Business and Technical Education, 7*(1), pp. 138–162. Reprinted with permission.

Image 1.7. Copyright © Bettmann/Corbis

Image 2.1. From Petty, B., *Bruce Petty's Australia—and how it works.* Melbourne: Penguin. Copyright © 1976. Reprinted by permission.

Image 3.2. From Halbak, C., *With Faith in their Hearts (1925–1950).* Copyright © 1950. Reprinted by permission of National Gypsum Properties, LLC.

Table 4.1. From *Research in Organizational Behaviour, 14,* Pennings, J.M., "Structural contingency theory: a reappraisal," copyright © 1992. Reprinted with permission of Elsevier.

Table 6.6. Reprinted by permission of Harvard Business School Press. From "Toxic Emotions at Work" by Peter J. Frost. Boston, MA, 2003, p.36. Copyright © 2003 by Peter J. Frost; all rights reserved.

Figure 7.1. From Blake, R.R., & Mouton, J.S., *The Managerial Grid III,* copyright © 1985. Reprinted by permission of Elsevier.

Figure 7.2. Situational Leadership® Model, Copyright © 2002, Center for Leadership Studies, Inc. All Rights Reserved. Situational Leadership® is a registered trademark of the Center for Leadership Studies, Inc.

Image 7.2. Copyright © Bettmann/Corbis

Table 7.3. From Boje, D.M., and Dennehey, R., *Managing in the Postmodern World.* Copyright © 1999, D.M. Boje. Reprinted by permission.

Table 7.5. From Bolman, L.G., and Deal, T.E., *Reframing Organizations: Artistry, Choice, and Leadership.* Copyright © 2003, Jossey-Bass. This material is used by permission of John Wiley & Sons, Inc.

ABOUT THE AUTHORS

Born and educated in England, **Stewart Clegg** migrated to Australia in 1976 and has worked as an academic for more than thirty years, not always in management (sometimes in humanities and sociology). He has also been a laborer on construction sites, worked in textile factories, been a shop assistant in a hardware store, an announcer on the radio (where he used to produce a couple of shows for Radio 4ZZZ in Brisbane, including *The Jazz Program*), and he has been a book series editor as well as a journal editor. He works at the University of Technology, Sydney, where he is a Professor of Management and the Director of ICAN (Innovative Collaborations, Alliances, and Networks) Research, a Key Research Centre of the university. He is also Visiting Professor at Aston Business School in the United Kingdom and Maastricht University in the Netherlands, as well as an International Fellow of the Centre of Comparative Social Studies of the Free University of Amsterdam. You can reach Stewart through s.clegg@uts.edu.au or the Web site for the book at www.ckmanagement.net.

Martin Kornberger was born in a small town in the west of Austria; after he moved a bit farther east—to Vienna, to study philosophy, humanities and management—he decided to move even farther east, and he came to Sydney. Originally, he planned to stay for a couple of weeks, but after a short intermezzo back in Europe (especially in a very cold Copenhagen), he bought a one-way ticket back to Sydney, where he has stayed for the past three years. Martin has had extensive experience of being managed, having worked for a rail cargo company, a hospital, a local council, a gas company, and as a social worker. These days, Martin is an INSEARCH Postdoctoral Research Fellow at the University of Technology in Sydney and also works on a research project with the University of Innsbruck. To conduct periodic reality checks to compare theory with practice, he cofounded a company called PLAY, which helps him to maintain a balance between writing and doing. You can reach Martin through martin.kornberger@uts.edu.au or the Web site for the book at www.ckmanagement.net.

Tyrone Pitsis came from Newtown in Sydney before moving to the Blue Mountains. He dropped out of school when he was 14 to start his first job working on construction sites, digging really big holes. At 16, he started working as a kitchen hand, and ended up being an executive chef until his late 20s. After one too many 70-hour workweeks, he decided to go back to college, where he completed his Higher School Certificate, and then studied Psychology at the University of New South Wales while supplementing his income teaching people to play the saxophone. Tyrone's friend, Adam Morgan, helped him start his academic career by recommending him for a job as a Research Assistant at the Australian Graduate School of Management; since then, Tyrone has never looked back. He now works as a senior researcher in ICAN (Innovative Collaborations, Alliances, and Networks) Research Centre at the University of Technology, Sydney, where he and Stewart have been researching together for six years. You can reach Tyrone through tyrone.pitsis@uts.edu.au or the Web site for the book at www.ckmanagement.net.